Integration of Information Systems: Bridging Heterogeneous Databases

OTHER IEEE PRESS BOOKS

A complete listing of IEEE PRESS books is available upon request.

Integration of Information Systems: Bridging Heterogeneous Databases

Edited by

Amar Gupta
Sloan School of Management
Massachusetts Institute of Technology

A volume in the IEEE PRESS Selected Reprint Series,
prepared under the sponsorship of the IEEE Computer Society.

**IEEE
PRESS**

The Institute of Electrical and Electronics Engineers, Inc., New York

Copyright © 1989 by
THE INSTITUTE OF ELECTRICAL AND ELECTRONICS ENGINEERS, INC.
345 East 47th Street, New York, NY 10017-2394
All rights reserved.

PRINTED IN THE UNITED STATES OF AMERICA

IEEE Order Number: PC0242-8

Library of Congress Cataloging-in-Publication Data

Integration of information systems: bridging heterogeneous databases
/ edited by Amar Gupta.
    p.   cm.—(IEEE Press selected reprint series)
  Includes bibliographies and indexes.
  ISBN 0-87942-251-3
  1. Data base management. 2. Computer networks. I. Gupta, Amar.
QA76.9.D3I547   1989   88-34425
005.75—dc 19   CIP

Contents

Dedicated to
ALOK and ANITA

Preface

ISLANDS of disparate information systems characterize virtually all large organizations today. The number and the size of these islands have grown over the years as organizations have invested in an increasing number of computer systems to support their growing reliance on computerized data. This has made the problem of integration more pronounced, complex, and challenging.

The integration of existing information systems involves a careful analysis of many technical, organizational, and strategic issues, and the surmounting of many technical and nontechnical barriers. These issues and barriers are delineated in this book, with special emphasis on the logical integration of information maintained in heterogeneous databases.

Existing information systems exhibit a wide range of heterogeneity in terms of hardware, systems software, application software, underlying semantics, and user interfaces. The evolving field of Distributed Heterogeneous Database Management Systems attempts to reconcile these dissimilarities, and to facilitate intelligent access to information maintained in such environments. All the major approaches that attempt to bridge heterogeneous databases are examined in this book.

Most researchers agree that in order to deal with the heterogeneity issue in a meaningful way, it is important that a critical mass of influential individuals participate in the development of solutions. In pursuance of this feeling, two symposiums were held at MIT during 1987. A number of distinguished experts from U.S. academic and research organizations, government agencies, computer companies, and other corporations presented their views at these symposiums. The papers received from all the invited speakers were professionally reviewed, and a subset of those papers are reproduced in this book.

Funds for organizing and conducting the two symposiums were provided by the U.S. Air Force, the U.S. Department of Transportation, IBM, and Citibank. I thank Major Paul Condit, Mark Hoffman (both of the U.S. Air Force), Dr. Frank Hassler, Bud Giangrande, and Bob Berk (all three of the Transportation Systems Center) for sponsoring the Knowledge-Based Integrated Information Systems Engineering (KBIISE) Project at MIT. I gratefully acknowledge the invaluable assistance provided by Professor Stuart E. Madnick; he and I jointly served as Principal Investigators for this project. I am indebted to all the individuals who contributed specifically authored material, and to my employer (MIT) which approved the use of such material in this book.

This is my seventh book to be published by the IEEE PRESS. I sincerely appreciate the support and encouragement provided by the staff of the IEEE PRESS on this book, and the preceding ones. Finally, I thank the readers for their interest in my books, for their comments and suggestions. Finally, I am indebted to Marilyn for keeping track of all the papers, and their different versions.

AMAR GUPTA
Massachusetts Institute of Technology
Cambridge, Massachusetts

Part 1
Introduction

THE proliferation of computer-based information systems and the huge effort involved in the implementation of large information systems make it imperative to develop new approaches that enable intelligent access to, and integration of, information spread over several independent information systems. Such access and integration offers the potential for significant technological, economic, and strategic benefits by facilitating the execution of functions not achievable using individual information systems.

The requirement for integrating information systems arises both in intra-organization and interorganization environments. Virtually all large organizations today rely on multiple computer systems to support their operations. The need for multiple systems is dictated by the:

- Level of required processing power and storage space;
- Desired level of reliability and fault tolerance;
- Geographic distribution of data collection, data manipulation, and data retrieval sites;
- Decentralized and functional structure of the organization; and
- Need to deal with different types of information, each of which may favor use of particular classes of computer hardware and software facilities.

Most organizations today depend on a portfolio of information processing machines ranging from mainframes to microcomputers, and from general purpose workstations to sophisticated CAD/CAM systems, to meet their computational requirements. While the individual hardware and software components in this growing array of computer systems may meet the objectives for which each was initially designed, their heterogeneity presents a major obstacle to ready access and assimilation of information. It requires tremendous amounts of time and effort to retrieve information from multiple systems today, and in many situations, it is simply not feasible to obtain integrated responses in desired timeframes.

As compared to the intra-organizational situation discussed above, the issues involved in integrating information on an interorganization basis are even more complex. First, there is greater heterogeneity in technical capabilities across organizations, as compared to a single organization. Second, there is less likelihood of reaching consensus on common goals and standards. Third, nontechnical issues, such as access rights and sharing of costs, acquire added importance when multiple organizations are involved. Integration of information systems is indeed a challenging task from all perspectives.

EXAMPLE SCENARIOS

The above issues can be better understood by looking at two different scenarios, one involving a single organization, and the other involving multiple organizations.

Scenario I

Imagine that a part of a factory manufacturing critical equipment suddenly becomes inoperational. In order to mitigate the resulting complications, it is necessary to:

(a) Investigate alternative plans that could potentially manufacture the equipment;
(b) Analyze the production schedules of these alternative manufacturing facilities;
(c) Retrieve information about suppliers who supplied components and materials to the inoperational site;
(d) Examine the transportation mechanisms for raw materials and finished components in the case of each alternative solution; and
(e) Examine time schedules and costs.

Information concerning the above aspects needs to be retrieved from several different systems. But it is not a simple database problem involving retrieval of data. Instead, coordinated access must be made to data as well as to program code.

Scenario II [1]

"A B-1B bomber flying in the European sector develops an operational problem. Although it is able to land safely at its base, it is determined that the problem is potentially serious. The overseas base uses electronic communication links to inform Dyess Air Force Base, which in turn alerts the 15th Air Force, SAC headquarters, Tinker Air Force Base, and the Rockwell International Support Control Center. Rockwell in turn contacts one or more of its subcontractors, depending on the nature of the problem. However, the Air Force receives weapon system technical information on paper and microfilm. The B-1B bomber continues to remain grounded until the relevant pieces of technical information can be identified, consolidated, and studied. Only then can a combined engineering/manufacturing/logistics effort be established to develop a field repair procedure."

It is difficult to put a price tag on the opportunity cost implicit in the delay in repairing the aircraft. This cost will be higher in wartime than in peacetime. It is clear that an accelerated pace of aircraft repair involves quick and efficient retrieval of information stored in different computers at geographically dispersed sites, and belonging to various organizations.

It should be emphasized that in both scenarios described above, the problem is not one involving data alone. Instead, process- or program-related information must be selectively retrieved to generate meaningful results. Present day systems are totally inadequate to handle either of the scenarios described above. Newer techniques must be developed to allow easy, efficient, intelligent access to information hosted on multiple systems, which are not identical to each other.

The various situations requiring such integration include the need to:

- *Span applications* such as integrating CAD/CAM and documentation systems;
- *Span functional areas* such as integrating procurement, engineering, and maintenance;
- *Span organizational boundaries* such as integrating project status information from Rockwell, TRW, and Lockheed; and
- *Span geographic separations* such as integrating warehouse stockpile information from systems in the U.S., Europe, and Asia.

Even though the motivation for integration may differ from domain to domain, many of the underlying issues are common for a broad range of applications.

FUNCTIONAL DEFICIENCIES

The problem of inefficient, incomplete, and time-consuming access to information can be traced, from a technical viewpoint, to functional deficiencies at several levels as described below:

- *Structured and Unstructured Applications*-Conventional computer-based information systems have been designed with specific applications in view. These systems are efficient for performing the originally intended application, but they are inefficient in dealing with ad hoc queries or new, unanticipated applications.
- *Information versus Knowledge*-Traditional database systems focus on retrieval of data, and on performing elementary operations (e.g., sorting and merging). Such systems cannot use both data and programs to respond intelligently to queries like "How many vehicles can be made available to evacuate people from the vicinity of a particular volcano within a specified period of time?" which require analysis of many factors.
- *Diverse Types of Information*-Different types of information (numerical, graphic, pictorial, speech, and video) are referenced in very different ways. During the 1960s, computers were designed to manipulate, store, and retrieve numerical information. During the 1970s, the focus was on textual information. Very little effort has so far been directed towards efficient storage and retrieval of pictorial information, and its combination with numerical and textual information.
- *Communications*-In spite of a continuing effort by a number of national and international institutions, it is still difficult to transfer complex information across computers of dissimilar architectures.
- *Granularity*-It is difficult to judge what volume of information should be made available, and how it should be arranged and tailored to meet the needs of the person requesting the information.
- *Security*-It is necessary to determine who can access the information, and what each person is permitted to modify. This aspect is especially important for defense applications involving more than one organization.

- *Semantics*-It is difficult to specify exactly the subset of information desired without knowing details of the systems being accessed. Further, a particular piece of information may possess different connotations on various systems. Conversely, the same item (such as a particular spare part) may be specified by different numbers on various systems.

The above list describes a few of the key technical problems. In addition, there are major nontechnical impediments that restrict integration. Because of the large number of issues and variables, a global solution to the problem of integrating distributed information systems has remained an elusive dream. However, partial solutions are now being developed.

LEVELS OF INTEGRATION

Integration of information resources can be visualized at different levels. At the least complex end of the spectrum, information can be exchanged across a network using basic facilities such as remote procedure call [13], and message passing. At the next higher level, a new layer of software can be created to insulate users from idiosyncrasies of different host machines. This layer can provide uniformity at the level of logically centralized file servers, as in the case of Andrew at CMU [2], or at the level of application programs, as in the case of Project Athena at MIT [3].

The approaches described in the preceding paragraph require a significant degree of user involvement. Also, they represent instances of integration of information. The focus of this book is, however, on integration of information systems. Further, our emphasis is on systems "dissimilar" from each other in terms of:

- Hardware: for example, one information system using an IBM mainframe, and a second system functioning on Unisys hardware;
- Operating systems: for example, one information system using OS/MVS, and the other using UNIX;
- Data models: for example, one system using network data models, and the other using relational data models;
- Database management systems: for example, one using INGRES, and the other using ORACLE database management systems, respectively.

Apart from the above differences arising from dissimilarities in hardware and software, different information systems use different sets of design decisions and underlying assumptions. For example, one system may be using the annual salary of employees, while another may be using monthly salary; further, the salary in one case may be gross salary (typical of systems used for computing total cost of production of a particular item), whereas, in the second case, it may be net salary (typical of systems used for printing checks). Similarly, a particular part may be specified by one part number at the time of design, and by a different part number at the manufacturing stage. All these differences must be reconciled when attempting to integrate dissimilar information systems.

There are two facets to integration—physical integration and logical integration. *Physical integration*, accomplished through physical connectivity, refers to the process of establishing actual communication links among disparate systems. This involves analysis of aspects such as bandwidths, security, availability, and internetwork protocol conversions. *Logical integration* refers to the process of accessing disparate systems in concert for generating integrated responses. This involves reconciliation of different assumptions and perspectives embedded in the systems being integrated. At the logical level, the integration system must:

- Know where all the information is stored, along with the data formats and the query languages of the local systems;
- Decompose the query into subqueries that can be executed by local systems;
- Accumulate the results from all the subqueries;
- Reconcile differences among the results accumulated; and
- Formulate integrated answers.

All the above tasks must ideally be carried out with no modification to existing systems. However, in practice, some approaches (discussed later in this book) involve some degree of changes to existing information systems.

Based on the level of integration achieved, and some additional characteristics, various types of integration approaches can be distinguished. These approaches, using the terminology of different researchers who have used dissimilar terms to refer to the same or similar ideas, include the following:

- Cooperation Systems for Heterogeneous Database Management System [4];
- Federated Database [5], [9];
- Composite Information System [6];
- Knowledge Based Integrated Information System [7], [11];
- Multidatabase [8], [10]; and
- Superdatabase [12].

Instead of attempting to cover all the views expressed by the individuals who coined these terms and phrases, the endeavor in this book is to encapsulate the main concepts and the emerging technologies that enable integration of dissimilar information systems.

ABOUT THIS PART

Part 1 of the book focuses on the importance of integration and the problems involved in such integration. Three different perspectives are presented.

In the first paper, Daniel S. Appleton distinguishes integration technology from interfacing technology. The key difference between them is in terms of data integrity. While there is no technological control over data integrity in the interfacing approach, data integrity is the major issue in the integration approach. As a consequence, while a two-schema approach suffices for the interfacing approach, a three-schema approach is highly desirable in the integration approach. The third schema is a conceptual schema which defines a consistent set of business rules that are needed to manage the integrity of shared information.

The second paper, by Richard Shuey and Gio Wiederhold, emphasizes the role of automated information systems. They highlight the fact that there are many situations in which the term "data" is used in a context where it might be more appropriate to use the terms "information" or "knowledge." Over time, information systems will evolve logically and physically into distributed computers and databases, with individual functional components of each information system being driven by information from companion components.

The third paper, by David Notkin *et al.*, embodies the opinions expressed at a forum, attended by an international group of fifty researchers, to discuss the technical issues relating to heterogeneous computing environments. Five styles of heterogeneity are identified in this paper. The key directions in many areas, such as interconnection, filing, authentication, naming, and user interfaces, are discussed. The paper stresses the fact that there is no single, correct way to address the problems of heterogeneity. Instead, there are many different styles, each driven by its own set of underlying assumptions and objectives.

Various solutions and potential solutions are examined in subsequent parts of this book.

REFERENCES FOR PART 1

[1] *IDS System Design*, Rockwell, May 1986, pp. 36–39.
[2] Morris, J. H., M. Satyanarayanan, M. H. Conner, J. H. Howard, D. S. H. Rosenthal, and F. D. Smith, "Andrew: A distributed personal computer environment," *Commun. ACM*, vol. 29, no. 3, Mar. 1986, pp. 184–201.
[3] Balkovich, E., S. Lerman, and R. P. Parmelo, "Computing in higher education: The Athena experience," *Commun. ACM*, vol. 28, no. 11, Nov. 1985, pp. 1214–1224.
[4] Adiba, M. and D. Portal, "A cooperation system for heterogeneous data base management systems," *Inform. Syst.*, vol. 3, 1978, pp. 209–215.
[5] McLeod, D. and D. Heimbinger, "A federated architecture for database systems," in *AFIPS Conf. Proc.*, vol. 49, National Computer Conf., 1980, pp. 283–289.
[6] Lam, C. Y. and S. E. Madnick, *Composite Information Systems—A New Concept in Information Systems*, Working Paper #35, Center for Information Systems Research, Sloan School of Management, MIT, May 1978.
[7] Gupta, A. and S. Madnick, *Knowledge-Based Integrated Information Systems Engineering: Highlights and Bibliography*, MIT, 1987. (NTIS/DTIC Accession # A 195850).
[8] Litwin, W. *et al.*, "SIRIUS systems for distributed data management," in *Distributed Databases*, H. Schneider, Ed. New York, NY: North-Holland Publishing Co., 1982, pp. 311–366.
[9] Heimbinger, D. and D. McLeod, "A federated architecture for information management," *ACM Trans. Office Info. Syst.*, vol. 3, no. 3, July 1985, pp. 253–278. Reprinted in this book.
[10] Thompson, G. R., *Multi-database concurrency control*, Doctoral Dissertation, Oklahoma State University, Stillwater, OK, 1987.
[11] Madnick, S. E. and Y. R. Wang, "Integrating disparate databases for composite answers," in *Proc. Twenty-first Annual Hawaii Int. Conf. Syst. Sci.*, vol. II, Jan. 1988, pp. 583–592.
[12] Pu, C., *Superdatabases for composition of heterogeneous databases*, Tech. Paper No. CUCS-243-86, Columbia University, NY, 1986.
[13] Gibbons, P. B., "A stub generator for multilanguage RPC in heterogeneous environments," *IEEE Trans. Software Eng.*, vol. SE-13, no. 1, Jan. 1987, pp. 77–87.

BIBLIOGRAPHY FOR PART 1

[1] Gupta, A. and S. Madnick, Eds., *KBIISE—Vol. 2: Knowledge-Based Integrated Information Systems Development Methodologies Plan*, MIT, Cambridge, MA, 1987 (NTIS/DTIC Accession # A 195851).

[2] ——, *KBIISE—Vol. 3: Integrating Distributed Homogeneous and Heterogeneous Databases: Prototypes*, MIT, Cambridge, MA, 1987 (NTIS/DTIC Accession # A 195852).

[3] ——, *KBIISE—Vol. 4: Object-Oriented Approach to Integrating Database Semantics*, MIT, Cambridge, MA, 1987 (NTIS/DTIC Accession # A 195853).

[4] ——, *KBIISE—Vol. 5: Integrating Images, Applications and Communications Networks*, MIT, Cambridge, MA, 1987 (NTIS/DTIC Accession # A 195854).

[5] ——, *KBIISE—Vol. 6: Strategic, Organizational, and Standardization Aspects of Integrated Informations Systems*, MIT, Cambridge, MA, 1987 (NTIS/DTIC Accession # A 195855).

[6] ——, *KBIISE—Vol. 7: Integrating Information Systems in a Major Decentralized International Organization*, MIT, Cambridge, MA, 1987 (NTIS/DTIC Accession # A 195856).

[7] ——, *KBIISE—Vol. 8: Technical Opinions Regarding Knowledge-Based Integrated Information Systems Engineering*, MIT, Cambridge, MA, 1987 (NTIS/DTIC Accession # A 195857).

[8] Wang, R. and S. Madnick, Eds., *Connectivity Among Information Systems*, CIS Project, MIT, 1988.

[9] Special Issue on Distributed Hetergeneous Systems, *Proc. IEEE*, vol. 75, no. 5, May 1987.

[10] Bachman, C. W. and R. G. Ross, "Toward a more complete reference model of computer-based information systems," in *Computers and Standards*, Vol. 1. New York, NY: North-Holland Publishing Co., 1982, pp. 35–48.

[11] Cole, R., "A method for interconnecting heterogeneous computer networks," *Software-Practice and Experience*, vol. 17, no. 6, June 1987, pp. 387–387.

[12] Gavish, B. and H. Pirkul, "Computer and database location in distributed computer systems," *IEEE Trans. Comput.*, vol. C-35, no. 7, July 1986, pp. 583–590.

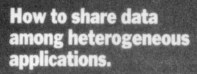

How to share data among heterogeneous applications.

by Daniel S. Appleton

THE TECHNOLOGY OF DATA INTEGRATION

Software integration is the Holy Grail of information resource management. What we want is efficient access, through a single query language and database schema, to data in preexisting, heterogeneous, distributed applications. We want to accomplish this without making changes to preexisting databases, their database management systems, or their application programs.

To the lay person, these may seem to be reasonable requirements: difficult, but not impossible. All that is

required is a software system that presents the user with the illusion of a single, integrated, consistent, nondistributed database. Simple. But no one, not even IBM, has succeeded in building such a software system, even though most information resource management professionals would give their left incisor for one.

The problem of building such a software system is so enormous that no one has been able to tackle the whole thing. Over the last five years, it has resolved itself into four separate but highly related subsets of technology: 1. user interface technology, 2. distributed heterogeneous data management technology, 3. network transaction management technology, and 4. interprocessor communication technology (see Fig. 1).

While the main focus of this article is on distributed, heterogeneous data management technology, a brief review of each of the four subsets of integration technology will prove helpful.

Interprocessor communication technology provides communications primitives (that is, the building blocks of protocols) that enable different computers to send and receive messages among themselves. This technology generally spans levels one through six of the OSI communications reference model.

This is the only subset of integration technology that exists below level seven of the OSI model. In fact, the emergence of the other three subsets gives rise to speculation that the seventh layer—the applications layer—should be redefined as the applications services layer, and that applications should be in an eighth lay-

er. Therefore, the remaining three subsets of integration technology contain most, if not all, of the functions of the applications services layer of the OSI model.

Network transaction management technology enables one process to send messages to another process, identified by a logical name, without specifying whether that process is on the same host or on a different host. Besides message transfer, it provides for functions such as job transfer and file transfer. Transaction management technology also provides many of the functions of a distributed operating system, including system-level resource accounting, recovery, security, and initialization.

User interface technology allows users to construct and use a wide variety of features, including windowing, searching, graphics, and report writing, using one standard language. A virtual terminal interface enables the user to use any terminal type to perform all of his language functions, regardless of what make or brand of terminal or terminal software he may have.

Distributed heterogeneous data management technology provides for the retrieval and update of data distributed throughout the environment. Through its data dictionary, it knows which data are where, what the logical and physical structures of those data are, and how to access them. It consists of a global, or neutral, data definition language that describes common data, and a global, or neutral, data manipulation language that manipulates those descriptions to provide access to the data, whether they are stored in a database management system (DBMS) or under a specialized file control system. The data dictionary can be either passive or active, i.e., it can be used to compile network programs or it can be active at run time.

A SPECIAL SOFTWARE SYSTEM

What does integration technology integrate? Two things. First, there is the current automated environment. Integration technology can be viewed as a special software system whose sole purpose is to integrate an existing environment of heterogeneous hardware, system software, DBMSs, file control systems, application systems, programs, databases, and data. When inserted into an existing environment, integration technology tends to stand out in that environment.

The second thing integrated by integration technology is the future automated environment. Future projects must use the technology as part of their development. In this way they share the integration technology. It is embedded within them. It constitutes the "parts they have in common." In

FIG. 1

THE FOUR SUBSETS OF INTEGRATION TECHNOLOGY

ISO/OSI LAYER 8 APPLICATIONS

PROPOSED REDEFINITION

ISO/OSI LAYER 7 "APPLICATIONS SERVICES"

DISTRIBUTED HETEROGENEOUS DATA MANAGEMENT

NETWORK TRANSACTION MANAGEMENT

INTERPROCESSOR COMMUNICATION MANAGEMENT

ISO/OSI LAYERS 1-6

future environments, integration technology will not be visible. It will just be there.

No one believes it is possible to build a single software system that will totally integrate all existing environments. Most researchers believe, however, that some degree of integration is possible for all existing environments. They also believe that if future additions and changes to the existing environments are implemented around such a software system, an optimum level of integration can be achieved. Environments exhibit varying degrees of hostility toward integration technology. Least friendly are those where specific hardware and data management technologies have been implemented just because they supported a given application. These environments can hardly be interfaced, much less integrated.

Environments built from a technology plan that standardizes DBMS software, as well as hardware and operating systems,

are much more friendly to integration technology. Network and relational database management technology are much more integratable than are hierarchical database management technologies or environments with no DBMS technology at all.

Progress has been made in all four areas of integration technology. The ISO/OSI reference model, for example, has helped in setting standards for interprocessor communication technology. In the area of user interface technology, concepts such as SQL, QBE, and lexical report writers have helped to transcend application particulars.

But to find the Holy Grail, the really tough problem of distributed, heterogeneous data management must also be solved. Reference models and standards must be established so that particular software systems can be designed and built.

Reference models and standards evolve from projects that invent and test possible solutions. To date, probably $50

The data dictionary is a major issue for integration technology.

The schema is a very special logical data model. It must be consistent, accessible, extensible, and transformable. It derives these qualities from the data model in which it is defined, and from the procedures used to build and maintain it.

Because the conceptual schema is in a well-defined entity relationship or semantic construct, it can be transformed into user views by a "global" data manipulation language that is very similar to relational or extended relational algebra. This transformation is called the conceptual-to-external transformation, and it generally is integrated into the user language of the software system.

The other transformation, conceptual to internal, is the hard part. Generally, transformations of both structure and form of the schema must be made to handle the wide variety of DBMSs and file control systems (FCSs) in the environment in which the schema is being implemented.

Since not all of the environment's DMBSs and FCSs are of equal quality, the conceptual-to-internal transformations are performed by software at each node, and data are moved through the network in the conceptual form. This is more economical anyway, since nodes can always expect to transmit and receive data in the same form.

The data described by the conceptual schema are viewed by many users as different external schemata. The data described by the conceptual schema are physically implemented in many databases, each described by an internal schema. In the IDEF1-Extended notation, each box represents an entity; each arc represents a relationship. A "big dot" indicates that the relationship is "one to many."

The conceptual schema describes a neutral, integrated view of the shared data resource. There is one global conceptual schema in an enterprise. It is independent of physical database structures and boundaries and is neutral to the biases of individual applications. Each internal schema represents a user or applications view of data. Requests are made against external schemata.

The following are the objectives of a conceptual schema:
• Data standardization—by defining a consistent, extensible, and transformable set of business rules to be used by all data projects.
• Data integration—by pulling together facts in multiple databases.
• Data sharing—by supporting multiple user views (i.e., external schemata) of the data resource.
• Data quality—by specifying and enforcing data integrity constraints.

• Data administration—by documenting the meanings in the data resource.
• Data independence—by isolating data structure changes (i.e., changes to internal schemata) from user views and programs.
• Data growth—by evolving consistently as its scope is extended.

The data dictionary is a major issue for integration technology. In fact, all four of the integration technology research projects determined that they had to build special data dictionaries to handle the distributed, heterogeneous data management problem. Existing commercial data dictionaries fell far short of their requirements.

All commercial data dictionaries are basically two-schema data dictionaries. They have little or no capability to define or store a conceptual schema and its transforms, much less to use them for anything. Most commercially available data dictionaries are designed for one DBMS only, and they are not even designed to handle physical distribution of the data in that DBMS.

All four integration technology projects are building and using three-schema data dictionaries. Typical of the three-schema data dictionary architecture is what IISS calls the CDM (Common Data Model) subsystem. The CDM subsystem consists of two software modules. The CDM dictionary is a database that describes shared data (the conceptual schema) and the network environment. The CDM processor is software that accesses the CDM dictionary and transforms users' data requests into transactions that can be processed by the local DBMSs or FCSs. The CDM processor is the distributed database manager of IISS.

All four technology projects have tackled what they call the retrieval problem. They all employ their data dictionaries to access data in the environment.

SCHEMA AS ROSETTA STONE

The objective, of course, is to use the conceptual schema as a Rosetta Stone to translate user queries that require data distributed over heterogeneous hardware nodes, DMBSs, and application databases. The user query is unaware of where and how the data are stored. These systems process both ad hoc and standard queries, and they have built-in security and access controls.

The retrieval problem is simple compared with the update problem, because retrievals do not affect database states; updates do. The three-schema data dictionary, therefore, has to worry about concurrency problems and about backup and recovery problems. These problems can be aggravated depending on how much the system uses redundancy

to improve efficiency.

IISS, IMDAS, and IDS are committed to attacking the update problems. To do this, they will use dependency and relationship constraint logic embedded in the conceptual schema to ensure the integrity of updates.

Obviously, the ideal is to have a three-schema data dictionary that controls updates and retrievals in a distributed, heterogeneous environment and that operates in-line with all application programs. To do so, it would have to operate at run time. Few commercial data dictionaries operate at this level today. Most of them are passive, i.e., a precompiler takes metadata out of the data dictionary and puts them into the source code of a program, which must subsequently be compiled into object code. Some of them are active, which means they are used by language compilers.

Three of the four research projects have requirements to develop run-time, three-schema data dictionaries for both update and retrieval. Today, however, they are content to achieve active status on retrievals (both ad hoc and standard) and on updates. In-line is still a ways away.

There is no doubt that the demand for integration technology is very high. This demand is driving all four subsets of the technology—interprocessor communications, network transaction management, distributed heterogeneous data management, and user interface technology—in clearly defined directions.

While progress is required in all four areas, individual businesses are attempting to assemble their own integration software subsystems from technological pieces that are currently available. Some organizations are attempting to build three-schema master data dictionaries using relational DBMSs or 4GLs. Others have chosen one of the many data dictionary products such as the IBM Data Dictionary, Data Manager, or the ADR Data Dictionary, and have performed surgery on it to turn it into a master data dictionary. Depending on the data dictionary, this surgery can be a simple appendectomy or a difficult quadruple heart bypass. The degree of difficulty is also dependent on what they want the final product to be: a two-schema or a three-schema master data dictionary, or both. Before this can be decided, some key architectural commitments must be made.

The first commitment is what I call the commitment to heterogeneity. Some businesses believe they can solve the integration problem by committing the future automated environment to one single hardware or software vendor. They believe they can solve their current integration prob-

9

A commitment to data integrity means a commitment to data management by thorough business rules.

lems by committing to build a homogeneous environment, e.g., a single "total integrated application."

MYOPIC BUSINESS PLANNING

Businesses that think and plan their automated environments in this way have no commitments to heterogeneity. They are, in my opinion, unrealistic and myopic. No environment is more dynamic than the information environment. No technology moves more quickly or in more directions. Businesses need to take advantage of these dynamics, not defend themselves. A commitment to heterogeneity will provide the context for taking advantage of all opportunities.

The second commitment is what I call a commitment to standards and the reuse of assets. Most businesses still see IRM standards as controls and constraints to creativity and progress. This is because of the way they have traditionally been developed and implemented by dp departments. Good standards enable creativity and prog-

ress. They are offensive, not defensive. Without a commitment to standards and reuse of assets, no concept of integration is even remotely feasible.

The commitment to standards and reuse of assets means first that special organizations, which I call asset engineering organizations, must be commissioned to build assets that are reusable. This requires an investment in asset development. Such an investment program requires significant changes in traditional IRM planning, system engineering, financing, performance management, staffing, project definitions, and project management processes.

The final commitment is what I call a commitment to data integrity. The most valuable information assets are data. In fact, today, the asset engineers in the IRM world are the database administrators and managers. (Maybe we should start calling them that.)

A commitment to data integrity does not mean standardizing the names of data elements. It means a commitment to

data management through business rules and a focus on common and shared data (see "Law of the Data Jungle," October 1983, p. 225). This commitment is what "data-driven" information resource management is all about.

Most businesses are stepping up to these commitments. The excuse I most often hear for deciding against making all three commitments is that "the technology is not here to support the commitments." But it is.

There are major technological movements in all four levels of integration technology. Some vendors even claim to have active three-schema data dictionaries, and more vendors are advertising that they have them in the works. But these technologies are not self-implementing.

Technology is holding nothing back. Cultural changes and changes to traditional IRM beliefs and processes are the real inhibitors to integration. But those are changing too—as I will explain in my next article. ◉

Data Engineering and Information Systems

Richard Shuey

Gio Wiederhold, Stanford University

Automated information systems will spearhead the penetration of computer technology into our society. Data engineering for these systems should focus on architectural alternatives and data service requirements.

The computer has made it possible to mechanize much of the information interchange and processing that constitute the nervous system of our society. The computerized systems that provide this mechanization, commonly called information systems, will be responsible for computer technology's long-term impact on society. We need to understand how the information requirements of the different segments of our society should influence the design and architecture of the information systems serving those segments.[1]

We have for some time been in a distributed computer era. This article discusses how the data requirements of information systems influence the structure of the distributed computer systems upon which they are often built. Many of the concepts, carried over into centralized systems, enable those systems to evolve in a distributed world.

Unfortunately, our current understanding of computer science does not include precise definitions of, or permit sharp boundaries among, data, information, and knowledge.[2] In this article, the orientation is on data; concepts touching on information and knowledge are introduced only as necessary. Consequently, the reader will find situations in which the term "data" is used in a context where it might be more appropriate to use the terms "information" or "knowledge."

Our two principal premises are

1. that a specific information system may involve logically and physically distributed computers and databases, and

2. that the individual functional components of an information system are driven by information from companion components and in turn provide information to other components through the transfer of data.

The term "component" here includes the interfaces as well as the internal parts of the systems, namely humans, displays, sensors, actuators, computers, and storage devices.

Both of these premises are likely self-evident. However, not so self-evident is that this interchange of data is far more than a data communication problem.

For example, we can describe the services provided by the post office from a pure data communication viewpoint. In the post office system, an envelope is delivered to the ad-

Reprinted from *IEEE Computer,* pp. 18–30, Jan. 1986.

11

dressee; the internal contents do not concern the postal service. If the languages of recipient and sender differ, the data of the message cannot be used. Problems in understanding the content must be resolved by cooperation between the sender and the recipient. Human beings are sufficiently flexible that this is usually not a major problem. Certainly, it is never the responsibility of the postal service to deliver intelligible messages.

In automated information systems, however, the equivalents of the sender and receiver are often relatively inflexible computers that must receive and at the same time interpret and act on the data. Thus, the designer of an integrated information system must consider factors that in our postal example lie outside the domain of concern of the system, and must take care of them in a disciplined way.

The definition of layers of responsibility, seen in communication protocols such as the OSI Reference Model,[3] is an aspect of such discipline. The lower levels of that model deal with communications questions in the sense of the post office example. They are in relatively good shape in that agreed-upon standards exist. The higher level protocols of the OSI model deal with data and information issues and standards that will make it possible for applications and information systems on different computers to work together. However, the lack of a needed understanding of a general solution and standards provides a promising opportunity for research.[4]

The storage of data and knowledge enables incremental learning and improvement of systems. Storage can be viewed as an asynchronous communications system that spans time and does not require that the addressee be known when the data are collected or processed. It is interesting that many common carriers are planning to include data storage facilities in their future networks.

Information systems include capabilities provided by hardware and software for computing, communications, control, data storage and retrieval, etc. The design of an information system must include all these functions. Even within an application the technologies cannot be separated. From an engineering standpoint, this breadth requirement makes it difficult to break a problem down into small, manageable subproblems. As the FCC learned during its computer inquiries, it is difficult to cleanly separate computer and communications technology or the business sectors that go by those titles. To be more explicit, the fields of computers and communications are merging. Two complementary aspects of the computer and communications interaction can be seen:

(1) Internal communications between the components of a computer are essential. Communications shortcomings often limit the performance of conventional computers and pose a serious problem in parallel computers. Communications technology, its capabilities, and its limitations are important factors in specifying the architecture of a computer system. Communications is a key to distributed computing. As a consequence, many computer companies, including IBM and DEC, are today expanding their activities in the communications business arena.

(2) Communications systems today contain a multitude of computers and stored program devices. The electronic switch in a central office is really a large computer[5,6] and the nationwide communications system, the world's largest distributed computer.[7] Signal processing within the nationwide network is increasingly performed by digital techniques utilizing stored program devices or microprocessors. Consequently, major communications companies, including AT&T, GTE, Northern Telecom, and the Bell Operating Companies, are entering parts of the computer and information processing market.

This article does not primarily report research results. A gap exists between the formal disciplines in many categories of data engineering and the formal overall discipline and design methodology needed to address large-scale distributed information systems in total. Applications will not, and have not, waited for that formal discipline. Many of today's large systems were created by a partial merger of individually developed applications, or if designed more as a whole, in the absence of adequate formal, integrated design methods. Engineers must deal with the evolution of those existing systems as well as the design of new systems. Moreover, they must do so in the absence of mature design methodology. We hope that this article will interest the design engineer faced with that problem. We also suggest areas of research to develop the needed methodology and stress the importance of a combined communications and computer viewpoint.

Although properly designed information systems might be viewed as black boxes, analysis and synthesis should break them down into reasonably separate components, or modules, with cleanly defined interfaces. This philosophy is also followed in describing computer architecture and large software systems. Fortunately, within an information system, the data services needed or provided by each component play a central role. They also provide a convenient structure within which to think about data-related questions. The field of data engineering primarily concerns the engineering of systems to provide those data services.

Our coverage of the impact of data engineering on overall information systems is structured as follows:

• The section on data engineering and data services emphasizes data services and the unifying role of those services in an information system. A model is suggested for such services in this context.

• The section on data attributes and parameters suggests a methodology, beginning with user needs, for organiz-

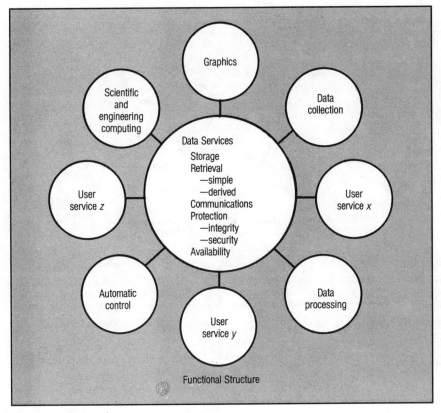

Figure 1. A view of information systems.

ing the information relevant to the design of data services for overall information systems. Only a core structure is presented. The objectives are more to outline good engineering practice in this field and set a framework for future research and development in data engineering than to report research results.

• With what we know today, we can extrapolate into the future and estimate what the architecture of a data-engineered information system environment might look like a few years from now. In the section on a university as an example of information system architecture, an architecture is suggested for a university campus as a whole. The suggested architecture represents a merger of computer and communications technology. Most of the components and features are being put in place today at certain universities and industrial installations.

Data engineering and data services

Data engineering can be defined as the engineering of systems that make data available when and where needed, in the required form. Providing the data in the right form requires selection and abstraction. In many cases, data must also be protected. The significance of the information obtained, and the actions taken because of it, are socially important, but not the primary concern of the engineer. More broadly, it is convenient to think in terms of a common set of data services that provide the data needed by functional systems and that accept data from them. Figure 1 presents such a generic view of an information system.

In such a functional view, however, understand that not all data operations

are performed in the data service function. Data operations occur within other functional units, just as within a distributed computer network computer operations are performed in the communications network serving those computers. The design objective is to logically separate out those operations primarily concerned with data, emphasizing data services that are common, shared, or global. If the data services required at this level of abstraction can be understood, there are far-reaching implications for overall information system architecture. The primary weakness in this approach is that in some cases the separation of, say, retrieving data from processing the retrieved data appears somewhat questionable. The field of artificial intelligence, or AI, is a case in point. In AI, inference engines and retrieval engines should perhaps be combined, but it is sometimes convenient to consider them separate entities performing different tasks. As in AI, a model like that in Figure 1, which admittedly is not entirely satisfactory, may nevertheless be useful.

Figure 1 is a logical functional diagram. All of the activities indicated could be performed within a general-purpose computer. At some point when establishing an architecture, we must begin to distinguish between the logical and physical alternatives that can provide the needed functional capability. Because the design tradeoffs are quite different in these two worlds, it is convenient to expand the model so that it better represents our distributed computer era. Figure 2 illustrates such an expansion. Note that this figure can be viewed as representing a logical distribution of information system functions, a physical distribution of those functions, or both. Specifically,

• if the figure represents a logical distribution of functions, those functions could still be performed in a single computer; and

• if the figure represents a physical distribution, the model encourages a focus on the capabilities and limita-

January 1986

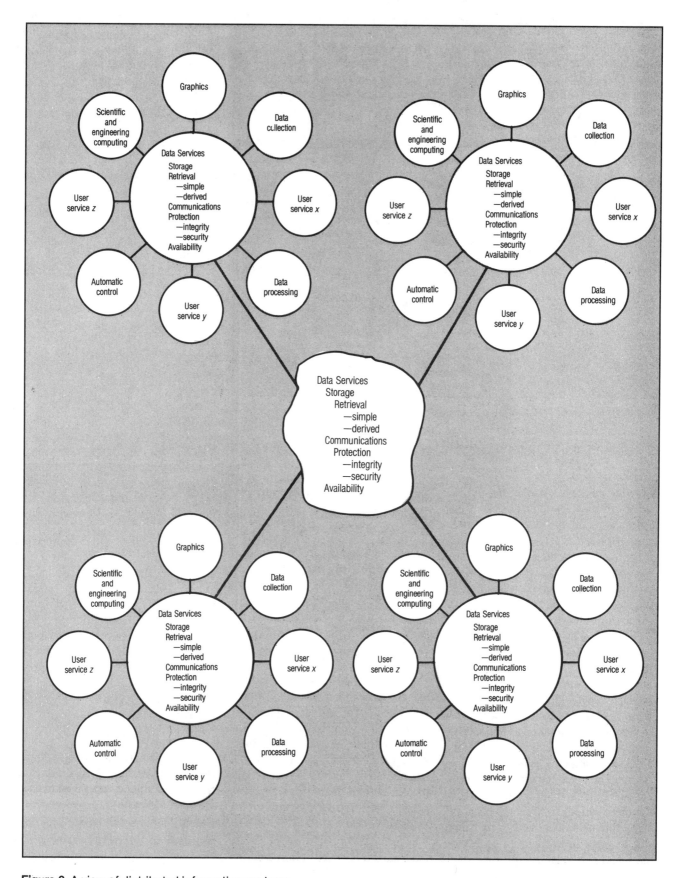

Figure 2. A view of distributed information systems.

tions of an actual physical configuration, including in that focus the associated communications network and equipment.

In the past, it was commonly considered that the primary central unifying services consisted only of a communications network and conventional data communication services. However, such a viewpoint is now too narrow. Placing all of the responsibility for data services, except data transport, at the distributed nodes corresponds to the post office problem. It is unrealistic in the computer world. Once the overall requirements and associated design tradeoffs are understood, then data services can be allocated throughout the distributed environment in a cost-effective way. This does not imply that a specific service is isolated at one logical or physical location. More likely the organization of the various services will be hierarchical in nature and distributed over the information system hierarchy. For example, the issue of data security should be addressed at all levels of the hierarchy and the architecture selected should support the distribution of security controls throughout that hierarchy.

The challenges are

• to provide the necessary data services in the context of today's information systems. It is not feasible to redo overnight the intricate information systems essential to the operation of many segments of society. Rather, more adequate data services must be introduced and evolved without disturbing the balance of the application environment.

• In the future, to select information system architectures within which it will be possible to support the required data services in a cost-effective way. Architectures should provide adequate flexibility to support the growing trend to distributed systems. Information systems grow and new ones are continuously added. The architecture must support such growth.

Data attributes and parameters

In this section we consider the attributes and parameters of the data exchanged between the different components and individuals of an organization. The objective is to establish a foundation for a more rational data-driven approach to the design of information systems.

Information systems must operate in an organizational environment. The degree to which the different components of an organization exchange information is illustrated in Figure 3, taken from the report on an academic study at Rensselaer Polytechnic Institute.[8] The study covered selected campus administrative information systems. The figure describes the complex information exchange between the administrative components of that institute. The pattern of data interaction shown on this small scale is typical of that in industrial and other organizations. In practice, it is usual for components of an organization to develop independent information systems only to learn at a later date that they use common data, that the systems are not properly interfaced, that the data cannot be maintained in a consistent manner, etc. And yet, it is the exchange of data between these components of the organization that drives the information systems serving the components and the organization as a whole. The proper creation, management, and control of shared data is essential if the component information systems of an organization are to provide accurate, consistent information. This makes it possible for all components to take consistent, integrated action.

At the lowest level of abstraction, it might be desirable to consider the data in an information system as data objects or data atoms, but the knowledge requirements of treating each object individually would be excessive. In practice, data objects with similar attributes are classified into data groups or sets. (Here we use the

conventional mathematical meaning of the term set.) Our concern is primarily with the management and control of data sets as distinct from the actual data instances.

From the standpoint of the user of a local information system, what parameters are important and what conditions must be met for the needed data sets and objects to be available when and where needed? From the standpoint of economics and overall system design, what are the information needs? Providing more data than is needed, faster availability of data, a higher level of security, sophisticated concurrency control for a static database, etc. can be very expensive. Clearly, the requirements are not uniform. They vary with the type of data and specific data sets and with the organizational and information system requirements. Most organizations are hierarchical. The corresponding information systems are often hierarchical. Consequently, it is sometimes convenient to describe requirements in the context of these hierarchies.

Some of the parameters important to the management and control of data are discussed below. The parameters are not necessarily independent or orthogonal.

• It helps to know whether a data object comes from a reference data set or a working data set. The data used during a calculation constitute a working data set during that calculation. The data obtained or referenced to initiate a calculation constitute a reference data set.

• Clearly, a working data set for one person may be a reference data set for another. Fast access to a working data set is generally required because its contents are the subject of immediate processing. An example is the large data set during reactor design calculations that contains a dynamic description of the state of a reactor core. On the other hand, in the distributed computer era, the focus is more on reference data sets, for which relatively slow access is adequate. The

Dept. \ Info.	Physical Facilities Systems: Prop. mgmnt.	Physical Facilities Systems: Space mgmnt.	Physical Facilities Systems: Prev. maint.	Physical Facilities Systems: Inven-tory	Physical Facilities Systems: White prints	Financial Systems: Work orders	Financial Systems: Purchase orders	Financial Systems: RPI payroll	Financial Systems: Accounting system	Academic Systems: Student Accounts	Academic Systems: Student records	Academic Systems: Alumni systems
Purchasing	M			R		R	Ⓜ		M			
Scheduling			Ⓜ	R	R	Ⓜ	R					
Accounts payable				R		M	M		M			
Receiving/ cen. stores				Ⓜ	R	M	M		R			
Risk mgmnt.	R	R	R	R	R	R	R					
Prop. mgmnt.	Ⓜ	R	R	R	R	R	R					
Housing	R	M	R	R	R	R	R		R	M	M	
Security/ safety	R	R	R	R	R	R	R				R	
Registrar		R		R	R	R	R		R	M	Ⓜ	M
Bursor				R		R	R	R	M	Ⓜ	M	
Admissions				R		R	R			M	M	
Medical				R		R	R				R	
Payroll				R		R	R	Ⓜ	M	M		
Personnel				R		R	R	M				
Academic campus	R	R		R	R	R	R		R		R	
Research accounting	R	R		R	R	R	R	M	M	R	R	
Dean of students				R	R	R	R	R	R	R	R	R
Planning	R	Ⓜ		R	Ⓜ	R	R					
Shops		R	M	R	R	M	R					
Comptroller	R			R		R	M	M	Ⓜ	M		
Cashier				R		R	R	M	M	R		
Alumni development				R		R	R				R	Ⓜ

R → read only → initiate transaction, inquiry
M → modify → selective information modification
Ⓜ → control → system controller

Figure 3. Information usage matrix.

It is important to establish standards, such as data dictionaries, that will be adhered to in describing data.

---

distributed computer or workstation occasionally needs new reference data, which it will process for some time. For example, a VLSI circuit designer working at a workstation needs the reference data on a specific chip, but will work on it locally for some time after the data are available. He can wait a reasonable length of time for the reference data. Another example is the downloading of recipes or control parameters to microprocessor control computers.

• Estimates should be made of the size of data sets and data objects. These estimates, when combined with response time requirements, make it possible to establish the data transmission rates needed. Such an analysis determines the communication rates required between a user or process and the source of the needed data. The designer should not be afraid to duplicate static data to reduce communication requirements. At the same time, be wary of allocating the working data sets required by a process over widely distributed computers. For example, performing relational database operations over widely-distributed tables can require the transfer of a great deal of data between computers.

• It is important to establish standards, such as data dictionaries, that will be adhered to in describing data.

The data descriptions are used whenever operations are performed on data. In too many organizations the interaction and integration of component information systems is limited by having similar data and activities designated by different names, by requests for data operations being described differently, and by having database structures so different that application programs written for one system cannot operate on data from another system. In more formal terms, it is important to establish or select a common data dictionary, collect in it all relevant knowledge, and then map this knowledge consistently into a data definition language (DDL) and a data manipulation language (DML).[9,10] Note that you can have a single data dictionary and multiple DBMs and DDLs. Despite the problems in implementing such an approach in a heterogeneous computer environment, the objective remains valid. However, satisfying the objective may require translation or interfacing tools.

• In a spatial sense, data needed for a specific task may be available locally or it may require remote access. If the information is distributed, the requirement may be for shared data or for derived data. For example, information about company policies usually represents shared data. On the other hand, a summary, by quantity and type of part, of material stored in a factory warehouse can be derived from local knowledge and detailed data about what is in that warehouse. The local people must know the location of a part. The person making requests of the warehouse only needs to know the summary data, which is very likely the only information made available outside the factory. In addition, data may be static or dynamic. In this example, the inventory is dynamic. There may be requirements that such data be updated and available on a defined time scale. The local detailed data and the derived global data must be concurrently updated in a consistent manner. More generally, dynamic data sets, and other data sets dependent on them, must be consistent throughout the system. Maintaining consistency can consume a large fraction of the computer and communications resources.

• Access rights to data are an important aspect of information system design. Included in access rights are the ability to read, append, and modify data, etc. Access rights may vary with the requester (individual, location, computer), service requested, and specific data set or object. Access rights vary over a distributed computer hierarchy and therefore need to be controlled at different points in the hierarchy.

• Similarly, data reliability is a significant design factor. More and more data are stored in machines without paper or manual backup. That data must be accurate, protected, and available. Protection must be provided in a hostile and malicious environment and provision made to guard against theft, modification, and system saturation. Encryption of selected data for communications and storage may need to be considered. Integrity and consistency of data must be maintained, and data services must be available and reliable.

• Data may be stored as an object, with no concern for content, or stored with linkages to semantically meaningful structures which will help with accessing relevant data, as in a library search. The former corresponds to placing a book on a shelf and requiring users to know the book's location. Automation of this type of storage is simple. Associative retrieval, on the the other hand, corresponds to visiting the library to find information on a given subject and finding the book through use of the cataloging and abstract system. This type of search is very difficult and requires additional effort at the times of data acquisition, data storage, and creation of the catalogs and abstracts. Furthermore, the latter are dynamic and must be modified as additional data are acquired.

The tradeoff between update and retrieval is a central problem of database management.

Considerations like those outlined above vary widely over any given system. Thus, to achieve effective control, objects and uses should be clustered into sets where, from a control standpoint, the members of a specific set may be treated alike. There will be large variations in the requirements over both the data sets and the user community.

Information system designers are generally aware of the factors and parameters discussed in the preceding paragraphs. To a large degree, these factors are considered intuitively during the design process. As distributed systems become more widespread and the need to integrate their components grows, it is increasingly desirable to have a more formal way of describing those attributes and parameters. Figure 4 suggests a way of recording in an organized way the data service requirements of a distributed system. At the very least, the preparation of such an analysis helps to organize the thinking of the design group. To the degree that computerized tools are available to handle the information, the approach provides many more services and permits the investigation of a large set of implementation alternatives.

In the data requirements matrix of Figure 4, the entries in the first column identify a data set or, if necessary, a data object. Entries in the second column describe the parameters of individual data sets important in managing and controlling the data set, not the contents of the data set. The third group of columns is divided into users, where the term user implies a single person or a class of individuals; a location; a computer application program; etc.; or any combination. The entries for a specific data set and user combination indicate the control parameters desired by the user and also which of the corresponding services can be provided or allowed within other constraints. At this point it may be neces-

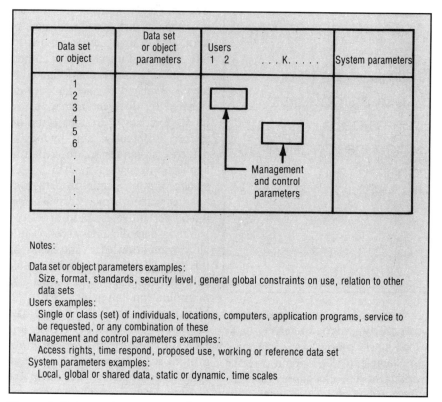

Notes:

Data set or object parameters examples:
  Size, format, standards, security level, general global constraints on use, relation to other data sets
Users examples:
  Single or class (set) of individuals, locations, computers, application programs, service to be requested, or any combination of these
Management and control parameters examples:
  Access rights, time respond, proposed use, working or reference data set
System parameters examples:
  Local, global or shared data, static or dynamic, time scales

Figure 4. Data requirements matrix.

sary to resolve any differences that arise between user desires and global constraints in the second column. A row entry in the fourth column considers all user entries in that row and summarizes the system parameters applicable to the data set represented by that row. At this stage it may be necessary to resolve inconsistencies in system parameters that result from conflicts between user desires. Inconsistencies in design can be managed by eventual definition of subsets of information and transformations of such information. To make such definitions feasible, no design information that defines these subsets should be lost in the process of conflict resolution.[11]

Within its original design structure or architecture, an information system evolves over a long period of time. Often assumed constraints can later be easily managed by improved technology; if so, all of the original design information may be needed.

At a later point it will be necessary to consider the impact of cost versus performance tradeoffs in the design. These tradeoffs will impact the entries in the third column and perhaps modify them. Clearly, Figure 4 suggests a procedure to help the engineer in the design process. If applied to existing systems, the procedure points out problem areas and areas needing attention when extending those systems.

We have touched on a comprehensive method of describing the data services required in an information system. As noted in the earlier discussion of Figures 1 and 2, we expect that those services will be distributed throughout the information systems hierarchy. Implicit in such a distribution is the desirability of distributing the data management and control functions indicated in Figure 4.

The discussion in this section has been in the context of large distributed information systems. Today we have

> Under practical implementation pressures, designers have not followed given methodologies.

neither the basic knowledge nor the computerized tools to fully apply the suggested methodology to entire large systems. However, the philosophy already applies to smaller systems and to computers themselves. In fact, computer architectures with access control lists, passwords, data dictionaries, etc., have already addressed some of the requirements.

Computers and information systems are becoming more distributed. At the same time, the integration and coordination of the individual information systems and computers in an organization are becoming more of a necessity. This introduces new requirements, design parameters, and tradeoffs. These considerations affect system issues ranging from the architecture of specific computers to the architecture of overall information systems. A comprehensive framework can provide a structure and standards that, if adhered to, make it possible to evolve systems from the bottom up, yet have those systems fit into an evolving global structure. Now is an opportune time to begin establishing methods supporting the collection and recording of detailed data requirements along the lines mentioned above. At the same time, we must be realistic, create the necessary tools, and first formulate requirements carefully at a component level. The ability to handle really large-scale projects comes with time. To reach that goal we must develop computerized engineering support systems.

In a sense, the steps we present are the steps a system designer would take naturally in dealing with small systems. They overlap concepts promul-

gated by papers and commercial consulting bureaus. Nonetheless, under practical implementation pressures, and in overall information systems on the scale of an entire business or university, designers have not followed given methodologies. As a result, problems exist in integrating the component subsystems. Certain industrial and business groups have carefully implemented large information systems, but the average leaves much to be desired.

A university as an example of information system architecture

For an example of a complex information system, consider a typical university campus a few years from now. A large industrial site or a governmental facility would do equally well. Because the example is a projection into the future, it utilizes technology and products, particularly in communications, just becoming available today (although they will be in widespread use a few years from now).

We assume that the use of computers and information systems is pervasive and includes administrative, instructional, and research work. Furthermore, the computers themselves are distributed throughout the campus in a hierarchical structure. We further assume that the data services analysis, discussed in an earlier section, has been at least partially completed. Pragmatically, however, many of the details of that analysis, and the action taken, on this time scale would be based on intuitive estimates of the university staff.

As might be expected, the campus computer complex includes a computing center that contains one or more large-scale computers, data storage facilities, and special purpose computers. (Supercomputers like the Cray II, large database machines, and so forth, are considered special-

purpose computers.) The computing center also contains a modern voice and data PBX, or private branch exchange electronic switch.[12,13] Scattered throughout the campus are minicomputers, some in clusters; process control and data collection machines; personal computers; word processors; workstations; etc. Information systems are scattered over these machines, as are the data essential to the overall operations of the university.

When the university made the decision to install a voice and data PBX, the responsibility for campus-wide voice and data communications was placed in one organizational component, Information Technology Services, reporting to the vice president of academic affairs. Earlier voice communications had been assigned to the administrative sector and given to those concerned with buildings and grounds. Those with the need and, pragmatically, those concerned with computers exercised responsibility for data communications. The decision to consolidate the responsibility for voice and data communications was taken because prior industrial and university experience indicated that this was almost a prerequisite for the successful cost-effective installation of a modern voice and data PBX. Decision makers assigned overall responsibility to the academic sector in order to better manage the dynamic high technology represented by the planned communication system and to insure that proper emphasis was given to serving academic needs. They realized that at a later date, and as the technology matured, it might be appropriate to shift the responsibility to the vice president of administration. Strictly speaking, a management issue of this type represents neither technology nor research. The resolution of this issue, however, may be a key to properly addressing the technical problems associated with the installation of a modern communications network, and does represent engineering.

Information Technology Services also received responsibility for the cen-

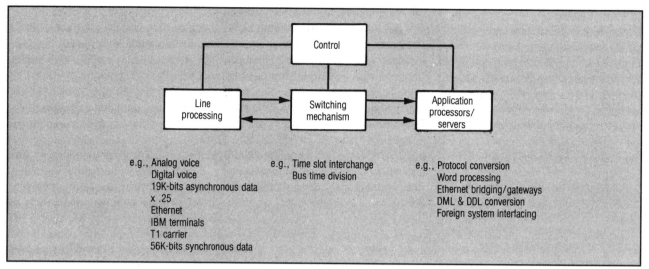

Figure 5. Private branch exchange (PBX) concepts.

tral computer complex and must evolve a strategy to meet long-term, campus-wide data-service needs. It was recognized at the very beginning that the data-service needs of distributed information systems would determine the requirements of the communications network.

• Information from a data services matrix such as that shown in Figure 4 was used to estimate data traffic requirements. It was determined that large working data sets would be concentrated in small systems such as workstations and workstation clusters, the central computer complex, and in some cases in computers associated with the control of experiments. Estimates indicated that access to reference data sets would be widespread, but that the expected data rates would be relatively low, for example below 100 Kbps.

• Data rate requirements seemed to fall into three regions: up to 100 Kbps; the region around 2 Mbps; and 50 to 100 Mbps. It appeared that the requirements in the first two categories are met by modern PBX technology utilizing multiple twisted-pair wiring. Requirements in the latter category require coaxial cable or fiber optics.

• Based on the above findings, the campus-wide core voice and data highway system would be based on a voice

and data PBX and the standard wiring installed concurrently with that PBX. In the communications industry, such wiring is commonly referred to as the wiring plant. For a variety of reasons, installing a PBX to replace central office services such as Centrex[14] almost always involves a new wiring plant. The cost of that wiring plant is justified by savings in telephone expenses. The incremental cost of adding additional wires for data services is small. The wiring plant design for the university specified six twisted pairs of wire to each office or work site. This configuration satisfies the requirements in the first two data-rate categories and provides the flexibility of terminal services. The use of other communications technology in local areas is expected. The decision to emphasize the PBX approach rested primarily on traffic estimates and cost, but security considerations also played a part. The cost avoidance associated with a reduced need for separate LANs proved significant.

The capabilities of modern PBXs are central to the architecture of the overall computer hierarchy. Figure 5 summarizes the salient features of combined voice and data PBXs coming on the market; see, for example, Northern Telecom's Meridian[15-17] and Rolm's CBXII.[18] As it is not the pur-

pose of this article to go into the details of PBX architecture, the figure takes some liberties with regard to the details of design. For example, the figure does not specify the switching mechanism. However, the services provided by the switch, as shown in Figures 5 and 6, typify what will be available. The data rates in the 2-Mbps region assume bus switching. Some additional operational properties and architectural features of the PBX are given below.

• There are microprocessors and minicomputers internal to the switch, which presumably exists in a controlled and limited-access environment. Consequently, a user of the communications system does not have access either to the software or to the mini- and microcomputers internal to the switch.

• The action taken on the inputs from the various lines to the outside world, or line processing, can come under microprocessor control on a per-line basis. Thus, the virtual channel properties available at a particular port can be strictly controlled. Control of access to equipment on a specific port can consequently take place on the basis of the originating port and vary with that port.

• Although the internal switching may occur on a time-division broadband bus basis, operating say at 1 Gbps, the bus is not a contention bus. Time slot assignments can be dynamic as assigned by the control processor. As indicated above, limits on virtual channels can be predefined on a per-port basis. From a security standpoint, the advantages over a broadcast system such as Ethernet are obvious. Superficially, one might think a centralized switch less reliable than a more distributed LAN broadcast network.

However, the distributed nature of the primary propagation path of the LAN is a disadvantage. Well-intentioned or malicious persons with access to the cable or port interfaces of the LAN can short, cut, overload, or jam the cable. For example, a shorted cable means the system is down; a shorted port on a PBX means that only that part of the communications system defined by the window on the port is down. In the case of the PBX, the

critical components of the communications network are at a controlled, centralized point. In addition, switches are designed for reliability; they utilize a great deal of redundant hardware and software. The experience with central office equipment is well documented[19,20] and typifies what can be expected of a modern PBX. Downtimes of around two hours in 40 years are common in the field. Electronic switches that meet communication industry standards and practice prove very reliable.

• Note that the application processors with access to the high-speed switching mechanism could perform many data service functions, as indicated by the examples given in Figure 5. Many mini- and microcomputer manufacturers are developing architectures based on a very high-speed parallel bus structure with a significant number of special-purpose, functional mini- or microprocessors attached to the bus. Bell[21] gives an excellent overview of the potential of coupling a large number of microprocessors through such a communications facility. Next-generation PBXs are well on the way to utilizing, internal to the switch, the technology described by Bell. With many functional processors on a very high-speed bus, the processors provide reliable centralized data services along the lines described here. In such a system, centralized data services are provided at the most central point of the distributed computer system, namely, the electronic switch.

• A comment on PBX throughput or switch bandwidth is in order. One can expect bandwidths measured in gigabits per second. Consequently, the PBX is unlikely to constitute a bottleneck in communications. For bandwidths of this order, the PBX is frankly more attractive than a network of interconnected LANs of comparable network connectivity and throughput.

Figure 6 shows the overall complex of campus computers. We should stress that this is not the only architecture possible for a campus environ-

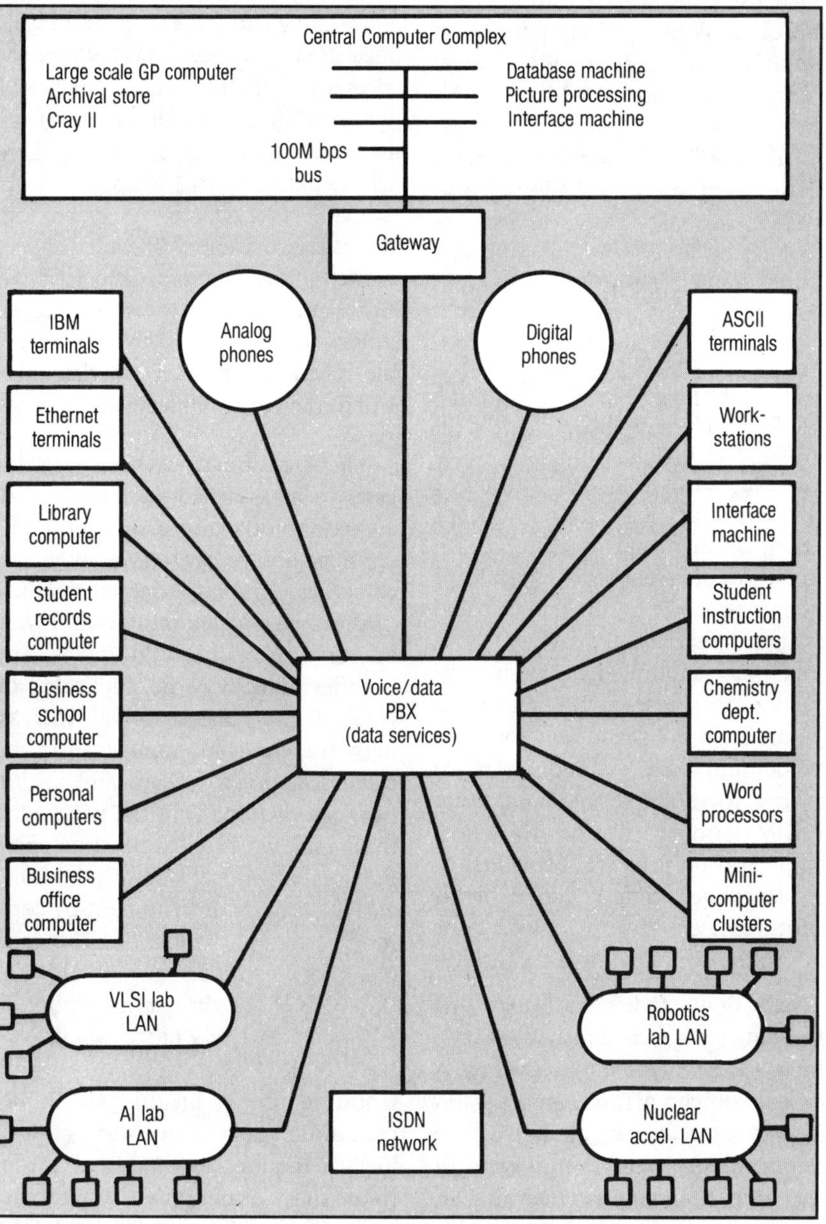

Figure 6. Campus computer system hierarchy.

ment, but that it seemed appropriate. To a large degree, the configuration is self-evident. The comments given below merely emphasize a few salient design decisions.

• The interfacing to foreign systems was considered a major problem. The university decided that to the degree possible the software running on the distributed computers would be left intact. Instead of changing vendor-supplied software, special interfacing machines and associated software would handle the interfacing between systems. Protocol converters and electronic mail bridges provide simple examples of interface machines. Interface machines can be actual hardware or in some cases application programs within a general-purpose machine. In Figure 6, interface machines lie at three levels: the central computer complex, external to the PBX, and internal to the PBX. The overall objective is to remove the problem of interfacing different data worlds from the individual user computers and address it as part of centralized data services.

• The services available at the central computer complex deal with large working data sets that must interact. Therefore, a 100-Mbps communications channel is specified and a gateway indicated to the PBX. Additional gateways and fiber optic links could be established to other points as needed, for example, to the nuclear accelerator for real-time data capture and analysis of experiments.

• Major information systems are developed on their own local computers as appropriate. Any decision should rely on a data matrix analysis and such factors as whether data requirements are largely local. For example, the data on library operations are largely localized to that library. Consequently, a local dedicated minicomputer provides a reasonable solution. On the other hand, another item in the matrix, security, can in some settings be a prime consideration. To allow strict control of access,

student academic records are best placed on a dedicated minicomputer and connected to a PBX port addressable only from specific terminals and with authorized passwords.

• The VLSI, robotics, and AI laboratories involve groups of people who share a great deal of semi-local data. Within those groups exist essentially no access control problems. Each laboratory has its own local area network for the transfer of data within that laboratory. The local area networks are bridged through the PBX, which exercises appropriate gateway control. Any authorized person on campus can address the ports on these LANs through virtual 2-Mbps LANs made available at a switch port. Note that the services seen by authorized persons are those of a 2-Mbps LAN, although in reality those services are provided by a very tightly-controlled window to a 1-Gbps noncontention bus or LAN.

Also note that the six twisted pairs per office play a significant role in the economics of the architecture shown. Analog and digital phones differ in cost. Line cards that can transmit 2 Mbps cost much more than 19.6 Kbps asynchronous cards. Although in some cases different services could be put on one pair (e.g., digital voice and 56-Kbps digital data), this may not be economical. Multiple pairs permit the selection on a case-by-case and port-by-port basis of an economic solution. In addition, pairs suit non-switched services, for example, the connection of IBM terminals or PCs to a host computer. Line drivers to provide such services are becoming available. In this regard, it is convenient to locate the PBX in the central computing facility.

Data flow studies indicated that most data services in a distributed system would be satisfied by 100 Kbps. A workstation can afford to wait a few seconds for reference data, which it then processes over a long period of time. Within a campus environment, there is essentially no limit on the length of a twisted pair that will meet

the 100-Kbps performance requirement. In the case of 2-Mbps services, a wiring limit forces devices to be within roughly 2000 feet of a switch port. However, although not shown, it is possible to distribute key parts of a switch; the requirement then limits a device to within 2000 feet of a distributed part of the switch.

It is important in a case like this to pick an architecture that provides alternatives in implementation and growth that respond to needs and technology that are to some degree uncertain. Thus, the mix of "local" local area networks and LAN-type services through the switch can be adjusted as dictated by the environment. Because of the pervasiveness of the wiring plant, up to 1 Mbps should be available everywhere. As technology drives the division of storage between workstations, servers, and archival stores, the network can adjust accordingly, and so forth. The goal: a flexible information system environment within the core architecture.

The discussion so far has treated the campus as a closed system. This of course is not realistic. For example, consider library operations, mentioned earlier. To a large degree members of the university community will want access to on-line databases and libraries unlikely to be duplicated on campus. Staff members will increasingly use electronic mail to their colleagues at other colleges and institutions. In the long run, the window to the outside world will be the Integrated Services Data Networks, or ISDNs currently under development by common carriers[22] worldwide. The campus bridge or window will be through the PBX[23] as shown in Figure 6. Although relatively narrow-band versions of ISDN services are being introduced today, meaningful implementation on a nationwide basis is likely to require ten years. In the meantime, the campus environment described is building a local set of integrated services, and in a way that will effectively couple to ISDN and the outside world.

This example has sketched an information system architecture that is data driven. Clearly, as far as the physical layout of such a system (for example, what is allocated to what location), the decisions required rely on data requirements and data service capabilities. In essence, data drive the entire system. The challenge of data engineering is the design and implementation of systems that provide the data services needed at all levels of the overall system. Thus, the scope of data engineering ranges from the details of database design on an individual computer to the communications system coupling the computers in the overall system.

It is generally understood that we are well into an era of distributed computing and that this trend will continue. To a large degree, we expect that, with regard to both hardware and software, distributed computer complexes will continue to be heterogeneous. Data services, the glue that holds together such complexes, will be the primary central service, although many of those services may themselves be distributed.

Specifically, we are concerned with information systems and computers that are distributed over a number of locations and yet must work together. In practice, most systems are special cases of this general model. It is important that we understand the general model and the engineering guidelines and practices that will support the development of successful systems within that global framework. Those same practices and guidelines when applied in the engi-neering of component information systems make it more likely that the components will work well together. This is particularly important in light of the trend for information system development itself to become distributed. □

References

1. R.L. Shuey, "Industry and Computer," *IEEE Trans. on Manufacturing Tech.*, Vol. MFT-4, No. 2, Dec. 1975, pp. 37-42.

2. G. Wiederhold, "Knowledge and Database Management," *IEEE Software*, Vol. 1, No. 1, Jan. 1984, pp. 63-73.

3. A.S. Tanenbaum, *Computer Networks*, Prentice Hall, 1981.

4. H. Zimmermann, "On Protocol Engineering," *Information Processing 83: Proc. IFIP 9th World Computer Congress*, North Holland, 1983.

5. L.G. Anderson, D.C. Dowden, H.H. So, and M.D. Soneru, "The Uncommon Family Of 5ESS Switches Has A Lot In Common," AT&T Bell Labs Record, Nov. 1983, pp. 4-10.

6. W.S. Hayward Jr., "The 5ESS Switching System," *AT&T Tech. J.*, Vol. 64, No. 6, part 2, July-Aug. 1985.

7. "Program Controlled Networks," *BSTJ*, Vol. 61, No. 7, part 3, Sept. 1982.

8. A.J. Bunshaft, "A View Of Administrative Information Flow and Usage: A Report Submitted to Rensselaer Polytechnic Institute," Sept. 1, 1983.

9. C.J. Date, *An Introduction To Database Systems*, 3d ed., Addison-Wesley, 1982.

10. E.B. Fernandes, R.C. Summers, and C. Wook, *Data Security and Integrity*, Addison-Wesley, 1981.

11. R. ElMasri and G. Wiederhold, "Database Model Integration Using the Structural Model," *Proc. ACM-SIGMOD Conf.*, ed. Bernstein, Boston, MA, June 1979, pp. 191-198.

12. J.C. McDonald, *Fundamentals of Digital Switching*, Plenum Press, 1983.

13. Wurzburg and S. Kelly, "PBX-Based LANs: Lower Cost Per Terminal Connection," *Computer Design*, Feb. 1984, pp. 191-199.

14. A.E. Joel, "A History of Engineering Science in the Bell System: Switching Technology (1925-1975)," Bell Telephone Labs, 1982.

15. A. Boleda, D. Lasker, and G. Stewart, "The Impact of New Technologies on Northern Telecoms's Office Communications Architecture," *ICC Conf. Record*, 1985, pp. 379-384.

16. T. Purdy, D. Thorsland, and N. Witchlow, "Meridian SL-1 Messaging: An Integrated Messaging Service," *2d Int'l Symp. Computer Message Systems*, Wash., DC, Sept. 5-7, 1985.

17. A. Boleda and D. Lasker, "The Architecture of Meridian SL Integrated Services Networks," *Telesis*, Vol. 12, No. 2, 1985, pp. 26-33.

18. J. M. Kasson and H. W. Johnson, "The CBX II Switching Architecture," *IEEE J. Selected Areas in Communications*, Vol. SAC-3, July 1985, pp. 555-560.

19. R. W. Foster, "NTC Field Experience on No. 1/1A ESS," *NTC Record*, 1981, pp. A6.5.1-4.

20. P.K. Giloth, "Reliability and Performance Assurance of the 4ESS Digital Switch," *ICC Conf. Record*, 1985, pp. 625-630.

21. C.G. Bell, "Multis: A New Class of Multiprocessor Computers," *Science*, Vol. 228, No. 26, Apr. 1985, pp. 462-467.

22. I. Dorros, "ISDN," *IEEE Communications*, March 1981, pp. 16.

23. J.L. Neigh, "ISDN in a PBX Environment," *ICC Conf. Record*, 1985, pp. 252-255.

HETEROGENEOUS COMPUTING ENVIRONMENTS: REPORT ON THE ACM SIGOPS WORKSHOP ON ACCOMMODATING HETEROGENEITY*

The ACM SIGOPS Workshop on Accommodating Heterogeneity was conducted in December 1985 in Eastbound, Wash., as a forum for an international group of fifty researchers to discuss the technical issues surrounding heterogeneous computing environments.

DAVID NOTKIN, NORMAN HUTCHINSON, JAN SANISLO, and MICHAEL SCHWARTZ

INTRODUCTION

A heterogeneous computing environment consists of interconnected sets of dissimilar hardware or software systems. Because of the diversity, interconnecting systems is far more difficult in heterogeneous environments than in homogeneous environments, where each system is based on the same, or closely related, hardware and software. Examples of heterogeneous environments include: a network with 3 VAXes, 16 SUNs, and 1 Symbolics LISP machine; a network with 1 DEC-2060, 1 IBM-4341, and 20 IBM PC-ATs; a network with 12 Xerox D-Machines, 6 of which are running Interlisp and 6 of which are running XDE. In contrast, examples of homogeneous environments include: a network of Macintoshes linked together with AppleTalk; a network of Micro-VAXes running Ultrix; a network of SUNs running UNIX and NFS; a network running Eden [1]; a network running Locus [12].

Heterogeneity is often unavoidable. It occurs as evolving needs and resources lead to the acquisition or development of diverse hardware and software. As a computing environment evolves, there is a tension between retaining homogeneity and acquiring new types of systems. Since some efforts are best conducted on systems different from those already available, this tension must at times be resolved in favor of heterogeneity. For example, research on constraint-based animation may be easier to perform on a Smalltalk engine than on a more conventional workstation environment.

Heterogeneity can be approached in many ways; each style arises from a specific set of underlying assumptions. Examples: Should a particular system characteristic, such as distribution, be hidden? Should a low-level facility, such as remote procedure call (RPC), be provided in all systems? Is a particular feature, such as transparent network file access, worth the added development cost? How much heterogeneity does the style anticipate? Different assumptions appropriate for each style of heterogeneity lead to different technical issues and problems.

Problems due to heterogeneity arise in several specific areas:

* A preliminary version of this report appeared in *Operating Systems Review* 20, 2 (Apr. 1986). 9–24, and also as Technical Report 86-02-01, Department of Computer Science. University of Washington (Feb. 1986). The report printed here is not a transcript: the order of the discussions has been changed, remarks have been paraphrased, and contents have been condensed. However, an attempt to remain faithful to the proceedings has been made.

Support for preparation of this report was provided in part by NSF grant DCR-8420945.

Interconnection.   How should heterogeneous systems communicate? Is message passing or remote procedure call the more suitable communication paradigm? How can systems and languages with different data representations (such as byte-ordering or record layouts) be accommodated?

Filing.   What kind of file system is needed in a heterogeneous environment? Should the file system support typing? When heterogeneous systems share data through a file system, where are the required translations done?

Authentication.   How is authentication supported in a heterogeneous environment? What are the sources of distrust and diversity in such an environment? How is local system autonomy over authentication provided in heterogeneous environments?

Naming.   How is naming provided in heterogeneous systems? What objects can be named across systems? How are they named? How does the environment evolve as new systems and naming approaches are incorporated?

User Interfaces.   How are varied user interfaces accommodated and shared between heterogeneous systems? Do you port an application? Do you provide a veneer so that it appears that an application is running on another machine? Do you split the user interface from the basic application and run these on separate systems?

STYLES OF HETEROGENEITY

There is not a single, correct way to address the problems of heterogeneity. Instead, there are many possible different styles, each driven by its own set of underlying assumptions and objectives. During the Workshop we identified basic assumptions and approaches participants use in their work. Without question, there are other styles of heterogeneity that were not represented by participants at the Workshop and are therefore not presented here.

Loose Integration Through Network Services

Accommodating heterogenous computer systems in this style is motivated by an environment of a large number of system types and a small number of instances of some of these types. For example, such an environment might have VAXes and SUNs running UNIX, one or two Symbolics LISP machines, and a number of prototypes of special purpose architectures. Here, the current cost of accommodating new systems is great.

A group at the University of Washington is investigating accommodating this style of heterogeneity [4]. Their approach to these problems is to reduce the cost of introducing a system and allowing it to use basic facilities (RPC, naming, and authentication) and services (filing, mail, printing, and remote computation). In general, transparent use of these facilities and services is not necessary in this approach, although it would be possible in cases where both economics and source code availability permit. Instead, the approach is to construct an environment based on simple clients and sophisticated servers. It should be inexpensive to develop a new client to take advantage of existing servers.

Sharing Among Different Languages Cultures

A second style of accommodating heterogeneity is based on a desire to share programs written in radically different programming languages, to increase the reuse of programs among groups of research programmers with different computing cultures, such as LISP and CLU. In particular, one culture's programs should be able to invoke another culture's programs in a transparent manner. This style expects a large number of instances of each system type. Hence, the effort spent on accommodating each system type can be greater than in the loose style of integration previously described.

A group at the Laboratory for Computer Science (LCS) at MIT is studying this style of accommodation. Their approach relies on two components: an invocation mechanism and a set of interfaces defining shared services. For invocation, the LCS group is considering an RPC facility that supports caller-initiated aborts, procedure parameters and callback, exception handling, failure semantics, atomicity, abstract types as parameters, a definition language for types and program interfaces, and authentication. For the second component, the LCS group plans to include name servers, object stores, archival stores, an authentication server, and a facility for cataloging programs, interface stubs, and abstract data types. This catalog contains converters and checkers in addition to object definitions.

Front-Ends for Multiple, Existing Systems

Another style of accommodating heterogeneity considers an environment in which there are multiple, existing systems over which there is no control and that cannot be changed, for example, using PCs to access an existing corporate database. By adding an understanding of the database to the PCs (which can be changed), the systems will be able to accommodate the database in the PC environment. A "protocol generator" for user interfaces might help in this style. Dave Reed of Lotus Development Corporation introduced this style at the Workshop.

Transparent Operating System Bridges

This style arises in an environment of several different types of workstations sharing resources via a common set of network backbone machines (e.g., a collection of PC-DOS machines, Macintoshes, and UNIX workstations served by a backbone of UNIX or Locus machines [12]). The capability of each type of workstation is extended by transparent access to remote resources, but the remote resources appear to be those of each particular workstation, rather than necessitating users of a particular type of workstation to understand the properties of the backbone machines. At the same time, the workstation user should be able to take advantage of the backbone machine's unique capabilities whenever desired.

The Distributed Systems Laboratory at UCLA is pursuing accommodating heterogeneity through transparent operating system bridges (TOSB). These objectives are achieved by intercepting operating system calls on the local system and passing appropriate calls to a server process on the remote system for fulfillment. Transparent access to remote resources implies that programs designed for a particular workstation environment can take advantage of remote resources without program modification. The most important case is transparent access to a remote file system; however, transparent operating system bridges can support a spectrum of services including local programs directly accessing remote files, local programs invoking remote processes, communication between local and remote processes, and remote processes directly accessing local files. There are some general principles for constructing a TOSB, but each pair of operating systems provides unique challenges, and solutions for them do not tend to be very general. Thus, the TOSB approach is best suited to environments with relatively few different types of operating systems.

Coherence

Coherence carefully defines a layer of software so as to enforce uniformity and permit implementation on diverse hardware to accommodate heterogeneity. Because the costs of providing coherence are great, coherence is feasible only in environments with a small number of system types with a large number of instances of each type. This style has been adopted in some instructional environments.

CMU's ITC project [8] and MIT's Project Athena [2, 6] exhibit coherence most clearly. In the ITC project, coherence is primarily at the level of the logically centralized file service. In Project Athena, coherence is primarily at the applications programming interface. Both projects rely on a uniform underlying operating system, UNIX, and on their window systems, each local products.

BASIC TOPICS IN HETEROGENEITY

The bulk of the sessions focused on specific areas that must be considered when dealing with heterogeneity. Distilled discussions on these topics—interconnection, filing, authentication, naming, and user interfaces—follow.

Interconnection

ISO transport was too low a focus. The discussion of interconnection of heterogeneous systems gravitated to a discussion of the proper way for processes running on different nodes to communicate. The two basic mechanisms for program communication, *message passing* and *remote procedure call* (RPC), were discussed. Message passing consists of passing a message asynchronously from one process to another, such that both the sending and receiving processes proceed concurrently. RPC, as defined by Birrell and Nelson [3, 10], provides semantics across a network that are nearly identical to those of procedure call in a standard programming language: the RPC is synchronous, the caller blocks until a reply is received or the call is aborted. In message passing, the data usually appear to the system as a stream of bytes, while in RPC the data have some structure and are type-checked. The sending or calling process is generally called the *client*; the receiving or called process is generally called the *server*.

Figure 1 illustrates how RPC usually works. The client is written as if it called the server directly using conventional procedure call mechanisms. To simulate this relationship across the network boundary (represented by the striped line down the center), two *stubs* are needed. The client stub's interface is identical to that of the server; the server stub's interface is identical to the client's. The client stub is responsible for translating the arguments into a suitable format for transmission over the network and also for passing the converted arguments to the transport mechanism. The server stub, conversely, is responsible for receiving the arguments from the transport mechanism and converting the arguments into the server's format. Multiple calls may take place between the stubs and the transport mechanisms, depending on the actual RPC implementation. Just as procedures must be linked before they can call one another, it is necessary to *bind* clients and servers together before RPC can take place.

Although the synchronous nature of RPC is suitable for many applications, a mechanism is needed to permit concurrent execution. *Light-weight processes* (LWPs), which permit a single program to define multiple threads of control, are the conventional solution. LWPs share a single address space, allowing context swaps between LWPs to be done much more quickly than traditional process swapping. Combining RPC and LWPs is natural: each remote call is embedded in its own LWP and when that call blocks, another LWP is scheduled. Hence, threads of control in both the calling and called process are active.

One point of view was that the RPC paradigm provides an appropriate level of abstraction for communicating between programs across nodes. Given this strict definition of RPC, the question became: "Are these semantics sufficient?" The answer was, in general, yes. However, there are times when a more flexible model of communication is mandatory. Examples of such instances are asynchronous operation when LWPs are not available, and a "no-reply" option when the reply would contain essentially no information. For instance, when a display is updated, the program sending the data need not wait for a reply from the output unit. There was some discussion as to whether pure semantics could be maintained given that light-weight processes were available. The answer was a qualified yes; however, performance will probably be reduced in "no-reply" situations.

The discussion of RPC as an acceptable communication paradigm then shifted to problems directly associated with heterogeneity. Several areas that require flexibility due to heterogeneity were identified. Transport protocols, such as TCP and XNS, differ across networks; how is it decided which protocol client and server processes will speak? Data representations, such as byte-ordering and the layout of structured data, differ from machine to machine and compiler to compiler; how are the necessary transformations identified and applied? Semantics and type systems vary from language to language; how can RPC semantics be maintained between languages that are dissimilar in this regard?

First consider data representation. There are at least three ways to select a data representation for transport. First, define and use a single standard representation. Second, send the data and require the receiving side to understand it. Third, negotiate a representation at bind time (i.e., when a specific client and server first decide to communicate). For transport protocols, variations of the first and third options are possible (the second is not possible for transport since a common transport is required to support the initiating conversation).

The problem with the single-standard approach is the potential for unnecessary inefficiency. The most obvious example is two systems with the same byte-ordering would be required to communicate by swapping and then unswapping bytes if their mutual byte-ordering differed from the standard. Experience with the DEC/SRC RPC system demonstrated the potential for selecting transport protocols and data

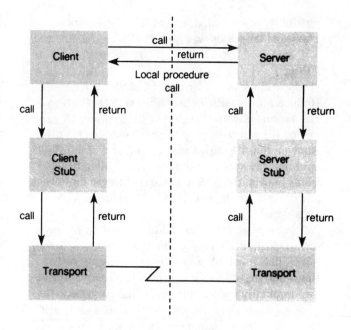

FIGURE 1. Remote Procedure Call

representations (within a limited domain) at bind time.

The relationship between efficiency and uniformity, with respect to data representation, was discussed at length. On one hand, some people were willing to accept a degree of ineffciency in the area of data representation as the price of simplicity. Bill Joy of SUN contended that the work required to minimize byte-swapping, for instance, is of little benefit since only as little as 5 percent of run-time is spent filling in data packets. On the other hand, in many cases it may be possible to reduce these costs quite easily.

The heterogeneity imposed by varying semantic and type models is usually addressed through the use of stubs to make RPC look like conventional procedure call, as shown in Figure 1. Stubs can be quite complex as they are usually responsible for packaging data and communicating with the transport layer. To relieve the user from writing complex stubs, stub generators are often provided with RPC systems. Although stub generation usually accounts for syntactic differences among languages, making the semantics compatible with all existing languages is at best difficult, and making them compatible with yet-to-be-developed languages is impossible.

Interface description languages (IDLs) are often a basis for generating stubs [7, 13]. Is it possible to define and use a single IDL? The adoption of a single IDL does not preclude hand-coding of stubs for particular applications or esoteric requirements. The possibility of several classes of IDLs for separate classes of languages was raised.

Filing

Andrew Black of the University of Washington introduced filing with a chart (Figure 2) that categorized some existing distributed file systems. (A survey on distributed file systems appears in [11].) He showed that the design space has many dimensions and that file system designers made different decisions in each dimension. Several of these dimensions with respect to the effects of heterogeneity were considered.

A large part of the discussion focused on file properties, particularly typing. On one hand, at a certain level, files are all the same "type"—simply collections of bytes or blocks. On the other hand, all files are implicitly typed in the sense that programs that access a file make assumptions about the nature of the data. If these assumptions are wrong, the data may be misinterpreted: this is a type error. If files are typed, then such an error can be detected before it leads to a rubble of bits.

The UNIX file system is an interesting study of file typing. The UNIX abstraction of an uninterpreted sequence of bytes is a great simplification; programmers must provide any further abstractions at a higher level. This abstraction makes some tasks easier but others harder. For instance, UNIX records must be constructed and shared by unenforced convention. On the other hand, generic utilities are easily written since there is only one file type.

Typing is more of an issue in a heterogeneous environment because different machines use different data formats, for example, different character codings and byte orders. Another reason is simply a larger number of file structures. If a file is typed, the file system can do the appropriate data conversion; if not, the client must do its own conversion. Another option is to provide self-describing data types, that is, objects that carry their type information with them. The advantage is that only the applications that deal with a specific type need to know about the type.

The relationship between file typing and the data representation problems of RPC were discussed. Files can be viewed as providing "time-shifted" communication, a little like RPC over a delay line. Because the reader and writer do not communicate with each other directly, the file system should have the responsibility of communicating the information an RPC system would exchange at bind time, and of typing the data in the same way an RPC system might. This can be achieved either by translating the file contents into a common intermediate format, or by recording the data in the sender's format and recording explicit formatting information.

The degree to which files are shared affects design decisions in a file system. To make these decisions properly, it must be determined whether the sharing supported by a file system is actual or just potential. In Multics, there is virtually no short-term sharing. Measuring sharing patterns before making decisions was suggested. Such measurements may be deceptive, however, since the infrequency of actual sharing does not imply a lack of need of actual sharing.

Several other questions were raised and briefly addressed. Files are usually addressed by name; how can heterogeneous file systems conform with diverse naming systems? What happens when applications demand more from a remote file system (e.g., locking and record access) than the remote system can provide? Is the notion of "file" too restrictive for the diverse environment we anticipate? (Although an object-oriented approach was suggested as more profitable, the fact remains that existing file systems are not, for the most part, object-oriented.)

Dave Reed of Lotus pointed out an anomaly. There is great diversity in file systems, but the Andrew system [8], in an approach shared by many other efforts, uses a single file system of its own design as the "glue" that connects heterogeneous components. This scheme relies on *replacing* the existing file systems with the new "glue" file system. But what is to be done at the next level up, when the Andrew file system needs to be connected to other similar systems? Presumably, at this level, we are not prepared to discard the file systems and build a new system that acts as "superglue." We may therefore be forced to provide remote access to a number of existing file systems rather than a single common file service where a file must live if it is to be shared.

Authentication

Discussions of authentication and authorization in heterogeneous computer systems focused on classes of problems rather than on specific authentication mechanisms. Three broad problem areas were covered: (1) sources of distrust and diversity with respect to authentication; (2) identifying the actual function of authentication and authorization systems; (3) accommodating the need for local system autonomy within global authentication environments.

Sources of distrust in heterogeneous systems include networks, gateways, hardware, operating systems, run-time systems, application programs, students, fellow researchers, family, and yourself. Sources of diversity include hardware (especially encryption support), programming environments, the

	Read Only?	Universal/FSF?	Transparent Access	Location Independent Names	Replication	Caching	Fetch Grain
Sesame	yes	Universal w/i Spice FSF for world	yes w/i Spice no for world	file id	optional	whole file	pages
IBIS	no, Unix locks	Universal	yes (library)	no, planned	on demand	yes	pages
Tilde	no, Unix locks	Universal	yes	at tree level	no	yes	pages
Xerox IFS	no (transactions added)	FSF	n/a	no	no (added)	n/a	pages and streams
Cedar	yes	FSF	yes	no	no	whole file	whole file
Sun NFS	no, no locks	FSF, but every Sun w/s can be FS	yes	no	no	no	pages
Vice/Virtue	no, locks	FSF	yes	file id	limited	yes, invalidate on read (now write)	file
Juniper (XDFS)	no, transactions	FSF	n/a	no	no		
Alpine	transactions	FSF	n/a	yes	n/a	no	n/a
Apollo	no, timestamp version consistency	Universal	yes	file id	no	V.M. Cache	pages
Glasser/Ungar	yes (really)	Universal	yes	no	no	no	pages
Eden	no, transactions	Universal w/i Eden	access from Eden only	file capa	yes	no	invocation
Amoeba	no, optimistic CC and locks	FSF	yes (through rose colored glasses)	file capa	yes	pages	var size pages
Roe	no, locks	FSF, stored on clients	no	yes	yes	migration	stream
8th Edn NFS	no, no locks	Universal w/i Unix	yes	no	no	no	stream
Locus	no, Unix locks	Universal	yes	yes	optional	pages	pages

The columns have the following meanings:

Read Only?   Are files read only (yes) or overwritable (no). If no, what mechanism is used to prevent conflicting writes?

Universal/FSF?   Does the file service provide universal access to files in existing file systems, or does it provide a new kind of file (a File Server File, FSF) that must be created explicitly?

Transparent Access.   Do the host operating systems hide the difference between accessing the local and distributed file systems?

Location Independent Names.   At what level (if at all) is the name of a file independent of its location?

Replication.   Is replication a standard feature, an option, or unavailable?

Caching.   Is caching performed? If so, what is the unit of caching?

Fetch Grain.   How is the file fetched from the server?

FIGURE 2.   Comparison of File Systems [4]

class of problems being solved, tolerance of costs, protocols for supplying and using authentication information, sheer size, and different administrations.

Although there was agreement on where problems originate, there was hot debate on whether the goal of an authentication mechanism was punishment or prevention. If punishment were the ultimate goal, then relatively passive mechanisms in conjunction with logging and auditing could be used to record information permitting the identification and apprehension of offenders. Prevention requires that more complex, active mechanisms be used to control execution of undesirable actions, malicious or inadvertent.

The punishment approach was criticized on the basis of the difficulties that arise in trying to track down operations spanning more than one "boundary." The moral and administrative implications of forming a "network police force" to implement punishment were also considered serious problems. It was suggested that the real world functions by auditing and logging, and that computer systems will have to fit to human systems, and not vice-versa. The problem of authenticating auditing information was mentioned in this regard.

As an example of a middle ground, Jerry Saltzer of MIT stated: "Project Athena is building an authentication server primarily because each private workstation is owned by a student, and each public workstation is captured by indivdiual students as superusers. Given this situation, there must be a way to protect the services, such as mail, printers, and file systems, from inadvertent errors. The goal is to halt mistakes but not necessarily malice."

The prevention approach requires pairwise agreement between each two communicating entities. Roger Needham of the University of Cambridge pointed out that this approach is cumbersome; he and Michael Schroeder showed how to optimize it in a homogeneous environment through the construction of a global authentication service with a distributed implementation [9]. Some problems, such as making sure to avoid using untrustworthy authentication services, become far more serious in a heterogeneous environment.

Other problems arise because different environments often have different views of the level of protection that is necessary or desirable. Further, different authentication or authorization boundaries may exist within a single system (e.g., within a university laboratory different rights might be provided depending on whether the user was accessing a research or an educational subnet). Deborah Estrin of USC observed that any authentication scheme for heterogeneous environments will require cooperation between autonomous administrative units. In this respect, there are very strong parallels between the problem of authentication and the problem of naming.

Authentication and authorization mechanisms are usually intimately related to the local operating system, relying on being "built-in" to both prevent and detect tampering. Is it possible to accommodate such low-level OS dependencies in a distributed, heterogeneous environment?

Rick Rashid of CMU enumerated classes of solutions to the authentication problem: building appropriate size barriers to discourage casual breaches; logging activities at each node; performing cross checks at intervals to ensure consistency; instituting a "network police force"; educating and applying social pressures to users; and punishing those found guilty.

Rashid also presented a short discussion of authorization. The key point was that providing a solution to the authentication problem is only half the battle. The authentication information must then be interpreted in a consistent manner across systems. A mechanism for performing this interpretation is a separate problem that is at least as hard as the original authentication.

Naming

John Zahorjan of the University of Washington identified four issues to be considered in naming in heterogeneous systems: accommodation of evolutionary growth, name resolution, transparency, and name acquisition. The discussion illustrated an underlying theme of the workshop: We know how to provide many styles of services, but which are the "right" ones? And, can multiple "right" approaches be combined smoothly?

In naming, several separate dimensions are apparent. One key issue is whether names should be *relative* or *absolute*. An absolute name refers to the same object regardless of the "context" (that is, the site, the user, and possibly the application) in which it is issued. Absolute names facilitate sharing since they provide a common vocabulary with which to refer to objects. A relative name is context dependent. A common example that illustrates the utility of relative names is mail nicknames. Each user creates a set of easily remembered nicknames to be used in place of more cumbersome, network-dependent mailbox names. The nickname `leach`, for example, is much easier to remember than the complete name of `apollo!pjl@uw-beaver.edu`. Another example of relative names is file names in a shared file system. A standard mechanism for providing these names imports or mounts a portion of a foreign name space and attaches it to a local "root." (E.g., this model has been used in the Andrew file system [8].) A major advantage of relative names is that convenient names for objects can be chosen within each context independently of other contexts. Particularly in a heterogeneous environment, this flexibility is a great asset since different contexts may have fundamentally different requirements of the naming scheme.

A notion closely linked to that of absolute and relative names is whether there is a single global, homogeneous name space or many local name spaces. A global name space appears to be desirable, but the cooperation and extent of changes required to implement it are considerable, especially in a heterogeneous environment. Indeed, the environment may be heterogeneous in part because individual subsystems in the environment might prefer or require their own naming schemes. It was observed, however, that if there is no global name space, then it is not possible to name all objects in all name spaces because some naming environments will have no way to translate some names.

Because sharing is so important, most existing name services provide absolute names. However, distributed, heterogeneous environments (among others) usually provide for some style of relative names as well. For example, in Locus a user may invoke a computation without knowing on which machine it will run. Thus, a mechanism is required whereby a single name can refer to any one of a number of executable files, each one appropriate to a different system type. Similarly, some names benefit significantly from being relative, such as the use of /tmp to refer to a temporary directory in a distributed UNIX system.

A number of short presentations on aspects of naming were given. David Cheriton of Stanford University described naming in the V system [5]. In contrast to most systems, which present a single logically centralized service, name management in V is distributed among the objects responsible for the named entities. This can be an advantage, especially in heterogeneous systems where name syntax and operations may differ significantly from one site to another.

Thomas Murtagh of Purdue University introduced his notion of *nice* names, that is, names that are location-transparent and symbolic, that can be used as syntactic sugar to insulate the user from the "nastiness" of the actual underlying naming scheme. Murtagh said that nice names are local, not global, and are required by the needs of application programs. Dave Clark of MIT suggested that nice names might work in a distributed, universal name service, assuming that they can be transported appropriately (that is, that they can really be kept location-independent). The possibility of using nice names is generally a function of facilities available in the command language, rather than the operating system primitives. Even then, nice names can suffer from the drawbacks of relativism, that is, path compression, and finding alternate paths may be difficult to do with nice names.

Karen Sollins of MIT discussed administrative issues that arise in handling name services. In a typical hierarchical name space human "managers" are responsible for subtrees of the name space at various levels in the naming tree. Because the name service provides some of the keys required to access the named resources (and in some cases all of the keys), it may be necessary to give control of access and update authority to the local manager. This makes managing the overall name service more difficult, as it may not be possible to make changes uniformly to all supporting servers.

Clark observed that so far little attention has been given to the dynamic aspect of naming. The autonomy that is characteristic of heterogeneous systems requires that there be provision for recovery from system failures and on-line changes to the name space (e.g., changed mailbox route or reincarnated object). In some sense, the discussion focused more on a name-management system than on a name space.

User Interfaces

Mark Weiser of the University of Maryland introduced this topic by observing that user interfaces are qualitatively different from the other basic topics: every system has one, they cannot, by definition, be hidden from users, and they are impossible to construct as a central service.

There are three ways to accommodate user interfaces. The first is porting, where an application is moved to the system being accommodated. The second is masking, where the application appears to have been ported, when in fact it is actually running entirely on another machine. The third is mapping, where the user interface is moved, but the heart of the application is not; the characteristics of each system must be mapped to the other.

Weiser defined four levels of user interface heterogeneity: (1) what the user sees, (2) what the application program sees and provides, (3) what the window system sees and provides, and (4) what the hardware provides. Different means of accommodation are more applicable at these different levels. For example, porting is a natural means of accommodating the interface between levels three and four, but mapping is more appropriate between levels two and three.

There was contention over the future of window systems in a heterogeneous environment. One side argued that they are too big and it is too difficult to integrate applications into a window system, stating that sophisticated applications almost always want to use the screen in a "raw" mode. This side continued by stating that every window system that goes into operation terminates work on user interfaces for at least one and a half years because most systems make too many decisions about the user interface, which locks out innovation. The other side responded that there are examples of sophisticated applications (such as Interleaf's WPS product on Apollos and SUNs) where raw mode was not needed to get the efficiency necessary for success.

Any window system that accommodates heterogeneity must be able to support different user interfaces (e.g., tiled and overlayed), different program interfaces (e.g., X and Sun Windows), and new input paradigms (e.g., natural language, speech, and images). The possibility of supporting all this by adopting a standard, extensible protocol is being explored.

Another approach, described by Keith Lantz of Stanford University, promotes the workstation as a front-end to all available resources, both local and remote. This way, the user is insulated from the underlying heterogeneous system. The interaction with all resources, since it is handled by local software, is consistent and natural. The user interface must support four levels of interaction: terminal management, command interaction and response handling, application specific interaction, and multi-application interaction. Additionally, the user must be permitted to configure the software components of the system to meet individual preferences.

Acknowledgments.   Ed Lazowska and John Zahorjan put much time and effort into helping create and revise this report for *Communications.* The other members of the Heterogeneous Computer Systems project at the University of Washington, including Andrew Black, Dennis Ching, Henry Levy, John Maloney, and Mark Squillante contributed as well. Dave Clark, Terry Gray, Paul Leach, and Mark Weiser supplied comments, suggestions, and (in some cases) text for the report. Peter Denning encouraged us to submit the report to *Communications* and then made several useful suggestions on how to improve the report. Thanks also to Andrew Birrell, Bill Joy, Jim Morris, and other members of the organizing committee. Of course, thanks go to the participants of the workshop.

REFERENCES
1. Almes. G.T.. Black. A.P.. Lazowska. E.D., and Noe. J.D. The Eden system: A technical review. *IEEE Trans. Softw. Eng. SE-11,* 1(Jan. 1985).
2. Balkovich. E.. Lerman. S.. and Parmelee. R.P. Computing in higher education: The Athena experience. *Commun. ACM 28,* 11(Nov. 1985). 1214–1224.
3. Birrell, A.D. and Nelson. B.J. Implementing remote procedure calls. *ACM Trans. Comput. Syst. 2,* 1(Feb. 1984).
4. Black. A.. Lazowska. E.. Levy. H.. Notkin. D.. Sanislo. J.. and Zahorjan. J. An approach to accommodating heterogeneity. Tech. Rep. 85-10-04. Dept. of Computer Science. Univ. of Washington. (Oct. 1985).
5. Cheriton. D.R. and Mann. T.P. Uniform access to distributed name interpretation. In *Proceedings of the 4th International Conference on Distributed Systems.* (May 1984).
6. Gettys. J. Project Athena. In *USENIX Summer Conference Proceedings.* (June 1984).
7. Jones. M.B.. Rashid. R.F.. and Thompson. M.R. Matchmaker: An interface specification language for distributed processing. In *Proceedings of the 12th ACM Symposium on Principles of Programming Languages.* (Jan. 1985).
8. Morris. J.H.. Satyanarayanan. M.. Conner. M.H.. Howard. J.H.. Rosenthal. D.S.H.. and Smith. F.D. Andrew: A distributed personal computing environment. *Commun. ACM 29,* 3(Mar. 1986). 184–201.
9. Needham. R.M. and Schroeder, M.D. Using encryption for authentication in large networks of computers. *Commun. ACM 21,* 12(Dec. 1978), 993–999.
10. Nelson. B.J. Remote procedure call. Ph.D. dissertation. Tech. Rep. CMU-CS-81-119, Dept. of Computer Science, Carnegie-Mellon Univ., (May 1981).
11. Svobodova, L. File servers for network-based distributed systems. *ACM Comput. Surv. 16,* 4(Dec. 1984).
12. Walker. B. et al. The LOCUS distributed operating system. In *Proceedings of the 9th ACM Symposium on Operating System Principles.* (Oct. 1983).
13. Xerox Corporation. Courier: The remote procedure call protocol. XSIS 038112. (Dec. 1981).

CR Categories and Subject Descriptors: C.2 [**Computer Systems Organization**]: Computer Communication Networks; D.4 [**Software**]: Operating Systems
   Additional Key Words and Phrases: distributed processing, heterogeneity

Contact: David Notkin. Department of Computer Science. FR-35. University of Washington, Seattle, WA 98195.

Part 2
Principles and Methodologies

THE design of an integrated information system is constrained by the following facts:

1) The new system must integrate existing information systems, each of which was designed independently with little premonition, if any, that the system would form part of a larger system at a future date.
2) Each existing information system must be fully understood in order to comprehend all underlying assumptions and semantics. Rarely are these systems fully and accurately documented.
3) The design must allow flexibility to add or remove individual systems into the integrated configuration. As such, it requires detailed knowledge of both immediate and long-term constituents of the integrated system.
4) The design must involve the least amount of changes to existing systems. Transactions, irrespective of whether they are queries or updates, involve retrieval or manipulation of information maintained in individual systems, each of which imposes its own set of requirements and standards, which must be reconciled by the new system.

The goal is to mitigate all the above-mentioned problems in an efficient and effective manner.

A Distributed Heterogeneous Database Management System (DHDBMS) attempts to meet the above goal by providing the facilities to access, to aggregate, and to update information maintained in multiple, distributed, heterogeneous systems. A typical DHDBMS approach is characterized by the following:

1) The use of a common data model, with appropriate mapping to data models of participating systems;
2) The support of a standard user language for retrieving data on a global basis in all cases, and also for storing data in some cases;
3) The ability to decompose a user request into an equivalent set of subqueries expressed in the format and manner required by participating systems;
4) The capability to resolve incompatibilities in semantics, data structures, and other parameters;
5) The mechanism to take the individual pieces of information provided by participating systems and to integrate them to provide a cohesive response to the original user request.

In addition to the above, some DHDBMS approaches facilitate implementation of sophisticated features, such as authorization control, and the ability to draw inferences in situations involving missing or conflicting data.

From a modeling viewpoint, a *global data model* is used to capture the complete meaning of all the information maintained in all the information systems. Based on this model,

data in the global environment are defined in a *global conceptual schema*. Similarly, the data in an individual information system form a *local schema;* a collection of such local models is referred to as a *local schemata*. In addition to these, there are user views of the stored information. Such *external schemata* form the third schema in the three-schema approach to information integration [1], [2]. The strategy used to map information between the three schemata determines the overall capability to mediate across dissimilar architectures and to meet user expectations.

In the first paper of this part, Virgil Gligor and Gary Luckenbaugh present an overall architectural model as a solution to the problem of interconnecting heterogeneous remote database management systems. Their model distinguishes between four major functional requirement areas: i) Global Data Management; ii) Distributed Transaction Management; iii) Structured Data Transfer Protocols; and iv) Data Communication Protocols.

In the second paper, Dennis Heimbigner and Dennis McLeod describe a federated approach in which multiple information systems are united into a loosely coupled federation for the purpose of sharing and exchanging information. A federation consists of a single federal dictionary and multiple components. The federal dictionary maintains the topology of the federation and oversees the entry of new components. The components represent individual users, applications, or workstations. The federated approach offers mechanisms for sharing information, for combining information, and for coordinating activities.

The third paper, by Batini, Lenzerini, and Navathe, provides a comprehensive comparison of methodologies for database schema integration. This paper begins with a unifying framework for analyzing the problem of schema integration, and then utilizes this framework to examine the strengths and weaknesses of twelve methodologies. The authors conclude that further work is needed in the areas of i) Extension of Integration Methodologies; ii) Knowledge Base Integration; iii) Process Integration; and iv) Use of Expert Systems for Schema Integration.

The fourth paper, by Gio Weiderhold *et al.*, examines the issue of knowledge integration. Information is produced by bringing together data, which consists of factual, observable, and verifiable descriptions of real-world events; and knowledge, which comprises higher level concepts used to structure, classify, and relate such real-world events. So far, researchers have concentrated on the data aspect alone. The KSYS architecture described in this paper deals with both data and knowledge, including the semantic mediation of operations across disparate domains.

The fifth paper, by Frank Manola, advocates the use of

object-oriented approaches. An object is a self-contained collection of data and procedures that can access that data. The data are private to the object, and cannot be accessed except via one of that object's procedures. The author contends that the encapsulation provided by the object paradigm allows internal details of individual components to be concealed. Further, he contends that thinking of the various components to be integrated as objects allows a common methodology to be applied to objects at all levels of granularity.

The sixth paper, by Yuri Breitbart *et al.*, focuses on the issue of transaction management. The authors emphasize the fact that virtually all approaches have so far concentrated on the retrieval aspect. A general transaction management strategy must provide equitable weight to both the retrieval and update aspects of the problem. The authors present an update algorithm for consistent execution of global transactions in the presence of local transactions.

The seventh paper, by Litwin, also deals with the concurrency control aspect. The author proposes the concept of a value date, which is sure only after its value date, and uncertain otherwise. By studying the relationship between the new method and classical methods, the author shows that locking, timestamp based methods, and the time warp mechanism can all be derived from a common concept.

The eighth paper, by Pu, proposes the concept of the superdatabase as a hierarchical composition of element databases. Each element database must provide local recovery and some kind of agreement protocol to recover from a global crash situation. Also, each database must offer local synchronization to enable global concurrency control. If these requirements are satisfied by all element databases, then it is possible to construct a consistent and adaptable superdatabase.

In the next part, actual examples of prototype systems are discussed.

REFERENCES FOR PART 2

[1] Appleton, D. S., "The technology of data integration," *Datamation,* Nov. 1985, pp. 106–116. Reprinted in this book.
[2] *The ANSI/X3 SPARC DBMS Framework Report of the Study Group on Database Management Systems,* AFIPS, 1977.
[3] Devor, C., *et al.*, "Five-schema architecture extends DBMS to distributed applications," *Electron. Design,* Mar. 1982, pp. ss27–ss32.

BIBLIOGRAPHY FOR PART 2

[1] Cardenas, A. F. and M. H. Pirahesh, "Data base communications in a heterogeneous data base management system network," *Inform. Syst.,* vol. 5, pp. 55–79.
[2] Ceri, S. and G. Pelagitti, *Distributed Databases Principles and Systems.* New York, NY: McGraw-Hill Book Company, 1984.
[3] Ceri, S., B. Pernici, and G. Wiederhold, "Distributed database design methodologies," *Proc. IEEE,* May 1987, pp. 533–546.
[4] Davor, C. *et al.*, "Five-schema architecture extends DBMS to distributed applications," *Electron. Design,* Mar. 1982, pp. ss27–ss32.
[5] Gavish, B. and H. Pirkul, "Computer and database location in distributed computer systems," *IEEE Trans. Comput.,* vol. C-35, no. 7, July 1986, pp. 583–590.
[6] Gibbons, P. B., "A stub generator for multilanguage RCP in heterogeneous environments," *IEEE Trans. Software Eng.,* vol. SE-13, no. 1, Jan. 1987, pp. 77–87.
[7] Gligor, V. D. and E. Fong, "Distributed database management systems: An architectural perspective," *J. Telecomm. Networks,* Computer Science Press, Inc., 1983, pp. 249–276.
[8] Schneider, H.-J., *Distributed Data Bases.* New York, NY: North-Holland Publishing Company, 1982.
[9] Schreiber, R. A. and W. Litwin, *Distributed Data Sharing Systems.* New York, NY: North-Holland Publishing Company, 1985.
[10] Smith, J. M., "Expert database systems: A database perspective," in *Expert Database Systems,* Larry Kerschberg, Ed. New York, NY: The Benjamin/Cummings Publishing Company Inc., 1986, pp. 3–15.
[11] Spaccapietra, S., "Heterogeneous data base distribution," in *Distributed Data Bases,* I. W. Draffen and F. Poole, Eds. Cambridge, MA: Cambridge University Press, 1980, pp. 155–193.
[12] Pu, C., "Superdatabases: transactions across database boundaries," *Data Eng.,* vol. 10, no. 3, Sept. 1987, pp. 19–25.
[13] Yu, P. S. *et al.*, "On coupling multi-systems through data sharing," *Proc. IEEE,* May 1987, pp. 573–587.

Today's remote, heterogeneous DBMSs do not effectively communicate with each other. With new application-level protocols and new data and transaction managers, intercommunication would improve.

Interconnecting Heterogeneous Database Management Systems

Virgil D. Gligor and Gary L. Luckenbaugh, University of Maryland

In spite of rapid advancements in the development of communication networks, there is still a great need for the development of improved communication between remote, heterogeneous database management systems, or DBMSs. At present, the lack of effective communication between distributed DBMSs is primarily due to the significant differences between local data managers, local data models and representations, and local transaction managers. A system of interconnected DBMSs that exhibit such differences is called a network of distributed, heterogeneous DBMSs.

In a closer analysis of these differences, it becomes evident that to achieve effective interconnection of remote, heterogenous DBMSs, the users must have uniform, integrated access to the different DBMSs. The importance of such an interconnection has been significantly demonstrated in many large organizations such as those of the US government,[1] which gather and maintain semantically related data in different DBMSs. The fundamental need for uniform, integrated access to such databases arises because users cannot be expected to learn the use of many different DBMSs and the operational differences between them.

This article is dedicated primarily to the analysis of the existing approaches to interconnecting heterogeneous DBMSs, to the review of four experimental DBMS projects in which effective interconnection of such systems was at least partially achieved, and to the discussion of the present alternatives for distributed transaction management and structured-data transfer protocols.

The architectural model

In establishing an overall architectural model as a solution to the problem of interconnecting heterogeneous, remote DBMSs, the features of existing, centralized DBMSs were extended to accommodate distributed systems and networks in a way similar to that used by

Gray.[2] The functional requirement for this model was that the processing functions of the global data manager, the distributed transaction manager, and the structured-data transfer protocol be clearly separated.

Common goals. The architectural model for interconnected, heterogeneous DBMSs was derived from three groups of goals that were common to various DBMS application environments in which experimental DBMS projects were being conducted.

The first group of goals aims at achieving the transparency of local DBMSs. These goals emphasize the need for both uniform and integrated access to remote DBMSs. Uniform access to remote DBMSs requires the existence of a common, global user view of all the data; a common, unified language for data manipulation; and a common, unified data dictionary. In addition, the integration of heterogeneous DBMSs requires a distributed data dictionary that includes the data of all local DBMSs and a set of name-resolution rules, and the inclusion of the results of user operations into the common user view.

The second group of goals is concerned with maintaining the autonomy of all DBMS sites. The requirements of this goal are as follows: (1) The local operations of each DBMS site must be unaffected by the addition of new mechanisms so that reprogramming of systems and/or user programs would be unnecessary. It also facilitates in the expansion of the DBMS network as new DBMSs are added; and (2) Each local DBMS optimization, such as that of access paths, must be unaffected by global operations, and global operations must not cause database reorganization.

The third group of goals suggests the use of standard communication protocols and existent networks. However, the need for special database-oriented protocols, such as structured-data-transfer protocols that use network communication protocols; is well recognized. An important operational issue of this group of goals is the allowance of distributed updates to remote DBMSs by

Reprinted from *IEEE Computer*, pp. 33–43, Jan. 1984.

global users. This issue has a major impact on the generation of features for both the database and for the database access protocol levels because it presents a number of semantic-integrity problems peculiar to the interconnection of heterogeneous DBMSs.

For example, the global semantic constraints in a system of heterogeneous DBMSs may not be identical to the constraints imposed locally by each data manager. Consequently, the global and the local updates may cause semantic conflicts. Such conflicts do not necessarily appear in distributed homogenous systems or in interconnected heterogeneous systems, where only uniform,

remote access to individual DBMSs is allowed. In the latter case, all local constraints can be used to determine the validity of an update. However, if heterogenous DBMSs are integrated for global accessibility by all distributed users, then semantic conflicts may arise; alternatively, changing local constraints to accommodate global ones violates the site autonomy requirement. Such semantic conflicts are illustrated by Kimbleton.[3]

In spite of the complexity of the distributed updates problem, it is important to allow distributed updates through the unified, global user view that do not destroy local DBMS constraints.

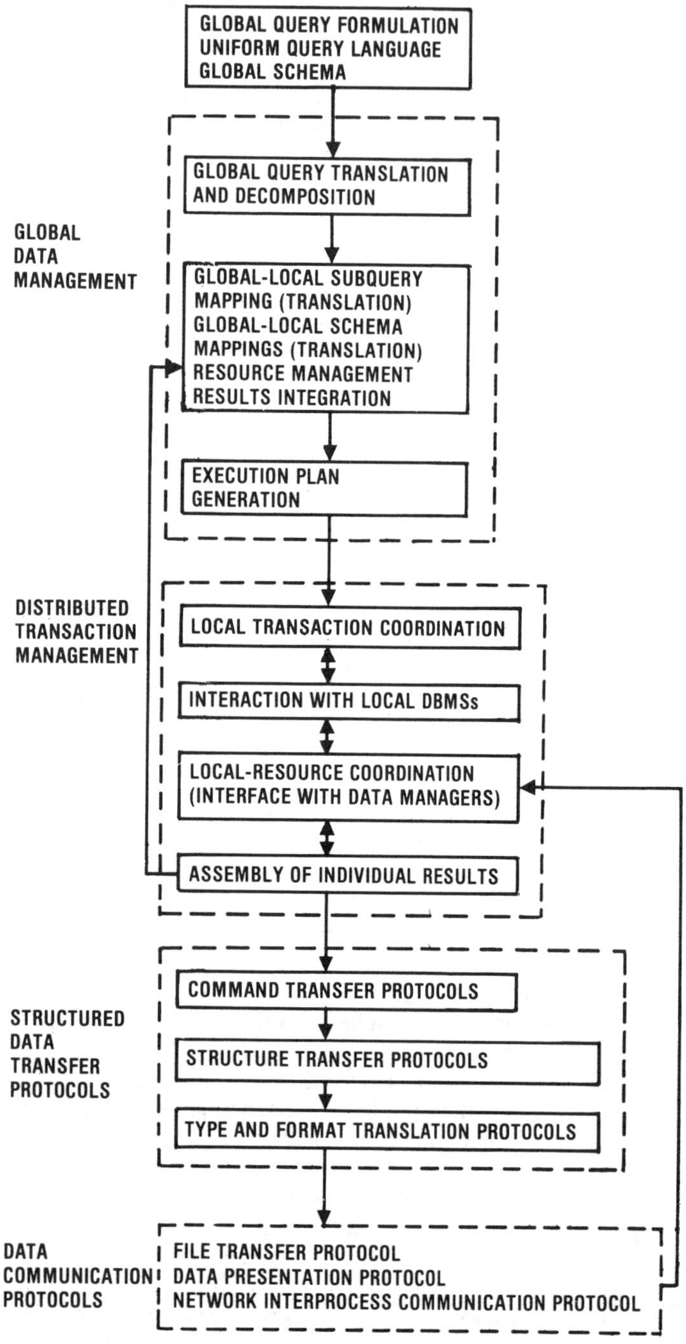

The model overview. The functional layering of the network of heterogeneous DBMSs, which refers only to the application layer of the ISO reference model described by the International Standards Organization,[4] consists of three sublayers: (1) the global data manager, or GDM, is the top-most sublayer that provides services directly to the end user; (2) the distributed transaction manager, or DTM, is the middle sublayer that supports the services of the GDM, and requires the services of the structured-data transfer protocols; and (3) the structured data transfer protocols, or SDTP, is the lower sublayer that supports the services of the DTM, and requires the services of the data presentation protocol, or DPP, and of other application layers, such as those of the file transfer protocol, or FTP. Each of these sublayers consists of several functional features, illustrated in Figure 1 and discussed in detail throughout the remainder of this article.

Features of the global data manager

The GDM of a distributed DBMS performs both the mappings between the global unified view of the data and the local DBMSs, and all relevant I/O operations.

Input. The initial input to the GDM is either a query or transaction formulated on the global schema. If the query or transaction is directed to an individual DBMS, then it is translated into the local query language and passed to the DTM. If a distributed query or transaction (which requires integrated, multi-DBMS access) is formulated, then the GDM transforms the original query or transaction into a collection of subqueries, each in a format acceptable to one of the local DBMSs.

Output. The GDM generates a plan of subquery execution, and passes these subqueries to the DTM. The DTM presents each subquery to the appropriate DBMS through the communications network and, when the results are available, it returns them to the GDM. Finally, the GDM assembles any individual results to produce the answer to the original query. The final result is presented to the user in terms of the global schema of the distributed DBMS. In this manner, the GDM communicates with the end user and with the DTM.

Functions. A GDM must include the following five functions: (1) global data model analysis, (2) query

Figure 1. Functional requirement areas.

decomposition, (3) query translation, (4) execution plan generation, and (5) results integration. These five functions, which are illustrated in Figure 1, are basic to the features of a GDM in both heterogeneous and homogeneous distributed DBMSs. However, in heterogeneous systems, the mapping between the uniform global data model and the specific local data models, the query translation, and the results integration are significantly more elaborate than in homogeneous systems.[5,6] As has been illustrated,[7] all distributed DBMSs include these functions in different ways, and the boundaries between these functions are not always distinct. Likewise, frequent interaction between the GDM and the DTM tends to blur the boundary between them in actual DBMSs.

The global data model. The global data model is central to the GDM of a distributed DBMS. It provides the global schema, which is the basis for both the distributed DBMS users' view of the data and the unified data accessing language. The global schema may be stored in a distributed data dictionary along with local schemas and other information about the local DBMS. The distributed data dictionary is frequently consulted by the GDM to provide information about the mapping between the global view of the data and the local DBMS. For instance, the query decomposer consults the dictionary to determine how to fragment the original query into appropriate subqueries, and the query translator consults the dictionary for local schema and naming information needed to translate subqueries properly.

Query decomposition. The query decomposer takes the original global query and fragments it into subqueries. In order to divide the global query into its local subquery components, the GDM uses the distributed data dictionary as a guide. A global query which references only a single local DBMS does not need to be decomposed at the global level, since its decomposition can be done by the local host. In principle, the decomposition strategy does not differ in heterogeneous systems from that of homogeneous ones.

Query translation. Query translation is a language-to-language translation which takes into account underlying data model differences. Query translation can take place at several points in the operation of the GDM. In a system of distributed homogeneous DBMSs, query-to-query translation is not required, since the same language is used for both the local and the global queries. In the heterogeneous case, this translation may be necessary in the following areas:

- global-local query translation,
- subquery translation, and
- subquery results interpretation.

It is assumed that the user issues the global query in the unified global query language. The global query translator may receive the original query that is formulated on a particular external view of the global database, and translate it into a global query that is based on the global schema of the database. After this is done, the translator translates each subquery based on the local

schemas, into the appropriate language for the local DBMS. Finally, the subquery results interpreter takes the subquery results and performs the translations necessary for results integration.

For specific examples of global-to-local schema mappings, subquery translations, and results integrations works by Jacobs,[5] Smith,[6] Chiang,[8] and Cardenas should be consulted.

Execution plan generation. The execution plan generator interacts with the DTM by passing subqueries to it. The execution plan generator decides which subqueries can be sent to the local DBMS in parallel, which queries must precede others, and what the relationships are among the intermediate results. The execution plan generator has the same function in both homogeneous and heterogeneous DBMSs.

Results integration. The results integrator combines the individual subquery results and represents them in terms of the global schema. Information from the distributed data dictionary and query decomposer will determine how the local DBMS results will be integrated into the global schema.[6]

GDMs: The approach of four projects

CSIN. The Chemical Substances Information Network,[1] which interconnects a group of remote, heterogeneous data base and file systems, was designed and implemented at Computer Corporation of America. CSIN ties together various existing databases scattered throughout the US with component information systems that are not necessarily general DBMSs. In this configuration, the subquery formulation process must be somewhat restricted, as the local query processors of some of the systems are more limited than those of general DBMSs. Consequently, each CSIN relation must be stored on a single component system. CSIN provides each user with a uniform way to access the individual DBMSs, but does not support the integration of these systems.

The global conceptual model in the CSIN project does not include all the data represented by the conceptual models of the component DBMSs. Certain data can be accessed only through the predefined query facilities or through direct contact with the local system, and not through CSIN's general query facility. The global data dictionary in CSIN, called the information resources directory, or IRD, is logically part of the CSIN processor but is located on a separate computer accessed through the communications network. Along with the global schema and local schemas, the IRD contains information used for query decomposition such as statistics on the local data and limitations of local query processors.

The CSIN query processor performs most of the duties of the global data manager. It uses information about the component systems, such as query capabilities and estimated result sizes, to generate a query execution plan. The CSIN access planner then considers a completely parallel strategy for processing subqueries. Actual execution of the subqueries is done by the component data interfaces.

Query decomposition is somewhat simplified in CSIN by the restriction of relations to a single component. Query translation and results integration are both performed by the CSIN query processor, the latter with the help of the transaction module's own DBMS. In addition, CSIN possesses a Script execution facility for selecting predefined queries or programs that allows a CSIN specialist to compile an optimal execution plan ahead of time, and is particularly helpful to the casual user who inputs a common request.

UCLA. The UCLA DBMS project[9] attempts to provide a uniform user view of a number of heterogeneous DBMSs. The UCLA approach includes both a global conceptual model and an internal model. The global conceptual model used is the entity-relationship model. A data-independent accessing model, modified to incorporate Codasyl syntax, is used for the global internal model. The user's request to this DBMS is based on a global external model known as the virtual database model.

Because of the large number of system layers, there are also many mappings and schemas which must be maintained in the distributed data dictionary, called the network catalog. The network catalog contains the virtual model, or VM, which is the global external model, the uniform global conceptual model, the uniform global internal model, the uniform local conceptual model, the uniform local internal model, and the local logical or data definition language model.

Query translation occurs at several points in the processing of a request. Initially, the query is translated into an appropriate form for the global conceptual and internal models based on the VM. After decomposition, the query translator converts the subqueries into the query or data manipulation language of the local systems.

The UCLA approach to DBMSs includes both a global conceptual model and an internal model, which uses Codasyl syntax.

Query decomposition in the UCLA project must provide for interdatabase relationships, that is, global relations defined over more than one component DBMS. Such relations were forbidden in the CSIN system. Interdatabase relationships in the UCLA project are implemented by explicit access paths reflected at the level of the uniform global internal models.[9]

The execution plan generation in the UCLA project is performed by the global query decomposer and the access path selector. The recomposer performs results integration.

XNDM. The XNDM project, which was initiated at the National Bureau of Standards,[3] interconnects several heterogeneous DBMSs that are running under the Multics, Tenex, and the Tops-10 operating systems through the Arpanet. XNDM uses the relational model as its global model and uses Sequel as the basic framework of the data language.

The distributed data dictionary used by XNDM is called the network wide directory system and is contained within the experimental network operating system of NBS.

The translation process in XNDM is a five-phase process: (1) lexical and syntactic analysis, (2) standardization, (3) static semantic processing, (4) dynamic semantic processing, and (5) code generation.

The two semantic processing phases perform the functions of query decomposition and execution plan generation, while the remaining phases perform the various stages of query translation. XNDM uses a common core translator, which takes custom-tailored front ends and back ends to handle the different translations needed for the different local DBMSs.

The first two phases of the translation process perform global query translation on the experimental network query language global query. The original query is converted to a source syntax tree representation and is put into a standard form for further processing. Each translation phase reshapes the tree until it represents a sequence of subqueries for the target local DBMSs. In the last phase, the code generator performs the subquery translation and outputs the DML statements for the component systems; the subqueries are first interpreted to produce call statements to primitive database operations on the local systems, and then these calls are translated to the appropriate DML statements for the target DBMSs.

Query decomposition begins in the static semantic processing phase with the data item renaming module and the record structure mapping module. This process prepares the tree representation for the decomposition into subtrees, a subsequent process which takes place in the dynamic semantic processing phase.

The dynamic semantic processing sequence module chains the subtrees together and determines the execution plan generation for the subqueries. The execution sequence that is selected will minimize the processing of intermediate records.

Results integration must be performed outside of the translation process of XNDM.

Multibase. The Computer Corporation of America's Mulitbase project[6] to interconnects and integrates preexisting, heterogeneous DBMSs. Multibase does not require any changes to the local databases or DBMSs. The GDM of the Multibase system consists of three main parts: (1) Query Translator, (2) Query Processor, and (3) Local Database Interface.

In Multibase, any of the local DBMS sites may have a global data manager. It is the only system mentioned that uses something other than the relational or the entity-relationship model as its global data model. A functional data model is used to define the global schema, and Daplex is the global query language. In addition to the global and local schemas, Multibase uses an integration schema which provides information used to resolve inconsistencies between the data of different local systems.

The query translator, according to Smith, "translates a global query over the global schema into a global query over the disjoint union of local schemata."[6] The local database interface also performs some query translation by translating local queries generated by the query processor into local queries in the DML of each local DBMS.

Query decomposition is performed by the query processor which decomposes the global query over the disjoint union of local schemata into individual local queries over local schemata. The query processor actually creates a query processing strategy from the query over the disjoint union of local schemata. This query processing strategy consists of a set of local subqueries together with move operations and local queries issued by the query processor. Taking this into consideration, it would be valid to say that the query processor includes the functions of execution plan generation. In addition, with its access planner and execution strategist, the query processor performs query optimization and coordinates local subquery execution.

In the Multibase project, a functional data model is used to define the global schema, and a local database interface is used for translation.

A local database interface stands between the execution strategist and each of the local DBMSs. The LDI may reside either with the GDM or at the local site. Besides translating subqueries, the LDI translates local subquery results into a uniform format for the query processor, which performs results integration.

Features of the distributed transaction manager

The distributed transaction manager is responsible for controlling the execution of distributed transactions in integrated, distributed DBMSs; these transactions will reference data at more than one site in a network.

A primary purpose of a transaction manager, whether it is distributed or centralized, is to help ensure the consistency of the database. In particular, a distributed transaction manager must extend the functions of local transaction managers[2] to maintain the global consistency of the distributed database. To do this, the DTM assumes that whenever a transaction runs in isolation and completes its task, it preserves the consistency of the database. However, when transactions are executed concurrently, or in the event that a system fails, there are two modules of the DTM that are designed to handle serializability and recovery. The concurrency control module makes sure that if transactions A and B reference shared data and are executed concurrently, the DTM ensures that the results will be the same if A was executed before B, or B before A. As it is imperative that intermediate results not be left in the database if the system crashes, the recovery control module makes sure that the distributed transactions will execute to completion, or not at all.

Concurrency control. The concurrency control module must schedule the subtransactions of concurrently executing transactions. This makes the concurrent execution of transactions equivalent to a serial or sequential execution of the transactions. There have been many algorithms published to solve this problem for centralized and homogeneous distributed systems.[10] However, very little work has been done to solve this problem in a heterogeneous, distributed environment. There are two basic alternatives for concurrency control in a heterogeneous, distributed DBMS.

Alternative 1. The first alternative is to coordinate the concurrency control mechanisms of the local transaction managers, or LTM. This requires that the LTMs be modified to recognize and respond to other LTMs.

This alternative is not an acceptable solution for two reasons. First, there are literally thousands of variations of concurrency control algorithms.[10] In order for this alternative to be useful, one would have to develop a general scheme for coordinating any combination of these algorithms; this would be very difficult, if not impossible. Second, the autonomy of the local DBMSs would be violated, as the local transaction managers would require extensive reprogramming in order to recognize and communicate with the other LTMs.

Alternative 2. The second and more appropriate alternative is to provide a hierarchy of concurrency control. This alternative to concurrency control does not violate the autonomy of the local DBMSs since the local systems are not modified in any way. All software is added on top of the existing systems whenever needed. The LTMs are not modified and are assumed to provide concurrency control for local transactions at each of the sites. The DTM, like the GDM, can view a distributed transaction as a collection of subtransactions, each of which runs on a single site.

The DTM is responsible for scheduling these local subtransactions for execution. Subsequently, it is the LTMs responsibility to schedule the individual operations of each sub-transaction. For example, suppose that there are two distributed transactions A and B that reference some of the same data and that there are two local DBMS sites. In order for the execution of A and B to be equivalent to the sequential execution of A and B in some arbitrary order, the DTM must ensure that either A effectively precedes B, or that B effectively precedes A at both sites. Let Ai (or Bi) represent the subtransaction of A (or B) that runs at site i and let $\rightarrow$ stand for "effectively precedes." In order for A and B to be serializable, the following condition must be satisfied: $(A1 \rightarrow B1)$ and $(A2 \rightarrow B2)$ or $(B1 \rightarrow A1)$ and $(B2 \rightarrow A2)$.

In this description, we have defined $\rightarrow$ as "effectively precedes" for two reasons. First, the requirement that $A \rightarrow B$ means that the net results must be the same as if A was executed to completion prior to executing B. However, the local transaction manager may execute A and B concurrently as long as the net results are the same as executing *A* and then *B*. Second, if *A* and *B* do not share any data, then the requirement $A \rightarrow B$ is met, since any order of execution will produce identical results. For example, suppose *A* and *B* are two distributed transactions that run at sites 1 and 2. Further suppose that *A*1 and *B*1 share some of the same data, but *A*2 and *B*2 do not share any data. The concurrency control condition can be trivially satisfied at site 2, since executing *A*2 and *B*2 in any order or concurrently will produce the same results.

A large number of algorithms have been published in the literature for concurrency control on such topics as two-phase locking, timestamping, and serialization graph checking.[10] The concurrency control mechanisms of the DTM can be based upon any variation of these algorithms. The only requirement is that the DTM must be able to tell which objects are being referenced by the subtransactions so that it can properly determine when synchronization between transactions is necessary. In centralized and homogeneous distributed systems, this information is usually provided by the local data managers. However, in a heterogeneous distributed system this information must be provided by the GDM so that the local data managers will not need to be modified.

For concurrency control, we can either coordinate the control mechanisms of local transaction managers—a nearly impossible task—or provide a control hierarchy.

Both distributed and centralized algorithms can be used by the DTM. Distributed algorithms are those whose components exist at several sites within the network. A centralized DTM would exist at only one site in the network. A distributed DTM would not necessarily violate the autonomy of the local DBMSs, since the DTM components would run on top of the local system as part of an application protocol.

The requirement for autonomy does place one minor restriction on the form that subtransactions may take. In order not to violate the autonomy of the local DBMSs, it must be possible to execute local transactions at the local sites without the DTM being aware of their existence. Furthermore, the DTM must continue to maintain the global consistency of the database even through it is unaware of these local transactions. This means that the DTM must serialize the distributed transactions together with the invisible, locally originated transactions. For example, suppose two subtransactions *T*11 and *T*12 are executed at site 1 on behalf of distributed transaction *T*, and that a locally originated transaction *L* is also being executed on site 1. There are two possible legal execution sequences: $L \rightarrow T11 \rightarrow T12$ and $T11 \rightarrow T12 \rightarrow L$.

It would be incorrect to allow the execution sequence $T11 \rightarrow L \rightarrow T12$, since inserting *L* between the two subtransactions of *T* may cause data inconsistencies.[2] The solution to this problem is to require that no more than one subtransaction per distributed transaction be executed at any given site. In other words, *T*11 and *T*12 in

the preceding example would have to be packaged into one transaction *T*1. With this restriction, there would be no way that an invisible local transaction could become inserted into the middle of a distributed transaction.

Recovery control. The purpose of recovery control is to provide data protection and recovery procedures for all transactions. Because it is desirable to build recovery mechanisms on top of the recovery mechanisms of the local DBMSs, we assume that all of the local systems provide methods for recovering local transactions in the event of system failure. The responsibility of the DTM is to provide such means of recovery for distributed transactions. In short, the DTM makes sure that either all of the subtransactions complete or that they all abort. The DTM does this by utilizing the two-phase commit protocol described by Gray[2] and by Lampson.[11]

In brief, this protocol relies upon a process that coordinates the completions of the subtransactions. The coordinator process goes through two phases. During the first phase, it prepares all the subtransactions, and during the second phase, it completes them all. In order for this scheme to work, the coordinator must be crash resilient.

Each subtransaction exists in one of four states: active, aborted, prepared, or committed. An active transaction is one that is running and contains no updates permanently stored in the database. An aborted transaction is one that has been terminated and has had all of its updates removed from the database. If the coordinator finds that a subtransaction has aborted due to a system crash, then it will abort the remaining subtransactions. A committed transaction is one that has terminated and has had all of its updates permanently stored. A prepared transaction is one that has had all of its updates saved in a safe place. This type of transaction can be either committed or aborted but, in the event of a system crash, can still be committed when the system recovers.

A major problem appears if this two-phase commit protocol is used in a heterogeneous DBMS. Most local DBMSs provide an external view of transactions as being in either an active, committed, or aborted state. There is usually no prepared state. Consequently, the local transaction managers would have to be modified in order to support this new state. Unfortunately, there does not appear to be a way around this problem. The most practical recovery algorithms for distributed systems are based on the two-phase commit protocol. Even so, it seems highly unlikely that a recovery algorithm could be designed that would not rely upon the existence of something like a prepared state.

Further problems can appear if the local systems do not provide full recovery measures in the event of a system failure. For example, many time-sharing systems provide data recovery measures only when a single file is being updated. Multiple file updates may not be recoverable. There does not appear to be an effective solution to this problem that would circumvent the modification of local transaction managers.

Summary of distributed transaction management. In summary, the DTM views a distributed transaction as a set of subtransactions. At most, only one subtransaction is allowed per site in the network. The DTM must make certain that two or more distributed transactions that reference shared data will execute in the same effective order at all sites in the network. This task can be done using existing algorithms such as two-phase locking, timestamping, and serialization graph checking.[10] We have not recommended any particular algorithm, or suggested that the DTM should be distributed. At the expense of throughput, the DTM could simply execute all distributed transactions in sequential order. This approach may be appropriate for distributed systems that must be brought on line quickly.

The most suitable recovery control algorithm is the two-phase commit protocol. However, the local DBMSs must be extended to allow transactions to exist in a

---

In distributed transaction management, a transaction is viewed as a set of subtransactions, with only one allowed per site in the network.

---

prepared, but not committed, state. Alternatively, the distributed system designer could choose not to support the data recovery measures that have been described.

The experimental systems developed to date[7] show that little research has been done on DTM in heterogeneous, distributed DBMSs. There are at least three reasons for this: (1) Some of the systems surveyed do not allow distributed updates or synchronized retrievals such as repeatable reads.[2] Without these features, there is no need for global recovery or concurrency control; (2) Some systems emphasize uniform access to individual DBMSs rather than integrated, distributed access. In other words, transactions reference only one remote site, and the LTMs can consequently ensure consistency without the help of a DTM; and (3) Most of the distributed, heterogeneous DBMSs are experimental in nature, and distributed transaction management was simply not included as part of the scope of the research project.

Features of the structured data transfer protocols

SDTPs are application-level protocols required for the interconnection of remote heterogeneous DBMSs.[12] The SDTPs are used by protocols and programs at higher levels which implement the interconnection of the remote DBMSs. These protocols and programs belong to the GDM and to the DTM. The SDTPs themselves use the data communication protocols. In fact, the SDTPs can be seen as extensions of the Data Communication Protocols, or DCPs, particularly since some of the DCP layers such as the file transfer protocol and the data presentation protocol layers assume the existence of the SDTPs. (The National Bureau of Standards draft proposals for the FTP and the DPP assume that the transformation of a file format from the file's native mode into the network-wide, virtual file format is performed externally at a level above them.)

The areas that are covered by the SDTPs are the command transfer protocols, the structure transfer protocols, and the type and format translation extensions to DPPs. The command transfer protocols deal with the transfer of commands to remote DBMSs. These protocols are particularly useful in cases where some of the transaction and data management protocols are implemented as remotely located servers rather than as application-protocol layers. As with the other SDTPs, the command-transfer protocols use a cannonical command format for command transfer across the network. Higher levels such as the GDM will perform the translation between local command formats and the cannonical form.

The most important SDTPs are the structure transfer protocols. A structure can be a Pascal or a Cobol record, a PL/I , or a C structure. It can contain a set of basic types such as integers, reals, and pointers, or it can contain other structures. The structure itself may have a specific type and, therefore, the types of a structure form a directed, acyclic graph. An example of a directed, acyclic graph in which a file is the base structure is shown in Figure 2.

The structure transfer protocols include two basic kinds of protocols: (1) protocols for pointer*- free structures, and (2) protocols for structures with pointers. The structure transfer protocol layer is a direct user of the FTP and DPP layers since files are most likely to be the representation type for most structures with or without

---

*"Pointer" is a generic term for the identifier of another structure. Pointers can identify structures within a host or structures located within remote hosts.

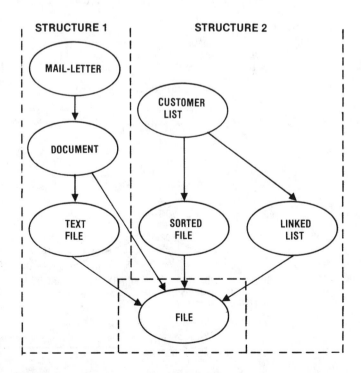

Figure 2. Two acyclic directed graphs illustrating the interrelationships among the types of two structures.

pointers. It is safe to assume that the protocols for the transfer of structures with pointers are significantly more complex than those which handle pointer-free protocols.

Other protocols for structure management, such as those used for space allocation and deallocation, are actually part of the data management protocols and are not considered at this level.

Type and format translation protocols are necessary for types of objects not included at the DPP level. Some structures may contain only basic types, such as integers, reals, characters and binary strings. Some other structures may contain other types, such as relations, documents, and lists, whose translation are not currently handled at the DPP level. Consequently, the structured transfer protocols require that the DPP level must be extensible, that is, the DPP must be prepared to handle a large variety of types in addition to the four that are currently specified.[13]

The need for SDTPs. The principal role of the SDTPs is the preservation of the meaning of transmitted data. The need for SDTPs is apparent, since the only potentially viable alternative to the use of SDTPs for communication among remote, heterogeneous DBMSs is that of using DCPs in various stylized ways. There are three alternatives for using DCPs as substitutes for SDTPs. However, none of the alternatives are adequate substitutes for SDTPs. A fourth alternative, which came close to being a specialized SDTP, is also presented together with its advantages and disadvantages are also discussed.

Alternative 1. First, the DCPs may be used as they are currently proposed, that is, the FTP, the DPP etc. Such use would require (1) that all structured data and commands of remote DBMSs be stored in the files of the various hosts, and (2) that the DCPs transfer the structures and commands as files across the network. The problem with this approach is illustrated in Figure 3. By storing a structure in a file, the meaning of the structure is lost, as the type "structure" is coerced downward to the type "file." Although the file may be delivered correctly from host H_i to host H_j, and although the representation of the file in host H_j would be correct because the DPP and FTPs were used, the DCPs (in this case, the FTP) cannot convert the file at host H_j into the correct structure at host H_j. In short, the DCPs cannot coerce the file at H_j into the structure at H_j because they do not understand the meaning and format of such things as structures and pointers. They are also unable to recognize the differences between the types "structure at H_i" and "structure at H_j." Consequently, direct reliance on DCPs to substitute for SDTPs is an inadequate way of bypassing the need for SDTPs.

Note that the implicit assumption in Figure 3 is that each host is equipped with the file presentation protocol which (1) transforms files at host H_i into the virtual file format (as expected by FTP/DPP), and (2) transforms the virtual files into files at host H_j. These transformations would be provided by SDTPs or directly by the architecture.

Alternative 2. Second, existent DCPs, such as those used by Telnet, may be augmented with mechanisms that could potentially eliminate the need for SDTPs. For example, each component DBMS can be equipped with a translator, like the CDI in CSIN,[1] which converts commands, messages, and structured data into terminal-oriented character strings (for example, strings ending with CR characters). As shown in Figure 4, these strings

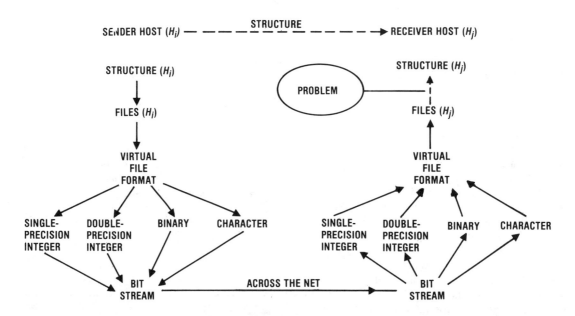

Figure 3. An example of the problem with alternative 1. Using standard DCPs, a structure at host H_i can be transported as a file to host H_j. At host H_j the file cannot become a structure.

would form the input to the Telnet protocols. Next, the Telnet protocols deliver the character strings to remote hosts where translators convert the character strings into commands, messages, and structured data.

In this approach, the translator parses the message strings using string-matching algorithms, performs data translation, and error detection and handling functions. This approach has the major disadvantage of imposing substantial translation overhead. The translators must convert complex data structures and types, commands, and messages into character strings intended for human-user inspection and processing. The more complex the data types to be transferred, the more overhead the translation process would impose. Such translation is necessary if DCPs such as those of Telnet are to be used, thereby making this second approach an inadequate substitute for the SDTPs.

Alternative 3. Third, the features of the DCPs may be augmented with selected mechanisms found in SDTPs. This approach differs from the second in that the augmentation is done internally to the DCPs, not externally. For example, the NBS draft proposal for the FTP* includes some nontransfer management functions that belong to SDTPs and higher level DBMS protocols. These functions include file management such as file space allocation on different hosts, file renaming, access-control modifications, and possibly file moves (as opposed to file copies or transfers). However, other management functions that belong to SDTPs, such as the transfer and recomputation of file indexes for index-sequential accesses, are not included.

Of course, significantly more complex functions performed by SDTPs could be included within various layers of DCPs. For example, the DPP layer might handle the transfer of more data types rather than just characters, or single- or double-precision integers and binary strings.

Further augmentation of DCPs with SDTP functions would not be beneficial for at least three reasons. First, further augmentation of DCPs with SDTP and DBMS functions would clutter the DCPs specifications with infrequently used, higher level functions. Second, this would also result in poor DCP layering and separation of concerns, and would violate the ISO model.[4] Third, further augmentation of DCPs would result in increased implementation cost and overhead. For these reasons, the augmentation of DCPs with SDTP functions is apparently an inadequate substitute for SDTPs.

Alternative 4. Let us assume that the translator of alternative 2 translates all structured data to and from a common format, called the structured data interchange form.[8] The SDICF then replaces the terminal-oriented character string as the common data format, which is transported across the network.

The SDICF is a file that consists of the structural data occurrences and a description of the structured data being interchanged among heterogeneous databases. The

---

*It must be noted, however, that the designers of the NBS draft proposals for the FTP and DPP have never suggested, nor intended, to replace the SDTPs by using DCPs.

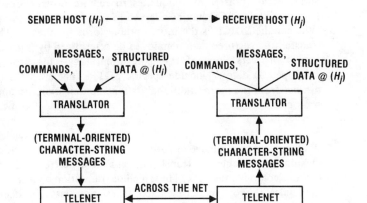

Figure 4. An example of alternative 2 illustrating the CSIN approach to the substitution of SDTPs with DCPs.

description section of the SDICF also defines the structure of the various data sections. A data section of the SDICF file contains the attribute values and additional information to allow the reconstruction of the structured data or of the database subsets within remote databases.

The translator transforms any portion of a DBMS into an SDICF file at a source DBMS host. The SDICF file, which is transported across the network by an FTP-like protocol, is translated by the remote host translator into a corresponding portion of the remote DBMS. Subsequently, the translated data is integrated within the remote DBMS.

Some details of the SDICF file contents and of the various components of what we call the "translator" are provided by Chiang.[8] Also provided are some examples of how structured data of a DBMS, which uses one data model, are transported and integrated into another DBMS, which uses a different data model.

This alternative is more suitable than the other alternatives for the transfer of structured data among remote heterogeneous DBMSs. However, it is not entirely suitable as a substitute for SDTPs for the following reasons. First, this alternative shares a major drawback with alternative 1. The SDICF is a structure itself; therefore, if it is coerced into a "sequential stream of ASCII characters,"[8] a mechanism or some protocol is required to make sure that the remote host is able to correctly coerce the sequential stream of ASCII characters back into the SDICF structure. No FTP can ensure the proper preservation of the meaning of the SDICF structure stored within a file. Consequently, some specialized protocol is still needed between the SDICF mechanism and the FTPs.

Second, this alternative does not seem to deal with the more complex problem of transferring structured data with pointers. The semantics for the transfer of structures with pointers (which may point to data located in remote hosts) are not defined, and the problems which appear in the transfer of such structures are not addressed.

Third, the SDICF format does not appear to be suitable as a canonical form for the transfer of commands, and for the transfer of subqueries to remote hosts. However, the SDICF may be adapted to that function. Whether the SDICF is the most suitable form for the transfer of structured data remains to be determined by future projects. Few of the experimental systems developed to date[7,12] include specific SDTPs that are distinct from the more traditional data communication protocols.

The need for a canonical format. There are several techniques available for translating data in a heterogeneous computer network. These include translation by the sender, the receiver, a centralized translation server, and translation by both the sender and the receiver through the use of a network wide canonical format.

The use of a canonical format appears to be the most appropriate method for translation. The primary reason is the ease with which a new host can be added to the network. The new host must have software written which can translate its internal representation for data to and from the canonical format. However, none of the other hosts in the network will be affected. Using this method each host needs two translators to translate to and from the canonical format. Consequently, if there are n dissimilar machines, only $2n$ translators are needed. On the other hand, translation only by the sender or by the receiver necessitates the use of $n(n-1)$ translators. The canonical format approach also has a minimal amount of host overhead, a minimal amount of message overhead, and is very reliable.[14]

The NBS draft proposal for the DPP provides data translation services between two communicating heterogeneous computer systems. The DPP entities operating on each host computer are responsible for translating local data to and from the network-wide canonical format. The DPP must be extensible to recognize any number of data types that might appear in different environments. The DPP is required to recognize these data types so that it could support the interconnection of remote, heterogeneous DBMSs.

Most DBMS systems make use of complex data structures containing pointers. It is desirable to allow these data structures, and fragments of a data structure, to be copied from one host to another. This permits a data structure to be distributed throughout the system.

As a result of data structure distribution, there must be a way to copy pointers from host to host, and to allow the pointers to point to structures located across machine boundaries. As currently specified in the NBS draft,[13] the DPP provides no services for handling pointers. Therefore, an additional protocol, such as the structure transfer protocol, is necessary for handling data structures with pointers. The structured transfer protocols are responsible for translating pointers just as the DPP is responsible for translating data. Pointers must be translated because of the differences in addressing architectures. Even if pointers are not allowed to point across machine boundaries, and all pointers are implemented as simple offsets into the data structure being copied, it is still necessary for them to be translated. Pointer translation is necessary because the length of the data items in the structure may change due to translation.

Consequently, the pointer offsets must be adjusted to compensate for these changes.

The best method for translating pointers is through the use of a canonical pointer format. The canonical format for pointers consists of the pointer itself and the context that is used for the pointer resolution. A context is a mapping from a pointer to an object. Thus, the canonical format of a pointer is a pair < integer, context >. The integer is a displacement within the context object which selects either a local object or a system-wide name (pointer). The system-wide name consists of a unique identifier of the remote context and an integer displacement within the remote context. The unique context identifier is usually structured as a < unique host identifier, context identifier >.

A detailed discussion of the various alternatives for contexts and for systemwide names is presented by Gligor[12] and Sollins.[15] Specific features of the protocols for the transfer of structures with pointers are also presented. The specific features are derived (1) from the canonical format for structure with pointers, (2) from the meaning of the transfer operation (such as copy vs. move operations), and (3) from the ability to preserve the sharing of components within the same structure with pointers.[12,15] The reader must be aware, however, that very few protocols exist for the transfer of structures with pointers. More experience with such protocols is necessary for the generation of a stable set of specific features.

An architectural framework that separates the activities of global data management, distributed transaction management, and structured-data transfer protocols is suitable for the analysis of existing systems as well as the design analysis of new systems. However, uniform, integrated access to autonomous, local DBMSs using standard communication protocols has been only partially achieved to date. Although the provision of a common, uniform user view of the database is fairly well understood, it is not as simple to integrate the systems to support distributed updates without violating the autonomy of the distributed DBMSs. The use of standard data communication protocols is always possible, provided that protocols such as those of the SDTP layer are added. However, very few real systems have provided such protocols because relatively little research has been done in DTMs and SDTPs. ∎

Acknowledgments

This work was supported in part by the National Aeronautics and Space Adminstration at the University of Maryland under contract NAS 5-27378, and by the National Bureau of Standards at International Software Systems, Inc., under contract NB80SBCA0367.

References

1. "A Prototype Chemical Substances Information Network," *Computer Corporation of America,* tech. report CCA-79-19, Cambridge, Mass., Aug. 21, 1979.

2. J. N. Gray, "Notes on Database Operating Systems," in *Operating Systems: An Advanced Course*, R. Bayer et al., eds., Vol. 60, Springer-Verlag, New York, 1978, pp. 394-481.

3. S. R. Kimbleton and P. Wang, "Application and Protocols", in *Distributed Systems: Architecture and Implementation*, Lecture Notes in Computer Science, Paul Lampson and Siegert, eds., Vol. 105, Springer Verlag, New York, 1981, pp. 308-370.

4. "Data Processing—Open Systems Interconnection—Basic Reference Model," *Int'l Standards Organization, ISO/TC97/SC16/537* rev., ANSI, New York, Dec. 1980.

5. B. E. Jacobs and T. E. Jacobs, "On the Functional Requirements of a Global Data Manager for a Set of Distributed Heterogeneous Databases I and II," University of Maryland tech. reports TR-1068 and TR-1069, Oct. 1981.

6. J. M. Smith et al., "Multibase-Integrating Heterogeneous Distributed Database Systems," *AFIPS Conf. Proc.*, Vol. 50, 1981 NCC, pp. 487-499.

7. V. D. Gligor and E. Fong, "Distributed Database Management Systems: An Architectural Perspective," *J. Telecommuncation Networks*, Vol. 2, No. 3, Nov. 1983, pp. 249-270.

8. W. P. Chiang, D. DeSmith, D. Leder, D. K. Nguyen, R. Perreault, and J. Fry, "Draft Specification for a Structured Data Interchange Form," University of Michigan Database Systems Research Group, working paper 80 DI 2.6. Feb. 1981.

9. A. Cardenas and M. H. Pirahesh, "Data Base Communication in a Heterogeneous Data Base Management System Network," *Information Systems,* Vol. 5, No. 1, 1980, pp. 55-79.

10. P. Bernstein and N. Goodman, "A Sophisticate's Introduction to Distributed Database Concurrency Control," *Proc. Eighth Conf. Very Large Databases,* Mexico City, Sept. 1982, pp. 62-76.

11. B. W. Lampson and H. Sturgis, "Atomic Transactions," *Distributed Systems: Architecture and Implementation,* Lecture Notes in Computer Science, Paul Lampson and Siegert, eds., Vol. 105, Springer Verlag, New York, 1981, pp. 246-265.

12. V. D. Gligor, "Features of Structured-Data-Transfer Protocols for Networks of Heterogeneous Database Management Systems," *Proc. Workshop on Self-Describing Data,* N. Roussopoulos, ed., University of Maryland, College Park, Md., Oct. 1982, pp. 229-270.

13. S. E. Clopper, "Features of the File Transfer Protocol (FTP) and the Data Presentation Protocol (DPP)" Institute for Computer Sciences and Technology, National Bureau of Standards report ICST/HLNP-80-6, Washington, DC, Sept. 1980.

14. P. Levine, "Facilitating Interprocess Communication in a Heterogeneous Network Environment," MIT Laboratory for Computer Science, tech. report TR-184, Cambridge, Mass., July 1977.

15. K. R. Sollins, "Copying Complex Structures in a Distributed System," MIT Laboratory for Computer Science, tech. report TR-219, Cambridge, Mass., May 16, 1979.

A Federated Architecture for Information Management

University of Colorado, Boulder

DENNIS McLEOD
University of Southern California

An approach to the coordinated sharing and interchange of computerized information is described emphasizing partial, controlled sharing among autonomous databases. Office information systems provide a particularly appropriate context for this type of information sharing and exchange. A federated database architecture is described in which a collection of independent database systems are united into a loosely coupled federation in order to share and exchange information. A federation consists of components (of which there may be any number) and a single federal dictionary. The components represent individual users, applications, workstations, or other components in an office information system. The federal dictionary is a specialized component that maintains the topology of the federation and oversees the entry of new components. Each component in the federation controls its interactions with other components by means of an export schema and an import schema. The export schema specifies the information that a component will share with other components, while the import schema specifies the nonlocal information that a component wishes to manipulate. The federated architecture provides mechanisms for sharing data, for sharing transactions (via message types) for combining information from several components, and for coordinating activities among autonomous components (via negotiation). A prototype implementation of the federated database mechanism is currently operational on an experimental basis.

Categories and Subject Descriptors: H.2.1 [**Database Management**]: Logical Design—*data models; schema and subschema*; H.2.4 [**Database Management**]: Systems—*distributed systems*; H.4.1 [**Information Systems Applications**]: Office Automation

General Terms: Algorithms, Design, Languages, Management

Additional Keywords and Phrases: Office information systems, distributed information management, federated databases

1. INTRODUCTION

The office information environment presents many new information management challenges [8, 28, 35]. In particular, the types of information and the patterns of information access are quite different from those of application

This research was supported in part by the Joint Services Electronics Program through the Air Force Office of Scientific Research under contract F49620-85-C-0071, in part by the National Science Foundation under grant MCS-8203485, and in part by the Defense Advanced Research Projects Agency under contract MDA903-81-C-0335.
Authors' addresses: D. Heimbigner, Computer Science Department, University of Colorado, Boulder, CO 80309. D. McLeod, Computer Science Department, Los Angeles, CA 90089-0782; ARPANET: McLeod@USC-ISIB.

Reprinted with permission from *ACM Trans. Office Info. Systems,* vol. 3, no. 3, July 1985.
© Copyright 1985 Association for Computing Machinery.

environments for which conventional database management technology and systems are intended. The integrated database system was primarily developed to support large, integrated, centralized databases. In a decentralized information environment there may not be a single, integrated database containing all of the organizational information under the control of a centralized data processing organization. Rather, databases tend to proliferate throughout an organization with little or no control by any one group. In such an environment there is a need for substantial information management flexibility, partial integration/ sharing, and autonomy [23].

A possible response to the decentralization of information is to attempt to return to centralization by reintegrating the data into a "composite database," sometimes called a "heterogeneous database." To form a composite database, a new, global/virtual conceptual schema is introduced, which describes the information in the databases being composed; database access and manipulation operations are then mediated through this new conceptual schema. This return to strict integration does, however, require centralization.

Inherent in the concept of integration is the existence of some authority (namely, a database administrator) responsible for designing and maintaining the conceptual and physical (implementation) schemas of the database. Thus, the process of integrating existing databases forces control over their structure to be ceded to some central authority. The users of the existing databases may have expended considerable resources (hardware, software, and human) in developing their databases and may be reluctant to lose control of them. Furthermore, changes to the structure of a database must pass through the database administrator, and they must be weighed against competing demands for change.

The integration of existing databases into a composite database is in general quite difficult. An important problem in this regard is that the same fact may be contained in several databases yet be represented using different conceptual structures. For example, one database may represent a memo by links/mappings among the writer, recipient(s), and memo content, while another database may represent the memo as a distinct object with links to the writer, recipients, and memo content. If a composite database approach is used, one or the other of these conceptual representations must be selected, and applications using the other representation may need modification. In sum, the composite structure may be difficult to construct, and if it can be constructed, it may be suboptimal for many users' needs.

In light of the difficulties posed by composite databases, it is appropriate to pursue an alternative architecture that allows the existing database systems to maintain their autonomy, yet provides a substantial degree of information sharing. The goal of this paper is to define an architecture and supporting mechanisms for interconnecting databases that minimizes central authority, yet supports partial sharing and coordination among database systems. This *federated database architecture* [10, 12, 13] allows a collection of database systems (*components*) to unite into a loosely coupled federation in order to share and exchange information. The term *federation* refers to the collection of constituent databases participating in a federated database.

Without the constraint of a central authority, the mechanisms provided for the federated architecture must balance two conflicting requirements: the components must maintain as much autonomy as possible; however, the components must be able to achieve a reasonable degree of information sharing. The first of these requirements, autonomy, specifically refers to four capabilities:

(1) A component must not be forced to perform an activity for another component. The role of centralized authority must be replaced by cooperative activity among components and supporting protocols.

(2) Each component determines the data that it wishes to share with other components. Since partial, controlled sharing is a fundamental goal of the federated approach, each component must be able to specify the information to be made available as well as to specify which other components may access it and in what ways.

(3) Each component determines how it will view and combine existing data. In a composite system, all access to the underlying data is mediated by a global schema. In a federation, each component must be able to, in effect, build its own "global" schema that is best suited to its needs.

(4) A component must have "freedom of association" with respect to the federation. Since the federation is a dynamic entity, components must be able to dynamically enter or leave the federation. Further, a component must be able to modify its shared data interface, adding new data and withdrawing access to previously shared data.

As a counterpoint to the capabilities required to support component autonomy, the federated architecture must provide mechanisms to support information sharing. Specifically, components can communicate in the following three ways:

—*Data communication.* Each component has a collection of data, and other components may be interested in accessing some portion of those data. Exchanging the data is the primary activity in a federation, and so a mechanism to support data sharing is essential to the operation of a federation.

—*Transaction sharing.* A component may not wish to share its data directly, but rather to share operations upon its data. This may be the case if the data are sensitive or have consistency constraints attached to them. In any case, components must be able to define transactions that can be invoked by other components.

—*Cooperative activities.* In a system of autonomous components, the only way that the federation can function correctly is by cooperation. Components must be able to initiate a potentially complex series of actions involving cooperation with other components. Cooperation in this context refers to negotiated data sharing.

Using these facilities, a collection of components in an office information system can collectively achieve a substantial amount of sharing while maintaining essential control over their data.

2. DISTRIBUTED DATABASE SYSTEMS

Databases, viewed as structured collections of information, can be roughly classified along two dimensions representing: (1) conceptual/logical structure (semantics), and (2) physical organization and structure. Each dimension may in turn be divided into two parts: centralized and decentralized. Using this framework, four classes of databases can be identified: (1) logically centralized and physically centralized databases, which include the conventional integrated databases; (2) logically centralized and physically decentralized databases, including *distributed databases,*[1] as well as a number of recent approaches to composite database support; logically decentralized and either (3) physically centralized or (4) physically decentralized databases, which represent the province of *federated databases.*

Integrated databases, distributed databases, and most approaches to composite databases represent the logically centralized approach: They provide a single conceptual schema for users and application programs. Multiple external schemas (views) may be provided in such systems, but a single central conceptual schema is nonetheless required. In this approach, an integration of the data associated with an application environment is attempted.

The distributed database architecture, for example, as described in [19], [29], [30], and [34], fits into the category of logically centralized and physically decentralized databases. In such a database the users and applications access data described through a single conceptual schema, but the data may be physically stored in many separate computers, typically the nodes of a computer network. This architecture is specifically designed to provide a unified system that is distributed across several interconnected computer systems. As such, it does not address the integration of preexisting databases except by discarding those databases and pacing their data into the new system. Thus the distributed database architecture does not address the same issues as the federated architecture.

Additional architectures have been proposed for databases, and these are more directly comparable to federated databases. The common feature of these *composite database systems* is that they attempt to combine a number of existing databases into a single, logically centralized entity. This is achieved by defining a global schema and then defining translation functions between the global schema and the local schemas of the constituent databases. In order to construct a composite database, two problems must be solved. First, the global schema must be defined in such a way as to integrate all the information in the local schemas and remove as much redundancy as possible. As indicated earlier, such integration is potentially very difficult. Second the translations must be defined so that operations on the global schema may be translated into equivalent operations on some set of the local schemas.

Composite database systems may be further classified as *homogeneous composite databases* and *heterogeneous composite databases.* The former is a composite database in which all of the local schemas as well as the global schema are defined using the same database model. Although this limits the complexity of

---

[1] The term "distributed databases" is used here as it has been mainly used in the literature, denoting a logically centralized, physically distributed system.

the translation functions, they are not trivial since two or more local schemas may structure the same information in different ways. Thus, no matter how the global schema structures the information, some transformation will be necessary to access one or the other of the local schemas.

A composite database is said to be *heterogeneous* if one or more of the constituent databases does not use the same database model as is used for the global schema. A heterogeneous composite database system inherits the difficulties associated with homogeneous composite database systems, and in addition must face the additional problem of translating between different data models. This problem is aggravated by the fact that constructs in one model may not exist in another model.

There are several existing and proposed composite database systems, including R* [20], XNDM [15, 16], Multibase [33], "superviews" [25], and the work of Litwin [21, 22]. A significant limitation of composite architectures is their basic centralized nature, and particularly the existence of a global schema. However, these approaches provide significant concepts and principles to address the problems of heterogeneity, integration, and, to some extent, autonomy (R*). Many of the ideas of these approaches have been incorporated into the federated architecture.

By contrast with composite systems, the federated database uses an organizational model based on equal, autonomous databases, with sharing controlled by explicit interfaces. The effect of modifications may be limited, and no database has authority over another. There is no global schema in a federation. Rather, each component has direct access to the original data provided by other components, and it is free to restructure that information into whatever form is most appropriate to its needs. The control of the sharing rests with the owner of the data, but the negotiation mechanism ensures that changes to the structure of the data proceeds in an orderly fashion.

The federated approach has some commonalities with the approach to "information object sharing" described in [23]; in fact, many of the basic concepts in [23] are derived from initial work on the federated architecture [12, 13]. The focus of [23] is to provide a small set of operations for object definition, manipulation, and retrieval in a distributed environment, modeled as a logical network of office workstations. Relationships among objects can be established across workstation boundaries, objects are relocatable within the distributed environment, and mechanisms are provided for access control. An object-naming convention supports location transparent object references, which means that objects can be referenced by user-defined names rather than by address. By contrast, the federated architecture is focused on a higher level than the object-sharing approach, in that it provides more explicit intercomponent interfaces, specific capabilities to support negotiation, and a "semantic" model of information vis-a-vis sharing.

3. THE FEDERATED DATABASE MODEL

Before discussing the details of the federated architecture, it is necessary to summarize the database model used to describe data in a federation. The architecture presented in this paper assumes that a common database model is used throughout the federation; that is, the federation is homogeneous. It is, of course, possible to have a heterogeneous federation if the components do not all use the same database model. "Hooks" exist in the architecture to deal with heterogeneity, although this paper does not consider them in detail; principles and techniques devised in research on composite database systems can be employed in this regard [15, 16, 21, 22, 25, 33].

The federated database model used in this paper is based on an object-oriented database model: the *event model* [17]. The event model is a characteristic "semantic database model" [1–3, 8, 11, 18, 26, 32]. Specifically, the federated database model is based on three basic data modeling primitives:

—*Objects.* The basic modeling element is an object, which corresponds to some (real world) entity or concept (e.g., the person Jane Smith or the number 5). Objects are divided into two categories: *descriptor objects* and *abstract objects.* Descriptor objects are atomic strings of characters, integers, or Booleans, and generally serve as symbolic identifiers in the database. Decriptor objects are the only directly displayable objects; thus all external references to objects in the database must ultimately be in terms of descriptor objects. All nondescriptor objects are abstract objects. They are not directly displayable, except in terms of related descriptor objects (such as unique identifiers).

—*Types.* Types are time-varying collections of objects that share common properties; the objects of a given type are called the *instances* of that type. Some types are designated descriptor types in that they may only contain descriptor objects. All other types are designated abstract types. A type may be a *subtype* of another (parent) type if it is defined so that its set of instances is always a subset of the instances of the parent type. Associated with any subtype is a *predicate* that determines which objects that are instances of the parent type are also instances of the subtype. A particular subclass of abstract types required in the federated architecture, termed *message types*, is described in Section 4.7.

—*Maps.* Maps are "functions" that map objects from some domain type to sets of objects in the power set of some range type. A number of simple integrity constraints may be specified with each map; for example, a map may be specified to be *single-valued* (i.e., its value for all objects in the domain type has cardinality of zero or one) or *multivalued*, and a map can be declared to be a *unique identifier* (*key*).

In addition to the data structuring primitives described above, the federated information model provides primitive operators for data retrieval and modification. In the federated model, data manipulation primarily involves traversing the directed graph of types and maps that constitutes a given database. The actions of the data manipulation operators are defined principally in terms of *cursors* [9], which in this model are abstract ordered sets of objects together with a pointer into that set. Each cursor refers to a unique sequence of objects and also contains some state information about that sequence. In particular, the cursor contains a marker that points to some specific element of the associated sequence. The model contains operators to create and destroy cursors, and to sequence through the elements of the cursor.

The database model also assumes the existence of *transactions*, which are procedures expressed in some programming language. The parameters to these procedures are objects in the database system. A transaction is integrated into the schema by representing its interface as a type and its parameters as maps associated with that type. Each invocation of a transaction creates an instance of the type associated with that transaction.

In a federated database, objects always reside in the component (database) in which they are created, but references to them may be passed to other components so that the objects can be manipulated remotely through a set of exported operators. Using this facility, a copy of any object can be created by any component, but the copy is a different object. This scheme requires that objects be given names that are unique with respect to an entire federation. Such unique names must themselves contain some tag indicating the component that contains the specified object. These unique names are generated by concatenating the component name with a local object name. The component name is guaranteed to be unique within the federation, and this is enforced by the federation system. A unique local object name (unique with respect to a component) can be generated by using a simple counter that is incremented whenever a new object is created. Alternatively, a clock of sufficient resolution can be used to generate unique names. Somewhat more general naming schemes can also be used, for example, as described in [23] and [28].

4. THE FEDERATED DATABASE ARCHITECTURE

The basic elements of the federated architecture are components, of which there may be any number; components represent individual information systems that wish to share and exchange information. Each federation has a single *federal dictionary*, which is a distinguished component whose information province is the federation itself. The federal dictionary supports the establishment, maintenance, and termination of a federation. The only difference between the federal dictionary and any other component is the database it contains. It has no direct control over other components, and it does not mediate communications among other components.

A component may be viewed as an autonomous database. A component has associated with it three schemas, each of which describes some class of information important to the proper functioning of the component. Each of the three schemas of a component is a collection of types and maps. The three component schemas are the private schema, export schema, and import schema; these are described immediately below.

4.1 Private Schema

The *private schema* describes that portion of a component's data that is local to (stored at) the component. The bulk of the private schema is devoted to describing the application data available in the database of a component. This portion of the schema, as well as the data it describes, corresponds to a normal database in a nonfederated environment. Although some of this information will remain local to the component, a portion of the application data and transactions will be exported to other components.

In addition to the application-specific data, the private schema contains a small collection of information and transactions relevant to the component's participation in the federation. This information is exported by the component for use by other components, particularly the federal dictionary. The federation-specific information falls into three categories:

(1) descriptive information about the component, such as the component name and network address;
(2) primitive operations for data manipulation, such as accessing a type and traversing a map;
(3) the import and export schemas.

4.2 Export Schema

The export schema portion of the component specifies the information that the component is willing to share with other components of the federation. The export schema consists of a collection of types and maps denoting the information to be exported to other components. As in the private schema, the exported information is divided among federation-specific information and application-specific information. The federation-specific information is much the same as the federation-specific information of the private schema and is explicitly derived from it. The application-specific information is analogously derived from the information in the application-specific portion of the private schema.

The export schema is actually a metaschema consisting of a set of types and maps in the component schema that contain the definitions of the types and maps that are to be exported. Other components import this export schema and peruse it like any other information. Not all exported types and maps are represented in the export schema. Certain primitive types and maps are always assumed to be exported, and it is not necessary for them to be explicitly included in the export schema.

Each type and map in an export schema must have certain properties associated with it. There are five properties for types: *category, definition, derivation, access list*, and *connection list*. For exported maps, there are six properties: the same five as for types plus a list of *constraints*. The category property specifies the kind of type or map: descriptor or abstract. The definition property indicates whether the type or map is derived; its actual derivation expression is specified by the derivation property. The constraint list for maps specifies whether the map is single valued, a unique identifier (key), etc. The access list and connection list are used to control access to exported types. The access list property specifies which other components may access this type. The connection list specifies which other components have imported this type and hence are potentially accessing it.

In a given federation each component will have certain types and maps that it is willing to share with every other component, but it will also have other elements that it is willing to share only with some specified subset of the components in the federation. In the federated architecture this is supported by placing access controls on types and maps in the export schema. Thus the first line of control over data access is the export/import mechanism, and the access controls provide a finer grain of control on top of that mechanism.

Access controls must be specified in terms of components rather than individual users of a component, because enforcement of user-level access controls is dependent on the proper operation of the component. If a component has errors that allow one user of the component to masquerade as another user, then a user may circumvent the access protections. It is possible for one component to enforce component-level access controls since it mediates every access to its data by another component, assuming proper operation of the underlying network.

An access list is a set of ordered pairs. The first element of each pair is a component identifier; the second element of the pair is an access right assigned to that component, specifying some type or map. Any component not contained in the access list has no right to access the type or map. There are two kinds of access rights: "read" and "write" (which implicitly allows read also). If a component has "read" access to a type, then it is allowed to "open" the type to sequence through the objects in that type. A component may only have "read" access to a map if it also has "read" access to the domain and range types of the map. If a component has "read" access to a map, then it can traverse ("apply") the map from a domain object to a set of range objects. A component with "write" access to a map allows a component to change the mappings for a given object, as well as perform "read" operations.

4.3 Import Schema

The import schema of a component specifies the information that component desires to use from other components. As for the other two schemas, the import schema deals both with federation-specific and application-specific information. Both the application-specific information and the federation-specific information are specified by a schema derived from the corresponding (accessible) portions of the export schemas of other components.

An imported type or map has the same properties as an exported type, except that it has no access list and no connection list. In addition, each imported element (type or map) has a derived definition property, specifying how the imported element is derived from the underlying exported element(s).

4.4 Schema Importation

Schema importation is the fundamental information-sharing operation in a federation. The term "importation" refers to the process of modifying a component's import schema as well as gaining access to some element of exported information. Before a component enters a federation, it imports nothing. As soon as it enters, it imports sufficient built-in information to function within the federation. This level of importation is essentially automatic. Beyond this, all importation of information is at the discretion of the component itself and must be explicitly negotiated with other components.

In order to import information, each component must know or discover what information is available in the federation. This is accomplished in two steps. First, through the federal dictionary each component may discover the names and network addresses of the other components. Second, each component contacts those components, using a predefined protocol. At this point a component is in a position to peruse the export schemas of the other components and engage in the schema importation process.

To illustrate the importation process, suppose that component c1 exports a type t1. Further suppose that component c2 wishes to import t1 for reading as its (c2's) type t2. C1 arranges the importation through the following negotiation:

(1) C2 requests c1 to give it read access to t1.
(2) C1 grants c2 the access, modifying the connection list.
(3) When c2 receives the affirmative reponse from c1, it adds a new type t2 to its import schema. The type t2 is defined to be derived with an initial derivation expression of "c1 > t1"; that is, it is a derivation of type t1 of component c1.

It is important to note that the importation of a type or map is separate from subsequent data access. The type is imported once, and then all subsequent accesses to the contents of that type are carried out directly, without the overhead of negotiation. The actual data transfers occur when the importer attempts to scan the contents of the type. This is completely analogous to access to a local type except that the data is transferred over a network.

When component c2 imports a schema element that is exported by another component c1, an implicit contract is established between c1 and c2. In this contract c1 guarantees that it will not modify the definition (structure or semantics) of the exported element unless it notifies the importer, c2. By this contract c2 also agrees to notify c1 when it no longer requires access to the element. This process of negotiated change is a key element of the federated architecture.

Three kinds of modification caused by evolving information sharing patterns require notification: giving the importer no access to the element, changing the importer's access right from "write" to "read," and changing the semantics of the element. In the first case, where the importer is denied any access to the element, the importer is obligated to relinquish the connection to the element. Of course, the importer cannot be forced to do this, but the implicit contract has been broken and further access would be denied. In the other two cases the importer has the option of either relinquishing access to the element or notifying the exporter that the modified element is an acceptable replacement for the original element, and so continue to use the element.

4.5 Type and Map Derivation Operators

Once some set of types and maps have been imported, a component can proceed to restructure that information to suit its purposes. To this end, the architecture provides a set of *derivation operators* for manipulating type and map definitions to produce new ones.

Before discussing the various type and map derivation operators, it is necessary to describe the concept of an *object equality function*. Such functions are essential for combining information across component boundaries. In the federated database model it is assumed that two objects from different components a priori refer to different objects. Often this is acceptable, but sometimes it is necessary to indicate that two objects owned by different components in fact do represent the same entity. Object equality functions are used to define this equivalence of objects.

An object equality function is a string (descriptor object) manipulation operation defined in a programming language.[2] The argument to the function is a string that is assumed to be an assigned name for an object. This string may be derived from the object via a series of key map traversals until a desriptor value is reached. The equality function takes that string and computes another string as a value. This string is assumed to represent some other object, which can be found via an additional series of traversals of key maps.

As an example, suppose that component c1 contains a type "employee" with a key map "employee-number" that is an encodng of the employee's social security number of the form "123456789." Also, suppose that component c2 contains a type "manager" with a map "social-security-number" of the form "123-45-6789." A possible equality function, denote it by ~, is a string funtion that takes a number of the form 123456789 and transforms it to 123-45-6789. Thus, given an employee, one constructively finds the equivalent manager by (1) obtaining the employee-number of the employee, (2) converting it to a social-security-number using ~, and then (3) finding the manager with that social-security-number.

The *type derivation operators* are used to construct new types as combination of existing types, which in turn may be derived types. These operators treat types as multisets of objects. There are four principal type derivation operators:

—*Concatenate* combines the instances of two types to create a new type. As a typical example, a unified type for airplanes might be constructed by concatenating the types for various makes of airplanes.[3]

—*Subtraction* subtracts the instances of one type from the instances of another type. Subtraction is most often used to obtain the complement of a type. For example, given types "airplanes" and "military-airplanes," one may obtain "commercial-airplanes" via subtraction.

—*Cross product* creates a type with one instance for every n-tuple of objects from some set of n types. This operation might be used for example to create a type "date" as the cross product of types "month," "day," and "year."

—*Subtype* allows a new type to be created via some predicate on another type. For example, given the type "airplanes" with a map "kind" specifying whether the airplane is commercial or military, the subtype "commercial-airplanes" is a subtype of airplanes where the map "kind" has the value "commercial."

As for types, it is possible to derive new maps from existing maps. Object equality functions are considered derived maps, although the derivation is by means of an arbitrary host-language procedure. Some type derivation operations (concatenate, cross product, and subtype) automatically induce new maps on the derived type.

In addition to object equality functions, there are the following eight *map derivation operators.*

---

[2] In the case of the prototype federated system, described below, this language is LISP.
[3] Since these operations generally involve types of two different components, it is typically necessary to specify an object equality function for defining common objects in the two types.

—*Composition* defines a new map as the composition of two other maps (e.g., *A* and *B*). If the map *A* and/or the map *B* are multivalued, then the composed map consists of all objects in the range of map *B* that are obtained by following an *A* map from the domain of *A* to the range of *A*, and then following a *B* map; if the result of applying either map is undefined, then so is the composition. For example, composing the map "manufacturer" of type "airplanes" with the map "name" of "manufacturer," the result is a new map specifying the name of the manufacturer of an airplane; if "manufacturer" and "name" are multivalued, then the composition consists of the set of all names of all manufacturers of airplanes.

—*Inversion* defines a new map as the inverse of another map. For example, inverting the map specifying the manufacturer of an airplane gives a map specifying the airplanes of a manufacturer.

—*Extension* extends the definition of a map from a type to its supertype. Even if the original map is total, its extension will be partial since it is undefined for objects in the supertype but not in the type. Extension is most commonly used with composition to allow a map on a subtype to be attached to the supertype. Thus if the type "commercial" airplanes had a map specifying the number of cabin attendants, composing this map with the extension map to type "airplanes" could provide the number of cabin attendants for all airplanes. Note, however, that the value of the map would be undefined for military airplanes.

—*Restriction* restricts the definition of a map from a type to its subtype. If the original function is total, then so is the restricted function. This derivation allows a map on a type to be attached to a subtype.

—*Cross product* creates a map whose value is the two-tuple of values produced by applying two other maps. It is most commonly used with the cross-product type derivation. Thus if the type "airplane" has maps specifying the year, month, and day of manufacture, these maps could be combined via cross product to create a map representing the date of manufacture.

—*Discrimination* maps are automatically defined for each type derived by concatenation. If *n* types are concatenated, then *n* discrimination maps are defined. The *i*th discrimination map is defined only on elements from the *i*th type, so it may be used with selection to test whether an object originated from a particular type. This derivation is usually used with the selection derivation.

—*Projection* maps, similarly to discrimination maps, are automatically defined for cross-product types. The *i*th projection map selects the *i*th element of any *n*-tuple of the cross product. This derivation can be used, for example, to choose the "month," "day," and "year" maps of the "date" type created via cross product.

—*Selection* allows a map to be one of a set of map expressions based upon a series of condition tests (viz., a "case statement"). The conditions are also map expressions. Each condition is evaluated, and if it results in a defined value, then the corresponding map expression is evaluated and returned as the result of the selection. When used in conjunction with discrimination maps, selection can be used to convert an operation on a concatenated type into an operation on one of types from which it was created.

This collection of type and map derivation operators is quite low-level (compared for example to [25] and [27]). In particular, it is important to realize that the derivation of a type is generally independent of the derivation of maps. For example, suppose two types, X and Y, are concatenated into a new type Z. Further, suppose that X and Y both have associated maps called "name." This does not mean that Z automatically is given a derived map called "name." Instead, that derivation, if it is desired, must be explicitly constructed. A higher level interface supporting such functionality, which, for example, automatically derives maps when new types are derived, can be constructed using the primitives provided here.

4.6 Data Update

In addition to providing read access to imported and derived data, the federated architecture must provide the capability for components to update such data. The update problem is complicated by the existence of derived types whose update requires updating the types from which it is derived (called "base types"). The problem of updating derived data is essentially the same as the view update problem [4, 7, 14], which has been principally studied in the context of the relational database model. Briefly, the problem is that the derived type is obtained by a mapping from a set of base types to the derived type. To update a derived type, it is necessary to invert the derivation function so that updates to the base types can be determined from the update to the derived type. In the most general case this inversion is impossible (it may be undefined or ambiguous), which means the derived type cannot be updated correctly.

The following approach to the update problem is adopted in the federated architecture. If the derivation is direct (i.e., renaming only), then update is allowed. Otherwise the data abstraction approach of Rigel [31] is used. In this method, all updates to derived types are funneled through an associated set of user-defined operations. Thus, the definer of the derived type also specifies all possible operations on that derived type, and specifically the update operations for the type. In practice, this method just transfers the problem to the definer of the derived type, who must choose operations and their parameters so that enough information is available to do the inversion. In the federation these operations are specified by means of a set of message types implementing transactions that perform the meaningful updates. The exporter is free to define the semantics of these transactions as desired.

4.7 Message Types

The decentralized nature of a federation dictates the need for many forms of communication among components. The capability for importing base types and maps is one form of communication, but other means are needed to support the exchange of higher levels of information. Specifically, the federation must allow components to import and invoke transactions defined by other components. Shared transactions are useful for two purposes. First, they can be used to control updates to shared data, much as in abstract data types. Second, they are needed to implement the negotiation subsystem (described in the next section).

The federated architecture allows components to share transactions through message passing. This facility is embodied in the *message type* construct, which serves as an interface specification for some transaction. The message type, like any type, can be exported by one component and imported by other components; it is this process that constitutes the sharing of a transaction among components.

The message type describes a class of intercomponent messages. Associated with the exporting component is a procedure that defines the transaction associated with that message type. The normal message-sending paradigm is transformed to the database paradigm of creating a new object: creating an object of the message type is equivalent to sending the object as a message. At the receiving component, the message is queued as an instance of the type. The message objects are scanned in arrival order, and the earliest one is passed to the transaction for processing. When the transaction is finished, the object is returned to the sender to signal the completion of one message passing cycle. If the object sender attempts to access the object before it is returned, the sender is delayed. Thus, to the sender the process is reasonably transparent and appears more or less as a normal object creation and access activity.

The maps associated with the message type allow parameters to be passed to the receiver and results returned to the sender. The maps associated with the type are partitioned into two kinds: *input maps* and *output maps*. The input maps define attributes of the messages that are intended to be inputs to the transaction associated with the message type. Similarly, the output maps represent results returned after the transaction processes the message.

A message actually consists of two objects. The importer of the message type creates a surrogate object locally and assigns values to all of the input maps. Each message type has two predefined input maps, "msg-surrogate" and "msg-source," whose values are assigned by the database system. The "msg-surrogate" map specifies a unique object name of the surrogate, while the "msg-source" map provides the name of the component sending the message.

For example, if component c1 exports the message type "order" with maps "part" and "quantity" as follows:[4]

order:
    part → partname
    quantity → integer

then c2 may import the type and maps as

c1/order:
    part → partname
    quantity → integer

The identifier "c1/order" is c2's local name for the imported version of c1's "order" type. An order message can be sent (by c2) using the following sequence:

1. let m = new (c1/order)

2. insert-map (m, c1/order.part, "wrench")

3. insert-map (m, c1/order.quantity, 100)

Here step 1 creates a new object of type "order," and steps 2 and 3 establish the input maps.

---

[4] Here the arrow separates a map name from its range type.

It is at the point when all the input maps have been assigned that the object is actually sent to the receiver. The originating component, c2 in this case, collects the name of the surrogate object, its own name (c2), and the input map values ("wrench" and 100), and converts them to a linear message suitable for shipping over the network. It should be noted that when the map value is an object, the value shipped is the unique name of that object (i.e., objects are transmitted by reference).

When the message is received by c1 (the exporter), c1 creates an instance of its message type ("order" in this case) and assigns the input map values taken from the message. The transaction of the message type is then invoked with this object as its argument. The transaction performs whatever action it desires, assigns values to the output maps, and returns. In the case where map values are objects (object references), accesses to these remote objects are converted to appropriate intercomponent messages. After the transaction is complete, the output maps are collected, linearized, and returned to the sender. The sender assigns the output values to its surrogate object and continues operation.

4.8 Negotiation

With the absence of a central authority, the federated architecture provides a mechanism to coordinate the sharing of information among components: the negotiation subsystem. A negotiation is a multistep, distributed dialogue among two components. For example, there is a built-in negotiation that sequences through the steps for importing a type that was exported by some component. Other negotiations control the entry and exit of components with respect to the federation. It is important to note that negotiation is distinct from the process of data access. Negotiation establishes the right to access some general kinds of data elements. Once this is established, the primitives of Section 3 are used to manipulate that data.

It is also possible for users to define new application-specific negotiations as well. As a corollary, the structure of negotiations must be accessible to the user, and hence they must be at least partially embedded in the database itself. The actual negotiation subsystem has two main parts: an interpreter and a negotiation language for writing negotiation procedures. The negotiation procedures (written in the negotiation language) are stored in the database of each component. Each negotiation procedure contains three elements: a set of *participant schemas*, a *negotiation schema*, and a *negotiation graph*.

Any particular negotiation is conducted between two participants, which are abstractions for components in the federation. Several of the same kind of negotiation may be in operation simultaneously but with different bindings of participant to component. Each participant has a participant schema, which when instantiated provides local memory during the negotiation. The schema may be parameterized, and the participant's state is initialized with actual values of these parameters when the negotiation is invoked.

To support the negotiation process, each participating component has a *negotiation database*. A negotiation database is described by a negotiation schema, which specifies a collection of types and maps; the database is in turn a collection of objects and map instances matching the format of the negotiation schema. It contains the actual state for any single instance of a negotiation. One of the types in the negotiation schema is called the *token type*; it represents the "root" type of the negotiation schema in that it serves as a handle to reach all other portions of the negotiation schema. The instance of the token type in the negotiation database is designated the *token*. During the steps of a negotiation, the token is exchanged between the participants until some final result is determined. The negotiation database is modified during the steps of the negotiation to reflect changes in the state of the subject of the negotiation.

The possible steps for each kind of negotiation are specified by the negotiation graph. If a negotiation is viewed as a program, then the negotiation graph serves as a representation of the major control flow of that program. A negotiation graph consists of a collection of nodes connected by arcs. Each negotiation node stands for a possible state of the negotiation, and each negotiation arc indicates a possible transition between states. A negotiation node has the following structure:

—the *node name* describes the state associated with that node.
—The *class* of the node indicates whether a node is *initial*, which means that it is the (unique) starting node for the negotiation, *terminal*, which means that it is a final node for the negotiation, or *other*. The three classes are mutually exclusive properties of the nodes.
—The *transitions* are the arcs from a given node leading to other nodes.
—Associated with each node is a procedure that defines the *semantics* of the node. It determines which transition is taken from the node on the basis of any criteria it chooses, for example, by interrogating one of the participants to the negotiation, or by some arbitrary computation.
—Each node of the graph is assigned to an *owning participant*, which "owns" that node.

A negotiation arc has the following structure:

—The arc has an *arc name* that is used as an input to the node semantics.
—The *source* and *destination* are the nodes connected by the arc.

One of the components in a federation initiates a negotiation by assigning itself as participant one and choosing another component as participant two. The use of "one" and "two" is arbitrary, but one of the participants must be identifiable as the initiator of the negotiation. Participant two is notified that a particular negotiation is to be initiated by means of an imported message type, specific to that negotiation. Each participant creates its local state and initializes it. In addition, participant two is responsible for creating the token and returning its unique name to participant one.

The negotiation starts with the participant that owns the initial node of the negotiation graph. It "places" the token upon the initial node of the negotiation graph via an arc with no name. Whenever the token is "located" at a given node, the owner of the node executes the procedure associated with that node. This procedure is given four arguments: its state, the token, the name of the current node, and the name of the last arc traversed. The procedure may examine and modify its local database and the negotiation database, and it may interact with the owner of the node. For nonterminal nodes the output of the procedure is an arc, which the system then traverses to reach a new node. For terminal nodes any output is ignored and the negotiation is terminated.

The success or failure of the negotiation is determined by the semantics of the terminal node. Many negotiations will have several terminal nodes, some representing success and some representing failure. It is important, however, that both participants know the outcome of the negotiation, and so as a special rule of notification, once the result of the negotiation is decided by one participant, the token must travel to a node of the other participant by the time it reaches a terminal state. In this way each participant knows the outcome of the negotiation.

As an example, consider the "access-type" primitive negotiation. In this negotiation, participant one requests access to (i.e., imports) some type exported by participant two. As data the negotiation requires access to an instance of the negotiation schema, a state for component one, and a state for component two. This information is defined by the following types:

```
access-type-info:
    type → string
    category → string
    definition → string
    excuse → string
access-type-state1:
    component → component-name
    type → string
access-type-state2:
    source → component-name
```

The type "access-type-info" is the sole type in the negotiation schema, so it is also the token type for the negotiation. It carries four items of information:

—The "type" is the name of the type to be imported.
—The "category" is either "descriptor," "abstract," or "message."
—The "definition" is either "base" or "derived."
—The "excuse" is an error message in case the access to the type is denied.

The two types "access-type-state1" and "access-type-state2" define the state information for each participant. Since the state and the token are the only items of information passed among nodes, the state must record any information at initiation that is needed by later nodes. In this case, each participant must record its binding to a particular real component, and participant one (the requester) must record the type to which access is requested.

The negotiation interpreter also requires information in order to track the state of the negotiation, and to this end, it uses the following negotiation-specific types:

access-type$participant1-negotiation:
    current-node → negotiation-node
    current-arc → negotiation-arc
    state1 → access-type-state1
    participant2 → component-name
    token → object-name

access-type$participant2-negotiation:
    current-node → negotiation-node
    current-arc → negotiation-arc
    state2 → access-type-state2
    participant1 → component-name
    token → access-type-info

The interpreter at each component maintains a collection of information about each instance of negotiation in process, specifically, "access-type$participant1-negotiation" and "access-type$participant2-negotiation." For both participants, the interpreter keeps a record of the node currently containing the token ("current-node") and the last arc traversed ("current-arc"). Additionally, links to the state information are maintained via "state1" or "state2," as appropriate. Further, the "token" is recorded, and hence a link is provided to the entire negotiation database. Finally, the interpeter records the identity of the component bound to the other participant.

A set of three message types is defined for each negotiation. These message types are used by the interpreters on each component to invoke action by the other component. The types are defined as follows:

access-type$initialize:
    input maps:
        graph → string
    output maps:
        token → access-type-info
    participant2-negotiation → access-type$participant2-negotiation

access-type$transition:
    input maps:
        graph → string
        participant2-negotiation → access-type$participant2-negotiation
        participant1-arc → string
    output maps:
        participant2-arc → string

access-type$finalize:
    input maps:
        graph → string
        participant2-negotiation → access-type$participant2-negotiation
    output maps:

The interpreter initializes the negotiation by first creating an instance of "access-type$participant1-negotiation" to stand for this instance of the negotiation. Next, the interpreter creates an instance of "access-type-state1," passes it to a negotiation-specific initialization procedure specified by the negotiation graph, and finally links that state object to the negotiation instance. The interpreter then sends an "access-type$initialize" message to the second participant to inform it to initialize for the specified negotiation. When the second participant receives the message, it creates an instance of "access-type-state2," an instance of the token type, and an instance of "access-type$participant2-negotiation." These latter two objects are returned to participant one as the output of the message. Upon receiving the response, the first participant begins to sequence through the graph.

Graph traversal is handled by repeated exchanges of "access-type$transition" messages between the two participants. The essential input from participant one is the arc that it is traversing; the output from participant two is the next arc. As a side effect of the message passing, the appropriate negotiation-specific node action is executed. After the negotiation reaches a terminal state and participant one gets a final response from participant two, the first participant sends an "access-type$finalize" message to the second participant to allow both of them to clean up the residue from the negotiation.

Textually, the negotiation graph for "access-type" is as follows:

```
access-type
    (token = access-type-info,
    state1 = access-type-state1,
    state2 = access-type-state2,
    init1 = save-atype, init2 = savesource,
    final1 = nofin1, final2 = nofin2)

request-access
    (type = start,
    semantics = get-atype,
    owner = 1):
    ready → receive-request

receive-request
    (type = other,
    semantics = test-type-access,
    owner = 2):
    ok → access-granted
    notok = access-denied

access-granted
    (type = terminal,
    semantics = finish-type-access,
    owner = 1):

access-denied
    (type = terminal,
    semantics = explain-type-access-failure,
    owner = 1):
```

The first part, labeled "access-type," is the header of the negotiation. It specifies the type which is the token, the two state types, and the names of the procedures that will handle initialization and finalization for each participant. Following the header is a series of node definitions. Each node specifies the node type (start, other, terminate), the procedure defining the semantics of the node, and the participant that owns the node. After that it specifies the names of the arcs from that node and the destination of each arc. For example, the start state has only one arc, named "ready," and it leads to the node names "receive-request."

The negotiation subsystem provides enough functionality so that it is relatively easy to add new negotiations to the system. It is only necessary to define the negotiation schema, the participant states, the negotiation graph, and the node semantics procedures. The interpreter then performs remaining functions automatically.

4.9 System-Level Issues

Underlying any instance of the federated architecture must be a real system of hardware and software, and certain system-level mechanisms are needed to support the proper operation of the federation. In [12] three particular system issues are addressed in detail: concurrency control, nested transactions, and object passing. The solutions proposed are straightforward modifications of known or obvious solutions (which is not to say that better solutions are not possible). Concurrency control is a variation on two-phase locking. Nested transactions are handled by associating locks of the inner transactions with the parent transaction. This solution is similar to that described in [24]. Finally, objects are only passed by reference, and all objects are given systemwide unique names derived from the unique name of the component in the federation.

4.10 The Initial Structure of a Federation

In order to function, the federated architecture assumes that each component shares a common set of descriptor types, base types, message types, and negotiations. There are seven primitive descriptor types: *string*, *boolean*, *integer*, *real*, *object name*, *component name*, and *path*. The first four are needed to represent descriptor objects. The type "object name" is a subset of strings representing a unique object name. "Component name" is a subset of strings representing the component names. "Path" is a subset of strings representing a unique type or map name; this unique name is formed from the concatenation of the component name and the type or map name.

Base types and message types may be grouped into three classes: (1) data manipulation, (2) negotiation support, and (3) import and export schemas. Data manipulation types allow a component to perform the data operations on remote objects analogously to operations upon local objects. As described previously, the basic access structure is the cursor. The base type "cursor" represents a set of primitive objects corresponding to cursors. It has no associated maps and can only be manipulated with primitive message types. The type "cursor" is used to access objects of other components.

The message types for data operations implement the operations of the federated database model. They are provided as message types so that they may be exported to other components. These components may in turn use them to navigate through their imported data. Cursors may be manipulated via the following operations: "cursor-create," "cursor-destroy," "cursor-reset," "cursor-next," and "cursor-more." Type-related operators are: "create-object" and "delete-object"; maps are manipulated via "apply," "apply-inverse," "insert-map," and "delete-map."

Most of the types and all of the operations associated with negotiations have been described in the context of the example negotiation "access-type." The only types not mentioned are those that store the negotiation graphs for the interpreter. The type "negotiation-graph" contains one object for every kind of negotiation in the system. Each such object refers to (via string names) the associated base and message types for each kind of negotiation. In addition, each graph refers to a set of nodes in the primitive type "negotiation-node," which in turn refers to the set of arcs in "negotiation-arc."

The import schema for each component is represented by a collection of types and maps defining the imported types and maps. In effect, there is a metaschema for defining the import schema. In this metaschema, the type "import-schema" has one object for each connected component. Each of these objects refers in turn to a set of "import-types," which in turn refer to a set of "import-maps." Associated with these imported types and maps is defining information (definition, category, and constraints).

The export schema is similar to but slightly simpler than the import schema. Since there is only one exporter (per component), there is no need for a type "export-schema." Thus only the types "export-type" and "export-map" are needed. These types differ from the import types by the addition of a connection list map specifying the names of the other components currently importing a given type or map.

Manipulation of the import schema and the export schema is carried out by a specific set of negotiations. One set allows the exporter to augment the export schema or to reduce it by withdrawing previously exported types and maps. Another set allows the importer to augment the import schema and to reduce it. The complete set is as follows:

—*Bootstrap* supports the initial negotiation between the federal dictionary and a component entering the federation.

—*Connect* links two components in the federation; it causes them to exchange import and export interface information so that each may determine what data is provided by the other.

—*Disconnect* unlinks two components; typically this is done as part of a sequence of actions when a component plans to leave the federation.

—*Withdraw-type* notifies others that a component plans to withdraw a type from its export schema.

—*Withdraw-map* notifies others that a component plans to withdraw a map from its export schema.

—*Access-type* requests access to a type exported by some component.

—*Access-map* requests access to a map exported by some component.

—*Release-type* notifies an exporter of a type that some component no longer wishes to import it.

—*Release-map* notifies an exporter of a map that some component no longer wishes to import it.

5. A PROTOTYPE IMPLEMENTATION

Completely implementing the federated architecture requires the use of a network of computers with each computer supporting a semantic database system. Neither the database nor the network was originally available when the federated architecture was designed. In consequence, a modest experimental prototype was produced. This existing prototype is a large program written in Franz-LISP under the Berkeley UNIX[5] operating system. The prototype supports a simple database implementing the federated information model, export and import schemas, message passing, and negotiations. In [12] an exhaustive, annotated transcript is provided of the execution of the prototype. The prototype has successfully executed access to imported data, simple derivations, message types, all of the built-in negotiations, and a sample negotiation based on a shared database of parts, suppliers, and consumers.

As a further test of its utility, the federated architecture is now being used as the basis for a distributed software engineering database [6]. A typical software project may involve a number of programmers each working on his or her own part of the software but also using certain pieces of code and data provided by other programmers. The federated architecture, with its emphasis on autonomy and partial sharing, is a natural structure for such programming environments.

This software engineering system prototype is a combination of the federated architecture with Odin [5], which is an extension of the UNIX "make" facility. The prototype runs on a network of Sun workstations running Berkeley UNIX 4.2, which provides both the hardware and software necessary to support distributed programs. In this prototype, there are three processes per machine: a user process (running Odin), a local database server process, and a federation server process. The user process provides the interface between the user and the local database server on one hand, and the user and the rest of the federation on the other hand. The local server performs requests generated by the user. The federation server handles requests from other components for exported information and negotiations. The local server and the federation server are designed to access the local database in parallel to provide better response for local requests. In consequence, requests from the local user are handled immediately. Requests from other components are multiplexed by the federation server. This means that intercomponent requests (e.g., for data transfer or negotiation) may not execute immediately. If a greater degree of concurrency is desired, then additional federation server processes can be added. In the extreme there may be one federation server for each known external component database.

6. CONCLUSIONS

While there is no production version of a federated architecture in use by a large body of users, it is nevertheless possible to assess how well the original goals are met by the architecture presented in this paper. It is also possible to see the parts of the architecture that are not completely successful and should be changed in some future version. Recall that in the absence of a central authority, the federated architecture has to resolve two conflicting requirements: (1) the components must maintain as much autonomy as possible, but (2) the components must be able to achieve a reasonable degree of information sharing. Autonomy specifically refers to four capabilities: control of data sharing, control of data viewing, cooperative activity, and support for structural evolution.

The principal architectural features in support of autonomy are the export and import interfaces of components. The export interface directly supports the

---

[5] UNIX is a trademark of AT&T Bell Laboratories.

requirement for control of data sharing. All accesses to some item of data must ultimately reference the component containing that item and hence are under the control of that component. The export interface also supports cooperation by providing a barrier between the private data of the component and all the other components. As long as a component maintains its interface contract with the federation, it is free to change the structure of its private data.

The role of the import interface is not as direct as that of the export schema. Its primary function is to support directly the requirement that each component be able to define its own view of the directly available data (i.e., without the use of a global schema). As a secondary function, the import schema focuses the attention of each component upon that exported data of immediate interest to it. If every component indiscriminately imported all the available information, which is equivalent to having no import schema, then it would be difficult for a component to deal with all of the information. It would also be difficult for other components to know who was a potential user of its data, thus inhibiting the evolution of a federation.

Once the concept of export and import interfaces is integrated with the database, the idea of importing simple data items follows immediately. But extending importation to include transactions is not quite so obvious, at least from the database point of view. Traditionally, databases have kept the transactions quite separate from the database structure. This is a result of the traditional emphasis on long-term data independence of the operations that manipulate it. The federated architecture, along with other work in office database systems (e.g., [35]), integrates communication facilities with the database.

Any discussion of sharing must also consider the exchange of metadata, namely, data representing the structure of the data, as opposed to the actual data. The federated architecture allows metadata to be exported so that other components may peruse the structure of exported data. Metadata are supported by a set of types in the built-in structures of the architecture. In this way, they may be shared using the normal export–import mechanisms.

Negotiation is another key feature of the federated architecture. Initially, the negotiation subsystem was to be a monolithic program that had all possible negotiations embedded within it. This approach, although feasible, does not allow the users easily to discern the structure of negotiations, and makes it difficult to add new kinds of negotiations. The negotiation subsystem has thus been divided into two parts: an interpreter, and a collection of procedures written in the negotiation language (negotiation graphs). A problem with the approach is that it does not go far enough. Currently, the semantics of a node is described as a string representing a host-language procedure to be executed. This means that a user must know that language in order to understand existing negotiations and to write new ones. Further, much information about the meaning of a negotiation state is hidden in those procedures. The system would be more uniform if the semantics was specified using the structures provided by the database model. In effect this would build in a programming language into the database model, and its programs would be manipulated in the same way as any other database structure.

The lack of multiparticipant negotiations is another problem with the current architecture. There are cases in which negotiations need to be carried out simultaneously by three or more participants. Modifying the system to handle n participants, for n fixed, is straightforward; the problem is handling negotiations that require varying numbers of participants or that need to be "quantified" over all the components currently in the federation.

An additional limitation of the negotiation system is its handling of exceptional conditions. Since it is operating in a distributed environment, many kinds of failures can occur: lost or duplicated messages, component failures, and network partitioning. At the moment, the only way to deal with these during a negotiation is to introduce explicit failure arcs to all the nodes in the graph. This seriously complicates the structure of such graphs. One alternative currently being explored is to introduce special nodes to the graph that can handle such errors, but need not have explicit arcs leading into them. Thus a typical negotiation graph would have the main graph plus a separate collection of graphs to handle various kinds of failures.

Finally, it is possible to compare the federated architecture with the list of the benefits of the logically centralized architectures (such as composite systems). A comparison shows two benefits that have been partially lost: removal of redundancy and providing a global resource. Since global data is directly counter to the goals of a federation, the latter loss seems inevitable. The redundancy problem has two essential aspects. First, two components may export the same information, kept separately. It may be desirable to relate these two versions by electing one of them to export the data and have the others keep their versions local. Second, for efficiency, it may be desirable to allow an importing component to keep a local copy of the shared data. It is clear from some work on federated software environments that this form of redundancy is desirable. To this end, new mechanisms (principally negotiations) are currently being added to support duplicated data.

ACKNOWLEDGMENTS

The authors would like to gratefully acknowledge the comments and suggestions of several individuals on earlier versions of this paper: Hamideh Afsarmanesh and Amihai Motro (USC); Robert Balzer, Neil Goldman, and David Wile (USC Information Sciences Institute); Roger King (University of Colorado, Boulder); Withold Litwin (INRIA); and Peter Lyngbaek (Hewlett-Packard Research Laboratories). The very useful recommendations of the *ACM Transactions on Office Information Systems* referees and editors are also most appreciated.

REFERENCES

1. ARITEBOUL, S., AND HULL, R. IFO: A formal semantic database model. In *Proceedings of the ACM SIGACT-SIGMOD Symposium on Principles of Database Systems* (Apr. 1984). ACM, New York, pp. 119–132.
2. BRODIE, M. L., MYLOPOULOS, J., AND SCHMIDT, J. W. (ED.). *On Conceptual Modelling.* Springer-Verlag, 1984.
3. BUNEMAN, P., AND FRANKEL, R. E. A functional query language. In *Proceedings of the International Conference on Management of Data* (Boston, Mass., May 30–June 1, 1979). ACM, New York, pp. 52–57.
4. CHAMBERLIN, D. D., GRAY, J. N., AND TRAIGER, I. L. Views, authorization, and locking in a

relational database system. In *Proceedings of the National Computer Conference* (June 1975). AFIPS Press, Reston, Va., pp. 425–430.

5. CLEMM, G. M. ODIN—An extensible software environment: Report and user's manual. CU-CS-262-84, Computer Science Dept., Univ. of Colorado, Boulder, Colo., March, 1984.

6. CLEMM, G., HEIMBIGNER, D., OSTERWEIL, L., AND WILLIAMS, L. Keystone: A federated software environment. In *ACM SIGPLAN Symposium on Programming Languages and Programming Environments* (Seattle, Wash., May 1985). ACM, New York.

7. DAYAL, U. AND BERNSTEIN, P. A. On the updatability of relational views. In *Proceedings of the 4th International Conference on Very Large Databases* (West Berlin, Sept. 1978). ACM, New York, pp. 368–377.

8. GIBBS, S., AND TSICHRITIZIS, D. A data modelling approach for office information systems. *ACM Trans. Office Inf. Syst. 1*, 4 (Oct. 1983), 299–319.

9. GRAY, J. N. Notes on data base operating systems. In *Operating Systems: An Advanced Course*, Lecture Notes in Computer Science, vol. 60. Springer Verlag, 1978, pp. 393–481.

10. HAMMER, M., AND MCLEOD, D. On database management system architecture. In *Infotech State of the Art Report: Data Design*, Infotech State of the Art Reports, vol. 8. Pergamon Infotech Limited, Maidenhead, United Kingdon, 1980, pp. 177–202.

11. HAMMER, M., AND MCLEOD, D. Database description with SDM: A semantic database model. *ACM Trans. Database Syst. 6*, 3 (Sept. 1981), 351–386.

12. HEIMBIGNER, D. M. A federated architecture for database systems. Ph.D. dissertation, Univ. of Southern California, Los Angeles, Calif., Aug. 1982.

13. HEIMBIGNER, D., AND MCLEOD, D. Federated information bases—A preliminary report. In *Infotech State of the Art Report: Database.* Infotech State of the Art Reports, vol. 9. Pergamon Infotech Limited, Maidenhead, United Kingdom, 1981, pp. 383–410.

14. KATZ, R., AND GOODMAN, N. View processing in multibase—A heterogeneous database system. In *An Entity–Relationship Approach to Information Modelling and Analysis*, ER Institute, 1981, pp. 259–280.

15. KIMBLETON, S. R., WANG, P. S. C., AND FONG, E. XNDM: An experimental network data manager. In *Proceedings of the Berkeley Workshop on Distributed Data Management and Computer Networks* (Berkeley, Calif., Aug. 1979). Pp. 3–17.

16. KIMBLETON, S. R., WOOD, H. M., AND FITZGERALD, M. L. Network operating systems—An implementation approach. In *Proceedings of the National Computer Conference* (June 1978), AFIPS Press, Arlington, Va., pp. 773–782.

17. KING, R., AND MCLEOD, D. A database design methodology and tool for information systems. *ACM Trans. Office Inf. Syst.1*, 1 (Jan. 1985), pp. 2–21.

18. KING., R., AND MCLEOD, D. Semantic database models. In *Database Design*, S. B. Yao, Ed. Prentice Hall, Englewood Cliffs, N.J., 1985.

19. LIEN, Y. E., AND YING, J. H. Design of a distributed entity–relationship database system. In *Proceedings of the International Computer Software and Applications Conference* (Chicago, Nov. 1978). IEEE, New York, pp. 277–282.

20. LINDSAY, B., AND SELINGER, P. G. Site autonomy issues in R*: A distributed database management system. Res. Rep. RJ2927, IBM Research Lab, San Jose, Calif., Sept. 1980.

21. LITWIN, W. A model for distributed data bases. In *Proceedings of the ACM 2nd Annual Louisiana Computer Exposition* (Feb. 1980). ACM, New York, pp. 1–36.

22. LITWIN, W. Logical design of distributed data bases. MOD-1-043, INRIA, Paris, France, July 1981.

23. LYNGBAEK, P., AND MCLEOD, D. Object sharing in distributed information systems. *ACM Trans. Office Inf. Syst. 2*, 2 (Apr. 1984), 96–122.

24. MOSS, E. B. Nested transactions: An approach to reliable distributed computing. Ph.D. Dissertation, Massachusetts Institute of Technology, Cambridge, Mass., Apr. 1981.

25. MOTRO, A., AND BUNEMAN, P. Constructing superviews. In *Proceedings of the ACM-SIGMOD International Conference on Management of Data* (Ann Arbor, Mich., Apr. 1981), ACM, New York, pp. 56–64.

26. MYLOPOULOS, J., BERNSTEIN, P. A., AND WONG, H. K. T. A language facility for designing database-intensive applications. *ACM Trans. Database Syst. 5*, 2 (June 1980), 185–207.

27. NAVATHE, S. B. Schema analysis for database restructuring. *ACM Trans. Database Syst. 5*, 2

(June 1980), 157–184.

28. OPPEN, D. C., AND YOGEN, Y. K. The clearinghouse: A decentralized agent for locating named objects in a distributed environment. *ACM Trans. Office Inf. Syst. 1*, 3 (July 1983), 230–253.

29. ROTHNIE, J. B., JR., BERNSTEIN, P. A., FOX, S., GOODMAN, N., HAMMER, M., LANDERS, T. A., REEVE, C., SHIPMAN, D. W., AND WONG, E. Introduction to a system for distributed databases (SDD-1). *ACM Trans. Database Syst. 5*, 1 (Mar. 1980), 1–17.

30. ROTHNIE, J. B., JR., AND GOODMAN, N. A survey of research and development in distributed database management. In *Proceedings of the 3rd International Conference on Very Large Databases* (Tokyo, Japan, Oct. 1977). IEEE, New York, pp. 48–62.

31. ROWE, L. A., AND SHOENS, K. A. Data abstraction, views, and updates in Rigel. In *Proceedings of the ACM-SIGMOD International Conference on Management of Data* (Boston, May 1979). ACM, New York, pp. 71–81.

32. SHIPMAN, D. The functional data model and the the data language DAPLEX. *ACM Trans. Database Syst. 2*, 3 (Mar. 1981), 140–173.

33. SMITH, J. M., BERNSTEIN, P. A., DAYAL, U., GOODMAN, N., LANDERS, T., LIN, K. W. T., AND WONG, E. Multibase: Integrating heterogeneous distributed database systems. In *Proceedings of the National Computer Conference* (June 1981). AFIPS Press, Reston, Va., pp. 487–499.

34. STONEBRAKER, M. R., AND NEUHOLD, E. A distributed database version of INGRES. In *Proceedings of the Berkeley Workshop on Distributed Data Management and Computer Networks*, (Berkeley, Calif., May 1977). University of California, Berkeley, pp. 19–36.

35. TSICHRITZIS, D. C. Integrating data base and message systems. In *Proceedings of the International Conference on Very Large Databases* (Cannes, France, Sept. 1981). IEEE, New York, pp. 356–362.

A Comparative Analysis of Methodologies for Database Schema Integration

C. BATINI and M. LENZERINI

Dipartimento di Informatica e Sistemistica, University of Rome, Rome, Italy

S. B. NAVATHE

Database Systems Research and Development Center, Computer and Information Sciences Department, University of Florida, Gainesville, Florida 32601

One of the fundamental principles of the database approach is that a database allows a nonredundant, unified representation of all data managed in an organization. This is achieved only when methodologies are available to support integration across organizational and application boundaries.

Methodologies for database design usually perform the design activity by separately producing several schemas, representing parts of the application, which are subsequently merged. Database schema integration is the activity of integrating the schemas of existing or proposed databases into a global, unified schema.

The aim of the paper is to provide first a unifying framework for the problem of schema integration, then a comparative review of the work done thus far in this area. Such a framework, with the associated analysis of the existing approaches, provides a basis for identifying strengths and weaknesses of individual methodologies, as well as general guidelines for future improvements and extensions.

Categories and Subject Descriptors: H.0 [**Information Systems**]: General; H.2.1 [**Database Management**]: Data Models; Schema and Subschema; H.2.5: [**Database Management**]: Heterogeneous Databases; D.2.1: [**Requirements/Specifications**]: Methodologies

General Terms: Management

Additional Key Words and Phrases: Conceptual database design, database integration, database schema integration, information systems design, models, view integration

INTRODUCTION

I.1 Schema Integration

Database management systems (DBMSs) have been developed in the past two decades using various data models and architectures. The primary data models used for implementation are the hierarchical, network, and relational data models. More recently, several so-called semantic data models, significantly more powerful than primary data models in representing the application of interest, have been proposed (e.g., see Smith's abstraction hierarchy model [Smith and Smith 1977], the Semantic Data Model [Hammer and McLeod 1981], the TAXIS data model [Mylopoulos et al. 1980], DAPLEX [Shipman 1980], and recently, the Galileo data model [Albano et al. 1985]).

C. Batini, M. Lenzerini, and S. B. Navathe

CONTENTS

Since semantic models allow data to be described in a very abstract and understandable manner, they are currently used in designing the conceptual structure of databases. This conceptual activity is called *conceptual database design*. Its goal is to produce an abstract, global view of the data of the application, called *conceptual schema*.

The introduction of a conceptual step in design methodologies is a fairly recent development. It allows designers and users to cooperate in collecting requirements and provides a high-level specification of the data involved in the application. Furthermore, it simplifies the integration of differing perspectives and expectations that various users have of the application.

One of the basic motivations for using the database approach instead of the traditional "data-processing-using-files" approach is that a database management system makes it possible to define an integrated view of relevant data for all applications. This eliminates duplication, avoids problems of multiple updates, and minimizes inconsistencies across applications. Whereas the above claims of the database approach are highly touted, database textbooks and survey literature to date have paid scant attention to this topic. At the same time, research on the problem of integration has proceeded, and most of the researchers have suggested performing the integration activity as a part of the conceptual design step. In this paper we refer to the integration activity by a generic term, *schema integration*, which is defined as the activity of integrating the schemas of existing or proposed databases into a global, unified schema. Schema integration, as defined here, occurs in two contexts:

(1) *View integration* (in database design) produces a global conceptual description of a proposed database.
(2) *Database integration* (in distributed database management) produces the global schema of a collection of databases. This global schema is a virtual view of all databases taken together in a distributed database environment.

The database technology has progressed to a level where thousands of organizations are using databases for their day-to-day, tactical, and strategic management applications. The distributed database management area is also becoming sufficiently well understood, and we expect to see a large number of organizations changing to distributed databases by integrating their current diverse databases.

The contributions to the state of the art of database design methodologies, and in particular schema integration, have been particularly significant in the last ten years. Our goal is to provide first a framework by which the problem of schema integration can be better understood, and second a comparative review of the work done thus far on this problem. Such a framework with an associated analysis of the prevalent approaches provides

(1) a conceptual foundation to the problem of schema integration;
(2) a basis upon which to identify strengths and weaknesses and the missing features about individual methodologies;
(3) general guidelines for future improvements and extensions to the present approaches.

In the next section we explain the view integration activity; Section I.3 is devoted to database integration. In Section I.4 we elaborate on the motivation for investigating integration. Finally, in Section I.5 we describe the general structure of the remainder of the paper.

I.2 View Integration in Database Design

The problem of *database design* is one of designing the structure of a database in a given environment of users and applications such that all users' data requirements and all applications' process requirements are "best satisfied." This problem has existed ever since DBMSs came into being.

The DBMSs that store and manipulate a database must have a definition of the database in the form of a schema. This is termed the *intension* of the database. The actual values of data in a database are called *instances* or *occurrences* of data. Sometimes they are termed the extension of a database, or just "the database." Whereas the extension of a database keeps changing with time, the intension of the database is supposed to be time invariant. The *database design* problem aims at designing the intension schema of the database, which includes logical specifications such as groupings of attributes and relationships among these groupings (*logical schema*), as well as physical specifications such as the type of access to records, indexes, ordering, and physical placement (*physical schema*). On the basis of this distinction, the corresponding database design activities are termed *logical schema design* and *physical schema design*. Logical schema design involves the problem of designing the conceptual schema and mapping such a schema into the schema definition language (or data definition language) of a specific DBMS. Figure 1 shows the phases of database design and the intermediate schema representations. The phases of database design are

(1) *Requirements Specification and Analysis*. An analysis of the information requirements of various areas within an organization resulting in a preliminary specification of the information needs of various user groups.
(2) *Conceptual Design*. Modeling and representation of users' and applications' views of information and possibly a specification of the processing or use of the information. The final result of this activity is a conceptual schema that represents a global, high-level description of the requirements.
(3) *Implementation Design*. Transforming a conceptual schema into the logical schema of a DBMS. The second and third phases taken together are called logical database design.
(4) *Physical Schema Design and Optimization*. Mapping the logical schema of a database into an appropriate stored representation in a DBMS, including new physical parameters to optimize the database performance against a set of transactions.

Typically, the application design activity proceeds in parallel with database design. Hence, Figure 1 also shows specifications related to applications as the outputs of the last two phases.

As shown in Figure 1, the activity of view integration can be performed at several points of the database design process. It usually is performed during conceptual design. In that case, its goal is to produce an integrated schema starting from several application views that have been produced independently.[1]

---

[1] There is a body of work that regards conceptual design as an activity that considers the application as a whole, thus producing a single schema. This includes Batini et al. [1984], Biller and Neuhold [1982], Brodie [1981], Brodie and Zilles [1981], Ceri [1983], Ceri et al. [1981], Chen [1983], Lum et al. [1970], Olle et al. [1982], Rolland and Richards [1982], and Sakai [1981].

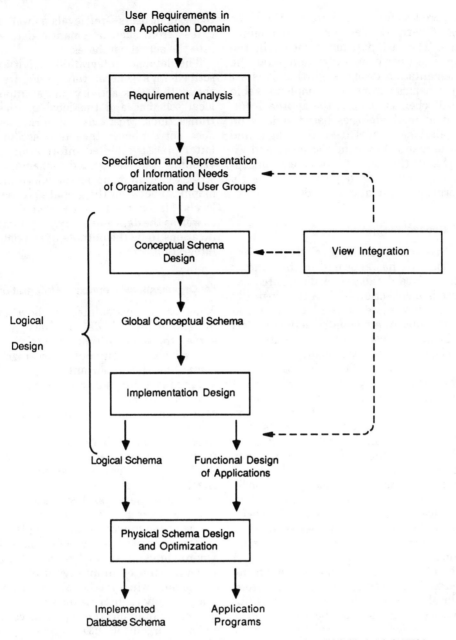

Figure 1. Phases of database design. (Adapted from Navathe and Schkolnick [1978].)

The reason for integration is twofold:

(1) The structure of the database for large applications (organizations) is too complex to be modeled by a single designer in a single view.

(2) User groups typically operate independently in organizations and have their own requirements and expectations of data, which may conflict with other user groups.

Another possibility (Figure 1) is to perform integration even before the "conceptual design" step is undertaken. In this case, view integration still occurs; however, views are less formal and are mostly in the form of narrative descriptions of requirements. The last possibility shown in the figure is to perform integration after the implementation design step, that is, start from schemas expressed as implementable logical schemas. This is the approach followed in methodologies based strictly on the relational model (see Al-Fedaghi and Scheuermann [1981] and Casanova and Vidal [1983]) that do not advocate a conceptual step and model requirements directly in terms of the relational model.

I.3 Database Integration

Database integration is a relatively recent problem that has appeared in the context of distributed databases. A distributed database is a collection of data that logically belong to the same system but are spread over the sites of a computer network [Ceri and Pelagatti 1984]. Distributed databases and distributed database management systems can be classified into two major categories: *homogeneous*, dealing with local databases having the same data model and identical DBMSs, and *heterogeneous*, having a diversity in data models and DBMSs. The term *Federated Database* is used (e.g., in McLeod and Heimbigner [1980]) to refer to a collection of databases in which the sharing is made more explicit by allowing *export schemas*, which define the sharable part of each local database. Each application is able to design its own global schema by integrating the export schemas.

The above contexts require that an integrated global schema be designed from the local schemas, which refer to existing databases. This too can be considered a database design activity. Existing work on database integration included in our survey implicitly addresses this problem. The authors of these works [Dayal and Hwang 1984; ElMasri et al. 1987; Mannino and Effelsberg 1984a; Motro and Buneman 1981] use a semantic data model as an intermediate model to facilitate the integration. Another implicit assumption they make is that the heterogeneous database management system is able to map the

requests of users—retrievals as well as updates—from such a semantic data model into the actual databases.

The database integration activity is described in a general way in Figure 2. It shows that this activity has as input the local schemas and the local queries and transactions. Most existing work, however, does not explicitly take into account the latter process-oriented information in developing the integrated schema. It is strictly used in mapping the queries (query mapping) between the global and the local levels. Hence, we show the global schema as well as the data and query-mapping specifications to be the outputs of the database integration activity.

I.4 Organizational Context for Integration

Thus far we have pointed out how schema integration arises in database design. As we survey the work on schema integration, it is worthwhile to point out an organizational context for this important area.

There is a growing trend to regard data as an autonomous resource of the organization, independent of the functions currently in use in the organization [National Bureau of Standards 1982]. There is a need to capture the meaning of data for the whole organization in order to manage it effectively. Because of this awareness, integration of data has become an area of growing interest in recent years.

One of the fundamental principles of the database approach is that a database allows a nonredundant, unified representation of all data managed in an organization. This is true only when methodologies are available to support integration across organizational and application boundaries. More and more organizations are becoming aware of the potential of database systems and wish to use them for integrated applications and not just as software for fast retrieval and updating of data.

Even when applications and user groups are structurally disconnected, as in most governmental and large administrative setups, there is something to be gained by having an enterprise-wide view of the data resource. This potentially affords individ-

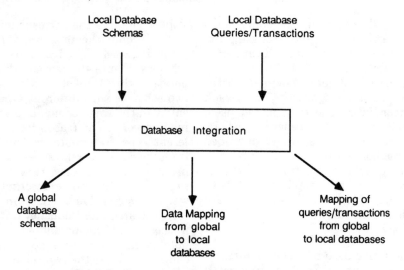

Figure 2. Inputs and outputs of database integration.

ual applications to "build bridges" among themselves and understand how the databases or files relate to one another.

With the increasing use of databases, we expect the integration problem to be more severe and pervasive. New technologies of networking, distributed databases, knowledge-based systems, and office systems will tend to spread the shared use of data in terms of number of users, diversity of applications, and sophistication of concepts. Design, manufacturing, and engineering applications are becoming centered around database management systems. The need for methodologies for integrating data in its diverse conceptual and physical forms is thus expected to increase substantially.

I.5 Structure of the Paper

As described in Section I.1, our main goals are to provide a conceptual foundation for schema integration and perform a detailed comparison of existing work in this area.

It is possible to classify the existing literature into two categories:

(A) *Complete methodologies* for schema integration. These include view integration and database integration.
(B) *Related works* addressing specific issues of schema integration.

In the References, the relevant literature is placed under Categories A and B.

In Section 1 we establish the general framework for a comparison of schema integration methodologies. An example introduces the aspects that influence the integration process; we then identify the activities usually performed during schema integration. These activities are used as a basis for comparing methodologies. Finally, we examine the influence of the conceptual model on the overall integration process.

Section 2 is devoted to a detailed comparative analysis of the methodologies. The results of the analysis are presented in the following format:

(1) Tables illustrating comparative features. The table entries are drawn from the original publications on the methodologies and are not exhaustively explained. However, we extract salient features and trends that are evident in these tables. We highlight the approach of a specific methodology when it explains a specific feature.
(2) Because of the diversity of the data models (entity–relationship, entity–category–relationship, functional, structural, Navathe–Schkolnick, relational, and generalized entity manipulator) used in the methodologies, we have adopted a uniform treatment of concepts primarily based on the entity–relationship model. The entity-relationship model is briefly summarized in Appendix 2.

In Section 3, we present the conclusions of this investigation, identify missing aspects and open problems, and indicate some research directions.

We compare 12 different complete methodologies. A summary description of each is in Appendix 2. The data model used, inputs and outputs, the general strategy, and special features are briefly described for each methodology.

In order to make the treatment of schema integration uniformly applicable to both the view integration as well as the database integration contexts, we use the following terminology:

General terms used for schema integration: Component Schema, Integrated Schema.

View integration context: user view, conceptual view.

Database integration context: local schema, global schema.

1. METHODOLOGIES FOR SCHEMA INTEGRATION

1.1 An Example

In order to introduce the reader to the main features and problems of schema integration, we present an example. In Figure 3, we show two descriptions of requirements and corresponding possible conceptual schemas that model them.

The following additional information applies to this example:

(1) The meaning of "Topics" in the first schema is the same as that of "Keyword" in the second schema.
(2) "Publication" in the second schema is a more abstract concept than "Book" in the first schema. That is, "Publication" includes additional things such as proceedings, journals, monographs, etc.

Figure 4 shows a set of activities that may be performed to integrate the schemas.

Let us look at the two schemas in Figure 4a. Topics and Keywords correspond to the same concept. Since we have to merge the schemas, the names should be unified into a single name. Let us choose the name

Topics. Observe the corresponding change in the second schema as we go from (a) to (b) in Figure 4. When we look at the new schemas (Figure 4b), another difference we notice is that Publisher is present in the two schemas with different types: It is an entity in the first schema and an attribute in the second. The reason for choosing different types (attribute vs. entity) comes from the different relevance that Publisher has in the two schemas. However, we have to conform the two representations if we want to merge them. Therefore we transform the attribute Publisher into an entity in the second schema and add a new attribute, Name, to it (see Figure 4c). We now can superimpose the two schemas, producing the representation in Figure 4d. We have not finished merging yet, since we have to look for properties that relate concepts belonging to different schemas, which were "hidden" previously. This is the case with the subset relationship between the concepts Book and Publication. We can add such a subset relationship to the merged schema, producing the result shown in Figure 4e. Now, to simplify the representation, we can restructure the schema by dropping the properties (relationships and attributes) of Book that are common to Publication. This is allowable since the subset relationship implies that all the properties of publications are implicitly inherited by Book. The final schema is shown in Figure 4f.

1.2 Causes for Schema Diversity

The example of schema integration used above is obviously a "toy example" that highlights some of the basic problems involved. That the integration of realistic sized component schemas can be a complex endeavor is amply evident from this example.

The basic problems to be dealt with during integration come from structural and semantic diversities of schemas to be merged. Our investigation of integration starts with a classification of the various causes for schema diversity, which are different perspectives, equivalence among constructs of the model, and incompatible design specifications.

C. Batini, M. Lenzerini, and S. B. Navathe

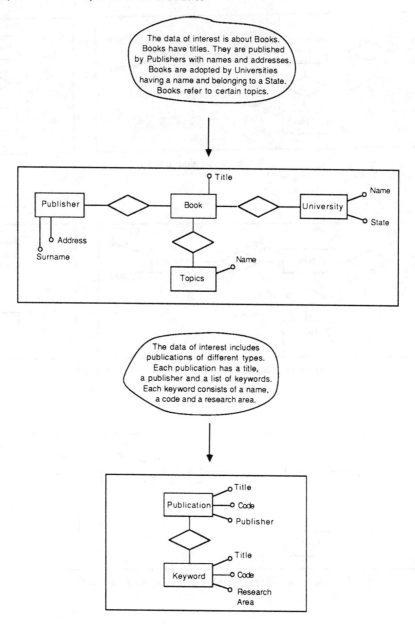

Figure 3. Examples of requirements and corresponding schemas.

1.2.1 Different Perspectives

In the design process, different user groups or designers adopt their own viewpoints in modeling the same objects in the application domain. For instance, in the example in Section 1.1, different names were attached to the same concept in the two views.

Another example is given in Figure 5, in which the two schemas represent information about employees and their departments. In Figure 5a information is modeled by means of the relationship E–D. In Figure 5b, relationship E–P relates the employees with projects, whereas relationship P–D associates projects with departments. It is assumed that an Employee "belongs to"

79

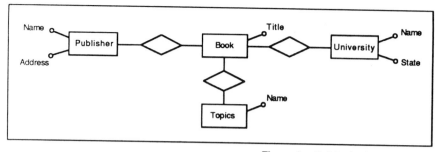
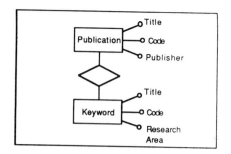

Figure 4a. Original schemas.

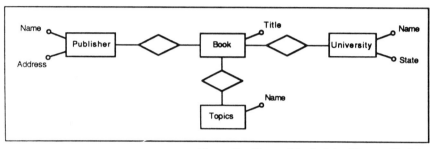
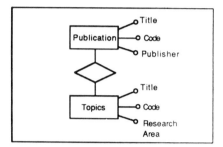

Figure 4b. Choose "Topics" for "Keyword" (Schema 2).

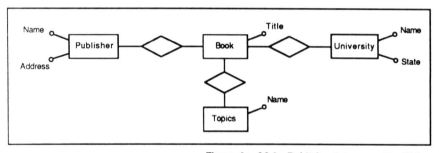
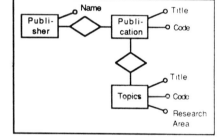

Figure 4c. Make Publisher into an entity (Schema 2).

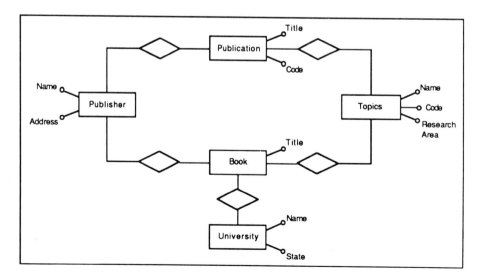

Figure 4d. Superimposition of schemas.

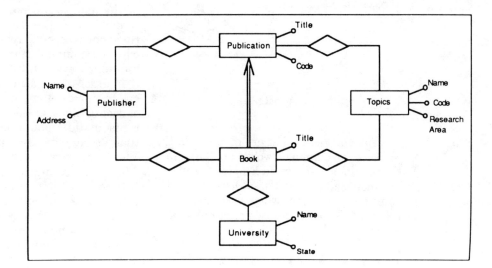

Figure 4e. Creation of a subset relationship.

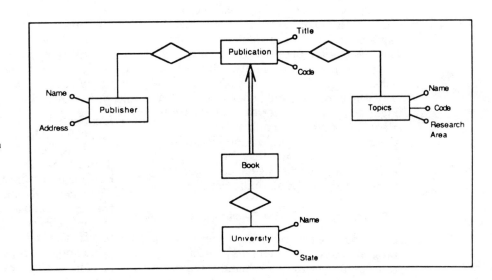

Figure 4f. Drop the properties of Book common
Publication.

Figure 4. An example of integration.

81

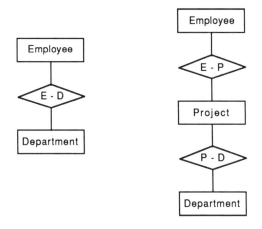

Figure 5. Different perspectives.

those departments that are involved in the projects the employee works on. Therefore the relationship between Employee and Department is perceived as a direct relationship in one schema, whereas it is seen via the entity Project and two relationships in another.

1.2.2 Equivalence among Constructs of the Model

Typically, in conceptual models, several combinations of constructs can model the same application domain equivalently. As a consequence, "richer" models give rise to a larger variety of possibilities to model the same situation. For example, in Figure 3, the association between Book and Publisher was modeled as an attribute of Publisher in one schema and as a relationship between Book and Publisher in the other. Figure 6 shows another example of equivalent constructs. Man and Woman are distinguished by a generalization hierarchy in the first schema, whereas in the second schema they are distinguished by the different values of the attribute Sex.

1.2.3 Incompatible Design Specifications

Erroneous choices regarding names, types, integrity constraints, etc. may result in erroneous inputs to the schema integration process. A good schema integration methodology must lead to the detection of such errors. Schema 1 in Figure 7 erroneously

shows that an Employee is always assigned to a unique project, since the cardinality constraint $1 : n$ has been specified. The correct situation (that an Employee may be assigned to many projects) appears in Schema 2.

These three aspects are concerned with what we can call the common part of the various schemas, that is, the set of concepts of the application domain that are represented in all of the schemas. In other words, the above aspects represent the reasons why the common part may be modeled in different ways in different schemas.

In order to perform integration, it is crucial to single out not only the set of common concepts but also the set of different concepts in different schemas that are mutually related by some semantic properties. We refer to these as *interschema properties*. They are semantic relationships holding between a set of objects in one schema and a different set of objects in another schema. In the rest of this section, we provide a further taxonomy to address correspondences among common concepts and concepts related by interschema properties.

1.2.4 Common Concepts

Owing to the causes for schema diversity described above, it may very well happen that the same concept of the application domain can be represented by different *representations* R_1 and R_2 in different schemas, and several types of *semantic relationships* can exist between such representations. They may be identical, equivalent, compatible, or incompatible:

(1) *Identical*: R_1 and R_2 are exactly the same. This happens when the same modeling constructs are used, the same perceptions are applied, and no incoherence enters into the specification.

(2) *Equivalent*: R_1 and R_2 are not exactly the same because different but equivalent modeling constructs have been applied. The perceptions are still the same and coherent. Several definitions of equivalence have been proposed in the literature (see Atzeni et al. [1982], Beeri et al. [1978], Biller [1979], Navathe and Gadgie [1982], Ng et al.

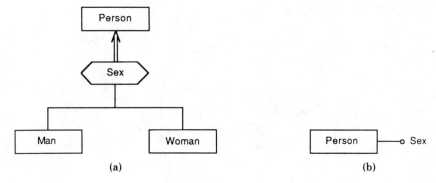

Figure 6. Equivalent constructs. (a) Generalization hierarchy. (b) A single entity.

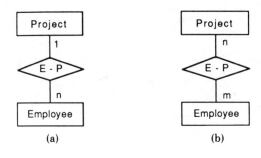

Figure 7. Incompatible design specifications. (a) Schema 1. (b) Schema 2.

[1983], Rissanen [1977]). Although several semantic data models are in existence today, the authors of these models do not provide any criteria for equivalence of concepts. Definitions are typically based on three different types of equivalence:

(a) *Behavioral*: R_1 is equivalent to R_2 if for every instantiation of R_1, a corresponding instantiation of R_2 exists that has the same set of answers to any given query and vice versa [Atzeni et al. 1982].

(b) *Mapping*: R_1 and R_2 are equivalent if their instances can be put in a one-to-one correspondence (e.g., see Rissanen [1977]).

(c) *Transformational*: R_1 is equivalent to R_2 if R_2 can be obtained from R_1 by applying a set of atomic transformations that by definition preserve equivalence. (Navathe and Gadgie [1982] call this "restructure equivalence.") This technique is common in other disciplines (e.g., program equivalence).

(3) *Compatible*: R_1 and R_2 are neither identical nor equivalent. However, the modeling constructs, designer perception, and integrity constraints are not contradictory.

(4) *Incompatible*: R_1 and R_2 are contradictory because of the incoherence of the specification.

Situations (2), (3), and (4) above can be interpreted as conflicts. Conflicts and their resolutions are central to the problems of integration. A general definition of the term conflict would be as follows:

A *conflict* between two representations R_1 and R_2 of the same concept is every situation that gives rise to the representations R_1 and R_2 not being identical.

1.2.5 Concepts Related by Some Semantic Property

Regarding the concepts in component schemas that are not the same but are related, we need to discover all the *interschema properties* that relate them. In Figure 8, we show two examples of interschema proper-

C. Batini, M. Lenzerini, and S. B. Navathe

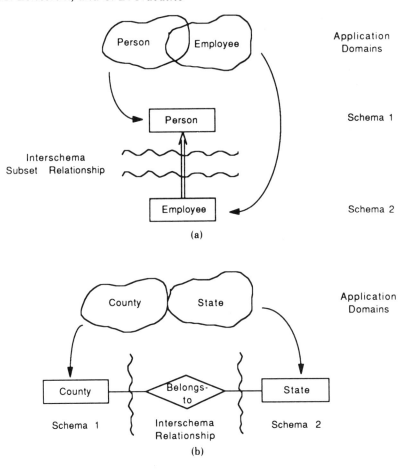

Figure 8. Interschema properties. (a) Example 1. (b) Example 2.

ties. The subset relationship among Person and Employee (Example 1) and the relationship "Belongs-to" between Country and State (Example 2) are interschema properties that could not be perceived in the original component schemas.

1.3 Steps and Goals of the Integration Process

Thus far, we have discussed the nature of the schema integration problem and identified the causes and implications of schema diversity. How do the methodologies accomplish the task of integration? Each methodology follows its own solution procedure. However, any methodology eventually can be considered to be a mixture of the following activities.

1.3.1 Preintegration

An analysis of schemas is carried out before integration to decide upon some integration policy. This governs the choice of schemas to be integrated, the order of integration, and a possible assignment of preferences to entire schemas or portions of schemas. Giving preference to financial applications over production applications is one example of an integration policy that could be set by management.

Global strategies for integration, namely, the amount of designer interaction and the number of schemas to be integrated at one time, are also decided in this phase. Collection of additional information relevant to integration, such as assertions or constraints among views, is also considered to be a part of this phase.

1.3.2 Comparison of the Schemas

Schemas are analyzed and compared to determine the correspondences among concepts and detect possible conflicts. Interschema properties may be discovered while comparing schemas.

1.3.3 Conforming the Schemas

Once conflicts are detected, an effort is made to resolve them so that the merging of various schemas is possible. Automatic conflict resolution is generally not feasible; close interaction with designers and users is required before compromises can be achieved in any real-life integration activity.

1.3.4 Merging and Restructuring

Now the schemas are ready to be superimposed, giving rise to some intermediate integrated schema(s). The intermediate results are analyzed and, if necessary, restructured in order to achieve several desirable qualities. A global conceptual schema may be tested against the following qualitative criteria:

- *Completeness and Correctness.* The integrated schema must contain all concepts present in any component schema correctly. The integrated schema must be a representation of the union of the application domains associated with the schemas.
- *Minimality.* If the same concept is represented in more than one component schema, it must be represented only once in the integrated schema.
- *Understandability.* The integrated schema should be easy to understand for the designer and the end user. This implies that among the several possible representations of results of integration allowed by a data model, the one that is (qualitatively) the most understandable should be chosen.

We make use of the above four phases of schema integration for analyzing and comparing different methodologies.

1.4 Influence of the Conceptual Model on the Integration Process

All of the above issues and activities are strongly influenced by the data model used to express conceptual schemas. The relationship between the comparison and conforming activity and the choice of data model is apparent in all the methodologies that perform these activities "by layers" [Batini et al. 1983; ElMasri et al. 1987; Kahn 1979; Navathe and Gadgil 1982; Teorey and Fry 1982; Wiederhold and ElMasri 1979; Yao et al. 1982]. These layers correspond to the different semantic constructs supported by the model; Table 1 makes an interesting point concerning the specific order of the layers of schema constructs used in the methodologies. The comparison activity focuses on primitive objects first (e.g., entities in the entity–relationship model); then it deals with those modeling constructs that represent associations among primitive objects (e.g., relationships in the entity–relationship model). Note that relational-model-based methodologies do not show up in this table because the relation is their only schema construct.

A few qualitative observations can be made concerning the relative merit of different models.

A simpler data model, that is, one with fewer data-modeling constructs, properties, and constraints has an advantage in conforming and merging activities. This stems from various factors:

- the possibility of type conflicts is smaller;
- the transformation operations are simpler;
- merging involves fewer primitive operations.

On the other hand, a simpler model constitutes a weaker tool in the hands of the designer in discovering similarities, dissimilarities, or incompatibilities. Models with a rich set of type and abstraction mechanisms have the advantage of representing predefined groupings of concepts and allowing comparisons at a higher level of abstraction.

Schema integration comes about when the design of a global schema is attempted

Table 1. Order of Schema Constructs Subjected to Integration

Reference	Phase 1	Phase 2
Batini et al. [1983]	Entities	Relationships
ElMasri et al. [1987]	Object classes	Relationship classes
Kahn [1979]	Entities	Relationships
Navathe and Gadgil [1982]	Objects	Connections
Teorey and Fry [1982]	Aggregations	Generalizations
Yao et al. [1982]	Objects	Functions
Wiederhold and ElMasri [1979]	Primary relations	Connections

using the "divide and conquer" philosophy. It is an inherent attribute or property of this philosophy that the "global characteristics" that cannot be captured by the individual views must be added when a global view becomes available. Consider the relative advantage of the entity–relationship model over the relational model in this respect.

Referring to the example in Section 1.1, adding the subset between Book and Publication allowed us to incorporate a "global characteristic" that was not evident in component schemas. The relational model lacks this modeling feature. Hence, it could only be captured by expressing and enforcing it as a part of the transactions that operate on the global schema or by defining new dependencies such as inclusion interdependencies (e.g., as in Casanova and Vidal [1983]).

The current body of work on the schema integration problem can be divided into two schools: one using the relational or functional models and one using semantic models. Among the semantic models, the entity–relationship model and its variants are dominant.

A few observations can be made when comparing these two schools:

(1) Methodologies using the relational model ([Al-Fedaghi and Scheuermann 1981; Casanova and Vidal 1983]) make the universal relation schema assumption; that is, every attribute name is unique, across the entire database. As a consequence, problems related to naming and contradictory specifications are ignored. Furthermore, they are not really able to state different perspectives (e.g., contradictory functional dependencies in two views at the start would not be allowed) and natu-

rally avoid dealing with a large subset of the possible conflicts. The semantic-model-based methodologies in general allow a larger amount of freedom in terms of naming, compatible and incompatible design perspectives, etc. Correspondingly, they deal with a much wider spectrum of conflicts.

(2) The more recent relational-model-based methodologies (e.g., Biskup and Convent [1986], Casanova and Vidal [1983]) use inclusion, exclusion, and union functional dependencies in addition to conventional functional dependencies. An inclusion (exclusion) dependency is used to constrain the set of values associated with a given attribute to be subset of (disjoint from) the set of values corresponding to another attribute. By making use of these dependencies, they claim to achieve the same semantic expressiveness as the semantic models. Owing to the well-defined semantics of the relational model in terms of set theory and dependency theory [Maier 1983; Ullman 1982], they are able to address the problem of minimal redundancy in a formal way.

2. A COMPARISON OF METHODOLOGIES

2.1 Introduction

There are 12 different complete methodologies that we consider (see Category A References). We have placed a summary description of each in Appendix 2, which include the data model used, inputs and outputs, the general strategy, and special features.

In this section, each methodology is analyzed and compared on the basis of some common criteria. In Section 2.2, we concen-

Table 2. Placement of Methodologies

Phases of database design	References
Between requirement analysis and conceptual design	Kahn [1979]
Conceptual design	Batini and Lenzerini [1984], ElMasri et al. [1987], Navathe and Gadgil [1982], Teorey and Fry [1982], Wiederhold and ElMasri [1979]
Implementation design	Al-Fedaghi and Scheuermann [1981], Casanova and Vidal [1983], Yao et al. [1982]

trate on the phases of database design, where the integration methodologies are most applicable. It is seen there that the different methodologies apply to different portions of the design process from requirements analysis to implementation design. We deepen the framework provided in Section 1 by first considering these methodologies as "black boxes" and examine their inputs and outputs. Then we deal with their general structure by examining the procedures that they follow in terms of the four main activities: preintegration, comparison, conforming, merging, and restructuring. Finally, we describe each of these activities in detail.

2.2 Applicability of Integration Methodologies

A majority of the methodologies being analyzed here fall into the class of view integration methodologies. In fact, all except those of Dayal and Hwang [1984], Motro and Buneman [1981], and Mannino and Effelsberg [1984a] belong to this class. That of ElMasri et al. [1987] belongs to both view integration and database integration.

There is little choice in terms of deciding when schemas are integrated in the case of database integration; it has to be performed on the basis of existing local database schemas when a global interface is desired to access them. In contrast, view integration can occur at different times (see Figure 1). It is therefore worthwhile to consider the correspondence between the phases of database design and the various view integration methodologies.

Table 2 shows the phases at which the various view integration methodologies can be considered to be best applicable.

Performing integration during the requirements analysis phase is difficult because user requirements are generally very poorly structured, and are difficult to deal with in terms of a formal methodology involving a semantic analysis. Among the methodologies, only that of Kahn [1979] can be considered applicable to the requirements analysis phase. There, a loosely structured data model is used that resembles those used for collecting requirements specifications.

On the other hand, performing integration during the implementation design phase is difficult because representations at that point do not allow one to make effective use of abstractions. Methodologies such as those of Al-Fedaghi and Scheuermann [1981] and Yao et al. [1982] are able to do integration as a part of the logical design phase by working with the relational (or a functional) data model and various types of dependencies. Pure relational synthesis algorithms (e.g., Bernstein [1976] and Biskup et al. [1979]) can also be considered examples of this approach. As such, they do not deal with the more powerful semantic constructs or abstractions.

The above observations suggest that the preferred phase for integration is the conceptual design phase, where the use of abstraction is very helpful in comparing and conforming different perceptions of the application domain by different user groups.

Another viewpoint regarding the phase when schema integration should be performed may be stated in terms of the following statements:

(1) Perform integration as early as possible because the cost of carrying erroneous/inconsistent data increases

during the life cycle of the database and the application.

(2) Perform integration only after complete, correct, minimal, unambiguous representations are available.

This again leads one to the conclusion that schema integration should be placed after requirements analysis but before implementation design. Methodologies [Batini and Lenzerini 1984; ElMasri et al. 1987; Navathe and Gadgil 1982; Teorey and Fry 1982; Wiederhold and ElMasri 1979] indeed confirm this position. We have placed these methodologies under "conceptual design" in Table 2 according to the present terminology. Database integration can be considered to apply more to the conceptual design phase rather than the other two. The above point of view is confirmed by [Dayal and Hwang 1984; ElMasri et al. 1987; Mannino and Effelsberg 1984a; Motro and Buneman 1981] in that for doing database integration they advocate translating heterogeneous logical schemas into conceptual data representations. Hence, all methodologies for database integration [Dayal and Hwang 1984; ElMasri et al. 1987; Mannino and Effelsberg 1984a; Motro and Buneman 1981] are placed in that category.

2.3 Methodologies Viewed as Black Boxes

The basic input to schema integration is a number of component schemas and the basic output is an integrated schema.

Table 3 shows the specific inputs and outputs taken into account by different methodologies. Since Navathe and Gadgil [1982] represented the view integration process with the most comprehensive listing of inputs and outputs, which roughly represent a union of all methodologies, we discuss their terminology:

- *Enterprise View.* Pertinent only to view integration, and not to database integration, this view is an initial conceptual schema which is the enterprise's view of the most important and stable concepts in the application domain. Having such a view at one's disposal makes the activities of comparing and conforming views easier.

- *Assertions.* These correspond to constraints. Intraview assertions are constraints defined on concepts within one schema, whereas interview assertions are constraints among concepts belonging to different views. Methodologies that assume interview assertions to be input implicitly require that some global knowledge pertaining to the diverse applications is supplied to the designer. Modified assertions in the output are revised constraints.

- *Processing Requirements.* These refer to the operations defined on component views. They may be specified in the form of a high-level data manipulation or query language.

- *Mapping Rules.* These define the mapping from queries (operations) applicable to component schemas to queries (operations) against the integrated schema.

- *Statement of Conflicts.* This is a set of conflicts that the designer is not able to resolve and is beyond the scope of the methodology to resolve automatically.

One issue deserving special attention is the treatment of processing requirements. Some methodologies [Al-Fedaghi and Scheuermann 1981; Batini and Lenzerini 1984; Casanova and Vidal 1983; Kahn 1979; Teorey and Fry 1982; Wiederhold and ElMasri 1979] ignore processing requirements totally. Navathe and Gadgil [1982] and Yao et al. [1982] refer to the transactions and queries on component schemas that have to be supported after integration. Navathe and Gadgil [1982] show that this support of processing requirements is provided by a set of mapping rules. In Dayal and Hwang [1984] and Motro and Buneman [1981] the query modification process is addressed in detail to deal with the processing of local queries on the global database. Batini et al. [1983] and Yao et al. [1982] consider the problem of query modification during view integration.

We can conclude that a complete treatment of processing requirements during integration is not present in any of the methodologies surveyed. Some recent proposals have been made to combine process design with database design [Carswell and Navathe 1986].

Table 3. Inputs and Outputs

Reference	Inputs	Outputs
Al-Fedaghi and Scheuermann [1981]	n External views	n External schemas Conceptual schema Mapping between external schemas and conceptual schema
Batini and Lenzerini [1984]	User schemas Weights for schemas Enterprise schema	Global schema
Casanova and Vidal [1983]	User views	Conceptual schema
Dayal and Hwang [1984]	Local schemas of existing databases Queries	Global interface to databases Modified queries
ElMasri et al. [1987]	Local schemas Interschema assertions	Global schema Mapping rules
Kahn [1979]	Local information structures	Global information structure
Motro and Buneman [1981]	Logical schemas Database queries	Superview Modified queries
Mannino and Effelsberg [1984a]	Local schemas Interschema assertions about entities and attributes	Global schema Mapping rules Definition of integration schema objects
Navathe and Gadgil [1982]	Enterprise view Local views Interview assertions Intraview assertions Processing requirements	Global view Mapping rules Modified assertions Conflicts
Teorey and Fry [1982]	Information, application, event, corporate perspectives Policy guidance and rules	Global information structure Conflicts
Yao et al. [1982]	Views Processing specifications	Global view Modified processing specification
Wiederhold and ElMasri [1979]	Two schemas	Global schema

The form in which the inputs and outputs exist in an integration system (which may be partly automated) is not stated explicitly by any of the authors considered. It is obvious that in order to process the schemas in an automated environment, they must be expressed in some well-defined language or some internal representation using data structures.

2.4 Gross Architecture of Methodologies

Let us consider the four activities of the integration process. In Table 4, we show the steps that are performed by each of the methodologies and the looping structure present in them.

It is possible to classify the methodologies into four groups on the basis of Table 4:

(1) Those that perform a repetitive comparison, conforming, and merging of schemas, and avoid the need to restructure later [Mannino and Effelsberg 1984a; Navathe and Gadgil 1982; Wiederhold and ElMasri 1979].

(2) Those that perform most of the activities during and after the merging of schemas. They include Steps 3 and 4 only and avoid comparison and conforming of the schemas [Al-Fedaghi and Scheuermann 1981; Casanova and Vidal 1983; Motro and Buneman 1981; Teorey and Fry 1982; Yao et al. 1982].

(3) Those that perform all four activities [Batini and Lenzerini 1984; Dayal and

Table 4. Schema Integration Activities

References	Preintegration (Step 1)	Compare (Step 2)	Conform (Step 3)	Merging (Step 4a)	Restructuring (Step 4b)
Al-Fedaghi and Scheuermann [1981]	—	—	—	X ⟷	X
Batini and Lenzerini [1984]	—	X ⟷	X →	X →	X
Casanova and Vidal [1983]	—	—	—	X →	X
Dayal and Hwang [1984]	—	X →	X →	X ⟷	X
ElMasri et al. [1987]	X →	X ⟷	X →	X →	X
Kahn [1979]	—	X →	X →	X →	X
Motro and Buneman [1981]	—	—	—	X ⟷	X
Mannino and Effelsberg [1984a]	X →	X ⟷	X →	X	—
Navathe and Gadgil [1982]	X →	X ⟷	X →	X	—
Teorey and Fry [1982]	—	—	—	X →	X
Yao et al. [1982]	—	—	—	X ⟷	X
Wiederhold and ElMasri [1979]	—	X ⟷	X →	X	—

Hwang 1984; ElMasri et al. 1987; Kahn 1979].

(4) Those that explicitly mention preintegration analysis [ElMasri et al. 1987; Mannino and Effelsberg 1984a; Navathe and Gadgil 1982].

On the basis of the looping structure alone, the following similarities can be observed:

(1) Casanova and Vidal [1983] and Teorey and Fry [1982] have a "no-feedback" approach to integration. They only perform the merging and restructuring steps.

(2) Al-Fedaghi and Scheuermann [1981]; Dayal and Hwang [1984], Motro and Buneman [1981], and Yao et al. [1982] are similar to the above group in that they perform only merging and restructuring; however, they allow a feedback between these two steps.

(3) Kahn [1979], Mannino and Effelsberg [1984a], Navathe and Gadgil [1982], Wiederhold and ElMasri [1979] provide a global loop from the end of the process to the initial comparison activity. Kahn [1979] includes the restructuring step, whereas the others do not.

(4) Finally, Batini and Lenzerini [1984] and ElMasri et al. [1987] cover all the steps; moreover, they provide an iterative execution of comparison and conforming steps before any merging is attempted. As such, they appear to have the maximum interaction with the user/designer.

2.5 Preintegration

As shown in Table 4, only three methodologies [ElMasri et al. 1987; Mannino and Effelsberg 1984a; Navathe and Gadgil 1982] explicitly mention preintegration. They basically propose a collection of correspondences among schemas in the form of constraints and assertions among component schemas. These specifications are used, for example, to relate names, to establish that an object in one schema is the result of some operation on a set of objects in another schema, etc.

For all methodologies, whether or not preintegration is explicitly mentioned, the sequencing and grouping of schemas for integration has to be considered. In this section we describe the different strategies that address this problem.

The first step, choice of schemas, involves processing component schemas in some sequence. In general, the number of schemas considered for integration of each step can be $n \geq 2$. Figure 9 shows four possible variations termed *integration-processing strategies*. Each strategy is shown in the form of a tree. The leaf nodes of the tree correspond to the component

90

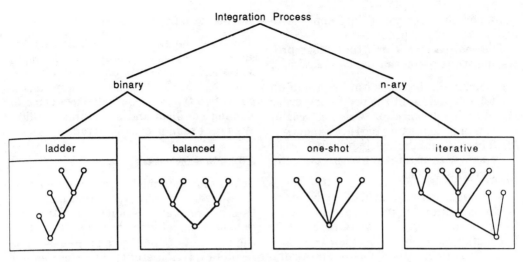

Figure 9. Types of integration-processing strategies.

Table 5. Integration-Processing Strategies

Reference	Type of integration-processing strategy	Balance of strategy
Al-Fedaghi and Scheuermann [1981]	One-shot *n*-ary	—
Batini and Lenzerini [1984]	Binary	Ladder
Casanova and Vidal [1983]	Binary	Balanced
Dayal and Hwang [1984]	Binary	No claim
ElMasri et al. [1987]	One-shot *n*-ary	—
Kahn [1979]	Binary	No claim
Motro and Buneman [1981]	Binary	No claim
Mannino and Effelsberg [1984a]	Binary among families	No claim
Navathe and Gadgil [1982]	Iterative *n*-ary	—
Teorey and Fry [1982]	Binary	Balanced
Yao et al. [1982]	One-shot *n*-ary	—
Wiederhold and ElMasri [1979]	Binary	Ladder

schemas, and the nonleaf nodes correspond to intermediate results of integration. The root node is the final result. The primary classification of strategies is binary versus *n*-ary.

Binary strategies allow the integration of two schemas at a time. They are called *ladder strategies* when a new component schema is integrated with an existing intermediate result at each step. A binary strategy is *balanced* when the schemas are divided into pairs at the start and are integrated in a symmetric fashion (see Figure 9, balanced).

N-ary strategies allow integration of *n* schemas at a time ($n > 2$). An *n*-ary strategy is *one shot* when the *n* schemas are integrated in a single step; it is *iterative* otherwise. The latter is the most general case.

Table 5 is a comparison of methodologies along two dimensions: binary versus *n*-ary and the nature of balancing.

We now comment on the specific features pertaining to the above classes of strategies.

The advantage of binary strategies is in terms of simplifying the activities of comparison and conforming at each integration step. It is evident from the table that most of the methodologies agree in adopting a binary strategy because of the increasing complexity of the integration step with respect to the number of schemas to be integrated. In general, the merging algorithm for *n* schemas can be shown to be n^2 in complexity. Hence, keeping *n* down is desirable from the standpoint of complexity. The disadvantages of binary strategies are an increased number of integration operations and the need for a final analysis to add missing global properties.

The motivation behind the ladder processing strategy comes from two reasons:

(1) Component schemas can be picked up for integration in the decreasing order of their relevance (or "weights," as Batini and Lenzerini [1984] call them);
(2) There is an inherent importance associated with an already existing partially integrated schema.

An integration step could take advantage of this situation by resolving conflicts in favor of the partially integrated schema. For instance, an enterprise view (see Section 2.3) is frequently viable in an organization. Choosing it as the initial schema makes the detection and resolution of dissimilarities more efficient.

A binary balanced strategy has been proposed only by Teorey and Fry [1982]. They justify it on the basis of minimizing the number of comparisons among concepts in the schemas.

The work of ElMasri and Navathe [ElMasri 1980; Navathe et al. 1984] are good examples of one-shot n-ary strategies. They consider that during Step 2, an analysis of the n schemas is performed together. After collecting, analyzing, and validating all the interview assertions, they perform the integration in a single step. The obvious advantages of n-ary integration are:

(1) A considerable amount of semantic analysis can be performed before merging, avoiding the necessity of a further analysis and transformation of the integrated schema;
(2) The number of steps for integration is minimized.

The recommended procedure given by Navathe and Gadgil [1982] is an iterative n-ary strategy where "equivalence groups" of user views are initially formed; the views within the groups are merged first, creating intermediate integrated schemas that are again analyzed and grouped iteratively.

Not all the analyzed methodologies state what strategy they adopt. Hardly any (except Teorey and Fry [1982]) make any statement about balancing.

2.6 Comparison of Schemas

The fundamental activity in this step consists of checking all conflicts in the representation of the same objects in different schemas. Methodologies broadly distinguish two types of conflicts (see Table 6): naming conflicts and structural conflicts. We now examine each in detail.

2.6.1 Naming Conflicts

Schemas in data models incorporate names for the various objects represented. People from different application areas of the same organization refer to the same data using their own terminology and names. This results in a proliferation of names as well as a possible inconsistency among names in the component schemas. The problematic relationships among names are of two types:

(1) *Homonyms*: When the same name is used for two different concepts, giving rise to inconsistency unless detected. Consider the two schemas shown in Figure 10. Both schemas include an entity named EQUIPMENT. However, the EQUIPMENT in Figure 10a refers to Computers/Copiers/Mimeographic machines, whereas in Figure 10b it refers to pieces of furniture as well as air conditioners. It is obvious that merging the two entities in the integrated schema would result in producing a single entity for two conceptually distinct objects.
(2) *Synonyms*: When the same concept is described by two or more names. Unless different names improve the understanding of different users, they are not justified.

An example appears in Figure 11, where CLIENT and CUSTOMER are synonyms; the entities with these two names in the two schemas refer to the same real-world concept. In this case, keeping two distinct entities in the integrated schema would result in modeling a single object by means of two different entities.

The motivation behind establishing naming correspondences and discovering

Table 6. Naming and Structural Conflicts

Reference	Naming conflicts	Structural conflicts
Al-Fedaghi and Scheuermann [1981]	—	—
Batini and Lenzerini [1984]	Homonyms Synonyms	Type inconsistencies Integrity constraints conflicts
Casanova and Vidal [1983]	—	—

Dayal and Hwang [1984]	Homonyms
	Synonyms
		Schema level conflicts:
		  Scale differences
		  Structural differences
		  Differences in abstraction
		Data level inconsistencies:
		  Various levels of obsolescence
		    and reliability

ElMasri et al. [1987]	Homonyms
	Synonyms
	Attribute equivalence assertions
	Entity class equivalence
		Open ended treatment of conflicts,
		  specifically:
		  Differences in abstraction levels
		  Differences in roles, degree, and
		    cardinality constraints of
		    relationships

Kahn [1979]	Homonyms Synonyms	Cardinality ratio conflicts
Motro and Buneman [1981]	—	—
Mannino and Effelsberg [1984a]	Use of qualified names Attribute equivalence specification	Differences in abstractions
Navathe and Gadgil [1982]	Homonyms Synonyms	Dependency conflicts Redundancy conflicts Modeling conflicts
Teorey and Fry [1982]	—	—
Yao et al. [1982]	—	—
Wiederhold and ElMasri [1979]	—	Cardinality ratio conflicts

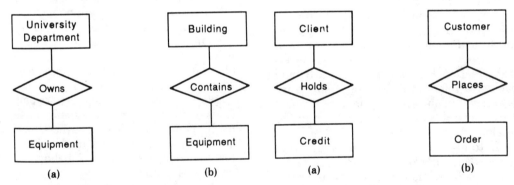

Figure 10. Example of homonyms.

Figure 11. Example of synonyms.

homonyms and synonyms is to be able to determine the four kinds of semantic relationships among component schemas that we introduced in Section 1.2. Note that whereas homonyms can be detected by comparing concepts with the same name in different schemas, synonyms can only be detected after an external specification.

Data dictionaries have been advocated as a useful adjunct tool to schema integration methodologies for a better management of names [Navathe and Kerschberg 1986].

Methodologies [Al-Fedaghi and Scheuermann 1981; Casanova and Vidal 1983; Motro and Buneman 1981; Teorey and Fry 1982; Wiederhold and ElMasri 1979; Yao et al. 1982] make no mention of naming correspondences, probably as a result of an implicit assumption that such correspondences are preestablished and thus no naming conflicts can arise (see also the discussion of the relational model in Section 1.4). In ElMasri et al. [1987] a full naming convention

schemaname.objectname

for objects and

schemaname.objectname.attributename

for attributes is adopted to assure uniqueness of names. As a consequence, homonyms cannot arise. The synonym problem still remains and must be dealt with via the establishment of attribute classes. There is also a cross-reference lexicon of names maintained to keep information on synonyms. In Batini and Lenzerini [1984] and ElMasri et al. [1987] the integration system automatically assigns a "degree of similarity" to pairs of objects, based on several matching criteria. Users are presented with the similarity information to help them detect synonyms.

A type of homonyms arises when for the same concept there is a match on names but no match on the corresponding sets of instances. They can occur at various levels of abstraction. For example, at the attribute level, size refers to dress size (a single integer code) in one schema, whereas it refers to trouser size (a pair of integers) in another schema. At the entity level, STUDENT refers to all students in the database kept in the registrar's office, whereas it refers to married students only in the married-student-housing database.

2.6.2 Structural Conflicts

We use the term *structural conflicts* to include conflicts that arise as a result of a different choice of modeling constructs or integrity constraints. They can be traced back to the three reasons for schema diversity described in Section 1.2. Table 6 lists the different kinds of structural conflicts that are taken into account in various methodologies. Here we present a classification of structural conflicts that is independent from the various terminologies and from the specific characteristics of the different data models adopted in the methodologies. Such a classification distinguishes the following kinds of conflicts:

(1) *Type Conflicts.* These arise when the same concept is represented by different modeling constructs in different schemas. This is the case when, for example, a class of objects is represented as an entity in one schema and as an attribute in another schema.

(2) *Dependency Conflicts.* These arise when a group of concepts are related among themselves with different dependencies in different schemas. For example, the relationship Marriage between Man and Woman is $1:1$ in one schema, but $m:n$ in another accounting for a marriage history.

(3) *Key Conflicts.* Different keys are assigned to the same concept in different schemas. For example, SS# and Emp_id may be the keys of Employee in two component schemas.

(4) *Behavioral Conflicts.* These arise when different insertion/deletion policies are associated with the same class of objects in distinct schemas. For example, in one schema a department may be allowed to exist without employees, whereas in another, deleting the last employee associated with a department leads to the deletion of the department itself. Note that these conflicts may arise only when the data model allows for the representation of behavioral properties of objects.

Another activity typically performed during the schema comparison step is the discovery of interschema properties. Methodologies usually consider this discovery to be a by-product of conflict detection. If any interschema properties are discovered during this step, they are saved and processed

Table 7. Schema Transformations Performed by Methodologies

Reference	Conform	Merge and restructure
Al-Fedaghi and Scheuermann [1981]	—	Removal of redundant dependencies
Batini and Lenzerini [1984]	Type transformations Restructuring Renaming	Subsetting Aggregation Restructuring
Casanova and Vidal [1983]	—	Optimization
Dayal and Hwang [1984]	—	Include Integration by generalization Define supertype Define subtype Scale unifying Renaming
ElMasri et al. [1987]	Modify assertions Renaming	Remove redundant relationships
Kahn [1979]	Renaming	Redundancy elimination
Mannino and Effelsberg [1984a]	Algebraic operations	Create generalization hierarchies Create subtype
Motro and Buneman [1981]	—	Meet Fold Aggregate Join Add Delete
Navathe and Gadgil [1982]	—	Attribute enhancement Attribute creation Restriction
Teorey and Fry [1982]	—	Aggregation Generalization
Yao et al. [1982]	—	Removal of functions
Wiederhold and ElMasri [1979]	—	Subsetting

during schema merging [ElMasri et al. 1987] or schema restructuring [Batini and Lenzerini 1984].

In general, both the discovery of conflicts and the interschema properties are aided by a strong interaction between the designer and the user. This is the position advocated by [Batini and Lenzerini [1984], ElMasri et al. [1987], Kahn [1979], Mannino and Effelsberg [1984a], and Navathe and Gadgil [1982].

2.7 Conforming of Schemas

The goal of this activity is to conform or align schemas to make them compatible for integration. Achieving this goal amounts to resolving the conflicts, which in turn re-

quires that schema transformations be performed. In order to resolve a conflict, the designer must understand the semantic relationships among the concepts involved in the conflict. Sometimes conflicts cannot be resolved because they arose as a result of some basic inconsistency. In this case, the conflicts are reported to the users, who must guide the designer in their resolution.

The concept of schema transformation is central to conflict resolution and therefore to the conforming activity. Since methodologies also perform schema transformations during merging and restructuring, in Table 7 we introduce a comprehensive taxonomy of all types of transformations.

From this table it is clear that a limited number of transformations are proposed

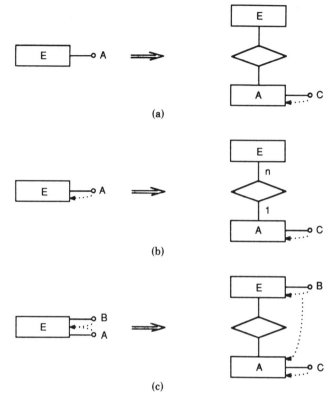

(a)

(b)

(c)

Figure 12. Transformation of an attribute into an entity.

for conflict resolution. Simple renaming operations are used for solving naming conflicts by most methodologies. With regard to other types of conflicts, the methodologies do not spell out formally how the process of resolution is carried out; however, an indication is given in several of them as to how one should proceed. For example, when dealing with equivalence, Batini and Lenzerini [1984] suggest that atomic concepts be transformed (i.e., transform entities/attributes/relationships among one another) to reach a common canonical representation of the schemas.

We show in Figure 12 three examples of transforming an attribute into an entity, as suggested by Batini and Lenzerini [1984]. The dashed lines in these figures specify identifiers. In Figure 12a attribute A is not an identifier. It is shown to be transformed into an entity. In Figure 12b, attribute A, which is an identifier, becomes an entity in the new schema; entity A now provides

identification to entity E (since $1:n$ means that every instance of A participates only once in the relationship with E). In Figure 12c attribute A is only a part of an identifier and so in the new structure, entity A becomes a part of a compound identifier for entity E.

It is interesting to note that among the methodologies surveyed, none provide an analysis or proof of the completeness of the schema transformation operations from the standpoint of being able to resolve any type of conflict that can arise.

All the methodologies take the goal of the conforming activity to be the construction of a single "consensus schema" by possibly changing some user views. This is consistent with the ANSI/SPARC [Klug and Tsichritzis 1977] three-schema architecture in which the conceptual schema is a unified representation of the whole application, whereas individual perspectives are captured by external schemas.

2.8 Merging and Restructuring

The activities usually performed by methodologies during this phase require different kinds of operations to be performed on either the component schemas or the temporary integrated schema. In order to establish a common framework for this phase, we assume that all methodologies first merge the component schemas by means of a simple superimposition of common concepts, and then perform restructuring operations on the integrated schema obtained by such a merging. Table 8 shows the transformations proposed in the methodologies for this step. Each transformation is performed in order to improve the schema with respect to one of the three qualities described in Section 1.3, namely, completeness, minimality, and understandability. We now analyze each quality separately.

2.8.1 Completeness

To achieve completeness, the designer has to conclude the analysis and addition of interschema properties that is initiated in previous design steps. In Figure 8 we showed examples of interschema properties. In Table 8 we present a comprehensive list of interschema properties mentioned in the methodologies. Note that "subsetting" is the interschema property used by most methodologies. In fact, it is considered to be the basis for accommodating multiple user perspectives on comparable classes of objects.

Batini and Lenzerini [1984], Dayal and Hwang [1984], Mannino and Effelsberg [1984a], Motro and Buneman [1981], Teorey and Fry [1982], and Wiederhold and ElMasri [1979] propose suitable transformations for introducing subset–generalization relationships in the integrated schema (subsetting, integration by generalization, define subtype, etc. are the names of such transformations). In Motro and Buneman [1981], "meet" is the transformation that produces a common generalization of two classes. Such a transformation is based on the existence of a common key for the two classes. On the other hand, "join" produces a common subtype for the two classes. It is used when a class is needed in the inte-

grated schema for the representation of the set of instances that are common to two different classes.

Other types of interschema properties are concerned with aggregation relationships among classes. Batini and Lenzerini [1984], Motro and Buneman [1981] and Teorey and Fry [1982], propose specific transformations for introducing new relationships in the integrated schema so that aggregation among classes coming from different component schemas can be represented.

Finally, there is a set of transformations that introduces new concepts in order to convey all the information represented in the component schemas. In Navathe and Gadgil [1982] "attribute creation" is the transformation that adds a new attribute to an entity in the integrated schema (a similar transformation is called "add" by Motro and Buneman [1981]). For example, the attribute Category for the class Student in the integrated schema may be used to distinguish among Graduate Students (the students represented in View 1) and Undergraduate Students (the students represented in View 2).

Note that the variety of interschema properties is strongly related to the repertory of schema constructs at the disposal of the data model. Among the semantic models, Wiederhold and ElMasri [1979] provide the richest set of interschema properties in the form of various subsets among different schema constructs. For every meaningful pair of constructs in their model, they show an exhaustive list of cases and show how to integrate each by adding interschema properties. Among the relational model based approaches, the richest set of interschema properties—inclusion, exclusion, and union functional dependencies—are provided by Casanova and Vidal [1983] and more recently in the extension of this methodology by Biskup and Convent [1986].

2.8.2 Minimality

In most of the methodologies, the objective of minimality is to discover and eliminate redundancies. A different approach is followed by Batini and Lenzerini [1984],

Table 8. Interschema Properties

Reference	Interschema properties
Al-Fedaghi and Scheuermann [1981]	—
Batini and Lenzerini [1984]	Subsetting Generalization Relationship
Casanova and Vidal [1983]	Inclusion dependencies Exclusion dependencies Union functional dependencies
Dayal and Hwang [1984]	Subsetting Subfunction
ElMasri et al. [1987]	Assertions related to extensions Clustering of attributes into classes
Kahn [1979]	—
Motro and Buneman [1981]	Subsetting
Mannino and Effelsberg [1984a]	Generalization Overlap and nonoverlap Attribute scope and meaning
Navathe and Gadgil [1982]	Categorization Subsetting Partitioning
Teorey and Fry [1982]	Generalization Aggregation
Yao et al. [1982]	—
Wiederhold and ElMasri [1979]	Subsetting

where it is stated that discovering the redundancies is a task of conceptual design, whereas their elimination has to be performed during the implementation design phase.

We motivate the minimality notion in Figure 13. There, three subset relationships are present, indicated by double-lined arrows; each arrow points from a subentity to a superentity.

The subset relationship between Engineering_manager and Employee is redundant since it can be derived from the other two. Keeping a minimal number of concepts in the global schema implies dropping the redundant relationship from it. Other typical situations sought are cycles of relationships, derived attributes [Batini and Lenzerini 1984; ElMasri et al. 1987; Navathe and Gadgil 1982], and composition of functions [Yao et al. 1982]. In the relational-model-based approaches, redundancies are related to derived dependencies of various types [Al-Fedaghi and Scheuer-

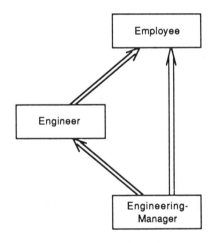

Figure 13. A schema with redundancy.

mann 1981; Casanova and Vidal 1983]. For these approaches, minimality is the driving force behind integration.

As seen from Table 7, most of the schema transformations during restructuring are geared for a removal of redundancy.

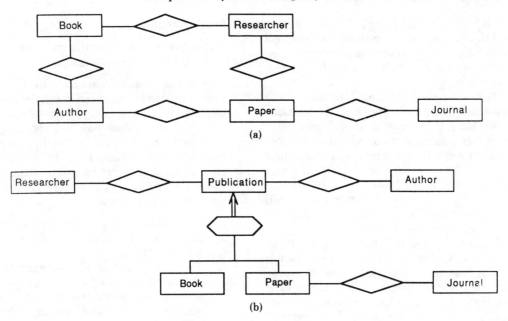

Figure 14. Improving understandability. (a) Schema A. (b) Schema B.

2.8.3 Understandability

Attention to the issue of understandability is diffused in all methodologies. The problem is addressed explicitly by Batini and Lenzerini [1984]. We reproduce an example in Figure 14, where they argue on qualitative terms that, while the two schemas are equivalent, Schema B is more understandable than Schema A. Schema B was obtained from Schema A by adding a generalization hierarchy relating Publication to Book and Paper. In general, for improving understandability, additional schema transformations are needed.

At present, to our knowledge, no quantitative and objective measures of conceptual understandability exist that can be applied here. If a graphical representation of the conceptual model is supported, the shape of the diagram, the total length of connections, the number of crossings and bends, and so forth may be used as parameters to define graphic understandability [Batini et al. 1986].

A specific activity performed during the restructuring step by database integration methodologies is query modification. We already have indicated in Figure 2 that the mapping of queries is an output of the database integration process. Dayal and Hwang [1984] develop query modification algorithms for modifying global queries into essential local subqueries with duplicate elimination.

3. CONCLUSIONS AND FUTURE WORK

3.1 General Remarks

A few general remarks about the methodologies are in order. The methodologies surveyed can be reviewed on the basis of some general criteria as follows.

3.1.1 Use

Most methodologies were developed as parts of research projects with low emphasis on developing full-scale automated systems. It is obvious that design tools can be built using the concepts from individual methodologies. If the size of the problem can be contained within manual means, however, methodologies also can be used manually.

Partial implementation of some of the methodologies (e.g., Batini and Lenzerini

C. Batini, M. Lenzerini, and S. B. Navathe

[1984], Teorey and Fry [1982], and Yao et al. [1982]) have been reported. Nothing has been reported, however, on the actual use of these methodologies to perform view integration.

The entity–relationship model, which provides a basis for the [Batini and Lenzerini 1984; ElMasri et al. 1987; Kahn 1979] methodologies, was reported to be the most widely used model in practice. Chilson and Kudlac [1983] report that the Navathe and Schkolnick model [Navathe and Schkolnick 1978], used in the Navathe and Gadgil [1982] methodology, was also known to the users surveyed.

Out of the methodologies for database integration, that of Dayal and Hwang [1984] has been used with modifications within the framework of the Multibase project at Computer Corporation of America. The Multibase system [Landers and Rosenberg 1982] has been designed and implemented to allow users access to heterogeneous databases in a single system. Several researchers [Hubbard 1980; Chiang et al. 1983; Data Designer 1981; Ferrara 1985] describe tools that allow an integration capability to a limited extent.

3.1.2 Completeness and Detailed Specification

Most of the surveyed methodologies do not provide an algorithmic specification of the integration activities, and they rarely show whether the set of conflicts or the set of transformations considered is complete in some sense. What they provide are general guidelines and concepts on different steps. Methodologies that address well-defined problems of logical design based on purely mechanized procedures such as Al-Fedaghi and Scheuerman [1981], Casanova and Vidal [1983], and Yao et al. [1982] are able to construct precise algorithms. But by their very nature, they cover more of the implementation design compared to conceptual design (according to Table 2).

A side effect of the above problem is that there is no easy way to guarantee convergence in these methodologies, especially for those involving looping structures (see Table 5). The termination of the loops is essentially left to the designer's discretion.

3.2 Missing Aspects

Several aspects are currently missing in methodologies for view integration.

(a) *Processing Specifications in View Integration.* This is the specification of the queries and transactions on component schemas. An initial position reported on view integration in the database design literature [Yao et al. 1982] was that a view integration methodology should have two goals with respect to processing specification:

  (1) *Feasibility.* The integrated schema supports any processes on the component schema.
  (2) *Performance.* The integrated schema is "optimal" with respect to a given set of component schema queries and transactions. Specifications of queries and transactions are not explicitly used in any methodologies except that of Yao et al. [1982], where an "optimal" structure is selected on the basis of a given set of transactions. We believe that performance analysis based on processing specifications is not meaningful at the conceptual design level since no reasonable performance predictions can be made. Such performance analysis is meaningful only when logical and physical schemas are fully defined in a DBMS. On the other hand, we stress that the real performance measures of conceptual schemas are the goals that we stated in Section 1.3, namely, completeness and correctness, minimality, and understandability.

(b) *Behavioral Specification.* This is the specification of the dynamic properties of objects in the schema (e.g., the value of the salary of an employee can never decrease).

None of the methodologies surveyed model behavioral properties fully. The models adopted by ElMasri et al. [1987] and Navathe and Gadgil [1982] allow them to formulate limited types of behavioral properties in the form of insertion/deletion constraints.

100

(c) *Schema Mappings.* To support the local views (i.e., external schemas according to the ANSI/SPARC [Klug and Tsichritzis 1977] terminology) of the users of component schemas on the basis of the integrated schema is a problem that is well addressed by the database integration methodologies [Dayal and Hwang 1984; Motro and Buneman 1981]. However, it is only hinted at by ElMasri et al. [1987], Mannino and Effelsberg [1984a], and Navathe and Gadgil [1982] in the form of recognizing "mapping rules" as an output of integration. Only Wiederhold and ElMasri [1979] have given a complete set of rules to support component schemas. Actually, various levels of mappings need to be addressed in going from (or building) external schemas of the integrated schema to (from) one or more external schema(s) of the component schemas.

3.3 Future Research Directions

From Sections 3.1 and 3.2, it is obvious that more work is required on incorporating processing specifications, behavior modeling, and schema mapping in the schema integration methodologies. More research is also required to settle open issues such as the choice of data models and levels of integrity constraint specification. Along with these, the following directions for future research are important.

3.3.1 Extension of Integration Methodologies

View integration methodologies need to be extended to be used in distributed database design. This would imply enriching the inputs by adding more information on the distribution preference of users as well as distributed processing requirements. The principle behind the integration process would remain practically unaltered, but a new set of problems would have to be considered in terms of materializing the so-called local conceptual schemas.

Another possible extension could be to address the design of databases with special properties, such as scientific and statistical databases and databases for computer-aided design (CAD). In the first case, the integration methodology has to deal with data at different levels of summarization. This leads to a greater complexity of the semantic analysis, an accompanying increase in conflicts, and a corresponding increase in the complexity of conflict-resolution strategies. In the case of CAD databases, problems arise as a result of multiple representations of the same data, as in very large scale integration design, top-down organization of design data, and the far-reaching update propagation.

The statistical and CAD databases are often subjected to database integration for allowing sharing of information. New methodologies of database integration for such cases need to be designed; the existing works seem limited in this area.

3.3.2 Knowledge Base Integration

Integration of knowledge bases has received attention in the literature only recently [Eick and Lockemann 1985]. Knowledge bases treat classes and their instances together: This implies that data and metadata coexist in the representation. Moreover, they provide richer linguistic mechanisms: Knowledge is often expressed in the form of logical assertions, productions, and inference rules. Rule integration is a problem in itself. These considerations bring a new set of issues that are not covered presently in the surveyed methodologies.

3.3.3 Process Integration

This refers to the activity of integrating and transforming a set of processes applicable to component schemas into a set of processes applicable to the integrated schema. It seems that many notions used for data schema integration can be transferred to process integration. For example, the goals (Section 1.3) are equally applicable; so are the concepts of equivalence, semantic analysis, conflict detection and resolution, and transformations. Tucherman et al. [1985] consider database design to be an integration of process modules. Some preliminary work is under way on the related problem of program transformation [Demo 1983; Demo and Kundu 1985].

3.3.4 Expert Systems for Schema Integration

As pointed out in the Introduction and Section 1, schema integration is a difficult and complex task. An expert system approach to database design in general and to schema integration in particular on the basis of the rules and heuristics of design is worth investigating. Projects have already been under way in this area (e.g., see Bouzeghoub et al. [1986] and Shin and Irani [1985]). Model dependent rules should be used in the comparison and conforming activities with the goal of improving the equivalence and/or compatibility of component schemas. Alternative schema transformations can be suggested or evaluated by the system when a conflict must be solved. Selection among alternative schemas for integration can be guided by system–designer interaction.

APPENDIX 1. A SUMMARY DESCRIPTION OF METHODOLOGIES

In the following, the methodologies surveyed in this paper are briefly described. The same categories of description are used for each methodology. These descriptions should only be treated as a quick reference guide and not as a substitute for the original descriptions of the methodologies. They are included here to highlight the fact that, although the general intent of all methodologies is very similar, the actual mechanics vary greatly. The terminology of the authors is used without modification. Words in parentheses refer to equivalent terms used in this paper.

Of the above methodologies surveyed, those of Dayal and Hwang [1984], Mannino and Effelsberg [1984a], and Motro and Buneman [1981] apply to database integration; the method of [ElMasri et al. [1987] is used for database integration as well as view integration, whereas the remaining methodologies apply to view integration only.

Al-Fedaghi and Scheuermann [1981]

Type: View integration methodology.

Model: Relational model.

Input: *n* external views (component schemas), given in terms of relations and functional dependencies.

Output: *n* external schemas, one conceptual schema (integrated schema), a mapping mechanism between external schemas and conceptual schema.

Processing specifications considered: No.

Integration strategy:

(1) Find sets of functional dependencies common to some set of external views.
(2) Eliminate in previous sets (local) redundant dependencies.
(3) Remove redundant dependencies due to transitivity in the global set of dependencies, thus producing a nonredundant cover of the conceptual schema.
(4) Identify dependencies that were eliminated in previous steps, but must now be readded to external views in order to minimize their effect on the mapping process; construct external views.

Special features:

(1) The main goal of the methodology is to obtain mappings that
   (a) preserve compatibility between relations and dependencies in external schemas and in the integrated schema;
   (b) reduce interferences between insert/delete operations in different external schemas.
(2) The methodology assures that all relations are projections of a universal relation.

Batini and Lenzerini [1984]

Type: View integration methodology.

Model: Entity–relationship model (see Appendix 2).

Input:
user schemata (component schemas),
enterprise schema,
weights for schemata.

Output: Global schema (integrated schema).

Processing specifications considered: No.

Integration strategy:

(1) Choose the enterprise schema as the base schema.
(2) While new schemas are to be integrated, do
    (2.1) Choose a new schema.
    (2.2) Find conflicts between the two schemas.
    (2.3) Amend the two schemas in order to conform them.
    (2.4) Merge the schemas.
    (2.5) Analyze the draft integrated schema in order to discover redundancies and simplify the representation.

Special features:

(1) Several indications are suggested to guide the designer in the investigation of conflicts (e.g., type inconsistencies, concept likeness/unlikeness).
(2) For every indication, several scenarios are proposed (i.e., typical solutions of the conflict).
(3) Several types of equivalence transformations are supplied to confirm the representation of concepts.
(4) A specific activity is suggested to improve understandability of the global schema.

Related references: Batini and Lenzerini [1983] and Batini et al. [1983].

Casanova and Vidal [1983]

Type: View integration methodology.

Model: Relational model. Besides functional dependencies, other types of dependencies are considered: inclusion, exclusion, and union functional dependencies.

Input: Two user views (component schema).

Output: Conceptual schema (integrated schema).

Processing specifications considered: No.

Integration strategy:

(1) Combine user views, merging relation schemas of the two different views and defining new inclusion, exclusion, and union functional dependencies.
(2) Optimize the temporary conceptual schema, trying to minimize redundancy and the size of the schema.

Special features:

(1) The relational model is enriched with interrelational dependencies useful for expressing how data in distinct views are interrelated.
(2) It is assumed that a preliminary integration process has been carried out to detect which structures of different views represent the same information and interrelational dependencies.
(3) The optimization procedure (Step 2) is shown to be correct for a special class of schemas, called restricted schemas; a restricted schema is essentially a representation of a collection of entities-relationships, identified by their keys.

Dayal and Hwang [1984]

Type: Database integration methodology.

Model: Functional model. The model uses two constructs: entities and functions (i.e., properties of entities, relationships among entities). Functions may be single valued or multivalued. Entities may be user defined (e.g., Person) or else constants (e.g., Boolean). A generalization abstraction is provided among entities and functions.

Input:
local schemas of existing databases, queries.

Output:
global interface to databases, modified queries.

Processing specifications considered: Queries.

Integration strategy:

(1) Solve conflicts among concepts in local schemas (naming, scale, structural, abstraction conflicts).
(2) Solve conflicts among data in existing databases (inconsistencies in identifiers, different degree of obsolescence, different degree of reliability).
(3) Modify queries and make them consistent with the global schema.

Special features:

(1) Generalization abstraction is uniformly used as a means to combine entities and resolve different types of conflicts.
(2) A detailed algorithm is given for query modification and is formally proved correct and nonredundant by Hwang [1982].

ElMasri et al. [1987]

Type: Both view integration in logical database design and database integration.

Model: Entity-Category-Relationship (ECR) model [ElMasri et al. 1985], which recognizes, besides entities and relationships, the concept of categories. Categories are used for two purposes: to show a generalization of a superentity into subentities and to simply allow for the definition of a subset of an entity based on some predicate.

Input:
n schemas, which represent either user views or existing databases represented in the ECR model;
attribute equivalence assertions;
object class extension assertions.

Output:
integrated schema,
mappings between integrated and conceptual schemas.

Processing specifications considered: Not to determine the result of integration. However, the problem of dealing with queries on the integrated schema is addressed in terms of mappings.

Integration strategy:

(1) Transform existing schemas into ECR if needed.
(2) Preintegration, which consists of an interleaved application of schema analysis and modification with assertion specification.
(3) Integration of object classes.
(4) Integration of relationship classes.
(5) Generation of mappings.

The above procedure is followed as an n-ary integration process.

Special features:

(1) A very detailed treatment of attribute and object extension assertions via consistency checking and verification of algorithms is included.
(2) The methodology uses the notion of extension of attribute types and object classes as a basis for comparison.
(3) The methodology applies equally to view integration and database integration.

Related references: ElMasri and Navathe [1984], Larson et al. [1986], Navathe et al. [1984], Navathe et al. [1986], Weeldreyer [1986].

Kahn [1979]

Type: View integration methodology.

Model: Entity–relationship model (see Appendix 2).

Input: Local information structures (component schemas).

Output: Global information structure (integrated schema).

Processing specifications considered: No.

Integration strategy:

(1) (Entity step) Aggregate entities.
    (1.1) Standardize names.
    (1.2) Aggregate entities to form a nonredundant collection.
    (1.3) Check entities against processing requirements.
    (1.4) Eliminate nonessential attributes.
    (1.5) Simplify the representation.

(2) (Relationship step) Aggregate relationships.

    (2.1) Standardize names.

    (2.2) Analyze consistency of relationship cardinalities versus entity cardinalities.

    (2.3) Aggregate relationships.

    (2.4) Determine conditional and existence-dependent relationship.

    (2.5) Eliminate all redundant relationships.

Special features:

(1) A rich set of heuristics is suggested to guide the designer in discovering conflicts.

(2) Several types of qualities are defined for the integrated schema, and strategies are suggested to achieve these.

Mannino and Effelsberg [1984a]

Type: Database integration.

Model: Generalized entity manipulator.

Input: Local schemas in a common data model, interschema assertions about entity types and attributes.

Output: Global view objects, global view mapping, integration schema objects.

Processing specifications considered: No.

Integration strategy:

(1) Transform each local schema into an easy-to-integrate form.

(2) Match the entity types and attributes of the local schemas.

(3) Define assertions about the entity types that can be generalized and then define assertions about equivalent attributes.

(4) Merge pairs of "generalizable" entity families as indicated by the assertions and designer preferences.

(5) Define global attribute formats and conversion rules for the global entity types.

Special features:

(1) The merging step uses entity families (collection of entity types related by generalization) rather than simple entity types.

(2) Companion global view definition language that uses the same set of integration operators as the methodology.

(3) Semantic equivalence and range of meaning of individual attributes, groups of attributes, and functions of attributes can be defined in attribute assertions.

Steps 2, 3, and 4 may be performed in sequence or iteratively with backtracking.

Related references: Mannino and Effelsberg [1984b], Mannino and Karle [1986], and Mannino et al. [1986].

Motro and Buneman [1981]

Type: Database integration methodology.

Model: Functional model. Constructs of the model are classes of objects, which may be related by two types of functions—att, by which one class becomes an attribute of another class, and gen, which establishes a generalization relationship.

Input:
Two logical (component) schemas with the corresponding databases, queries.

Output:
superview (global schema), modified queries.

Processing specifications considered: Queries.

Integration strategy:

(1) Merge the two (independent) logical schemas by combining initially primitive classes.

(2) While new restructurings can be applied to the temporary integrated schema, do

    (2.1) Choose a restructuring primitive and apply to the integrated schema.

Special features:

(1) The main feature of the methodology is to provide a large and powerful set of restructuring primitives while no

heuristics are given to discipline their use.

Related references: Motro [1981].

Navathe and Gadgil [1982]

Type: View integration methodology.

Model: Navathe–Schkolnick model. The main construct of the model is the object (type), representing either an entity or an association, which can be recursively defined in terms of entities or associations. Other concepts are connectors, which model insertion/deletion properties of associations and subsets between objects. Associations are divided into three types: subsetting, partitioning, and categorizing associations.

Input:
enterprise view,
local views (component schemas),
integration strategy,
interview and intraview assertions,
processing requirements.

Output:
global view,
mapping rules,
unresolved conflicts,
modified assertions.

Integration strategy:

(1) Divide views into classes of

equivalent views,
identical views,
single views.

(2) Integrate classes checking for conflicts (among names, keys, etc.) and solving them on the basis of assertions and order of preference.
(3) While new view assertion operations are applicable, do
    (3.1) Perform new integrations between intermediate and semiintegrated views in a way similar to Step 2.
(4) Generate mapping rules determining how each of the component views can be obtained from the integrated view.

Special features:

(1) Equivalence and containment relations among information contents of user schemas are assumed as input to the design.
(2) A taxonomy is given for types of comparisons among objects, conflicts, and view integration operations.
(3) Conflicts are generally resolved by adopting the most restrictive specification.
(4) Attention is given to the problem of automating the view integration process, distinguishing activities that can be solved automatically and activities that ask for interaction with the designer/user.

Teorey and Fry [1982]

Type: View integration methodology.

Model: Semantic hierarchical model. Constructs are classes of objects, aggregation abstractions among objects by which an object is seen as an abstraction of the set of its properties, and generalization abstractions.

Input:
information perspective (component schemas),
application perspective,
event perspective,
corporate perspective,
policy guidance and rules.

Output:
global information structure (integrated schema),
conflicts.

Processing specifications considered: No.

Integration strategy:

(1) Order local views as to importance with respect to the specific design objectives.
(2) Consolidate local views, two at a time (the order is determined by Step 1).
(3) Solve conflicts that have arisen in Step 2.

Special features:

(1) Attention is given to the problem of integration of processing specifications, but no specific strategies and methods are proposed.
(2) Different types of integration processing strategies (see Section 2.5) are compared. The binary balanced strategy is claimed to be the most effective.

Wiederhold and ElMasri [1979]

Type: View integration methodology.

Model: Structural model. Such a model is constructed from relations that are used to represent entity classes and several types of relationships among entity classes. Other types of relationships are represented by connections between relations.

Input: Two data models (component schemas).

Output:
Integrated database model (integrated schema),
database submodels.

Processing specifications considered: Only primitive operations on concepts (insertion, deletion).

Integration strategy:

(1) Find all compatible pairs of relations.
(2) For each pair of relations, integrate the connection between them.
(3) Integrate compatible relations.

Special features:

(1) Owing to the rich variety of modeling constructs of the structural model, an extensive set of conflicts is presented and analyzed, and solutions are provided.
(2) Mapping rules are derived from the integration process to express data models consistently with the integrated database model.

Related references: ElMasri [1980] and ElMasri and Wiederhold [1979].

Yao et al. [1982]

Type: View integration methodology.

Model: Functional model. Constructs of the model are nodes, classified into simple nodes representing atomic data elements and tuple nodes, representing nonfunctional (i.e., many-to-many) relationships among nodes, and functions among nodes.

Input: Two schemas.

Output: The integrated schema.

Processing specifications considered: Yes, in language TASL.

Integration strategy:

(1) Merge nodes with same values.
(2) Merge nodes that are subsets of other nodes.
(3) Remove redundant functions and modify corresponding transaction specifications.

Special features:

(1) The main aspect dealt with in the methodology is to determine and remove redundancy.
(2) Paths to be removed are found by using processing specification information.
(3) A transaction specification language (TASL) accompanies the methodology.

APPENDIX 2. THE ENTITY–RELATIONSHIP MODEL

The original model, known as the entity–relationship Model (E–R), was proposed by Chen [1976]. Further extensions of the model appear in Dos Santos et al. [1980] and Scheuermann et al. [1980]. The following concepts are defined in the model.

An *entity* is a class of objects of the real world having similar characteristics and properties. A *relationship* is a class of elementary facts or associations among entities. An attribute is an elementary property either of an entity or a relationship. An entity E_1 is a *subset* of an entity E_2 if every object belonging to E_1 also belongs to E_2. An entity E is a *generalization* of entities $E_2, E_2, \ldots, E_n$ if

(1) every E_i is a subset of E, and
(2) every object belonging to E belongs exactly to one of the E_i's.

A diagrammatic representation is widely used with the E–R model. In Table 9 we show the correspondence between the concepts of the model and the diagrammatic symbols.

An example of a schema appears in Figure 15, which describes information of interest in a data processing department of a company.

The information is about employees (which includes programmers, managers, and senior programmers), projects, and languages. The entities and their corresponding attributes are as follows:

Employee: Employee#, Last_name, Age
Project: Project#, Name
Language: Name, Version
Manager: Budget
Programmer: none
Senior_programmer: Years_of_experience

The relationships among the above entities are:

"Works_on," connecting Employee and Projects.
"Uses," connecting Programmer, Project and Language.

The Works-on relationship has an attribute %_of_time.
Senior-Programmer is a subset of Programmer, and Employee is a generalization of Programmer and Manager. The resulting hierarchy among Employee as a generic entity and Programmer and Manager as its specialized entities is denoted by the name Rank. Note that, by virtue of the generalization hierarchies, Manager and Program-

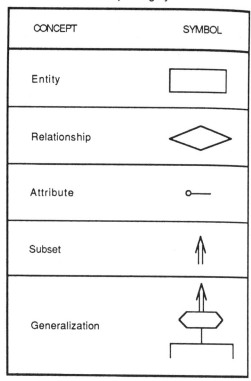

Table 9. Concepts of the Entity–Relationship Model and Corresponding Symbols

CONCEPT	SYMBOL
Entity	▭
Relationship	◇
Attribute	○—
Subset	⇑
Generalization	(generalization symbol)

mer inherit all properties (attributes and relationship types) of Employee, which include attributes of Employee and relationship "Works_on." Owing to the subset relationship, Senior_programmer inherits all the properties of Programmer, which include relationship "Uses" and all attributes from Employee.

Various types of constraints have been specified to go with the E–R model. Here we only refer to the cardinality constraints. The cardinality constraint restricts the number of relationships in which a specific entity can participate. In the example, the cardinality constraint governing the "Works On" relationship is many to many $(m:n)$; that is, an employee may Work on many projects, and a project may have many employees who Work on it. Common cardinality constraints are: one to one $(1:1)$, one to many $(1:n)$, many to one $(n:1)$, and many to many $(m:n)$.

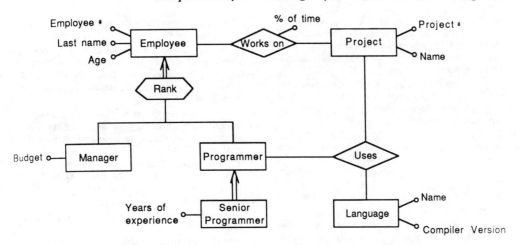

Figure 15. An entity–relationship schema.

ACKNOWLEDGMENTS

Navathe's research was partly supported by National Science Foundation grant No. INT-8400216. Batini's and Lenzerini's research was partly supported by Progetto Finalizzato Informatica and Progetto Finalizzato Transporti, CNR, Italy.

We gratefully acknowledge the patience and cooperation of Sharon Grant and Claudio Dollari in preparing this manuscript. The comments of anonymous referees were very helpful in revising an earlier draft of the paper.

REFERENCES

A. Complete Methodologies for Schema Integration

AL-FEDAGHI, S., AND SCHEUERMANN, P. 1981. Mapping considerations in the design of schemas for the relational model. *IEEE Trans. Softw. Eng. SE-7*, 1 (Jan.).

BATINI, C., AND LENZERINI, M. 1984. A methodology for data schema integration in the entity relationship model. *IEEE Trans. Softw. Eng. SE-10*, 6 (Nov.), 650–663.

CASANOVA, M., AND VIDAL, M. 1983. Towards a sound view integration methodology. In *Proceedings of the 2nd ACM SIGACT/SIGMOD Conference on Principles of Database Systems* (Atlanta, Ga., Mar. 21–23). ACM, New York, pp. 36–47.

DAYAL, U., AND HWANG, H. 1984. View definition and generalization for database integration in multibase: A system for heterogeneous distributed databases. *IEEE Trans. Softw. Eng. SE-10*, 6 (Nov.), 628–644.

ELMASRI, R., LARSON, J., AND NAVATHE, S. B. 1987. Integration algorithms for federated databases and logical database design. Tech. Rep., Honeywell Corporate Research Center (submitted for publication).

KAHN, B. 1979. A structured logical data base design methodology. Ph.D. dissertation, Computer Science Dept., Univ. of Michigan, Ann Arbor, Mich.

MANNINO, M. V., AND EFFELSBERG, W. 1984a. A methodology for global schema design, Computer and Information Sciences Dept., Univ. of Florida, Tech. Rep. No. TR-84-1, Sept.

MOTRO, A., AND BUNEMAN, P. 1981. Constructing superviews. In *Proceedings of the International Conference on Management of Data* (Ann Arbor, Mich., Apr. 29–May 1). ACM, New York.

NAVATHE, S. B., AND GADGIL, S. G. 1982. A methodology for view integration in logical data base design. In *Proceedings of the 8th International Conference on Very Large Data Bases* (Mexico City). VLDB Endowment, Saratoga, Calif.

TEOREY, T., AND FRY, J. 1982. *Design of Database Structures.* Prentice-Hall, Englewood Cliffs, N.J.

WIEDERHOLD, G., AND ELMASRI, R. 1979. A structural model for database systems. Rep. STAN-CS-79-722, Computer Science Dept., Stanford Univ., Stanford, Calif.

YAO, S. B., WADDLE, V., AND HOUSEL, B. 1982. View modeling and integration using the functional data model. *IEEE Trans. Softw. Eng. SE-8*, 6, 544–553.

B. Related Work

ALBANO, A., CARDELLI, L., AND ORSINI, R. 1985. Galileo: A strongly typed, interactive conceptual language. *ACM Trans. Database Syst. 10*, 2 (June), 230–260.

ATZENI, P., AUSIELLO, G., BATINI, C., AND MOSCARINI, M. 1982. Inclusion and equivalence between relational database schemata. *Theor. Comput. Sci. 19*, 267–285.

BATINI, C., AND LENZERINI, M. 1983. A conceptual foundation to view integration. In *Proceedings of the IFIP TC.2 Working Conference on System Description Methodologies* (Kecskmet, Hungary). Elsevier, Amsterdam, pp. 109–139.

BATINI, C., LENZERINI, M., AND MOSCARINI, M. 1983. Views integration. In *Methodology and Tools for Data Base Design*, S. Ceri, Ed. North-Holland, Amsterdam.

BATINI, C., DEMO, B., AND DI LEVA, A. 1984. A methodology for conceptual design of office data bases. *Inf. Syst. 9*, 3, 251–263.

BATINI, C., NARDELLI, E., AND TAMASSIA, R. 1986. A layout algorithm for data flow diagrams. *IEEE Trans. Softw. Eng. SE-12*, 4 (Apr.), 538–546.

BEERI, C., BERNSTEIN, P., AND GOODMAN, N. 1978. A sophisticate's introduction to database normalization theory. In *Proceedings of the 4th International Conference on Very Large Data Bases* (West Berlin, Sept. 13–15). IEEE, New York.

BERNSTEIN, P. A. 1976. Synthesizing third normal form relations from functional dependencies. *ACM Trans. Database Syst. 1*, 4 (Dec.), 277–298.

BILLER, H. 1979. On the equivalence of data base schemas: A semantic approach to data translation. *Inf. Syst. 4*, 1, 35–47.

BILLER, H., AND NEUHOLD, E. J. 1982. Concepts for the conceptual schema. In *Architecture and Models in Data Base Management Systems*, G. M. Nijssen, Ed. North Holland, Amsterdam, pp. 1–30.

BISKUP, J., AND CONVENT, B. 1986. A formal view integration method. In *Proceedings of the International Conference on the Management of Data* (Washington, D.C., May 28–30). ACM, New York.

BISKUP, J., DAYAL, U., AND BERNSTEIN, P. A. 1979. Independent database schemas. In *Proceedings of the International Conference on the Management of Data* (Boston, Mass., May 30–June 1). ACM, New York.

BOUZEGHOUB, M., GARDARIN, G., AND METAIS, E. 1986. Database design tools: An expert systems approach. In *Proceedings of 11th International Conference of Very Large Databases* (Stockholm, Sweden). Morgan Kaufmann, Los Altos, Calif.

BRODIE, M. L. 1981. On modelling behavioural semantics of data. In *Proceedings of the 7th International Conference on Very Large Data Bases* (Cannes, France, Sept. 9–11). IEEE, New York, pp. 32–41.

BRODIE, M. L., AND ZILLES, S. N., EDS. 1981. In *Proceedings of the Workshop on Data Abstraction, Databases, and Conceptual Modelling. SIGPLAN Not. 16*, 1 (Jan.).

CARSWELL, J. L., AND NAVATHE, S. B. 1986. SA-ER: A methodology that links structured analysis and entity relationship modeling for database design. In *Proceedings of the 5th International Conference on the Entity Relationship Approach*, S. Spaccapietra, Ed. (Dijon, France, Nov.), pp. 19–36.

CERI, S., ED. 1983. *Methodology and Tools for Database Design*. North-Holland, Amsterdam.

CERI, S., AND PELAGATTI, G. 1984. *Distributed Databases: Principles and Systems*. McGraw-Hill, New York.

CERI, S., PELAGATTI, G., AND BRACCHI, G. 1981. A structured methodology for designing static and dynamic aspects of data base applications. *Inf. Syst. 6*, 1, 31–45.

CHEN, P. P. 1976. The entity-relationship model—Toward a unified view of data. *ACM Trans. Database Syst. 1*, 1 (Mar.), 9–36.

CHEN, P. P. 1983. English sentence structure and entity–relationship diagrams. *J. Inf. Sci. 29*, 127–150.

CHIANG, W., BASAR, E., LIEN, C., AND TEICHROEW, D. 1983. Data modeling with PSL/PSA: The view integration system (VIS). ISDOS Rep. No. M0549-0, Ann Arbor, Mich.

CHILSON, D., AND KUDLAC, C. 1983. Database design: A survey of logical and physical design techniques. *Database 15*, 1 (Fall).

DATA DESIGNER 1981. Data designer product description. Database Design Inc., Ann Arbor, Mich.

DEMO, B. 1983. Program analysis for conversion from a navigation to a specification database interface. In *Proceedings of the 9th International Conference on Very Large Data Bases* (Florence, Italy). VLDB Endowment, Saratoga, Calif.

DEMO, B., AND KUNDU, S. 1985. Modeling the CODASYL DML execution context dependency for application program conversion. In *Proceedings of the International Conference on Management of Data* (Austin, Tx., May 28–30). ACM, New York, pp. 354–363.

DOS SANTOS, C. S., NEUHOLD, E. J., AND FURTADO, A. L. 1980. A data type approach to the entity relationship model. In *Proceedings of the International Conference on the Entity Relationship Approach to System Analysis and Design*, P. Chen, Ed. (Los Angeles, 1979). North-Holland, Amsterdam, pp. 103–120.

EICK, C. F., AND LOCKEMANN, P. C. 1985. Acquisition of terminological knowledge using database design techniques. In *Proceedings of the International Conference on Management of Data* (Austin, Tx., May 28–30). ACM, New York, pp. 84–94.

ELMASRI, R. 1980. On the design, use and integration of data models. Ph.D. dissertation, Rep. No. STAN-CS-80-801, Dept. of Computer Science, Stanford Univ., Stanford, Calif.

ELMASRI, R., AND NAVATHE, S. B. 1984. Object integration in database design. In *Proceedings of the IEEE COMPDEC Conference* (Anaheim, Calif., Apr.). IEEE, New York, pp. 426–433.

ELMASRI, R., AND WIEDERHOLD, G. 1979. Data model integration using the structural model. In

Proceedings of the International Conference on Management of Data (Boston, Mass., May 30–June 1). ACM, New York.

ELMASRI, R., WEELDRYER, J., AND HEVNER, A. 1985. The category concept: An extension to the entity-relationship model. *Data Knowl. Eng. 1*, 1 (June).

FERRARA, F. M. 1985. EASY-ER: An integrated system for the design and documentation of data base applications. In *Proceedings of the 4th International Conference on the Entity Relationship Approach* (Chicago, Ill.). IEEE Computer Society, Silver Spring, Md., pp. 104–113.

HAMMER, M., AND MCLEOD, D. 1981. Database description with SDM: A semantic database model. *ACM Trans. Database Syst. 6*, 3 (Sept.), 351–386.

HUBBARD, G. 1980. *Computer Assisted Data Base Design.* Van Nostrand-Reinhold, New York.

HWANG, H. Y. 1982. Database integration and optimization in multidatabase systems. Ph.D. dissertation, Dept. of Computer Science, Univ. of Texas, Austin, Oct.

KLUG, A., AND TSICHRITZIS, D., Eds. 1977. The ANSI/X3/SPARC Report of the Study Group on Data Base Management Systems. AFIPS Press, Reston, Va.

LANDERS, T. A., AND ROSENBERG, R. L. 1982. An overview of Multibase. In *Distributed Databases,* H. J. Schneider, Ed. North-Holland, Amsterdam.

LARSON, J., NAVATHE, S. B., AND ELMASRI, R. 1986. Attribute equivalence and its role in schema integration. Tech. Rep., Honeywell Computer Sciences Center, Golden Valley, Minn.

LUM, V., GHOSH, S., SCHKOLNICK, M., JEFFERSON, D., SU, S., FRY, J., AND YAO, B. 1979. 1978 New Orleans data base design workshop. In *Proceedings of the 5th International Conference on Very Large Data Bases* (Rio de Janeiro, Oct. 3–5). IEEE, New York, pp. 328–339.

MAIER, D. 1983. *The Theory of Relational Databases.* Computer Science Press, Potomac, Md.

MANNINO, M. V., AND EFFELSBERG, W. 1984b. Matching techniques in global schema design. In *Proceedings of the IEEE COMPDEC Conference* (Los Angeles, Calif.). IEEE, New York, pp. 418–425.

MANNINO, M. V., AND KARLE, C. 1986. An extension of the general entity manipulator language for global view definition. *Data Knowl. Eng. 2*, 1.

MANNINO, M. V., NAVATHE, S. B., AND EFFELSBERG, W. 1986. Operators and rules for merging generalization hierarchies. Working Paper, Graduate School of Business, Univ. of Texas, Austin, April 1986.

MCLEOD, D., AND HEIMBIGNER, D. 1980. A federated architecture for data base systems. In *Proceedings of the AFIPS National Computer Conference,* vol. 39. AFIPS Press, Arlington, Va.

MOTRO, A. 1981. Virtual merging of databases. Ph.D. dissertation, Tech. Rep. #MS-CIS-80-39, Computer Science Dept., Univ. of Pennsylvania, Philadelphia, Pa. 1981.

MYLOPOULOS, J., BERNSTEIN, P. A., AND WONG, H. K.T. 1980. A language facility for designing database-intensive applications. *ACM Trans. Database Syst. 5*, 2 (June) 185–207.

NATIONAL BUREAU OF STANDARDS 1982. Data base directions: Information resource management—strategies and tools. Special Publ. 500–92, A. Goldfine, Ed. U.S. Dept. of Commerce, Washington, D.C., Sept. 1982.

NAVATHE, S.B., AND SCHKOLNICK, M. 1978. View representation in logical database design. In *Proceedings of the International Conference on Management of Data* (Austin, Tex.). ACM, New York, pp. 144–156.

NAVATHE, S. B., AND KERSCHBERG, L. 1986. Role of data dictionaries in information resource management. *Inf. Manage. 10*, 1.

NAVATHE, S. B., SASHIDHAR, T., AND ELMASRI, R. 1984. Relationship matching in schema integration. In *Proceedings of the 10th International Conference on Very Large Data Bases* (Singapore). Morgan Kaufmann, Los Altos, Calif.

NAVATHE, S. B., ELMASRI, R., AND LARSON, J. 1986. Integrating user views in database design. *IEEE Computer 19*, 1 (Jan.), 50–62.

NG, P., JAJODIA, S., AND SPRINGSTEEL, F. 1983. The problem of equivalence of entity relationship diagrams. *IEEE Trans. Softw. Eng. SE-9*, 5, 617–630.

OLLE, T. W., SOL, H. G., AND VERRIJN-STUART, A. A., Eds. 1982. Information systems design methodologies: A comparative review. In *Proceedings of the IFIP WG 8.1 Working Conference on Comparative Review of Information Systems Design Methodologies* (Noordwijkerhout, The Netherlands). North-Holland, Amsterdam.

RISSANEN, J. 1977. Independent components of relations. *ACM Trans. Database Syst. 2*, 4 (Dec.), 317–325.

ROLLAND, C., AND RICHARDS, C. 1982. Transaction modeling. In *Proceedings of the International Conference on Management of Data* (Orlando, Fla., June 2–4). ACM, New York, pp. 265–275.

SAKAI, H. 1981. A method for defining information structures and transactions in conceptual schema design. In *Proceedings of the 7th International Conference on Very Large Data Bases* (Cannes, France, Sept. 9–11). IEEE, New York, pp. 225–234.

SCHEUERMANN, P., SCHIFFNER, G., AND WEBER, H. 1980. Abstraction capabilities and invariant properties modeling within the entity relationship approach. In *Proceedings of the International Conference on Entity Relationship Approach to System Analysis and Design,* P. Chen, Ed. (Los Angeles, 1979). North-Holland, Amsterdam.

SHIN, D. G., AND IRANI, K. B. 1985. Knowledge-based distributed database system design. In *Proceedings of the International Conference on*

Management of Data (Austin, Tex., May 28–30). ACM, New York, pp. 95–105.

SHIPMAN, D. W. 1980. The functional data model and data language DAPLEX. *ACM Trans. Database Syst. 6*, 1 (Mar.), 140–173.

SMITH, J. M., AND SMITH, D. C. 1977. Database abstraction: Aggregation and generalization. *ACM Trans. Database Syst. 2*, 2 (June), 105–133.

TUCHERMAN, L., FURTADO, A. L., AND CASANOVA, M. A. 1985. A tool for modular database design.

In *Proceedings of the 11th International Conference on Very Large Data Bases* (Stockholm, Sweden). Morgan Kaufmann, Los Altos, Calif.

ULLMAN, J. D. 1982. *Principles of Database Systems*, 2nd ed. Computer Science Press, Potomac, Md.

WEELDREYER, J. A. 1986. Structural aspects of the entity–category–relationship model of data, Tech. Rep. HR-80-251, Honeywell Computer Sciences Center, Golden Valley, Minn.

KSYS: An Architecture for Integrating Databases and Knowledge Bases

GIO C. M. WIEDERHOLD, MICHAEL G. WALKER, WAQAR HASAN, SURAJIT CHAUDHURI, ARUN SWAMI, SANG K. CHA, XIAOLEI QIAN, MARIANNE WINSLETT, PETER K. RATHMANN, AND LINDA DeMICHIEL

1. INTRODUCTION

As systems using artificial intelligence grow in size and importance, it behooves us to consider the data and software engineering required to implement such substantial systems. We define here *data engineering* as the approach which focuses on the structure of the data, while *software engineering* focuses on the computing procedures. In artificial intelligence (AI) systems, these two aspects of system design are characterized on one hand by a concern about the representation of knowledge, and on the other hand by the capabilities of the interpreters which operate on the knowledge [1].

Knowledge representation is recognized as a major concern in AI systems. The encoding of knowledge is difficult because of the intrinsic complexity of knowledge. This complexity is evidenced by the many and varied relationships we can define among the conceptual units needed to represent knowledge. On the other hand, structures intended to deal with large quantities of factual data tend to be simple and regular; and much of the recent progress in dealing with large databases is due to the structural simplification provided by the relational model [2].

In order to deal with demands as posed by growing AI systems, a substantial research effort is now devoted to introducing more flexible support structures into databases, as indicated by the collections in [3], [4]. Many researchers in the intersection of AI and databases expect that database techniques will provide the necessary assistance to deal with the problems encountered as knowledge bases grow [5], although this belief is far from universal [4]. No convincing demonstration of the benefits of such an integration can yet be shown.

1.1. Motivation

Why should problems arise with large knowledge bases? We see first of all that the number of candidate relationships grows rapidly with the number of nodes in the knowledge base. Nodes in knowledge bases represent concepts that are linked to many other concepts and instances in the knowledge base. Those concepts represent abstractions at a variety of levels and classifications. Many conceptual nodes also apply to many instances. The nodes we classify as being conceptual are linked to many other concepts, while the nodes classified as being factual need only be hierarchically linked to their descriptor nodes. These descriptors define the entity being described and the attribute defining the describing value.

Traditional databases, being concerned with facts, can use relational tables effectively for the representation of their contents. The relational table provides a regular linkage structure in two dimensions, namely to the attribute and to the entity represented by the key. Maintenance of such a database is fairly straightforward [6]. In time-oriented databases a third dimension, time, is added, and this seemingly simple extrapolation, although long recognized as being useful [7], is just now being dealt with formally [8]. Things get worse when more structural relationships are to be considered, such as derived views which join multiple database structures [9].

Updating of the arbitrary structures used in AI is more difficult yet; in general it is probably n.p. hard as discussed by [10] for rule-based representations. Knowledge base maintenance is rarely addressed in current systems, primarily because so few knowledge-based systems of significant size have moved from the lab into practical use. Thus, issues of updating and consistency that are familiar to database managers still require solutions in knowledge base applications. Changes in the knowledge base require considerable retesting. Even then, correctness is rarely provable in substantial systems.

In the discussion above we have casually introduced our definition of what is knowledge versus data. We will restate this definition now, since it is the basis for one of the two strategies we are trying to exploit in the research described in this paper. We define *data* as the factual, observable and verifiable descriptions of real-world events, and *knowledge* as the higher level concepts used to structure, classify, and relate such real world events. When the two are brought together, we can produce information [11]. A system which applies encoded knowledge to formalized collections of data, or databases, is defined to be a *knowledge-based system*.

These definitions have to be interpreted with some practical engineering sense. For instance, the data describing the contents of a bank account are not visually verifiable: there is no pile of money in the bank with a name on it, and yet, this information is certainly best classified as data. Also, records of events which occurred in the past are no longer verifiable, but are still considered to be data. Some other examples will be harder to classify. For instance, derived data are not dealt with in this classification. This issue is not discussed in this paper, although it is of concern to us.

1.2. Our Approach

Our Knowledge SYStem project (KSYS) is intended to demonstrate methods towards a systematic approach to deal with large knowledge bases. Given the semantic distinction we make between knowledge and data, we make a corresponding engineering distinction. The notions underlying our approach are largely based on a variety of previous research in the KBMS and RX groups, initiated in 1977. Projects related to these data engineering issues of KSYS were described in [12], [13], [14], [15], [16], [17], [18]. An overview of earlier KBMS work is provided in [19].

First of all, we will use in KSYS simple, regular structures for data, while supporting the complexity of the stored knowledge with a more general structure. The benefits expected from this dichotomy are that now the costly maintenance of complex structures is only required for a fraction of other stored information, and that well-established, efficient algorithms can be applied to the database. This benefit is only significant if the volume of information that can be classified as data is large. Our understanding of the few large knowledge-bases now in existence, such as R1/XCON [20] is that this is indeed the case. We believe in fact that for all large AI systems, the amount of complex stored knowledge, by our definition, is quite modest, especially in systems which require regular updating.

There are obviously also liabilities associated with the use of two distinct representations. The processing system has to provide an interface, so that for a user needing information from the system, the knowledge and data are tightly coupled.

Since the user will always access the data via the knowledge-base, we believe we will find solutions to the user interface issue. In current database management systems, all accesses are already mediated by the a database schema. The traditional schema focuses on data attributes, their representation, and on access paths. Stored knowledge in the knowledge base can be viewed as a generalization of such a schema. The extension to the schema in a knowledge-based system can encompass concepts not directly represented in the database, for example overall health status in a medical record. The knowledge base will also permit effective storage of interrelational constraints and processing rules.

The interface must also not reduce performance excessively, so that the benefits obtained from the specialized storage management can overcome this potential liability. We are not addressing in KSYS the problems of persistent storage of the conceptual frames within a DBMS. This is a real issue, and is being addressed by many researchers [21]. We expect these efforts to be successful and solve our problem.

The problem of operational efficiency in access is being addressed by keeping the knowledge in (real) memory. We assume that the memory capacity of modern computers is adequate to hold all of the required knowledge once the more voluminous data are separated. For transactions where accessed data is reused, such data can be cached, and also retained in memory. For best use, the data, once retrieved, should be bound into the knowledge structure, as explored in [22]. (See also [23] and the section below on binding and query optimization).

We now come to the second of the two strategies for knowledge management: the use of multiple hierarchies. Although computer memory hardware is now adequate to store large amounts of knowledge, this does not address the problem of how to manage that knowledge. The complexity of interactions among the knowledge grows rapidly with the size of the knowledge, eventually overwhelming the access advantage gained from the use of a large memory. Much of this complexity of interaction can be mitigated through the use of a hierarchical organization, in which all interactions flow through well defined parent-child links. However, a single hierarchical organization is an inadequate paradigm for the representation of knowledge bases, especially those which involve sharing of knowledge.

1.3. Sharing

A large system, and hence the representations used to demonstrate KSYS, must support a diversity of usage. It is desirable to share knowledge as well as data, since knowledge acquisition is even more costly than data collection [24]. Sharing of knowledge is also motivated by the objective of consistency. We expect many applications to work on different aspects of the problem. Database technology has enabled data sharing, so that factual observations used by distinct applications will be identical. But if these applications interpret the same facts differently, because of differences in their encoded knowledge, we will not have achieved the objective of consistency among applications.

To enable sharing we see multiple hierarchical classifications of knowledge structures as a solution. Specific AI and database systems, which use general processing strategies, most often are constrained to operate in hierarchical structures, and have great difficulty in dealing with cycles. These hierarchies are closely related to the concepts of views, as further discussed below.

1.4. KSYS Research Projects

In the following sections we describe research projects within the KSYS project that are related to the theme of artificial intelligence and data engineering. Each project addresses an aspect of the theme such as simplifying the design, implementation, or maintenance of databases, knowledge bases, or programs, or providing user interfaces that reduce the need for programmer involvement.

The overall KSYS architecture is shown in Fig. 1. The persistent store is a relational database (RDB from DEC in our prototype). The KSYS Frame System (KFS) is described in the first section following the introduction. The binding layer seeks to make optimal use of a moderately large main memory (8 megabytes), and is described in the section below on binding and optimization. Components of KSYS that use knowledge for dealing with views, semantic mediation of operations across disparate domains, integrity control and constraint management, and user interfaces are described in succeeding sections, and we conclude with work on knowledge acquisition from databases.

2. THE KSYS FRAME SYSTEM

The KSYS Frame System (KFS) is intended to be part of an experimental Knowledge Base Management System (KBMS). The KFS will provide a base on which ''intelligent'' database applications may be built. We plan to use the frame system

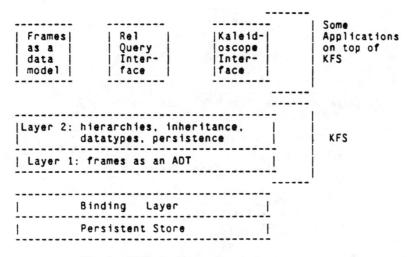

Fig 1: KBMS Architecture

with connections to a persistent store as the bottom layer for supporting such applications. Frames were proposed by Minsky [25] as part of a scheme for making intelligent machines. Commercial frame-based systems like KEE [26] are widely available and familiar to most system developers. Since we wish to experiment with various novel concepts, we are building our own frame system, rather than use one of the commercial systems.

The KFS consists of two layers. Layer 1 provides a very general and flexible framework on top of which layers with tighter semantics may be built. It implements frames as an abstract data type and supports object-identity in the standard way. A frame is an extensible record structure. It has a name and consists of a set of *slots,* and each slot has a set of facets. Facets contain data. The semantics of the representation depend on how the higher layers or programs interpret the data in the facets. Data in a facet may be interpreted as values, references to other frames, or procedures, to mention some possibilities. Layer 2 organizes frames into hierarchies and provides data-types and support for persistence. The hierarchical structuring helps control the complexity of the design process [27]. We will now briefly discuss our design decisions and contrast them with alternative approaches.

2.1. Class and Instance Frames

Frames may be of two kinds, *class* and *instance.* As an example, a class frame may define the class **Ships** and its properties, and an instance frame may represent the ship **Queen Elizabeth** (see Figs. 2, 3).

A given frame is of exactly one kind. Class frames are defined by the user to model the prototypical objects in the world being represented. Slots in a class could represent properties of either the class as a whole or that of its instances. For example, the **Ships** class may have the slot **ShipName** which specifies the structure of the instances, and the slot **NumberofShips** which is an exclusive property of the class. Any slot in a class frame is required to have the **type, value** and **inheritance** facets. It is expected that there will be a moderate number of class frames. We also find it useful to distinguish certain frames as *system frames.* System frames

are those class frames which define the system. For example definitions of data types and hierarchy types are system frames. View definitions are another example of system frames. The instance frames represent individuals or the instances of the prototypes. In instance frames, the only facet a slot is required and permitted to have is the **value** facet. It is expected that there will be a large number of such frames. They may be generated as needed from information in the database, as described in the section below on binding and optimization. The *instance* frames need to be implemented carefully from both space and access-time viewpoints.

2.1.1. Inheritance Hierarchies: Frames may reference each other. In addition, the class frames may be organized into *hierarchies.* However, a frame may belong to more than one hierarchy at the same time. The **Ship hierarchy** is shown in Fig. 2. **NavyShips** and **CommercialShips** are subclasses of the ships class and may inherit slots from it. Note that each frame in the hierarchy has the slots ships-parent and ships-children. These are used by the system to store the links to the ancestor and children, and are modifiable only through certain functions.

A hierarchy is defined by creating a hierarchy definition frame in the special hierarchy called Hierarchies. A hierarchy definition frame has the following slots: The **parent-slot** stores the name of the parent slot. This slot is required to contain exactly one frame with the exception of the root frame in which it is empty. The **children-slot** gives the name of the children slot. The **root-frame-slot** provides the name of the root frame of the hierarchy. The **hierarchy-slots** are the definitions of all slots which may be inherited through this hierarchy. The **required-instance-slots** are the names of slots which every frame in the hierarchy must possess. Instance frames which are instances of classes in the hierarchy must have values for these slots as a necessary condition for being instances. The **class-slots** give the names of slots which may not be inherited by instance frames. A class-slot cannot be a required-instance-slot. The defining frame for the **Ship hierarchy** is shown in Fig. 4. Any frame belonging to a hierarchy possesses the parent-slot, children-slot, and all the required-instance-slots for that hierarchy.

```
                          Ships
                         /     \
                        /       \
                       /         \
                  NavyShips   CommercialShips
                  /   |   \
                 /    |    \
                /     |     \
        Destroyers NuclearSubs Frigates
        ( Ships
              ( Ship-parent
                     ( Value ))                    ; since no parents
              ( Ship-children
                     ( Value NavyShips CommercialShips ))
              ( ShipName
                     ( Type Symbol )
                     ( Value )
                     ( Inheritance Yes ))
              ( NumberOfShips
                     ( Type Integer )
                     ( Value 1105 )
                     ( Inheritance No ))
              ( Instances
                     (value G582)
                     (persistence ship-persistence)))

        ( NavyShips
              ( Ship-parent
                     ( Value Ships ))
              ( Ship-children
                     ( Value Destroyers Frigates))
              ( #Marines
                     ( Type Integer )
                     ( Value )
                     ( Inheritance Yes )))


        ( CommercialShips
              ( Ship-parent
                     ( Value Ships ))
              ( Ship-children
                     ( Value ))
              ( CargoCapacity
                     ( Type Integer )
                     ( Value )
                     ( Inheritance Yes ))

           Fig 2: The Ship hierarchy and class frames


        ( G582
           (Shipname
                 ( Value QueenElizabeth )))


           Fig 3 : The instance frame for the QueenElizabeth
```

Hierarchy Types: Hierarchies may have various semantics. For example, a hierarchy may be a generalization hierarchy. We may further specify properties like disjointness and completeness of subclasses. Hierarchies need not always be generalization hierarchies. For example, a hierarchy could be an aggregation (part-of) hierarchy or a view hierarchy. Such semantics will be enforced by the upper layers in the KBMS.

Inheritance: Any hierarchy-slot may be inherited by a child from its parent in the hierarchy. Inheritance makes it easier to specify similar classes. It often saves the trouble of redefinition, resulting in space saving and ease of maintenance. When we say "slot *s* is inherited" it means that the slot, all its facets, and the data in the facets are also applicable to the child. In general, it may not be appropriate to inherit the slot exactly as it is; we may wish to make changes to the data in some of the facets. This is achieved by updating the desired facets in the child to override the inherited value. The **Inheritance** facet of the slot specifies whether the slot is to be inherited or not. The possible values for this facet are "Yes" and "No."

We now consider the question at which level the inheritance facet should be specified. There are several choices. The inheritance could be specified **Globally** (with slot definition), at the **parent frame**, or at the **child frame**. We will opt for a **Hybrid** scheme, such that inheritance is specified in the parent frame, which may be overridden by specification at each child. Since a frame may be a child as well as a parent at the same time, an additional **Inheritance-Override** facet is needed to implement the hybrid scheme. In some hierarchies the inheritance may be globally controlled, to simplify automatic interpretation.

```
( Ship-hierarchy
    ( parent-slot
            ( Type Symbol )
            ( Value ship-parent )
            ( Inheritance Yes ))
    ( children-slot
            ( Type Symbol )
            ( Value ship-children )
            ( Inheritance Yes ))
    ( root-frame
            ( Type Frame )
            ( Value ships )
            ( Inheritance Yes ))
    ( hierarchy-slots
            ( Type Symbol )
            ( Value ShipName NumberOfShips #Marines
                        CargoCapacity)
            ( Inheritance Yes ))
    ( required-instance-slots
            ( Type Symbol )
            ( Value ShipName )
            ( Inheritance Yes ))
    ( class-slots
            ( Type Symbol )
            ( Value NumberOfShips )
            ( Inheritance Yes )))

            Fig 4 : The definition of the Ships hierarchy


(Ship-persistence

    ( persistence-parent
            (Value Rdbmap))
    ( mapping
            ( Type slotattributemap)
            ( Value
                (shipname = ships. shipname)))

            Fig 5 : Example of a Persistence-frame

    -------
```

A frame may simultaneously belong to multiple hierarchies. However, slots are local to a hierarchy. This defines away the problem of multiple inheritance. The restriction that the hierarchy be a tree structure ensures that there is a single parent of a frame in a hierarchy. An interpreter can switch among the multiple hierarchies, in effect changing interpretive strategy. Such a switch would typically take place when some subgoal has been satisfied: some data have been located, or an intermediate conclusion has been drawn.

What happened to Multiple Inheritance? Multiple inheritance in its full generality is that a frame may have several parents and the value of a slot in a frame is a function (call this function the *inheritance policy*) of the value of the slot in all ancestors of the frame and some other factors (e.g., distance from an ancestor, etc.). For example, the value of the completion-date slot in a projects hierarchy may be specified to be the minimum of the values in all superclasses.

However, multiple inheritance adds dangerous complexity to the system. The attempt to isolate functions which are useful as inheritance policies is an open ended process and degenerates to allowing the user to write his own inheritance policies as LISP functions, to be executed by a nonsharable interpreter. In general, a dividing line has to be found between what inheritance policies are sharable and defined and those that are left to an interpreter implementing higher level view definitions or application programs. A problem with arbitrary

functions as inheritance policies is that they make optimization by the system difficult.

These problems are better dealt with at a higher level. On the other hand, there are often cases when the same object has different and perhaps apparently contradictory values for a query depending on how we look at it. As an example, we may consider an individual's financial-condition to be poor when he is accessed through the **UniversityEmployees** hierarchy. But it makes sense for his financial condition to be considered rich when accessed through the **Students** hierarchy. The problems of management of such information motivated the design decision to consider slots to be local to a hierarchy.

2.2. The Class-Instance Connection

Instance slot: Class and Instance frames are connected by the **Instances** slot in the class frame. Let i be an *instance* frame and c be a *class* frame. A sufficient condition for i to be an *instance-of* c is the occurrence of i in the value facet of the instances slot of c. A necessary condition for i to be an *instance-of* c is that in i, values are assigned (*not* inherited) to all the required-instance-slots of the hierarchy to which c belongs. Another useful facet of the instances slot is the *persistence* facet which is discussed below.

Class-Instance inheritance: The value facet is the only facet of slots in instance frames. However, we would like an instance frame to inherit the default value from the class frame, if the slot value in the instance is a null value. But we would like inheritance to be suppressed if, for example, the null value has the interpretation *not applicable*, due to the specific structure of the information. It suffices to partition the null values into two sets, the **inheritance-nulls** and **structural-nulls**. As far as this layer is concerned the only relevant semantics of the structural nulls is that they suppress inheritance, and therefore it suffices to *not* distinguish them from normal data values. We permit the specification of the inheritance-nulls as a facet called inheritance-nulls with each slot. The operational interpretation of this facet is: If the value of a slot in an instance frame is an inheritance-null, then replace value with inherited value.

2.3. Persistence

We need to provide a mechanism to store and materialize frames from a persistent secondary store. One could use various storage systems for persistence, like files or relational databases. A **Persistence Hierarchy** provides the information about different available storage systems. The implementation of persistence for instance and class frames will have to be different. We will have a common systemwide mechanism to store and materialize the class frames. However, the structures of instance frames for different classes may vary widely. Therefore, the information about the persistence mapping is best kept on a class by class basis. The **persistence** facet in the instance slot of the class frame refers to a **persistence-frame** which stores this information.

3. BINDING AND QUERY OPTIMIZATION

The persistent data of applications built using the KSYS system are stored in a conventional relational database system. The data must be initially accessed by executing queries to external storage. However, in typical knowledge-based (KB) applications, it does not appear that satisfactory performance can be achieved by simply replacing each subsequent access to the same persistent data by a database retrieval [22]. Such applications can be expected to make many more references to facts during the inferencing process than are made by the typical database query.

Thus, the brute force solution of collecting information from secondary storage whenever the application refers to it is too expensive. Our approach is to save accesses to external storage by various techniques; e.g., never repeating the same query (as far as possible). The important idea behind this and other techniques discussed below is **binding** [28], e.g., keeping data in memory within an efficient data structure and establishing links with related data. The various kinds of binding we consider are influenced by our query processing system whose architecture is described below. In particular, the *query optimizer* has many novel characteristics and will be discussed in greater detail.

3.1. Kinds of Binding

To support the goal of accessing the external database as little as possible, we plan to keep information about the past interaction with the database (a query log). We also need to keep track of various kinds of data already available in main memory. As a special case, the binding of data instances to their parent knowledge frames serves to remind the system that these data are already available in memory, and helps to eliminate redundant accesses to secondary storage.

Some relations may be accessed often enough to justify binding them in their entirety in memory. The relations in which the *metadata* is kept are a good example of this. Generalizing, results of queries are kept in memory as long as it is beneficial. To handle conflicting demands on real memory space (which is finite), it is necessary to use the query log for deciding on the cost/benefit tradeoffs. For transactions which run only for a limited time, memory overflow problems should be rare.

An important kind of binding is the *prejoining* of data. Joins along connections as in the *structural model* [29] are good candidates for prejoining, as are joins seen frequently in queries. The resulting join could be kept on external storage, but we plan to only keep them bound in memory. If kept in memory, the join does not need to be materialized by catenation, i.e., by copying of the data into new, contiguous, tuples. Instead, we use pointers to the tuples as retrieved into memory from the original relations, along with a descriptor for the result to allow interpretation of the pointers [30]. Such structures are not only space-efficient, but also save on the CPU cost of copying data which has been shown to be significant in memory resident databases [31].

3.2. Query Processor Architecture

The query processor can be distinguished as a module which provides the interface between the frame system and the database system where the persistent data is stored. It consists of three components: Preprocessor, query optimizer, and query interpreter.

Requests for data *queries* posed by the frame system are processed in the following fashion. The preprocessor transforms the query into a relational algebra query (if it is not already in that form). The query optimizer transforms the relational algebra query into an efficient execution plan (this plan is called the Query Evaluation Plan, or QEP). The query interpreter carries out the QEP to produce the results.

The database system is used to perform relation scans and indexed retrievals of data on disk, and some selections and projections. It is *not* used to perform joins; all join processing is done by the query interpreter. The query interpreter manages the memory available to the query processor; it takes hints from the query optimizer, e.g., the query optimizer could request that certain relations should be kept memory resident.

Unlike conventional query optimizers, the QEP generated by the query optimizer not only takes advantage of the database structure and the access methods available but also makes use of data bound in memory. This is the reason that the query optimizer must be able to provide hints to the query interpreter.

3.3. Memory Residency

When a large amount of the data needed for query processing is memory resident, we have to take into account a whole new set of costs and goals. In our modeling of costs, it is not sufficient to take only disk accesses into account. It is necessary that CPU costs (comparisons, data movement, evaluation of predicates, hashing) are estimated carefully. As noted above, real memory may not be sufficient to keep all data resident, and virtual memory may gain us little versus well-managed secondary storage access. Especially with increasingly large main memories, memory costs are important, and will be taken into account in the cost estimation.

With these considerations, we have developed a comprehensive cost model which can be used by the query optimizer. The cost model spans the range from entirely disk-based query processing strategies to wholly memory resident strategies. The part of the cost model dealing with memory resident processing is described in [23]. We have identified the important parameters of the cost model, and have developed a cost formula which can be used to account for CPU costs, memory costs, and I/O costs with dynamic weights to reflect changing conditions.

To demonstrate the use of the cost model, we have derived cost equations for various important methods for evaluating a two-way Select-Project-Equijoin on memory resident relations. Analysis of these cost equations leads to some interesting results which are summarized in [32].

3.4. Use of Application Knowledge

Query optimizers must use of a lot of knowledge in their decision making. Some of this knowledge is independent of the particular application, e.g., the strategy of performing selection as early as possible is considered to be usually efficient. However, as shown in [17], some of the most effective knowledge used in optimization is application-dependent.

We can classify the knowledge used in query optimization in five broad categories:

- Knowledge which is independent of the database context, e.g., $\neg \, (x > 40) \Rightarrow (x \leq 40)$.
- Knowledge which depends only on the database context, but is independent of the particular database, e.g., performing selections as early as possible is usually efficient.
- Knowledge about the application database schema or intension, e.g., a relation has a clustered index.
- Knowledge about the actual database contents or extension, e.g., cardinality of a relation.
- Knowledge which is dependent on the application, e.g., integrity constraints.

The knowledge in the last three categories can be further classified based on the database units it mentions. This classification is given in [23], where we also give examples of each class of knowledge illustrating their use in query optimization. Some of the application knowledge is given in the form of *integrity constraints*.

3.5. Future Work on Optimization

We are currently validating the cost model for query processing with memory resident data. We are doing experiments to derive accurate values for the parameters of the cost

model. The query optimizer of the KSYS system will use this cost model. Continuing with our work in utilizing application knowledge, we are currently studying how the query optimizer can uniformly use these kinds of application knowledge along with more domain independent knowledge. We are also setting up an experimental testbed to investigate the utility of various kinds of knowledge.

4. VIEWS

Partitioning of knowledge bases by views is a concept motivated by many of the same considerations which led to the development of views for databases. Knowledge bases will grow to be too large to be conveniently comprehensible to a single person, particularly a casual user. Presenting only a focused subset of the data is a good way to reduce this complexity. Aside from complexity, different groups of users will desire data in a form customized to their own particular needs and interests. Both of these considerations affect the software engineering process. It is much simpler for a program to deal with only the information it needs, without having to sift through irrelevant detail. Also, it is easier for a program to deal with data in a customized, usually object-oriented, format, while, for purposes of sharing, it may be best to store the data in a more general purpose representation. There are several possible approaches to extend the concept of database views to knowledge bases. Since KSYS is an experimental project, we shall probably try several of them.

A special type of hierarchy provides the most direct implementation of views. This type of hierarchy uses somewhat different semantics than those described in Section 2, in order to facilitate sharing across different views. In a universe of persons, there may be hierarchies of taxpayers, family members and employees—representative of the numerous associations in which people engage. KSYS would represent each of these as a separate logical hierarchy, while a given frame will be in as many of these hierarchies as apply. The complications of multiple inheritance are avoided by a restriction that, although frames may participate in many hierarchies, each slot, for purposes of inheritance, may only be in one. Thus, an individual would inherit his salary from the employee hierarchy, his marital status from a family hierarchy, and so on. Although this is formally less general than a full multiple inheritance scheme, it is our hypothesis that the KSYS scheme will suffice for most applications.

Constraining interpretation by interposing hierarchical views greatly simplifies the design of the interpreters. The construction of an interpreter to operate on general graph structures is very difficult, and must rely either on user guidance [33] or on heuristics [34]. Our interpreters need only be able to process a hierarchy, as opposed to having to navigate through a general graph structure.

Different hierarchies will deal with different sets of frames, organized in different ways, but the frames themselves will always have the same slot values, independent of hierarchy. A given view hierarchy need only focus on a subset of the slots in the frame, but the interpreters have a consistent base to build upon.

Each hierarchy will be a different view of the data, and each user will use whichever hierarchy (or set of hierarchies) corresponds to her interests and needs. While multiple hierchies provide a structure on which to build a convenient user interface, this is not a complete answer to the view problem. Additional theory and structure is needed to facilitate sharing of information across the hierarchies, to ensure consistent updates, and to provide access to the database.

We plan to incorporate the relational model as much as possible in order to take advantage of the existing theory and formalized structure. We incorporate the syntax of relational algebra, letting individual frames represent the various relational operations of **select, project, join,** and **set difference,** as well as extensions that may be needed for aggregation, temporal inference, and recursion.

Subsidiary views may be constructed by means of ordinary relational algebra, at least so far as the data are concerned. However, we also need to be able to find an appropriate translation of the nonrelational knowledge so that it also is available from the view. A main focus of this part of the project is how to effect such translations. If the additional knowledge is represented as a theory in first order logic, we may take advantage of the duality between relational algebra and logic. The view specification may be written as a set of logic formulas defining new predicates. The theory applying to the view is then that obtained by augmenting the original theory with this new set of formulas. If we wish to manage knowledge, such as uncertainty information, which is not easily represented by first order logic, the translation is less direct, and the subject of ongoing research.

In many software engineering and design applications, it is often convenient to use an *object-oriented* paradigm for representing information. However, different classes of users (or the same users at different times) may need this information organized quite differently. Since we hope to share this information, we will have problems with redundancy and update anomalies. It is because of these problems that we feel that objects are not well suited for long term storage of data which must be shared among diverse classes of users [35]. Rather, we wish to use the view facility to create objects as they are needed. Updates to an object must then be translated into updates on the underlying database. This is an example of the view update problem, to which partial solutions exist, either using predefined semantics [16] or ad-hoc techniques suitable for planning-type applications [13].

5. SEMANTIC INTEGRITY CONSTRAINTS

One important type of knowledge in an integrated knowledge-base system such as KSYS is the collection of semantic integrity constraints controlling persistent data. Two closely related issues arise: the representation of constraints in the semantic hierarchies, and the validity maintenance of constraints in knowledge base evolution. There can be several semantically equivalent representations of a piece of knowledge which may have quite different computational characteristics in terms of knowledge manipulation. There has been little help from the system on how knowledge should be represented for efficient manipulation. We must be concerned about representing integrity constraints effectively in the hierarchies, taking advantage of the structure information about the organization of the hierarchies and other domain knowledge, such that the validation of constraints will be efficiently performed.

The validity or consistency maintenance of constraints during knowledge-base evolution is vital for the proper functioning of the system. On one hand, it is a data engineering issue: the management of the knowledge-base evolution to preserve certain semantics; on the other hand, it is also a software engineering issue: the management of the computations (transactions) which manipulate the knowledge-base such that the semantics are preserved. Constraint maintenance has been very difficult to implement efficiently because there is a need for implementation-independent, formal specification of both the constraints and the transactions that may potentially affect the validity of the constraints, while a straightforward evaluation of formally specified constraints against a large volume of knowledge and data is very expensive. Furthermore, it is unrealistic to expect that users or programmers understand the semantics of all constraints completely, and program them correctly in transactions. We are specifically working on automatic transformations of formal transaction specifications into efficient programs which guarantee the validity of the knowledge-base.

In order to achieve the joint goals of clear specification and efficient execution, we concentrate on the following two processes [36], [37]:

1. The reformulation of formal constraint specification into representations with better evaluation efficiency;
2. The synthesis of transactions which preserve the integrity constraints of the knowledge base.

We expand now on these two concepts.

5.1. Constraint Reformulation for Improved Representation

We are developing a framework to exploit knowledge about the application domain and knowledge base organization to reformulate programmer-specified integrity constraints into representations which are syntactically different, but semantically equivalent, given the application semantics, and which are more efficient to evaluation in the current knowledge base configuration. Such a knowledge-based approach provides great potential for more effective constraint representation because: 1) logically equivalent representations can have very different computational characteristics, and 2) after reformulation, constraints are specialized to the current computational environment with more optimization opportunities.

Constraint reformulation is accomplished with the technique of antecedent derivation. An inference engine serves as a search space generator of all alternative reformulations. Reformulation is formalized as a tree-search process guided by cost function and control strategies.

5.2. Transaction Synthesis for Efficient Constraint Enforcement

Our approach to the efficient integrity control of large knowledge-bases has several properties: 1) the transactional interface to the knowledge base is formalized by providing a high-level transaction specification language whose semantics can be formally defined; 2) a formal logic system is developed to reason about the effect of a transaction on the validity of a set of integrity constraints; and 3) transactions are modified to incorporate a constraint validation code by efficiently using the property of transaction atomicity and knowledge about transaction control flow and knowledge-base structure.

This approach has many advantages. First of all, both the integrity constraints and the transactions that access the knowledge-base are specified in high-level languages which facilitate knowledge base programming and software maintenance. Second, synthesized transactions are guaranteed to preserve the validity of the knowledge-base, without going through a tedious transaction verification process. Finally, the efficiency of the resulting transaction code is greatly improved by taking advantage of the properties of specific transaction and knowledge base implementation.

A prototype implementation of constraint reformulation is under development. A generalized theorem prover is used as an inference engine. We have implemented the cost model for estimating the evaluation cost of integrity constraints and a set of control strategies for controlling the reformulation process for single constraints. We have just started working on transaction synthesis, and have designed algorithms for constraint regression through primitive update operations.

6. The Semantic Mediation of Operations Across Disparate Domains

It is often necessary for a decision-making support system to obtain data from a variety of sources so that decisions can be based on a fusion of a broad range of information. These sources may include relations and relation fragments within a single distributed database system, to several homogeneous or heterogeneous databases, or multidatabase systems. Particularly where information must be obtained from several database systems owned by distinct user groups, it may not always be represented in forms that are directly comparable.

Within all of these contexts, as well as within a single database system, it remains desirable to be able to perform operations across domains that are seemingly incompatible, for example, because of type conflicts, but that are in some fundamental sense semantically similar or the same. While this requirement is most clearly pronounced in the multidatabase situation [38], the need sometimes also arises within a single database system, as, for example, when its conceptual design is not adequate to the demands placed upon it for generating information according to new views being imposed on the old data.

At the same time, such situations also point to the need for some sort of constraint system to guard against semantically meaningless operations in cases where domains may superficially appear to be the same, but in fact are not. If a user who is unaware of the semantic intention of the implementation performs operations across disparate domains, the results may not be meaningful. Domain mismatch occurs when two attributes are not of the same types, or when they are of the same types, but the types have a different semantics in some of the relations involved in the operation.

This aspect of KSYS investigates methods for the correct performance of relational database query operations despite data domain mismatch. It addresses problems related to distributed database systems, and applications where information must be extracted from heterogeneous domains. One means of ameliorating this problem is through the use of an abstract type facility; this can provide a semantic classification of domains, independent of their representation. An abstract type facility can thus be used to exclude meaningless operations between semantically incompatible domains when these are represented by different types. The extent to which a type system can perform this function depends on the notion of type equivalence that it uses; we assume that name equivalence is used, so that two data types are considered equivalent only if they are from the same database system and bear the same name.

The question naturally arises as to how one may allow for operations between types that are not equivalent, but that do have a common core of semantic meaning. The traditional varieties of type conversion in programming languages are insufficient for this task. Our model for the semantic mediation of operations across *disparate domains* is based on the notion of *virtual attributes*. A virtual attribute denotes the property of some entity and is associated with a particular domain. The virtual attribute need not be physically present in the database, although it might be materialized for efficient processing. Virtual attributes are derived from real attributes by invoking functions or mappings which embody knowledge of the semantic relationships between domains.

Our work is proceeding in the following directions:

- A formalization of operations across disparate domains in terms of operations in the presence of incomplete information. We propose an extension of the relational operators to handle operations across virtual attributes. Theoretical and practical limitations of these extended operations are being considered.
- A consideration of the impact of virtual attributes and domain mediation on query-processing efficiency, including means for avoiding loss of performance.
- In view of the theoretical limitations on the performance of operations across disparate domains, we are also examining heuristic approaches for use when more formal methods fail.
- Future work will also address the implementation of a frame-based system residing at a level above the database schema to provide a virtual attribute facility. This system is intended to embody both a functional encoding of knowledge of domain relationships in terms of a virtual attribute facility, and a heuristic component to handle problems of incompleteness.

7. Kaleidoscope: Open-Ended Menu Interface for Data Access

The large data collections that the KSYS approach envisages are difficult for a user to understand. The use of a formal language, such as SQL, provides a formal and clean interface, but does nothing to mitigate the underlying complexity. We wish to exploit knowledge about the data to help the users. A user's difficulties in accessing a database often causes additional programming effort, requiring an intermediary programmer, who hand-crafts a solution to deal with the user's inability to extract the desired information. The Kaleidoscope project is concerned with providing an open-ended knowledge-driven menu interface that ultimately reduces the work load for software engineers.

Using an artificial query language for problem solving, whether it is formal like SQL or whether it mimics natural English, involves scheduling of two cognitive processes: 1) the *planning process* that formulates the mental propositional content of a query and produces it in a query language, and 2) the *delivery process* that ships the outcome of the planning process to the system. Human short term memory is not big enough to hold a query of typical length and becomes a major bottleneck to these processes. In addition, the unreliability process of human long-term memory retrieval [39] interferes with users in planning and delivery of queries. Naive users are further subject to the difficulties [40] associated with learning a new language, and the logical data organization of a system. Some knowledge-based systems have incorporated menu-driven dialog interfaces, but these interfaces are typically geared to a particular task, and their capability is prespecified by an articulated task model. The open-ended nature of problems to be solved demands maintaining interfaces that allow arbitrary access and manipulation of data.

Kaleidoscope is a query interface using a knowledge-driven, context-dependent menu system. A linear syntax query language is the medium for casting a system's underlying semantic power over menus. The system predictively generates a collection of choices on a menu, and the user constructs a query incrementally via a sequence of guided selections. Kaleidoscope provides two alternatives for the user query language: 1) SQL for direct manipulation of database objects, and 2) a subset of natural language for access of the interpreted data at a high level. Kaleidoscope's use of menus is based on previous work on NLMenu [41] and INGLISH [42]. Menus guide the users within an acceptable boundary of the system's limited syntax and semantics.

7.1. Linear Menu-Guided Query Creation

The simplest way of creating a query is to follow the menu guidance linearly. To illustrate, shown below is a SQL query created in 12 successive mouse clicks on selected choices. Numbers indicate the sequence of selections.

SELECT$_1$ Ship-Name$_2$ *Owner$_3$* Weight$_4$ *FROM$_5$* *Ships$_6$* *WHERE$_7$* Weight$_8$ $\geq_9$ 100000$_{10}$ ORDER BY$_{11}$ Weight$_{12}$

Each choice comes from a different state of a dynamically changing menu window. SQL delimiters like commas and parentheses are automatically inserted by the system, whenever it is obvious, by later selections. A small status window is allocated on the screen to display a partial query being constructed, and a cursor indicating where the next action will take place. To create terminal symbols such as database

values, number constants, and database object identifiers (like tuple variables and view names) that should be created by the users, Kaleidoscope follows NLMenu's approach by generating a set of demons on the menu, each of which, once selected, prompts a nested interaction with the user. These demons form a special class of preterminal symbols.

7.2. The Interpreter

To generate choices predictively on the menu, the Kaleidoscope interpreter operates over a domain-independent grammar, which is coupled tightly to the domain-specific semantics stored in a knowledge base. At run time, the interpreter maintains a *dynamically changing forest* of parse trees with shared terminal and nonterminal nodes. Most of the trees in the forest are incomplete during query construction. As the user makes a choice, the interpreter aborts the trees that cannot incorporate the new choice as part of their body, and then expands the forest to find the next set of choices. If there are new complete trees in the forest, the interpreter enables query execution. For an unambiguous query language, the number of such complete parse trees is at most one. It is this dynamically changing forest of trees that distinguishes Kaleidoscope from the conventional menu system which stores its choices in a predetermined hierarchy, and gives the expressive power of a context-free language to Kaleidoscope.

7.3. More Flexibility in Menu Interaction

So far, we have introduced a style of menu interaction that is linear with respect to the terminal symbols of acceptable queries. However, this style of interaction burdens the users with navigation in a limited choice space, since mental query planning does not necessarily match the left-to-right linearity of a query. We see two ways of handling this problem: 1) accommodating a limited range of syntactic variety for natural language queries, and 2) providing more flexibility in menu interaction. A full range of syntactic variety is avoided in favor of keeping the grammar for natural language queries small. Two specific functions for flexible menu interaction are presented next.

Kaleidoscope allows a choice selection to be deferred until the later part of a query is constructed. The system recognizes how far to go in deferment by the nonterminal path to current choices in the forest. When the user returns to the deferred point by a system command, the interpreter takes into account the additional selections made in between. For example, it is often convenient in SQL to defer the choice of projection attributes in a SELECT clause until the relations are specified in a FROM clause or later. When the user returns to the SELECT clause after completion of the FROM clause, the system considers only the attributes of the selected relations to be generated. The user can also move the cursor back to an arbitrary point of the current query to redo previous selections. Consistency checking is triggered for the rest of the modified query. This is also a way to create quickly a query whose structure is similar to one of the previous queries. The system maintains a history of recent queries, and allows the user to retrieve a query into the status window.

7.4. Activation of Stored Knowledge

Activation of semantic constraints in predictive choice generation is essential for effective menu guidance. Syntactic knowledge of a language, for instance a BNF definition of SQL, does not provide enough constraining power. The result is a flood of irrelevant choices on menus, and creation of semantically anomalous queries. To make the knowledge base accessible to the interpreter, arbitrary constraint predicates are attached to context-free grammar rules. Demons which can access database values use stored information to guide users in creating database values in query, by presenting a list of values for the user to choose, or asking the user to enter a value based on a suggestion on its range.

7.5. Benefits and Status

Currently, we are implementing the interpreter of Kaleidoscope. Written in Common Lisp, the interpreter will be integrated to operate on top of the KSYS frame system.

We conjecture that Kaleidoscope will replace human lower level query planning and delivery process by menu choice search and selection. This means the human users are guarded from the trivial errors [40] in planning and delivery. In addition, once structural misconceptions are filtered, the post-query cooperative response can focus on the other types of misconceptions due to erroneous assumptions of content [15], [12]. In Kaleidoscope, the semantics of the underlying system are pushed upward to the process of generating surface query fragments on the menu. This contrasts with the typical approach of formal and natural language query interfaces, in which the flow of control follows a top-down translation, and the semantic power of a system is not visible to users. Kaleidoscope needs only a small number of syntactic rules and vocabularies. This distinguishes Kaleidoscope from the approach of relatively passive natural language interfaces like TEAM [43] that require a large number of syntactic rules and vocabularies.

8. KNOWLEDGE ACQUISITION FROM DATABASES

The development of knowledge bases is a serious data engineering problem, hindered particularly by the bottleneck of knowledge acquisition and validation. Building knowledge bases is expensive, time consuming, and often yields unsatisfactory results. In addition, knowledge base maintenance is difficult because modifications to a knowledge base may cause cases that previously were handled correctly to fail. We need new data engineering tools to help break the knowledge acquisition bottleneck, and to simplify knowledge base management. We are currently developing a program to assist in knowledge acquisition and management by using databases of case examples.

The knowledge acquisition subsystem is intended to assist in expert system applications in which domain experts give estimates of the probabilities of events, and the probabilistic relationships between events. There are many applications where probabilities are necessary or desirable. The notion of uncertainty may apply to either the likelihood of occurrence of an event or the strength of a relationship as indicated by the measures used to record an event. Knowledge engineers have found difficulty in implementing systems using uncertainty, because experts have great difficulty providing reliable estimates of probabilities. Estimates are often inconsistent among experts, individual experts are often not self-consistent, and often experts cannot provide any quantifiable estimate at all, particularly for joint probabilities of multiple events.

Integrating databases which record cases of events with knowledge acquisition methods can help solve these problems. After a domain expert has entered initial knowledge, if databases containing case examples are available, a computer program can examine the database to validate the knowledge entered by the expert, and, where appropriate, propose additional knowledge to incorporate. Databases usually contain more cases than any one expert has seen. Programs can analyze a case database to determine probabilities more accurately and completely than the expert.

The 1986 Banff Workshop on Knowledge Acquisition for Knowledge-Based Systems [44] provided an overview of knowledge acquisition research. Research in automated discovery has been particularly concerned with using empirical databases for knowledge acquisition; we reviewed these systems in [45]. The RX and RADIX projects [46], [47] were earlier projects from our group that are predecessors of our current work. In the RX and RADIX projects, we developed a program to discover and confirm medical knowledge from databases by a combination of statistical and knowledge-based methods. RX performed as follows. It generated a hypothesis relevant to the database (using simple correlation), e.g., "the drug prednisone increases serum cholesterol." It evaluated the hypothesis by extracting appropriate data from the case database, and designing and executing a statistical analysis. It interpreted the results to determine validity, and incorporated validated knowledge in the knowledge base.

RX was a relatively successful experiment. It rediscovered medical relationships not previously known to the project participants. It provided new, independent evidence of suspected relationships. It accurately confirmed known medical relationships. Most important, it demonstrated that a combination of statistical and knowledge-based methods are effective in finding and confirming relationships from a case database.

We plan to apply and extend these capabilities to the specific problem of knowledge validation and acquisition. The current design is to perform as follows.

1. The domain expert and knowledge engineer create a preliminary knowledge base which includes probability estimates for relationships.

2. The system either automatically or jointly with the user selects relationships from the knowledge base to confirm against the database of case experience. Relationships may be selected for confirmation because of their high frequency of use in rules, because of low confidence indicated by the user, or for their importance in reaching conclusions (e.g., as indicated by sensitivity analysis). There are usually probabilities that the developer does not know; he may tell the system to determine these.

3. The program designs an appropriate statistical study to confirm or find the probabilities. This includes deter-

mining if there is sufficient data in the database to perform the analysis, determining if confounding variables are known, determining methods to control for confounding variables, and selecting a suitable statistical method (e.g., cross sectional analysis, longitudinal regression, etc.).

4. The program carries out the design specified in step three by extracting the relevant cases from the database and performing the statistical analysis.

5. Finally, the program reports those relationships that were found to be accurately described, those that differed from the expert, and those that the expert did not specify which it was able to determine.

In addition to helping in initial knowledge acquisition, this capability is useful for validating knowledge bases that have been modified. When new knowledge is added, it is difficult to confirm that the system still runs correctly for cases that previously worked. It would be useful to provide a simple method to validate knowledge base modifications; to test them by some automated means. This is a capability we plan to include; to use the case database as a reservoir of test cases to validate additions or modifications to the knowledge base.

Performing such knowledge validation and acquisition within KSYS should strengthen the confidence that users must have if KBMSs are to be widely accepted.

9. POSTSCRIPT

The engineering of AI systems remains a major problem. Our KSYS project is intended to elucidate and demonstrate methods to deal with the encoding and interpretation of conceptual knowledge and factual data. It is important to develop techniques that will engender trust in systems using knowledge based techniques. Shared use of knowledge is important for economy, but also as a means of sharing concepts, and assuring consistency of interpretation of the large database on which modern planning systems are based.

To have any hope of success the structures must be composed of simple and understandable components, as we have learned from our experience in dealing with large quantities of factual data. The knowledge problem is harder. The methods still must not demand such a level of sophistication of the users that the systems cannot be understood or properly managed. We hope not to give up too much power to achieve this goal.

The focal concept guiding our research is the imposition of views on knowledge and databases. These views define application areas, object structures, and the scope for automated inference procedures. Integration of these views will lead to a complexity which will be hard to manage, so that we plan to always restrict maintenance and control effort to one active view at a time. We hope to be able to demonstrate within KSYS that such a partitioning will permit retention of most of the power of fully general knowledge networks, while introducing reliability, maintainability, and adaptability.

10. ACKNOWLEDGMENTS

Basic research in the Management of Knowledge and Databases is supported by DARPA under contract N39-84-C-211, managed by SPAWAR. Research on theory and computation for natural language processing was supported by NSF-IST grant 8023889 and was in part aided by Texas Instruments. Related work on RADIX was supported by the National Library of Medicine through grant LM-04334. Earlier funding was provided by the National Center for Health Services Research through grant HS-04389. Computing resources are partially supported in Intellicorp, DEC ISTG, and by SUMEX-AIM, which is funded by NIH grant RR-00785 from the Biotechnology Resources Program. As always, our conclusions do not reflect official positions of any of our sponsoring agencies.

REFERENCES

[1] Barr, A. and E. A. Feigenbaum, *The Handbook of Artificial Intelligence*, vol. 1. Stanford, CA: HeurisTech Press, 1981.

[2] Codd, E. F., "A relational model for large shared data banks," *CACM*, vol. 13, no. 6, 1970, pp. 377–387.

[3] Kim, W., D. Reiner, and D. Batory, *Query Processing in Database Systems*. New York, NY: Springer-Verlag, 1985.

[4] *On Knowledge Base Management Systems: Integrating Artificial Intelligence and Database Technologies*. Brodie, Mylopoulos and Schmidt, Eds. Springer-Verlag, 1987, Proc. Islamorada Workshop, Feb. 1985, Computer Corporation of America.

[5] Kerschberg, L., *First Workshop on Expert Database Systems (EDBSW)*, 1986. Also in *Expert Database Systems*, L. Kerschberg, Ed. Benjamin Cummins, 1986.

[6] Schkolnick, M. and M. Tiberio, "Estimating the cost of updates in a relational database," *ACM TODS*, vol. 10, no. 2, 1985, pp. 163–179.

[7] Weyl, S., J. Fried, G. Wiederhold, and F. Germano, "A modular self-describing databank system," *Comput. Biomedical Res.*, vol. 8, 1975, pp. 279–293.

[8] Gadia, S. K., "Towards a multi-homogeneous model for a temporal database," in *Proc. IEEE Data Eng. Conf.*, Feb. 1986.

[9] Bancilhon, F. B. and N. Spryatos, "Update semantics of relational views," *ACM TODS*, vol. 6, no. 4, 1981. pp. 557–575.

[10] Suwa, M., A. C. Scott, and E. H. Shortliffe, "An approach to verifying completeness and consistency in a rule-based expert system," *AI Magazine*, vol. 1, Fall, 1982, pp. 16–21.

[11] Wiederhold, G. C. M., R. L. Blum, and M. G. Walker, "An integration of knowledge and data representation," in *On Knowledge Base Management Systems: Integrating Artificial Intelligence and Database Technologies*. Brodie, Mylopoulos and Schmidt, Eds. Springer-Verlag, 1987, Proc. Islamorada Workshop, Feb. 1985, Computer Corporation of America.

[12] Corella, F., S. J. Kaplan, G. Wiederhold, and L. Yesil, "Cooperative responses to Boolean queries," in *Proc. IEEE Data Eng. Conf.*, Apr. 1984, pp. 77–93.

[13] Davidson, J. and S. J. Kaplan, "Natural language access to databases: interpreting update requests," *Amer. J. Computational Linguistics*, Apr.–June 1983, pp. 57–68.

[14] Finkelstein, S., "Common expression analysis in database applications," *Int. Conf. Management of Data*, ACM-SIGMOD, June 2–4, 1982, pp. 235–245.

[15] Kaplan, S. J., "Cooperative responses from a portable natural language query system," *Artificial Intelligence*, 1982, pp. 165–187.

[16] Keller, A. M., "The role of semantics in translating view updates," *Computer*, vol. 19, no. 1, Jan. 1986, pp. 63–73.

[17] King, J., "QUIST: A System for Semantic Query Optimization in Relational Databases," in *Proc. of the 7th Conference on Very Large Data Bases*, Zaniolo and Delobel, Eds., 1981, pp. 510–517.

[18] Rowe, N., "An expert system for statistical estimates on databases," in *National Conf. Artificial Intelligence*, Mar. 1983.

[19] Wiederhold, G. C. M., "Knowledge and database management," *IEEE Software*, vol. 1, no. 1, 1984, pp. 63–73.

[20] McDermott, J., "R1: A rule-based configurer of computer systems," *Artificial Intelligence*, vol. 19, no. 1, 1982.

[21] Stonebraker, M., "The design of the POSTGRES Storage system," in *Proc. 13th VLDB Conference*, Sept. 1987.

[22] Ceri, S., G. Gottlob, and G. Wiederhold, "Interfacing relational databases and prolog efficiently," in *Proc. First Int. Conf. Expert Database Syst.*, 1986, pp. 141–153.

[23] Swami, A., "Application knowledge and its use in query optimization," Tech. Rep., Stanford University, 1987.

[24] Duda, R. O. and E. H. Shortliffe, "Expert systems research," *Science,* vol. 220, 1983, pp. 261-276.

[25] Minsky, M., "A framework for representing knowledge," in *Mind Design,* Hangeland, J., Ed. Cambridge, MA: The MIT Press, 1981, pp. 95-128.

[26] Fikes, R. and T. Kehler, "The role of frame-based representation in reasoning," *CACM,* vol. 28, no. 9, Sept. 1985, pp. 904-920.

[27] Dijkstra, E. W., "The structure of the THE multiprogramming system," *CACM,* vol. 11, no. 5, 1968, pp. 341-346.

[28] Wiederhold, G. C. M., "Binding in information processing," Tech. Rep., Stanford University, 1981, Report STAN-CS-81-851.

[29] Wiederhold, G. C. M. and R. El-Masri, "The structural model for database design," in *Proc. Int. Conf. Entity-Relationship Approach,* 1979, pp. 247-267.

[30] Lehman, T. J. and M. J. Carey, "Query processing in main memory database management systems," in *Proc. ACM-SIGMOD Int. Conf. Management Data,* 1986, pp 239-259.

[31] Bitton, D., M. B. Hanrahan, and C. Turbyfill, "Performance of complex queries in main memory database systems," in *Proc. IEEE Data Eng. Conf.,* 1987, pp. 72-81.

[32] Swami, A., "A validated cost model for memory resident databases," *Proc. ACM Sigmetrics,* 1989.

[33] Stonebraker, M. and J. Kalash, "TIMBER: A sophisticated relation/browser," in *Proc. 8th VLDB Conf.,* McLeod and Villasenor, Eds., 1982, pp. 1-10.

[34] Korth, H. F., G. M. Kuper, J. Feigenbaum, A. vanGelder, and J. D. Ullman, "System/U: A database system based on the universal relation assumption," *ACM TODS,* vol. 9, no. 3, 1984, pp. 331-347.

[35] Wiederhold, G. C. M., "Views, objects, and databases," *IEEE Computer,* vol. 19, no. 12, Dec. 1986, pp. 37-44.

[36] Qian, X., and D. R. Smith, "Constraint reformulation for efficient validation," in *Proc. 13th Int'l. Conf. VLDB,* Sept. 1987, pp. 417-425.

[37] Smith, D. R., "Derived preconditions and their use in program synthesis," in *Sixth Conference on Automated Deduction,* D. W. Loveland, Ed. New York, NY: Springer-Verlag, 1982, pp. 172-193, Lecture Notes in Computer Science 138.

[38] Litwin, W. and P. Vigier, "Dynamic attributes in the multidatabase system MRDSM," in *Second Int. Conf. Data Eng., IEEE CS,* 1986.

[39] Card, S. K., T. P. Moran, and A. Newell, *The Psychology of Human-Computer Interaction.* Lawrence Erlbaum Associates, 1983.

[40] Reisner, P., "Human factors studies of database query languages: A survey and assessment," *ACM Computing Surveys,* vol. 13, no. 1, 1981, pp. 13-31.

[41] Thompson, C. W., K. M. Roth, H. R. Tennant, and R. M. Saenz, "Building usable menu-based natural language interface to databases," in *9th Conf. VLDB,* 1983, pp. 43-55.

[42] Phillips, B., and S. Nicholl, "INGLISH: A natural language interface," *Foundation for Human-Computer Communication,* K. Hopper and I. A. Newman, Eds., IFIP WG 2.6 Working Conference on The Future of Command Languages, 1985, pp. 7-26.

[43] Grosz, B., D. E. Appelt, P. Martin, and F. Pereira, "TEAM: An experiment in the design of transportable natural language interfaces," Tech. Rep. 356, SRI AI Center, Aug. 1985.

[44] *Knowledge Acquisition for Knowledge-Based Systems Workshop,* Banff, Alberta, Canada, 1986.

[45] Walker, M. G., "How feasible is automated discovery?," *IEEE Expert,* vol. 2, no. 1, Spring 1987, pp. 70-82.

[46] Blum, R. L., "Discovery, confirmation, and incorporation of causal relationship from a large time-oriented database: The RX project," *Computers Biomed. Res.,* vol. 15, no. 2, 1982, pp. 164-187.

[47] Walker, M. G. and R. L. Blum, "Towards automated discovery from clinical databases: the RADIX project," in *Proc. Fifth World Congress on Medical Informatics (Medinfo).* New York, NY: Elsevier Science Publishers, 1986, pp. 32-36.

Applications of Object-Oriented Database Technology in Knowledge-Based Integrated Information Systems

FRANK MANOLA

Abstract—Knowledge-based integrated information systems denote a class of systems that involve the integration of heterogeneous information sources. These information sources may include heterogeneous distributed database systems, knowledge-based systems (such as expert systems) involving heterogeneous knowledge representations, and conventional application programs, and their associated processors. This paper briefly describes several applications of object-oriented database technology in knowledge-based integrated information systems, including the integration of heterogeneous (and distributed) system components, and heterogeneous data and knowledge representations, and identifies some future research directions for the underlying technology.

INTRODUCTION

GENERALITY and flexibility are increasingly important system design criteria, for practical, not theoretical, reasons. The need for generality is increasingly motivating the integration of pre-existing systems within organizations, both to enable better use to be made of existing data, and to enable management to assert greater control over valuable data resources. The need for flexibility arises because organizations must be adaptive to changing business situations, hence their systems must be adaptive. In addition, flexible systems allow for reduction of system life-cycle costs in the face of inevitable changes in technology.

Database Management Systems (DBMSs) were originally introduced to provide generality and flexibility in the context of business data processing. Prior to the introduction of DBMSs, data were dispersed among multiple applications, organized according to the specific needs of individual applications, and were inaccessible except through those applications. This meant that it was difficult to gain access to data, or to organize them, for new and unanticipated purposes. There was also considerable redundancy, both of data, and of program code required to manipulate and maintain the multiple application files. The database substituted a central data repository, and accompanying data management facilities were equally accessible by multiple applications. This reduced data redundancy, as well as the redundant data manipulation program code previously required within the applications. *Object-oriented database technology* is being developed to extend this generality and flexibility to "unconventional" types of data, and associated processing, including text, graphics, and voice data, that cannot currently be handled by DBMSs, and that thus cannot be integrated in the same way as conventional data.

OBJECT-ORIENTED CONCEPTS

Object-oriented concepts were originally introduced in the programming language and artificial intelligence communities. While there are many variations of the object-oriented approach, a typical description (using typical terminology [2]), is as follows. The phrase *object-oriented* generally refers to the idea of decomposing a system into a collection of logical or physical entities called *objects*. Conceptually, an object is a self-contained collection of data and procedures that can access that data. The data is private to the object, and cannot be accessed except via one of that object's procedures. The procedures support a set of operations (the object's *protocol*) that are visible outside the object. Users invoke an operation by sending a *message* to the object effectively asking it to perform the operation. On receiving a message, the object selects and performs one of the procedures, called a *method*, corresponding to the message. This involves dynamic binding of the name of the operation (the *selector*) with the code to be executed. Objects with the same methods are grouped into *object classes*, and the methods are often physically grouped with the object class definition in order to reduce redundancy. However, the data associated with a particular object (called the *instance variables*) remains with the object. An object-oriented system may be extended by defining new object classes, and these new object classes may be defined in terms of existing object classes. A particular form of definition of a new object class in terms of existing ones is when a new object is defined as a *specialization* of an existing one. In this case, the object classes are said to form an *inheritance hierarchy*, and the specialized class is said to *inherit* the methods of the more general class (i.e., the methods of the general class also apply to the specialized class). Methods may also be defined for the specialized class that apply only to that class, or that extend or replace the methods it inherits.

Fig. 1 illustrates some simple objects in an object-oriented model. The top left object represents a **Part** object class that might be defined for a CAD application. The object class has **display, weight, specification,** and **part number** methods. The top right object represents a **Part** object (instance), with its associated method calls and instance variables. The bottom left object represents the object class for a specialized type of **Part** object, a **3Dsolid** object. The **3Dsolid** object class defines two additional methods that apply to **3Dsolid** objects, **union** and **intersection** operations. When

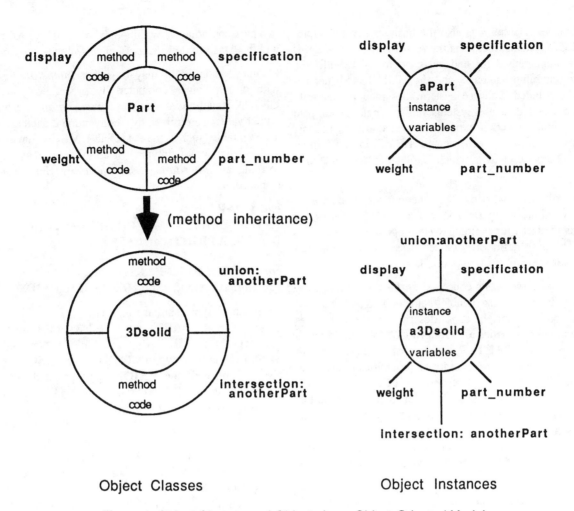

Object Classes

Object Instances

Figure 1 Object Classes and Objects in an Object-Oriented Model

directed at a given **3Dsolid**, these operations return the **3Dsolid** that represents the union or intersection, respectively, of the given object and the **3Dsolid** object supplied as a value of the **anotherPart** parameter. Only the two new methods are defined for object class **3Dsolid**. However, because it is a specialization of object class **Part**, the **3Dsolid** object (instance) on the bottom right is shown as inheriting all the method calls that apply to **Part** objects, together with the specialized ones defined for **3Dsolid** objects.

Object-oriented DBMSs [10], [5] generally attempt to capture these same concepts, but also emphasize certain additional characteristics necessary to support large, shared, persistent object stores. These characteristics include efficient processing of set-oriented requests (query optimization), efficient processing over large secondary storage organizations, concurrency control, and recovery.

Compared to a conventional relational DBMS, a typical object-oriented DBMS differs primarily in trying to support user-defined operations on object classes, and (method) inheritance. Other aspects found in object-oriented DBMS descriptions include support for the concept of *object identity* (the object has an identity independent of the values of its instance variables), and *direct object relationships* (objects related to a given object are accessed by invoking a method of the given object, as if the related objects were part of the given

object's internal data). Representative examples of current OODBMS work include EXODUS [1], GEMSTONE [13], PROBE [4], [11], [12], [14], CACTIS [6], GARDEN Object Server [16], and POSTGRES [19]. With the exception of GEMSTONE, none of these systems is an announced product.

AN EXAMPLE OBJECT-ORIENTED DATABASE SYSTEM

We briefly describe the characteristics of CCA's PROBE system, currently under development, in order to illustrate the capabilities of one specific object-oriented database system. PROBE was primarily intended to support applications involving such "nontraditional" data types as spatial, image, and time data. PROBE incorporates an object-oriented data model that allows integration of programs implementing object behavior together with data, is extensible, and allows the use of special-purpose processors for new data types. It provides efficient recursive query processing (for use in queries on parts hierarchies or task precedence networks), as well as spatial and temporal query processing (using special object types).

PDM, PROBE's data model, is an extension of the Daplex (functional) model [15]. Daplex already contained the concept of "entities" (objects) to which "functions" (messages), could be applied in a dynamic way, inheritance hierarchies of entity types, and other characteristics similar to those of an object-oriented model. Daplex was also the basis of several implemented CCA systems, including the ADAPLEX LDM/DDM, a DBMS implemented in, and designed to work with, the Ada* programming language, and the MULTIBASE heterogeneous distributed database system, designed to integrate multiple existing database systems into a single system, so there was implementation experience available with at least some aspects of an object-oriented DBMS in developing PROBE. The basic areas in which Daplex has been extended in PDM are:

- multiargument and computed functions are supported
- a collection of operations, called *PDM algebra,* is defined as the basis for defining system operations
- the ability to define new object classes with specialized operations (extensibility) is supported.

PDM contains two basic concepts: *entities* and *functions.* An entity is a construct that denotes some individual thing (and thus corresponds to an object, as described earlier). Entities with similar characteristics are grouped into collections called *entity types* (e.g., **PART**). Properties of entities, relationships between entities, and operations on entities (behavioral aspects) are all uniformly represented in PDM by *functions* (which correspond to methods). In order to access properties of an entity or other entities related to an entity, or to perform operations on an entity, one must evaluate a function having the entity as an argument. The examples below illustrate some of the aspects of PDM functions (the syntax used is illustrative only):

- The single-argument function **PART_NUMBER-(PART)→STRING** allows access to the value of the part number attribute of a **PART** entity.
- The multi-argument function **COLOR(X,Y,PHOTO)→COLOR_VALUE** allows access to the color values at particular points in a photograph.
- The function **LOCATION(CONNECTION,LAYOUT)→(X,Y)** allows access to the value of the coordinates of a connection in a diagram (note that a function can return a complex result).
- The function **UNION(3DSOLID,3DSOLID)→3DSOLID** provides access to a union operation defined for 3-dimensional solid models of parts.
- The set-valued function **COMPONENTS(PART)→set of PART** allows access to the component parts of a group part (assembly).

Functions may also be defined that have no input arguments, or that have only Boolean (truth-valued) results. For example:

- the zero-argument function **PART()→set of ENTITY** is implicitly defined for entity type **PART**, and returns all entities of that type (a corresponding function is implicitly defined for each entity type in the database).
- the function **ADJACENT(PART,PART,ASSEMBLY)→BOOLEAN** defines a predicate that is true if

two parts are adjacent within a given assembly. All predicates within PDM are defined as Boolean-valued functions.

Functions in PDM may be either *intensionally-defined,* with output values computed by procedures (such as the **UNION** function above), or *extensionally-defined,* with output values determined by a conventional database search of a stored table (such as the **PART_NUMBER** function above).

Specializations (subtypes) of entity types may be defined, forming an *inheritance (isa) hierarchy.* For example, the declarations:

entity PART
function PART_NUMBER(PART)→STRING
function WEIGHT(Part)→REAL

entity 3DSOLID isa PART
function UNION(3DSOLID,3DSOLID)→3DSOLID

define entity types similar to the object classes shown in Fig. 1. They define a **PART** entity type having two functions, and a subtype **3DSOLID** having an additional function. Because **3DSOLID** is a subtype of **PART**, any **3DSOLID** entity is also an entity of the **PART** supertype, and automatically ''inherits'' the **PART_NUMBER** and **WEIGHT** functions.

Generic operations on objects (entities and functions), such as selection, function application, set operations, and formation of new derived function extents, have been defined in the form of an algebra [12] similar in many respects to the algebra defined for the relational data model. Like the relational algebra, this *PDM algebra* provides a formal basis for the definition of general database operations. In particular, the algebra serves to define the semantics of expressions in PROBE's query language, *PDM Daplex,* involving functions and entities, such as:

for P in PART, for D in DRAWING
print(PART_NUMBER(P)) where
WEIGHT(P)>5 and
SQ _INCHES(AREA(P,D))<10

INTEGRATION OF HETEROGENEOUS COMPONENTS USING THE
OBJECT-ORIENTED APPROACH

Object-oriented approaches provide a very natural framework for use in integrating heterogeneous components. As a *design approach,* thinking of the components to be integrated as objects allows a common methodology to be applied to objects at all levels of granularity. Whether the objects to be integrated are entire systems, or individual object classes within a single system, the approach has a number of important effects:

- It focuses attention on the definition of the message protocols that give access to the object behavioral semantics, as implemented by the object methods. In a distributed environment, development of such protocols and support for them would have to be done anyway, whether the components were heterogeneous *or* homogeneous.
- It focuses attention on the definition of *mutually understandable* message protocols so that the objects can communicate.

* Ada is a trademark of the Department of Defense (Ada Joint Program Office).

direct way of implementing these required capabilities.

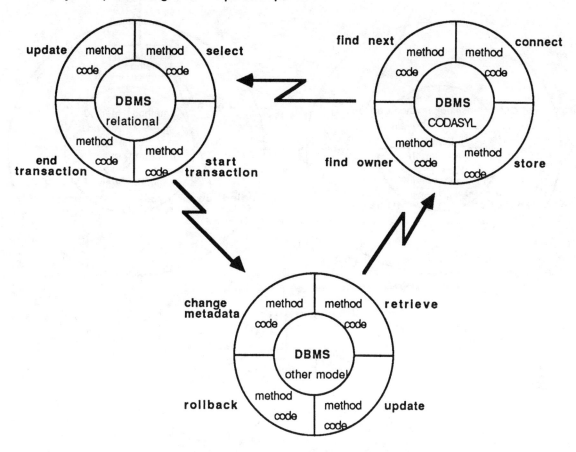

Figure 2 Heterogeneous Database Systems Encapsulated As Objects

• It directs attention away from arbitrary syntactic differences among the components (e.g., among the query languages if the components are heterogeneous database systems).

As an *implementation approach,* the encapsulation provided by the object paradigm allows internal details of individual components to be concealed. Moreover, the object provides a framework for procedures required in interobject communication to be incorporated directly in the objects, such as procedures for data conversion. Also, the method inheritance concept provides a valuable facility for "homogenizing" heterogeneous components. The examples below illustrate these points.

Figs. 2 and 3 shows the steps involved in integrating heterogeneous DBMSs using an object-oriented approach. Fig. 2 shows "objects" defined to encapsulate each of three entire heterogeneous DBMSs. The object encapsulation allows the operations provided by each DBMS to be invoked by messages from other objects. Clearly, nothing very exciting has happened so far with regard to integration; all that has been done is to establish communications among the components. Since the systems implement different data models, a given system will be unable to understand messages sent by the others. This illustrates the fact that thinking about, or implementing, components as objects is not an automatic

solution to any problem. The *design* of the objects is an important consideration, too.

Fig. 3 illustrates the second step in the process, which involves defining (and implementing) object methods that implement messages whose semantics are mutually understandable by the various components. The approach is basically to surround the DBMS with a layer of software that implements a common interface, using the object concept to encapsulate this software. In this case, the common interface has been chosen to be relational, and to implement the relational **select** operation on all systems. While this involves no translation on the relational system, it requires a translation method to be implemented on the other systems. (This "translation method" may, of course, be a very substantial piece of software if it is required to implement a complete relational interface on another form of DBMS!) A component playing the role of the translation method is frequently found in heterogeneous distributed DBMS architectures, such as that of CCA's MULTIBASE system [9], where it is referred to as a *Local Data Interface* (LDI). The point is thus not to claim that the object-oriented approach provides entirely new capabilities in this case, but rather to illustrate that it provides a natural way to think about how the components fit into an overall design approach, as well as to show how, as an implementation approach, object-orientation provides a direct way of implementing these required capabilities.

129

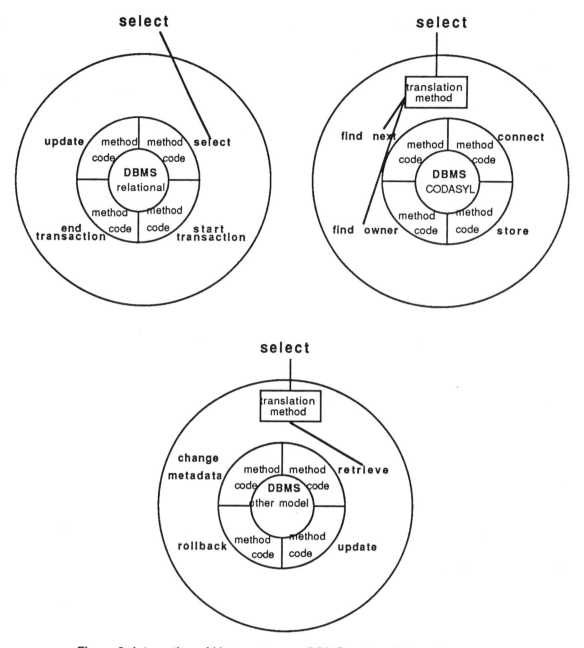

Figure 3 Integration of Heterogeneous DBMSs using Object Encapulation

Fig. 4 shows the definition of objects at a smaller level of granularity. In this case, a part object class has been defined on each of two heterogeneous DBMSs. Note that while both classes implement a **part_number** method, the other methods are different. In the case of the **display** and **show** methods, the semantics are the same, but the names of the methods are different. In the case of the other methods, the semantics are different as well. This makes it difficult to integrate parts from the two systems. For example, without additional system facilities, the user would have to know what system a part came from in order to know how to display it (i.e., whether to issue the command **show** or **display**).

Fig. 5 shows the use of the *inheritance* mechanism to define a generic type of part object class that permits integration of the two part object classes. The generic object class is defined as a supertype of the existing object classes, and as having

methods that correspond to the methods possessed in common (at least semantically) by the two existing object classes. This technique of using inheritance to integrate heterogeneous object classes has also been used in CCA's MULTIBASE system [3], utilizing the inheritance capabilities of its DAPLEX data model.

Fig. 6 shows the use of object encapsulation to implement the generic part object class defined in Fig. 5. The translation method that implements the **part_number** operation on the generic part object class has only to dispatch the operation to the right underlying part, since this operation is supported by both underlying part object classes. However, the translation method that implements the **output** operation must determine whether the **display** or **show** operation should be sent to the underlying part.

As in the previous example, the translation methods are

130

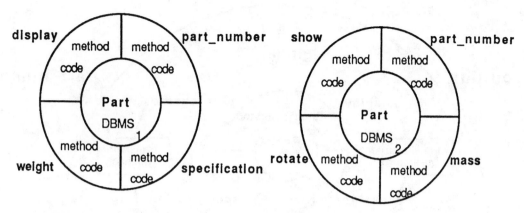

Figure 4 Part Object Classes on Two Heterogeneous Database Systems

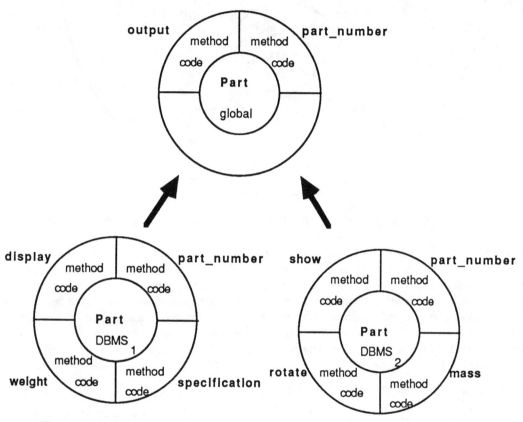

Figure 5 Definition of Generic **Part** Object Class Using Inheritance Concept

effectively implementing what in conventional database technology would be called a *view*. Basically, a *view* consists of a set of data objects derived or transformed from stored data in the database, the purpose being to allow a user or application to "view" the data in a way that is more useful to it than the way the data was originally stored. Views are generally defined in database systems using the facilities of the database's query language, but views defined in this way have a number of important limitations [8]. Work such as [3] in heterogeneous distributed database technology has established that integration of these systems is basically similar to a view mapping problem. By allowing arbitrary procedures to be integrated into the model as object methods, the object-

oriented approach provides a convenient way to provide increased view mapping capability. While some level of these facilities can be provided in more conventional approaches, it is often difficult and clumsy to do.

These examples illustrate that the object-oriented approach can be valuable in integrating heterogeneous systems (and data types), but is not a panacea. The conceptual advantages of object-oriented approaches must be backed up by implementation of facilities that support it. Moreover, protocol standardization and rationalization is vital, since without this objects may not understand the messages directed to them, or be able to direct messages to other objects in appropriate ways. Users and designers of object-oriented systems will still require

131

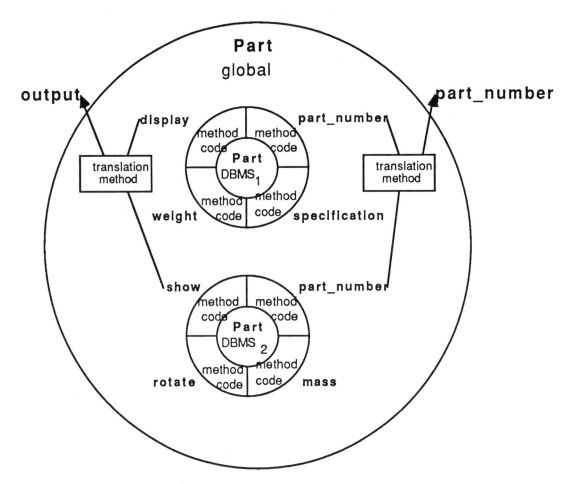

Figure 6 Integration of Part Object Classes Using Object Encapsulation

considerable interface support, since they must now understand a large set of objects in order to make use of the system. Finally, research and experience is needed in realizing the object-oriented approach in a heterogeneous environment. Current research on object-oriented database systems is addressing some of these issues, but little work exists that combines both elements of object-oriented research *and* heterogeneous distributed DBMS research.

INTEGRATION OF KNOWLEDGE-BASED PROCESSING USING THE OBJECT-ORIENTED APPROACH

In integrated information systems, knowledge-based processing will be important in a number of ways:

- providing assistance to users and designers
- resolving differences in data semantics
- implementing advanced concurrency control mechanisms
- providing improved efficiency (through techniques such as "semantic query optimization")
- implementing application-specific rules
- versioning, configuration management, and security.

Integrating this knowledge-based processing into a DBMS object model could be useful for a number of reasons. First, the generality, flexibility, and extensibility provided by the object-oriented approach should be extended to knowledge-based processing as well. For example, it is reasonable to expect that, over the system life cycle, existing knowledge-based components will have to be modified, and new knowledge-based components added. Moreover, these knowledge-based components may use heterogeneous knowledge representation techniques, either because the different techniques are more adapted to specialized requirements, or because advances in technology create new knowledge representation techniques that are included in new components. It seems likely that object-oriented techniques for the integration of heterogeneous components can also be used for the integration of heterogeneous knowledge-based components.

A second reason to integrate knowledge-based processing time into the object model is that it enables the behavior of objects in the model to be derived from knowledge-based processing. In many cases, it may be irrelevant to outside objects whether the behavior of a given object is based on conventional processing, or on knowledge-based processing. The nature of the processing may thus be encapsulated within the object, and only the external behavior revealed. This provides a flexible way to integrate both conventional and knowledge-based components within the same system.

Finally, integration of knowledge-based processing into the object model allows the object-oriented DBMS to provide persistent object support for knowledge-based applications. It is anticipated that knowledge-based applications will increasingly require database support facilities, either because they are dealing with database-sized knowledge bases, or because the raw data they use as input to their processing are stored in databases so as to provide for access by other application programs. The coupling of knowledge-based and database systems is currently a very active area of research, and attempts have already been made to "loosely-couple" existing knowledge-based and database systems (by embedding database calls where database data are required). However, it is believed that performance considerations will demand a much tighter degree of integration of knowledge-based and database processing than can be achieved by such loose-coupling techniques (see, e.g., [7]).

An example of research aimed at integrating knowledge-based processing with object-oriented database management is CCA's HiPAC project, which is just underway. The project is based on CCA's PROBE object-oriented DBMS described earlier. The intent is to enhance PROBE with a number of high-impact incremental facilities that increase support for knowledge-based applications. Specific enhancements being investigated include:

• Capturing heterogeneous knowledge-representations to enable knowledge-based applications to use PROBE as persistent storage.

• Support for condition monitoring over the database (the active DBMS paradigm). This enables a knowledge-based application to download situation-action (production) rules to the DBMS, so that the DBMS can notify the application of "interesting" situations in the database (a simple version of this capability is described in [18]. The action triggered by the condition becoming true could also involve more complex processing, including uploading of data from the database into an application's workspace, for knowledge-based analysis of the details of the situation.

• Representation of plans to support time-constrained scheduling. This is important to enable the DBMS to give priority to processing that might be extremely urgent, or to take compensating action when the time requirements of applications cannot be satisfied.

Work in these areas can build to some extent on existing work in multiparadigm knowledge programming systems, such as LOOPS [17], which integrates conventional, object-oriented, and rule-based programming styles with condition monitoring (triggers, active values).

FUTURE DIRECTIONS

Object-oriented approaches create the potential for changes in the way data models evolve. Data models originally involved relatively few constructs. This forced users to do most of the work in mapping from the real world they wanted to model to the constructs provided by the data model. A more recent trend in data model development is to define more and more special-purpose constructs directly in the data model. Recent examples include various proposals for "version" constructs (for use in engineering information systems), and various forms of space and time data types. The advantages of defining such constructs in the data models is that their special semantics can be directly captured in the DBMS implementation, thus making it possible to optimize processing of requests involving those data types. However, while such constructs

provide extended, tailored facilities to the users of the data model, these constructs are fixed by the data model designer. Thus, they may not exactly capture the semantics required by the particular application involved, and in any event cannot adapt to changing requirements. The object-oriented approach provides the best of both worlds, since new constructs can be user-defined, and thus highly tailored to particular application requirements, but the new constructs can behave as if they were "part of the data model."

Object-oriented approaches also identify required data model research directions. For example, to take full advantage of the ability to support user-defined types, required implementation support, such as extensible query optimization facilities, must be present in the underlying system. Methods of defining procedural information within object-oriented data models also require investigation. The ability to define procedures in conventional programming languages and invoke them from the object is one approach, but in general we expect "tighter coupling" of procedural and conventional DBMS capabilities, so as to support query optimization and concurrency. Adding persistent objects to an object-oriented programming language, as in the GEMSTONE DBMS [13], is a possible approach. However, this does not address the fact the DBMSs conventionally support multiple programming languages. Architecturally, this raises the issue of where one draws the line between "database system" and "application program" in such a framework (or whether such lines are still appropriate). Optimization to achieve good performance in such architectures is a challenge, since it involves closely integrating DBMS and programming language forms, smart staging over a large "object memory," and dealing with complex and possibly large objects. Ultimately, this may lead to new organizations of "operating system," "programming language," and "DBMS" facilities, in order to support these advanced requirements.

ACKNOWLEDGMENTS

The author wishes to thank Michael Brodie, Umesh Dayal, and the other members of CCA's PROBE project, for their contributions to this paper.

This work was partially supported by the Defense Advanced Research Projects Agency and by the Space and Naval Warfare Systems Command under Contract No. N00039-85-C-0263. The views and conclusions contained in this paper are those of the author and do not necessarily represent the official policies of the Defense Advanced Research Projects Agency, the Space and Naval Warfare Systems Command, or the U.S. Government.

REFERENCES

[1] Carey, M. J., et al., "The architectures of the EXODUS extendible DBMS," in [5], pp. 52–65.
[2] Cox, B. J., Object Oriented Programming. Reading, PA: Addison-Wesley, 1986.
[3] Dayal, U. and H. Hwang, "View definition and generalization for database integration in a multidatabase system," IEEE Trans. Software Eng., vol. 10, no. 6, pp. 628–645, 1984.
[4] Dayal, U. and J. M. Smith, "PROBE: A knowledge-oriented database

133

management system," in *On Knowledge Base Management System: Integrating Artificial Intelligence and Database Technologies,* M. L. Brodie and J. Mylopoulos, Eds. New York, NY: Springer-Verlag, 1986.

[5] Dittrich, K. and U. Dayal, Eds. *Proc. Intl. Workshop on Object-Oriented Database Systems.* Washington, DC: IEEE Computer Society Press, 1986.

[6] Hudson, S. E. and R. King, "CACTIS: A database system for specifying functionally-defined data," in [5], pp. 26–37.

[7] Jarke, M., J. Clifford, and Y. Vassiliou, "An optimizing prolog front-end to a relational query system," *Proc. SIGMOD '84,* Boston, MA, June 1984.

[8] Keller, A., "Choosing a view update translator by dialog at view definition time," *Proc. Twelfth Intl. Conf. on Very Large Data Bases,* Kyoto, Japan, Aug. 1986.

[9] Landers, T. and R. L. Rosenberg, "An overview of MULTIBASE," in *Proc. 2nd Intl. Symp. on Distributed Databases,* H. J. Schneider, Ed. Berlin, W. Germany, Sept. 1982.

[10] Lochovsky, F., Ed., *Database Engineering,* vol. 8, no. 4, Special Issue on Object-Oriented Systems, IEEE Computer Society, 1985.

[11] Manola, F. and J. Orenstein, "Toward a general spatial data model for an object-oriented DBMS," *Proc. 12th Intl. Conf. on Very Large Databases,* 1986.

[12] Manola, F. and U. Dayal, "PDM: An object-oriented data model," in [5], pp. 18–25.

[13] Maier, D., J. Stein, A. Otis, and A. Purdy, "Development of an object-oriented DBMS," *Proc. ACM Conf. Object Oriented Programming Systems, Languages, and Applications,* Portland, OR, Sept. 1986.

[14] Rosenthal, A. *et al.,* "Transversal recursion: A practical approach to supporting recursive applications," *Proc. ACM-SIGMOD Intl. Conf. on Mgmt. of Data,* 1986.

[15] Shipman, D., "The functional data model and the data language DAPLEX," *ACM Trans. Database Systems,* vol. 6, no. 1, pp. 140–173.

[16] Skarra, A. H., S. B. Zdonik, and S. P. Reiss, "An object server for an object-oriented database system," in [5], pp. 196–204.

[17] Stefik, M. J., D. G. Bobrow, and K. M. Kahn, "Integrating access-oriented programming into a multiparadigm environment," *IEEE Software,* vol. 3, no. 1, Jan. 1986.

[18] Stonebraker, M., "Triggers and inference in database systems," in *On Knowledge Base Management Systems,* M. L. Brodie and J. Mylopoulous, Eds. New York, NY: Springer-Verlag, 1986, pp. 297–314.

[19] ——, "Object management in POSTGRES using procedures," in [5], pp. 66–72.

Transaction Management in a Multidatabase Environment

YURI BREITBART,[1] AVI SILBERSCHATZ,[2] AND GLENN THOMPSON[3]

Abstract—A new update algorithm that ensures the consistent execution of any system of global transactions in a multidatabase system in the presence of local transactions is presented. The model considered in this paper does not make any assumptions about local concurrency control mechanisms. We also assume that local database management systems are not aware of each other and cannot exchange their concurrency control information (such as, for example, local schedules, local wait-for-graphs, etc.). The algorithm is being integrated into the production version of the Amoco ADDS multidatabase system.

1. INTRODUCTION

IN recent years we have witnessed the development of new database applications that often require data from a variety of preexisting databases located in various heterogeneous hardware and software environments. Manipulation of information located in a heterogeneous database requires an additional software layer on top of existing data management systems (DBMS). This software layer is called a multidatabase system (MDBS). Local DBMSs may employ different logical models, data definition and data manipulation languages, and differ in their concurrency control and transaction management mechanisms. An MDBS creates the illusion of logical database integration without requiring physical database integration.

A multidatabase system offers many advantages to the users. It significantly extends user capabilities enabling them to access and share data without the added burden of learning the intricacies of different DBMSs. Preexisting programs and procedures remain operational in the integrated multidatabase environment.

Research related to data retrieval (that is, no updates are permitted) using MDBS systems has been active for several years now [2], [3], [4], [5], [6], and several retrieval systems have recently been developed. Among them are MULTIBASE developed at Computer Corporation of America [7]; DDTS developed at Honeywell [8]; SIRIUS-DELTA and MRDSM developed at INRIA [9], [10]; ADDS developed at the Amoco Production Company Research Center [11]; and MERMAID, developed at UNISYS [5]. None of these systems, however, provides a general transaction management scheme (that is, one that allows both retrieval and updates).

[1] Department of Computer Science, University of Kentucky, Lexington, KY 40506.
[2] Department of Computer Science, University of Texas, Austin, Texas 78712.
[3] Amoco Production Company Research Center, P.O. Box 3385, Tulsa, OK 74102.

The problems associated with providing a general transaction management scheme in the multidatabase environment were first identified in [18]. The authors extensively discussed the inherent difficulties associated with the problem, but did not propose a particular solution. Following this, a number of different solutions were proposed which are briefly discussed below.

Pu [12], [13] and Elmagarmid [14] assumed that the multidatabase system is aware of local transactions. The assumption requires making changes to local DBMSs, and thus violates the local autonomy of the DBMS.

In [19] an update and a deadlock avoidance algorithm was presented for a restricted set of global transactions that can have no more than one local site at which the transaction can read and write. At any other site, the transaction either reads or writes, but cannot do both. The author's deadlock-avoidance algorithm, however, identifies some transaction configurations as deadlock-free when, in fact, the potentiality of a deadlock exists as demonstrated in Example 4 in [17].

In [15] the update problem was considered under the assumption that the MDBS is not aware of local transactions, and local DBMSs are not aware of each other. An "altruistic" locking scheme was presented that increases concurrency by allowing early lock release, subject to constraints. The authors, however, do not guarantee global database consistency in all cases.

Litwin and Tirri [20] proposed a new paradigm for a concurrency control that uses the concept of value date. They show the applicability of their concept to a multidatabase environment. Their approach avoids data locking for prolonged periods of time and, thereby, seems to be very promising.

A formal model of data updates and a theory of serializability in a multidatabase environment in the presence of local transactions was developed in [17]. In [16], a new protocol was developed that allows the concurrent execution of a set of global transactions in the presence of local transactions. In this paper, we develop a transaction manager algorithm for a distributed multidatabase system. Our algorithm allows the MDBS to update semantically-related data items retaining global database consistency in the presence of local transactions. The remainder of the paper is organized as follows. Section 2 describes our model assumptions and the multidatabase transaction manager system architecture. In Section 3 we outline the theoretical background that the transaction manager

Manuscript received January 3, 1989.

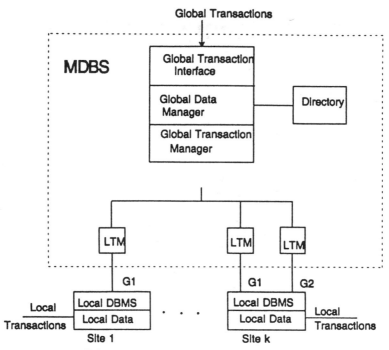

Figure 1. MDBS Architecture

algorithm's correctness is based on. Section 4 contains two versions of a site selection procedure that is used by the global transaction manager (GTM). The global transaction manager algorithm's implementation issues are discussed in Section 5. Section 6 concludes the paper.

2. MULTIDATABASE UPDATE ARCHITECTURE

Fig. 1 illustrates the layered architecture of the MDBS system. Interactions with a global (local) database are carried through global (local) transactions. A transaction is a sequence of read and write operations defined on a database. A global transaction is one that is submitted to the MDBS and is executed under its control. Each such transaction is divided into a number of subtransactions that are executed at the local sites under the control of the various DBMSs. A local transaction, on the other hand, is one submitted to a local DBMS, outside of the MDBS control. Global transactions can be submitted at any node. One of the sites in a distributed system is a master site, and all global transactions submitted to the system are reported to the master site's MDBS system.

The MDBS model discussed in this paper is based on the following assumptions:

1. No changes can be made to the local DBMS software to accommodate the MDBS. Modifying a local DBMS software creates significant development and maintenance problems.

2. No changes can be made to the local application programs to accommodate the MDBS. Local application programs are not aware of the MDBS.

3. Each DBMS retains the local autonomy of the database it controls. The concept of local autonomy requires that the local DBMS, local transactions, and local database administrator perform as if the MDBS does not exist.

The local DBMSs perform their operations without any knowledge of other DBMSs and the MDBS. The implication of this assumption is that the local DBMS that execute parts of the same global transaction cannot synchronize their operations to ensure global database consistency.

4. Global subtransactions running at any local site are treated by local DBMS as any other local transaction. The DBMS does not have the ability to distinguish between local and global transactions. As a result, global transactions are not supplied with any DBMS control information, such as schedules, lock tables, etc., that can help in transaction synchronization at different local sites.

5. A local DBMS ensures the serializability and freedom from local deadlocks for any system of global and local transactions that are active at the site.

A high level nonprocedural language is used for user interaction with the system. For example, SQL and SQL-like query languages are widely used in many multidatabase systems [20]. User requests, either in the form of programs with embedded MDBS statements, or online MDBS statements, are submitted to the system's global transaction interface (GTI). The GTI parses the request, optimizes it based on the statistical information contained in the MDBS directory, and generates an execution plan. This execution plan is integrated with other execution plans for the currently active user requests, and the resulting plan serves as an input to a global data manager (GDM).

The global data manager is responsible for managing all intermediate data received from the GTM during transaction execution. The MDBS model discussed here uses the relational approach for both the global database application design

136

and multidatabase data management. Transaction intermediate results are stored as relations, and those relations are used as operands for the subsequent relational operations in the transaction execution plan. Thus, the GDM analyzes an execution plan to derive the needed temporary relations. Temporary relations are allocated by the GDM and recorded in the directory for the duration of the transaction.

Local DBMS may have different operation capabilities. For instance, some DBMS may not be capable of executing join operation, while some other may not be able to execute nested queries. A priori, the MDBS is not aware of the exact operational capabilities of each local DBMS. It assumes, however, that each DBMS can do at least as much as can be expressed in the MDBS language. Thus, an attempt to execute the next step of the execution plan may result in the situation where the local DBMS is not able to execute the required operation. In this case, the request is returned to the GDM that subdivides the request into more elementary operations. These are integrated with the global execution plan and, if needed, additional temporary relations are allocated.

An operation that cannot be executed by a local DBMS is executed at the MDBS level, after the local DBMS prepares required operands for the operation. Therefore, the MDBS should have complete database management capabilities, and these capabilities are implemented at the GDM level.

3. TRANSACTION GRAPHS

In order to describe the update algorithm, it is necessary to define the concept of a transaction graph.

A transaction graph for a system of global transactions G is a bipartite graph whose set of nodes is a set of sites (site nodes) and a set of global transactions (transaction nodes). Edges exist only between site and transaction nodes. If a site S_j was selected to perform at least one operation of the transaction G_i, then an edge is drawn between G_i and S_j. To illustrate this concept let us consider the following example.

Example 1: Consider a global database that contains data item a—at sites S_1 and S_2, b—at sites S_1 and S_3, and c—at sites S_2 and S_3. Let us define global transactions G_1 and G_2 as follows:

$$G_1: r_1(a) w_1(b)$$

$$G_2: r_2(b) w_2(c).$$

The GTM may generate one of the following sequence of local operations for each transaction:

$$G_1: r_1(a_1) w_1(b_1) w_1(b_3)$$

$$G_2: r_2(b_3) w_2(c_2) w_2(c_3)$$

or

$$G_1: r_1(a_1) w_1(b_1) w_1(b_3)$$

$$G_2: r_2(b_1) w_2(c_2) w_2(c_3).$$

The transaction graphs for a system of global transactions G_1 and G_2 for each site selection are shown in Fig. 2(a) and 2(b), respectively. The following theorem formulates the global

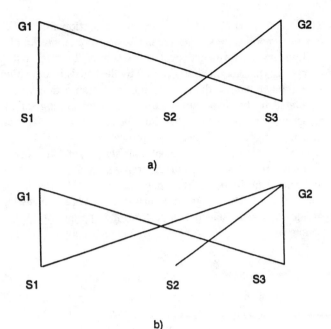

Figure 2: Transaction Graph

database consistency conditions and constitutes the basis for correctness of the algorithm given in the next section.

Theorem 1: Let G and L be a set of global and local transactions, respectively. The consistency of a global database is assured if the following conditions hold:

1. Any local transaction from L is a read-only transaction or can write only nonreplicated data items.
2. There exists at least one selection of sites for executing global operations for transactions from G such that the corresponding transaction graph for G is acyclic.

The proof of the theorem is given in Appendix 2.

4. SITE SELECTION ALGORITHM

The main objective of the site selection algorithm is to select data sites for each operation in such a way that a transaction graph for a system of global transactions will be acyclic. If such site selection is not possible, then the global transaction whose operation caused by a cycle in a graph is aborted. The correctness of this strategy is assured by virtue of Theorem 1.

We will describe two versions of the site selection algorithm. The first one ensures that if for a sequence of global transaction operations there is an acyclic transaction graph, then such a graph will be found. It may, however, take an exponential amount of time in the number of global transactions and data sites. Based on results in [17] and Theorem 1, it follows that the problem of finding an acyclic transaction graph for a system of global transactions is NP-complete. Therefore, there is little hope that a polynomial time algorithm that finds an acyclic transaction graph will ever be found.

The second algorithm, on the other hand, only requires a polynomial execution time, and uses a heuristic approach. The algorithm, however, may not find an acyclic transaction graph for a system of global transactions even if such graph exists.

This, in turn, may lead to unnecessary transaction aborts. For practical applications, the second algorithm is preferable. Preliminary performance evaluation results indicate that a number of transaction aborts caused by the heuristic algorithm is not much larger than the number of transaction aborts generated by the exhaustive search site selection algorithm. Consequently, the second algorithm behaves sufficiently well in generating acyclic transaction graphs.

For both algorithms, the input consists of a global transaction identifier—TID, the current transaction operation—OP, and the data item—X that the operation OP should be performed on. The algorithm returns the set $SITE$, consisting of sites that were selected to perform the operation OP. We denote by $S(X)$ a set of sites that contain a copy of the data item X.

4.1. Site Selection Algorithm—Version One

This algorithm uses an exhaustive search to find a set of sites for a system of global transactions in such a way that there are no cycles in a transaction graph. For each global transaction G_i that is currently active, the algorithm builds and maintains a set of site set alternatives. This set is denoted by $ALT(G_i)$, and it includes those site sets that could have been selected to execute transaction G_i operations that have been processed by the GTM so far. To illustrate this, consider the following example:

Example 2: Consider the global database and the set of global transactions of Example 1. Assume that the global transactions operations are executed by the global transaction manager in the following order:

$$r_1(a)r_2(b)w_1(b)w_2(c).$$

After $r_1(a)$ has been processed, $ALT(G_1) = \{\{S_1\}, \{S_2\}\}$ and $ALT(G_2) = \varnothing$.

After $r_2(b)$ has been processed, $ALT(G_1)$ has not changed, but $ALT(G_2) = \{\{S_1\}, \{S_3\}\}$.

Finally, after $w_1(b)$ and $w_2(c)$ have been processed, $ALT(G_1) = \{\{S_1, S_3\}, \{S_1, S_2, S_3\}\}$ $ALT(G_2) = \{\{S_1, S_3\}, \{S_1, S_2, S_3\}\}$.

Let G_i be a global transaction and $ALT(G_i) = \{A_1, A_2, \cdots, A_k\}$ its current set of site set alternatives. After execution of each operation from G_i, $ALT(G_i)$ is updated. There is no alternative in selection sites from $S(X)$ to execute a write operation: all sites must be selected. There are, however, as many alternatives to select a site to read the data item X as the number of sites in $S(X)$. Therefore, if the operation is a write, then each site set alternative $A_i (1 \leq i \leq k)$ is expanded to include all sites that contain copies of the data item X. Let $S(X) = \{S_1, \cdots, S_p\}$ and let OP be Read(X). The new $ALT(G_i)$ may include as many as $k*p$ sets $A_1, \cdots, A_{k*p}$ where each A_t is obtained as follows:

$$A_t = A_i \cup \{S_j\}, \quad (1 \leq i \leq k, \ 1 \leq j \leq p).$$

We are now in a position to describe the algorithm. Let G be a system of global transactions. The site selection to execution $OP(X)$ of the transaction G_i will be performed as follows:

1) Generate the new $ALT(G_i)$ as described above.

2) For each G_j from G select one A_{jp} from $ALT(G_j)$. Use these sets to construct a transaction graph as described in Section 3.

3) If the transaction graph obtained in step 2) is acyclic, then the site(s) to perform $OP(X)$ is obtained from the A_{ip} that was used in the construction of the graph for the transaction G_i.

4) If the transaction graph obtained in step 2) contains a cycle, then step (2) should be repeated. If all possible selected combinations have been exhausted then the transaction G_i is aborted.

The algorithm may select different site set alternatives during transaction processing. It may require changing sites for reading data items that have been already read prior to the site selection for the operation $OP(X)$.

Suppose that Read(Y) from transaction G_i was executed before $OP(X)$, and for Read(Y) the algorithm selected site S_1. Let us further assume that for $OP(X)$ such site set alternative was selected that does not contain S_1, but contains another site, say S_2 that also has a copy of Y. If at site S_2 the transaction G_i did not execute any write operations prior to $OP(X)$, then changing site for Read(Y) from S_1 to S_2 cannot destroy a global database consistency. However, if the transaction G_i happened to execute at S_2 some write operations prior to $OP(X)$, then changing site for Read(Y) may potentially result in a global database inconsistency. The next theorem establishes that the outlined algorithm will never change reading sites if the transaction has done any writing at the site prior to the execution of $OP(X)$.

Theorem 2: Let Read(Y) and $OP(X)$ be two operations of G_i with Read(Y) preceding $OP(X)$. Let S_k be a site that was selected to execute Read(Y). If a site set alternative A_j was selected for $OP(X)$, and S_k is not in A_j, then the transaction G_i did not execute any write operation at the site S_k prior to the operation $OP(X)$.

Proof: Assume by contradiction that G_i has executed Write(Z) at site S_k. Therefore, the site set of the data item Z includes S_k. From the construction of the site set alternatives for G_i it follows that every member of the site set alternatives must contain S_k after execution Write(Z). Once a site is in a site set alternative, it is never removed from it. Therefore, any site set alternative constructed after execution Write(Z) contains S_k, and consequently A_j also contains s, which contradicts the condition of the theorem.

The described algorithm for a given system of global transactions G and a global schedule $O_1 O_2 \cdots O_k$ finds an acyclic transaction graph by considering all possible site set alternative combinations for each transaction from G. Therefore, if for G and for $O_1 O_2 \cdots O_k$ an acyclic transaction graph exists, the algorithm will find it.

4.2. Site Selection Algorithm—Version Two

The algorithm presented in this section uses a heuristic approach in selecting sites in such a way that a transaction graph is acyclic. We do not conduct an exhaustive search of all possible site alternatives in order to find an acyclic transaction graph. Rather, we use the following heuristic:

1. If a transaction has already processed data at a site that contains a copy of the data item to be read, then that site will be selected.
2. A copy of the data item to be read is always selected from the sites that the transaction has to write to.

The input for the algorithm is the same as the input for the general update algorithm. If the site selection algorithm finds a site (or a set of sites) to execute the operation without causing a cycle in the transaction graph, then the algorithm returns these sites in the *SITE* set. If no such site can be found, then *SITE* is empty.

The site selection algorithm is formally presented in Appendix 1. Here we only present the basic ideas behind the algorithm.

The algorithm for Read(X) operation on behalf of the transaction G_i works as follows:

1. If the transaction G_i has already processed data at some site S_k from $S(X)$, then the site S_k is selected. If there are several such sites, then the site where the transaction has already executed a write operation is selected.
2. If transaction G_i has not accessed a data item at any site from $S(X)$, then a site from $S(X)$ is selected such that an addition of such a site does not generate a cycle in a transaction graph. If no such site exists, then the site selection was not successful.

The site selection algorithm for a Write(X) operation on behalf of the transaction G_i works as follows:

1. Add all the sites from $S(X)$ to the transaction graph.
2. For any read operation, Read(Y), of the same transaction executed prior to the write operation, we replace the site S_i that was selected to perform Read((Y) with one of the sites from $S(X)$, if such a replacement is possible (i.e., if $S(Y) \cap S(X) \neq \varnothing$).
3. If the resulting transaction graph has a cycle, then the site selection is unsuccessful; otherwise it successfully completes.

The algorithm always selects a new site in such a way that it does not cause a cycle in a transaction graph. However, unlike the first version of the algorithm, this algorithm may report that the site selection was not successful even though an acyclic transaction graph actually exists.

Example 3: Consider a global database consisting of data items a and b at sites S_1 and S_2, and c at site S_3. Let G_1 and G_2 be two global transactions defined as follows:

$$G_1: r_1(a) w_1(c)$$

$$G_2: r_2(b) w_2(c).$$

Consider the following global schedule:

$$r_1(a) r_2(b) w_1(c) w_2(c).$$

The algorithm generates the transaction graph shown in Fig. 3. This graph contains a cycle.

However, there exists a site selection which results in the transaction graph being acyclic. Our algorithm, however, will not be able to find it.

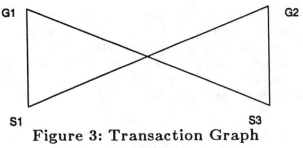

Figure 3: Transaction Graph

5. GLOBAL TRANSACTION MANAGER ALGORITHM

The GTM controls the execution of global transactions. For each global operation, the GTM calls the site selection algorithm described in Section 4 to select a local site (or a set of sites) where the operation should be executed. To execute the operation, a local transaction manager (LTM) must be allocated by the GTM at the selected local sites. A local transaction manager could be either a process in the UNIX-like environment, or a virtual CPU in the VM-like environment. Consequently, one may assume that the GTM either has an unlimited number of LTMs in the UNIX-like environment, or a limited number of LTMs in the VM-like environment. In this paper we assume that the GTM has unlimited number of LTMs, so that any transaction's request for the LTM is always satisfied. The case of a limited number of LTMs and problems associated with this assumption will be discussed elsewhere.

The algorithm uses the following data structures:

- ACTIVE_QUEUE—A queue consisting of those global transactions that are active in the MDBS. Each queue element is a triple $\langle TID, OP, X \rangle$, where TID is a transaction identifier, OP is the next operation to be performed by the transaction, and X is the data item that the operation is to be performed on.
- RESTART_QUEUE—A queue consisting of those global transactions that were aborted by the MDBS. The transaction is aborted by the GTM if the site selection algorithm fails to select a site (or sites) to execute the operation OP, i.e., that attempt to execute OP will cause a cycle in the transaction graph.
- SITE—A set of sites that were selected for by the site selection algorithm for the execution of the operation OP. If no site was found, then the set is empty.

The GTM synchronizes the execution of global transactions ensuring consistency of the database in the presence of local transactions. It selects the next transaction from the ACTIVE_QUEUE and executes the current operation of the transaction. If the next operation is commit, then the Commit process is called to commit the results of the transaction permanently in each local database.

The Commit process uses a two-phase commit protocol [1]. We do not require any specific commit protocol to be supported by the local DBMSs. We assume, however, that any local DBMS is capable of committing the results of local transaction.

All LTM's allocated to the transaction are deallocated. Edges between the transaction and all sites that the transaction was active at may or may not be removed from the transaction graph, depending on whether removing the edges will create a

139

possibility of inconsistent database while processing other active transactions remaining in the system. To illustrate this point let us consider the following example.

Example 4: Consider a global database that contains data items a and b at site S_1, and c and d at site S_2. Let us consider the following global transactions:

$$G_1: w_1(a)w_1(c)$$

$$G_2: w_2(b)w_2(d).$$

In addition to that, the following local transactions L_3 and L_4 are active at site S_1 and S_2, respectively.

$$L_3: r_3(a)r_3(b)$$

$$L_4: r_4(c)r_4(d).$$

The global transactions operations are submitted to GTM in the following order:

$$w_1(a)w_2(d)w_1(c)c_1w_2(b)c_2,$$

where c_1 and c_2 are commit operations for the transactions G_1 and G_2, respectively.

Let the local schedules at sites S_1 and S_2 be as follows:

$$S_1: w_1(a)r_3(a)r_3(b)c_3c_1w_2(b)c_2$$

$$S_2: w_2(d)r_4(c)r_4(d)c_4w_1(c)c_1c_2.$$

The combination of both local schedules does not retain a global database consistency. On the other hand, if after the completion of c_1, the algorithm removes edges pertaining to the transaction G_1 from the transaction graph, the site selection algorithm will not report the possibility of the global inconsistency.

There are two ways to deal with the problem illustrated in Example 4. First, only require that each local schedule will be a strict one [1], subject to conditions 1 and 2 of Theorem 1. However, this is very strong restriction on the set of local DBMSs. The second approach is based on the premise that at some point in time all edges from committed transactions are completely removed from the transaction graph. Such removal requires completion of all currently active transactions without allowing any new transactions to become active.

The GTM inspects then RESTART_QUEUE to check to see whether there is any transaction that can be restarted after the TID transaction completion. A transaction G_i can be restarted if and only if at least one of the transactions that caused abort of the G_i has become inactive.

If a global transaction aborts, the GTM instructs the LTM to rollback the updates at local sites. All LTMs allocated to the transaction are deallocated, the transaction graph edges incidental to the aborted transaction are removed from the transaction graph along with TID node of the graph, and, finally, the RESTART_QUEUE is inspected to check whether any transaction there can be reactivated.

If the global operation is Read/Write, then the GTM invokes the site selection process that selects the local site(s) to perform the operation without a possibility of causing either a global inconsistency or a global deadlock. If no such site(s) exists, the transaction is aborted and placed at the RESTART_ QUEUE. A set of global transactions that, along with the transaction TID comprise a loop in the transaction graph, is

recorded, and the RESTART_QUEUE entry for the transaction TID contains a pointer to that list.

If the site selection is successful, LTMs are requested and allocated at the sites at which the transaction was not yet active, and the GTM generates messages to be sent to local sites instructing them to perform the operation at those sites. Only one LTM for a global transaction at the local site may be allocated. Each LTM translates global read and write operations into the languages of the local DBMSs. It also transfers the retrieved data to the GTM.

Once execution messages are sent, the GTM processes a response queue that contains data and/or responses from local transactions managers reporting the progress of their operations submitted by the GTM. If a local LTM reports that the transaction has been aborted by the local DBMS, the Abort command for the transaction TID is generated, and eventually Abort will be executed by the GTM as described above.

6. Conclusions

We have presented a new update algorithm that ensures the consistency of a multidatabase. The algorithm allows the performance of consistent multidatabase updates in the presence of both local read-only transactions and local transactions that can only update nonreplicated data items at local sites.

We presented two versions of the site selection algorithm. We proved that the site selection algorithm does not generate cycles in the transaction graph, and thereby retains global database consistency.

One drawback of the proposed update algorithm is that it may generate a large number of transaction aborts. To overcome this drawback, a different update strategy is needed which we are currently pursuing. It is, however, important to emphasize that the algorithm proved to be practical and will be shortly used on the production level in the ADDS multidatabase system [11].

Acknowledgments

This material is based in part upon work supported by the Texas Advanced Research Program under grant No. 4355 and by the National Science Foundation under Grant no. IRI-8805215.

Appendix 1

In this appendix we formally present the second version of the site selection algorithm described informally in Section 4.

The algorithm uses the following structures:

- *READ_SITES*—The set of all sites at which transaction G_i performs only read operations (that is no writes) prior to the operation *OP*.
- *WRITE_SITES*—The set of all sites at which the transaction G_i writes and possibly reads data items prior to the operation *OP*.
- *CURRENT_SITE*—A temporary variable that is used to keep site values.
- *TRANSACTION_GRAPH*—an $K \times N$ adjacency matrix defining the transaction graph, where K is the number of active transactions in the system, and N is the number of local sites in the multidatabase. TRANSACTION_GRAPH$(i, j) = 1$ if and only if transaction TID is active at site S_j.

Procedure: Site_Selection(TID, OP, X, $SITE$)

  If OP = 'WRITE'

  then **Begin**

       For any $CURRENT\_SITE$ **from** S(X)

        $TRANSACTION\_GRAPH(TID, CURRENT\_SITE) = 1$

       If $TRANSACTION\_GRAPH$ **is acyclic**

       then **Begin**

            $SITE = $ S(X)

            $WRITE\_SITES = WRITE\_SITES \cup$ S(X)

            For any $CURRENT\_SITE$ **from** $READ\_SITES$

            Do

            If the read operation at $CURRENT\_SITE$

            can be executed at one of the sites from $SITE$

            then Do

                $READ\_SITES = READ\_SITES - \{CURRENT\_SITE\}$

                $TRANSACTION\_GRAPH(TID, CURRENT\_SITE) = 0$

               End

           End

          Return

         End

       else /* $TRANSACTION\_GRAPH$ contains a loop */

        Begin

         $SITE = \varnothing$

        For any $CURRENT\_SITE$ **from** S(X)

        $TRANSACTION\_GRAPH(TID, CURRENT\_SITE) = 0$

        Return

        End

      End

    else if OP = 'READ'

    then **Begin**

       If S(X) $\cap$ ($READ\_SITES \cup WRITE\_SITES$) $\neq \varnothing$

       then Begin

          If S(X) $\cap$ $WRITE\_SITES \neq \varnothing$

          then select $SITE$ **from** (S(X) $\cap$ $WRITE\_SITES$)

          else select $SITE$ **from** (S(X) $\cap$ $READ\_SITES$)

          Return

         End

       else /* No site from S(X) was used by TID */

         Begin

         If there is $CURRENT\_SITE$ **from** S(X) **such that**

         adding edge $<TID, CURRENT\_SITE>$ **does not**

         create a cycle in $TRANSACTION\_GRAPH$

         then Do

             $SITE = CURRENT\_SITE$

             $READ\_SITES = READ\_SITES \cup \{SITE\}$

             For each $CURRENT\_SITE$ **from** $READ\_SITES$

             Begin

$$\text{If read can be performed at } SITE$$
$$\textbf{then Do}$$
$$READ\_SITES = READ\_SITES -$$
$$\{CURRENT\_SITE\}$$
$$TRANSACTION\_GRAPH(TID,CURRENT\_SITE) = 0$$
$$\textbf{Return}$$
$$\textbf{End}$$
$$\textbf{End}$$
$$\textbf{End}$$

else /*adding any site from S(X) results in loop in the transaction graph*/

$$\textbf{Begin}$$
$$SITE = \varnothing$$
$$\textbf{Return}$$
$$\textbf{End}$$
$$\textbf{End}$$
$$\textbf{End}$$
$$\textbf{End} \text{ /* procedure*/}$$

APPENDIX 2—PROOF OF THE THEOREM 1

In order to prove the theorem, it is necessary to define the notion of a site graph [16].

A site graph for a global transaction G_i is a graph whose nodes are sites that are accessed as a result of the execution of G_i. These nodes are connected by undirected edges, labeled with the transaction name G_i, in any order that forms an acyclic graph. Let G be a set of global transactions. A site graph for G is formed by taking the union of site graphs for each global transaction from G. Note that the site graph for any global transaction G_i as well as for a system of global transactions G is not unique. Fig. 4 depicts site graphs for each site selection for a system of global transactions G_1 and G_2 of Example 1.

The following theorem formulates the global database consistency conditions.

Theorem [17]: Let G and L be a set of global and local transactions, respectively. The consistency of a global database is assured if the following conditions hold:

1. Any local transaction from L is a read-only transaction or can write only nonreplicated data items.
2. There exists at least one selection of sites for executing global operations for transactions from G such that the corresponding site graph for G is acyclic.

In order to complete the proof of the theorem we will need the following lemma.

Lemma 1: For any system of global transactions G, a site graph for G does not contain a cycle if and only if a transaction graph for G does not contain a cycle.

Proof: Let $G_1 S_1 G_2 S_2 \cdots G_k S_k G_1$ be the smallest cycle in the transaction graph, where $k \geq 2$, $G_i(i \geq 1)$ is a transaction node, and $S_j(j \geq 1)$ is a site node. For any $m(m > 1)$, a transaction G_m is active at sites S_{m-1} and S_m, and a transaction

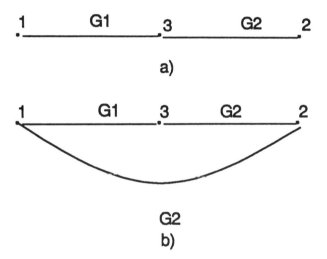

Figure 4: Site Graph

G_1 is active at S_1 and S_k. Thus, the site graph for G contains a cycle.

Let us assume now that a site graph contans a cycle. Let C: $S_1 S_2 \cdots S_k S_1$ be the smallest cycle in the site graph, where $k \geq 2$. Each edge in the cycle is labeled with a transaction name from G. Since a site graph for a single transaction is acyclic, by definition, then there are at least two different transaction names that label edges from C. Since C is the smallest, all edge's labels in the cycle are different. Inserting the transaction name that labels an edge between two sites in the cycle, we obtain a cycle in the transaction graph.

Since an absence of cycles in the transaction and site graphs for G are equivalent conditions, Theorem 1 is proven.

REFERENCES

[1] Bernstein, P., V. Hadzilacos, and N. Goodman, *Concurrency Control and Recovery in Database Systems*. Addison-Wesley, 1987.
[2] Landers, T. and R. Rosenberg, "An overview of Multibase," in *Distributed Data Systems*, H. Schneider, Ed. North-Holland, 1982.

[3] Litwin, W., J. Boudenant, G. Escullier, A. Ferrier, A. Gloriex, J. La Chimia, K. Kabbaj, G. Moulinoux, P. Rolin, and C. Stranget, "SIRIUS system for distributed data management," in *Distributed Data Bases*, H. Schreiber, Ed. North-Holland, 1982.

[4] Motro, A. and P. Buneman, "Constructing Superviews," in *Proc. ACM SIGMOD Int. Conf.*, 1981.

[5] Templeton, M., D. Brill, A. Hwang, J. Kameny, and E. Lund, "An overview of the Mermaid System—a front-end to heterogeneous databases," in *Proc. EASCON, 1983*, IEEE Computer Society.

[6] Breitbart, Y. and L. Tieman, "ADDS - Heterogeneous distributed database system," in *Distributed Data Sharing Systems*, F. Schreiber and W. Litwin, Eds. North-Holland, 1985.

[7] Dayal, U., "Processing queries over generailized hierarchies in a multidatabase system," in *Proc. 9th VLDB Conf.*, 1983.

[8] Devor, C. and J. Weeldreyer, "DDTS: a testbed for distributed database research," Honeywell Rep. HR-80-268, 1980.

[9] Ferrier, A. and C. Stranget, "Heterogeneity in the distributed system SIRIUS-DELTA," in *Proc. 8th VLDB Conf.*, 1982.

[10] Litwin, W., "An overview of the multidatabase system MRDSM," *ACM 85*, 1985.

[11] Breitbart, Y., P. Olson, and G. Thompson, "Database integration in a distributed heterogeneous database environment," in *Proc. Int. Conf. Data Eng.*, 1986. Reprinted in this book.

[12] Pu, C., "Superdatabase for composition of heterogeneous systems," Columbia University Tech. Rep. CUCS-243-86, 1986.

[13] Pu, C., "Superdatabases: Transactions across database boundaries," *IEEE Data Eng.,* vol. 10, no. 3, Sept. 1987.

[14] Elmagarmid, A. and Y. Leu, "An optimistic concurrency control algorithm for heterogeneous distributed database systems," *IEEE Data Eng.*, vol. 10, no. 3, Sept. 1987.

[15] Alonso, R., H. Garcia-Molina, and K. Salem, "Concurrency control and recovery for global procedures in federated database systems," *IEEE Data Eng.*, vol. 10, no. 3, Sept. 1987.

[16] Breitbart, Y., A. Silberschatz, and G. Thompson, "An update mechanism for multidatabase system," *IEEE Data Eng.*, vol. 10, no. 3, Sept. 1987.

[17] Breitbart, Y. and A. Silberschatz, "Multidatabase update issues," in *Proc. SIGMOD*, 1988.

[18] Gligor, V. and R. Popescu-Zeletin, "Concurrency control issues in distributed heterogeneous database management," in *Distributed Data Sharing Systems*, F. Shreiber, W. Litwin, Eds. North-Holland, 1985.

[19] Elmagarmid, A. and A. Helal, "Supporting updates in heterogeneous distributed database systems," in *Proc. Int. Data Eng. Conf.*, 1988.

[20] Litwin, W. and H. Tirri, "Flexible concurrency control using value date," Reprinted in this book.

Flexible Concurrency Control Using Value Dates

W. LITWIN AND H. TIRRI

Abstract—A new paradigm for concurrency control is proposed based on the concept of a value date. A data value is sure only after its value date and uncertain otherwise. We show that among the family of value date based concurrency control policies, there exists an application semantics independent method which guarantees that transaction executions are serializable, as well as deadlock and livelock free. We also show that without changing the value date paradigm, a scheduler design may take into account specific properties of a class of applications to enhance the efficiency of the concurrent processing within this class. After studying the relationship between value date method and classical methods, we show that locking, timestamp based methods and the time warp mechanism can all be derived from this same concept. Value dates also exhibit an interesting relationship to the concept of commitment as they constitute an implicit commit operation without any special negotiation protocols. All these properties, together with the simplicity of the implementation, make the paradigm attractive, especially for multidatabase management in a distributed environment.

1. INTRODUCTION

AFTER the introduction of the notion of serializability by Eswaran *et al.* [4] database concurrency control has become a widely studied field. There are currently hundreds of algorithms [2] for the concurrency control in databases. Most of the known methods are based on locking [4] or on timestamping [1]. The former methods are sometimes called pessimistic, the latter optimistic[1] according to the mechanism to enforce consistency, i.e., blocking or restarting. In practice, the most widespread of the locking methods is two-phase locking [4], probably due to its simplicity both conceptually and from the implementation point of view. In addition most methods are usually coupled with commitment protocols, i.e., algorithms that guarantee the atomicity property [6] of transactions.

A closer analysis of these algorithms show that they are all based on a common principle of transparency, i.e., each user of the database or the application program should feel as being the single user of the system. Thus the system should be totally transparent with respect to concurrency, and the application program should not be concerned with conflicts which may occur with other users of the database. The current assumption is that when the transaction is executed in a concurrent environment, it should not require any additional logic with the possible exception of lock, unlock, or commit statements. The concurrency control module should handle all the occurring conflicts. At the implementation level a conflict means that at least one of the transactions is forced to wait or alternatively to restart, all in a way invisible to the user.

However, there are various fundamental problems with these principles which make it difficult or impossible to apply them in practical applications such as a large multidatabase system [10], particularly in a distributed environment [11]. In a multidatabase system (e.g., viable for banking or travel business related applications) there typically exist a large set of interconnected databases. It seems that there is no way to find an acceptable method for concurrency control starting from the concept of locking, due to the nature of the method. As the transactions are varying in length (i.e., from seconds to days) it is totally unacceptable to keep data locked for a long period of time, thus blocking the access of many other transactions. Similar observation has already been discussed in [3] in the context of engineering applications (CAD) and recently in [5], where the concept of sagas was introduced. In locking, additional problems are caused by deadlocks, which are very hard to detect and solve in distributed systems.

The other basic mechanism based on timestamps seems to suffer from similar problems; long transactions are bound to be restarted, and the overall effect in the system may well be that very few transactions will ever be finished as a result of continuous restarting. An interesting (and a very little studied) additional feature in a multidatabase environment is the fact that data might be sometimes unavailable, not only because of failures but due to natural causes; for example, a database may only be open during business hours. As far as we know this unavailability aspect of data has not been addressed in any studies of transaction modelling or database concurrency control.

Due to all the reasons discussed above, a new paradigm is needed. In the following we will discuss such a concept, its consequences, and implementation issues. Our underlying fundamental assumption is that the total transparency requirement has to be relaxed in the sense that the transactions (i.e., applications issuing transactions) know that they are operating in a concurrent environment. This idea will be realized by requiring transactions to use value dates, a concept well known in the banking business environment. A value date is the date from which on the value is official, i.e., valid. It is established precisely to let a user know that some concurrent operation is or was going on until this date. An important observation is that it may, and usually does, differ from the actual time of the operation setting up the value. If the value date follows the operation date, the value is considered unsafe in the meantime. For instance, the value date of a check received is usually a day after the actual date of the check processing. The value date may also precede the actual date, meaning that some time was necessary for the concurrent processing that physically has delayed the value definition.

---

[1] There is some confusion in the literature about the term *optimistic*; it is sometimes associated with certification methods such as [8]; sometimes the scope of the term is extended to cover any method that uses restarts to enforce correct executions. Here we adopt the latter view.

Manuscript received January 3, 1989.

This may be useful in some applications, such as interest rate computations.

In this paper we will analyze the concurrency control principles based on value dates. We will introduce a set of rules that a well-formed transaction using value dates has to satisfy. For these safe transactions there exists a value date policy called VDAS which will guarantee that all the concurrent executions are serializable, deadlock, and livelock-free. These properties, together with the simplicity and extensibility of the scheme, make the value date based approach highly promising, both conceptually and pragmatically. In fact we are able to show that classical concepts like locking and timestamp methods can be conceptually derived from our notion of a value date. Through this general relationship the limitations of these classical methods can be more easily understood.

This paper is organized as follows. Section 2 presents the basic concepts, and Section 3 discusses a special class of transactions using value dates that we call safe transactions, and the VDAS policy for them. In Section 4, we discuss different ways to relax the assumptions of safe transactions. The corresponding policies for unsafe transactions may be more efficient, while remaining correct for some particular classes of applications. Section 5 presents a comparison of the value date concept to classical methods, and Section 6 concludes the discussion.

2. BASIC CONCEPTS

In the literature the notion of a transaction is understood as a collection of consistency preserving database operations which realizes a set of queries expressed in a database manipulation language, such as MSQL [11]. We will now proceed by giving rigorous definitions for the concepts needed.

Definition 1. A *transaction* T is an intention leading to manipulation of some data in database(s). The intention is generally formulated in a high-level language, but is represented by a multistatement program with operations of form T:read(D) or T:write(D). In particular, T may consider that some data may sometimes be unavailable for a while, or even during the lifetime of the whole transaction. This may happen even if T is alone in the system. Transaction T may then switch to access some other data. If no choice exists, T may issue a T:undo operation which would restore all the values the transaction has modified to the state they were before T started. It may also ask for a restart later on. We assume that any T:write(D) operation is preceded with T:read(D), so there are no "blind" writes. Notice that, although for simplicity, only read and write operations are considered, no descriptive power is lost as the delete operation corresponds to T:read(D) followed by T:write(Null), while insertion can be described with a sequence T:read(Null) and T:write(D).

How the conformity of program T to its intention is achieved is outside the scope of this paper. As a practical example of a transaction T considering unavailability, one could consider a "rent any car" transaction. This transaction may be required to switch to the Hertz database if the Avis database is shut down for some reason (and vice versa). Note that this notion of unavailability was not considered in the properties of a classical transaction [6]. We consider that an execution where the unavailability of a data entity D due to a conflict triggered an alternative choice in transaction T is correct, provided that the unavailability of D triggers the same choice for T when it is executed alone in the system.

Definition 2. A *conflict* between concurrent transactions T_1 and T_2 occurs when read-sets and write-sets of these transactions intersect. By solving a conflict we mean that after the execution of both T_1 and T_2, the results (both the database state and information acquired by the transactions[2] are correct according to the correctness criteria adopted, e.g., serializability.

There exist numerous canonical examples where a conflict can lead to an undesirable result. Examples of such conflicts are the well-known conflict in two elementary sequences realizing transactions T_1 and T_2 manipulating the same data entity D, i.e., T_1:read(D) T_1:write(D) and T_2:read(D) T_2:write(D). It is obvious that if nothing is assumed about the intentions of the transactions there are cases where the result of the execution

$$T_1: read(D)\ T_2: read(D)\ T_1: write(D)\ T_2: write(D)$$

could wipe out the update by T_1, and the result would be incorrect.

Another well-known problem caused by the conflict is one variant of the phantom problem [4]. If T_1 performs a sum of accounts D_i; $i = 1, 2, \cdots, k$, and T_2 performs a fund transfer of size 1000\$ from D_2 to D_k after T_1:read(D_2), but prior to T_1:read(D_k), then this particular 1000\$ would be summed twice, which obviously is incorrect. To be of general interest the method for concurrency control has to universally address solving all types of conflicts.

Our purpose is to propose a scheme for concurrency control with all the above properties (managing unavailability of data, viable in a distributed multiple linked database environment, long transactions) which is both conceptually simple and easy to implement. In the literature the term "locking method" means in fact a family of different locking policies. Similarly, we also introduce a family of methods, which we call the *value date algorithms (VDA)*. This general method is more in the tradition of timestamp algorithms [1] than locking, but as we will see it provides much more flexibility than either of these methods.

Definition 3. A *value date* V_d is an attribute appended (virtually or physically) to a data entity D subject to an operation by a transaction T. Value date has the semantics of declaring the moment in time after which the value is valid. Hence as long as the actual date A_d is such that $A_d < V_d$, then D is safe for the transaction T only. It may remain unchanged until $A_d = V_d$, but it may change as well, being in particular subject to an undo operation. Given A_d one may define V_d as either $V_d > A_d$, $V_d = A_d$, or even sometimes $V_d < A_d$.

The basic idea in transactions using value dates is that each T receives from the scheduler[3] the pair $(D, V_d(D))$. If the data

[2] If serializability is chosen as the correctness criteria as in Section 3, we adopt the stricter notion of view serializability [13] rather than state serializability [12].

[3] Following the common tradition in concurrency control literature, we call the concurrency control module scheduler.

entity D is safe, transaction T is allowed to manipulate it. If D is unsafe, transaction T is allowed to decide whether it still uses D, switches to an alternative D', or asks the scheduler to solve the conflict. The last alternative means that T asks either a restart later on, or possibly a safe value of D which can be provided by undoing the transaction whose value date is in D. This new freedom allows transactions to enhance their performance and flexibility with respect to all classical schemes. However, due to the power of the mechanism, one must be careful to avoid errors in case of some conflicts, as well as deadlocks, livelocks, etc.

3. SAFE TRANSACTIONS

We will first show that there exists a value date algorithm which works independently of the application semantics. This can be achieved by assuming that all the concurrent transactions respect some basic safety rules, with respect to value dates, and disregard unsafe values. Later on we will present examples of situations where these rules may be gracefully relaxed for specific classes of applications.

Definition 4. A *transaction T is safe* if:

(i) T is of finite execution length.

(ii) T starts with getting from the system some value date $V_d(T)$.

(iii) T disregards all unsafe D's it could get. If needed and possible, T can reissue T:read(D) after $A_d > V_d(D)$, as value of D could have changed in the meantime.

(iv) if D is safe then T validates it with $V_d(T)$ at the first read operation T:read(D). Any further operations from T on D do not change $V_d(D)$, i.e., D keeps $V_d(T)$.

(v) if T is not terminated by $V_d(T)$, then T is undone before A_d is V_d. This means that all the values T has written become as they were before T was started.

We will deal with the rules for choosing a suitable value date $V_d(T)$ later on. Obviously, this date should usually be at least far enough in the future to allow T to terminate in a nonconcurrent environment. We further assume that no two safe transactions can have the same V_d (this can easily be guaranteed). Thus V_d value is also an identifier for a safe transaction.

Definition 5. A transaction is safely undone if no value it has written has been used by another transaction. Such an undo is called safe as well.

Undoing a transaction can have a "domino effect" in an unsafe environment where the values not yet validated have already been used by other transactions. Therefore unsafe undo's should generally be avoided.

3.1. Value Date Algorithm for Safe Transactions (VDAS)

With safe transactions it will be easy to develop a policy that guarantees the widely accepted correctness notion called serializability [4] for any type of applications.

Definition 6. An execution (also called a schedule in the literature) of a transaction set $T = \{T_1, T_2, \cdots, T_n\}$ is *serializable* if, after finishing the execution, all the information used in transactions in the set T and the final database state

is the same as in some serial (one-by-one) execution of the same transaction set.

Notice that according to our model of transaction, in the case of unavailable data, the equivalence of the execution is tested against the behavior of the corresponding transaction when executed alone in the system. Hence, serializability requires that if the transaction is prepared to handle the unavailability, it will do it similarly in both the concurrent execution and in some serial execution.

We will first note that a set of safe transactions behaves well with respect to undoing.

Proposition 1. If all transactions are safe, then any transaction T may be safely undone anytime during its execution.

Proof. T will validate with $V_d(T)$ any data entity D it writes. No $T' \neq T$ will then use a data entity D stamped by T, until $A_d = V_d(T)$. As undo T may occur at most at $V_d(T)$, any undo of transaction T is safe.

Definition 7. *(Value date algorithm for safe transactions (VDAS))* Assume that some transaction T_1 issues T_1:read(D_1) to data D_1 already validated by $T_2 \neq T_1$. If T_1 behaves in the following way

(i) if $A_d \geq V_d(T_2)$ then T_1 obtains D_1.
Otherwise, i.e., if $A_d < V_d(T_2)$ then

(ii) if $V_d(T_1) > V_d(T_2)$, then T_1 is scheduled after the end of T_2 that continues its execution.

(iii) if $V_d(T_2) > V_d(T_1)$ and D_1 unavailability was not considered by the transaction description, then T_1 or T_2 is undone, otherwise

(iv) if D_1 unavailability was covered by the transaction description, then T_1 continues without accessing $\bar{D_1}$,

then T_1 is said to follow VDAS policy.

Theorem 1. All executions of a transaction set T that follow VDAS are serializable.

Proof. Consider that T_1 and T_2 have started concurrently. If their datasets do not intersect, then there is no conflict, and the execution is serializable. If they conflict on a data entity D_1, consider that T_1 access was scheduled to follow T_2, the other case being symmetric. Then, there cannot be a data entity D_2 requested further on concurrently by T_1, and for which the conflict resolution would lead T_1 to precede T_2. Indeed, consider T_1 reading the data entity D_1 validated with $V_d(T_2)$. In the case (i) above there is no conflict, as D_1 value is safe, and so T_2 has already terminated. The only case when T_1 may be scheduled to follow T_2 is case (ii). Consider this case, and that now T_2 reads the data entity D_2 already validated by T_1. But, then $V_d(T_1) > V_d(T_2)$, and so either T_2 or T_1 is undone, unless the unavailability of D_2 was programmed to transaction T_2. In all the cases, T_1 would not be scheduled to precede T_2.

Theorem 1 simply means that VDAS guarantees serializability because of the order imposed by value dates on the termination time of safe transactions. It is easy to see that only the transaction with the later value date may be scheduled to wait until the other terminates. If the other transaction requests access to data already validated by the first one, then either it can continue in presence of unavailability of this data, or one of the two transactions has to (and also can be) safely undone.

Thus the serial order of conflicting operations is always preserved.

It can be easily demonstrated that this simple policy solves the basic conflict types correctly. For example consider the case of our basic conflict, assuming that T_1:read(D) validates D. The operation T_2:read(D) could occur only after T_1:write(D), or one of the read operations would be undone, and so the conflict would be solved. Similarly, in the variant of the phantom problem, T_2 would be unable to execute T_2:read(D_2), as $A_d < V_d(D_2) = V_d(T_1)$ holds. Depending on the relationship between $V_d(T_2)$ and $V_d(T_1)$, this read would be delayed adequately, or either T_2 or T_1 would be undone and restarted later on.

3.2. Deadlock and Livelock Freedom of VDAS

Unlike the timestamping mechanism, VDAS forces transactions sometimes to wait until A_d exceeds the value date V_d of the conflicting data entity (Definition 7 (ii)). However, as opposed to, e.g., two-phase locking, it can be shown that VDAS does not cause a deadlock.

Proposition 2. Transaction set T following VDAS does not deadlock.

Proof. For any two T_1 and T_2 that run concurrently, either $V_d(T_1) > V_d(T_2)$ or vice versa (Definition 4). Consider the first case, the other one being symmetric. Let us assume that D_1 has $V_d(T_1)$ and $D_2 \neq D_1$ has $V_d(T_2)$. If the request T_1:read(D_2) is issued, it is delayed until $A_d \geq V_d(T_2)$. If during this delay the request T_2:read(D_1) is also issued, then T_2 will be undone, unless it has a strategy for D_2 unavailability. In both cases T_1 will terminate and no deadlock occurs. A similar situation would occur for any longer cycle $T_1, T_2, \cdots, T_k, T_1$, with T_1 waiting for T_2, etc., leading to an undo of T_k.

Proposition 3. Consider a safe transaction T_1 following VDAS whose V_d is sufficiently far in its future for T_1 to terminate in the absence of conflicts. There are executions that may successfully terminate any such T_1 in progress in the presence of any number of conflicts.

Proof. By Theorem 1 any T_2 in progress that has validated data T_1 needs can be undone. In such an execution, T_1 neither needs to wait for the successful end of T_2, nor needs to be undone if $V_d(T_1) < V_d(T_2)$.

A normal way to solve a conflict when T_1 requests data with $V_d(T_2)$, while $V_d(T_2) < V_d(T_1)$, is to execute the corresponding request once T_2 terminated. These conflicts may nevertheless delay T_1 enough to make it unable to terminate at $V_d(T_1)$. It could happen any number of times when T_1 restarts, leading in the worst case to a livelock, i.e., the situation where no transaction terminates, since they are undone and restarted all the time. However, Proposition 3 states that fortunately there are executions avoiding this danger. If needed, for instance, after a fixed limit of n restarts, any current transaction may be executed until its end. Note that it is not the case in any execution of safe transactions. For instance, it would not be the case in an execution undoing only T in case of T:read(D) with $V_d(D) > V_d(T)$.

3.3. Further Advantages of VDAS Policy

Serializability, absence of deadlock and of livelock are the most important properties of safe transactions following VDAS. In addition, VDAS has many other properties highly useful for practical applications, such as multidatabases that were discussed in the Introduction.

The proposed scheme is much simpler to implement than many of the schemes proposed in the past. It is likely that it is even easier to implement than the two-phase locking accompanied with some protocol for the deadlock and livelock resolution.

When a transaction T requests for an unsafe D, it basically receives $V_d(D)$. Hence, as opposed to locking methods, it will know how long it should wait and whether it may get a safe value at all before $V_d(T)$, unless the scheduler undoes the other transaction. Transaction T may use this information to enhance its performance. For instance, it may do some processing in the meantime, including access to other "non-blocked" data. It may also avoid to use D at all if the delay is too long, or $V_d(D) > V_d(T)$, and some alternative D' is available. Finally, it may also use this information for trying to convince the scheduler to arbitrate in its favor.

3.4. Examples

Example 1. To show the flexibility of our approach, consider the following examples. Let us assume an interactive transaction T whose goal is to rent a car from one of databases: Avis, Hertz, National, . . . preferably from Avis. In this case transaction T can adopt the following approach:

$$T$$

get $V_d(T)$;
T:read(Avis), if $A_d > V_d(Avis)$, then /* the scheduler puts
   then $V_d(Avis) = V_d(T)$ start to discuss with the
   customer; if the discussion finishes positively at $A_d < V_d(T)$, then
T:write(Avis)
   else if $V_d(Avis) - A_d < 1$ min then wait else read
   (Hertz), etc.

Example 2. Consider a transaction T with the goal to rent a car, and a corresponding hotel H giving a reduced rate to the car rental company. Knowing the value dates, T may rent a car, then try to book a room from hotel H. At that moment T may have several choices:

(i) to simply book the room.
(ii) to wait for some time, if $V_d(H) > A_d$.
(iii) to ask for arbitration, if $V_d(H) > V_d(T)$.

In the last case, the scheduler may undo T or the other transaction T', if T' is just a hotel reservation, i.e., without the associated car rental, or if it is the nth restart of T, etc. In particular, T could also start with the hotel booking in the case of temporary unavailability of the car rental data.

3.5. Estimating Value Dates and Other Implementation Issues

As we have shown above, the value date approach allows various application based solutions to conflicts, enhancing the efficiency of the concurrent processing with respect to the automatic classical approach. Nevertheless, it leaves room for automatic (re)scheduling. In particular, if T_1 finds D with $V_d(D) > A_d$, the difference $V_d(D) - A_d$ is small, and $V_d(D)$

$\preccurlyeq V_d(T_1)$, then the system may by itself decide to put T_1 into the wait state until $A_d \geq V_d(D)$. On the other hand, generally, the decisions to start a transaction and arbitrations are under the scheduler responsibility. An attractive property of the approach is that the scheduler is now able to know in advance the probable length of a transaction. Therefore, there exist possibilities for flexible usage of various priority rules. The scheduler may give the priority to shorter transactions, or may avoid to undo the longest ones when they are close to their end, etc.

We have not yet addressed the problem of finding a suitable value date for the transaction at start time. Obviously, it should be based on the estimation of the transaction length in normal, i.e., nonconcurrent execution. At least for interactive transactions, it will usually be dependent on the semantic of the application, and on human response time. The conflict frequency may have an effect that has to be taken into account, but the processing speed factor should be negligible. For short, batch oriented transactions, the estimation may in contrast also include the estimation of the current system work load, etc.

Value dates may be physically attached to data or they may exist only in dedicated tables of the scheduler. The detailed study of both approaches remains to be done. In particular, one may consider two special value dates, noted Min and Max: Min is assigned to available data found without any V_d; Max is assigned to currently unavailable data without any V_d. As we will show, even with this binary valued scheme, concurrency control can be implemented (which is in fact an exclusive locking policy).

4. RELAXING THE SAFETY CONDITIONS

There are two basic ways to relax VDAS assumptions:

(i) transaction T or the scheduler is allowed to change value dates during the transaction,
(ii) transaction T is allowed to use unsafe values.

Both choices may also be combined and are very attractive in practice. Notice that it is always safe to change $V_d(T)$ before the expiration date once it has been assigned, although this may complicate implementation issues. This alternative may be particularly useful when the length of a transaction may vary greatly. However, in general the correctness of relaxed rules will depend on the application context. The transaction programmer may be aware of the effects that may occur, and may be the best person to define the correct rules. On the other hand, a systematic study of various cases is needed and remains to be done. For the time being and the purpose of discussion, we will illustrate this extended approach only through examples showing enough of its practical flexibility.

Example 3. A bank may wish to keep the amount of a check cashed unsafe for a day, although to process the check takes only minutes. One solution to model this is to define a safe transaction that lasts a day. Another alternative is to define a short safe transaction, but to terminate it in case of check preacceptance by the extension of the value date to the next day. Furthermore, the bank policy may be to add the check amount to the customer account amount only after the value date. But it might be also that the amount of the check should enter the account with the date of the check reception, the delay for verification being the bank's internal affair. A natural solution may be to set back the value date to that date which is the end of the verification delay. In this particular case the value date would then be behind the actual time. It could be useful, for instance, to virtually undo an actual negative balance that appeared in the meantime without the customer's fault. The new condition for the corresponding scheduler is in this case to be able to pass to the transaction the existing value date before the transaction marks its own value date.

Example 4. A transaction may know that some of its results are safe no matter how it terminates, and may wish to make them available as soon as possible. One technique may be to allow the value date for the corresponding data to be advanced with respect to $V_d(T)$. It may be useful for longer transactions. An example of this type of an application is an airline reservation system, since frequently a customer who finished with the reservation may still spend time on noncritical requests about the type of plane, of meal, etc. Similarly, this can also be the situation in engineering databases, where some subdesigns are already stable although the whole design is not.

Example 5. Consider again the transaction T to rent a car and a hotel giving a reduced rate to the car rental company. It may happen that transaction T has rented a car, and tries to book a room from the corresponding hotel H, but $V_d(H) > V_d(T)$. If, nevertheless, the number of free rooms F is large, then there is a very high chance of booking being successful. In this case transaction T may confirm the booking to the user and issue a compensating transaction only for the hotel booking, to be launched at $A_d \geq V_d(H)$.

5. VALUE DATE METHODS VS. CLASSICAL METHODS

Consider the special case of choosing $V_d(T) = Max$ (currently unavailable) for all transactions. Hence, we can construct an exclusive locking policy based on value dates, with a special invoking mechanism that informs a waiting transaction when the data comes available again. Thus algorithms for locking and two-phase locking in particular are special cases of our approach. The deadlock problem with the locking occurs since the deadlocked transactions T_1 and T_2 have, in fact, the same value date that, in addition, is ahead of both transactions. Unlike the safe transactions, the scheduler has therefore *a priori* no information to decide which transaction should be undone. The value date method provides higher flexibility and efficiency than locking since it carries more information for both transactions and the scheduler. Similarly, shared locks are special cases of $V_d(T) = Max$ where the safety rules of the usage of unsafe values are relaxed for some classes of operations, such as retrievals.

Timestamping may also be seen as a particular case where, for all value dates, one has $V_d(T) = A_d$ of the transaction start operation. They are then used to detect conflicts in a similar way than our value dates, but they provide very little flexibility to solve the conflict if one occurs. The value date approach is thus inherently more efficient than the timestamping when conflicts occur. When there are no conflicts, the value date-based schedule works with the same efficiency as the timestamp method. Similar observation holds also for Jefferson's time warp mechanism [7], although the mechanism itself is much more complicated than our approach. Notice also that the certification methods such as in [8] can be derived from value date paradigm as methods that allow unsafe transactions.

A very interesting observation is that the value date may also be considered as a commitment point of the safe transaction as a whole, and also for each manipulated value. The corresponding relationship is interesting, as value dates provide an implicit commit, while the classical notion corresponds to some explicit negotiation protocol. This property seems to make value dates a potentially useful tool for protection against failures (this was one of its initial intentions in banking). As the commit point may be implicit and set up to an arbitrary future date, our paradigm should be especially useful for distributed environments. The method is in particular a solution for those contexts when classical commitment protocols are clearly inapplicable, e.g., when a single update concerns very many databases (20–100) which, in addition, are geographically distributed (see Example 6). In this case the unreliability of both the data communication links and systems themselves does not in practice allow for an atomic update for all the databases simultaneously, as, due to the high probability of failures, some of the databases are bound to be unavailable at any particular moment. Value data may then be a unique vehicle for both concurrency control and online or delayed commitment, guaranteeing the overall consistency at a given date.

Example 6. Consider a safe transaction T that performs a multidatabase update U on some set B of distributed databases. The databases are expected to be mutually consistent only by the date $V_d(U)$ associated with U. The choosing of V_d may take into account the number of sites involved, their opening hours, type of the net, etc. The date may then be chosen far enough to make reasonably certain that all sites finished the operation, or an appropriate compensating action could be done. The update may be safely incorporated into each B_i because of the existence of $V_d(U)$, unlike in the classical approach, where it has to be kept until the commit outside B_i (note the simplification of the corresponding processing). A number of efficient strategies to guarantee the consistency appear for consideration, depending on the expected reliability of the communication system, the number of databases involved, etc.:

(i) An update of B becomes valid by default, i.e., unless a message invalidates it or increases value date V_d.

(ii) Vice versa, an update is undone at V_d unless a message confirms it prior to V_d or increases V_d.

(iii) Each site confirms the reception of the update by a message sent upon the reception (or upon the demand of the source site), like in a two-phase commit protocol.

It is likely that the first strategy will be the most popular for multidatabases with large numbers of databases. Notice also that values of V_d's may be chosen to be different from site to site.

6. CONCLUSIONS

Value dates are a new paradigm that are proposed for concurrency control problems. We have shown that the concept leads to important practical advantages, with the simplicity of the basic scheme competing with that of two-phase locking. The usage of the concept is furthermore highly flexible through the possibility of manipulating value dates and uncertain values by the transaction itself. The corresponding knowledge of the semantics of transactions may therefore be incorporated into a concurrency control scheme. In many practical situations it then allows enhancing the degree of concurrency with respect to the classical application independent methods.

Further research should concern, on the one hand, experiments with value date based schemes in practical environments (e.g., multidatabases), and on the other hand, more detailed quantitative comparison between VDAS and other basic methods which is needed. Furthermore, many useful schemes with relaxed safety rules, but correct for particular classes of applications, remain to be specified and analyzed. Any scheme in tradition of the classic methods where one replaces $V_d = Max$ with a finite V_d and eventually provides access to uncertain values, could be an interesting starting point.

REFERENCES

[1] Bernstein, P. and N. Goodman, "Concurrency control in distributed database systems," *ACM Computing Surveys,* vol. 13, no. 2, 1981, pp. 185–221.

[2] Bernstein, P., V. Hadzilacos, and N. Goodman, *Concurrency Control and Recovery in Database Systems.* Addison-Wesley, 1987.

[3] Banchilhon, F., W. Kim, and H. Korth, "A model of CAD transactions," *Proc. 11th Int. Conf. Very Large Databases,* 1985, pp. 25–33.

[4] Eswaran, K., J. Gray, R. Lorie, and T. Traiger, "The notion of consistency and predicate locks in a database system," *Commun. ACM,* vol. 19, no. 11, 1976, pp. 624–633.

[5] Garcia-Molina, H. and K. Salem, "Sagas," *Proc. ACM Conf. Management of Data,* 1987, pp. 249–259.

[6] Gray, J., "A transaction model," IBM Res. Rep. RJ2895, IBM Research Laboratory, San Jose, CA, 1980.

[7] Jefferson, D. and A. Motro, "The time warp mechanism for database concurrency control," *Proc. IEEE Int. Conf. Data Eng.,* 1986, pp. 474–481.

[8] Kung, H. and J. Robinson, "On optimistic methods for concurrency control," *ACM Trans. Database Systs,* vol. 6, no. 2, 1981, pp. 213–226.

[9] Litwin, W., A. Abdellatif, A. Zeroual, B. Nicolas, and P. Vigier, "MSQL: A multidatabase language," *Information Sci.,* vol. 48, no. 2, July 1989.

[10] Litwin, W. and A. Abdellatif, "Multidatabase interoperability," *IEEE Computer,* vol. 19, no. 12, 1986, pp. 10–18.

[11] Litwin, W. and A. Zeroual, "Advances in multidatabase systems," *European Conf. Telecommun.* EUTECO'88, R. Speth, Ed. 1988, pp. 1137–1152.

[12] Papadimitriou, C., "The serializability of concurrent database updates," *J. ACM,* vol. 26, no. 4, 1979, pp. 631–653.

[13] Yannakakis, M., "Issues of correctness in database concurrency control by locking," in *13th ACM Symp. Theory of Computing,* 1981, pp. 363–367.

Superdatabases
for Composition of Heterogeneous Databases

Calton Pu

Department of Computer Science
Columbia University

Abstract

Superdatabases are designed to compose and extend databases. In particular, superdatabases allow consistent update across heterogeneous databases. The key idea of superdatabase is hierarhical composition of element databases. For global crash recovery, each element database must provide local recovery plus some kind of agreement protocol, such as two-phase commit. For global concurrency control, each element database must have local synchronization with an explicit serial order, such as two-phase locking, timestamps, or optimistic methods. Given element databases satisfying the above requirements, the superdatabase can certify the serializability of global transactions through a concatenation of local serial order. Combined with previous work on heterogeneous databases, including unified query languages and view integration, now we can build heterogeneous databases which are consistent, adaptable, and extensible by construction.

1 Introduction

For both efficiency and extensibility, integrated and consistent access to a set of heterogeneous databases is desirable. However, current commercial databases running on mainframes are, by and large, centralized systems. Physical distribution of data in distributed homogeneous databases has been demonstrated in several systems, such as R* [15] and INGRESS/STAR [18]. Nevertheless, the research on integrated heterogeneous databases has been limited to query-only systems.

Good examples of heterogeneous database research on unifying query languages and data view integration are MULTIBASE and MERMAID. MULTIBASE [5,13] is a retrieve-only system, developed at the Computer Corporation of America. Through the functional language DAPLEX, MULTIBASE provides uniform access to heterogeneous and distributed databases. The prototype implemented at CCA supports a CODASYL database and a hierarchical database. The focus of MULTIBASE is on query optimization and reconciliation of data, and consistent updates across databases were not part of their goals. More seriously, no global concurrency control was employed in the retrievals, so inconsistent data (from the global point of view) may be obtained in a query.

MERMAID [3,25] is also a retrieve-only system, but developed at the System Development Corporation (now part of UNISYS). Unlike MULTIBASE, MERMAID supports the relational view of data directly, through a query language, the ARIEL, which is a superset of SQL and QUEL. Another project providing a common query language to access databases using different data models is SIRIUS-DELTA [8].

In contrast to the relative success of research on query processing and optimization over heterogeneous databases, few results have been reported on consistent *update* across heterogeneous databases. To the best of our knowledge, only one paper [10] has discussed the properties of concurrency control mechanisms in heterogeneous database systems.

Our answer to this challenge is the building of *superdatabases*. Unlike earlier works on uniform query access through a single language, our emphasis is on consistent update across heterogeneous databases. A superdatabase is conceptually a hierarchical composition of element databases, which may be centralized, distributed, or other superdatabases.

Update support in homogeneous databases relies on two sets of fundamental techniques: concurrency control and crash recovery. We propose the construction of a superdatabase through hierarchical composition of concurrency control and crash recovery. Many years of research on nested transactions [16,19,22,27] have produced several particular ways to implement nested transactions organized into a hierarchy. Systematic use of hierarchical composition has been used to derive the design and implementation of a nested transaction mechanism in the Eden system [21]. Work reported here applies hierarchical composition to general databases.

In Section 2 we summarize the general architecture of superdatabases. In Section 3 we describe some sufficient conditions to make element databases composable. In Section 4, we explain the design of a superdatabase capable of gluing the element databases together. Section 5 sketches an implementation plan. In Section 6 we summarize related work on many different aspects of heterogeneous databases, comparing and constrasting them with ours. Finally, Section 7 concludes the paper.

2 Hierarchical Composition

2.1 General Structure

The superdatabase composes element databases hierarchically. In figure 1, DB_j (the leaves) represent different element databases glued together by superdatabases (the internal nodes). A transaction spanning several element databases is called a *supertransaction*. When participating in a supertransaction, the local transaction on each element database is called a subtransaction. For simplicity of presentation, we assume that there is only one subtransaction per element database for each supertransaction. Although this is a standard assumption [10], there are cases (e.g. element databases running strict two-phase locking) in which this assumption is not necessary.

Reprinted from *IEEE 1988 Data Engineering Conference,* pp. 548–555, 1988.

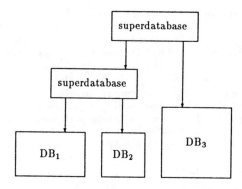

Figure 1: The Structure of Superdatabases

The main reason for the tree-structured organization is to minimize amount of data transfer, both in terms of message size and quantity. Since we will show in section 5.2 that we only need to piggyback a small amount of information on messages already required for distributed commit protocols, this goal has been achieved. Research to distribute the functions of superdatabase is outlined in section 5.4.

We divide this hierarchical composition into two parts. In section 2.2, we summarize the conditions an element database must satisfy, so the superdatabase can handle it. These conditions are described in further detail in section 3. In section 2.3, we outline the design ideas of the superdatabase to connect composable element databases. The design is detailed in section 4.

2.2 Composable Element Databases

An element database is said to be *composable* if it satisfies two requirements. The first is on crash recovery: the element database must understand some kind of agreement protocol, for example, two-phase commit. As we will see in section 4.1, this necessary requirement is a consequence of distributed control, not heterogeneity.

The second requirement is on concurrency control: the element database must present an explicit serial ordering of its local transactions. This may seem a serious requirement, demanding extensive modifications on the concurrency control mechanisms on the element databases. Actually, as we will see in section 3.3, all major concurrency control methods (two-phase locking, timestamps, and optimistic concurrency control) provide an easy way to capture the serial order they impose on the transactions. Furthermore, since any agreement protocol implies communication between participants, passing the explicit serial order of subtransactions (local to each element database) may piggyback on these messages, reducing the performance impact of the second requirement.

For consistent updates, these two are the only requirements we make on the element databases. An element database may be centralized, distributed, or as we shall see, another superdatabase. Unfortunately, in practice most centralized databases do not support any kind of agreement protocol. Similarly, most distributed databases do not supply the transaction serial order. Consequently, our results cannot be applied directly to existing databases without modification. Nevertheless, we believe that these relatively mild requirements, once identified, can be feasibly incorporated into current and future database systems. The pay-off is significant: extensibility and accommodation of heterogeneity.

2.3 The Superdatabase Glue

We have three design goals for the superdatabase that glue the composable element databases together. The main function of the superdatabase is to support consistent update across heterogeneous element databases.

1. Composition of element databases with many kinds of crash recovery methods.

2. Composition of element databases with many kinds of concurrency control techniques.

3. Recursive composibility; i.e. the superdatabase must satisfy the requirements of an element database.

The realization that we need only an agreement protocol for crash recovery made the first goal easy. The key idea that achieved the second goal is to use the explicit serial ordering of transactions, the common denominator of best known concurrency control methods. The third goal was accomplished through careful design of the agreement protocol and explicit passing of the serial order.

The superdatabse itself does not contain data, which are stored in the element databases. However, it does have to maintain the information to recover from crashes and serialize supertransactions. In Section 4.1, we describe the log management to guard the structure of the supertransaction against crashes. For concurrency control, we describe in section 4.4 the certification of serial order of each subtransaction involved in a supertransaction.

3 Composibility Conditions

3.1 Declarative Interface for Superdatabase

Since the superdatabase is a general-purpose glue to connect element databases of different construction, the interface to the superdatabase must be declarative and independent of particular implementation methods. It should specify what is needed, instead of what to do. The two requirements on the interface are that it should be simple enough to minimize adaptation effort on existing database systems, and general enough to allow composition of heterogeneous databases.

Currently, we use the following tentative interface, divided into two groups, the *Transaction* group and the *Resource* group.

- BeginTransaction(in: ParentID, out: TID)

- CommitTransaction(in: TID)

- AbortTransaction(in: TID)

- OpenResource(in: TID, ... other parameters ...)

- CloseResource(in: TID, ... other parameters ...)

The Transaction declarations bracket the extent of the transaction, which starts at BeginTransaction, and ends in CommitTransaction or AbortTransaction depending on the outcome of the transaction. These declarations are standard except for the ParentID parameter in BeginTransaction to allow run-time composition.

The Resource declarations correspond to the first and last access of a specific resource, defined as a portion of the database. These declarations are redundant, in that the information in them usually can be deduced from a mechanical analysis of the program. We make these declaration explicit for two reasons. First, we can avoid mentioning actions specific to particular concurrency control methods, for example, lock and unlock. Second, declarations bracketing the resource access seem to be sufficient for the implementation of superdatabase. Since these declarations may be generated by a pre-processor on the transaction program, we can preserve the compatibility of the superdatabase with the application programs.

3.2 Distributed Transaction Commit and Recovery

The usual model of a distributed transaction contains a coordinator and a set of subtransactions. Each subtransaction maintains its local undo/redo information. At transaction commit time, the coordinator organizes some kind of agreement with subtransactions to reach a uniform decision. The two-phase commit protocol is the most commonly used because of its low message overhead. In phase one, the coordinator sends the message "prepare to commit" to the subtransactions, and these vote "yes" or "no". If all votes are "yes", the coordinator enters the phase two, sending the message "committed" to all subtransactions. Otherwise the coordinator decides to abort and sends "aborted" to all subtransactions.

The distributed database system R* [15] provides a tree-structured computation, which refines the above flat coordinator/subtransactions model. Subtransactions in R* are organized in a hierarchy, and the two-phase commit protocol is extended to the tree structure. At each level, the parent transaction serves as the coordinator. During phase one, the root sends the message "prepare to commit" to its children. The message is propagated down the tree, until a leaf subtransaction is reached, when it responds with its vote. At each level, the parent collects the votes; if all its own children voted "yes", then it sends "yes" to the grand-parent. If every subtransaction voted "yes", the root decides to commit and sends the "committed" message, propagated down the tree. Between the sending of its vote and the decision by the root, each child subtransaction remains in the *prepared* state, ready to either undo the transaction if aborted, and to redo the transaction if the child crashed and the root decided to commit.

Since heterogeneous databases are distributed by nature, it is necessary that each element database maintains the undo/redo information locally. Since the superdatabase stores only the global information, it has to rely on element databases for local recovery. In addition, it is necessary that each element database understands some kind of agreement protocol, such as the two-phase commit outlined above, three-phase commit, and the various flavors of Byzantine agreements. The following simple example demonstrates that the need for agreement comes from distribution, not heterogeneity.

Consider a distributed transaction T with two subtransactions, T_1 and T_2. Suppose that T commits if and only if both T_1 and T_2 commits, and that there is no agreement protocol between T_1 and T_2 at commit time. Therefore, one of them will decide to commit before the other. As soon as the first one decides to commit, the other crashes, aborting. Consequently, T cannot commit, since one subtransaction aborted. However, T cannot abort either, since the other subtransaction committed. Having shown the necessity of agreement protocol for distributed databases, including the heterogeneous ones, we proceed to compose different concurrency control methods.

3.3 Explicit Serialization for Concurrency Control

We assume the element databases maintain serializability of local transactions. The question is whether the superdatabase can maintain global serializability given local serializability. The answer is yes, if the superdatabase certifies that all local serial orders are compatible in a global serial order. One way to implement the

superdatabase certification is to require that each element database provide the ordering of its local transactions to the superdatabase. Please note that this assumption provides a sufficient condition for composition of heterogeneous databases, but it is not necessary, since implicit serialization is possible under restricted circumstances (section 5.3). The serial order of each local transaction is represented by an *order-element*, or O-element for short. In Section 4, we shall describe the composition of O-elements for certification. Here, we only discuss how the concurrency control methods produce the O-elements.

First, we consider element databases with two-phase locking concurrency control. Locking says that a lock on a resource must be acquired before it may be accessed. Transactions using two-phase locking acquire all locks in a growing phase, and then release them during a shrink phase, in which no additional locks may be acquired. Eswaran et al. [7] showed that two-phase locking guarantees serializability of transactions because $SHRINK(T_i)$, the timestamp of transaction T_i's lock point, indicates T_i's place in the serialization. We take advantage of this fact and designate $SHRINK(T_i)$ as the O-element for element databases with two-phase locking.

The second most popular concurrency control method uses timestamps for serialization. Since transactions serialized by timestamps have their serialization order explicitly represented in their timestamps, these serve well as O-elements. Timestamp intervals [1] or multidimensional timestamps [14] can be passed as O-elements as well. The important thing is to capture the serialization order of committed local transactions.

As another alternative, optimistic concurrency control methods also provide an explicit serialization order. Kung and Robinson [11] assign a serial transaction number after the write phase, which can be used directly as O-element. Ceri and Owicki [4] proposed a distributed algorithm in which a two-phase commit follows a successful validation. Taking a timestamp from a Lamport-style global clock [12] at that moment will capture the serial order of transactions. Since the write phase has yet to start, all following transactions will have a later timestamp. Similarly, all preceding transactions must have obtained their timestamps before the validation phase has ended.

There is no constraint on the format of the O-element. Each element database may have its own representation. We only require that two O-elements from the same element database be comparable, and that this comparison recover the serialization guaranteed by local concurrency control methods. More formally, let the serialization produced by the concurrency control method be represented by the binary relation *precede* (denoted by $\leq$). We require that O-element$(T_1) \leq$ O-element(T_2) if $T_1 \leq T_2$ in the local serialization.

If an element database is centralized, its O-element can be easily obtained as described above. If an element database is distributed in nature, the timestamp will have to come from a global clock to assure total ordering. Ceri and Owicki's distributed optimistic algorithm is an example.

4 Algorithms Used in Superdatabase Design

Having established the composibility conditions in the previous section, now we proceed to use them in the superdatabase. For crash recovery, we describe a hierarchical commit protocol and its use in the recovery of supertransactions. For concurrency control, we describe a hierarchical certification algorithm that guarantees serializability given the O-vectors.

152

4.1 Hierarchical Commit

Given that some form of agreement is necessary (section 3.2), the question is whether it is sufficient for hierarchical commit. In R*, two-phase commit implements hierarchical commit. Since the only function of two-phase commit protocol is to reach agreement, and no recovery information is involved, we conclude that any agreement protocol will do. Examples we have mentioned in section 3.2 include three-phase commit and Byzantine agreements. All these agreement protocols have a natural extension to tree-structured computations. The important thing is that for each element database, the superdatabase must understand and use the appropriate protocol. If all element databases use the same protocol, the superdatabase has the obvious role in the hierarchical protocol. Interesting cases arise when element databases support different kinds of agreement protocols. In the discussion below, references on the Byzantine agreements can be found in the several PODC Proceedings; the other protocols are described in the recent book by Bernstein et al. [2].)

To simplify the discussion, we divide the distributed agreement protocols into two groups: symmetric and asymmetric. Symmetric protocols such as Byzantine agreements and decentralized two-phase commit give all participants equal role. In asymmetric protocols, a distinguished coordinator decides the outcome based on information supplied by other participants. For example, in the centralized and linear two-phase commit, as well as the three-phase commit, a coordinator initiates the protocol and decides whether the transaction commits or aborts.

If an element database supports an asymmetric agreement protocol, the superdatabase assumes the role of coordinator with respect to that element database. Notice that the superdatabase may have to act as the coordinator for different protocols. Compared to symmetric protocols, this situation is relatively simple since no information needs to be sent to the participants except for the final decision.

If some element databases employ symmetric protocols, in order to reach agreement each participant needs to send more information to all the others. We have two choices for the superdatabase. First, it can simulate the protocol by translating the information received from "asymmetric" element databases and retransmitting it to the "symmetric" participants. This method makes it easy to prove the correctness of the combined algorithm, but sends unnecessary messages without additional crash resiliency. Second, the superdatabase may act as a *representative* of the "asymmetric" participants, sending the result of the asymmetric protocols in one round of messages. The second method decreases the number of messages, but may increase the response time slightly. These two choices exist also for the communication between "symmetric" participants using different protocols.

In summary, the superdatabase functions both as a coordinator for the asymmetric agreement protocols and as a translator for the symmetric protocols. It collects sufficient information for supertransaction commit, and provides enough information for participants using symmetric protocols to reach their own conclusion that matches the superdatabase's.

4.2 Superdatabase Recovery

Since the superdatabase is the coordinator for the element databases during commit, it must record the transaction on stable storage. Otherwise, a crash during the window of vulnerability would hold resources in the element databases indefinitely.

Of the known recovery methods, logging is the best for superdatabase recovery. Since no before-images or after-images need to be saved, versions are of little utility. Conceptually, the superdatabase log is separate from the element database logs, just as the superdatabase itself. In actual implementation, the superdatabase log may be physically interleaved with an element database log, as long as the recovery algorithms can separate them later.

For each transaction, the superdatabase saves the following information on the log:

- Participant subtransactions.

- Parent superdatabase, if any.

- Transaction state (prepared, committed, or aborted).

The superdatabase should remember the participant subtransactions because the transaction does not necessarily abort when the superdatabase crashes. Suppose that the superdatabase crashes, but is brought back online quickly, before its subtransactions have finished. Since the superdatabase performs no computation, the supertransaction may still commit. To carry out two-phase commit after such glitches, the participant subtransactions should be remembered in the log, which is read at restart to reconstruct the superdatabase state before the crash.

The transaction state is written to the log during the agreement protocol. If a transaction was in the active state when the superdatabase crashed, the superdatabase simply waits for (re)transmission of two-phase comm't from the parent. In case it is the root, it (re)starts the two-phase commit. If a transaction was in the prepared state when the superdatabase crashed, the superdatabase inquires the parent about the outcome of the transaction. If the transaction has been committed, the results are retransmitted to the subtransactions.

4.3 Concurrency Control: An Example

Consider the following example, in which subtransactions $T_{1.1}$ and $T_{1.2}$ run on element databases DB_1 and DB_2, respectively.

```
BeginTransaction(Top-level, T_1)
    cobegin
DB_1.BeginTransaction(T_1, T_1.1) ... actions ... CommitTransaction(T_1.1)
DB_2.BeginTransaction(T_1, T_1.2) ... actions ... CommitTransaction(T_1.2)
    coend
CommitTransaction
```

If both DB_1 and DB_2 use *strict* two-phase locking, we have no problem. Since no lock will be released before the commit time, the lock point for all data access in the supertransaction happens when the supertransaction commits at phase two of two-phase commit. Consequently, the supertransaction is two-phase and the superdatabase needs to take no action for concurrency control.

However, if locks may be released before commit agreement, then in the above example $T_{1.1}$ may start releasing locks while $T_{1.2}$ has not reached its lock point. Consequently, the supertransaction T_1 may lose its two-phase property and become non-serializable. Although there are other reasons to avoid early lock releases such as cascading of aborts, this case reveals the crucial problem in hierarchical composition of two-phase locking mechanisms: we need to synchronize the lock points of the participating subtransactions. If element databases use strict two-phase locking, the synchronization comes for free at commit time. Otherwise, an explicit synchronization is necessary, which may be pessimistic or optimistic. In the pessimistic case, unlock requests in the element databases are blocked. It is only after all subtransactions have reached their lock points, indicated by a commit vote or an unlock request, that the superdatabase allows the element database to proceed.

Alternatively, the synchronization may be optimistic. The subtransactions may be allowed to run independently, without preventive synchronization. Since two-phase locking provides dynamic atomicity [26], the subtransactions from two different supertransactions may interleave in a non-serializable manner. To check the serializability of all subtransactions, we use the explicit serialization order of two-phase locking, captured by the O-elements.

4.4 Hierarchical Certification with O-vectors

The main problem that the superdatabase has to detect is when subtransactions from different element databases were serialized in different ways. In our example, this happens when a second transaction T_2 with the same subtransactions produces the ordering: O-element$(T_{1.1}) \leq$ O-element$(T_{2.1})$ and O-element$(T_{2.2}) \leq$ O-element$(T_{1.2})$.

To prevent this kind of disagreement from happening, we define an order-vector (O-vector) as the concatenation of all O-elements of the supertransaction. In the example, O-vector(T_1) is (O-element$(T_{1.1})$, O-element$(T_{1.2})$). The order induced on O-vectors by the O-elements is defined strictly: O-vector$(T_1) \leq$ O-vector(T_2) if and only if for all element database j, O-element$(T_{1.j}) \leq$ O-element$(T_{2.j})$. If a supertransaction is not running on all element databases, we use a wild-card O-element, denoted by $*$ (star), to fill in for the missing element databases. Since its order does not matter, by definition, O-element(any) $\leq *$, and, $* \leq$ O-element(any).

From this definition, if O-vector$(T_1) \leq$ O-vector(T_2) then all subtransactions are serialized in the same order, ordering the supertransactions. Therefore, we can serialize the supertransactions by checking the O-elements of a committing supertransaction against the history of all committed supertransactions. If the new O-vector can find a place in the total order, it may commit.

The comparison with all committed supertransactions may be expensive, both in terms of storage and processing. Fortunately, it is not necessary to compare the O-vector with all committed supertransactions. Since a transaction trying to commit cannot be serialized in the ancient history, it is sufficient to certify the transaction with a reasonably "recent history" of committed supertransactions.

The part of the serialization history we have to look at is limited by the oldest active transaction in each element database. Suppose we are certifying an O-vector whose subtransactions are older than the currently oldest active transaction on all element databases. Comparing this O-vector to the history of all committed supertransactions, we may not be able to certify this O-vector because of some other older transaction, in which case it must be aborted. Alternatively, we may find a place in the serialization history for the O-vector. Once we find such an O-vector(T_0) preceding all active subtransactions, it must precede the O-vectors of all serializable supertransactions that have yet to commit.

The above claim follows from the observation that any subsequent O-vector must have one component preceded by the corresponding component in T_0. (The component that was active when T_0 was certified.) Consequently, either the new O-vector cannot be serialzed with respect to T_0 and is aborted, or all its components are preceded by T_0, QED. From this claim, in the certification process we need only to compare the new O-vector with T_0 and O-vectors more recent than T_0. Therefore, the O-vectors preceding T_0 are not necessary and can be released.

From the composition point of view, the key observation is that the certification based on O-vectors is independent of particular concurrency control methods used by the element databases. Therefore, a superdatabase can combine two-phase locking, timestamps, and optimistic concurrency control methods in any way. As long as we can make the serialization in element databases explicit, the superdatabase can certify the serializability of supertransactions.

More importantly, the certification gives the superdatabase itself an explicit serial order (the O-vector) allowing it to be recursively composed as an element database. Thus we have found a way to hierarchically compose database concurrency control, maintaining serializability at each level.

The certification method is optimistic, in the sense that it allows the element databases to run to completion and then certifies the serial ordering. In particular, the O-vector is constructed only after the subtransactions have committed. Since some concurrency control techniques (such as time-interval based and optimistic) decide the transaction ordering only at the transaction commit time, it is difficult for the superdatabase to impose an ordering during subtransaction execution. In other words, the superdatabase has to be as optimistic as its element databases.

5 Implementation and Performance

5.1 Superdatabase

Although in principle a superdatabase must check the serializability of all subtransactions, there are important cases that permit some optimization. As we have observed in section 4.3, if all element databases use strict two-phase locking, the lock points of the subtransactions are synchronized by the agreement protocol, and no certification will be necessary. However, the certification algorithm should be used if simple two-phase locking, timestamps, or optimistic concurrency control is introduced into the superdatabase.

In crash recovery, since in practice all distributed databases use two-phase commit, the introduction of more sophisticated agreement protocols into the superdatabase will await their use in the element database first.

Currently, several groups of students are implementing parts (query translation and execution, concurrency control and storage management) of an element database and a prototype superdatabase. Another prototype based on the Camelot transaction system [24] is under way. Camelot runs on top of Mach, a Berkeley/Unix-compatible operating system. Transaction functions supported by Camelot include a full nested transactions mechanism, fast and reliable logging, and many utility packages.

Taking advantage of Camelot's Unix compatibility, we intend to adopt existing distributed databases running on Unix, for example, the public domain INGRES. In this case, we need to add both O-element passing and two-phase commit. Another candidate element database is the one mentioned above being implemented by project students on top of the Synthesis operating system [20].

5.2 Run-Time Cost

We have argued in Section 4.4 that the certification process is limited to the recent history of committed supertransactions. Since the certification occurs in a central location (the superdatabase), and is limited by the recent history, the message overhead is small. Postponing the question of distributing superdatabase to the next section, we turn our attention to possible sources of delay in the element databases or communications.

In the element databases, we require only that the serial order of transactions be made explicit. With some concurrency control methods, such as timestamps, this is trivial. If the element database is centralized, then the cost of taking a timestamp is also low. However, if the element database is a distributed database with internal concurrency control, then a global clock will be necessary to capture the serial order. Fortunately, the maintenance of a global clock is independent of the number of transactions, and therefore can be amortized.

Finally, the additional piece of information that the superdatabase requires from the element databases is the O-element. Since we have demonstrated the necessity of an agreement protocol for recovery purposes, at least one message must be exchanged between the superdatabase and each element database at commit time. The certification occurs only at commit time, so the subtransaction serial order information can piggyback on the commit vote message. Therefore, the superdatabase does not introduce any extra message overhead during transaction processing.

5.3 Transaction Concurrency

The superdatabase design using O-vectors in section 4 is minimal in the sense that it receives only the explicit serialization order from the element databases. Consequently, supertransactions that are in reality unrelated, but apparently conflict due to their serialization order, will be aborted.

Fortunately we have found methods to increase concurrency in the superdatabase by taking into account the particular information provided by each concurrency control method. Two examples are two-phase locking and timestamps.

In the first place, element databases using strict two-phase locking do not have to participate in the certification. Since they hold their locks, and their lock points are synchronized by the hierarchical commit protocol, they are serialized with respect to each other and all other component transactions. This observation applies even to the minimal design.

Second, we can avoid unnecessary aborts involving element databases using general two-phase locking concurrency control. All it takes is an agreement protocol to synchronize the lock point of participating component transactions. If a supertransaction has several component transactions under general two-phase locking, it could use two-phase agreement once to synchronize the lock points, and a second time to commit the supertransaction. However, we have to be careful and take into account the ordering of these component transactions with respect to other component transactions synchronized through different concurrency control methods.

Third, timestamp-based element databases could provide the superdatabase with additional information. For example, time-interval based concurrency control methods would allow the superdatabase to serialize some transactions that would have been aborted in the minimal design.

Finally, we observe that serializability is itself more restrictive than optimal scheduling. We use serializability as the best trade-off in overhead and number of transactions unnecessarily aborted. Similarly, in the design of supertransactions, we strive for a good trade-off between run-time overhead and the additional restriction on concurrency.

5.4 Symmetric Distribution

As we have seen in previous sections, hierarchical organization of superdatabases results in low message overhead. However, the main disadvantage of the hierarchical structure is its centralized organization. Shutting down any of the internal nodes will isolate part of the tree. More concretely, if any node running a superdatabase crashes, all element databases connected to that superdatabase will remain inaccessible.

We are investigating two research directions to distribute the functions of superdatabase, which consists of participation in agreement protocols for recovery and serialization certification for concurrency control. On the recovery side, any node can assume the different roles in different agreement protocols, so distributing crash recovery seems relatively straightforward. The situation is more complicated for concurrency control.

First, we can replicate the superdatabase nodes, resulting in higher message overhead to keep the replicas consistent. Simple replication comes close to being the "brute force" method to distributed functions in a distributed system. In principle, just about any program or data can be distributed this way, provided that they are kept consistent. Unfortunately, consistent replication is expensive and this approach then loses the low-overhead advantage of hierarchical superdatabase.

Second, we can circulate the concurrency control certification information among several sites. This approach is similar to the work by Ceri and Owicki [4] in distributing the optimistic concurrency control certification algorithm. Again, higher message overhead will be necessary. Perhaps the hierarchical organization with low overhead functions best under normal situations, and a distributed algorithm should be added if more fault-tolerance is desired in the heterogeneous database.

6 Comparisons

6.1 Crash Recovery

The hierarchical commit algorithm described in section 4.1 is a direct descendent of distributed commit protocols such as R* [15] and commit protocols for nested transactions [21]. Our conclusion is that heterogeneity does not introduce additional difficulty, compared to homogeneous distributed databases.

Gligor and Luckenbaugh [9] have described the recovery problem in heterogeneous databases. Using a terminlogy based on two-phase commit protocol, they suggested that the prepared state may be necessary for any recovery algorithm. Since we know that the window of vulnerability always exists in distributed commit, and that the prepared state of two-phase commit corresponds to the window of vulnerability, we have confirmed their conjecture. In addition, our work shows that any agreement protocol will do, not just two-phase commit.

6.2 Concurrency Control

Gligor and Popescu-Zeletin [10] studied concurrency control in heterogeneous databases with emphasis on deadlock detection. Through an example, they showed that there exist some deadlocks which escape hierarchical distributed deadlock detection algorithms. Consequently, either we employ some deadlock avoidance mechanism such as time-outs, or we must pass local dependency information to global deadlock detection algorithms. They also specified five conditions which should be satisfied by any concurrency control mechanisms for heterogeneous databases.

Their first condition says that all local concurrency control (of component databases) must provide local synchronization atomicity. We also make this assumption. Their second condition says that all local concurrency control must preserve the relative order of execution determined by the global transaction manager. This corresponds to a pessimistic approach. In contrast, the superdatabase certifies the serializability after the execution in an optimistic manner. Their third condition says that each site can run only one subtransaction. Although we also make this assumption for simplicity, we are working to relax this restriction. Their fourth condition says that the global transaction manager must be able to identify objects referenced by all subtransactions. Using explicit serialization order in O-elements, we have eliminated the need to check object references. Finally, their fifth condition refers to global deadlock detection. Deadlocks remain a problem for further research.

Elmagarmid and Leu [6] have studied the use of a centralized optimistic concurrency control to validate each subtransaction based on its readset and writeset. Readset and writeset of subtransactions are sent to the Global Data Manager for validation at global transaction commit. Their approach allows more concurrency between transactions since their validation is sophisticated. In compensation, the superdatabase requires a much smaller amount of data transfer for concurrency control and the work necessary for validation is simple.

6.3 Partial Integration

In contrast to our "strongly consistent" database composition, significant work has been done based on weaker consistency constraints. Two examples of this approach are MRDSM [17] and ADMS± [23]. Being developed at INRIA, the prototype multi-database system MRDSM provides a relational interface to independent databases. Instead of global schemas, special "dependency schemas" define interdatabase relationships. Since they avoid integration by design, no consistent updates are included in MRDSM.

ADMS± takes advantage of current hardware advances to integrate a mainframe database (ADMS+) with workstation databases (ADMS−) downloaded from the mainframe. Since each user typically uses only a portion of the database, local queries on ADMS− data are very efficient. Updates occur only on ADMS+ and they are incrementally propagated to ADMS− databases offline. In summary, ADMS± can be seen as a systematic decomposition of a centralized database.

6.4 Other Issues

Deadlock detection is non-trivial for a hierarchical approach. Simple examples have been exhibited in which distributed deadlocks cannot be detected in a hierarchical way [10]. More work on deadlock detection and avoidance will be necessary to determine the advantages and disadvantages of each. Since time-out mechanisms are necessary for network communications, it seems reasonable to use it to avoid deadlocks in distributed systems connected through superdatabases.

7 Conclusion

We have described the design of superdatabases and the algorithms used to compose consistent databases out of both homogeneous and heterogeneous elements. There are four good characteristics in the superdatabase approach to building heterogeneous databases.

First, superdatabases guarantee the atomicity of global updates across the element databases. This atomicity includes both reliability atomicity through an agreement protocol, such as two-phase commit, and concurrency atomicity through the certification of serialization provided by the element databases.

Second, the design of superdatabase is adaptable to a variety of crash recovery methods and concurrency control techniques used in the element databases. We have established the necessity for an agreement protocol for supertransaction commit. However, the protocol is independent of particular crash recovery methods used to undo and redo local transactions in the element databases. We have also shown that as long as the element databases use concurrency control methods which easily supply an explicit serial order of their transactions, they can be included under the superdatabase.

Third, databases built with superdatabases are extensible by construction. Element databases may be added or deleted without changing the superdatabase. In additon, many interesting applications can take advantage of the extensibility. For example, a replicated database can be constructed by connecting two identical element databases with a superdatabase. Another example is that given a database X, satisfying the requirements of section 3 for crash recovery and concurrency control, a superdatabase delivers the distributed version of X.

Fourth, transactions local to element databases run independently of the superdatabase, which intervenes only when needed for synchronization or recovery of supertransactions across different element databases. In other words, the additional overhead introduced by the indirection through superdatabase is paid only by the direct users of its services. The only interference happens when a component transaction of a supertransaction conflicts with a local transaction.

Even though we described the serialization of supertransactions using O-vectors, the hierarchical approach admits other methods that explore the properties of particular concurrency control methods. For example, using an agreement to synchronize lock points of two-phase locking elements databases and distributing global timestamps to timestamp-based element databases are techniques that may improve the concurrency in the superdatabase.

Global deadlock detection and resolution remains a research challenge, since it is immune to hierarchical approaches. Observing that the time-out mechanism is inherent in distributed systems, we expect it to be useful in avoiding deadlocks.

Many years of research on heterogeneous databases have achieved impressive and substantial progress, especially in query language translation and view integration. We hope the combination of our results with previous work on heterogeneous databases will produce superdatabases which are consistent, adaptable, and extensible.

References

[1] R. Bayer, K. Elhardt, J. Heigert, and A. Reiser.
    Dynamic timestamp allocation for transactions in database systems.
    In H. J. Schneider, editor, *Distributed Data Bases*, North-Holland, 1982.

[2] P.A. Bernstein, V. Hadzilacos, and N. Goodman.
    Concurrency Control and Recovery in Database Systems.
    Addison-Wesley Publishing Company, first edition, 1987.

[3] D. Brill, M. Templeton, and D. Yu.
    Distributed query processing strategies in MERMAID, a frontend to data management systems.
    In *Proceedings of the First International Conference on Data Engineering*, 1984.

[4] S. Ceri and S. Owicki.
On the use of optimistic methods for concurrency control in distributed databases.
In *Proceedings of the Sixth Berkeley Workshop on Distributed Data Management and Computer Networks*, pages 117–129, Lawrence Berkeley Laboratory, University of California, Berkeley, February 1982.

[5] U. Dayal.
Processing queries over generalization hierarchies in a multidatabase system.
In *Proceedings of the Ninth International Conference on Very Large Data Bases*, October-November 1983.

[6] A. Elmagarmid and Y. Leu.
An optimistic concurrency control algorithm for heterogeneous distributed database systems.
Data Engineering Bulletin, 10(3):26–32, September 1987.

[7] K.P. Eswaran, J.N. Gray, R.A. Lorie, and I.L. Traiger.
The notions of consistency and predicate locks in a database system.
Communications of ACM, 19(11):624–633, November 1976.

[8] A. Ferrier and C. Stangret.
Heterogeneity in the distributed database management system SIRIUS-DELTA.
In *Proceedings of the Eighth International Conference on Very Large Data Bases*, Mexico City, September 1983.

[9] V. Gligor and G.L. Luckenbaugh.
Interconnecting heterogeneneous database management systems.
Computer, 17(1):33–43, January 1984.

[10] V. Gligor and R. Popescu-Zeletin.
Concurrency control issues in distributed heterogeneous database management systems.
In F.A. Schreiber and W. Litwin, editors, *Distributed Data Sharing Systems*, pages 43–56, North Holland Publishing Company, 1985.
Proceedings of the International Symposium on Distributed Data Sharing Systems.

[11] H. T. Kung and John T. Robinson.
On optimistic methods for concurrency control.
Transactions on Database Systems, 6(2):213–226, June 1981.

[12] L. Lamport.
Time, clocks and ordering of events in a distributed system.
Communications of ACM, 21(7):558–565, July 1978.

[13] T. Landers and R.L. Rosenberg.
An overview of MULTIBASE.
In H.J. Schneider, editor, *Distributed Data Bases*, North Holland Publishing Company, September 1982.
Proceedings of the Second International Symposium on Distributed Data Bases.

[14] P.J. Leu and B. Bhargava.
Multidimensional timestamp protocols for concurrency control.
In *Proceedings of the Second International Conference on Data Engineering*, pages 482–489, Los Angeles, February 1986.

[15] B. Lindsay, L.M. Haas, C. Mohan, P.F. Wilms, and R.A. Yost.
Computation and communication in R*: a distributed database manager.
ACM Transactions on Computer Systems, 2(1):24–38, February 1984.

[16] B.H. Liskov and R.W. Scheifler.
Guardians and Actions: linguistic support for robust, distributed programs.
In *Proceedings of the Ninth Annual Symposium on Principles of Programming Languages*, pages 7–19, January 1982.

[17] W. Litwin and A. Abdellatif.
Multidatabase interoperability.
Computer, 19(12):10–18, December 1986.

[18] R. McCord.
INGRES/STAR: a distributed heterogeneous relational DBMS.
Vendor Presentation in SIGMOD, May 1987.

[19] J.E.B. Moss.
Nested Transactions: An Approach to Reliable Distributed Computing.
PhD thesis, Massachusetts Institute of Technology, April 1981.

[20] C. Pu, H. Massalin, J. Ioannidis, and P. Metzger.
The Synthesis System.
Technical Report CUCS-259-87, Department of Computer Science, Columbia University, February 1987.

[21] Calton Pu.
Replication and Nested Transactions in the Eden Distributed System.
PhD thesis, Department of Computer Science, University of Washington, 1986.

[22] D.P. Reed.
Naming and Synchronization in a Decentralized Computer System.
PhD thesis, Massachusetts Institute of Technology, September 1978.

[23] N. Roussopoulos and H. Kang.
Principles and techniques in the design of ADMS±.
Computer, 19(12):19–25, December 1986.

[24] A. Spector, J.J. Bloch, D.S. Daniels, D. Duchamp, R.P. Draves, Eppinger J.L., S.G. Menees, and D.S. Thompson.
The Camelot Project.
Technical Report CMU-CS-86-166, Computer Science Department, Carnegie-Mellon University, December 1986.

[25] M. Templeton, D. Brill, A. Hwang, I. Kameny, and E. Lund.
An overview of the MERMAID system – a frontend to heterogeneous databases.
In *Proceedings of EASCON 1983*, pages 387–402, IEEE/Computer Society, 1983.

[26] W.E. Weihl.
Specification and Implementation of Atomic Data Types.
PhD thesis, Massachusetts Institute of Technology, March 1984.
Tech.Report MIT/LCS/TR-314.

[27] M. Weinstein, T. Page, B. Livezey, and G. Popek.
Transactions and synchronization in a distributed operating systems.
In *Proceedings of the Tenth Symposium on Operating Systems Principles*, pages 115–126, ACM/SIGOPS, December 1985.

Part 3
Example Systems

IN THE preceding part, the basic principles of integration and the methodologies employed to accomplish such integration were discussed. Now, in this part, we see how those principles and methodologies have been utilized in experimental systems.

The first paper, by John Smith *et al.,* describes the Multibase software system [1], [2], [3] designed by Computer Corporation of America. Multibase represents the first serious attempt in the U.S. to develop a commercial product that provides integration of heterogeneous database systems. Its design provides an integrated scheme for uniform query access to dissimilar systems, as well as for global query optimization.

The second paper, by V. Krishnamurthy *et al.,* describes the IMDAS architecture which has been implemented as part of an experimental facility at the Automated Manufacturing Research Facility of the National Bureau of Standards. This architecture has been designed to demonstrate the feasibility of supporting the manufacturing and production environment for factories of the future.

The third paper, by S. M. Deen *et al.,* describes the PRECI* prototype system developed in the United Kingdom [4], [5]. This system differs from others in its concept of inner and outer nodes to suit different user requirements. Only the inner nodes contribute to the global database schema.

The fourth paper, by Marjorie Templeton *et al.,* describes the MERMAID data access system being developed by UNISYS. This system allows information stored on different machines under various relational database management systems to be manipulated using a common language.

The fifth paper, by Witold Litwin and Abdelaziz Abdellatif, describes Multics Relational Data Store Multidatabase (MRDSM). In the interoperability approach adopted by the authors, the user is not provided with a single global schema, but rather with a set of functions for manipulating data in visibly distinct schemas.

The sixth paper, by Yuri Breitbart *et al.,* describes the Amoco Distributed Database System (ADDS). The authors contend that their system is capable of integrating all types of databases, and even files that are not managed by any database management system. One interesting feature of ADDS is its ability to provide a range of query capabilities for users with different levels of sophistication.

In the seventh paper, W. Staniszkis describes the Multidatabase Management System (MDBMS) which is closely related to the Network Data Management System (NDMS). This paper provides details about both these systems, and highlights their capabilities in relation to other research initiatives.

In the eighth paper, Alfonso Cardenas describes the UCLA HD-DBMS project. The author stresses the fact that, in contrast to other systems which provide only a monolingual interface to heterogeneous distributed databases, HD-DBMS has been designed to provide a multilingual interface to such databases.

In the ninth paper, M. P. Reddy *et al.* compare and contrast the query processing capabilities of eight prototype systems, and categorize them into three main groups. Their assessment reveals interesting merits and demerits of each system.

The various prototype systems described in this part represent the broad spectrum of approaches being researched around the world. While many of these prototype systems may hold little potential for use in commercial applications today, these systems are harbingers of commercial products which will become available in coming years. Also, these prototypes serve as the foundation for building systems for specific domains, such as IMDAS for computer integrated manufacturing (CIM) environments, and ADDS for oil exploration applications. Because of these reasons, the main specifications of all the different prototypes are summarized in Table 1 [7], [8], [9].

In the next and final part of this book, a number of important auxiliary issues are examined.

REFERENCES FOR PART 3

[1] Landers, T. and R. L. Rosenberg, "An overview of multibase," in *Distributed Data Bases,* H. J. Schneider, Ed. North-Holland, 1982, pp. 311–366.
[2] Dayal, V., "Processing queries over generalization hierarchies on a multidatabase system," in *Proc. of 9th Int. Conf. on Very Large Databases,* Italy, 1983.
[3] Shipman, D., "The functional data model and the data language DAPLEX," *ACM Trans. Database Syst.,* Mar. 1981.
[4] Deen, S. M., R. R. Amin, and M. C. Taylor, "Implementation of a prototype for PRECI*, *Computer J.,* vol. 30, no. 2, 1987.
[5] ——, "Data integration in distributed databases," *IEEE Trans. Software Eng.,* vol. SE-13, no. 7, July 1987, pp. 860–864.
[6] Yu, C., *et al.,* "Query processing in a fragmented relational distributed system: Mermaid," *IEEE Trans. Software Eng.,* vol. SE-11, no. 8, Aug. 1985, pp. 795–810.

TABLE I

	MULTIBASE	IMDAS	IISS	PRECI*	MERMAID	MRDSM	ADDS	NDMS	HD-RDBMS
ACRONYM DERIVED FROM	None	Integrated Manufacturing Database Administration System	Integrated Information Support System	Prototype of a Relational Canonical Interface	None	Multics Relational Data Store Multibase	Amoco Distributed Database System	Network Data Management System	Heterogeneous Distributed Relational Database Management System
ENVIRONMENT	General	Manufacturing	Manufacturing and Logistics	General	General	General	General (mostly scientific and engineering databases relating to data collected from oil wells)	Transportation	General
ORGANIZATION	Computer Corporation of America (US)	National Bureau of Standards (US)	Air Force (US)	University of Keele (UK)	UNISYS	INRIA (France)	Amoco Production Company, Research (USA)	CRAI (Italy)	University of California, Los Angeles
LOCAL DATA MODELS SUPPORTED	Hierarchical, Relational, Network	Relational	Relational, Network	Any model via relational algebra interface	Relational or Relational Interface	Relational or Relational Interface	Relational, Hierarchical Networks	Relational, Network	Relational, Hierarchical, Network
LOCAL DBMS SUPPORTED (Current Version)	CODASYL database, Hierarchical database	Relational-INGRES, RIM, and DB2 (planned)	Network-IDMS on IBM 3081, IDS/II on Honeywell level 6, IDBMS on VAX, Relational-ORACLE on VAX	Under development	IDM (Britton-Lee) on VAX, INGRES on SUN 170 and SUN 120, MISTRESS on SUN 120, M204 under development.	Multiple MRDS on Honeywell	Hierarchical (IMS, INQUIRE) Relational (SQL/DS, RIM, FOCUS) and some sequential file formats	Network-IDMS DB/DC and ADABAS on IBM; Relational-RODAN on IBM, INGRESS on VAX	Prototype implementation to follow
GLOBAL DATA MODEL	Functional Data Model	Semantic Association Model (SAM*)	IDEF, (ER Based)	Canonical Data Model	Relational	Extended Relational	Relational	Relational	Generalized Data Access Graph (GDAG)
GLOBAL DATA MANIPULATION LANGUAGE	DAPLEX. Local host may not support all capabilities provided by DAPLEX.	SQL-like. Supports interactive access and programs through attachment to local interprocess communication	No interactive query language. Query statements embedded in COBOL and precompiled.	PAL (PRECI Algebraic Language) which is relational algebra based	SQL or ARIEL (SDC query language)	MDSL which is an SQL like, extended version of DSL. (the data manipulation language of MRDS)	Extended Relational Algebra Language, plus a subset of the ANSI SQL language	Modified version of SQL	Global Conceptual language—a calculus type language.
LOCAL DATABASE SCHEMA CONVERSION	Local database schema called Local Host Schema (LHS) in any model needs to be redefined/extended into Functional Data Model to enforce uniformity. New schema is called Local Schema (LS). Local host schema remains intact.	Local database schema redefined/extended into relational model with system utilities. Mapping work which would leave local host schema intact is progressing.	Redefined using Neutral Data Definition Language (NDDL). (No information about the structure of NDDL is available. It has been mentioned that it is capable of supporting relational and network schemas, entities and relations, and mapping.)	Local database schema must be redefined to support relational algebra or PAL.	Needs conversion into relational form. System does not provide help for conversion from local data model to relational form or from relational form to local data model. Can map user relational view to repeating groups in local database.	No conversion required. The system is designed to serve databases implemented with MRDS DBMS on Honeywell machines. The aim is to deal with semantic heterogeneity in order to provide uniform access to these databases.	Needs conversion to relational form. The schemas of the local databases are described as: a) Base relations, and b) Semantic information mapping. Base relations are constructed with objects from underlying database schema. Semantic and manipulation information about these objects is represented with Mapping Definition Language.	Needs conversion to relational form. Has two parts: a) Base relations, described as Physical Databases (PDBs). PDBs are comprised of Physical Database Components (PDBCs). A PDBC for a relational database is a relation. A PDBC for a hierarchical database may represent a path from the root segment of the database to a leaf segment.	Needs conversion to ER form. This is accomplished using the global conceptual language. Objective is to develop a DDL/DML compiler-compiler workbench.
DATA INCOMPATABILITIES AND SEMANTIC MISMATCHES	Resolved through an integration Database Schema (called IS) for all the Local Schemas. Extent of coverage is not sufficient, but it can take care of differences like kilometers and miles, age in years and in qualitative form, (young, old), etc.	Performs conversions, maintains relationships between dependent relations and parent relations. Resolved by Global Schema.	Performs data format and unit conversion operations.	Local database schemas, converted to the relational form are placed directly in Global Schema. Integration data are also placed separately in Global Schema. Unlike MULTIBASE, users can refer to incompatible information (e.g., kilometers and miles) through Global External Schema separately rather than as one unit. Mapping is provided by Global Schema	Deals with two types of data translation schemes: functional type and enumerated type. Functional translation deals with problems like unit conversions (e.g., kilometers and miles) and format conversions (e.g., date) etc. Enumerated type translation deals with converting sets of values through a table lookup (e.g., codes and names).	Handles three types of interdatabase dependencies. They are a) manipulation dependencies; b) privacy dependencies, c) equivalence dependencies. Equivalence dependencies handle data incompatibilities and semantic mismatches.	Supports different names and characteristics (e.g., data types and units) assigned to semantically equivalent fields located in different databases through the system data definition language. Data conversion is performed as the physical data are loaded into the logical temporary relations.	Maintains information along with Global Schema in System Encyclopedia. Further details are not available.	Allows single mappings and nested mappings to overcome certain differences. Also, the query composer is responsible for combining responses to subsequences. Further details are not available.
GLOBAL SCHEMA CONSTRUCTION	Uses the Functional Data Model to define the global schema and the associated query language DAPLEX as the global data manipulation language. The local DBMS and their Local Host Schema (LHS) are mapped into local schema (LS) which are expressed in terms of the Global Data Model. The local schema are merged into global schema with an auxiliary Integration Schema (IS) which contains information needed for reconciling inconsistencies between the local schemas.	On line SAM* Dictionary utilities for defining Global Schema, Views, Site capabilities, Fragmentation, and Partitioning.	The structure of NDDL is unknown. It is not clear how various local schemas, redefined in NDDL, are merged.	Converted Local Schemas in relational form are placed in Global Schema with node information. Integration data and meta-data are maintained in relational form in the Global Schema. Merging of relations and mappings are maintained in Global External Schemas (Views).	All the relations from different local schemas are grouped through a schema translation mechanism. Schema translation deals with name changes, partitions, one-to-many and many-to-one mappings of relations (e.g., a global relation 'ship' can be mapped to a relation with name 'boat' in one database and a join of two relations in another database). Local database schemas subject to schema and data translation mechanisms are maintained in Global Schema in relational form.	A single Global Schema does not exist. Instead, a conceptual schema known as multischema with elements from local database schemas along with one or more dependency schemas to handle interdatabase dependencies. The elements of multischema created by the user are: (i) one or more dependency schema, or (ii) explicit enumeration of local databases to compose a multidatabase.	A Global Schema does not exist. Users can create one or more Composite Data Base. Schema (CDB) definition is used to describe the subset of all the physical databases that may be appropriate for an application. Many CDBs may be defined depending on the number of applications. A CDB is comprised of one or more Logical Data Bases (LDBs) and an LDB is comprised of one or more Physical Databases (PDBs). An LDB is the set of PDBs that are managed by a single DBMS at a single site. All the CDBs are defined in a directory. A user can choose a CDB, define a view and query on this view. Also a user can define his or her own CDB schema.	Local database schemas converted to relational form are further analyzed for naming conflicts and type conflicts. Equivalent base relations are integrated together.	Uses a global conceptual model (network wide highly logical model of data) and a global internal model (access-path oriented model of the structure of the integrated system) of data. The global internal model identifies major elements outside the realm or interests of each local DBMS; relationships between entities in different DBMS, logical replication, and perhaps physical replication of entities and relationships in heterogeneous databases.

TABLE I *(Continued)*

	MULTIBASE	IMDAS	IISS	PRECI*	MERMAID	MRDSM	ADDS	NDMS	HD-RDBMS
QUERY PROCESSING (Retrieval)	A query on Global External View is modified and converted to queries on Global Schema. If Global Schema cannot process the query, it is passed to the Master Schema Manager (called MDAS) for further processing; otherwise, it is translated into queries on local schemas.	A query on Global Schema is translated into queries on Global Schema. These are further translated into Local DML queries. Adopts "no two variables in a query range over the same entity type" strategy to generate queries on Local Schemas. Adopts data reduction and data movement techniques in Global Query optimization strategy. Merging and final processing takes place at Global Schema result node.	Currently, query statements in Neutral Data Manipulation Language (NDML) on Global Schema are embedded in COBOL and precompiled. On precompilation, source code files are sent to their respective hosts for compilation.	This system follows the same strategy as MULTIBASE except in the final processing. The designers have aimed at a higher degree of parallelism. While in MULTIBASE, final processing is done at a result node, PRECI facilitates parallel processing at multiple nodes.	A query in SQL or ARIEL on Global Schema is translated into queries in an intermediate language called DIL (Distributed Intermediate Language), and later translated from DIL to the Local DBMS language. Currently translators are available for IDL, QUEL and SQL Query Processing supports fragmented and replicated relations. Final post processing is done by one of the hosts.	A query on multischema is decomposed into queries on local DBs after removing interdata dependencies that cannot be handled locally. Then a working DB is created to collect data from different DBs. The collection process is optimized by performing projection and selection operations on source DBs. Finally queries are generated on the working DB to combine data.	Queries can be submitted against any number of Composite Data Bases (CDB). A query is optimized for minimal communication cost and a subquery schedule is produced. The steps of the subquery schedules are processed by server processes against a base relation is translated into the language of the local DBMS.	An Application Schema is defined at each node over internal schema that represents a group of users at that node. Users at that node define their views on this Application Schema. Queries posed on Application Schema are translated to local database language through internal schema. Query processing strategy has three parts: intermediate storage structure, query optimization and query execution.	Application program query (DML) enters the virtual layer at each node over internal schema that is transformed into a unified virtual layer (UVL) query, which is then mapped into a unified global layer (UGL) query. The UGL query is transformed into a set of one or more unified local layer (ULL) queries and an access plan. A ULL query is transformed into a local layer (LL) DBMS dependent query and then sent to the local DBMS for processing to the precedence established by the access plan.
GLOBAL UPDATE AND TRANSACTION MANAGEMENT	Not supported	Contains Transaction Manager, to handle integrity, concurrency control and recovery. Allows Global update on base relations only. Recovery limited to cancel/restart. More work is in progress.	Committed to supporting global updates.	Allows global update on base relations only. If data are replicated, update is done only on the original copy and broadcasted to other copies. (Not fully implemented as yet)	Update to single database is permitted.	Limited Multidatabase Update facility exists.	Retrieval system is being modified to evaluate new concurrency control algorithm.	Updates are done through co-ordinated (Composite Data Bases) processing applications. Transaction programs need to be implemented as application programs of the host DBMS. Co-ordinated by Transaction Processor.	Under examination
NETWORK SERVICES	Global Data Manager (GDM) and Local Data Interface (LDI) incorporate network interface for establishing communication.	Token bus, Ethernet LAN. TCP/IP, HDLC. Plan to use MAP Compatible network. Inter-process communication through shared memory.	LAN and wide area communication. A kernel known as Network Transaction Manager (NTM) has been implemented to provide sophisticated services on the network. Interprocess communication through message passing.	Designers propose to develop a standard message oriented protocol for communications between distributed databases.	Ethernet, TCP/IP. Plan to use MAP and DODIIS protocols for interprocess communication.	The system uses inter-Multics communication facilities over X.25 TRANSPAC Net (French national net).	SNA, Ethernet (TCP/IP), Bisync. Uses a Logical network approach to provide a common interface to the physical networks.	X.25 protocol. Interprocess communication through message passing.	Protocols allow transactions on data within the system; aborts on certain transactions; delayed updates; broadcasting and handling system status (as in up/down/recovering).
CURRENT STATE LIMITATIONS AND FUTURE DIRECTIONS	Internal prototype ready. U.S. Air Force has showed an interest in using it on an experimental basis in their applications. Currently permits READ-ONLY access and local updates.	Global Schema Manager (called DDAS) and local schema manager (called BDAS) exist on UNIX and VMS. Work is in progress on Master Schema manager. Research is on for coordination and synchronization of distributed transaction management functions.	Feasibility demonstrated using a scenario selected by 22 contractors. Further work on interactive query facility and global update is pending.	Basic design is complete. Currently implementing a pilot system. Initial plan is to have two nodes at Aberdeen on Honeywell, one node at Belfast on VAX, and a fourth in Dublin on another VAX.	Not a commercial product. In use within DOD systems developed by UNISYS. Operates only on top of multiple relational DBMSs. Tested on a navy database that contains ships, positions, weapons installed on the ships, etc. The database is distributed to four sites. Plan to extend into the areas of object management, security, and integration with deductive inference engine.	Investigating application of knowledge processing techniques in the area of query processing to simplify query expressions.	Current version operates under VM/CMS and access data controlled by IMS, SQL/DS, RIM, FOCUS, and INQUIRE databases. The system includes a remote user interface and programming language interface for use on workstations. Future directions include supporting update transactions. ADDS-to-ADDS communication, tools for automatic CDB creation, and support for additional DBMSs such as DB2.	Current prototype interfaces with DBMSs on IBM and VAX. Future extensions include graphic query interface, distributed application design tools and performance monitoring. Testing on Transportation Information System.	Several papers have been published. It is now intended to implement a prototype system.
REMARKS	Further work suspended due to lack of funds.	Designed to achieve a high level of automation for factory environment.	Designed to provide a high level of support for automated Manufacturing and Logistic environment.	Designed to handle replication of databases.	Claims to offer one of the most complete query optimization algorithms that has been implemented and tested. Supports replicated and fragmented relations.	Operate in a specialized domain. Not a 'true' heterogeneous system. Heterogeneity is dealt at semantic level by providing uniform access to all the databases implemented with same DBMS.	Has been designed to work in the specialized environment of databases relating to oil wells. Current version is being enhanced for corporate wide deployment	Designed for meeting the requirement of National Transport Information System of Italy.	Long range project
CONTACT PLACE (Person)	Computer Corporation of America Four Cambridge Center, Cambridge, MA 02142 (D. Smith)	Integrated Systems Group, National Institute of Standards and Technology, Gaithersburg, MD 20899 (M. Mitchell, E. Barkmeyer, D. Libes or Howard Bloom)	Material Laboratory, Air Force, Wright Aeronautical Labs, Air Force Systems Command Wright-Patterson AFB, OH 45433	Dept. of Computer Science, University of Keele, Staffs, ST5 5BG, England (S. M. Deen)	UNISYS, 2525 Colorado Ave., Santa Monica, California 90406 (M. Templeton)	INRIA BP 106, 78153 Le Chesnay Cedex, FRANCE (W. Litwin)	Amoco Production Company, Research, P. O. Box 3385 Tulsa Oklahoma 74102 (Glenn R. Thompson)	CRAI Via Bernini S., Localita'S. Stefano, 87036 Rende (Cosenza), ITALY (W. Staniszkis)	Computer Science Department, University of California, Los Angeles, CA 90024, USA (Alfonso F. Cardenas)

[7] This table has evolved over a 3 year period. The first version was compiled by B. E. Prasad and Amar Gupta in 1986 at MIT, and a copy was sent to the principal researcher for each of the projects seeking their inputs. Subhash Bhalla and Jaideep Ganguly assisted in revising the original table. Interim versions have appeared in [8], [9].

[8] Bhalla, S., B. E. Prasad, A. Gupta, and S. E. Madnick, "A technical comparison of distributed heterogeneous database management systems," in *Integrating Distributed Homogeneous and Heterogeneous Databases: Prototypes,* A. Gupta and S. Madnick, Eds. MIT, Cambridge, MA, 1987, pp. 159–218. (NTIS and DTIC Accession Number A 195852).

[9] ——, "A framework and comparative study of distributed heterogeneous database management systems," Working Paper #1981–88, Sloan School of Management, MIT, Cambridge, MA, Feb. 1988.

BIBLIOGRAPHY FOR PART 3

[1] Alonso, R., H. Garcia-Molina, and K. Salem, "Concurrency control and recovery for global procedures in federated database systems," *Data Eng.,* vol. 10, no. 3, Sept. 1987, pp. 5–11.

[2] Black, J. P., L. F. Marshall, and B. Randell, "The architecture of UNIX united," *Proc. IEEE,* May 1987, pp. 709–718.

[3] Brietbart, Y., A. Silberschatz, and G. Thompson, "An update mechanism for multidatabase systems," *Database Eng.,* vol. 10, no. 3, Sept. 1987, pp. 12–18.

[4] Cardenas, A. F. and G. W. Wang, "Translation of SQL/DS data access/update into entity-relationship data access/update," *IEEE Proc. Fourth Int. Conf. on Entity-Relationship Approach,* Chicago, IL, Oct. 28–30, 1985, pp. 256–267.

[5] Dayal, U. and H.-Y. Hwang, "View definition and generalization for database integration in a multidatabase system," *IEEE Trans. Software Eng.,* vol. SE-10, no. 6, Nov. 1984, pp. 628–645.

[6] Elmagarmid, A. and Y. Leu, "An optimistic concurrency control algorithm for heterogeneous distributed database systems," *Data Eng.,* vol. 10, no. 3, Sept. 1987, pp. 26–32.

[7] Gilgor, V. and R. Popescu-Zeletin, "Transaction management in distributed heterogeneous database management systems," *Inform. Syst.,* vol. 11, no. 4, 1986, pp. 287–297.

[8] Lee, Wen F. *et al.,* "A remote user interface for the ADDS multidatabase systems," in *Proc. of Second Oklahoma Workshop on Applied Computing,* pp. 194–204.

[9] Litwin, W. and A. Abdellatif, "An overview of the multi-database manipulation language MDSL," *Proc. IEEE,* May 1987, pp. 621–632.

[10] Litwin, W. *et al.,* "SIRIUS systems for distributed data management," in *Distributed Data Bases,* H. J. Schneider, Ed. New York, NY: North-Holland, 1982, pp. 311–366.

[11] Navathe, S., R. Elmasri, and J. Larson, "Integrating user views in database design," *IEEE Computer,* Jan. 1986, pp. 50–62.

[12] Neuhold, E. J. and B. Walter, "An overview of the architecture of the distributed data base system Porel," in *Distributed Data Bases,* H. J. Schneider, Ed. New York, NY: North-Holland, 1982, pp. 247–290.

[13] Belcastro, V., *et al.,* "An overview of the distributed query system DQS," in *Advances in Database Technology—EDBT '88.* Berlin, Germany: Springer-Verlag, pp. 170–189.

[14] Su, S. Y. W., "Modeling integrated manufacturing data with SAM*," *IEEE Computer,* Jan. 1986, pp. 34–49.

[15] Takizawa, M., "Heterogeneous distributed database system: JDDBS," *Database Eng.,* vol. 2, 1984, pp. 58–62.

[16] Templeton, M., E. Lund, and P. Ward, "Pragmatics of access control in Mermaid," *Data Eng.,* vol. 10, no. 3, Sept. 1987, pp. 33–38.

Multibase—integrating heterogeneous distributed database systems*

by JOHN MILES SMITH, PHILIP A. BERNSTEIN, UMESHWAR DAYAL, NATHAN GOODMAN, TERRY LANDERS, KEN W. T. LIN, and EUGENE WONG

Computer Corporation of America
Cambridge, Massachusetts

ABSTRACT

Multibase is a software system for integrating access to pre-existing, heterogeneous, distributed databases. The system suppresses differences of DBMS, language, and data models among the databases and provides users with a unified global schema and a single high-level query language. Autonomy for updating is retained with the local databases. The architecture of Multibase does not require any changes to local databases or DBMSs. There are three principal research goals of the project. The first goal is to develop appropriate language constructs for accessing and integrating heterogeneous databases. The second goal is to discover effective global and local optimization techniques. The final goal is to design methods for handling incompatible data representations and inconsistent data. Currently the project is in the first year of a planned three year effort. This paper describes the basic architecture of Multibase and identifies some of the avenues to be taken in subsequent research.

1. INTRODUCTION

What is Multibase?

The database approach to data processing requires that all of the data relevant to an enterprise be stored in an integrated database. By "integrated," we mean that a single schema (i.e., database description) describes the entire database, that all accesses to the database are expressed relative to that schema, and that such accesses are processed against a single (logical) copy of the database. Unfortunately, in the real world many databases are not integrated. Often, the data relevant to an enterprise is implemented by many independent databases, each with its own schema. Such databases are nonintegrated. Furthermore, these databases may be managed by different database management systems (DBMS), perhaps on different hardware. In this case, in addition to being nonintegrated the databases are distributed and heterogeneous. Thus, the real world of nonintegrated, heterogeneous, distributed databases differs greatly from the more ideal world of an integrated database.

Nonintegrated, heterogeneous, distributed databases arise for several reasons. First, many of these databases were created before the benefits of integrated databases were well understood. In those days, total integration was not a principal database design goal. Second, the lack of a central database administrator for some enterprises has made it difficult for independent organizations within an enterprise to produce an integrated database suitable for all of them. Third, the large size of many data processing applications has made distribution a necessity, simply to handle the volume of work. Since integrated distributed DBMSs have not been available, it has been necessary to implement applications on different machines. Since different applications often have different performance and functionality requirements, different DBMSs were often selected to run on these machines to meet these different requirements. Many data processing organizations have experienced these problems, so there are many nonintegrated, heterogeneous, distributed databases in the world.

A principal problem in using databases of this type is that of integrated retrieval. In such databases, each independent database has its own schema, expressed in its own data model, and can be accessed only by its own retrieval language. Since different databases in general have different schemata, different data models, and different retrieval languages, many difficulties arise in formulating and implementing retrieval requests (called queries) that require data from more than one database. These difficulties include the following: resolving incompatibilities between the databases, such as differences of data types and conflicting schema names; resolving inconsistencies between copies of the same information stored in different databases; and transforming a query expressed in the user's language into a set of queries expressed in the many different languages supported by the different sites. Implementing such a query usually consumes months of program-

* This research was jointly supported by the Defense Advanced Research Projects Agency of the Department of Defense and the Naval Electronic Systems Command and was monitored by the Naval Electronic Systems Command under Contract No. N00039-80-C-0402. The views and conclusions contained in this document are those of the authors and should not be interpreted as necessarily representing the official policies, either expressed or implied, of the Defense Advanced Research Projects Agency or the Naval Electronic Systems Command or the U.S. Government.

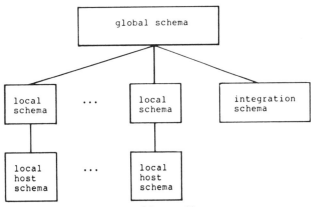

Figure 1—Schema architecture

ming time, making it a very expensive activity. Sometimes, the necessary effort is so great that implementing the query is not feasible at all.

Multibase is a software system that helps integrate non-integrated, heterogeneous, distributed databases. Its main goal is to present the illusion of an integrated database to users without requiring that the database be physically integrated. It accomplishes this by allowing users to view the database through a single global schema and by allowing them to access the data using a high level query language. Queries posed in this language are entirely processed by Multibase as if the database were integrated, homogeneous, and non-distributed. Multibase uses the Functional Data Model[1] to define the global schema, and the language DAPLEX[1] as the high level query language.

Implementation Objectives

There are many approaches to the design of the Multibase system. In deciding which approach to choose, we begin with the following design objectives.

1. Generality: we do not want to design an application-specific Multibase system. Instead, we want to provide powerful generalized tools that can be used to integrate various database systems for various applications with a minimum of programming effort.
2. Extendability: we want a design that allows expansion of functionality without major modification. There are areas in the Multibase design where substantial research effort is still required, so we must be able to add additional features to the Multibase system as we learn more about the problems.
3. Compatibility: we want a design that does not render existing software invalid, because such software represents a very large investment. Thus, we must leave the existing interface to the local DBMS intact.

The proposed architecture of the Multibase system consists of two basic components: a schema design aid and a run-time query processing subsystem. The schema design aid provides tools to the "integrated" database designer to design the glob-

al schema and to define a mapping from the local databases to the global schema. The run-time query processing subsystem then uses the mapping definition to translate global queries into local queries, ensuring that the local queries are executed correctly and efficiently by local DBMSs. The schema design aid is discussed first.

Schema Architecture

The Multibase architecture has three levels of schemata, a global schema (GS) at the top level, an integration schema (IS) and one local schema (LS) per local database at the middle level, and one local host schema (LHS) per local database at the bottom level. These components and their interrelationships are depicted in Figure 1.

The local host schemata are the original existing schemata defined in local data models and used by the local DBMSs. For example, they can be relational, file, or CODASYL schemata. Each of these LHSs is translated into a local schema (LS) defined in the Functional Data Model. By expressing the LSs in a single data model, higher levels of the system need not be concerned with data model differences among the local DBMSs. In addition, there is an integration schema that describes a database containing information needed for integrating databases. For example, suppose one database records the speed of ships in miles per hour, while the other records it in kilometers per hour. To integrate these two databases, we need information about the mapping between these two scales. This information is stored in the integration database.

The LSs and IS are mapped, via a view mapping, into the global schema (GS). The GS allows users to pose queries against what appears to be a homogeneous and integrated database. Roughly speaking, the LHS to LS mapping provides homogeneity and the LS and IS to GS mapping provides integration. The schema design aid provides tools to the database designer to define LSs, the GS, and the mapping among them and the LHSs.

Query Processing Architecture

The architecture of the run-time query processing subsystem consists of the Multibase software and local DBMSs.

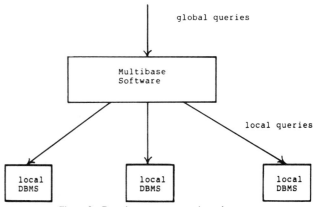

Figure 2—Run-time query processing subsystem

These components and their interrelationships are depicted in Figure 2. The users submit queries over the global schema (called global queries) to the Multibase software, which translates them into subqueries over local schemata (called local queries). These local queries are then sent to local DBMSs to be executed.

Since the global queries are posed against the global schema without any knowledge of the distribution of the data and the availability of "fast access paths," the Multibase software must optimize queries so they can be executed efficiently. In addition, the translation process must also be correct; that is, the local queries must retrieve exactly the information that the original global query requests.

Meeting the Objectives

The proposed architecture meets the objective of generality. The only component of the Multibase system that is customized for the application is the global schema and its mapping definition to the local schemata. The only component of Multibase that is customized for the local DBMSs is the interface software that allows Multibase to communicate with the heterogeneous DBMSs in a single language. These are only small components of the Multibase system. Thus, most of Multibase is neither application-specific nor DBMS-specific. Multibase also meets the objective of compatibility, because local databases are not modified; therefore, existing application programs can still access local databases through local DBMSs. And as the details of the architecture are discussed in later sections, it will become clear that the objective of extendability is also met.

Project Status

The Multibase project is a three-year effort. Within the first two years, the research problems in the system design will be resolved and evaluated, using a "breadboard" implementation of the system. In the final year, a revised design will be developed and implemented in ADA. The ADA version will be made available for experimental testing within the Navy "Command and Control" environment.

It is anticipated that the major research problems are

1. basic architecture of the system,
2. global and local optimization, and
3. handling incompatible data.

At the time of this writing, an architecture has been designed that supports a restricted version of DAPLEX with reasonable efficiency and that can be tailored to handle certain kinds of data incompatibility. This basic architecture is currently being implemented as a breadboard system. Subsequently, research will be devoted to removing the restrictions on DA-PLEX and investigating algorithms for processing incompatible data. The breadboard system will then be enhanced to include the new capabilities. This paper describes the basic architecture developed to date.

Organization

The architecture of the Multibase system is expanded in more detail in Section 2. The process of mapping each LHS to a LS and merging LSs into a GS is discussed in Section 3. Section 3 also discusses the problem of data incompatibility and inconsistency. The method by which user queries are translated into efficient local queries is discussed in Section 4. Section 5 is a summary.

2. QUERY PROCESSING ARCHITECTURE

The architecture of the Multibase run-time subsystem consists of

1. a query translator,
2. a query processor,
3. a local database interface (LDI) for each local DBMS, and
4. local DBMSs.

A global query references entity types and functions defined in the global schema. Before it can be processed, it must be translated by the query translator into a query referencing only entity types and functions defined in the local schemata. In other words, the query translator translates a global query over the global schema into a global query over the disjoint union of local schemata. The query processor decomposes the global query over the disjoint union of local schemata into individual local queries over local schemata. The query processor also does query optimization and coordinates the execution of local queries. The LDI translates local queries received from the query processor into queries expressed in the local DML and translates the results of the local queries into a format expected by the query processor. These components and their interrelationships are depicted in Figure 3.

The User Interface

The global schema is expressed in the functional data model.[1] In this data model, a schema is composed of *entity types* and *functions* between entity types. Each entity type contains a set of entities, so functions map entities into entities. Functions can be *single-valued* or *multi-valued*, and can be *partially defined* or *totally defined*.

The functional data model was selected because it embodies the main structures of both the flat file data models, such as the relational model, and the link structured data models, such as CODASYL. Entity types correspond roughly to relations in the relational model or record types in the CODASYL model. Functions correspond to owner-coupled sets in the CODASYL model.

The query language that we use with the functional data model is called DAPLEX. DAPLEX is a high level language that operates on data in the functional data model and is designed to be especially easy to use by end users.

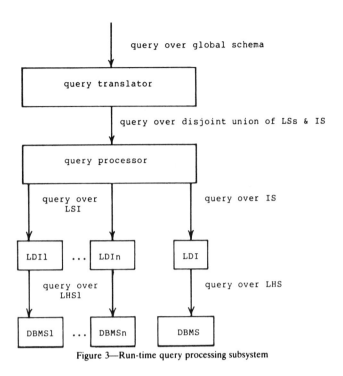

query over global schema

query translator

query over disjoint union of LSs & IS

query processor

query over
LSI

query over IS

LDI1 ... LDIn

LDI

query over
LHS1

query over LHS

DBMS1 ... DBMSn

DBMS

Figure 3—Run-time query processing subsystem

Query Translator

The query translator receives global queries expressed in DAPLEX over the GS and translates them into queries expressed in an internal language over the disjoint union of LSs and IS.

To perform the translation, the query translator must use the mapping that defines how entity types and functions of the GS are constituted from the entity types and functions of the LS and the IS. The query translator uses these mapping definitions to substitute global entity types and global functions in the global query by their mapping definitions. The substitution results in a query containing only entity types and functions of the LSs and the IS. Therefore references by the global query to entities in the GS are now expressed as references to the actual entities at particular sites that implement the global GS. Any extra data needed from the integration database to resolve incompatibilities among LSs is now explicitly referenced in the translated query.

The query produced by the query translator only references data in the LS and the IS. Thus, we can imagine that this query is posed against a database state that is the disjoint union of the LSs together with the IS. This disjoint union is a homogeneous and centralized view of the distributed heterogeneous database.

The language used for defining the mapping between schemata must be compatible with the global DML. Otherwise, it would be awkward to translate the query from the GS to LSs and IS using conventional query modification techniques. (Query modification composes the given query, which is a function from GS states to answer states, with the mapping from LS and IS states to GS states, to produce a query from LS and IS states to answer states.[2]) Therefore, we propose to

use the same language DAPLEX as both the query and mapping language. The process of constructing the global schema from the local schemata is discussed in Section 3.

Query Processor

The query processor translates a query over the disjoint union of LSs and IS into a *query processing strategy*. This strategy includes the following: a set of queries, each of which is posed against exactly one LS or the IS; a set of "move" operations to ship the results of these queries between the local DBMSs and the query processor; and a set of queries that is executed locally by the query processor to integrate the results of the LS and IS queries. The main goal of this translation is to minimize the total cost of evaluating the query, where cost is measured by local processing time and communication volume.

A query processing strategy is produced in two steps. First, the query is translated into an internal representation called a *query graph*. Using this representation, the query processor isolates those subqueries of the given query (which are essentially subgraphs of the query graph) that can be entirely evaluated at one local DBMS. Thus, the result of the first step is the set of single-site subqueries of the given query.

The second step is to combine the single-site queries with move operations and local queries issued by the query processor. Move operations serve two purposes. First, they are used to gather the results of the single-site queries back to the query processor. These results can be integrated by the query processor by executing a query local to itself. The integrated results may be the answer to the query, in which case they are returned to the user. Second, they may be used as input to other single-site queries. In this case, a move operation is issued to ship the data to the local DBMS that needs it. The method by which single-site queries, move operations, and queries local to the query processor are sequenced to produce a correct and efficient strategy is discussed in Section 4.

Local Database Interface (LDI)

Local queries posed against the LSs are sent by the query processor to the LDIs in an internal format. The LDI translates these local queries into programs in the local DML and programming language over the local host schema (LHS). This translation is optimized to minimize the processing time of the translated query. When the local DBMS uses a high level (i.e., set-at-a-time) language, such as DAPLEX, this translation is fairly direct. However, when the local DBMS uses a low level (i.e., record-at-a-time) language, such as CODASYL DML embedded in COBOL, this translation may be quite complex and may require nontrivial optimization. Translation methods for a file system and CODASYL language are described in Section 4.

To do the translation, the LDI must have information about how entity types and functions in the LS are mapped to objects in the LHS. These mappings are defined using the rules discussed below.

3. SCHEMA INTEGRATION ARCHITECTURE

"Schema Integration" is the process of defining a global schema and its mapping from the existing local schemata. The general architecture of this design process is discussed in this section.

There is one local host schema (LHS) for each local database. Each LHS can be expressed in a relational, CODASYL, or a file language. To merge these LHSs we must convert them into a common data model first. Otherwise, we would be mixing relations from a relational model with record types and set types from a CODASYL model. Thus the first step of schema integration is to translate LHSs into Local Schemata (LS) defined in the Functional Data Model of DAPLEX.

The second step is to merge LSs into a GS. To do this, an integration schema which defines an integration database is often needed. An integration database contains: information about mapping between different scales used by different LSs for the same entity type; statistical information about imprecise data; and other information needed for reconciling inconsistency between copies of the same data stored in different databases. The integration schema and LSs are then used to define a global schema.

The overall architecture of schema integration consists of

a) a global schema,
b) a mapping language,
c) local schemata (LS) and an integration schema (IS),
d) a mechanized local-to-host schema translator, and
e) local host schemata (LHS) and local DBMSs.

These components and their interrelationships are depicted in Figure 4. The local host schemata are translated into local schemata by the mechanized local host schema translator, and local schemata and the IS are mapped into the GS by using the mapping language facility.

Mapping between LHS and LS

Since an LHS can be defined in the relational, CODASYL, or file model, how an LHS is mapped into an LS depends on the data model used.

CODASYL model

If an LHS is defined in the CODASYL model, then it consists of record types and set types. The functional data model consists of entity types and functions on entity types. So, to map the LHS into an LS one simply maps record types and set types into entity types and functions respectively.

The concept of record type in the CODASYL model is very similar to that of entity type in the functional data model. A record in the CODASYL model has a record ID, and one or several attributes. The record ID uniquely identifies the record, and the attributes describe properties of the record. Similarly, in the functional data model, an entity is an object of interest, and the functions defined on the entity return values that describe the properties of the entity. Therefore, a

record type corresponds to an entity type, and the attributes of the record type correspond to functions defined on the entity type.

If an attribute of a record type is a key (in CODASYL terminology, a key is the data item(s) declared "NO DUPLICATE ALLOWED") then the corresponding function must be a totally defined one-to-one mapping. If the attribute is a repeating group (declared to have multiple occurrences in a CODASYL model), then the corresponding function is a set-valued function.

A set type in the CODASYL model is a mapping between an owner record type and one or several member record types. A set type maps an owner record to a set of member records, or, conversely, a set type maps a member record to a unique owner record. Therefore, a set type resembles a function that maps an owner entity to a set of member entities, or, conversely, maps a member entity to a unique owner entity.

In a CODASYL model, a set type implies not only certain semantic information but also the existence of access paths. For example a set type "work-in" between "department" and "employee" record types implies that the employees owned by a department work in that department. But it also implies that there is an access path from a department record to the employee records owned by that department and another access path from each employee record to its own department record. Since the LSs will be used for query optimization, we

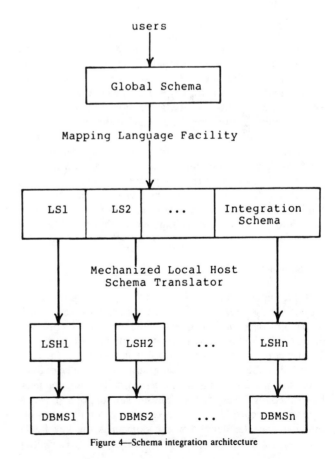

Figure 4—Schema integration architecture

must capture all this access path information in the LSs. Therefore, for each set type in an LHS, not only a set-valued function from the owner entity type to the member entity type, but also a single-valued function from each of the member entity types to the owner entity type must be defined in the corresponding LS.

In a CODASYL model, a record type can be declared to have a "LOCATION MODE CALC USING KEY." This means that an index file is created for the key, and the record type is directly accessible through the indexed key. Therefore, for each record type with "CALC KEY" in the LHS, a system set function of which the domain is the key value and the range is the entity type (corresponding to the record type) must be defined in the LS. This system set function will be used only for query processing optimization. It is not visible to the database designer. Therefore, it cannot be incorporated into the global schema. This restriction is imposed to preserve the data independence of the global schema.

For example, the CODASYL schema shown in Figure 5 is translated into the schema in the functional data model shown in Figure 6. In Figure 6, the inverse of a function F is denoted by "F-inv."

Relational model

A relational database schema consists of a set of relation definitions. To translate a relational LHS to a functional LS we essentially map each relation to an entity type. A tuple of a relation in a relational model is similar to an entity in a functional data model. A tuple is uniquely identified by its primary key and has one or more attributes, just as an entity has one or more functional values. Therefore, to map a relational model LHS into a functional data model LS, for each relation in the LHS an entity type is defined in the LS, and for each attribute of the relation a function is defined on the corresponding entity type. The range of the function is the domain of the attribute. If the attribute is a primary key, then the function must be totally defined and one-to-one. If it is a candidate key, then the function can be partially defined, but it must still be one-to-one. In any case, due to the relational format, the function must be single-valued, not set-valued. For example, the relational LHS shown in Figure 7 is translated into the functional data model LS shown in Figure 8.

File model

A file model consists of record files and indexed fields (keys) in those files. A record file consists of a set of records of the same type, which is similar to the concept of record type in the CODASYL model or a relation in the relational model. To map a file LHS to a functional data model LS, for each record file in LHS a corresponding entity type must be defined in the LS, and for each field of the record file a function must be defined on the entity type. Since a key supports an access path to the record file, for each key of a record file, a system function must be defined whose domain is the key field's entity type and whose range is the entity type corresponding

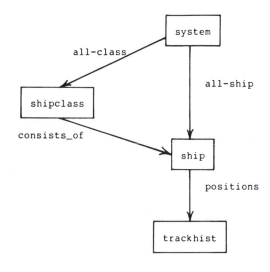

```
Shipclass Record                    Trackhist Record
*classname    char(24)        **  DTG        char(10)
 length       char(6)             speed      char(3)
 draft        char(2)             latitude   char(5)
 beam         char(3)             longitude  char(6)
 displacement char(5)             course     char(3)
 endurance    char(3)

*    primary key
**   key within a set

Ship Record
*    UIC          char(6)
     VCN          char(5)
     name         char(26)
     type         char(4)
     flag         char(2)
     owner        char(2)
     hull         char(4)
```

Figure 5—A CODASYL schema

to the record file. This system function is not visible to the database designer; it is used only for query optimization.

Integration of LSs

To integrate LSs into a global schema, the database designer designs an integration schema that defines an integration database. He then designs a global schema and defines it in terms of the LSs and the Integration Schema by using the view support facility.

An integration database contains information needed for merging entity types and their functions. For example, two entity types, E1 and E2, from two schemata are shown in Figure 9. These two entity types represent information about ships. There are two functions defined on each entity type; one function returns the ship-id of a ship and the other returns the ship-class of the ship. The ship-class of E1 and E2 are coded differently. A sample of entities and their functional values are also shown in Figure 9. To merge E1 and E2 into a single entity type, a uniform code must be defined, and the two existing codes must be mapped to the new code. Definitions of the new code and the mapping function are shown in Figure 10, and a sample of the function is shown in Figure 11.

```
type shipclass is entity
   classname    : string(1..24);
   length       : string(1..6);
   draft        : string(1..2);
   beam         : string(1..3);
   displacement : string(1..5);
   endurance    : string(1..3);
   consists-of  : set of ship;
end entity;

type ship is entity
   UIC   : string(1..6);
   VCN   : string(1..5);
   name  : string(1..26);
   type  : string(1..4);
   flag  : string(1..2);
   owner : string(1..2);
   hull  : string(1..4);
   positions : set of trackhist;
   consists-of_inv : shipclass;
end entity;

type system is entity
   all-class : set of shipclass
   all-ship  : set of ship;
end entity;

type trackhist is entity
   DTG       : string (1..10);
   speed     : string (1..3);
   latitude  : string (1..5);
   longitude : string (1..6);
   course    : string (1..3);
   positions_inv : ship;
end entity;
```

Figure 6—A schema in the functional data model

The definitions of the new code and the function are stored in the integration database. A global schema defined on the two local schemata and the integration schema is shown in Figure 12.

As the discussion above indicates, integration of local schemata which are not disjoint involves two activities: merging of entity types and merging of their functions. These activities are discussed in the next section. Two special problems relating to schema integration, the creation of new entity types,

and the integration of incompatible data, are discussed in subsequent sections.

Merging Entity Types and Functions

To merge two entity types, say E1 and E2 in Figure 9, into an entity type, say E in Figure 12, the database designer must first determine whether the set of entities of type E1 is disjoint from the set of entities of type E2. If E1 and E2 are disjoint, then E is simply the union of E1 and E2. If E1 and E2 are not disjoint, then the condition under which two entities from E1 and E2 respectively are identical must be specified. To specify the condition under which entities are identical, entities of E1 and E2 must be able to be identified by their attributes. Therefore, for each entity type to be merged, a function or combination of functions of the entity type must be a primary key. Two entities from two entity types being merged can then

```
type platform is entity
   VesselName :string (1..26);
   class      :string (1..25);
   type       :string (1..6);
   hull       :string (1..6);
   flag       :string (1..2);
   category   :string (1..4);
   PIF        :string (1..4);
   NOSICID    :string (1..8);
   IRCS       :string (1..8);
end entity;

type position is entity
   PIF       :string (1..4);
   NOSICID   :string (1..8);
   DTG       :string (1..10);
   latitude  :string (1..5);
   longitude :string (1..6);
   bearing   :string (1..3);
   course    :string (1..3);
   speed     :string (1..3);
end entity;
```

Figure 8—A schema for the functional data model

```
Relation Platform
   VesselName          char(26)
   class               char(25)
   type                char(6)
   hull                char(6)
   flag                char(2)
   category            char(4)
    ⎧ PIF               char(4)
 * ⎨ NOSICID            char(8)
    ⎩ IRCS              char(8)

Relation Position
    ⎧ PIF               char(4)
 * ⎨ NOSICID            char(8)
    ⎩ DTG               char(10)
   latitude            char(5)
   longitude           char(6)
   bearing             char(3)
   course              char(3)
   speed               char(3)

 * primary key
```

Figure 7—A relational model

```
type E1 is entity            type E2 is entity
   shipid1 : integer;           shipid2 : integer;
   class1  : code1;             class2  : code2;
end entity;                  end entity;
```

E1	shipid1	class1
e11	1212	c1
e12	1240	c3
e13	2341	c5

E2	shipid2	class2
e21	3440	d2
e22	3651	d3
e23	4411	d4

Figure 9—Local schemata

```
type code is entity
end entity;

Define a new function
   f : (code1 union code2)  -> code.
```

Figure 10—Integration database

169

```
           Sample of function f
--------------------------------------------------
 code1,code2 c1  c2  c3  c4  c5  d1  d2  d3  d4
--------------------------------------------------
 code         1   2   3   4   5   6   7   8   9
--------------------------------------------------
```

Figure 11—Sample of function f

```
type E is entity
      shipid : integer;
      class  : code;
end entity;
```

Figure 12—Global schema

be specified as identical if and only if they have identical primary key values.

In Figure 13, entity types E1 and E2 (which are assumed to overlap), are merged into an entity type E. The syntax used is a subset of DAPLEX. Notice that "shipid1" and "shipid2" are assumed to be primary keys of E1 and E2 respectively. Further, it is assumed that an E1 entity and an E2 entity are identical if and only if they have the same primary key values.

Creation of a New Entity Type and its Functions

Merging two entity types into a single entity type is a special case of creating a new entity type. Essentially, a new entity type may be created which is a combination of the existing entity types. However, this combination does not create new objects in the database. Rather, it simply presents many existing objects of different types as objects of a single type to the global schema users. Properties of the new global entities are simply those that previously existed in the local schemata.

However, in some cases, a database designer may want to design a more sophisticated global schema in which new (virtual) objects derive their properties (attributes) from many dissimilar existing objects. An example is used to illustrate this process, and general principles can be drawn from the example.

```
        type E is entity
           shipid : integer;
           class  : code;
        end entity;

for each  x in E1 where not (shipid1(x) isin
                                  shipid2(E2))
loop
create new E(shipid => shipid1(x)
                  class  => f (class1(x)));
end loop;

for each x in E2

loop

create new E(shipid => shipid2(x),

                  class  => f(class2(x)));

end loop;
```

Figure 13—The mapping definition of entity type E

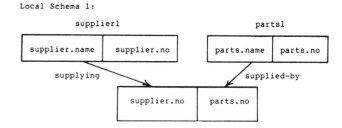

Local Schema 1:

```
type supplier1 is entity
     sname       : string(30);
     sno         : integer;
     supplying   : set of supply1;
end entity;

type parts1 is entity
     pname       : string(15);
     pno         : integer;
     supplied-by : set of supply1;
end entity;

type supply1 is entity
     sno    : integer;
     pno    : integer;
end entity;
```

Local schema 2:

```
          supply2
|---------|--------------|
|  sno    |     pno      |
|---------|--------------|

type supply2 is entity
     sno    : integer;
     pno    : integer;
end entity;
```

Figure 14—Two local schemata

Suppose a global schema with two entity types, "supplier" and "parts," is to be designed from two local schemata shown in Figure 14. The global schema must capture all the information contained in both schemata. Notice that in the second schema, "supplier" and "parts" entities do not exist, but their existence is implied by the presence of supplier numbers and part numbers: "sno" and "pno." To capture this information, virtual "supplier" and "parts" entities corresponding to those "sno" and "pno" must be created in the global schema. A definition of the global schema is shown in Figure 15. Notice that in the definition primary keys "supplier.no" and "parts.no" are used to map the new entities to existing entities in the first schema and the implied entities in the second schema.

Data Incompatibility

Several sources of data incompatibility are discussed in this section. The objective of the discussion is to show how the proposed architecture allows us to incorporate our present understanding of incompatible data into Multibase. The details of solutions to the problem are to be fully investigated later in the project.

Some sources of data imprecision are:

1. *Scale difference*. For example, in one database four values (cold, cool, warm, hot) are used to classify climates

```
type supplier is entity
     sno     : integer;
     supplying : set of parts;
  end entity;

type parts is entity
     name: string(15);
     no  : integer;
  end entity;

for each x in (sno(supplier1) union sno(supply2))
 loop
  create supplier (sno => x);
  end loop;

for each y in (pno(parts1) union pno(supply2))
 loop
  create parts (pno => y);
  end loop;

for each s in supplier loop
supplying(s) .+ (p in parts where (for some y1 in supply1:
     sno(s) = sno(y1) and pno(p)= pno(y1)) or
     (for some y2 in supply2 :
     sno(s) = sno(y2) and pno(p) = pno(y2)));
  end loop;
```

Figure 15—A global schema

of cities, while in another database the average temperatures in Fahrenheit may be recorded.

2. *Level of Abstraction.* For example, in one database "labor cost" and "material cost" may be recorded separately, while in another they are combined into "total cost." Another example is recording an employee's "average salary" instead of his or her "salary history" for the previous five years.

3. *Inconsistency Among Copies of the Same Information.* Certain information about an entity may appear in several databases, and the values may be different due to timing, errors, obsolescence, etc.

There are many other sources of data incompatibility. Data incompatibility must be resolved if different databases are to be integrated. The architecture of schema integration developed previously can be extended to handle the problem.

Let E1 and E2 be two entity types, and f1 and f2 be functions defined on E1 and E2 respectively. If E1 and E2 have been merged into an entity type E, then f1 and f2 can be merged into the function f defined on E as follows,

$$f(e) = \begin{cases} T1(f1(e)) & \text{if e in E1-(E1 intersect E2)} \\ T2(f2(e)) & \text{if e in E2-(E1 intersect E2)} \\ g(f1(e),f2(e)) & \text{if e in (E1 intersect E2)} \end{cases}$$

The transformations T1 and T2 are typically used to map the ranges of f1 and f2 into a common range as discussed in the section "Merging Entity Types and Functions." On the other hand, the function g is used to reconcile any inconsistencies between the values of f1 and f2 over the same entity. Typically, g will involve accessing data described in the integration schema.

For example, in Figure 16, the entity types E4 and E5 are merged into the entity type E6 by using functions IS2 and IS3 of the integration database. In the figure, the data values of the entities and functions are shown in tabular form. In this example, T1 and T2 transform the climate of cities from two

different scales, (cold,cool,warm,hot) and Fahrenheit, into a unified scale (temperature range, probability) by combining E4 with IS2 and E5 with IS3. The function g could return all the (temperature range, probability) pairs from the two databases without any further processing, as is shown in Figure 16.

Alternatively, g could use some statistical technique to process sets of (Temp range, probability) pairs, and return a simpler but descriptive summary of those pairs. For example, the function g could return the average value and the standard deviation of the distribution represented by these pairs; it can make statistical estimation and return a confidence interval; or it can do time series analysis and return information about the spectral function.

The above examples are merely illustrative of potential data integration problems and their solutions. More complete approaches to the problem will be fully investigated later in the project.

4. RUN-TIME QUERY PROCESSING SUBSYSTEM

Overall Architecture

Now we will show how the schema mappings developed during schema integration are utilized to drive query processing over the global schema. As we explained in Section 2, the run-time subsystem consists of a query translator and a query processor. Here we will expand these two components in further detail.

A "Global Database Manager" (GDM) is that part of the Multibase System which consists of the query translator, and the query processor. A query over the global schema is normally sent to the nearest site that has a Global Database Manager (GDM). There may be one or more GDMs in a Multibase system. A GDM stores a copy of global schema,

E4 (of LS1)			IS2 (of integration database)		
city1	climate		climate	range of temp	probability
Boston	cold		cold	0 - 20 F	20%
Norfolk	cool		cold	20 - 40 F	40%
Dallas	warm		cold	40 - 60 F	25%
Miami	hot		cold	60 - 80 F	10%
...	...		cold	80 - 100F	5%
			cool	0 - 20 F	10%
			cool	20 - 40 F	20%
			...	...	...

E5 (of LS2)			IS3 (of integration database)		
city2	mean temp		mean temp	range of temp	probability
Denver	52 F		52 F	0 - 20 F	20%
Chicago	54 F		52 F	20 - 40 F	35%
Los Ang	75 F		52 F	40 - 60 F	30%
...	...		...	...	...

E6 (of global schema)		
city	temp range	probability
Boston	0 - 20 F	20%
Boston	20 - 40 F	40%
...	...	...

Figure 16—Example of data incompatibility

local schemata, integration schema, and the mapping definitions among them. It uses this information to parse, translate, and decompose queries over the global schema into local queries over local schemata, and coordinates execution of the local queries. The structure of a GDM and its interface with local DBMSs is shown in Figure 17.

A query expressed in DAPLEX over the global schema is first parsed by the parser and a parse tree is generated. Components of the parse tree, which are entities and functions of the global schema, are then replaced by their corresponding definitions, which are expressed in terms of the local schemata LSs. The result is a parse tree consisting of entities and functions of the local schemata. The parser is part of the query translator.

The parse tree is then simplified to eliminate the inefficient boolean components. For example, the boolean expression "$(a > 5) or (a < 20)$" is reduced to "true," and "$(a > 5) and (a < 2)$" is reduced to "false." The query simplifier is also part of the query translator.

The parse tree is then decomposed by the decomposer into subtrees. Each subtree represents a local query referencing only entities and functions of a single local schema.

The "ACCESS PLANNER" transforms the local queries into "data movement" and "local processing" steps. Depending on the memory size and processing power of each individual site, and the capacity of the communication channels, the "ACCESS PLANNER" may move data and distribute the computing load among several sites, or it may move

data to a central site which has large memory and computing power and do most of the processing there. In doing this planning, the "ACCESS PLANNER" tries to produce steps which minimize the cost of processing the query. The meaning of "cost" depends on the individual systems being integrated. It may mean the amount of data moved between sites, or the amount of processing time.

The execution of the access plan is coordinated by the "EXECUTION STRATEGIST." It sequences the steps of the access plan and it makes sure that the data needed by a step are there before the step is initiated.

The "EXECUTION STRATEGIST" communicates with local DBMSs through the Local Database Interface (LDI). The LDIs receive "data move" and "local processing" steps from the "EXECUTION STRATEGIST," translate these steps into programs in the local query language or Data Manipulation Language (DML), or call local routines to process these steps, and translate the results of these steps into the format expected by the "EXECUTION STRATEGIST." The LDI may reside in a GDM if the local site does not have enough memory or cpu power; otherwise it resides with the individual local DBMS at the local site.

The query processor to be described in this section is oriented towards the initial breadboard system. It is designed to handle restricted versions of the user interface language and view mapping language with reasonable efficiency. Subsequent research is needed to extend the query processor to efficiently handle the unrestricted languages.

Within the "Query Processor," the database is modelled as a collection of *entity types* and *links*. A link L from entity type R to entity type S is a function from entities of S to entities of R; S is called the *owner* entity type and R is called the *member* entity type relative to L. We assume that if L links R to S, then L, R, and S are all stored at the same site. We also assume that there is a database schema describing the entity types and links of the database.

We will sketch the Multibase query processing strategy in three steps. First, we define the set of queries that can be posed. Second, we define the set of basic operations that Multibase is capable of executing. Third, we describe how to translate a query into a sequence of basic operations that solve the query. Finally, we describe how to translate a local query posed over a CODASYL local host schema into a program in a low level Data Manipulation Language.

Queries

A *query* consists of a target list and a qualification. A *target list* consists of a set of *function terms* of the form A(R) where R is an entity type and A is a non-link function of R. A *qualification* is a conjunction of selection clauses, join clauses, and link clauses. A *selection clause* is a formula of the form $(A(R) \text{ op } k)$ where A(R) is a function term, op is one of $\{ =, \leq, <, >, \geq, \neq \}$ and k is a constant. A *join clause* is a formula of the form $(A(R) = B(S))$ where A(R) and B(S) are function terms. A *link clause* is a formula of the form $(L(R) = S)$ where L is a link from R to S.

Let r and s be entities in R and S respectively. We say that

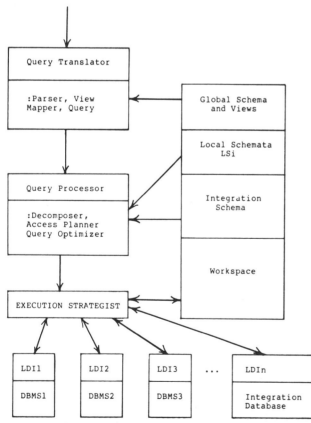

Figure 17—Run time query processing subsystem

r *satisfies the selection clause* (A(R) op k) if the A-value of r is op-related to k (i.e., (A(r) op k)). We say that r and s *satisfy the join clause* (A(R) = B(S)) if the A-value of r equals the B-value of s (i.e., A(r) = B(s)). And we say that r and s *satisfy the link clause* L(R) = S if L connects r and s (i.e., L(r) = s).

Let R1,..., Rn be the entity types referenced by qualification q, and let r1,...,rn be entities in R1,...,Rn respectively. We say that r1,...,rn *satisfy the qualification* q if r1,...,rn satisfy all of the clauses of q.

Let Q be a query consisting of target list T = ((Aj1(Ri1), ...,Ajm(Rim)) and qualification q. Let R1,...,Rn be the entity types referenced in T and q. The *answer* to Q is the set of all tuples of the form ((Aj1(ri1),...,Ajm(rim))) such that r1,...,rn are in R1,...,Rn (respectively) and r1,...,rn satisfy q. Given a database R1,...,Rn and a query Q, our goal is to compute the answer to Q efficiently.

The subset of DAPLEX that we have just described makes the following simplifications:

1. Set expressions in range predicates and qualifications have been "flattened out," and quantifiers eliminated. This allows us to utilize existing view algorithms for relational databases. Further research will be devoted to handling the novel aspects of view processing in the DAPLEX functional model.
2. The type-subtype hierarchy is not explicitly handled. This hierarchy will be useful in the schema integration step. However, the mechanics of interpreting queries against the hierarchy require further research.

A query graph QG(N,E) is an undirected labelled graph that represents a query Q. The nodes, N, of QG are the entity types referenced in Q. Each node is labelled by the entity type name of the node, the non-link functions of the entity type that appear in the target list, and the selection clauses of Q's qualification that reference the entity type. The edge set E of QG contains one edge (R,S) for each join clause or link clause that references R and S. Each edge is labelled by its corresponding clause(s).

A query is called *natural* if (a) join clauses are of the form (A(R) = A(S)), that is, the functions referenced in both terms of a join clause have the same name; and (b) if A is a non-link function of two entity types R and S, then A(R) and A(S) are "connected" by a sequence of join clauses. There is a simple and efficient algorithm that, given a database description and a query Q, renames the functions of the entity types where necessary to produce an equivalent natural query Q'; Q and Q' are equivalent in the sense that they produce the same answer for any database state (up to the renaming of fields). We will therefore assume, without the loss of generality, that our queries are natural. Given that we deal only with natural queries, the edge labels corresponding to join clauses are unnecessary. Also target lists need only contain function names, instead of function terms.

Given a join clause (A(R) = A(S)) and a selection clause (A(R) op k), we can deduce that (S(A) op k). We assume that the qualification of each query is augmented by all clauses that can be deduced in this way. A simple and efficient transitive closure algorithm is sufficient for performing such deductions.

Basic operations

There are three types of sites in the breadboard Multibase: File, CODASYL, and GDM. Each type of site is capable of executing a different set of basic operations. This section describes these basic operations.

1. *File Select.* If record type R is stored at a File site S, then the only operation that can be applied to R at S is a selection of the form

   R[(A1 = k1) and (A2 = k2) and ... and (An = kn)].

   The result of the selection is a record type consisting of the set of all records r in R such that r[Ai] = ki for i = 1,...,n; this result is always transmitted to the GDM.
2. *File Semijoin.* In principle, File select can be generalized into File semijoin by performing selections iteratively. Let R be a File file and S a GDM file, and suppose A1,...,An are fields of R and S. Then the semijoin of R by S on A1,...,An, denoted R[A1,...,An]S, equals

   {r in R | (there exist s in S)
   $$(r.A1 = s.A1 ... r.An = s.An)\}.$$

   This can be computed by the following program.

   ```
   Result: = 0;
   for each s in S
   loop
     k1: = s.A1,...; kn: = s.An;
     Result: = Result ∪ R[(A1 = k1)...
         (An = kn)];
   end loop;
   ```

   In practice, this operation may place an unacceptable load on the File system and hence may not be usable.
3. *CODASYL tree queries.* The basic operation that can be performed at a CODASYL site S is to solve a natural tree query (defined below), returning the result to the GDM. A *natural tree query* Q at site S has two properties: (1) All record types referenced in Q must be stored at S. (2) Let Q' be Q minus its join clauses (i.e., all clauses of Q' are selections or links), and let QG' be the query graph of Q'; then QG' must be a tree.

   To solve a tree query Q using CODASYL DML, one essentially expands the cartesian product of the record types referenced by Q and evaluates the qualification on each element of the cartesian product. We describe how this cartesian product can be systematically generated in the section "Processing CODASYL Tree Queries."
4. *CODASYL Tree Semijoins.* The preceding operation can be generalized into a semijoin-like operation. Let Q be a CODASYL tree query and S a GDM record type, and suppose A1,...,An are fields of S and fields of record types of Q. Let Q' have the same qualification as Q, and the target list augmented by A1,...,An. Finally, let R' be the result of Q'. The semijoin of Q by S on A1,...,An, denoted Q < A1,...,An], equals

   {r' in R'| (there exist s in S)
   $$(r'.A2 = s.A2) ... (r'.An = s.An)\}.$$

This can be computed as follows. Suppose A1,...,An are fields of R1,...,Rn respectively where R1,...,Rn are record types of Q. (R1,...,Rn need not be distinct.) Augment the qualification of Q' by adding the clauses (R1.A1 = k1)...(Rn.An = kn). And execute the following program.

```
Result: = 0;
for each s in S loop
  k1: = s.A1;...; kn: = s.An;
  Result: = Result ∪ Q';
end loop;
```

5. *GDM Queries*. The GDM can process any natural query Q provided (1) all entity types referenced in Q are stored at the GDM, and (2) Q contains no link clauses. Suppose Q references entity types R1,...,Rn. Q is processed by constructing a request to the local DBMS (the Datacomputer for the initial breadboard system) of the form:

for each r1 *in* R1 *where* (selection clauses on R1)
for each r2 *in* R2 *where* (selection clauses on R2)
                    and (join clauses on R1 and R2)

.
.
.

for each rn *in* Rn *where* (selection clauses onRn)
                    and (join clauses on R1 and Rn)
                    and (join clauses on R2 and Rn)

.
.
.

                    and (join clauses on Rn-1 and Rn).
                    print (target list).

It is important that the "for" statements be in a "reasonable" order for performance reasons. Optimization techniques developed by Wong for the SDD-1 DM[3] are directly applicable.

Query Decomposition

To solve a query Q, we must decompose it into a sequence of basic operations. Our basic strategy is to find subqueries of Q that can be entirely solved at File and CODASYL sites, move the results of these subqueries to the GDM, and solve the remainder of the query at the GDM.

To follow this strategy, we must isolate File and CODASYL subqueries of Q. File subqueries are easy to find. We simply find entity types in Q that are stored at File sites. For each such entity type R, we produce a subquery consisting of the selection clauses on R.

Let QG be the query graph of Q. To find CODASYL subqueries, we begin by deleting from QG all entity types not stored at a CODASYL site and all join clauses. Each connected component of the resulting graph includes entity types and links that are stored at the same site, because no link can connect two entity types stored at different sites (c.f., the section on "Overall Architecture"). If a connected component is a tree, then it corresponds to a tree query and can be solved by the CODASYL site. If it has a cycle, then it must

be further decomposed into two or more tree queries. (In the breadboard version of Multibase, we will only handle queries whose CODASYL subqueries are tree queries; if some CODASYL subquery is cyclic, the query cannot be processed.)

Having extracted the File and CODASYL subqueries, we must now choose an order for these subqueries to be executed. As a first-cut solution, we propose to solve all File and CODASYL subqueries before processing the results of any of these subqueries at the GDM. This strategy will be an especially poor performer if a File or CODASYL subquery has no selection clauses. For such cases, we recommend use of File and CODASYL semijoin operations, so that the results of some subqueries can be used to reduce the cost of other subqueries. However, this tactic brings us into the realm of new query optimization algorithms and will require further research.

Processing CODASYL Tree Queries

Let Q be a CODASYL tree query and QG its tree. The following algorithm compiles Q into a program that solves Q. The program contains statements of the form:

1. *for* r *in* set(s) *loop*...*end loop* ; where S owns R via set ;
2. r: = set_inv(s) ; where R owns S via set. Note that set-inv is the inverse function of set and is always a function.

Algorithm

1. Do a pre-order traversal of QG. The result is a list of the nodes of QG. Call this list P.
2. Let R and S be nodes of QG; with R the parent of S. *Cases*
   R is the root of QG; replace "R" by "*for* r *in* R *loop*" in P.
   R owns S: replace "S" by "*for* s *in* set(r)" in P.
   S owns R: replace "S" by "s: = set_inv(r)" in P.
3. Push loop independent assignments up as high as possible.
4. Add an "output (target list)" statement, add selections, and joins as high as possible, tack on enough *ends* to balance the *fors*.

As an example let QG be the query graph of Figure 18.

1. Preorder traversal: R,S,T,U,V.
2. *for* r *in* R *loop*
      for s *in* L1(r) *loop*
         t: = L2_inv(r)
            for u *in* L3(t) *loop*
               v: = L4_inv(t)
3. Push up T and V; add an output statement; add *ends* to balance the *fors*.
      for r *in* R *loop*
         t: = L2_inv(r);
         v: = L4_inv(r)
         for s *in* L1(r) *loop*

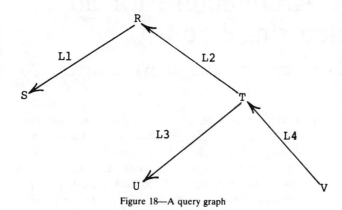

Figure 18—A query graph

```
for u in L3(t) loop
    output (target list);
    end loop;
  end loop;
end loop;
```

5. SUMMARY

This report describes the architecture of the Multibase system. Details of the components of the architecture to be implemented in the initial breadboard version are also described. Although additional research is required to fill in the details of optimization and incompatible data handling, the architecture already contains several innovative ideas in integrating distributed heterogeneous databases. These include the following:

1. the idea of using an integration database to resolve data incompatibility;
2. the idea of using a mapping language to uniformly define the global schema in terms of the local schemata and the integration schema; and
3. the idea of using query modification and query graph decomposition to transform a global query into local queries and queries over the integration database.

REFERENCES

1. Shipman, D., "The Functional Data Model and the Data Language DAPLEX", *SIGMOD 79*, Boston, MA, 1979.
2. Stonebraker, M.R.: "Implementation of Integrity Constraints and Views by Query Modifications." *Proc. ACM-SIGMOD Conf.*, San Jose, CA, 1975, pp. 65-78.
3. Wong, E., "Retrieving Dispersed Data from SDD-1: A System for Distributed Databases," *1977 Berkeley Workshop on Distributed Data Management and Computer Networks*, Univ. of CA, Berkeley, CA, May 1977.

A Distributed Database Architecture for an Integrated Manufacturing Facility

VISHU KRISHNAMURTHY, Y. W. SU, HERMAN LAM, MARY MITCHELL, AND ED BARKMEYER

1. INTRODUCTION

Computer Integrated Manufacturing (CIM) includes activities for supporting, planning, and controlling the manufacture of products. The objective of CIM is to improve the acquisition and delivery of manufacturing information, thus improving manufacturing effectiveness and resource utilization. Computer aided systems do exist at this time. However, most of these systems and methods have been designed and used independently to support specific CIM functions. The result is a limited interaction among the different component functions of CIM. The totally integrated manufacturing system is still nonexistent.

A survey of CAM [12], and a more recent discussion on Engineering Information Systems [11], stresses that software integration is the technology in CIM with the greatest potential to improve productivity. To realize the full benefits of CIM, the fully integrated manufacturing system must 1) link the activities on the shop floor with the design, factory planning, and manufacturing engineering functions; 2) provide accurate and timely feedback from the factory floor; and 3) modify and replan activities based on actual performance feedback.

The design of a system to support the information requirements of automated manufacturing [29] is affected by the environment in which it operates. The general requirements applicable to any CIM system are the following:

a) Integration of Heterogeneous Systems: The use of different systems for CAD having different database management systems is not uncommon. Manufacturing components such as robots, machine tools, vision systems, measurement systems, etc., are produced by different vendors, and have diverse control protocols, capabilities, and interface protocols.

b) Flexible Manufacturing: A CIM system should provide the ability 1) to adjust for future production demands, 2) to meet dynamically changing states in the production environment, and 3) to expand with some degree of modularity. It should also provide the capability to logically or even physically regroup the equipment or reassign resources to meet changing production requirements.

c) Local Autonomy and Integrated Operation: In the development stage of the integrated facility, whenever new equipment is introduced to the factory data network, the factory control must provide for independent testing and integration. The data must remain consistent, and an independent set of data and data manipulation capabilities must be provided for the subsystem.

d) Time Critical Operations: Many systems that direct equipment on the factory floor are real-time control systems, which make use of sensory data to perform their functions. In an automated environment, these sensory and other forms of feedback are data resources that need to be shared. Real time control systems imply that delays imposed by data sharing and communications will not be tolerated.

e) Adaptive Control: The control systems in an automated factory are able to make use of the sensory inputs and other feedback to intelligently react to failures, discrepancies, and unexpected events.

It is evident from the CIM requirements listed above that data sharing is a principal requirement in a CIM environment. Therefore, central to a fully integrated manufacturing system is a data administration system that manages the shared data resources throughout the design, planning, and manufacturing processes [24]. Other manufacturing integration efforts, such as NASA's IPAD, and the Air Force's ICAM projects [10], [13], [14] have recognized the importance of data management in CIM by concentrating on the study and development of distributed database management techniques. The issues of representation, integration [3], and administration of CAD/CAM data have been identified as some of the major problems in CIM [31].

This paper focuses on the design of a distributed database management system architecture to support integrated manufacturing. A prototype system has been implemented and is being used in the National Institute for Standards and Technology's Automated Manufacturing Research Facility (AMRF).[1] The AMRF is being developed as a testbed for automated small batch manufacturing [1], [20], [21], [23], in an effort to examine the requirements and features of CIM in more detail, and to identify measurement and standard needs for CIM.

This paper is organized as follows. Section 2 describes the overall architecture of the Integrated Manufacturing Data Administrative System (IMDAS). Sections 3 and 4 briefly describe the global data model (OSAM*) and the global data manipulation language designed and prototyped for the distributed database system, respectively. Section 5 then details the various modules of the IMDAS. In Section 6, we present a processing scenario of the IMDAS. Finally, in Section 7, we conclude with some notes on our future efforts in this project.

[1] The National Institute for Standards and Technology was previously known as the National Bureau of Standards.

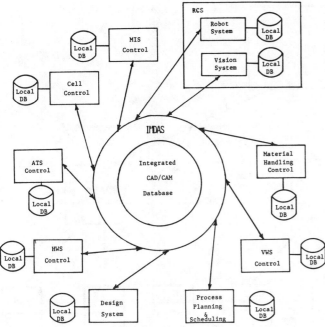

Fig. 1. The integration of heterogeneous component systems in a factory network.

2. THE ARCHITECTURE OF THE INTEGRATED MANUFACTURING DATABASE ADMINISTRATION SYSTEM (IMDAS)

IMDAS supports an integrated database which is physically distributed over a number of component systems (see Fig. 1). In order to map from the logically integrated database to physically distributed databases, IMDAS provides three levels of view definition. They are 1) global external views, 2) global conceptual view, and 3) fragmented views. A global external view defines a portion of the integrated database as seen by a single user, typically a control process. It identifies the data objects and their associations useful to the user. The global conceptual view represents the integrated database and is a comprised view of all enterprise data required to manage the CIM. The fragmented views represent the physical partitioning or replication of the conceptual objects across the component systems. Each fragmented view represents the data objects residing on a component system.

2.1. Considerations in Architecture Selection

Distributed database architecture [9] falls into two basic categories: centralized control, and distributed control. In the centralized architecture, a single central data administration system handles all the control and management functions. Data are stored in distributed databases, but all database requests are routed to a central control module. Although the architecture is straightforward to develop and easy to manage, it suffers from the lack of autonomous operation, predictable service times for time critical operations, and adaptive recovery and reliability due to single point of control—all of which are critical issues in CIM.

In a fully distributed architecture, every component system has a data administration that can control and manage distributed execution of database requests originated by its own processes, and is also capable of servicing requests coming from other component systems. This architecture makes the system more reliable and provides each component system with maximum autonomy. Unfortunately, fully distributed control of database integrity, concurrency, and recovery is far more difficult to achieve than a centralized control. Most fully distributed database systems manage homogeneous databases on similar component systems. In contrast, a CIM system generally contains heterogeneous databases that reside in dissimilar component systems. Therefore, the considerations that led to the selection and use of distributed control for homogeneous distributed database management systems such as Distributed INGRES, System R*, SDD-1, and POREL [7], [8], [22], [30] are not necessarily valid for the CIM environment. Moreover, implementing a totally distributed database software on every heterogeneous component system in a CIM environment is not as feasible, technically or economically, as implementing it on many homogeneous systems. A significant overhead is imposed in a fully distributed system by the handshaking required by the distributed control, and this has a negative impact on the performance of real time operations.

The IMDAS design pursues a third possibility [5], [27]: a hybrid architecture which has the features of both centralized and distributed controls, thus possessing the advantages of both control strategies and, at the same time, avoiding some of their individual drawbacks. The IMDAS consists of three levels of control, each of which is responsible for a defined set of distributed database management functions. These functions are distributed over the CIM component systems according to their computational capabilities. The different levels of control cooperate to establish, manipulate, and control the distributed databases.

2.2. The Three-Level Architecture of IMDAS

The IMDAS provides each component system with one or more classes of data management services. These classes are referred to as basic, distributed, and master services.

The basic data management services include command translation, data translation, and network communication. They are required by the control processes residing on every component system. These services are provided by a Basic Data Administration System (BDAS), which is implemented and installed on every component system.

The distributed database control and management functions include query translation, distributed query execution, and final data assembly. They are handled by the Distributed Data Administration System (DDAS). This software resides on those component systems that are powerful enough to support it. Not every component system has a DDAS, but each has access to one.

The "master" class of data management services are required when different component systems or subgroups of them (some containing more than one DDAS) are integrated into an operating segment of the factory data network. For each independently operating segment of the factory, there is exactly one Master Data Administration System (MDAS), which carries out such services as network initialization, managing the master data dictionary, and resolving concurrency problems between DDASs. The MDAS resides on one of the DDAS component systems.

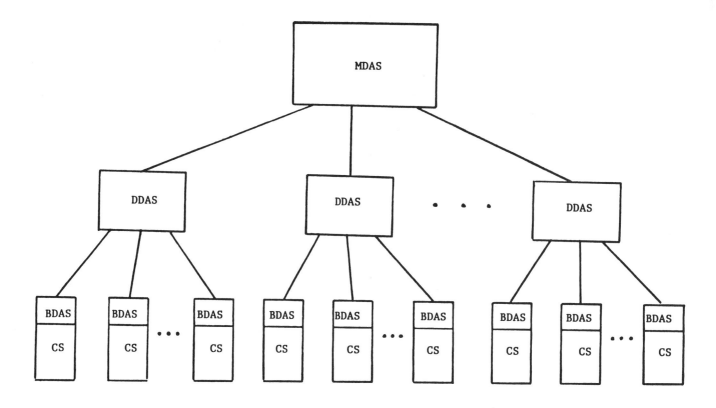

MDAS — Master Data Admininstration System

DDAS — Destributive Data Administration System

BDAS — Basic Data Administration System

CS — Component System

Fig. 2.   The three-level architecture of IMDAS.

A three-level hierarchy exists among the BDAS, DDAS, and MDAS modules of the IMDAS (see Fig. 2). As illustrated in Fig. 1, the integrated database is physically distributed on different component systems, and the BDAS, DDAS, and MDAS modules serve as a central core through which all the CIM subsystems interact and communicate.

3. A GLOBAL DATA MODEL FOR IMDAS

Within the various levels of the AMRF control hierarchy, the control processes access the integrated database through the IMDAS. For the purpose of providing a uniform interface to the integrated database, the integrated database is modeled using a common global data model, and the database requests are made using a common global DML. In this project, the common global data model used is the Semantic Association Model (SAM*) [25], [26] and its more recent extension to an Object-oriented SAM*, or OSAM* [28].

The OSAM* models objects found in an integrated CAD/CAM database in terms of complex data structures, rules, and constraints. An OSAM* database is a collection of object classes. Each object class consists of an object-type definition and its instances. An OSAM* class is defined by the following:

1) Name—This is the name of the class or the object-type it represents;

2) Structure—This is defined by the associations of the class to other classes. The various possible associations[2] are Membership (M), Aggregation (A), Interaction (I), Composition (C), Cross-product (X), Generalization (G), and data type constructors such as Set, Bag, Ordered-set, Vector, Matrix, etc.;

3) Operations—These are all the valid operations (or methods) that are associated with the class or the instances of the class;

4) Knowledge Rules—These are general inference rules, expert rules, and semantic constraints associated with the class or the instances of the class.

The OSAM* model recognizes two different types of classes: 1) *entity object* class, and 2) *domain object* class. An *entity object* class represents a class of instances, which are entities in an application domain and are, therefore, explicitly created by the user of the database. A *domain object* class is a class that strictly represents a domain of data values for some attribute used to describe an object in the database.

A detailed description of the OSAM* data model is beyond

---

[2] Note that the Summarization Association type discussed in [25], [26] has been dropped, and its semantics are incorporated in the descriptive attributes associated with a class as described in [28].

178

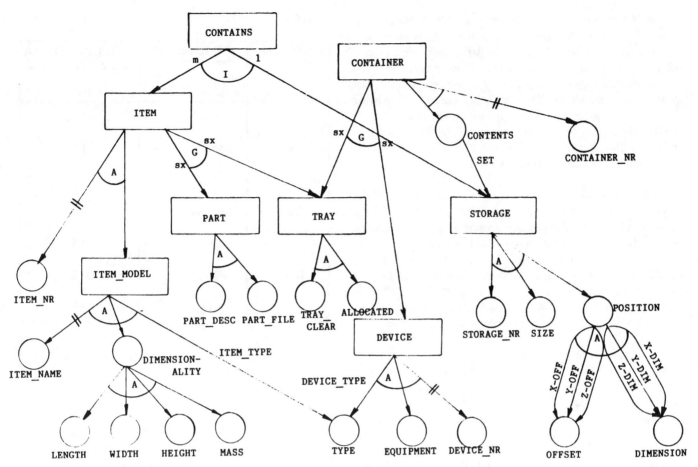

Fig. 3. Schema of a portion of an integrated manufacturing database.

the scope of this paper. For a detailed discussion of OSAM*, refer to [25], [26], [28]. In this paper, we shall briefly describe some of the features of OSAM* and illustrate some of its capabilities with an example.

The OSAM* model provides, besides the schema, two additional representations of the database: 1) Semantic diagram (S-diagram), and 2) Generalized relation (G-relation). The S-diagram depicts the structure and some of the constraints of the object classes in the database by means of a network of labeled nodes and links. For example, the S-diagram in Fig. 3 illustrates a portion of an integrated manufacturing database, which describes items, trays, parts, devices, containers, and storage locations, and the relationship that a storage location may contain an item. In the S-diagram, nodes stand for object classes. A rectangular node represents an entity object class, while a circular node represents a domain object class. Links emanating from a node represent the structural attributes of the class. A link drawn from class A to class B stands for an association of an object in A to some object in B. The type of association is indicated by labeling the link as one of the following: M, A, I, C, X, G, set, bag, ordered set, vector, or matrix. An object class is defined by its associations with other object classes. The associations are represented by labeled attributes. Each attribute is assigned a name, which can be the same as the object class from which it draws its members (i.e., the domain). For example, the attribute DEVICE_NR of the class DEVICE (i.e., the link) has the same name as its domain DEVICE_NR. The name of

an attribute can be different from that of its domain. In this case, the link representing the attribute is explicitly named in the S-diagram (e.g., the attribute DEVICE_TYPE of class DEVICE). In order to uniquely identify an instance of a class, an attribute whose values uniquely identify the instances of the class is designated as the object identifier. The object identifier is indicated in the S-diagram by an attribute link with double dash-marks across it. For example, DEVICE_NR of class DEVICE is an object identifier.

The example shown in Fig. 3 illustrates five types of OSAM* associations: Membership, Aggregation, Interaction, Generalization, and Set. The Membership association type (not shown in the diagram) associates objects of a domain object class with some primitive domain object class such as a STRING, INTEGER, REAL, etc. These primitive domain object classes contain atomic data values and are system-predefined. For example, in Fig. 3, the object class ITEM_NAME is a domain of item names of data type STRING.

The Aggregation association type models the semantics that each object of a class is described or characterized by an aggregation of objects of some other classes. In the S-diagram, the attribute links of a class, which point to the class's constituent classes, are grouped together by an arc designated by the letter A for aggregation. For example, in Fig. 3, an instance of the class STORAGE is defined by an aggregate of objects drawn from the classes STORAGE_NR, STORAGE_SIZE, and POSITION.

An interaction between or among a set of objects is itself an

179

object. An object class, which represents a set of interactions, is said to enter an interaction association with its participant object classes. In the S-diagram, the participant object classes of an interaction are connected to the defined class by attribute links, which are grouped together by an arc designated by the letter I for interaction. The cardinality constraints existing between participant classes are depicted on the arc. In Fig. 3, CONTAINS is an object class with an interaction association with the classes ITEMS and STORAGE. The class CONTAINS models a class of facts that some storages contain some items.

A class may contain generic properties of objects, while another class may contain more specialized properties of those objects. The class which contains generic properties is called a superclass, and the class which contains more specialized properties is called a subclass. A superclass may have a number of subclasses. The subclasses are connected to their superclass by attribute links in an S-diagram. These attribute links are explicitly labeled by the letter G for Generalization. An object in the subclass also belongs to its superclass, and thereby it "inherits" all the properties (i.e., attributes, operations, and rules) of the superclass. The example in Fig. 3 contains two generalization associations among object classes. First, the object classes PART and TRAY are subclasses of the class ITEM. This indicates that some subset of items are trays or parts. The set exclusion (SX) constraint between the classes TRAY and PART (shown flanking the arc between the structural attributes in the figure) precludes any tray from being a part and vice-versa. Second, the superclass CONTAINER contains DEVICE and TRAY as its subclasses. The generalization association models the fact that a device or a tray is also a container. The generic properties of trays and devices are captured in the class CONTAINER.

The set association between two object classes A and B is modeled in an S-diagram by an attribute link connecting A to B. The link is explicitly labeled by SET for set association. Each instance of A is a set of instances of B. The set association is a data-type constructor, which constructs sets out of the domain B. For example, in Fig. 3, the class CONTENTS represent a class whose instances are sets formed from the instances of the class STORAGE.

We now turn our attention to the other representation of a database. A G-relation is a tabular representation of the instances of an object class. The first row of a G-relation contains the object class attributes, and the rest of the rows represent the object instances. A G-relation is defined recursively, and results in a nested tabular structure. In other words, it is a relation (in the relational model sense) in which the attributes themselves can be relations. It has a set of distinct attributes: the object identifier, which is distinguished from the others by an underlined attribute name, and structural attributes, which are explicitly labeled by their association types. The G-relation is the standard format in which the result to a user's query is presented. The data associated with the instances of classes are stored internally as G-relations, which represent the logical storage structure of the instances of a class.

Fig. 4 shows the G-relational representation of the example

ITEM

OID : G	ITEM_NR : A	ITEM_MODEL : A
		OID
05	part_1	012
06	part_2	014
07	part_3	012
08	part_4	014
09	tray_1	013
010	tray_2	013
011	tray_3	013

PART

OID	PART_DESC : A	PART_FILE : A
05	blank	PF_1
06	T_joint	PF_2
07	L_joint	PF_3
08	crank	PF_4

TRAY

OID	TRAY_CLEAR : A	ALLOCATED : A
09	6	yes
010	4	no
011	10	no

Fig. 4. G-relations for entity object classes shown in Fig. 3.

in Fig. 3. Every entity object class in the S-diagram has a G-relation representation. Every entity object class instance is assigned by the system a unique object identifier, which is referred to as OID. An object class instance is referred to by the instances of other object classes through its OID. For example, in the G-relation representation of ITEM, the attribute ITEM_MODEL contains the OIDs of the instances stored in the G-relation of the object class ITEM_MODEL. In

STORAGE

OID	STORAGE_NR : A	POSITION : A						SIZE : A
		X_OFF	Y_OFF	Z_OFF	X_DIM	Y_DIM	Z_DIM	
015	S0	*	*	*	*	*	*	10
016	S1	*	*	*	*	*	*	20
017	S2	*	*	*	*	*	*	10
018	S3	*	*	*	*	*	*	20
019	S4	*	*	*	*	*	*	20
020	S5	*	*	*	*	*	*	10
021	S6	*	*	*	*	*	*	10
022	S7	*	*	*	*	*	*	10
023	S8	*	*	*	*	*	*	20

CONTAINS

OID	ITEM : I	STORAGE : I
	OID	OID
031	05	015
032	09	019
033	07	015
034	06	020
035	011	021

Fig. 4.   (*Continued*).

181

ITEM_MODEL

OID	ITEM_NAME : A	ITEM_TYPE : A	DIMENSIONALITY : A			
			LENGTH : A	WIDTH : A	HEIGHT : A	MASS : A
O12	BLANK	PART	10	5	3	15
O13	TRAY	TRAY	20	10	10	40
O14	BLANK_1	PART	15	10	5	30
O15	GRIPPER	R_GRIP	20	5	3	15

CONTAINER

OID : G	CONTAINER_NR : A	CONTENTS : A
		STORAGE : SET
		OID
O1	cart_1	015 016 017
O2	unit_1	018 019
O9	tray_1	020
O10	tray_2	021
O11	tray_3	022
O3	end_effec	023

DEVICE

OID	DEVICE_NR : A	EQUIPMENT : A	TYPE : A
O1	cart_1	V_MTOOL	cart
O2	unit_1	H_TOOL	unit
O3	end_effec	V_ROBOT	end_effector

Fig. 4. (*Continued*).

processing a query, the user specified DML is converted into a query tree consisting of operations on G-relations.

4. A GLOBAL DATA MANIPULATION LANGUAGE FOR IMDAS

Database requests in the IMDAS are posed in a common, global data manipulation language (GDML). The GDML is modeled after SQL [2], which is a high level, nonprocedural, set-oriented language for relational databases. Features of the GDML include simple structures, powerful operators, short initial learning period, improved data independence, and integrated data and metadata manipulation. Additional features of the GDML for supporting CAD/CAM applications are:

1) High level specification of the database request; the user

182

RESULT

DEVICE_NR : A	EQUIPMENT : A	CONTENTS : A		
		STORAGE : SET		
		STORAGE_NR : A	CONTAINS : A	
			ITEM : SET	
			ITEM_NR : A	
cart_1	V_MTool	S0	part_1 part_3	
		S2	-	

Fig. 5. Result of the example query.

need not specify the traversal path of the query since it is already represented by the semantics of the database.

2) Support for complex and abstract data types, which facilitates the modelling of engineering/manufacturing data.

3) Strong data type checking for complex and abstract data types.

4) Provision for the expression and execution of knowledge rules, thus providing the infrastructure for knowledge base management.

5) Automatic enforcement of constraints. For example, based on the semantics specified in the OSAM* schema, an update request can trigger additional database operations automatically to maintain the consistency in the database.

6) Support the attribute inheritance property of the OSAM* generalization association.

A query is posed by viewing the S-diagram. The language allows the user to formulate a query by naming the objects and attributes of his/her interest. Since the interrelationships among objects are already explicitly represented in the database, no explicit joins need be specified in the GDML. This is unlike the relational SQL, in which the effect of joins is achieved by nesting SELECT_FROM_WHERE blocks. All that is necessary in the GDML is the specification of the object classes, about which information (attributes and values) is to be retrieved, along with the condition of retrieval. The attributes and values to be retrieved can either be those of the class itself, or can be derived through the associations between the object class and other object classes. A detailed discussion on the GDML is beyond the scope of this paper. Interested readers may refer to [16], [17]. We shall illustrate some of the capabilities of the GDML with an example:

QUERY:

SELECT   device_nr, equipment,
                (**SELECT** storage_nr, (item_nr **IN**
                CONTEXT OF Contains)
                FROM   Contents
                WHERE size = 10)

FROM   Device
WHERE   device_nr = 'cart_1'
USE MEMORY   Device_contents

The above query is based on the S-diagram shown in Fig. 3. Its intent is to retrieve the device_nr and the equipment of device 'cart_1', and, for that device, retrieve the storage_nr of its storage whose size equals 10, and the item_nr of the item contained in that storage location. The result of this query is presented in a G-relational form shown in Fig. 5. Some of the features of the GDML illustrated in this query are:

1) Transparent paths: If there is no ambiguity present in the S-diagram, i.e., there are no multiple paths between them, it is not required that a complete path from a class or a complex attribute to its nested attributes be specified in the GDML. For example, in the given query, the path from CONTENTS to attributes SIZE is derived from the interconnections of the S-diagram of Fig. 3. Since the semantics of the database have been defined in the schema, the user should not have to restate them in the query.

2) Property inheritance: CONTENTS is an attribute defined for the CONTAINER. Since a DEVICE is a CONTAINER, this property is inherited by DEVICE.

3) Complex projection list: Further database operations can be performed on nonatomic attributes (e.g., CONTENTS) in the projection list of the query.

4) Data delivery specifications: In a CIM application, most of the queries to the database are issued by application programs. Hence, the data retrieved from the database must be delivered to some location that is easily accessible by these programs. In AMRF, two such delivery locations are possible: the common memory[3] and the disk. In the example query, the USE MEMORY clause indicates that the data is to be delivered to a common memory location named by the user as Device_contents. If the results are to be delivered to a disk file,

[3] A shared memory scheme [19], in which a process stores information of a particular type for a particular type of recipient.

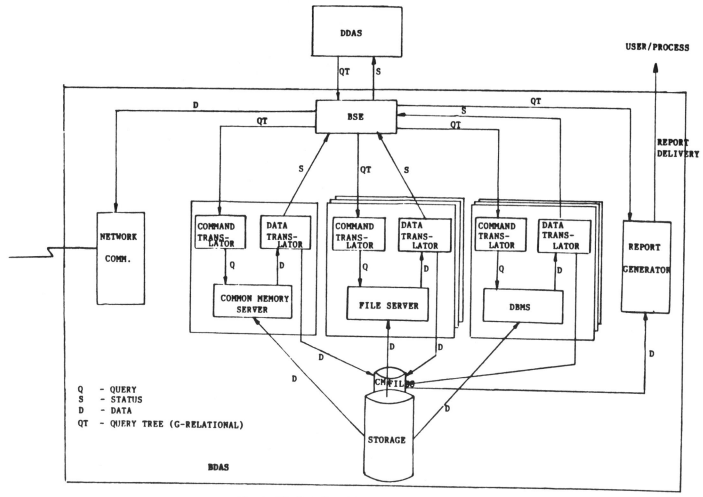

Fig. 6. The Basic Data Administration System (BDAS).

then the USE FILE clause is used. In general, the USE clause can be expanded to specify the format of the result, and the delivery mode of the data such as simple, stream, or block.

5. Functional Description of the IMDAS Modules

The IMDAS architecture's hierarchical structure (Fig. 2) has no direct relationship to its control topology. There are three levels of software which form the fully functional distributed IMDAS. These are the Basic Data Administration System (BDAS), the Distributed Data Administration System (DDAS), and the Master Data Administration System (MDAS).

5.1. Basic Data Administration System (BDAS)

The BDAS provides a uniform interface between the data residing on each component system and the integrated database. Since the component computer systems have widely different processing capabilities, the BDAS provides only the essential data management and communication functions. These functions may be implemented differently on each component system in order to cater to the idiosyncrasies of that system. The different functional modules of the BDAS illustrated in Fig. 6 are: a) Basic Service Executive (BSE), b) Database Management or File Management, c) Report Gener-

ator, d) Command Translation (CT), e) Data Translation (DT), f) Interprocess Communication, Common-memory (CM), and g) Network Communication.

a) Basic Service Executive (BSE)—The function of this element is to provide a single point of contact between the DDAS and BDAS data services. The BSE accepts commands from DDAS and routes them to the appropriate BDAS modules, which perform the command translation, data manipulation, and data translation functions. It also constructs data delivery paths, sequences the execution of query tree operations, and reports completions and problems back to the DDAS transaction manager.

b) Database Management or File Management—The BDAS on each component system must provide, through the local database or file management system, the actual access to and manipulation of the local databases. The database manipulation and management capabilities vary substantially from system to system, depending on the facilities provided by the software. For example, in small systems, the local database may be implemented only in the main memory, and managed by a shared memory management process; in others, a file manager may meet all local requirements, giving the system little more than "read" and "write" operations. In larger systems, sophisticated database management systems may provide the actual database services. Moreover, there may be

184

more than one such facility on a single component system. The data manager must also be capable of cooperating in distributed consistency, concurrency, and recovery control.

c) Command Translation (CT)—In IMDAS, a query issued in the Global Manipulation Language (GDML) by a component system is translated into a tree of primitive operations by a DDAS. The DDAS then sends these primitive operations to the appropriate BDASs. The BDAS then uses the Command Translator to convert the received primitive operations into a sequence of operations in the language of the local data or file manager.

d) Data Translation (DT)—Whenever data is moved from one component system to another, it has to be translated from the source representation to the target representation. In a heterogeneous complex, a source-to-common, and then common-to-target conversion of the data is more economical. In IMDAS, the common representation of data is the standard Generalized relation (G-relation). Also, the data element exchanged between the various IMDAS modules is in the standard G-relation. The Data Translator (DT) therefore has to do the following tasks: 1) Once the primitive operations are executed by the local data manager or file manager in a BDAS, the retrieved data conforms to the representation used by that local data manager. The DT has to convert this data to its global format, i.e., to the standard G-relation; 2) conversely, when a BDAS receives data to be inserted into its local database, the DT translates the data from its G-relation format to the format used by the local data manager.

e) Report Generator—The requesting process receiving the data may want it to be formatted according to certain format specifications as specified either in the GDML or in the external view definition of that process. Every BDAS has a report generator to perform this operation.

f) Interprocess Communication—If the component system houses multiple control and sensory processes, or if the communications and data management services are implemented as separate processes, a mechanism for communications among these processes is needed. This mechanism can either be process-to-process message passing or some kind of shared memory, depending on the capabilities of the local operating system. The AMRF uses a common memory scheme [18], [19], in which an originating process stores information of a particular kind for a particular recipient into a designated area of the common memory, and the process interested in this information retrieves it from this designated area. This scheme is implemented on different systems by either a hardware shared memory, a message passing to a memory manager process, or a process which copies the information between each process's local memory areas and a background common memory [4]. The common memory approach permits data to be used by more than one process without any explicit action by the originator to deliver the data to all consumers. The common memory not only serves as a communication vehicle, but also serves as a database. This approach is effective in equipment level functions which perform real-time operations where the system response time requires much of the data to be memory resident.

g) Network Communication—Every component system must have access to the factory data network, and must implement sufficient protocols to enable it to communicate with the other component systems. The IMDAS architecture presumes that the factory data network utilizes a bus or ring local area network technology, thereby providing a peer relationship between component systems. The four lowest layers of the ISO/OSI reference model must be implemented for each component system, either within the system or with network appliances. These basic protocols allow reliable communication between any two systems on the network. In addition, the interprocess communication mechanism chosen within a system must be reflected in the interprocess communication between systems. It can be either direct message passing or a simulated global shared memory.

In the AMRF, the network communication function is performed by a Network Interface Process (NIP) in each component system [19]. The NIP maps the needed areas of a conceptual "global" common memory into the local common memory by replicating areas of its local common memory into the common memory areas of remote components requiring copies. This is done with the assistance of the network and the remote NIP. The NIP is table-driven, so that mappings can be dynamically modified by creating or destroying entries in the delivery table. The advantage of this scheme and the local common memory is that they are distributed database mechanisms, and therefore can both contribute to and profit from other database techniques in the IMDAS.

5.2. Distributed Data Administration System (DDAS)

The DDAS provides uniform access to the integrated database for the control and user processes. In a CIM environment, in each separable group of component systems, i.e., each group capable of independent operation, at least one component system must contain a DDAS. The functions of the DDAS are: data manipulation language service, query mapping service, data assembly, dictionary initialization, and distributed transaction management. Fig. 7 illustrates the various DDAS modules and their interrelationships. The functions of each module are described below.

Distributed Service Executive (DSE)—The DSE acts as a single point of contact between the DDAS and the MDAS. The function of the DSE is to coordinate the activities of the various DDAS modules. It first initializes its data dictionary to reflect only the data which is resident in the local BDAS. It then creates connections to its subordinate remote BDASs, and incorporates their data dictionary information. Any inconsistencies within the dictionary are resolved. Then, on request from the MDAS, a connection to the designated MDAS is established, and it transmits dictionary entries containing a model of its local fragment of the global conceptual view. It then executes MDAS directed recovery transactions, if any. Finally, it initializes the interface to control processes served by the DDAS. However, it has to wait for the MDAS to acknowledge a "READY" state before it can begin accepting requests for service.

The DSE then receives the user or process issued GDML through local or networked interprocess communications, and forwards it to the Data Manipulation Language Service

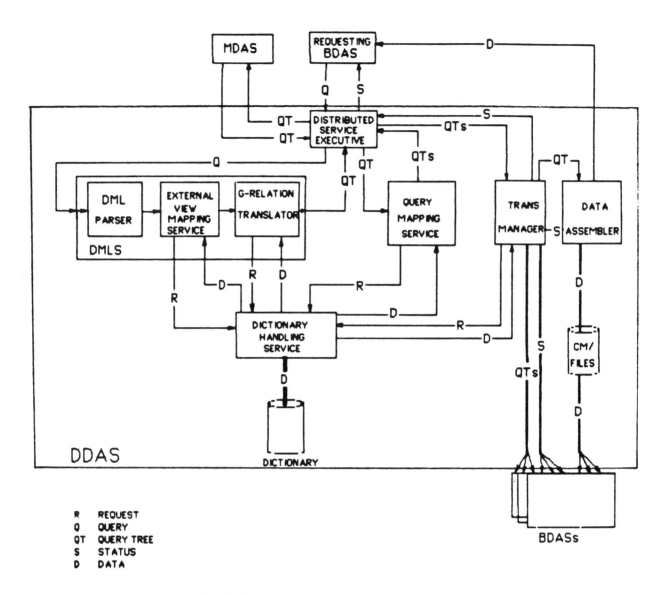

R   REQUEST
Q   QUERY
QT QUERY TREE
S   STATUS
D   DATA

Fig. 7.   The Distributed Data Administration System (DDAS).

(DMLS). It then routes the parsed and translated query returned by the DMLS to the Query Mapping Service (QMS). And finally, it passes the list of subqueries returned by the QMS to the distributed Transaction Manager.

Data Manipulation Language Service (DMLS)—GDML queries are issued against global external views of the integrated database. The DMLS is responsible for composing from the query expressed in GDML, which is a high level language, a query tree of primitive operations. This query tree can either first materialize the external view specified and then perform the operations, or modify the query tree into an equivalent query on the global conceptual view. The query tree is further modified to incorporate integrity and security constraints defined on the underlying data structures. The DMLS then obtains from the DDAS dictionary information on where the data requested in the query resides. Based on this information, it determines whether the query can be satisfied by the DDAS or if it requires the cooperation of other DDASs. If other DDASs are required, the query tree is forwarded to the MDAS for processing. Otherwise, the query tree is passed

to the Query Mapping Service (QMS) for further processing.

Query Mapping Service (QMS)—The QMS accepts the modified query tree pertaining to the global conceptual view of the integrated database and performs its mapping to the fragmented views. From the dictionary, it accesses the information pertaining to the partitioning and replication of global conceptual data in the local BDASs, and modifies the query tree to incorporate fragments of the data referred therein. Based on the site allocation of the data fragments and the sites' capabilities, it decomposes the query tree into subquery trees, each involving operations on a single BDAS. The decomposition is done in an optimized way so that each subquery consists of an optimum sequence of operations. Each subquery is tagged with its delivery information (i.e., source and destination areas, buffer sizes, and delivery modes) and a list of identifiers of other subquery trees which must be completed before this one. The list of subquery trees generated is directed to the Transaction Manager (TM).

Transaction Manager (TM)—The TM controls and manages the distributed query execution and distributed consist-

186

ency, integrity, and recovery. When the TM receives the list of subquery trees from the QMS, it initializes the transaction as the atomic unit of recovery, and realizes a serializable schedule for the operations. It then analyzes the transaction and checks for any concurrency conflicts with any currently executing transactions. If conflicts are detected, the TM defers the transaction until all involved BDASs finish the transaction which was in conflict. If the transaction was received from the MDAS, the TM must notify the MDAS, and wait for the MDAS to direct aborting or stalling the query execution. When necessary, the TM inserts concurrency controls into the transaction to ensure consistency among the BDASs activities, and transmits the operation sequences along with directions for constructing delivery paths to the proper BDASs using the local or networked interprocess communication. When the final results of the transaction are correctly received by the requesting process, or when the data is properly updated, the TM identifies the transaction to be complete.

The TM is responsible for the recovery of executing transactions and the integrity of all data being modified. The TM performs transaction and database recovery by selectively delegating recovery actions to the BDASs, properly maintaining distributed checkpoints, and directing parallel activities of the BDASs using the two-phase commit protocol.

Data Assembler (DASM)—The DASM [15] performs selections, joins, assembly, merging, sorting, and other final operations on the data retrieved from the different BDASs. It is required in the DDAS to provide these services for BDASs which have only very basic data management capabilities. It is also required when data from multiple sources are to be assembled into the final result.

Data Dictionary Service (DDS)—The data dictionary in DDAS includes the following metadata: 1) the schema and mapping information for the conceptual-to-fragmented and the fragmented-to-local external views of the data residing on subordinate BDASs; 2) the mapping information for the external-to-conceptual views referenced by the control processes, which this DDAS supports; 3) the security and integrity constraints associated with the data in subordinate BDASs; 4) data delivery information and site information; and 5) the information representing the capability of each subordinate BDAS. When requested by the various software modules of the DDAS, the DDS performs a lookup of the dictionary and provides the necessary information.

5.3. Master Data Administration System (MDAS)

There is one MDAS in each independently operating partition of the factory. When the partition is initialized, one of the DDASs is designated as the MDAS, and other DDASs are directed to report to it. The function of the MDAS is to coordinate the activities of the multiple DDASs. The coordination consists of managing the master data dictionary, resolving concurrency problems between DDASs, directing initialization, integrity, and recovery. The software needed to accomplish these functions is resident in every DDAS. Hence, the MDAS is primarily DDAS software that operates on different subordinate components, i.e., DDASs instead of BDASs, with a master layer dictionary that contains the integrated view of the global database together with the mapping of this global database to its fragments represented by the DDASs.

6. IMDAS PROCESSING SCENARIO

A processing scenario of a typical integrated database access within a DDAS is shown in Fig. 8. All retrievals from the database are based on the external views defined for the integrated database. In this illustration, a control process within a component system (represented by requesting BDAS in Fig. 8) is requesting an access to some data. The request is in the form of a GDML query. This query is forwarded to the DDAS which controls the requesting BDAS.

Within the DDAS layer, the Data Service Executive (DSE), which acts as a liaison between the various modules of the DDAS, forwards the GDML query to the Data Manipulation Language Service (DMLS). The DMLS first parses the GDML query, and generates an equivalent query tree consisting of operations on the internal G-relational representation of the schema. The operators in the query tree are G-relational algebra operators [17]. The query tree is then evaluated against the information present in the data dictionary to determine whether all the data elements requested are contained in the underlying BDASs; if not, the DSE then routes the query tree to the MDAS. However, once the data elements are determined to exist in the underlying BDASs, the query tree, which pertains to some external view of the database, is modified with the help of the external view mapping information present in the dictionary to conform to the global conceptual view of the database. The query tree is then further modified, if necessary, to take care of specifying complete paths to the attributes in the query tree. Finally, the query tree is optimized and returned to the DSE. The DSE then forwards the fully grown tree to the Query Mapping Service (QMS).

The main task of the QMS is to handle the fragmentation of the G-relations pertaining to the conceptual schema that is present in the underlying BDASs. The QMS makes use of the fragmentation mapping information present in the dictionary to modify the query tree so that it contains operations on the fragment G-relations. The next task of the QMS is to fragment the query tree itself based on 1) the allocation of the fragmented G-relations to the various underlying BDASs, and 2) the operational capabilities of the BDASs involved so that each tree fragment can be sent to the appropriate BDAS for processing. The QMS attaches input or output delivery nodes at the point of "cut-off" of the tree fragment, so that the processor, which will execute a tree fragment, will know where to deliver or retrieve the data. The delivery nodes in the query tree essentially carry information as to where and how the data should be delivered or obtained. The process of fragmenting the query tree may result in a tree fragment that has to be sent to the Data Assembler (DASM), either to assemble the data returned from the individual BDASs involved, or to perform further operations on them, if necessary. Since there may be an order of precedence involved in the processing of the fragmented query trees, the QMS clearly marks each tree with its precedence number, including the information about its destination BDAS. This information is essential for the Transaction Manager (TM) in scheduling

187

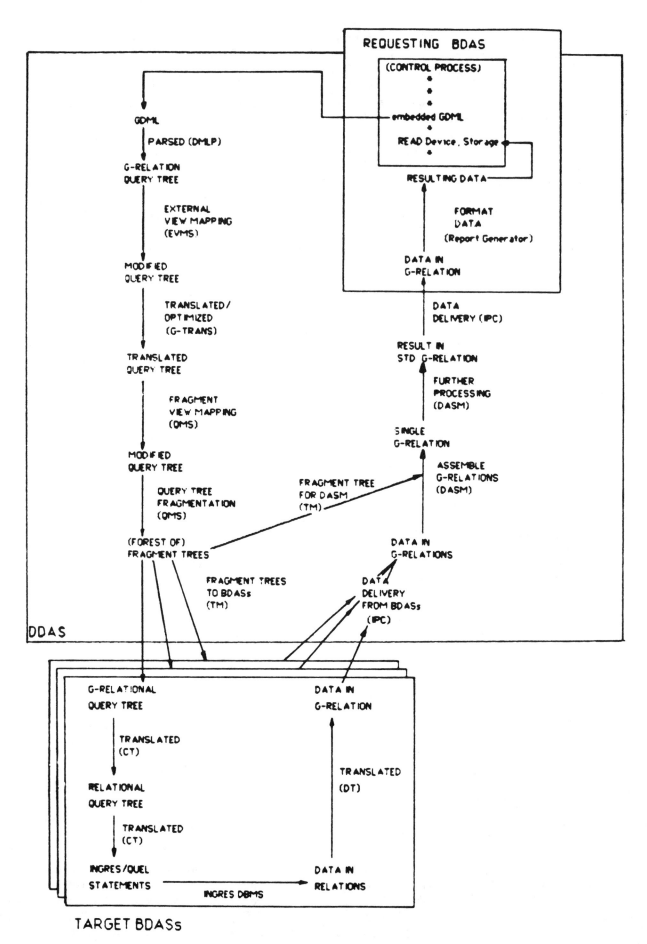

Fig. 8. A typical IMDAS processing scenario.

188

and dispatching the query trees for execution. The forest of fragment trees thus generated is then returned to the DSE.

The Transaction Manager (TM) obtains the forest of fragmented query trees from the DSE and schedules them for execution. The entire forest of fragmented query trees is handled as a single transaction, and the two-phase locking scheme is adopted by the TM to exercise concurrency control. Standard "distributed" recovery and rollback schemes [8] are used.

Once the DDAS has finished producing the appropriate query tree for execution at a BDAS, the Basic Service Executive (BSE) of the BDAS, based on the information provided by the DDAS, calls the appropriate Command Translator (CT) to translate the query to the appropriate language that the designated data management system can understand. For example, if INGRES is the data management system, then the query tree of G-relational operations is mapped to an equivalent set of operations on relations [6], [15]. The information for mapping between the G-relational schema to the relational schema is stored in the local dictionary. The query tree of relational operations is then translated into QUEL statements(s), which is then executed by the INGRES DBMS. Once the data are returned by the local data management system, the Data Translator (DT) for that system converts the data format to the standard G-relational format. The data elements are then delivered to the designated area specified by the delivery node in the query tree. Once this is done, the BSE informs the DDAS Transaction Manager of the completed assignment. If no further processing was required, and if only one BDAS was involved in processing the query, the DDAS would have instructed the BDAS to deliver the resulting data directly through interprocess communications to the requesting BDAS. Otherwise, once all the BDASs involved in processing a query return the data, the TM in the DDAS instructs the Data Assembler (DASM) to assemble the data and further process them if necessary. Finally, the resulting data in the standard G-relational form are delivered to the requesting BDAS.

The above description of IMDAS processing is typical for any retrieval from the integrated database. For certain database updates, however, the scenario changes somewhat. Here, by database updates we mean "insertion," "deletion," and "update" of instances in a G-relation. (In the DML, this would be expressed as insertion, deletion, and update of instances in OSAM* class). Database updates that contain a condition for selecting the tuples to be updated are carried out in two phases. Due to horizontal and vertical partitioning of data in the fragment G-relations, the data to be updated may be in one or more fragments, and the update conditions may be based on attributes present in different fragments. However, every fragmented G-relation of a conceptual G-relation contains the common instance identifier field. Hence, in the first phase, the DDAS creates a retrieval query tree to select the instance identifiers from the relevant fragments that satisfy the given conditions in the update query. In the second phase, updates are performed on the relevant fragments for those instances whose identifiers were selected in the first phase.

7. Conclusion

A prototype of the IMDAS architecture has been developed and integrated with the AMRF testbed facility of the National Institute of Standards and Technology [20]. The description of an earlier prototype can be found in [27]. Extension to the SAM* model and the SAM*DML have been made since then to provide better modeling power and expressive capabilities. These changes are being incorporated in a new system under implementation.

Our future research will continue to concentrate on CAD/CAM data modelling and a better interface for design/manufacturing systems. Distributed techniques for query processing, optimization, concurrency control, system initialization, and error recovery, which are critical for integrated factory networks, will also be improved. Knowledge in the form of rules, constraints, and operations is a critical commodity in an integrated manufacturing environment. It needs to be shared by the various components of CIM. Therefore, we are looking into techniques for combining data and knowledge management supports for the CIM. We are also investigating an object-oriented approach to the integration of distributed systems.

Acknowledgments

This research is supported by the Navy Manufacturing Technology Program through the National Bureau of Standards grant number 60NANB4D0017. We acknowledge the contributions of the following persons to this project: Mohammad Khatib and Don Libes of the National Institute for Standards and Technology; Ashish Kumar and Chong Soo of University of Florida.

References

[1] Albus, J. S., A. J. Barbera, and R. N. Nagel, "Theory and practice of hierarchical control," in *Proc. 23rd IEEE Computer Society Int. Conf.*, Sept. 1981, pp. 18–39.

[2] American National Standard Database Language SQL, doc. no. X3H2-87-8, ANSI working draft, Dec. 1986.

[3] Appleton, D. S., "The technology of data integration," *Datamation*, pp. 106–116, Nov. 1985. Reprinted in this book.

[4] Barbera, A. J., M. L. Fitzgerald, and J. S. Albus, "Concepts for a real-time sensory interactive control system architecture," in *Proc. 14th Southeastern Symp. Systems Theory*, Apr. 1982.

[5] Barkmeyer, E., M. Mitchell, K. P. Mikkilineni, S. Y. W. Su, and H. Lam, "An architecture for distributed data management in computer integrated manufacturing," U.S. Dept. Commerce rep. no. NBSIR 86-3312, Jan. 1986.

[6] Blumenthal, D. F., "An algorithm to translate relational algebra queries into QUEL," Master's Thesis, Dept. Computer and Information Sci., University of Florida, May 1985.

[7] Bray, O. H., *Distributed Database Management Systems*. Lexington Books, 1982.

[8] Ceri, S. and G. Pelagatti, *Distributed Databases: Principles and Systems*. New York, NY: McGraw-Hill Co., 1984.

[9] Ceri, S., B. Pernici, and G. Wiederhold, "An overview of research in the design of distributed data bases," *Database Eng.*, vol. 7, no. 4, pp. 46–50, 1984.

[10] Fullerton, G., "Integrated program for aerospace vehicle design (IPAD)," NASA rep. no. TM-81874, 1980.

[11] Gadient, A. J., "Engineering information systems: implementation approaches and issues," in *Proc. Third Int. Conf. on Data Eng.*, pp. 576–578, Feb. 1987.

[12] Hatvary, J., M. E. Merchant, K. Rathmill, and Yoshikawa, *World Survey of CAM*. Kent, U.K.: Butterworth & Co. Ltd., 1983.

[13] ICAM Program Prospectus, Air Force Systems Command, Wright-Patterson Air Force Base, OH, USA, Sept. 1979.

[14] ICAM Project, "Computer program development specification (DS) for ICAM integrated support system (IISS) configuration item: Precompiler," prepared by Control Data Corporation and D. Appleton Company, Dec. 1983.

[15] Khatib, M., "Data assembly in a distributed heterogeneous data base management system," Master's Thesis, Electrical Eng. Dept., University of Florida, May 1986.

[16] Krishnamurthy, P., "A data manipulation language for the semantic association model SAM*," Master's Thesis, Electrical Eng. Dept., University of Florida, Dec. 1985.

[17] Krishnamurthy, V., Internal Report, Database Systems Research and Development Center, University of Florida, Apr. 1987.

[18] Libes, D., "User-level shared variable," in Proc. of Summer 1985 USENIX, Portland, OR, June 1985.

[19] Mitchell, M. and E. Barkmeyer, "Data distribution in the NBS automated manufacturing research facility," in Proc. Nat. Symp. on Advances in Distributed Data Base Management for CAD/CAM, NASA Publication 2301, Apr. 1984.

[20] McLean, C. R., M. Mitchell, and E. Barkmeyer, "A distributed computing for small batch manufacturing systems," IEEE Spectrum, May 1983.

[21] Nanzetta, P., "Update: NBS research facility addresses problems in setups for small batch manufacturing," Industrial Eng., pp. 68–73, June 1984.

[22] Neuhold, E. J., "Distributed database systems with special emphasis toward POREL," IPAD II, Proc. National Symp., NASA Conference Publ. 2301.

[23] Simpson, J. A., R. J. Hocken, and J. S. Albus, "The automated manufacturing research facility of the National Bureau of Standards," J. Manufacturing Syst., vol. 1, no. 1, 1982.

[24] Smith, B., "PDES project: Objectives, plans and schedules," Internal Memo. on Product Data Exchange Specification, National Bureau of Standards, June 1986.

[25] Su, S. Y. W., "SAM*: A semantic association model for corporate and scientific-statistical databases," Info. Sci., vol. 29, 1983, pp. 151–199.

[26] ——, "Modeling integrated manufacturing data using SAM*," in Proc. of Data Base Systems for Office, Eng. Sci., Karlsruhe, W. Germany, Mar. 1985; and IEEE Computer, Jan. 1986.

[27] Su, S. Y. W., H. Lam, M. Khatib, V. Krishnamurthy, A. Kumar, S. Malik, M. Mitchell, and E. Barkmeyer, "The architecture and prototype implementation of an integrated manufacturing database administration system," Spring COMPCON, 1986.

[28] Su, S. Y. W., V. Krishnamurthy, and H. Lam, "An object-oriented semantic association model (OSAM*) for engineering and manufacturing databases," in preparation.

[29] Wedekind, H. and G. Zoerntlein, "Conceptual basis for database application in flexible manufacturing systems (FMS)," in Proc. IEEE Int. Conf. Robotics and Automation, vol. 1, pp. 551–557, Mar. 1987.

[30] Williams, T., et al., "R*: An overview of the architecture," in Proc. Int. Conf. Database Systems, Jerusalem, Israel, June 1982.

[31] Yoshikawa, H., K. Rathmill, and J. Hatvany, Computer-Aided Manufacturing: An International Comparison. Washington, DC: National Academy Press, 1981.

The Architecture of a Generalised Distributed Database System – PRECI*

S.M. DEEN, R. R. AMIN, G. O. OFORI-DWUMFUO AND M. C. TAYLOR

PRECI PROJECT, *Department of Computing Science, University of Aberdeen, Aberdeen AB9 2UB, Scotland*

A research prototype of a generalised distributed database system called PRECI* is currently being developed at the University of Aberdeen in collaboration with a number of research centres, mainly in Britain. The system is fully decentralised, with both retrieval and update facilities, permitting heterogeneous and even pre-existing databases as nodes and supporting links to other (external) distributed databases. The system supports both location transparent and transaction-oriented queries to fulfil differing user requirements. Nodal autonomy, data integration, metadata and staged binding of queries may be seen as its other main features. The basic design of the system is now complete, and a partial implementation is in progress.

1. INTRODUCTION

PRECI(Prototype of a relational canonical interface) is a database research project which was originally undertaken at Aberdeen[1] in order to provide a framework for research in all aspects of databases. To date the project has produced a research prototype called PRECI/H which is a generalised DBMS, based on a canonical data model supporting relational, network and other data models as user views. It uses the ANSI/SPARC architecture, its ' conceptual schema' (called canonical schema) being written in a relational form. The principal data manipulation language used includes an extended relational algebra called PRECI Algebraic Language (PAL), which supports all the traditional relational commands (including functions) and a number of special commands for data integration. The result of any of these commands is another relation, thus all operations have the closure property.

PRECI*(pronounced presi-star) is a research prototype within the PRECI project for a generalised distributed database management system (DDBMS), which is being developed in collaboration with a number of research centres. Its principal architectural characteristics are:

(1) A decentralised control system with heterogeneous databases (including pre-existing databases) as nodes.
(2) Both inner and outer nodes to suit differing user requirements (see later).
(3) Retrieval and update facilities for global users, with full location transparency for the inner nodes.
(4) Ability to allow new nodes to join.
(5) Ability to link with other distributed databases (external DDBs) at peer level.
(6) Maximal nodal autonomy as described below:
(i) A nodal database retains its nodal users, independent of the distributed database management system (DDBMS).
(ii) A database can join the DDB as a node by contributing only a logical subset of its data, the subset containing none to all of the data.
(iii) Each nodal database retains full control of itself, with means to withdraw itself or its data. It can specify who can update and retrieve its data, and under what conditions.

(iv) Data contributed by a nodal database (home node for these data) to a DDB can be replicated and distributed by the DDBMS to other nodes (foreign nodes for those replicated data), if so permitted by the home node. This facility applies only to the inner nodes.
(v) A database may participate as a node in several DDBs and can itself be a DDB.

These characteristics have been discussed initially in reference 14, and taken together they distinguish PRECI* from the current prototype implementations[2][13]. It should be noted that we have used the term node to imply a logical site, one for each nodal database and its associated global module.

The architecture of PRECI* is meant to support the characteristics listed earlier. In Section 2 we present a five-level schema architecture, followed by a discussion of nodal and global control systems in Section 3. For a clearer understanding of the architecture and its impact, we have outlined the elements of the global query processor in Section 4. A conclusion is given in Section 5.

2. ARCHITECTURAL LAYERS

We define a distributed database as a database representing a logical collection of data from other inter-linked databases. It is possible for the same computer to support several databases, and hence several nodes. Therefore the nodes of a DDB may not necessarily be connected via data communications links. We categorise DDBMS broadly into two classes: closed and open. A closed DDBMS permits only a purpose-built DDB where all nodal DBs are designed to suit the requirements of the DDB. Typically this could be a homogeneous system with the DDBMS having the final control over all data distribution. In contrast, an open DDBMS allows pre-existing databases, ideally of any data model, to join the DDB – potentially at any time. Thus the interfaces provided by an open DDBMS are open to all. An open DDB is typically a confederation of nodes, each node retaining full control over its data. PRECI* is intended as an open DDBMS.

The architectural framework used in PRECI* can be viewed as an extension of the ANSI/SPARC model by

Reprinted with permission from *The Computer Journal*, pp. 282–290, vol. 28, no. 3, 1985.

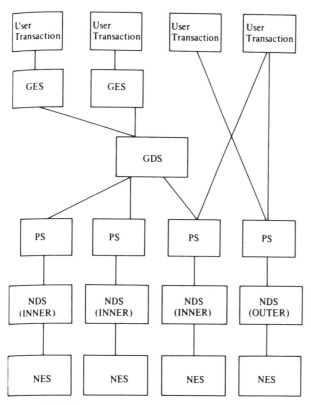

Figure 1. PRECI* schema levels

two additional layers: the global conceptual schema referred to as global database schema (GDS) and the global external schema (GES)(figure 1).

Although a nodal database can be a DDB, we shall generally assume a node to be a leaf node supporting a leaf database (ie a non-distributed data base) except where indicated otherwise. A nodal database in PRECI* is fully autonomous, with its independent nodal DBMS (NDBMS) and nodal external schemata (NESs). It must however provide a relational, preferably a PAL interface to the DDB which uses PAL as the standard language for communications. The DDB may be assumed to be a nodal user via a relational external schema to the nodal database, called the participation schema (see later). A node can participate in a PRECI* DDB in one of two ways:

(i) as an inner node : which contributes to the GDS
(ii) as an outer node : which does not contribute to the GDS

We describe them more fully below.

2.1 Inner Nodes

In general, the inner nodes provide the best available service to their global users (inner users), through the global database schema and global external schemata. The special facilities not available to the outer users (the users of the outer nodes) are:

Integrated data
Meta data
Location transparency
Replicated data (for faster queries)
Easier query formulation

Global Database Schema (GDS)

The GDS is formed by the participation schemata (PSs) of the inner nodes, each relation in the GDS retaining the identity of its home nodes by means of a logical node name. The presence of this logical node name is not intended to curtail location transparency. It rather enables the user to find the node name of a relation, should he require it. However the user does not have to specify node names in a query unless he wishes it (see also GES). We have chosen a relational representation mainly because of its simplicity and decomposability[15].

The GDS supports integration data and meta data, which are assumed to be stored in a subsidiary database (discussed later). The need for data integration arises chiefly from the different practices at different nodes for expressing the same information. For instance one nodal database may represent distance in miles, and another one in kilometres. Likewise one database may store the price and sales tax of an item separately, while another one might store only the sum of the two as the total price. To take another example, one node may represent three exam marks in a relation R as R(STUDENT EXAM1 EXAM2 EXAM3) while another may use a ternary relation R(STUDENT EXAMNO MARKS) for the same information. The GDS itself does not provide an integrated view, say by converting all distances to miles. Instead we represent the total information at the GDS level without any loss, but recording additionally as integration data, the necessary units, conversion factors and other relevant information. The desired integration can thus be carried out at the global external schema as needed, eg permitting one GES to express distance in miles and another in kilometres. Therefore our GES and not GDS is closer to the global schema of Multibase[3].

Figure 2 shows a sample global database schema, where we have deliberately chosen the university names to be absent in node 1 and node 2, thus making communications with node 3 difficult. This difficulty is removed by creating a new relation UNODE as integration data. EID means entity identifier or primary key, which can be composite. The non-EID attributes are identified as ATT. If an attribute is a foreign key, then its type is FKEY qualified by the name of the relation where this attribute is the EID. Unit gives the unit in which a numerical value is expressed, eg £ for pounds sterling.

The meta data described in the GDS represents optional information typically held in a data dictionary. This facility can be used to declare semantic groupings of selected relations, attributes, domains and so on. Thus in figure 2, we have declared a meta relation R (relationnames, attributenames). The user can access these meta relations like any other relations except that their update is restricted.

There is a global mapping schema (GMS) associated with the global database schema. It has two functions:

(i) to distribute (ie replicate) permitted relations to other nodes (foreign nodes).
(ii) to associate node names with their participation schema names (including those for subsidiary databases).

```
ITEM      NAME              TYPE       UNIT


NODE      NODE1(UNIVERSITY)


REL       DEPT
EID       DNO               INTE 4
ATT       DNAME             CHAR 20


REL       TEACHER
EID       TDN               FKEY DEPT      /*TDN is teacher's department
EID       TNO               CHAR 4            number*/
ATT       SAL               INTE 5       £



NODE      NODE2(UNIVERSITY-B)


REL       DEPT
EID       DNO               INTE 5
ATT       DNAME             CHAR 25


REL       TUTOR
EID       TNO               CHAR 6
ATT       SAL               INTE 5          $
ATT       DNO               FKEY DEPT
ATT       GRADE             CHAR 10



NODE      NODE3 (STUDENT-UNIONS)


REL       UNION
EID       UNIVERSITY        CHAR 20
ATT       POPULAION         INTE 5
ATT       FEE               INTE 2          £



NODE      INT (INTEGRATION-DATA)


REL       UNODE
EID       UNIVERSITY        CHAR 20
ATT       NODE              CHAR 6



NODE      META (META DATA)


REL       R
EID       REL-NAME          CHAR 10
EID       ATT-NAME          CHAR 10
```

```
In relation TEACHER the EID is <TDN><TNO>
whereas in relation TUTOR, the EID is TNO alone.
```

Figure 2. Global Database Schema

Global External Schema (GES)

The global external schema can support relational and possibly other user views, provided that the data model and the language are convertible into our standard form (that is PAL). The GES with the help of its mapping entries can support additional meta data description and an integrated, location transparent view. As indicated earlier PAL is intended to provide powerful data integration commands and to be used both as a data manipulation and description language. An indication of these facilities is given in Figure 3 which is derived from the GDS of Figure 2. The entry ATT* implies that the attribute concerned can have null values and hence cannot be used for, say calculation of an average. The Mapping Division given shows some PAL commands for data integration. A publication on PAL data integration and data manipulation facility is under preparation.

Participation Schema (PS)

The participation schema describes the nodal data along with various authorisation controls. An example is shown in Figure 4 where the global users of the NODE

```
DATA DIVISION


REL   DEPARTMENT
EID   DNO               INTE 5
ATT   DNAME             CHAR 25


REL   TEACHER
EID   DNUM              FKEY DEPARTMENT
EID   TNO               INTE 6
ATT   SAL               INTE 6
ATT*  GR                CHAR 10      /*ATT* implies that this attribute can
                                        have null values*/


MAPPING DIVISION

DEPARTMENT == NODE1..DEPT ++ NODE2..DEPT

TEACHER == (NODE1..TEACHER::REP(TDN BY DNUM),    EXT (GR=NULL)
           ++(NODE2..TUTOR:: REP(DNO BY DNUM),   REP(GRADE BY GR)

where N..R indicates relation R of node N ;
R.A indicates attribute A of relation R ;
R::EXT(A) indicates relation R extended by new attribute A
R::REP(B BY C) indicates relation R with attribute B replaced by new
attribute C
and "++" and "==" are the symbols for union and definition respectively.
```

Figure 3. A Sample GES and its Mapping

```
    PS        NODE1-PS

    REL       DEPT
    REPLICATION ALLOWED TO NODE2, NODE3
    RETRIEVAL   ALLOWED TO NODE2, NODE3
    UPDATE NOT ALLOWED
    EID       DNO            INTE 4
    ATT       DNAME          CHAR 20


    REL       TEACHER
    REPLICATION NOT ALLOWED
    RETRIEVAL ALLOWED TO NODE3
    UPDATE ALLOWED TO NODE2
    EID       TDN            FKEY DEPT      UPDATE NOT ALLOWED
    EID       TNO            CHAR 4
    ATT       SAL            INTE 5
```

Figure 4. A Participation Schema

have a general permission to update relation Teacher but not its attribute TDN. Each participation schema has a version number which is updated every time the PS is changed.

Subsidiary database

Since we allow a DDB to support pre-existing databases, it is unreasonable to expect that they will be changed to incorporate replicated data. We therefore associate with each inner node a small database, to be called a subsidiary database (SDB), to be managed by an SDBMS (subsidiary database management system) under the control of the DDBMS at this node. The basic contents of the SDB are:

(1) Integration data of the GDS
(2) Metadata of the GDS

could be the same in all inner nodes, subject to nodal authorisation.

194

(3) Metadata of the GES
(4) replicated data

} vary from one inner node to another.

The SDBMS is expected to support a fuller set of PAL commands, with the ability to process external data (see later).

The database schema of the subsidiary database is assumed to act as the participation schema as well, there being no separate participation schema defined for it.

2.2 Outer Nodes

If the number of nodes in a DDB is large, say in the tune of several hundreds, and if the expected usage frequency of the DDB is low, so that a user accesses only a few of those hundreds of databases at any one time, then the overhead of the creation and maintainance of the GDS and GES could be too high. What we require, therefore is a transaction-oriented facility, which permits the user to formulate his query through a suitable language for specific nodes. He could also be allowed, if he needs, to navigate through the nodes until he finds his node of interest. This we may refer to as the seek and search approach.

The need for such a facility without any elaborate GDS and GES has been re-emphasised in a recent EEC feasibility study for a distributed facility to seek and search medical records in the community[17]. Typically a doctor in Aberdeen might need to access a medical database in Capri. The doctor might know about his need to access the Capri database, from another database or from an exogeneous source such as the patient. In this case the location transparency is not relevant, the doctor would only want a simple capability to send his query to Capri. We provide this capability within the PRECI* architecture by what we call outer nodes (cf. reference 6).

Our outer nodes do not contribute to the GDS, but they must provide participation schemata in a relational form like any other node; however there is no structural difference between the participation schemata of inner and outer nodes. The outer user can access several participation schemata directly and address queries to one or more of them. The outer user does not normally get meta-data, data integration or replicated data, although he can create a partially integrated view by PAL commands.

Note that, although the outer nodes do not contribute to the GDS, the DDBMS has to maintain the necessary control information on them. Subsidiary databases are optional for outer nodes, but can be used to provide additional PAL commands (see below).

3. NODAL AND GLOBAL CONTROLS

3.1 Nodal Controls

As mentioned earlier, each node is independent and is expected to have its nodal users independent of the DDBMS. By insisting on a node to provide a relational view, we are localising the problem of heterogeneous mappings to the sphere of the nodes but have not resolved it. Some of the issues of such mappings have been discussed in reference 14, and are currently being studied

by us. To minimise the changes in a node we basically require a node to support the following minimal set of operations:

Selection
Join
Division
Projection

either in a relational algebra, or in a calculus, but preferably in PAL. It is recognised that an NDBMS may not be able to process external data, that is, relations not stored in this database, but sent to it over the communications lines for processing. The capability to process such external data, and other PAL commands, is provided by the local SDBMS. However, due to machine restrictions or other limitations, a given SDBMS might not be able to handle all PAL commands. In that event, the DDBMS of this node would despatch the relevant data and the query to the SDBMS of another node which can process the required command.

If a node withdraws from a DDB, then the relevant participation schemata are made inoperative with a null version number. Each node has essentially a bilateral arrangement with other nodes, thus stipulating in the participation schema the conditions under which the data can be accessed. Since the participation schemata are controlled by the node, and not by the DDB, the latter cannot violate the authorisation stipulation of the former. It is recognised that a node may change its data. Any such change should cause the NDBMS to alter the version number of the relevant participation schema.

3.2 Global Control

The decentralised control system of PRECI* is shown in Figure 5, except that the outer nodes do not necessarily have any subsidiary databases. The DDBMS together with SDBMS and SDB, if present, constitutes what we call the global module. An initial description of the functions of a global module is given in reference 14.

PRECI* also supports interactions with other distributed databases. This is done in two ways:

(i) a subordinate node: in this case the DDB in question acts as a PRECI* node (either inner or outer) complete with a participation schema and a global module. Thus this DDB becomes an internal DDB

(ii) an external DDB: in this case the other DDB, called an external DDB, behaves like an outer node but without having the global module of the PRECI* However an external DDB can provide to PRECI* more than one PS, each being treated as if it were an outer node. Conversely PRECI* can provide suitable external schemata to the other DDB. All commands and data between PRECI* and the external DDB are converted into an intermediate standard form via what is called an external protocol (see also later).

4. TRANSACTION PROCESSOR

All global transactions are compiled and executed in three stages, the compiled version normally being retained for subsequent execution. In order to ensure the integrity of

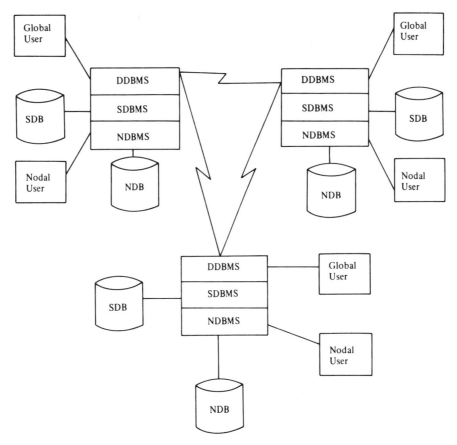

Figure 5. Decentralised Controls with subsidiary database

:he DDB, global update is permitted only on base relations. It is assumed that a participation schema will not grant update permission on a relation unless it is a base relation. The queries however can be more complex and operate on any set of authorised relations or their derived views. The basic query processing steps are sketched below:

4.1 Global Query Preprocessor (GQP)

Each user query at the originating node (ie the requester) is validated by the GQP against the GES in the case of inner nodes (inner queries) and against the PS in case of outer nodes (outer queries), along with appropriate authorisation checks. The query is then resolved, where appropriate, into a set of intermediate queries, one or more such queries for a given node (execution node). The intermediate queries are further subdivided, eventually into subqueries, by an optimiser, taking into account:

i) replicated data where available and relevant
ii) availability of operations. For instance if an intermediate query has an operation that cannot be performed by either the NDBMS or SDBMS of the designated execution node, then the subquery would be divided into secondary subqueries which can be performed at the designated node. The results of these secondary subqueries would be sent to another execution node to evaluate the original subquery.
iii) communications cost

The original global query is now transformed into a tree, made up of subtrees, a subtree representing a global subquery, with one or more subqueries for each selected execution node. As the first stage of compilation the GQP produces a global query plan (Q-plan) containing:

(1) the tree
(2) addresses of the execution and destination nodes (where the result should be sent after the execution of a query)
(3) version numbers of the GES, GDS and PS
(4) input/output data structures and parameters and, where relevant, a list of actions to be invoked on specified execution conditions.

Note that all inner queries are mapped against the PS entries via the compiled version of the GES and GDS, whereas all outer queries and external queries are mapped directly against the relevant PS.

From the Q-plan, the GQP prepares subquery execution plans (S-plans) one for each subquery. S-plans contain:

(1) the subtree
(2) pre-execution instructions
(3) post-execution instructions (ie what to do with the result)
(4) relevant input/output data structures and other parameters (such as version numbers of the involved schemata)
(5) a list of actions to be invoked on specified execution conditions.

S-plans form part of PRECI* protocols, of which there are two:

(i) internal protocol for communicating with PRECI* nodes, and hence understood by all PRECI* DDBMS.
(ii) external protocol for communicating with external DDBs. Such protocols are currently being studied in collaboration with several European research centres under EEC grants.

4.2 Global Subquery Preprocessor (GSP)

The principal task of the GSP is to transform a subquery in the S-plan into one or more nodal queries and submit them to the next stage for compilation. There are two reasons why a subquery may require splitting/modifications:

(i) If an operation of the subquery can be performed only by the SDBMS, but not by the NDBMS.
(ii) If the NDBMS does not support a PAL interface, in which case the subquery has to be transformed into the relational language supported at that node. This part of the GSP will vary from one node to another.

The GSP eventually generates a nodal query plan (N-plan) which includes compilation/execution instructions.

4.3 Nodal Query Preprocessor (NQP)

NQP is a part of the NDBMS, beyond the control of the DDBMS and hence implementation-dependent. We assume here only its conceptual existence as part of the nodal query processor which must compile/translate each nodal query. (The NQP should not distinguish between a query from a global user and one from a nodal user.) Similar compilation also takes place in the SDBMS, but under the control of the global module.

After a successful compilation, the Q-plan, S-plans and N-plans are suitably updated making them ready to be used for execution. We recognise that some nodal DBMSs may translate and execute a query at the same time, without retaining a compiled version for subsequent use. This requires only a trivial modification to our strategy and hence is not discussed here.

4.4 Query Execution

The execution of a query also proceeds in three stages (via a global query executor (GQE), a global subquery executor (GSE) and a nodal query executor (NQE), paralleling the preprocessing stages. At every execution, the version numbers of GES, GDS and PS are matched where relevant, rejecting the query with an appropriate message in the case of a mismatch. If the query is not affected by the new versions, it can be recompiled immediately without any change. We however, do not expect too many changes of version numbers.

This architecture permits the use of an intermediate node of the DDB to execute subqueries if so required by the optimiser. In Figure 6, the requester node A asks execution nodes B and C to forward relations R1 and R2 respectively to node D, which is required to perform

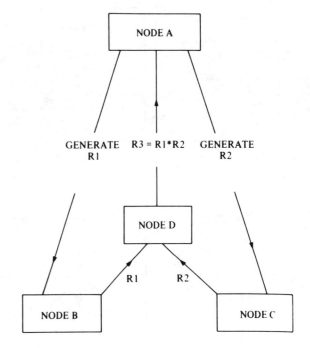

Figure 6. Use of an intermediate node D

a join on them – with the help of its SDBMS if necessary – and to transmit the result back to A.

4.5 Internodal Integrity

By internodal integrity, we mean the consistency of data among the participating nodes. There are two possible sources of inconsistency[1a].

(i) Replicated data: if data is replicated over several nodes, then the database will be inconsistent if all the copies are not updated every time.
(ii) Dispersed update-unit: if the data in the read/write set of an update transaction is dispersed over several nodes then we have a dispersed update-unit. Such a situation would occur if the employee salary details are maintained in the branches (nodes), and total salary expenditure in the department record at the head office (another node).

Consistency can be weak or strong. If weak, the database can remain in a transient inconsistent state without corrupting the data, whereas if strong, the database must be maintained in a consistent state at all times. Strong consistency must be enforced in the case of dispersed update-units, but not necessarily so in the case of replicated data.

Data is generally replicated for ease of access in cases where the frequency of retrieval exceeds that of update. It seems to us that the retrieval requests do not always need the latest version of the data, and in those cases (referred to as retrieval Mode A) a weak consistency should suffice. Thus our Mode A transactions use replicated data if it is cheaper, but all update transactions, and those retrieval transactions which require the latest data (retrieval Mode L), are directed to the home node which always maintains the latest version of data. Once an update is performed, the home node immediately broadcasts the update message to all

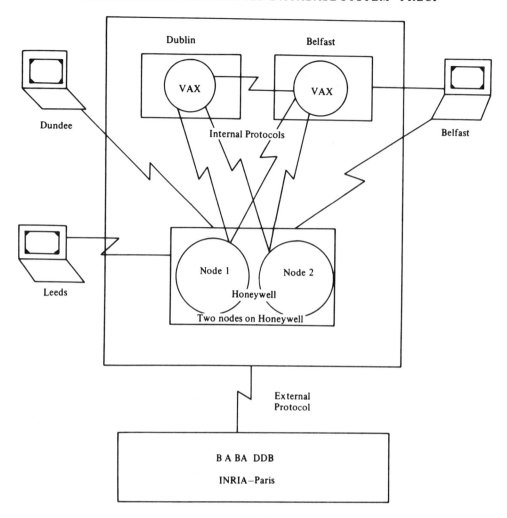

Figure 7. PRECI* Environment

relevant foreign nodes which then copy the update in their databases with the highest priority. The delay in effecting the update in the foreign nodes is expected to be very short, and hence most retrieval users should be satisfied in the transaction Mode A.

A nodal user may not be allowed to update data given to foreign nodes or those which form part of dispersed update-units. This must be enforced at the nodal level, transforming all such nodal transactions into global transactions either manually or automatically.

We assume that each node maintains a set of mail boxes, one for each node in the DDB. The mail boxes are used for holding messages sent out to those nodes but not yet acknowledged. When a node starts a session or restarts after a breakdown, it must first take two recovery actions. It reads its mail boxes at other nodes, and takes action on the messages, such as completing lost updates. Then it broadcasts all its outstanding messages to other nodes, and these messages include those which have been sent out earlier, but their acknowledgements were not received. Such retransmission of a message does not cause any update problem to replicated data, since the update version numbers of replicated data units are always checked before an update is effected. Strong consistency based on what we call a delayed two-phase commit protocol is being planned for dispersed update-units.

5. CONCLUSION

The architecture presented here is meant to capture many of the facilities of an open and generalised DDB, in particular the ability to provide location transparency and transaction-oriented queries, the former providing data integration and meta data. An associated activity is the development of a standard protocol for communications between distributed databases, mentioned in the text as external protocol. The basic design of PRECI* is now complete and we are implementing a pilot system, with only a subset of the design features described above. The pilot system is expected to include an initial version of an external protocol for linking to EEC countries over national data-communication networks. In the implementation we plan to have two nodes at Aberdeen co-existing in the same Honeywell computer, one node at Belfast in a VAX and another one in Dublin, in another VAX, with an external link to Litwin's Multidatabase project (Figure 7). Connections to our collaborators at Leeds and Edinburgh are also envisaged.

Acknowledgements

We wish to thank the British SERC, and the EEC COST 11 BIS for supporting this project by several grants. We also wish to thank all our internal and external collaborators, for suggestions, discussions and comments, in particular to David Bell of Ulster Polytechnic, Jane Grimson of Trinity College, Dublin, W. Litwin of INRIA (France) and Peter Apers of Vrije University (Amsterdam).

We are grateful to R. Carrick, and D. Kennedy of Aberdeen University for suggesting improvements to the earlier version of this paper.

REFERENCES

1 (a) S.M. Deen et al, The design of a canonical database system (PRECI), *The Computer Journal*, Vol.24, No.3, (1981)
(b) S.M. Deen et al, The run — time system of PRECI, *Proc of the Second British National Conference On Databases*, July 1982, ed. Deen & Hammersley, J. Wiley, (1982).

2 J.B. Rothnie et al, Introduction to a System for Distributed Databases (SDD — 1), *ACM TODS* Vol 5:1, (March 1980) p1. There are a number of other articles on SDD — 1 in the same issue of TODS.

3 T. Landers and R.L. Rosenberg, An overview of Multibase, *Distributed Databases*, (Proc. of the Second International Symposium on Distributed Data Bases, Berlin, 1982), ed. by H.J. Schneider, (North — Holland) p153.

4 R. Williams et al, R*: An overview of the architecture, RJ3325, IBM San Jose, California.

5 W. Litwin et al, SIRIUS systems for distributed data management, published in the *Proceedings of the Second International Symposium on Distributed Databases*, Berlin Sept 1 — 3, 1982, ed. H.J. Schneider, North — Holland (1982), p311.

6 Litwin et al, reference 5 includes a section on the B A BA project.

7 (a) K.C. Toth, et al, The ADD System: An architecture for DDBs, *Proc. of the 4th VLDB*, Berlin 1978.
(b) K.C. Toth, et al, Query Processing Strategies in a distributed database architecture, as in reference 14, p11.

8 E.J Neuhold and B. Walker, An Overview of the Architecture of the DDBs POREL, as in reference 3, p24.

9 R. Munz, Realisation, synchronisation and restart of update transactions in a DDBs, *Distributed Data Bases* (Proc. of the first International Symposium on DDB, Paris 1980), edited by C. Delobel and W. Litwin (North — Holland), p173.

10 A.J. Borr, Transaction monitoring in ENCOMPASS *Proc. of the 7th VLDB*, Cannes 1981, p155.

11 R. Elmasri, et al, Notes on DDRs — an apparatus for experimental research in DDBMS, Tech Rep HR — 81 — 252, Honeywell CCSC, Bloomington, Minnesota, February 1981.

12 M. Adiba, et al, Polypheme — ...., as in reference 9, p6.

13 P.R. Tillman, ADDAM — the ASWE DDBMS, as in reference 3, p185.

14 S.M. Deen, A general framework for the architecture of distributed database systems, *Proc. of International Seminar on Distributed Data Sharing*, Amsterdam, June 1981, edited by W. Litwin and R. Van de Riet (North — Holland), p153.

15 E.F. Codd, Relational database: A practical foundation for productivity, *Comm. ACM*, Vol.25, No.2, Feb 1982 (ACM Turing Award Lecture).

16 ISO/TC97/SC5/WG3, Report on Concepts and Terminology for the Conceptual Schema and the Information base, ed. J J van Griethuysen, N. V. Philips ISA — TMF — ET, Geb.Hsk, 5600 MD EINDHOVEN THE NETHERLANDS

17 David Bell, EEC Medical Project, Ulster Polytechnic (private communications).

Mermaid—A Front-End to Distributed Heterogeneous Databases

MARJORIE TEMPLETON, DAVID BRILL, SON K. DAO, ERIC LUND, PATRICIA WARD,
ARBEE L. P. CHEN, MEMBER, IEEE, AND ROBERT MacGREGOR

Invited Paper

Mermaid is a system that allows the user of multiple databases stored under various relational DBMSs running on different machines to manipulate the data using a common language, either ARIEL or SQL. It makes the complexity of this distributed, heterogeneous data processing transparent to the user. In this paper, we describe the architecture, system control, user interface, language and schema translation, query optimization, and network operation of the Mermaid system. Future research issues are also addressed.

I. Introduction

Distributed database management systems (DDBMS) require the integration of technology from other fields such as operating systems, networks, and for Department of Defense systems, security and formal verification. Two factors moving the field toward DDBMS are the development of networks which make DDBMS possible and the migration of users away from large central CPUs toward powerful workstations. Data may reside in different computers for many reasons such as ownership, security classification, performance, or size. Data may be stored redundantly in different computers for reliability or survivability.

SDC (now UNISYS Corporation) has developed a prototype named Mermaid that is a front-end to three relational database management systems (DBMS) that runs on a network of computers. It appears to the user to be a DDBMS. This prototype has demonstrated the feasibility of the concepts and has been used to experiment with different optimization algorithms and system control strategies. The basic system is now being developed into a product while research continues on extensions in the areas of object management, security, and integration with a deductive inference engine.

The current Mermaid configuration consists of four computers running UNIX 4.2[1] and connected with an Ethernet. Each computer contains a DBMS: a VAX11/780 which is host to a back-end Britton-Lee IDM database machine [2], a Sun 120 with INGRES, a Sun 170 with INGRES, and a Sun 120 with Mistress [18]. Mermaid, which may reside at any of the computers in the network, operates on top of these DBMSs which can also be used independently. The advantage of this "front-end" approach is that each DBMS may operate autonomously to achieve local control over access, accounting, and resource allocation. Moreover, this approach makes it possible to access existing databases stored under various DBMSs running on different computers.

Section II of this paper discusses similar efforts and previous SDC work in this area. Section III examines the Mermaid system in detail, Section IV shows examples of operation, and Section V outlines our project plans and future directions.

II. Related Technology

Many technical problems must be solved in order to provide a front-end system which can provide transparent access to existing databases. The Mermaid project has made maximum use of related technology. The related technologies may be categorized as:

- standard user language and data model
- query optimization
- distributed operating systems.

A. Standard User Language and Data Model

Transparent access to a variety of DBMSs requires the definition of a data model and data manipulation language which can be used to mediate between different DBMSs. The language and model need to be broad enough to cover all potential models used in target DBMSs and all func-

Manuscript received October 15, 1985; revised October 15, 1986.
M. Templeton, D. Brill, S. K. Dao, E. Lund, and P. Ward are with the UNISYS Corporation, Santa Monica, CA 90406-9988, USA.
A. L. P. Chen is with Bell Communications Research, Inc., Morristown, NJ 07960, USA.
R. McGregor is with the Information Science Institute, Marina del Rey, CA 90292, USA.
IEEE Log Number 8714296.

[1]UNIX is a trademark of AT&T.

Reprinted from *Proc. IEEE*, pp. 695–708, vol. 75, no. 5, May 1987.

tionality of the target language, or at least a subset of the target language which will be supported in the distributed system.

There are two stages of solution to the problem of multiple database access. The first is to provide a standard view of single databases stored under different DBMSs and to provide access to a single database at a time through a standard query language. The second is to provide an integrated view of multiple heterogeneous databases and to provide the capability to access and integrate data from several databases to answer one query.

The solution to the first problem, that of a common language, is being addressed by the DODIIS NQL-DD/D Project [29], the SAFE Project [19], the ADAPT Project [14], and FOCUS [12]. SDC is developing a DODIIS (Department of Defense Intelligence Information System) Query Language (DQL) and a common data dictionary and directory (DD/D) for locating data. The goal is to provide a common functionality and language that includes some features not found in the target systems, and it does not attempt to provide all features found in all target systems.

The next step beyond common access to a single database at a time is common access to multiple databases. CCA (Computer Corporation of America) developed the language ADAPLEX [21], [22] and the system Multibase [23], [13] which is a front-end distributor to heterogeneous DBMSs. Their goals are the same as those for Mermaid although their implementation differs significantly. CCA actually built their own DBMS, called the "Local Data Manager" that manipulates data and does postprocessing. Mermaid uses one or more existing DBMSs to do manipulation and postprocessing. CCA has put more emphasis on access to nonrelational DBMSs and translation than Mermaid has and less emphasis on query optimization. Another difference is that Mermaid is stressing a separation of the data model, the user query language, and the intermediate language. All communication between Mermaid processes is via an intermediate language which is independent of the user language and the semantic model of the data.

Another system, NDMS (Network Data Management System) [24], is being developed at CRAI in Italy. Its goals and architecture are very close to those of Mermaid. NDMS uses SQL for the user language and has the concept of an intermediate language. The user model is the relational data model with semantic extensions, and schemata of the underlying databases are integrated into a federated schema with different user views.

The U.S. Air Force has sponsored development of a prototype heterogeneous front-end system called IISS (Integrated Information Support System) [11]. It has a goal of accessing databases on three types of hardware (VAX, IBM, and Honeywell) and many DBMSs. Their approach is batch-oriented. There is no ad hoc query language and all retrieval requests must be precompiled.

B. Query Optimization

Access to data in multiple databases requires careful planning to control the time that is required to process the query. This is important in local DBMSs, but it becomes even more important when data must be moved across a network. Query optimization algorithms have been developed

for DDBMS such as SDD-1 [1], distributed INGRES [7], Encompass [27], and R* [31], [15].

The Mermaid system started with ideas from SDD-1 and distributed INGRES when developing the optimization algorithms that are currently running. These algorithms will be discussed further in Section III-C6.

C. Distributed Operating Systems

BBN has developed a prototype called Cronus [20]. Cronus provides a level above host operating systems that appears to be a distributed operating system to application programs. It provides uniform mechanisms for operating system functions including communication, access control, naming, and data storage and retrieval. The IISS system has an operating system component called NTM (Network Transaction Manager). The NTM is started as an operating system above the existing operating systems and supports the application programs. Communication between processes in NDMS is done through mail messages sent between computers connected with a network that uses the X.25 protocol. The system control and network protocol of the Mermaid system will be discussed in Sections III-C7 and III-C8.

III. MERMAID ARCHITECTURE

A. Assumptions

Mermaid is expected to operate in an environment where there is a federation of pre-existing databases. Ad hoc users and application programs will access individual databases directly, and Mermaid will be used primarily for ad hoc access to the federation. Mermaid must operate above the pre-existing databases without changing the DBMS or the design of the databases. Mermaid cannot require changes to the database structure for compatibility of data types or for optimizations.

Mermaid must provide a query optimization algorithm which can adjust to a wide variety of data distributions. In some environments, there may be closely coupled databases in which a relation from one database may be replicated in another database or in which some relations may be fragmented with fragments stored in different databases. In other environments, the databases may be basically disjoint, although there must be some attributes that can be used to join relations across the databases or there would be little reason to treat them as a federation.

It is assumed that processing costs and communications costs will not be uniform. There will be different data management systems which will have different operational characteristics even when running on the same hardware, and there will be different types of computers. The network will also be nonuniform. There may be multiple local networks, possibly different types of networks, connected by gateways.

Since it is assumed that users of Mermaid will tend to use it interactively, minimization of response time is important. The response time includes the time to develop the plan for answering the query as well as the time to execute it. Therefore, a major objective has been to design an optimization algorithm that runs quickly even if the plan is not necessarily the optimum. Plans are not compiled and saved

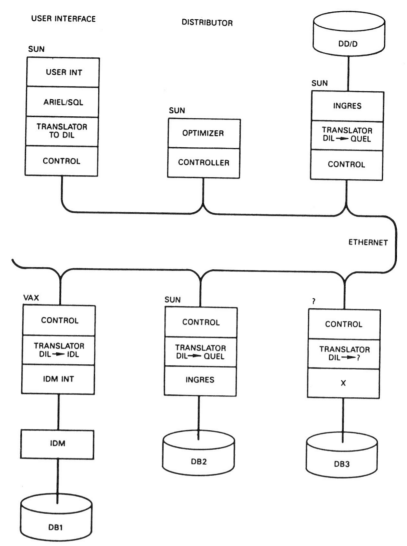

Fig. 1. Mermaid processes.

because *ad hoc* use is expected, but, in the future, plans could be saved if queries are saved in the query library or executed from application programs.

Since relational databases are becoming prevalent and relational interfaces are being developed for nonrelational DBMSs, Mermaid has emphasized access to relational DBMSs. Mermaid assumes the existence of a local optimizer which determines which indices to use, how to perform a join, and the order of joins if multiple joins are required.

Most of the expected users will not be doing updates through Mermaid. The majority of updates will be made by existing application programs. Some updates may be made interactively, but the updates will be made by the owner of the data to a single database. Since Mermaid is expected to be a front-end system to existing databases, we expect few conflicting updates and little need for transactions that cross databases in this environment.

B. Overview

The development of Mermaid started in 1982. It was initially implemented on a single VAX running UNIX 4.1. The emphasis the first year was on query optimization and translation of queries to IDL which is the language of the IDM database machine. ARIEL (which is an SDC-developed user-friendly query language) [16] and the user interface environment were added in 1983. The Ethernet was acquired in 1984 and the entire system was moved to UNIX 4.2 and the network of Suns as well as the original VAX.

The major processes in the system are shown in Fig. 1 and described as follows:

• *The user interface process:* The user environment has an embedded ARIEL or SQL parser and a translator that produces DIL (Distributed Intermediate Language).

• *The distributor process:* It contains the optimizer and the controller. The user interface process and the distributor process could be on the same computer or different computers.

• *One DBMS driver process for each database to be accessed.* The driver also contains a translator that translates from DIL to the DBMS query language. It interfaces to the DBMS through a DBMS supplied procedural interface.

All information about schemata, databases, users, host

computers, and the network is contained in a DD/D (Data Dictionary/Directory) which is stored in a database and accessed through a special driver. Either of the DBMS drivers could be the DD/D driver. The translator and the optimizer access the DD/D in order to do translation and query planning.

The following paragraphs will describe the flow of a query through the system.

The user builds an ARIEL or SQL query in the user environment. This query is then parsed and validated by the translator. If the query is valid, it is sent to the distributor.

The controller reads the query and passes it to the optimizer which plans the execution. The DIL query may have to be decomposed into several subqueries and the controller sends them to one or more DBMS drivers for execution. The controller then waits for responses from the DBMS drivers.

Each DBMS driver will process the DIL (sub)query by calling the translator to translate the query into the DBMS query language, sending the query to the DBMS, reading the status (tuple count, error messages), and then retrieving the response if any. The result returned to the driver may be just a status if the operation does not retrieve data, it may be a report, or it may be a relation that must be sent to another driver.

When the final report has been assembled at a site, the controller directs the driver at that site to send the report to the user interface.

C. Component Discriptions

1) Data Dictionary/Directory: The information about the databases, the users, the DBMSs, the host computers, and the network is contained in the DD/D. The layers of schema supported in the DD/D are shown in Fig. 2 and described

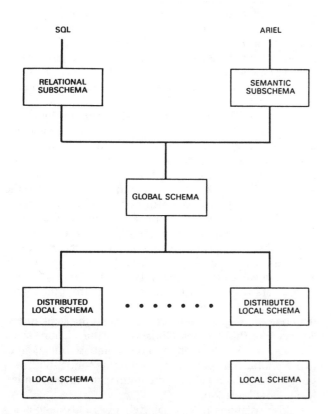

Fig. 2. Mermaid schema architecture.

as follows:

• *Subschema Layer:* This layer represents the user view based on the global schema. The user view can be represented in the relational or semantic model.

• *Global Schema:* This schema represents the global (federated) view of all the data defined in the distributed local schema. It is represented in the relational model.

• *Distributed Local Schema:* This schema represents the relational view of the local schema.

• *Local Schema:* This schema corresponds to the external view of the local database. It can be represented in any data model.

The relational model is being used as the global data model. The local schemata currently supported are all relational, i.e., there is no distinction between the distributed local schema and local schema. However, we maintain this four-layer schema architecture for the future expansion to include nonrelational DBMSs.

Much of the friendliness of the ARIEL language results from its exploitation of new modeling constructs that become available when a semantic model is defined above the global schema. For example, in many or most cases the system will be able to infer from the semantic subschema how to join a pair of relations on which pair of columns. This will allow a user to specify queries which omit references to joins.

There could also be multiple global schemata defined over the same set of underlying databases to provide different application views or different security views, but each different global schema is a different "database" that the user opens and each is stored separately in the DD/D.

In addition to the schema information, the DD/D contains data describing physical characteristics, both of the data in the local databases (such as the size in bytes of a relation) and of the system (such as the number of sites in the system). It also includes the performance characteristics of the network connecting the various sites and the capabilities of the different DBMSs which are needed for the optimizer.

2) Languages:

a) User languages: Because of its modular structure, Mermaid can use a variety of user interfaces. Each specific user interface requires a translator to translate the user language into DIL. Currently there are translators that accept ANSI standard SQL or ARIEL. If an application requires another type of interface, such as forms, a specific interface could be written to produce DIL and the full power of Mermaid would be available.

b) Distributed Intermediate Language: DIL is a highly structured language which is designed for ease of translation. The user language can be flexible with a rich syntax, but it is translated into DIL before it is given to the query optimizer. The use of DIL has many advantages:

• DIL supplies the functionality of a large class of database query languages. New translators can be easily written for new user languages without impacting the existing system.

• DIL can be entered directly into the distributor or into the driver so that either module can be tested independently.

• DIL is a better representation of the query than a tree form for transmission across a network because it contains only ASCII characters.

• Nested queries and aggregates in the qualification are difficult for the optimizer and may be difficult for the translator because many DBMSs do not support these features. We solve this problem by using the translator to translate the queries into a multi-step DIL query which contains no nested queries or aggregates in the qualification.

We have found from experience that the intermediate language must be human-readable. It allows the system administrator and the users to check the functioning of the system via the run-time journals that our system produces. It also simplifies the development of the programs, because each module can be tested independently by entering its input in DIL and looking at its DIL output.

The DIL parser will enforce the rule that every relation referenced in a query must appear in a join clause. This restriction is motivated by the desire to avoid the growth of data via a cross-product. It may have to be relaxed so that a warning is given rather than actually forbidding it. However, in our experience, cross-products are generally obtained accidentally when the user forgets a join clause.

c) DBMS languages: All of the DBMSs that are currently accessed are relational. We have translators within the DBMS drivers that translate DIL into IDL, QUEL, and SQL.

3) Query and Data Translation: There are three types of translation that take place within Mermaid. They are language translation from ARIEL or SQL to DIL, DIL to QUEL or SQL or IDL; data translation; and schema translation. The mapping information used for schema and data translation is stored in the DD/D.

a) Language translation: The user language may be SQL or ARIEL, and the DBMS language is whatever is supported by the *ad hoc* interface to the DBMS. Problems occur when the languages do not have the same functionality. The developer of each translator must have a detailed understanding of the semantics of various operations. Problems can occur with duplicate tuple removal, with building new relations, and with aggregates.

Most relational systems leave duplicate tuples in sets returned unless the user specifies that duplicates are to be removed. For example, INGRES allows the user to say "retrieve (A.x)" or "retrieve unique (A.x)". However, a system built on pure relational algebra would automatically remove duplicates.

Mermaid builds new relations during query processing to hold temporary results. Dynamically created relations are not allowed in systems that do not have a data dictionary that can be accessed and updated during operation. Even those systems that do allow building new relations have different methods for doing so. For example, ORACLE's [17] SQL does not support "select . . . insert into" which is used to build new relations from old in Mistress SQL. The DIL "retrieve into" must be translated into two commands for ORACLE, one to CREATE a new relation and another to INSERT into it.

Aggregate processing is not supported in a uniform manner across systems. Even in the current Mermaid system, which is all relational, there are differences between Mistress and the other DBMSs. IDM allows different qualification on each aggregate while Mistress has a global qualification. INGRES and IDM allow aggregates in the qualification clause as well as the target list, but Mistress allows aggregates only in the target list.

There is no simple solution to the problem of different functionality across systems. Our current solution in Mermaid is to define a basic set of functions that will be supported. DBMSs which cannot perform the minimum func-

tions will not be supported in the Mermaid system. Other DBMSs may be supported on a retrieve-only basis, that is, they cannot be used to perform *ad hoc* joins or report generation.

Queries are simplified as much as possible when translated into DIL. The translator from the user language to DIL generates a sequence of DIL subqueries for all queries that contain aggregates in the qualification, nested queries, or disjunctions. This procedure is called "query flattening." The sequence of subqueries builds temporary relations which are referenced in later subqueries. This simplifies the queries which in turn makes it easier for the optimizer to plan the query execution and for the translator to translate each subquery into DBMS languages.

Other features such as quantifiers, set-operators, trigonometric functions, user defined functions, and report generation are not supported by the user interface. Instead they are handled in other ways. For example, report generation functions are added in a post-processor. Output may be stored in relations or files for further processing.

b) Data translation: The user views the federated database as a single database with a common representation for the data elements that are of the same domain. However, data may have different representations in different databases. The data used in the qualification of the query are translated from the global representation, as input by the user, into the local representation. The data that are retrieved for joining between databases or for the final report are translated into the global representation.

Two basic types of translation are supported: functional translation and enumerated type translation. Functional translation is used for any algorithmic translation such as from miles to kilometers or from one date format to another. Enumerated type translation converts sets of values through a table lookup such as from internal codes to names.

c) Schema translation: Schema translation is closely related to data translation but it affects the relations and fields named in the query rather than the data. The names of fields may be changed, joins may be added or removed, predicates may be added, and fields may be concatenated or substringed. If fields in the qualification are concatenated or substringed, then the data in the qualification will have to be modified.

Schema mapping may be at the relation or the field level. At the relation level, the types of translation include name changes, horizontal partitions, projections, and one-to-many or many-to-one mappings. Horizontal partitions are defined with a predicate. Each partition may be in a different database or a partition may be excluded from the federated view. Projections require no translation because the excluded fields are simply not known to the global view. One-to-many mappings from the global to the local view require the addition of a join in the query and can be done only within a single local database. When the global view is defined we exclude global relations that require a join across databases. Many-to-one mappings from the global to the local view may mean the removal of a join if more than one of the global relations is used in the same query. For example, the relational global view of the relation "ship" may map to a single relation in one database but a join of two in another database. The "submarine" and "ship" relations in the global view may actually map to the same underlying "boat" relation.

Field translations include name changes and one-to-many or many-to-one mappings on character fields only. For example, a date may be stored in a single field as "YYMMDD" in one database but as three fields "month," "day," and "year" in another database.

Our translation design supports another translation from the distributed local relational schema to the corresponding local nonrelational schema. This data model translation is currently not supported in the Mermaid system.

4) User Interface: The user interface appears to the user to be a DBMS because it provides a set of commands similar to those provided by most DBMSs. This includes support for query libraries, query editors, debugging, help, synonym replacement, spelling correction, report manipulation, and options for customizing the system.

The current version of the user interface runs on either a standard CRT terminal or on a Sun bit-mapped display. With both types of terminal, there are "windows" that represent different functions. When running with the standard CRT, the function windows overlay each other. When running with the multiple-window version for the Sun bit-mapped display, the user is able to format and edit queries in one window, receive traces from Mermaid in another window, get output in a third window, and bring up additional windows as needed for help and synonym editing. The implementation uses the standard set of window management tools provided by Sun (the SunTools) which allows the user to move windows around, use pop-up menus and the mouse, and organize the windows so that multiple functions can be viewed simultaneously.

With any terminal type, the user interface provides three screen modes: the standard command mode, the help mode, and the report mode. The standard command mode screen has three windows: the data window, the command window, and the message window. The current query is shown in the data window, the commands to edit or run or validate the query are given in the command window, and messages are given in the message window. For instance, if the user enters "run query01" in the command window, the query named "query01" is loaded from the current query library and is displayed in the data window. While it is running, messages like "parsing of query in progress" appear in the message window.

The user can enter help mode by entering the command "help" in the command window. He then gets a new screen, either on top of the command screen or as an additional window, and works in the help window until exiting from the help mode. The help screen, at the user's discretion, allows the user to step backwards and forwards through various levels of help information.

When the report is returned, the user enters into report mode. The report mode screen lets the user scroll or page, as well as search, the report.

The user interface also supports synonym replacement for any word or string of words in a query as well as spelling correction. Spelling correction requires close integration with the ARIEL and SQL parsers because unrecognized words must be sent to the spelling corrector during parsing and, if the spelling can be corrected, the correct word must replace the invalid word in the parse tree.

With these capabilities and facilities, the user is able to manage his own Mermaid system environment.

5) Data Distribution: Mermaid is designed to operate as a front-end to existing DBMSs. This means that, generally, each database will be disjoint. However, there may be databases with the same or similar schema but different data at different sites, and there may be relations that are replicated at sites other than their originating site for performance and reliability.

Four types of data distribution are supported:

1) A "local" relation exists in its entirety at one site.
2) A "replicated" relation exists in its entirety at more than one but not necessarily all sites.
3) A "fragmented" relation is located at several sites; each site contains a subset of the relation's tuples and no tuple exists at more than one site.
4) A "dependent fragmented" relation is fragmented and the location of a tuple depends upon the location of a tuple in another fragmented relation; "dependency" means that tuples in a fragment at a site can only join to tuples in another fragment at the same site to generate nonempty results.

The concept of the "dependent fragment" or of "placement dependency" is a semantic concept which can be used to achieve faster query processing. Placement dependencies exist in databases whether they are recognized and used or not. For example, in an employee database, records about an employee may be located at the headquarter of the employee's division. This results in a logical dependency between the employee's record and the division records.

6) Query Decomposition and Optimization: The simplest but possibly most "expensive" method of answering a query is to move all of the data to a single site and then process the entire query at the site. This is not acceptable because large amounts of data might need to be moved across the network and large amounts of temporary storage might be needed at the receiving site. Therefore, the query must be decomposed and many subqueries run at individual database sites before the final report is assembled at a single site. A high-level description of this process is contained in this section. Details may be found in [3], [32]–[35].

The Mermaid query optimization algorithm is one of the most complete algorithms in the current literature according to [15] and one of the few that has been implemented and tested. In 1982 the first algorithm, the semijoin algorithm, was developed and tested. It is an extension to the SDD-1 algorithm which assumes that the most important cost is the number of bytes transmitted between processes. The algorithm was extended to support fragmented and replicated relations. In 1983 the replicate algorithm was developed and tested. It is derived from distributed INGRES. It assumes that CPU overhead dominates network costs and uses fragmented relations to maximize the amount of parallelism in operations. In 1984 we began work to support nonuniform processor speeds, nonuniform network speeds, better aggregate processing, and a combined algorithm which uses the best of the semijoin and replicate algorithms [5].

a) Semijoin algorithm: The semijoin algorithm assumes that the cost of transferring data between sites greatly outweighs the local processing costs at each site. The basic idea, therefore, is to reduce relations as much as possible before sending them across the network. This is accomplished by a combination of local operations and intersite semijoins. The algorithm contains four stages: 1) site selection, 2) local reduction, 3) global reduction, and 4) assembly. These are briefly discussed in the following.

Site selection is concerned with locating the relations that are relevant to the current query. In contrast to the replicate strategy described below, this algorithm chooses exactly one copy of each relation. Since we are attempting to minimize network traffic, it is desirable that these relations reside at as few sites as possible. Therefore, site selection finds the minimal site set that covers all relevant local relations and fragments, and at least one copy of each relevant replicated relation. Note that within a minimal site set there may still be more than one copy. In this case, an arbitrary choice is made, except that a copy at the result site is preferred.

The second stage of the semijoin algorithm is local reduction. In this phase, each relation is reduced by a) projecting out the attributes referenced in the target and join clauses of the query, and b) selecting tuples by applying predicates from the qualification. Local reduction can be performed at all sites in parallel. The distributor sends one command to each driver for each relation at the site controlled by that driver. After this is done, the relations are as fully reduced as possible without interrelation processing.

In the global reduction stage, the reductive effect of the query's join clauses is achieved through a series of semijoins. A semijoin selects the tuples from one relation which are capable of joining with tuples in another relation on some specified attribute. One advantage of semijoins is that they necessarily reduce the total amount of data, whereas this might not be true with a join. Also, fewer data need to be transferred across the network to perform a semijoin than a join. Instead of moving the whole sending relation, the joining attribute(s) of this relation are projected off, leaving only a set of unique values to be copied to the receiving relation's site.

The central problem in global reduction is finding the best sequence of semijoins. Mermaid uses a hill-climbing algorithm to determine such a sequence. The algorithm evaluates the costs and benefits of each possible semijoin and selects the most profitable one, that is, the one whose benefit most exceeds its cost. This semijoin is executed and the procedure is then iterated until no further profitable semijoins can be found.

The cost of semijoining relation $R1$ with $R2$ is assumed as a function of the size of the joining attribute in $R2$ which must be copied to $R1$'s site. Since duplicate values are removed in the course of projecting this attribute from $R2$, the cost is estimated from the expected number of unique values and the width of the joining attribute. The benefit is the amount by which $R1$ is reduced as a result of the semijoin. Benefit is estimated from the total size of $R1$ and the selectivity of the joining attribute.

The selectivity of an attribute is a measure of the variability of the values of that attribute, that is, whether the attribute has few or many of the values it could possibly assume. The selectivity is calculated by dividing the actual number of distinct values in the attribute by the possible number of distinct values, that is, by the size of the attribute's domain. If a relation is joined with a highly variable attribute it will be less reduced than if joined with an attribute having only a small fraction of the different values in the domain. If the joining attribute contains all the values in the domain, no reduction will occur.

Since the estimation of the cost and benefit is imperfect, the selection of semijoins is performed dynamically. The best semijoin is performed and a tuple count is returned. Then the costs and benefits are recomputed and the best remaining semijoin is selected and performed. This process continues until no semijoin is found whose benefit is greater than its cost.

The final stage in this algorithm is assembly. After global reduction, the reduced relations are gathered at a single result site. Currently this is the site where the user's query originates. Not all of the referenced relations need to be copied to the result site. Somtimes, the full reductive effect of a relation is achieved in the semijoin stage and the relation is of no further use. Once the relations are assembled, the distributor sends a query to the result DBMS driver to produce a report. This query may specify that aggregation, arithmetic operations, joins, and sorting are to be performed by the DBMS. The report is then sent by the distributor to the user interface.

b) Replicate algorithm: In contrast to the semijoin algorithm, the replicate algorithm assumes that local processing costs dominate network delay for most queries. Since transmission costs are of less concern, the replicate algorithm does not reduce relations. Instead, it finds an optimal set of sites at which the query can be executed in parallel, and it then combines the partial answers produced at these sites. The main features of this strategy are that it enhances parallelism, reduces the number of intermediate objects which must be built, permits the local DBMS to perform more local optimization, and is conceptually simple and easy to implement. There are four stages in the replicate algorithm: 1) site selection, 2) replication, 3) query execution, and 4) assembly. We will outline these below.

Site selection is the first, and most important, stage of this algorithm. As in the semijoin method discussed above, it serves to choose that set of sites at which query processing will be performed. There is a significant difference, however, in the handling of replicated relations. Whereas semijoin site selection has the effect of picking only one copy of a relation for consideration, the algorithm outlined here makes full use of all available copies. In fact, the greater the degree of replication, the more efficient this strategy will tend to be.

The replicate algorithm seeks to execute the user's query at several different sites in parallel. All sites containing relations referenced by the query are potential processing sites. However, the set that is actually chosen will have the following characteristics: a) not more than one relation will remain fragmented, i.e., have fragments at the selected sites, and b) there will be complete copies of all other referenced relations at each selected site. Since there will often be no set of sites that initially meets these requirements, fragments or full relations may have to be copied between sites. The chosen set is simply the one which requires the least data transfer.

The procedure for selecting processing sites is similar to that originally specified for distributed INGRES. The procedure first chooses the relation which is to remain fragmented. This is simply the relation having the largest total size. Then, weighting functions are used to evaluate the relative desirability of each site on the basis of global data transfer requirements. A site is selected if the data it receives as a processing site are less than the additional data it would have to send if it were not a processing site.

In Mermaid, the site selection process has been generalized to take placement dependencies into account. The site selection algorithm does not actually operate on relations but rather on classes of relations. Within each such class all relations have valid placement dependencies, but there are no dependencies between relations in different classes. Essentially, a class of relations can be treated as a single fragmented relation, and this substantially reduces transmission costs.

The second stage in this algorithm is replication. Here certain relations or fragments are copied to the sites which have been selected for query processing. The action taken for any given relation R depends on whether R is fragmented and, if so, whether it has been chosen to remain fragmented. If R is not fragmented, it is copied to all processing sites (where it does not already exist). If R is fragmented and is to remain so, then all fragments of R not currently at a processing site are copied to one. Otherwise, all fragments of R are copied to each processing site (where they do not already exist).

Query execution is the next stage. Once the processing sites contain the necessary data, the user's query is sent to each of these sites and is executed in parallel to provide a set of partial answers. Actually, the query may be modified somewhat before it is sent. Queries which specify sorting provide a simple example. Sorting done at the processing sites would only have to be repeated at the result site when the partial answers were combined. Another example involves aggregation. There are certain situations in which operations such as count and average cannot easily be performed in a distributed manner. In such cases, the aggregation operator may be modified or removed from the user's query before it is sent to the processing sites. These operations are delayed until after the partial answers have been assembled at the result site.

The fourth and final stage of the replicate algorithm is assembly. The query is executed in parallel and yields a partial answer at each of processing sites. These partial answers are then moved to the result site where they are unioned into a temporary relation. This relation may constitute the complete answer or it may require further processing, as in the sorting and aggregation cases mentioned above. In either case, a report is generated and sent back to the user interface for display to the user.

c) Combined algorithm: The replicate and the semijoin algorithms are based on different assumptions about the network and the database. Since we are operating in a heterogeneous environment with predefined databases, we need to operate efficiently when there are extensive replicated data as well as when there are basically disjoint databases. The replicate algorithm performs better in the first case while the semijoin algorithm performs better in the second case. We need to operate on fast local networks as well as across internet gateways. The replicate algorithm was designed for operation on local networks while the semijoin algorithm was originally designed for the ARPAnet. Therefore, we have designed and are implementing a combined algorithm that is further described in [5].

The new algorithm is basically an extension of the replicate algorithm. However, selection clauses are applied to individual relations or fragments and some semijoins may be performed to reduce large relations or fragments before they are moved across the network. In addition, processing cost is considered as well as data transmission cost, and the transmission cost may be different between each pair of computers. This algorithm will perform well even when there are no replicated or fragmented relations in the database because it degenerates to a variation of the semijoin algorithms.

7) System Control: The controller does process initialization of the drivers at local or remote sites, sets up interprocess communication, and handles the asynchronous I/O between the distributor and drivers.

The controller and the communication mechanism provide the functionality of a distributed operating system, above the independent UNIX 4.2 operating systems. The controller has four major functions and is contained within the distributor process:

- configuration control
- DIL parsing
- DIL generation
- I/O control.

These provide the central control of the Mermaid system. They are wrapped around the query optimizer and provide services for it.

The configuration control determines what options are to be used for a run and where the databases are to be found. The options control the amount and type of debugging information which varies when the system is running in different modes. The configuration control journals the options that are in effect for the run, and carries out the necessary remote log-ins and starts the DBMS driver processes. It also provides for the detection and handling of internal errors.

The DIL is transformed by the controller from its external, human readable format, into internal structures that are used by the optimizer. As the optimizer plans the query execution, it gives pieces of the query to the DIL generator which turns the internal form back into an ASCII form. This text is sent to DBMS drivers for execution.

The distributor process is the only process that may be handling multiple outstanding commands, but only one command may be outstanding to any driver process. The I/O control maintains read and write queues for each DBMS driver. As the optimizer writes a command to the DBMS driver, the write request is enqueued. If the site is available, the actual write is performed, the request is dequeued, and the control is returned to the optimizer. As the optimizer requests that an acknowledgment be read from any site, the I/O control requests any messages from the DBMS drivers. As messages are received from the DBMS drivers, the read queues are emptied of their outstanding work, and the corresponding write queue is checked for any other work that the optimizer may have requested. Thus many DBMS driver processes may be running in parallel, and the optimizer does not block on every command that it writes.

A handshake mechanism with the supposedly active DBMS drivers is provided. The maximum time for completion of a handshake is so small that it is not noticed by the users, and a failed site can be detected in a matter of seconds instead of in minutes.

8) Network Protocol: TCP/IP is the DoD standard protocol and is therefore the first one selected for use by Mermaid. A main reason for selecting the Sun computers is that

UNIX 4.2 comes with an implementation of TCP/IP. However, TCP/IP is designed mainly for terminal-to-host communication and not for distributed application program communication.

Mermaid's concept of operation does not fit the TCP/IP model. In the Mermaid model, a master process is started when a user logs in. The master starts slave processes on the same or remote computers. Any process may communicate with any other process so many-to-many communication connections are needed. All of the processes are operating on behalf of the user and therefore are owned by him. This is necessary for security so that the DBMS access controls can check permissions for the specific user and for accounting so that users can be billed for the resources used.

To support remote process management in Mermaid, at least the following capabilities need to exist within the network or the combination of the network and the operating system.

• Remote process initiation.

The user interface has to start the distributor process and then the controller starts a local or remote driver process for each database that is to be accessed.

• Out-of-band messages.

The controller needs to send a software interrupt to the remote process to kill it or to determine whether or not it is still operational.

• Permanent communication channels.

A permanent I/O channel must be set up between the user interface and the distributor process and between the controller and each driver process.

• Dynamic communication channels.

Any two processes located anywhere in the network must be able to set up a communication channel between them.

• Nonblocking read.

It should be possible for the controller to read the various I/O channel connections to the driver processes in an asynchronous, nonblocking fashion. Otherwise, a synchronous polling scheme must be used, with degraded performance due to the (sometimes) unnecessary waiting for data to arrive.

We have developed a communication mechanism which provides Mermaid with two types of network-related activities to facilitate the operation of the system. They are remote process creation and interprocess communication between any distinct pair of processes at arbitrary locations in the network.

The communication mechanism is layered and has evolved over the course of the project. Initially, we used the standard UNIX 4.2 Socket Interface with TCP as the underlying transport protocol. This is a low-level interface which is relatively nonportable. In the current system, we have moved to the Sun Remote Procedure Call (RPC) facility. This allows Mermaid programs to use function call semantics for networking, and it provides a uniform external data representation. RPC implementations are available for several different machines and operating systems. To take advantage of the emerging OSI network standards, future releases of Mermaid will use the MAP [8] and DODIIS (Department of Defense Intelligence Information System) protocols for interprocess communication. This will support access to computers beyond the local network.

9) DBMS Drivers: Since the DBMS driver does low-level process control that is very dependent upon particular operating system calls and acts as the user of the DBMS, a driver must reside at each DBMS site. A different version of the driver is needed for each DBMS and operating system type.

The driver is initiated by the controller when the first query is made. It is started as a local or remote process that is owned by the user of Mermaid. The first message sent to the driver includes the database name and information about the network configuration. The driver establishes a connection with the DBMS and opens a database as a user. It then stores the network configuration table for future reference.

Intersite transfer of relations is done by retrieving a relation, translating the data into global units, and storing them in a buffer or buffers in a standard format. The receiving driver translates the form to the restore format for the particular DBMS and executes a bulk load. If the relation already exists, the "restore" appends tuples rather than replacing them, which allows Mermaid to gather fragments of relations from several sites into a single relation at a single site.

D. Testing and Measurement

Tests were conducted using a database that exists in a centralized version as well as in different distributed configurations. The test database contains seventeen relations which range from four tuples to 19 000 tuples.

The test database is a Navy database that has ships, positions, information about weapons installed on the ships, characteristics of the ships, battle groups which are temporary groupings of ships, and visits to ports by the ships. The database is distributed to four sites which correspond to the second, third, sixth, and seventh U.S. Naval Fleets. Some relations are fragmented, some are replicated, some are dependent fragmented, and some are single-site relations.

A set of test questions was developed to test access to different data distributions, different numbers and types of join, and different features of the query language. Each new release of Mermaid has been tested with this set of test questions.

We have done system tests to compare the operation of the semijoin and replicate algorithms and to compare the operation of the centralized version of the database with operation on four databases on a single computer and on three different computers. The results of the early testing are given in [28]. Results of testing on the network are given in [30].

IV. EXAMPLE TO ILLUSTRATE OPERATION

We will trace the operation of one query to illustrate the operation of the system. First, we will show how the query is answered using the semijoin algorithm, and then we will show the same query using the replicate algorithm.

A. Semijoin Algorithm

In this example, we will be concerned with three relations in a naval database, namely, the ship, weapon, and install relations. The first two describe various characteristics of the ships and weapons systems in the database, and the third specifies which weapons are installed on which ships. There are four sites, $S2$, $S3$, $S6$, and $S7$, each of which corresponds to a fleet. The ship relation is fragmented at all four of these sites. Thus ships in the second fleet, for example, are described in the fragment at $S2$. The install relation is also fragmented at the four sites, and it is dependent on ship. That is, install tuples at a given site can only join with ship tuples at the same site to produce a nonempty result. The weapon relation is replicated in its entirety at two sites, $S2$ and $S3$.

We assume that a query "Which US destroyers carry Harpoon weapons?" is submitted at $S2$. The user might express this query in ARIEL as follows:

```
retrieve name of ship
where type = "DD"
and flag = "USA"
and name of weapon = "Harpoon"
and ship.num = install.shipid
and install.weapon = weapon.id
```

The translator in the user interface translates the ARIEL query into DIL as follows:

```
BEGIN
VARIABLES
  ship IS ship,
  install IS install,
  weapon IS weapon
RETRIEVE
  name (ship.name)
SELECT
  ship.type = "DD"
  ship.flag = "USA"
  weapon.name = "Harpoon"
MERGE
  ship.num = = install.shipid,
  install.weapon = = weapon.id
END
```

The user interface sends this DIL query to the distributor. The first stage in the optimization process is site selection. Because the ship and install relations are fragmented at sites $S2$, $S3$, $S6$, and $S7$, all four of these sites must be chosen. Furthermore, the copy of weapon at $S2$ is chosen over the one at $S3$ because $S2$ is the result site where the user resides.

The goal of the semijoin algorithm is to reduce the size of relations as much as possible before assembling them at the result site. This is accomplished in the local and global reduction stages of the optimization process. For this query, there are two local reduction operations, which we refer to as LOCAL1 and LOCAL2, and two global reduction operations, GLOBAL1 and GLOBAL2 (as discussed below). Table 1 demonstrates the progressive reduction of all the relevant relations at the four sites. For example, the ship fragment at $S2$ initially contains 370 tuples, but after LOCAL1 it is reduced to 20 tuples. Similarly, there are initially 772 tuples in install at $S2$, but the GLOBAL1 and GLOBAL2 operations reduce this fragment to 111 and then 14 tuples.

In the local reduction phase, the selection clauses found in the user's query are applied to the relations, and these relations are then projected on their joining and target attri-

Table 1: Progressive Reduction

SITE	RELATIONS	INITIAL	LOCAL1	LOCAL2	GLOBAL1	GLOBAL2
$S2$	ship	370	370	20	20	20
	install	772	772	772	111	14
	weapon	51	1	1	1	1
$S3$	ship	361	361	22	22	22
	install	763	763	763	109	16
$S6$	ship	140	140	5	5	5
	install	184	184	184	13	0
$S7$	ship	140	140	4	4	4
	install	181	181	181	14	0

butes. The LOCAL1 operation reduces the weapon relation. It is accomplished by sending the following command to the driver at site $S2$:

```
retrieve into weapon1 (weapon.id)
where weapon.name = "Harpoon"
```

The LOCAL2 operation involves sending the following command to the drivers at $S2$, $S3$, $S6$, and $S7$:

```
retrieve into ship1 (ship.name, ship.num)
where ship.type = "DD"
and ship.flag = "USA"
```

This command is executed in parallel at the four sites. The distributor waits until all acknowledgments have been received before proceeding.

In the global reduction stage, semijoins are used to further reduce relations. Initially, four semijoins are possible. These are as follows:

```
SEMIJOIN ship BY install
SEMIJOIN install BY ship
SEMIJOIN weapon BY install
SEMIJOIN install BY weapon
```

The cost and benefit of each of these semijoins is computed, and the most profitable over a certain threshold is selected for execution. The most profitable semijoin turns out to be reducing install by weapon. Normally, performing the semijoin would require projection of weapon onto its joining attribute, weapon.id. In this case, however, the projection has already been done in LOCAL1. Therefore, weapon1 can be copied directly to the other sites at which install is fragmented:

```
COPY weapon @ S2 → weapon1 @ S3, S6, S7
```

Now, in operation GLOBAL1, we actually perform the semijoin by sending the following command to $S2$, $S3$, $S6$, and $S7$:

```
retrieve into install1 (install.shipid, install.weapon)
where install.weapon = weapon1.id
```

This command is executed in parallel at the four sites and acknowledgments are sent to the distributor. After they are all received, the distributor examines the remaining semijoins. There are now three possibilities:

```
SEMIJOIN ship BY install
```

SEMIJOIN install BY ship
SEMIJOIN weapon BY install

This time the cost/benefit analysis determines that install should be reduced by ship. Because install and ship are fragmented at all four sites and a placement dependency exists between them, it is not necessary to project off the ship.num attribute or to copy this attribute between sites. Instead, the semijoin operation GLOBAL2 is achieved by simply sending the following command to S2, S3, S6, and S7:

retrieve into install2 (install.shipid, install1.weapon)
where install1.shipid = ship1.num

Again, the semijoins are executed in parallel and each driver returns an acknowledgment. At this point, two further semijoins are still possible, but the optimizer decides that neither is worthwhile. Thus the global reduction phase is over. The install relation has been twice reduced and, in fact, Table 1 shows that the fragments at S6 and S7 have no more qualifying tuples at all.

The next stage in the semijoin algorithm is assembly. We build a complete copy of the reduced ship relation at result site S2 by copying the remote ship fragments to S2 and appending them to the fragment already there. This assembly process is then repeated for the install relation. Note that there are only two nonnull fragments of install after global reduction. Also, we do not need to assemble weapon because S2 already contains a complete copy of that relation.

COPY ship1 @ S3 → ship1 @ S2
COPY ship1 @ S6 → ship1 @ S2
COPY ship1 @ S7 → ship1 @ S2

COPY install2 @ S3 → install2 @ S2

After all relevant relations have been reduced and assembled at the result site, a report is produced and sent to the user interface. This is done by sending the following command to the driver at S2:

retrieve (ship1.name)
where ship1.num = install2.shipid

The select clauses in the original query are absent here because they have already been applied during local reduction. Also, it is unnecessary to specify the join between install and weapon because GLOBAL1 has reduced install by weapon as completely as possible.

After the user has received the report, the final step is to send each driver a command to destroy all the temporary relations that have been built during processing. The distributor then waits to receive the next query from the user interface.

While the semijoin algorithm produced satisfactory results in the above example, it should be noted that an even better strategy could have been followed. This would have been to reduce ship by install in GLOBAL2 instead of reducing install by ship. Doing so would have made it unnecessary to move any fragments of install to S2 during assembly. This is because install does not contain target attributes and it could have no further reductive effect on ship during the report stage. Thus the command to generate the report would simply be:

retrieve (ship1.name)

There are two reasons why this preferred strategy was not followed. First, to compensate for ignoring processing costs, we are currently using a benefit threshold in selecting semijoins. That is, we will not perform a semijoin that can only eliminate a few tuples because its DBMS cost usually outweighs its data transmission benefit. Thus ship was not further reduced because its largest fragment only contained 22 tuples. Second, the algorithm did not recognize the advantage of reducing ship because it was unable to look ahead to the assembly stage. During global reduction, semijoins were chosen for their immediate benefit and the longer range possibility of eliminating unnecessary assembly steps was missed. These problems will be addressed in future versions of the optimizer.

B. Replicate Algorithm

In order to contrast the operation of the semijoin and replicate algorithms, we will use the same query and database environment as above.

The first stage in the replicate algorithm is site selection. This involves choosing a relation (or class of relations) to remain fragmented, and then deciding which of the sites containing these fragments will be used for processing. Table 2 shows the initial distribution of the relations at the four sites, with the symbol F denoting fragments and C denoting copies. The size of each fragment and copy is specified accordingly. Table 2 also shows weights that are used in choosing the processing sites.

Table 2 Site Selection

Site	Ship	Install	Weapon	Weight
S2	F 370	F 722	C 51	1142
S3	F 361	F 763	C 51	1124
S6	F 140	F 184		273
S7	F 140	F 181		270

Because there is a placement dependency between the ship and install relations, these two relations form a class. Normally the largest class is chosen to remain fragmented but, in this case, there is only one possibility (since weapon is not fragmented). Therefore, its members, ship and install, will remain fragmented at some subset of their initial four sites.

Each site that is chosen for processing needs to contain a copy of the weapon relation. If weapon does not already exist there, it has to be sent from another site. We will select the set of sites that minimizes data transmission. This could be done by calculating the total transmission cost for every subset of the four sites, but it is more efficient to compute a single weight for each site. These weights represent the size difference between the fragmented data already at a site and the other data needed there. For example, the weight for S6 is calculated as: 140 + 184 − 51 = 273. Table 2 shows that all the weights are positive, and therefore all four sites are chosen to be processing sites.

The next stage of this algorithm is replication. Each processing site must have complete copies of all relations except the one that is to remain fragmented. In this case, we send a copy of weapon to sites *S*6 and *S*7:

COPY weapon @ S2 → weapon @ S6, S7

Once all necessary data are present at the processing sites, the query can be executed in parallel at each of these sites. This is accomplished by sending the following command to the drivers at *S*2, *S*3, *S*6, and *S*7:

retrieve into result (ship.name)
where ship.type = "DD"
and ship.flag = "USA"
and weapon.name = "Harpoon"
and ship.num = install.shipid
and install.weapon = weapon.id

Execution of this command results in a partial answer at each processing site. After receiving acknowledgments from all of these sites, the distributor gathers the partial answers into a single complete answer at the result site.

COPY result @ S3 → result @ S2
COPY result @ S6 → result @ S2
COPY result @ S7 → result @a S2

The next stage in the replicate algorithm is to produce the report at the result site and write it to the user interface. We do so by sending the following command to *S*2:

retrieve (result.name)

Finally, as in the semijoin algorithm, the distributor destroys all the temporary relations it has created and then waits for another query.

Since the above example is fairly simple, we should briefly consider a more complex case. Referring to Table 2, suppose the sizes of the fragments of ship and install at *S*7 are 20 each. Then we would obtain a negative weight at *S*7 and this site would not be selected for processing. That is, it would be more costly to move weapon to *S*7 than to move the fragments at *S*7 elsewhere and do the processing at three sites. This latter option, then, is exactly what is done. The fragments of ship and install at *S*7 are sent to *S*2 and unioned with copies of *S*2's ship and install fragments. Then weapon is sent to *S*6 and the query is executed in parallel at the three processing sites, *S*2, *S*3, and *S*6.

V. Conclusions and Future Research

A. Conclusions

Mermaid is an operational prototype which has demonstrated the feasibility of operating as a front-end to distributed heterogeneous databases. It has been used for testing and improving query optimization algorithms and system control strategies. A user language, ARIEL, has been defined which incorporates basic relational functionality with relaxed syntax (compared to relational languages such as QUEL, SQL, IDL), and extended semantics. An internal language DIL has been implemented to support basic relational functionality and network commands.

Mermaid supports heterogeneity at many levels:

- Different DBMSs and computers containing databases.
- Data translation including function conversions and enumerated type conversions.

- Schema translation including relation and field mapping.
- Different network protocols and configurations.

The current Mermaid prototype is being enhanced to provide the following features:

- Support for updates.
- New query optimizer that combines the semijoin and replicate algorithms.
- More user interface features such as a forms/menu interface.
- Provision of a program interface.
- Mermaid communications package calls to isolate the programs from the network protocol in order to make protocol conversion more transparent.

A schema design tool is also being developed which supports the user when developing the global view of the databases from existing schemata.

B. Future Research

The major research efforts are in the areas of:

- Expert systems.
- Secure systems.
- Object management systems.

1) Expert Systems: Supporting a semantic data model not only opens the possibility for more sophisticated user interfaces and aids in the translation process, but it provides a basis for enforcing a much higher degree of data integrity than is possible in a purely relational system. Also, we envision that an expert system should be able to tie directly into the semantic model, and thus add inference capabilities to the system. UNISYS is currently developing a Flexible Deductive Engine (the FDE) [36] which can use Mermaid to access external databases. The FDE runs on a Xerox 1100 and is connected to the Ethernet. It can produce a query in DIL and send it to Mermaid for execution. We have proposed to add the capability to send queries from Mermaid to the FDE so that inference capability may be added to the Mermaid system.

2) Secure Systems: An ultimate goal of the Mermaid project is to develop a system that can be evaluated at the B1 security level. This is an NSA security rating as specified in the "Orange Book" [6]. A security model has been developed, and the current Mermaid system is being evaluated against the model. The results of the evaluation will influence the future design of the Mermaid system.

3) Object Management Systems: A longer term research issue is the development of an object management system that will provide integrated management and sharing of structured data objects, text, images, and voice. Current object oriented systems such as the Xerox PARC SMALLTALK [9] and Apple Lisa [26] are not integrated with full DBMS capabilities. In the meanwhile, object oriented machines such as the INTEL iAPX 432 [10] offer new architectures for object management, and new developments in database management such as the CCA Local Data Manager (LDB) [4] and Berkeley's Postgres [25] support new data types. In order for the Mermaid system to integrate different object types, the basic functionality supported by ARIEL and DIL will need to be extended beyond relational operators to support operators for the additional object types.

REFERENCES

[1] P. Bernstein, N. Goodman, E. Wong, C. Reeve, and J. Rothnie, "Query processing in a system for distributed databases (SDD-1)," *ACM Trans. Database Syst.*, Dec. 1981.

[2] Britton Lee Inc., *IDM 500 Software Reference Manual*, Version 1.7, Nov. 1984.

[3] D. Brill, M. Templeton, and C. Yu, "Distributed query processing strategies in Mermaid: A frontend to data management systems," in *Proc. IEEE Data Engineering Conf.*, Apr. 1984.

[4] A. Chan, U. Dayal, S. Fox, N. Goodman, R. Ries, and D. Skeen, "Overview of an ADA[2] compatible distributed database manager," in *Proc. ACM SIGMOD*, May 1983.

[5] A. Chen, D. Brill, M. Templeton, and C. Yu, "Distributed query processing in Mermaid: A frontend system for multiple databases," submitted for publication, 1986.

[6] DoD Computer Security Center, "Trusted computer system evaluation criteria," Tech. Rep. CSC-STD-001-83, Aug. 1983.

[7] R. Epstein, M. Stonebraker, and E. Wong, "Distributed query processing in a relational database system," in *Proc. ACM SIGMOD*, May 1978.

[8] General Motors Technical Center, *Manufacturing Automation Protocol Specification*, Version 2.1, Mar. 1985.

[9] A. Goldberg and D. Robson, *SMALLTALK80: The Language and Its Implementation*. Reading, MA: Addison-Wesley, 1982.

[10] J. Hemenway and R. Grappel, "Intel's iAPX 'Micromainframe'," Mini-Micro Systems Rep., May 1981.

[11] "Integrated Information Support System (IISS)—An evolutionary approach to integration," AF Wright Aeronautical Lab. Rep., 1985.

[12] Information Builders Inc., *FOCUS General Information Guide*, 1985.

[13] T. Landers and R. Rosenberg, "An overview of multibase," in *Proc. Int. Symp. on Distributed Database*, 1982.

[14] Logicon Inc., "ADAPT I: Final functional and system design specification," Rep. 76-C-0899-2, Jan. 1978.

[15] G. Lohman, C. Mohan, L. Haas, B. Lindsay, P. Selinger, and P. Wilms, "Query processing in R*," IBM Res. Rep. RJ 4272, Apr. 1984.

[16] R. MacGregor, "ARIEL—A semantic frontend to relational DBMSs," in *Proc. VLDB Cont.*, Aug. 1985.

[17] Oracle Corp., *ORACLE SQL/UFI Reference Manual*, Version 4.0, June 1984.

[18] Rhodnius Inc., *Mistress: The Query Language*, Version 2.2, July 1982.

[19] "SAFE Project user interface requirements specification," TRW Tech. Rep. CE-7200E, Feb. 1983.

[20] R. Schantz and R. Thomas, "The architecture of the Cronus distributed operating system," BBN Lab. Rep., Apr. 1985.

[21] D. Shipman, "The functional data model and the data language DAPLEX," *ACM Trans. Database Syst.*, Mar. 1981.

[22] J. Smith *et al.*, *ADAPLEX Reference Manual*, Computer Corp. of America, Jan. 1981.

[23] J. Smith, P. Bernstein, U. Dayel, N. Goodman, T. Landers, K. Lin, and E. Wong, "Multibase—Integrating heterogeneous distributed database systems," in *Proc. AFIPS*, 1981.

[24] W. Staniszkis, M. Kowalewski, G. Turco, K. Krajewski, and M. Saccone, "Network data management system—General architecture and implementation principles," in *Proc. Int. Conf. on Engineering Software*, Apr. 1983.

[25] M. Stonebraker and L. Rowe, "The design of Postgres," in *Proc. SIGMOD*, May 1986.

[26] G. Stewart, "A first look at Lisa," *Popular Computing*, Mar. 1983.

[27] Tandem Computers Inc., *Distributed Database Management*, 1981.

[28] M. Templeton, D. Brill, A. Hwang, I. Kameny, and E. Lund, "An overview of the Mermaid system—A frontend to heterogeneous databases," in *Proc. IEEE EASCON*, Sept. 1983.

[29] M. Templeton and J. Kendall, "Solving the DODIIS database interoperability problem," in *Proc. AFCEA*, Mar. 1985.

[30] M. Templeton, D. Brill, A. Chen, S. Dao, and E. Lund, "Mermaid—Experiences with network operation," in *Proc. IEEE Data Eng. Conf.*, Feb. 1986.

[31] R. Williams *et al.*, "R*: An overview of the architecture," IBM Res. Rep. RJ3325, Dec. 1981.

[32] C. Yu, C. C. Chang, M. Templeton, D. Brill, and E. Lund, "Query processing in a fragmented relational distributed system: MERMAID," *IEEE Trans. Software Eng.*, vol. SE-11, pp. 795–810, Aug. 1985.

[33] C. Yu, K. Guh, C. Chang, C. Chen, M. Templeton, and D. Brill, "Placement dependency and aggregate processing in a fragmented distributed database environment," in *Proc. IEEE COMPSAC*, Nov. 1984.

[34] ——, "An algorithm to process queries in a fast distributed network," in *Proc. Real Time System Symp.*, Dec. 1984.

[35] C. Yu, C. Chang, M. Templeton, D. Brill, and E. Lund, "On the design of a query processing strategy in a distributed database environment," in *Proc. ACM SIGMOD*, May 1983.

[36] D. Van Buer, D. Kogan, D. McKay, L. Hirschman, R. Whitney, and R. Davis, "FDE: A system for experiments in interfaces between logic programming and database," in *Proc. NATO Advanced Study Workshop*, July 1985.

[2]Ada is a trademark of the Department of Defense (Ada Joint Program Office).

Multidatabase Interoperability

Witold Litwin and Abdelaziz Abdellatif

Institut National de Récherche en Informatique et en Automatique

Many users now have an interest in simultaneoulsy accessing several databases. We present the main features of a prototype relational system designed specifically for this purpose.

The development of database systems, or DBSs, has given rise to many databases. Frequently, dozens of databases exist on a large computer and thousands of databases are accessible through computer networks. In particular, videotex systems, like Prestel, Teletel, Telidon, etc., provide hundreds of databases on almost any subject such as cinema, train, and airline schedules; banking services; and restaurant fare. An increasing number of users have an interest in simultaneously accessing and manipulating data from several databases. A user may search for restaurants through several restaurant guides or may check several airlines for the cheapest flight, or may need to extract data from a public database for his personal database, etc.

The basic property of such databases is that they are independently created and administered.[1-3] Since each administrator of a database has his own database needs, databases differ physically and logically. The physical differences may concern data formats, login procedures, concurrency control, etc.[4] The logical differences may concern data manipulation languages or even entire data models. Even if the participating databases all use the same data model, they usually present mutual semantic conflicts.[4] These conflicts are differences, redundancies, or incompatibilities with respect to names, values, and meanings among similar data. They result from different perceptions of the same reality by different people. In the sidebar on page 13, we show examples of differences that may occur.

This situation calls for a new type of system designed to manage multiple databases. Such systems have been called multidatabase (management) systems or MBSs[5]—a term now rather widespread. One may attempt to base the design of such a system on the idea of global schema. This schema should define from all databases a logically single, integrated database. Users should then manipulate only data of the global schema or of an external schema derived from it. In both cases, they should feel as if they were in front of a classical database for which the global schema would constitute the classical conceptual schema. This is the approach taken, for instance, in MULTIBASE.[6]

However, it appears that the creation of a global schema is usually difficult.[1,4,7,8] This is the case even if the participating databases constitute only a small number and present the same data model for the common usage. The main reason is the lack of a general solution for the semantic conflicts in a situation in which the autonomy of each of the constituent databases is preserved. In particular, if the databases disagree about a value, then there is no single integrated value satisfactory for all users. Furthermore, no general technique for updates through the global schema seems to exist. Finally, even for organizational reasons alone, a single schema for the thousands of databases on future open systems is a dream.[2]

A more general approach may be to assume that the databases the user may access basically have no global schema.[1,2,7,9] The user will then in general know that he faces multiple databases. The system should provide him with functions for manipulating data that may be in visibly distinct schemas and may be mutually nonintegrated. One may say that the con-

Reprinted from *IEEE Computer*, pp. 10–18, Dec. 1986.

stituent databases would then become interoperable, instead of being manipulable only separately or only as if they were components of a single global database.

Interoperability looks appealing for several reasons. At first, it may of course facilitate manipulation of multiple databases when a global schema does not exist. On the other hand, one still may use such a schema when it may be specified (as the schema of a particular view of the entire collection of interoperable databases[5]). Furthermore, because interoperability does not require integration, it should be convenient for administrators, who usually like to remain autonomous (this is often the reason why they choose to create separate databases). Finally, interoperability should also be appreciated by users, who usually like to face a variety of views of reality of, for example, the ratings or opinions given by several independent restaurant guides.

In this article we present a prototype multidatabase system, called Multics Relational Data Store Multidatabase or MRDSM, that is representative of the interoperable approach. The system renders interoperable the databases that are relational or present a relational view for the common usage. The use of the relational model as the common one seems a reasonable choice, as most of the future databases are expected to be of this type or are expected to be provided with the relational interface. The testbed databases are those of the well-known MRDS, or Multics Relational Data Store, database system.[10] For MRDS, MRDSM is a user among others. In particular, databases manipulable through MRDSM remain accessible directly through MRDS. Also no change to the MRDS system was introduced. The functions for the translation of other data models into the relational one have not been studied. See for instance Brodie et al.[11] for several papers on these issues.

The functions for multidatabase interoperability that MRDSM proposes at present are mainly of two types:

• The administrators of the databases who are cooperating in such a system may define, at the data definition level, names for collections of databases and interdatabase dependencies. The dependencies link the schemas provided for the cooperative usage. These dependencies are outside these schemas, in dependency schemas that define interdatabase relationships with respect to the interdatabase integrity, privacy, or data meanings. Different groups of administrators may define dependencies independently.
• Users have at their disposal the multidatabase manipulation language Multidatabase Data Sublanguage, or MDSL. Unlike the present manipulation lan-

guages, MDSL makes it possible to express retrievals and updates, addressing jointly data in distinct database schemas, as well as to exchange data between databases. The language design is particularly oriented toward the simplicity of a multi-datadase query expression. "Simplicity" here means that the user intention becomes a single (formal) query (statement), despite eventual semantic conflicts between the participating schemas. At present, the manipulations the MRDSM user may perform are basically as follows:

• the joining of data in different database schemas;
• the broadcasting of user intentions over a number of database schemas with the same or different naming rules for data with similar meanings;
• the broadcasting of user intentions over a number of databases with data similar in meaning, but with different decomposition into relations;
• the dynamic transforming of actual attribute meanings, units of measure, etc., into user-defined value types;
• allowing data to flow between databases (interdatabase queries); and
• the dynamic aggregating of data from different databases using various new standard (built-in) functions.

Experience with the MRDSM system and everyday use of Teletel databases show that all the above possibilities, at both the data definition and manipulation levels, are highly desirable. Most of them are still unique to MRDSM.

Data definition level

Database schemas. Each database schema presented to MRDSM for multidatabase use is defined through the MRDS data definition language. A schema may be a conceptual schema of an MRDS database, its data model in MRDS terminology, or a database view schema, also called a data submodel. In the latter case, the administrator can hide some parts of the conceptual schema from MRDSM users. The submodel may in particular be secured.[10]

Following the terminology of Heimbigner and McLeod,[4] all such schemas are called export schemas. For the users, export schemas constitute the conceptual schemas of the databases. The users have at their disposal commands enabling them to instantly display the export schemas of databases they wish to acquire knowledge of.

Database access. A database is visible to MRDSM users only after its declaration to the system. The perception the users then have of the database is defined by the export schema. In particular, the access

rights that any user can have to the database are then bound by those defined in the schema. These rights are defined by the administrator through standard MRDS facilities. The administrator retains total control over these rights and, in particular, may change them at any moment. He also may at any moment withdraw the database from MRDSM. The database then becomes invisible again to the MRDSM users.

Multidatabase naming. An administrator or a group of administrators using MRDSM may define for any collection of databases a collective name called a multidatabase name. For instance, the databases Michelin, Kleber, and Gault_M may collectively get the name Rest_guides. Collective names are popular with public database servers. Such names may also simplify the expression of some commands. Otherwise, these commands may require an enumeration of the corresponding databases. A multidatabase name may itself be an element of a larger collection provided with the multidatabase name, etc.

Database identification. Different users may choose the same database or multidatabase name for different databases. The corresponding MRDSM identification rules extend those of MRDS. The MRDSM rules are as follows:

• Any collection of databases managed by MRDSM is called a multidatabase. All databases and, possibly, named multidatabases of the same user implicitly constitute a multidatabase called user multidatabase, the name of which is the user's name. Then, all user multidatabases of the same Multics project implicitly constitute the project multidatabase named as the project is. Furthermore, all project multidatabases in the same MRDSM site constitute a site multidatabase, named INRIA for instance, etc.
• Names given to (multi)databases when they are created are called relative names. The user may refer to his own (multi)databases using only the relative names. To refer to a (multi)database of another user in the same project, the user may prefix the relative name with the corresponding user name. Another possibility is to move into the other user directory, in which case relative names suffice. Similar rules govern access to databases of other projects, etc.

Interdatabase dependencies. The administrators may at present define three types of dependencies:

• manipulation dependencies,
• privacy dependencies, and
• equivalence dependencies.

Manipulation dependencies. A manipulation dependency triggers a query to a database when a given query to another database occurs. For instance, an insertion of data about a new restaurant to one user database may trigger the insertion of the same data to his friend's restaurant database. Manipulation dependencies may thus act as a kind of message passing system. In particular, a triggered query may in turn become the source of another query, etc.

The triggered queries are called complements of the original query. To declare a complement one has to indicate (1) the relation name to be concerned by the source manipulation, (2) the type of the source query (insertion, deletion, etc.), and (3) the name of the Multics segment with the complement itself.

Manipulation dependencies may be defined independently. Through transitivities, a manipulation may then lead to complements outside the original administrator's knowledge. Long and even infinite chains of complements may then appear. MRDSM does not prevent such a situation. However, it limits to a predefined value the number of complements to be processed. The set of complements is determined before the query execution. If the limit, let it be N, is exceeded, a warning is issued. In any case, at most N complements are processed.

While defining the complement, the administrator may indicate whether its execution should precede or should follow the source manipulation. In the former case, the source manipulation is performed only if the complement execution could take place. In the latter case, the administrator may ask for a deferred execution.

Privacy dependencies. The aim of these dependencies is to prohibit manipulations that would match data from different databases in a way that would disclose confidential information. The declaration of such dependencies is similar to that for the manipulation dependencies. However, the privacy dependencies may access the user identification data. They may further correspond to arbitrary checks whose detailed principles are outside the MRDSM design goals. Their basic action is nevertheless to include selections and projections with every query posed by a designated user about a designated relation. These selections and projections have the effect of making certain values invisible.

Equivalence dependencies. These dependencies identify in different databases the primary or candidate keys whose equality of values corresponds to the same real object. For instance, such a dependency could be declared for the restaurant names and corresponding street names in the case of our example databases. They are useful for formulation of some multidatabase queries with implicit joins. We will present these types of queries in the next section.

MRDSM data manipulation language

An overview. The MRDSM data manipulation language called MDSL extends DSL,[10] the data manipulation language, or DML, of MRDS. Like SQL and QUEL, DSL is based on tuple calculus. New functions within MDSL are mainly intended for multidatabase queries. Some auxiliary functions are designed for query editing, help, and displaying of schemas. Also, any Multics command may be called. Thus, text editors may be called, programs may be compiled or executed, etc. The main functions are designed to make it possible to formulate multidatabase queries of the types discussed earlier. Only these functions will be presented in the following discussion.

Query form. The general form of a MDSL query follows:

open name1 [mode1] name2 [mode2]...
-db (abbrev1 name1) (abbrev2 name2)...
< auxiliary clauses >
-range (tuple_variable relation)...
-select < target list >
-where < predicates >
-value value_list
< query commands >
close name1 name2...

As usual, the open command opens the databases for processing. The mode argument specifies the opening mode (r for retrieve, u for update in shared mode, and either er or eu [default mode] in exclusive mode). Names may be database names or multidatabase names. The "close" command closes the databases. Both commands are optional if the databases to be used are already open or should remain open for further queries.

The -db clause is also optional. It makes it possible to define abbreviations that may be easier to use. It also makes it possible to define the set of the databases the query should refer to, without closing unused ones (to close a database is usually a heavy manipulation). The databases that a query refers to are called the scope of the query. Open databases constitute the maximal and default scope.

The auxiliary clauses are clauses that do not exist in DSL. They are introduced specifically for the multidatabase environment and will be presented below. The clauses -range, -select, and -where are main clauses. Their syntax is basically similar to those of DSL. The semantics will be presented below. The -value clause exists only for updates. The value_list is a list of new values. Finally, the query commands are: retrieve, modify, store, delete, copy, move, and replace. The first four commands are DSL compatible. The last three are used for interdatabase queries. Commands may have parameters or clauses, which will be discussed later on.

The names that a query uses for referring to data types are called designators.[12] In DSL and generally in the existing DMLs, designators are unique (unequivocal) identifiers of data types (an attribute, a relation, an entity type, a record type, etc.). If several attributes bear the same name, then the corresponding designators use relation names as prefixes providing unique identifications. If therefore one calls *designator scope* the set S of designated types, then the general rule for relational languages is card(S) = 1 for all S. This is not always the case in MDSL, where one may have card(S) > 1. The reasons will be shown later on.

Elementary queries. An MDSL query is an elementary query if all designators are unique identifiers of data types within the scope. The result of an elementary query is a relation, or an update to a database relation. DSL queries, as well as queries formulated using known relational DBSs, are all elementary monodatabase queries. An elementary multidatabase query differs from a DSL query in that designators may concern relations in different schemas. The -where clause of any elementary multidatabase query then involves interdatabase joins. The corresponding implementation issues in MRDSM are presented in Litwin.[8]

Unlike a DSL query, an elementary MDSL query makes it possible to use database names as prefixes for unique identification of relations. In the multidatabase environment, it may indeed happen that two relations in different databases bear the same name.

Example 1. Retrieve from My_rest and Cinemas the names of restaurants and of cinemas that are on the same street.

open My_rest Cinemas er
-db (m My_rest)(cn Cinemas)
-range(x R)(y cn.C)
-select x.rname y.cname
-where (x.street = y.street)
retrieve

The designated relation C is prefixed in order to distinguish it from the relation C within the database My_rest. The mode er is valid for both databases.

Multiple queries

The concept. Multiple queries are intended for situations where various databases model the same universe. The user may then need to broadcast the same manipulation to several databases (e.g., project any relation describing restaurants on the attribute expressing the restaurant type). Present relational languages do not allow one to simply express such intentions. If only elementary queries are available, then the user needs to formulate as many queries as there are databases. Furthermore, these queries may differ from database to database. In contrast, multiple queries allow one to broadcast the intention through a single query. This may be a considerable simplification, especially for larger scopes. Multiple query has also been called diffusion query or broadcast query.[7]

Formally, a multiple query is a query where some designators designate more than one data type. Basically, these types are in different databases, but they may be in the same database as well. The query is considered as a set of all elementary queries, called subqueries, that may result from all choices of unique identifiers within the designator scopes. A choice may lead to a subquery that cannot be executed. We call the executable subqueries pertinent. The result of a multiple query is basically the set of relations produced by all and only pertinent queries. In MDSL, multiple queries are basically formulated through the application of the new concepts of (1) multiple identifiers, (2) semantic variables, and (3) options on the target list.[12]

Multiple identifiers. A multiple identifier is a name shared by several attributes, relations, or databases. For instance, if the scope of the query is Michelin and Gault_M, then the designator R is the multiple identifier of both R relations and type is the multiple identifier of both type attributes. A multiple query with multiple identifiers is an equivalent of the set of pertinent subqueries resulting from all the combinations of the unique identifiers in the scope of the multiple ones. This function is intended for the broadcast of manipulations of data bearing the same names. Syntactically, the queries are basically formulated as elementary queries. However, the meaning of designators that are multiple identifiers is different.

Example 2. (Q1) Retrieve from Michelin or Gault_M restaurants that are Chinese according to a guide.

```
open Michelin Gault_M er
-range (x R)
-select x
-where (x.type = "Chinese")
retrieve
```

This query would be the equivalent of the following two queries:

```
open Michelin er
-range (x R)
-select x
-where (x.type = "Chinese")
retrieve
open Gault_M er
-range (x R)
-select x
-where (x.type = "Chinese")
retrieve
```

The result would be the set of two relations. Each relation would inherit the database(s) name(s) its attributes come from. The relations would not be union compatible, since their arities and attributes would differ. As guides may disagree upon the type of a restaurant, a restaurant could figure in both or in only one of the relations. The location would then be

---

Example databases

The schemas that follow define the databases we use throughout the examples. The relations are defined according to the MRDS data definition language. We avoided the domain and attribute declarations, which are mandatory for actual MRDS schemas. The character * identifies key attributes.

DB Cinemas:
C(c#*, cname, street, tel), Cinemas
M(m#*, mname, kind), Movies
P (c#*, m#*, hour, price); Projections

DB Michelin:
R(r#*, rname, street, type, stars, avprice, tel), Restaurants
C(c#*, cname), Courses
M(r#*, c#*, price); Menus

DB Kleber:
REST(rest#*, name, street, type, forks, t#, owner, meanprice),
C(c#*, cname, ncal),
MENU(rest#*, c#*, price);

DB Gault_M:
R(r#*, rname, street, qual, tel, type, avprice),
C(c#*, cname, ncal),
M(r#*, c#*, price);

DB My_rest:
R(r#*, rname, street, qual, tel, type, avprice),
C(c#*, cname, ncal),
M(r#*, c#*, price);

The schemas model actual applications, essentially on the French public videotex system Teletel. The database Cinemas models a public database describing the current cinema programs in a city. Michelin, Kleber, and Gault_M model public databases defined upon famous French restaurant guides with the same names (the full name for Gault_M is Gault-Millau). My_rest is a personal database in which a user stores the restaurants of his choice, using as a reference the Gault_M model and data. Some of My_rest restaurants may nevertheless be unknown to Gault_M. Then, some of the restaurants in both databases may be characterized by different values. This would mean that the user replaced in My_rest the Gault_M opinion about a restaurant of his own. Of course he could not do it if he did not have his own database.

The relations within the restaurant databases model respectively restaurants, courses (dishes), and menus. The attributes are based upon the actual guides. All data are data model homogeneous, as all databases are relational. However, data are to some extent semantically heterogeneous. This is because of the following properties, modeling those of the actual guides and due to the databases' autonomy:

1. Guides partly disagree upon (a) the choice of attributes that should model the universe of restaurants and (b) the names modeling the same concepts.

2. A restaurant may be recommended by more than one guide, but not all restaurants are recommended by all the guides. The situation is similar with respect to courses.

3. Despite the same names, primary key values modeling the same object in different databases are independent.

4. The units and scales of restaurant quality ratings differ from guide to guide. Michelin rates restaurants from none to three stars (***). Kleber ratings are from zero to four forks. Gault_M rating is m/20, where m = 1,...,20. There is no objective specific rule for ratings correspondence. Nevertheless, it is frequently clear that guides disagree about a restaurant.

5. The guides may also disagree on the average price of a meal or on a restaurant type. For instance, a restaurant may be Chinese for one guide and Vietnamese for another. The guides may disagree also on the phone number, although it is a candidate key within each database.

6. In particular, Michelin and Gault_M disagree on the meaning of attributes dealing with prices, despite the same attribute names. Michelin prices are without the 15 percent tip, mandatory in France, while Gault_M prices include the tip.

7. In contrast, the guides always agree on a restaurant name and the corresponding street name. This property thus identifies the same restaurant in different guides. Likewise, course (dish) names are the same in different guides.

Similar properties will be typical of the general multidatabase environment. Multiple databases relative to the same universe will usually resemble each other, but will also present numerous semantic differences like those above.

semantically meaningful, as it would implicitly indicate the guide that considers the restaurant Chinese.

Example 3. Delete from Michelin the restaurant with the key r# = "456".

```
open Michelin eu
-select r#
-where (r# = "456")
delete
```

The query would delete the tuples from all relations in Michelin that have attribute r. It would thus replace two classical relational queries. In addition, it would automatically preserve the referential integrity. This is not the case with queries one may formulate using known relational languages.[13]

Semantic variables. We call a semantic variable a variable whose domain is data type names. In MDSL the domain may be explicit, which means that names are enumerated in an auxiliary clause, or implicit, which means that they result from the variable name. The aim in the concept is to enable the user to broadcast his intention over data named differently. A query may invoke several semantic variables, together with multiple identifiers. Each semantic variable means that the query concerns all the names in its domain. The names may in particular be multiple identifiers. The query is equivalent to the set of pertinent subqueries resulting from possible substitutions of semantic variables and multiple identifiers by unique identifiers.

Explicit domains. The corresponding clause is

$$\text{-range\_s } (x_1.x_2. \ldots .x_k \, n_{1,1}.n_{2,1}. \ldots \\ .n_{k,1} \, n_{1,2}.n_{2,2}. \ldots n_{k,2}\ldots)\ldots$$

Each x is a semantic variable. Each n is a name. The i-th subquery corresponds to the simultaneous substitutions of $n_{j,i}$ to x_j; $j = 1,\ldots,k$.

Example 4. (Q2) Retrieve from Rest_guides, i.e. from Michelin, Kleber, and Gault_M databases, restaurants that a guide considers to be Chinese.

```
open Rest_guides r
-range_s (x R REST)
-range(y x)
-select y
-where (y.type = "Chinese")
retrieve
```

x is a semantic variable whose values are names R and REST. Since REST is a unique identifier, the corresponding substitution produces an elementary query. In contrast, since R is a multiple identifier, it leads to two elementary queries, equivalent together to (Q1). All three resulting relations are not union compatible. As for (Q1), they may also contain different restaurants.

Example 5. Retrieve from Cinemas and from My_rest the restaurants and the cinemas that cost less than 30 francs.

```
open Cinemas r My_rest r
-db (cc Cinemas)(mr My_rest)
-range_s (x.y.y# R.M.r# C.P.c#)
-range (z x) (v y)
-select z
-where (z.y# = v.y#)&(v.price < 30)
retrieve
```

The query will lead to two differently formulated subqueries, one per database in the scope.

Example 6. Change to "123" the phone number "876" in all example databases.

```
open Rest_guides Cinemas My_rest eu
-range_s ( t tel t#)
-select t
-where (t = "876")
-value "123"
modify
```

The query will replace five elementary queries. It could in fact replace any number of such queries, provided the database owners agree to name telephone either tel or t#. Thus it is not even necessary for all administrators to agree upon a common name.

Implicit domains. Here, a variable name contains one or more special characters that at present are: *, designating any string of digits, including the empty string, and ?, designating any but only one digit. The domain is then implicitly constituted from all data names in the scope (not data values, like in SQL) that match the resulting pattern. For instance, the domain of x = R* is all names in the scope that start with R. The subqueries correspond to all pertinent substitutions of data names within the domains. If the characters * and ? are parts of data names themselves, as in R* for instance, then they should be preceded by the character \. Thus x = R* would include all names starting with the string R*.

Example 7. The expression of query (Q2) from Example 4 may be simplified to the following one:

```
open Rest_guides er
-range(y R*)
-select y
-where (y.type = "Chinese")
retrieve
```

This formulation would remain valid for any number of databases in the scope, provided that all and only restaurant relation names start with the character R. The corresponding query with the explicit domain would then be usually more complex, as it would require a range_s clause with as many identifiers as there are different names.

Options. Current relational DMLs assume implicitly that all the attributes in the -select clause target list are in the schema of the addressed database. As the

examples below will show, it is useful to relax this assumption in the multidatabase environment. The concept of options[12] is intended for this purpose. The corresponding syntax is as follows.

Let d be an attribute designator within the -select clause. Let q be a subquery resulting from some substitutions and a the unique identifier corresponding to d in q.

- If d is preceded by a space, as is usual in DSL, then q is pertinent only if there is attribute a in its scope. Thus, by default a is mandatory.
- d, written ~d, means that q may be pertinent without an attribute named a in the scope. q is then considered as equivalent to a query formulated like q without a in the -select list. The attribute a is thus optional.
- A list $d_1|d_2|\ldots|d_n$ means that the pertinent form of q should contain one and only one a_i. The choice follows the list order. A list preceded with ~ means that the whole list is optional.

Options deal with the existence of attribute names in schemas and not with null values within tuples. However, one may extend this concept to null values as well.

Example 8. Retrieve from Rest_guides name, street, and owner, if any, of all restaurants.

```
open Rest-guides er
-range(x R*)
-select x.*name x.street ~x.owner retrieve
```

Since the attribute owner is optional, all three databases will be addressed. If owner were mandatory, the tuples would be retrieved only from the Kleber database.

Example 9. Assume that Gault_M does not have the attribute tel. Retrieve from Rest_guides restaurant names and either phone numbers if available else the corresponding streets.

```
open Rest-guides er
-range (x R*)
-select x.*name, x.t*|x.street
retrieve
```

The query will provide the telephone number from Michelin and Kleber, and the address from Gault_M.

Incomplete queries

The concept. While formulating MDSL queries, the user may avoid specifying some equijoins. Basically, one may avoid equijoins linking primary or foreign keys that share a domain. Such queries are called incomplete queries. A subquery of a multiple query may in particular be an incomplete query. Omitted joins are called implicit joins.[14] They are deduced by the system from database schemas. The result is called a complete query. The completion algorithm is described in detail in Litwin.[14]

It is shown that this process leads to the intuitively expected result in more cases than the present algorithms for the universal relation interface.[13] A major consequence is also that updates may be performed.

This function has as goals (1) to further simplify query formulation and (2) to allow multiple queries to databases modeling the same universe, but different through decompositions into relations. Indeed, there is sometimes no way to express an intention in a single query, if one has to formulate all equijoins corresponding to different decompositions.

Example 10. Retrieve from Michelin the address of all restaurants that serve "confit d'oie".

The incomplete query could be

```
open Michelin er                    (Q3)
-select street
-where (cname = "confit d'oie")
retrieve
```

The complete query would be

```
open Michelin er                    (Q3')
-range(x R)(y M)(z C)
-select x.street
-where (z.cname = "confit d'oie") &(x.r#
  = y.r#)&(y.c# = z.c#)
retrieve
```

Example 11. Consider now that instead of three relations Gault_M contains only one (universal) relation with all attributes in Gault_M. Assume further that the user wishes to broadcast the query about "confit d'oie" to both Michelin and Gault_M. The formulation (Q3) will then remain valid, provided both databases are open. The clauses will, however, define a multiple query. The query will be the equivalent of two subqueries differing by equijoins. These are (Q3') and the query

```
open Gault_M er
-select street
-where (cname = "confit d'oie")
retrieve
```

Example 12. Delete from My_rest all the courses whose ncal > 2,000.

```
open My_rest eu
-select C
-where (ncal > 2,000)
delete
```

This will delete the appropriate tuples from both C and M.

Dynamic attributes. Dynamic attributes are transforms of actual attributes. They are dynamically defined within a query and unknown to any schema. Except for eventual update limitations, they may be manipulated as the actual attributes.[9] This function makes it possible for the user to dynamically and subjectively transform data values. Such a need will be frequent in the multidatabase environment. In particular, it will be frequently necessary for interdatabase joins, as joins are meaningful only for data with the same meaning and unit of measure.

The MDSL user may declare a dynamic attribute by means of the following auxiliary clauses:

```
-attr_d [hold] a : C/R
-define by MT(s) = m
-updating s' by MT(s'') = m'
```

a is the dynamic attribute name with value type either C (character) or R (real). If there is no hold argument, then a is known only within the query that defines it. Otherwise, further queries from the user may also refer to a, until the end of the session.

The clause -define by defines the mapping m of actual attribute(s) s on a. It is mandatory for retrievals. MT denotes the mapping type. It may be D for a dynamically defined dictionary (table), F for a formula, or P for a program. The corresponding clause forms are respectively as follows:

```
-define by D(s) = (a₁, s₁),...,(a_k, s_k)
```

$$\text{-define by } D(s) = (a_1, s_1),...,(a_k, s_k)$$
$$\text{-define by } F(s) = \text{arithmetical\_formula}$$

```
-define by P(s) =
  Multics_segment_name
```

s_i are actual values and a_i the corresponding dynamic ones. Formulas are arithmetical formulas. The Multics segment contains the program that may be written in any programming language.

The clause -updating defines the mapping of a on an actual attribute s', which is needed when the user updates a. The attribute s' should be one of the actual attribute(s) in s, and s'' are all the other attributes in s, if there are any. This clause is currently mandatory if MT in the -define by clause is P or F. It is optional for D type mappings. The default option is then that a given a value, let it be a', corresponds to the first s_i such that $a' = a_i$. In all cases, mapping types in both clauses have to be the same.

A dynamic attribute may share the name of an actual one. If some of the actual attributes defining a are not in the scope of the (sub)query, the name in the (sub)query then designates the actual attribute. Otherwise, it designates the dynamic attribute.

The user may also wish to refer to an actual attribute n that shares the name of a dynamic one, previously defined using the hold argument. Then, the -select clause has to be preceded by the clause -actual n.

Example 13. Assume that the '****' rating of Michelin corresponds to Gault_M.qual ≥ 19/20 and '***' corresponds to 17/20 ≤ qual ≤ 18/20. Retrieve from Michelin and from Gault_M restaurants rated ***.

```
open Michelin Gault_M er
-range (t R)
-attr_d stars : C
-define_by P(qual) = star
-select t
-where (t.stars = '****')
retrieve
```

This query leads to two subqueries. The first one to Michelin will select the actual attribute, since the attribute qual, used for the definition of the dynamic attribute star, is not in this subquery scope. The second subquery will produce the values of the dynamic attribute and will use these values for -where clause evaluation with respect to Gault_M. The overall result of the query will be homogenized with respect to the Michelin scale of rating, arbitrarily transposed by the user to the Gault_M database. Note that there is no objective integration rule for Michelin and Gault_M scales or for subjective scales in autonomous databases in general.

star is the program that dynamically computes through the Multics execute command the values of stars. It expresses, in an arbitrary host language, the algorithm:

```
if qual ≥ 19/20: stars = '****' else if
qual ≥ 17/20: stars = '***' endif;
```

The same mapping could also be formulated using the D type declaration as follows:

```
-define_by T(qual) = (***, 20),
  (***,19), (**, 18), (**, 17)
```

Example 14. Retrieve from Michelin restaurants that have the same average price in Michelin and Gault_M.

```
-db (m Michelin) (g Gault_M)
-range (t m.R) (v g.R)
-attr_d price : R
-define_by F(m.r.avprice) = m.r.avprice *
  1.15
-select t
-where (t.price = v.avprice) &(t.name =
  v.name) &(t.street = v.street)
retrieve
```

The function here renders meaningful the interdatabase join on price, as the meanings of the concept of price differ in both databases. The clauses referring to name and street may be implicit, if the corresponding equivalence dependency was defined. More examples of dynamic attributes as well as the discussion of their implementation in MRDSM are in Litwin and Vigier.[9]

Interdatabase queries. The general form of interdatabase queries is as follows:

```
copy / move
< source selection expression >
store / modify / replace
-target <db_name>.[<relation_
  name>]
<mapping clauses>
```

The commands copy and move define the action on the source database(s). The copy command copies source data, according to the source selection expression, while the move command also deletes the source data. Its selection expression has then to designate all attributes of a relation. In both cases, if data values are to be converted, the source selection expression should contain the definition of appropriate dynamic attributes. The meaning of these attributes should be that of the corresponding target attributes. Type conversions, like that of integers to reals, are automatic.

The commands store, modify, and replace define the action on the target. The clause -target identifies the target database or relation. The mapping clauses define the matching of the incoming attributes to the corresponding target attributes. The syntax of the mapping clauses is as follows:

```
<mapping clauses> : = -mapping
[<rule>][<matching_list>]
<rule> : = by order / by name
<matching_list>  :  =  (<option>
[, <option>])
<option> : = source_name —>
target_name / target_name /
source_name —> 'new'
```

The source names are the attribute names within the source -select clause. The rule "by name" means that source attributes should be mapped onto target attributes with the same names by default, unless specified otherwise within the matching list. The rule "by order" means in contrast that the attributes should be matched in order of their listing in the source -select clause, to the attributes in the matching list if one is present, or those of the target schema; otherwise, in the prescribed order. In the former case, the elements in the matching list must be target names only.

The matching list alone specifies an arbitrary correspondence. In particular, the option 'new' means that the source attribute does not exist in the target and should be added to the target schema. For security reasons, source attributes without the target counterparts and not declared 'new' are disregarded. Conversely, if a target attribute has no source counterpart, then the corresponding values are set to null or are preserved, depending on the command. Finally, except for the replace command, the query is assumed valid only when the key attributes of the incoming relations correspond to the key attributes of the target relations.

The store command inserts tuples that do not share key values of existing target tuples and preserves those target tuples that share incoming key values. The modify command also inserts incoming tuples without target key counterparts, but it modifies target tuples that share incoming key values. The modification concerns only the attributes that have counterparts within incoming tuples. Neither command affects target tuples whose keys do not share incoming key values. In contrast, the replace command replaces the whole content of the target with the incoming one.

Example 15. Copy to My_rest restaurants considered as good by Gault_M, as well as the associated courses and menus.

```
copy
-db (g Gault_M) (m My_rest)
-range_s (x g.R g.C g.M)
-range (t x)
-select t
-where qual > 14/20
store
-target m
```

The copy command will produce three subqueries. Two of them will require completion of implicit joins. The whole query will copy three relations, containing respectively the selected restaurants, courses, and menus. The result will automatically preserve the referential integrity. The selected relations and attributes will be mapped on those with the same names within the target. Only tuples that do not share key values already in My_rest will be stored. Thus the user's opinion about a restaurant, a course, or a menu, will have priority. The inverse effect would appear if the modify command were used.

This query represents the case we spoke about in the overview of MRDSM, where source data in several relations should enter several target relations. Some other instances where such a case would arise are a supplier and his parts, a student and his courses, a customer and his accounts, etc.

Example 16. Replace the content of My_rest with the restaurants, the related courses, and menus that correspond to the '***' rating in Michelin. Convert the meaning of the Michelin prices to those with tip included.

```
copy
-db (m Michelin) (my My_rest)
-range_s (x m.R m.C m.M)
-attr_d price : R
-define_by F(m.r.*price) = m.r.*price*1.15
-range (t x)
-select t
-where stars = '***'
replace
-target my
-mapping by name (stars —> qual)
```

Example 17. Consider that the user has changed the schema of the relation C into the following one:

C (c#*, origin, cal, name),

where the new attribute origin denotes the region or country the course (dish) comes from, if any. The query "copy to My_rest the courses in Gault_M" may be expressed as follows:

```
copy
-db (g Gault_M) (m My_rest)
-range (x g.c)
-select x
store
-target m
-mapping in order(c#, name, cal)
```

The values of origin will be null.

Example 18. Consider that the user wishes to keep in My_rest only the best restaurants (those rated more than 16/20). However, he also wishes to save in a separate database, let it be My_rest_archives, the content of relation R. The corresponding query may be as follows:

```
move
-db (m My_rest) (a My_rest_archives)
-select m.R
-where qual < 17/20
store
-target a
```

Standard functions. Standard functions, such as avg, sum, max, etc., may be declared in MDSL in two ways:

(1) Inside the clauses, being then enclosed within square brackets. The function is then evaluated independently for each subquery.

(2) As independent clauses. The function applies then to all the tuples of the query.

Some functions may be applied only to subqueries, some have meaning only as independent clauses, and some may be applied in both manners.

Example 19. Retrieve the average price of meals according to each database in Rest_guides.

```
open Rest_guides er
-select [avg(price)]
retrieve
```

This query returns three values, one for each database. The following returns just one value.

Example 20. Retrieve average price of all meals within Rest_guides databases.

```
open Rest_guides er
-avg
-select price
retrieve
```

In addition to the well known standard functions, the user will need new functions, specific to the multidatabase environment. The following functions should prove particularly useful.

name function. Let n be a designator. Then name(n) provides the name of data designated by n, name(.n) provides the name of the container of data (relation for an attribute, etc.) designated by n, name(..n) refers to name(.name(.n)), etc.

This function results from the need for relational operations not only on data values, but also on data names. It may be applied instead of an attribute name within -select and -where clauses. The result is then considered as if it had been an actual attribute value.

Example 21. Retrieve the names of Chinese restaurants and of the guides that recommend them.

```
open Rest_guides er
-range(x R*)
```

```
-select x.*name, x.[name(.R*)]
-where (x.type = "Chinese")
retrieve
```

Each tuple will then contain the name of a restaurant and the name of the database the tuple comes from. As may be seen, in the multidatabase environment, database names may bear logical information.

norm function. This function merges into one tuple all tuples corresponding to the same real object. The correspondence results from the equality of the keys indicated by the user. Keys may be the primary keys or the candidate keys, if the values of the primary keys within different databases differ. The norm function has the following syntax:

```
-norm ((id_att) tuple_var).
```

Here id_att are designators of keys identifying the same object. The function appears only as an independent clause. The result is the natural outer join of the designated relations.

Example 22. Retrieve from Rest_guides Chinese restaurants, creating one tuple per restaurant.

```
open Rest_guides er
-range(x R*)
-norm((*name, street) x)
-select x
-where (x.type = "Chinese")
retrieve
```

The result would be a single relation R whose attributes would be all those of involved relations, prefixed with the database name in the case of a name conflict. The id_att would figure only once, according to the definition of natural joins. To any restaurant would correspond exactly one tuple. The values of the attributes corresponding to databases that do not recommend the restaurant would be null. Absence of null values in at least some columns corresponding to attributes from a database would thus be an implicit indication that the corresponding guide recommends the restaurant.

Outer joins are unknown to MRDS. Algorithms for efficient processing of such operations have therefore been investigated. Discussion of such algorithms may be found in Dayal.[15]

upto function. This function appears only as an independent clause. It limits the multiplicity of information that may come from several databases. For instance, a query to 10 restaurant databases may ask for at most two recommendations of a restaurant. In particular the user may give priority to databases he trusts more than others. The function syntax is as follows:

```
-upto (n (A) [B]).
```

The function provides at most $n \geq 1$ tuples sharing the values of attributes designated in the list A. Priorities correspond to the order of the list B that designates database names. A, n, and B

are optional. If A is not specified, the query processing stops after a non-null response from n databases. The default value of n is 1. Finally, empty B means that the user has no preference.

Example 23. Retrieve the number of calories of "confit d'oie", preferably according to Kleber.

```
open Rest_guides er
-upto (1 (cname) [Kleber])
-select ncal
-where (cname = "confit d'oie")
retrieve
```

The result will come from another database only if Kleber does not describe confit d'oie.

Example 24. Retrieve all Chinese restaurants from Rest_guides, but limit the number of descriptions of each restaurant to two. Give the priority to Michelin and Kleber descriptions.

```
open Rest_guides er
-range(t R*)
-upto (2 (t.*name t.street) [Michelin Kleber])
-select t
-where(t.type = "Chinese")
retrieve
```

A restaurant will figure in the output from Gault_M only if it was not in the output from Michelin or Kleber.

As databases become easily accessible on computers and networks, more and more users face multiple databases. New functions for data manipulation languages are then needed, as present languages were designed for manipulations of single databases. These functions should especially allow users to manipulate autonomous databases. MRDSM offers some such functions for relational databases. Most future distributed databases will be of this type or will at least present a relational view. Numerous examples show that the MRDSM functions should prove useful for a large variety of user needs. This is because of their flexibility and open nature with respect to the accommodation of autonomous names, values, and structures. Most of these functions are not yet available in other languages and systems. The functions designed for MRDS databases can also be added to other relational languages. The corresponding extension of SQL is under study. The concepts of multiple identifiers, semantic variables, interdatabase queries, etc., may further be applied to other data models. They may thus form a useful basis for the design of distributed systems using other popular models.

In particular, several functions have also proved useful in a single database context. Thus, the concept of the multiple identifier may help in preserving the referential integrity. Implicit joins simplify the formulation of most relational queries. Dynamic attributes are useful for applica-

tions where subjective or frequently changing value mapping rules render the traditional concept of view too static. It should thus be worthwhile to incorporate similar functions in any relational system.

The functions discussed lead to many open problems at the implementation level. Also, new functions may be added. A function currently studied for implementation concerns multidatabase views, to be defined through stored MDSL queries, in the manner similar to those of DB2 and of INGRES. Knowledge processing techniques are also investigated, as they should prove particularly useful in the multidatabase environment.[2,9] In particular, they should enlarge the class of intentions expressible as a single query and should make it possible to further simplify the expression of some queries.□

References

1. D. Heimbigner and D. McLeod, "A Federated Architecture for Information Management," *ACM-TOIS*, Vol. 3, N3, 1985, pp. 253-278.

2. C. Hewitt and P. De Jong, "Open Systems," *On Conceptual Modeling: Perspectives from Artificial Intelligence, Databases, and Programming Languages*, eds. M. L. Brodie, J. Mylopoulos, and J. W. Schmidt, Springer-Verlag, Berlin, 1985, pp.147-164.

3. P. Selinger et al., *The Impact of Site Autonomy on R*. Databases-Role and Structure*, Cambridge Univ. Press, New York, 1984, pp. 151-176.

4. S. Ceri and G. Pelagatti, *Distributed Databases Principles & Systems*, McGraw-Hill, New York, 1984.

5. W. Litwin et al., "SIRIUS Systems for Distributed Data Management," *Distributed Databases*, ed. H. Schneider, North-Holland, New York, 1982, pp. 311-366.

6. T. Landers and R. L. Rosenberg, "An Overview of MULTIBASE," *Second Symp. Distr. Databases*,. Berlin, Sept. 1982, North-Holland, New York, 1982, pp. 153-184.

7. P. Lyngbaek and D. McLeod, "An Approach to Object Sharing in Distributed Database Systems," *VLDB 83*, Florence, Oct. 1983, pp. 364-376.

8. W. Litwin, "An Overview of the Multidatabase System MRDSM," *ACM Nat'l Conf.*, Denver, Oct. 1985.

9. W. Litwin and Ph. Vigier, "Dynamic Attributes in the Multidatabase System MRDSM," *IEEE-COMPDEC-2*, Los Angeles, Feb. 1986.

10. *Multics Relational Data Store (MRDS) Reference Manual*, CII-Honeywell bull. ref. 68 A2 AW53 REV4, Jan. 1982.

11. *On Conceptual Modeling: Perspectives from Artificial Intelligence, Databases, and Programming Languages*, eds. M. L. Brodie, J. Mylopoulos, and J. W. Schmidt, Springer-Verlag, New York, 1984.

12. W. Litwin, "Concepts for Multidatabase Manipulation Languages," *JCIT-4*, Jerusalem, June 1984, pp. 433 and 442.

13. J. D. Ullman, *Principles of Database Systems*, second ed., Computer Science Press, Rockville, Md., 1983.

14. W. Litwin, "Implicit Joins in the Multidatabase System MRDSM," *IEEE-COMPSAC*, Chicago, Oct. 1985.

15. U. Dayal, "Query Processing in a Multidatabase System," *Query Processing; Database Systems*, ed. Kime et al., Springer-Verlag, New York, 1985, pp. 81-108.

DATABASE INTEGRATION IN A DISTRIBUTED HETEROGENEOUS DATABASE SYSTEM

YURI BREITBART - PETER L. OLSON - GLENN R. THOMPSON

AMOCO PRODUCTION COMPANY, Research Center
P.O. Box 3385, Tulsa, Oklahoma 74102

ABSTRACT

This paper describes the approach to data-base integration in a heterogeneous distributed database environment utilized by the Amoco Distributed Database System (ADDS). We start with the definition of the extended relational data model that is used by ADDS for database integration. We demonstrate various aspects of resolving possible data conflicts occurring in the database integration process. The ADDS query and data definition languages are defined and their expressive power is discussed. We conclude with presentation of a query conversion algorithm to convert a user data request into a set of queries against supported physical databases.

1. INTRODUCTION

Current scientific and engineering applications require data from a wide variety of independent databases. These databases may exist at different geographic locations, use different database schema architectures expressed as different database models (i.e., hierarchical, network, relational, etc.). Each model may employ its own DBMS with its own database query and manipulation languages. Generating queries that require data from various preexisting databases presents some difficult problems for users.

Let us consider a user who requests data on test results performed on rock samples taken from oil wells at a certain depth. Information about the samples and test results performed on the samples is distributed among three different databases. The first database is an INQUIRE database containing information about permeability, porosity, and water saturation of a rock sample. The second is an IMS database containing information about well name, well owner, and rock sample compressibility. The third database is a RIM database containing information about porosity and grain density of a rock sample. These sample databases are shown in Figure 2.

Suppose our hypothetical user wishes to find oil wells owned by his company and test results conducted on samples taken from these wells at depths between 1500 and 1550 feet. In the absence of an integrated database system, the user needs to determine:

1. Physical database locations, database names, data item names, data item formats, units of measure for each data item, and query language and data manipulation languages of each of the three DBMS's.

2. How to translate the original query into queries and/or transactions and submit them for execution to each physical database system. In this example, the original query must be translated into queries addressed to INQUIRE, RIM, and IMS.

3. How to access the indicated databases in a way that minimizes the potential data transfer. Results of each query are to be accumulated at one site.

4. How to merge data retrieved from different databases.

Current database technology provides users with two methods of solving most of the problems listed above.

1. Develop a homogeneous distributed database system, such as R*, and redesign preexisting applications as logically integrated distributed database applications running under this system.

2. Develop a heterogeneous distributed database system to logically integrate preexisting applications without redesign using an integrated data model.

The Amoco Distributed Database System (ADDS) is a database system of the second type. The system has been designed and is being developed at the Amoco Production Company Research Center. The project was initiated in late 1982.

ADDS is a software system that provides a uniform interface to various preexisting heterogeneous databases which are distributed among nodes of a computer network. Databases that contain related information are described as an

Reprinted from *IEEE Conf. Data Engineering*, pp. 301–310, Feb. 1986.

integrated database using a uniform data
definition language and no changes are required
to the preexisting databases or to the application programs. The integrated database permits a
user to retrieve data simultaneously from several
databases using a common language without knowing
the specifics of the underlying DBMS's.

ADDS is capable of integrating relational,
network, and hierarchical databases. The ADDS
user is provided with a logically integrated view
of data stored under different databases. User
data requests are formulated in terms of the
integrated data model and then translated into
supported physical database queries. The information required to resolve various data conflicts
is stored in the ADDS directory. The ADDS directory also contains information about composite
database schemas that describe uniform views of
the various preexisting databases that are components of the composite database, an equivalent
description of the local databases in terms of
the ADDS data model, and various users' views of
the composite database. The ADDS schema architecture is represented in Figure 1. The concep-

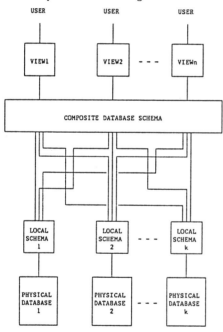

Figure 1
ADDS Schema Architecture

tual architecture of ADDS and a general description of its basic modules are described in (10).

In this paper we are primarily concerned
with database integration issues and how they are
resolved in ADDS. The most significant data
integration problems within ADDS are:

- resolution of naming conflicts, which typically
  involves either semantically equivalent data
  items named differently in different databases,
  or semantically different data items which have
  the same name in different databases;

- resolution of data representation conflicts for
  the same data item in different databases. For
  example, well depth in the INQUIRE database
  could be defined as a character data type,
  while in the IMS database it is defined as
  real;

- resolution of data scaling conflicts, when the
  same data item is stored in different databases
  using different units of measure. For example,
  well depth in one database is measured in
  meters and in the other one in feet;

- resolution of data structure conflicts caused
  by using various data models by different
  DBMS's;

- resolution of data inconsistencies for the same
  data item residing in several databases.

DB1 - INQUIRE DATABASE

| WELLID | DEPTH | PERM | POROS | SATUR |

DB2 - IMS DATABASE

| WELLID | WELLNAME | WELLDEPTH | WELLOWNER |

| ROCKCOMPR |

DB3 - RIM DATABASE

| WID | DEPTH | PERM | POROS | GRDEN |

COMPOSITE DATABASE

Data Items

WELLID, DEPTH, PERM, POROS, SATUR, RCOMP, WOWNER, GRDEN, WELLNAME

Relations

LR1(WELLID, DEPTH, PERM, POROS, SATUR)
LR2(WELLID, DEPTH, WOWNER, RCOMP, WELLNAME)
LR3(WELLID, DEPTH, PERM, POROS, GRDEN)

CDB = OJOIN * (
         LR1
         OJOIN * (LR2, LR3)
         WHERE LR2.WELLID = LR3.WELLID and LR2.DEPTH = LR3.DEPTH)
      WHERE LR1.WELLID = LR2.WELLID and LR1.DEPTH = LR2.DEPTH

Figure 2
Data Integration Example

We are using an extended relational model
(8, 12) for the database integration in ADDS and
argue that this model is rich enough to resolve
most of the integration issues in the heterogeneous database environment. Our model differs
from the model used by the MULTIBASE system (1,
5, 11), which uses a functional data model. We
believe that using our approach one can integrate
any databases that can be integrated using
MULTIBASE.

Database integration issues in the heterogeneous database environment were extensively analyzed (2-7, 11). Most of the research effort was
directed in applying operation generalization and
aggregation to database integration. Data conflicts are resolved using an auxiliary database
containing information required to provide the
user with a consistent database view. The func-

tional data model was largely used to describe an integrated database.

In the DDTS project (6) the Entity-Category data model was used for the data integration. This model is capable of integrating relational and CODASYL databases.

ADDS is capable of integrating all types of databases, and even files that are not managed by any DBMS, distributed among nodes of a computer network.

Section 2 describes the extended relational model (8, 12) and ADDS operations used for database integration. Section 3 discusses issues involved in capturing the semantics of different databases in the process of integration. Section 4 briefly discusses the ADDS query language and we show that this language is more expressive than an extended relational algebra. The ADDS data definition language and some details of the ADDS data model are also discussed. Section 6 contains a discussion of a view definition in ADDS and its role in data integration within ADDS. In Section 7 we present a query conversion algorithm to convert a user data request into a set of queries to local databases. In section 8 we conclude with a brief summary of our results.

2. EXTENDED RELATIONAL MODEL

We assume that the reader is familiar with the notions of a relation, a relational schema, an attribute, and a domain. An extended relational model, by definition, is a relational algebra with operations join, outer join, natural join, natural outer join, difference, and select. For the sake of completeness, let us briefly cover the definitions of these operations.

Let R1 and R2 be relational schemas defined on some set of attributes A. Let r1 and r2 be relations defined on these schemas. Let·F be a subset of attributes from a multiset (R1, R2). Finally, let P be a logical condition, which is a boolean combination of elementary predicates defined on attributes from A.

Each elementary predicate takes one of the following forms:

1. <Attribute_name> <Relational_operator> <Attribute_name>

2. <Attribute_name> <Relational_operator> <Constant>

Elementary predicates of the first type are called join conditions, provided that <Attribute_name>'s on both sides of <relational_operator> are from different relational schemas. Elementary predicates of the second type are called non-join conditions.

In the ADDS system, we introduce for each domain a special value called a null value. The presence of a null value for an attribute in a tuple of a relation indicates that the value for the attribute is not known or not present. Nulls from different domains are not equal and a null is not equal to any non-null value. If a functional dependency X -> Y exists and two tuples contain equal non-null values for X and one tuple contains a non-null value for Y, then the null value for Y in the other tuple is replaced by the non-null value from the opposite tuple.

a. JOIN F (R1, R2) WHERE P
    The result of this operation is the projection on F of all tuples from the cartesian product of the relations r1 and r2, which satisfy P.

b. OJOIN F (R1, R2) WHERE P
    The result of the outer join operation is the result of the join of r1 and r2 expanded with unmatched tuples from r1 (r2) padded with null values for the attributes R2 (R1).

Example 1
    Let R1(x, y) and R2(x, z) be two relational schemas.

r1:	x	y		r2:	x	z
	1	3			1	6
	1	5			2	3
	2	7			5	7
	4	6				

Let R3(x, t, y, z) = OJOIN R1.x, R2.x, R1.y,
                           R2.z (R1, R2)
                      WHERE R1.x=R2.x

    Then

r3:	x	t	y	z
	1	1	3	6
	1	1	5	6
	2	2	7	3
	4	-	6	-
	-	5	-	7

c. NJOIN F (R1, R2) WHERE P
    The result of the natural join operation is the projection on F of all tuples from the natural join of R1 and R2 that satisfies P. The logical condition P may not contain any join conditions and F is a subset of attributes from R1 union R2. If F = R1 = R2 and P is empty then NJOIN of R1 and R2 is a set theoretic intersection of r1 and r2. The NJOIN operation can be easily expressed as a JOIN of R1 and R2.

d. NOJOIN F (R1, R2) WHERE P
    The result of the natural outer join is a natural join of r1 and r2 expanded with unmatched tuples from r1 (r2) padded with null values for attributes from R2 / (R1 R2) (R1 / (R1 R2)). P may not contain any join conditions. If F = R1 = R2 and P is empty then the natural outer join of R1 and R2 is a set theoretic union of r1 and r2.

e. DIFF F (R1, R2) WHERE P
    The result of the difference of two relations R1 and R2 is the projection on F of all tuples from r1 that are not in r2 that satisfy P. P may not contain any join conditions and R1 should be equal to R2.

223

f. SELECT F (R1) WHERE P

The result of the select operation is a projection on F of all tuples from r1 that satisfy P. P may not contain any join conditions.

It can be proven that the operations listed above can be expressed using only two operations: OJOIN and SELECT and these operations are independent.

3. ADDS COMPOSITE DATABASE DEFINITION.

The composite database definition in ADDS is normally prepared by a database administrator (DBA). The DBA introduces the semantics necessary to allow each local database to interpret incoming queries. Before introducing the definition of a composite database, let us consider several examples.

Example 2

Let

R1(wellid1, depth, porosity, permeability)
                                            and
R2(wellid2, depth, porosity, permeability)

be two relational schemas to be integrated into a composite database. Both relations contain information about porosity and permeability results of tests performed on rock samples taken from oil wells at certain depths. However, well identifiers in both relations have different semantic values. Here we define a composite database as a natural outer join of relations R1' and R2', where R1' (R2') is a relational schema R1 expanded by the data field wellid2 (wellid1) with null values substituted in this field in r1 (r2).

Functional (or any other) dependencies existing in local databases may not be valid for a composite database as the next example demonstrates.

Example 3

Let

R1(wellid, depth, formation)
                                        and
R2(wellid, depth, formation)

be two local databases defined on the same set of attributes. In each of these relations the following functional dependency is valid: (wellid, depth) --> formation.

For the same well and depth, different geologists may assign different formation names. However, each local database contains a unique formation name determined by a given well and depth. If R1 and R2 are to become components of a composite database, then both values for the formation contained in different local components should be considered as valid. A composite database can be defined as the outer join of R1 and R2 where R1.wellid = R2.wellid and R1.depth = R2.depth. Then a functional dependency existing in each local database separately would not exist in their outer join.

It should be noted, however, that when designing a composite database, the database administrator could consider the formation attributes in R1 and R2 semantically different and assign them different logical data item names. In that case the composite database could be defined as a natural outer join of R1 and R2. (And moreover, each functional dependency existing in local databases will also be valid in the integrated model.)

In our data model each local database is equivalently represented as a set of relations and a composite database is represented as the union of relations representing local databases.

An integrated composite database will be considered as a view defined on this set of relations. Our definition of an integrated composite database is, therefore, as follows:

Definition

An integrated composite database is an algebraic expression defined on the set of relations equivalently representing local databases using operations of an extended relational algebra and satisfying the following conditions:

1. Separate logical data items represent semantically different physical data items.

2. Every logical data item that is present in at least one relation must be defined to the composite database.

3. A projection of an integrated composite database on the attributes of a logical relation corresponding to the database-component should contain all tuples of that relation-component.

To illustrate the last point of our definition let us consider the following example.

Example 4

Let

R1(name, salary)   and

R2(salary, grade)

be two relational schemas and r1 and r2 are as follows

r1:	name	salary		r2:	salary	age
	John	15k			15k	33
	Mary	20k			40k	40

Let us further assume that an integrated composite database is defined as a natural join of R1 and R2.

Then a projection of the integrated composite database on attributes of R1 generates relation r1 that contains only one tuple: <John, 15k> and therefore the above construction of the integrated database violates condition 3 of the definition and thereby can not be considered as a valid integrated composite database.

224

In the sequel we will only consider integrated composite database definitions that satisfy conditions 1-3.

4. ADDS QUERY LANGUAGE

The query language that is used by the ADDS system is a variant of an extended relational algebra (ERA) that includes the operations defined in Section 2. The ADDS query language provides the user with two options. The first option is to formulate queries using the extended relational algebra against logical relations. The second option is to formulate universal queries against a universal relation defined on a set of logical fields. Queries of the second kind are simple retrieval statements of the form

```
RETRIEVE <field_list>
FROM <view_name>
WHERE <restrictions>.
```

The RETRIEVE command is similar to that found in the SYSTEM/U language. The reader may observe that our definition is more restrictive than the SYSTEM/U definition. We do not allow implied or natural joins to be a part of the restrictions. We believe the "naive" user, at whom the universal view is primarily directed, will not be able to generate queries with join operations. The user who is capable of doing so can define relational queries against the CDB or define his own view.

Queries formulated using the extended relational algebra are sets of statements of the following form.

Relation (attn_1, ..., attn_k) = <Query_expr>

Each Query_expression can be defined as follows.

```
<Query_expr>    := <Select_query>
                := <Join_query>

<Select_query>  := SELECT <Attname_list>
                   FROM <Relation_name>
                   WHERE <Boolean>

<Join_query>    := <Join_op> <Attname_list>
                   (<Operand>,<Operand>)
                   WHERE <Boolean>

<Join_op>       := JOIN
                := NJOIN   /* natural join */
                := OJOIN   /* outer join */
                := NOJOIN  /* natural outer
                              join */
                := DIFF    /* set difference*/

<Operand>       := <Select_query>
                := <Join_query>
                := <Relation_name>
```

In <Select_query>, <Boolean> may not contain any join conditions.

Example 5.
Let R(x,y) be an arbitrary relation. Let us consider the following query.

```
S(x,y) = R(x,y)
S(x,y) = JOIN R.x,R.y (R,S) WHERE R.y = S.x
```

The query defines a relation S which is the transitive closure of the relation R. This example shows that the ADDS query language is more expressive than a conventional relational algebra.

The interpretation of a universal query in ADDS can be described in the following terms.

1. Retrieve the view definition from the ADDS directory.

2. Merge the field list from the RETRIEVE statement with the field list specified in the view.

3. Merge the WHERE restrictions from the RETRIEVE statement with the WHERE restrictions specified in the view.

After these transformations, a universal query becomes an extended relational algebra query and is interpreted as such. Figure 3 provides an example of a universal query against the composite database view defined in Figure 2. Figure 4 shows the universal query translated into a relational algebra query.

Retrieve well names and results of grain density tests conducted for wells owned by Amoco at a depth between 1500 and 1550 feet.

```
RETRIEVE WELLNAME, GRDEN
FROM CDB
WHERE WOWNER = 'AMOCO' &
      DEPTH >= 1500 &
      DEPTH <= 1550
```

Figure 3
Universal Query Example

```
OJOIN WELLNAME, GRDEN
    (SELECT WELLID, DEPTH
     FROM LR1
     WHERE DEPTH >= 1500 &
           DEPTH <= 1550,
     OJOIN WELLID, DEPTH, GRDEN, WELLNAME
        (SELECT WELLID, DEPTH, WELLNAME
         FROM LR2
         WHERE DEPTH >= 1500 &
               DEPTH <= 1550 &
               WOWNER = 'AMOCO',
         SELECT WELLID, DEPTH, GRDEN
         FROM LR3
         WHERE DEPTH >= 1500 &
               DEPTH <= 1550)
     WHERE LR2.WELLID = LR3.WELLID &
           LR2.DEPTH = LR3.DEPTH)
 WHERE LR1.WELLID = LR2.WELLID &
       LR1.DEPTH = LR2.DEPTH
```

Figure 4
Merging retrieval query from Figure 3
into a relational query.

The result of the merge process is a query parse tree of the relational algebra expression.

5. ADDS DATA DEFINITION LANGUAGE

Let us start by defining several notions that are fundamental to the ADDS data definition language.

Physical Database (PDB)
: All, or some semantically related subset, of a physical database that exists somewhere in a communications network. Examples of PDB's are: an SQL relation, a physical and/or logical IMS database, etc. Within ADDS, PDB's are assigned unique names corresponding, whenever possible, to the actual physical database name.

Logical Database (LDB)
: One or more PDB's that can be accessed using network facilities. Each LDB is defined by:

1. A physical network node identification.
2. A database management system type used by all PDB's in the LDB.
3. A unique name assigned by the database designer.

Logical Data Field (LF)
: A data field that corresponds to one or more semantically equivalent data fields from the physical databases that are components of a composite database (CDB) definition.

Base Relation
: Defined on a set of logical fields belonging to the same CDB.

Each logical field can be viewed as an attribute of a CDB and is characterized by a name, a length, a data type and a unit of measure. The ADDS data types include CHARACTER, CHARACTER VARYING, INTEGER, FIXED POINT DECIMAL, FLOATING POINT DECIMAL and ARRAY of the previously mentioned data types.

As mentioned earlier, each composite database can be viewed from two different standpoints:

1. As a set of attributes organized into relations describing the composite database. This is the traditional viewpoint of the relational approach to database applications.

2. As a set of logical database components each one consisting of physical databases. Each logical component is characterized by a DBMS and the network node where the logical component resides.

In addition, physical databases consist of fields that are organized into some database structure (i.e., relational, hierarchical, network, etc.). Each physical field is mapped into one, and only one, logical field.

Figure 5 depicts the CDB structure as it is

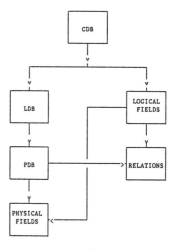

Figure 5
Composite Database Structure in ADDS

defined in ADDS. To define an internal ADDS CDB schema, the following data definition statements are supported.

1. Statements defining a CDB as a set of logical fields and as a set of logical databases.

2. Statements defining a PDB with its set of physical data fields.

3. Statements defining basic relations for a CDB and connecting them to corresponding physical databases.

```
<ddl_stat> := DEFINE CDB <cdb_info>
                 (<fname>, <ftype>, <flen>;
                  <fname>, <ftype>, <flen>; ...
                  <fname>, <ftype>, <flen>)
              LDB
                 (<ldbname>, <dbms>, <node>;
                  <ldbname>, <dbms>, <node>; ...
                  <ldbname>, <dbms>, <node>)
           := DEFINE PDB <pdb_info>
                 (<pfname> AS <fname>;
                  <pfname> AS <fname>; ...
                  <pfname> AS <fname>)
              FOR CDB <cdb_name>
              FOR LDB <ldb_name>
           := DEFINE RELATION <rel_info>
                 (<fname>, <fname>, ... <fname>)
              FOR CDB <cdb_name>
              FOR LDB <ldb_name>
              FOR PDB <pdb_name>
```

Figure 6
ADDS Data Definition Statements.

The ADDS data definition statements are shown in Figure 6. The DEFINE CDB statement contains a list of logical data fields and characteristics, as well as, a list of logical databases and characteristics. LDB characteristics include network node name and supporting DBMS name.

The DEFINE PDB statement contains information concerning the disposition of a physical database, containing a list of the physical data fields and corresponding logical data fields.

The DEFINE RELATION statement defines a set of relations for a CDB and the characteristics of the logical fields for the relations.

For the system to adequately translate a relational query into supported DBMS subqueries, ADDS needs to know the relationship between the base relations specified in the user query to the corresponding logical databases. This information is kept in the ADDS directory.

Relational design of a CDB is accomplished by performing the relational design of each LDB for the CDB. We could, however, assume that the design of a CDB is based only upon user data requirements. This would lead to the creation of base relations that span more than one physical location. In designing ADDS, we chose to apply the following three restrictions to eliminate unnecessary complications in handling distributed relations.

1. Base relations may not span more than a single network location.

2. Preexisting databases may not be changed.

3. The characteristics and structure of the physical data fields must correspond to the logical data fields specified in a user query. This condition is very important because the tools used for actual database retrieval, in many cases, reflect the underlying structure of the database.

To define a new CDB, a user prepares a set of ADDS data definition statements describing a CDB schema (see Figure 1). The CDB schema is stored in the ADDS directory and is used for user query interpretation. ADDS generates subqueries from the original user query that are directed to the supported DBMS's.

6. ADDS VIEW INTEGRATION

The schema definition described in the previous section is analogous to a logical database schema in a homogeneous database environment. To provide specific database applications in a homogeneous database environment with their view of data, the DBA generates view definitions for them. Similarly, in ADDS, a user or a group of users can be provided with data using the view facilities of ADDS. The ADDS statements that define a view are as follows:

```
<VIEW_DEF>    := DEFINE VIEW <VIEW_NAME> AS
                 <VIEW_TEXT> FOR CDB <CDBNAME>

<VIEW_TEXT>   := <QUERY_EXPRESSION>
```

The outer join and natural outer join operations play an important role in view definitions. These operations are used extensively to express operation generalization and aggregation (3) in the ADDS environment, as further examples will demonstrate.

Example 6

Let

R1(ssno, name, age)   and

R2(ssno, name, address)

be two relatoinal schemas. Then a relation

R3(ssno, name) = NOJOIN ssno, name (R1, R2)

is a generalization of R1 and R2 and a relation

R4(ssno, name) = NJOIN ssno, name (R1, R2)

is an aggregation of R1 and R2.

Local databases in ADDS are defined as a set of relations and no application and/or view schema is provided in ADDS at the local level. This is to allow greater flexibility in processing user queries. Otherwise, in our view, local semantics would be imposed on the user.

The remainder of this section discusses various schema and data conflicts occurring during the database integration process and their solution in ADDS.

6.1 NAMING CONFLICTS

Naming conflicts can occur as one of two types. First, when two semantically equivalent data items in different physical databases are named differently and second, when semantically different data items in different physical databases are named the same. Both of these conflicts can easily be handled by renaming, using the ADDS data base definition language.

In the first case the same logical data item name is assigned to the semantically identical physical data item names. In the second case, different logical data item names are assigned to the semantically different physical data item names. In the example of Figure 7, well identi-

WELLS

APIWELL	LATITUDE	LONGTITUDE

OILWELS

WN	LATITUDE	LONGTITUDE

```
DEFINE CDB OIL (WELID,...)
       LDB ( WEL1, WEL2)
DEFINE PDB WELLS (APIWELL AS WELID,...)
       FOR CDB OIL
       FOR LDB WEL1
DEFINE PDB OILWELS (WN AS WELID,...)
       FOR CDB OIL
       FOR LDB WEL2
```

Figure 7
Naming Conflicts Resolution

fier is named diffe~ently for the two physical databases WELLS and OILWELS. The corresponding

227

logical data item, WELLID, is defined in the DEFINE CDB statement. The correspondence between WELLID and its physical counterparts in WELLS and OILWELLS is established in the DEFINE PDB statements.

Figure 8 illustrates the resolution of a

WELL

WELLNAME	WELDEPTH

OILWELL

WELLNAME	WELDEPTH

```
DEFINE CDB OIL ( WELNAME, OILDEPTH, CURDEPTH)
       LDB   (WEL1, WEL2)
DEFINE PDB WELL (WELDEPTH AS OILDEPTH,...)
       FOR CDB OIL
       FOR LDB WEL1
DEFINE PDB OILWELL (WELDEPTH AS CURDEPTH,...)
       FOR CDB OIL
       FOR LDB WEL2
```

Figure 8
Naming Conflicts Resolution

naming conflict of the second type. Local databases WELL and OILWELL in Figure 8 have an attribute WELDEPTH that has different semantic meaning for each database.

6.2 DATA REPRESENTATION CONFLICT

The same data item stored in several local databases could have different data types and/or data lengths. To resolve this conflict in ADDS, a logical data item with its logical data type and length is defined. This data item corresponds to the physical data items from the local databases. A data conversion from a physical data type and length to a logical data type and length will be performed during the data extraction from the local databases by the ADDS system.

6.3 DATA SCALING CONFLICT

The same data item may be stored in different databases using different units of measures. This conflict is resolved in ADDS by defining a logical data item with its unit of measure and matching it with the corresponding physical data items supplying the rules for converting a physical data item value to a logical data item value. Figure 9 demonstrates one of

WELLS

WELLID	DEPTHF

OILWELL

WELLID	DEPTHM

```
DEFINE CDB WELL ( WELLID, DEPTH)
       LDB   (WEL1, WEL2)
DEFINE PDB WELL (WELID AS WELLID, DEPTHF AS DEPTH)
       FOR CDB WELL
       FOR LDB WEL1
DEFINE PDB OILWELL (WELLID AS WELLID, DEPTHM AS DEPTH/3.33)
       FOR CDB OIL
       FOR LDB WEL2
```

Figure 9
Scaling Conflict Resolution

the ways to resolve the conflict in ADDS.

In some cases the data definition language will not be able to resolve a data conversion problem (such is the case when the data item DEPTH is encoded in one database and measured in meters, for example, in another database). In this case, ADDS will call a conversion routine during the data extraction from a local database. The name of the routine is stored in the ADDS directory.

6.4 DATABASE SCHEMA STRUCTURE CONFLICT

Structural differences between local databases can result for several reasons. Among these are:

1. Missing data items; data items present in one local database are not present in another. Figure 10 depicts an example of possible conflict resolution in this case.

```
        EMP1(SSN, NAME, AGE)

        EMP2(SSN, NAME, ADDRESS)

DEFINE CDB EMPLOYEE (SSNO, NAME, AGE, ADDRESS)
       LDB (CHICAGO_EMP, BOSTON_EMP)
DEFINE PDB EMP1 (SSN AS SSNO, NAME AS NAME, AGE AS AGE)
       FOR CDB EMPLOYEE
       FOR LDB CHICAGO_EMP
DEFINE PDB EMP2 (SSN AS SSNO, NAME AS NAME, ADDRESS AS ADDRESS)
       FOR CDB EMPLOYEE
       FOR LDB BOSTON_EMP
DEFINE RELATION CHI_EMP(SSNO, NAME, AGE)
DEFINE RELATION BOS_EMP(SSNO, NAME, ADDRESS)
DEFINE VIEW EMP AS
       OJOIN CHI_EMP.SSNO,CHI_EMP.NAME, AGE, ADDRESS
                  (CHI_EMP, BOS_EMP)
       WHERE CHI_EMP.SSNO = BOS_EMP.SSNO
```

Figure 10
Data Structure Conflict Resolution

2. Different Data models used by different DBMS's. An example of conflict resolution for the two local database models - relational and hierarchical is given in Figure 11.

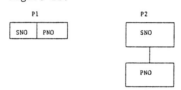

```
DEFINE RELATION R1 (SNO, PNO)
       FOR CDB SUPPLIER_PART
       FOR LDB CHICAGO_SUPPLIER
       FOR PDB P1
DEFINE RELATION R2 (SNO, PNO)
       FOR CDB SUPPLIER_PART
       FOR LDB BOSTON_SUPPLIER
       FOR PDB P2
DEFINE VIEW S_P AS
       NOJOIN * (R1, R2)
```

Figure 11
Schema Structure Conflict Resolution

3. Local schemas of integrated databases are not isomorphic. A possible conflict resolution for Example 2.4 from (5) is shown in Figure 12.

6.5 DATABASE IDENTIFIER CONFLICT

This conflict arises when otherwise semantically and structurally identical local databases have semantically different database record identifiers. Example 2 provides one out of several possible alternatives of conflict resolution in this case.

228

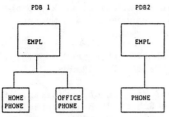

```
DEFINE CDB EMP (EMPL, PH)
        LDB (L1, L2)
DEFINE PDB PDB1 (EMPL AS EMPL, HOMEPHONE AS PH, OFFICEPHONE AS PH)
        FOR CDB EMP
        FOR LDB L1
DEFINE PDB PDB2 (EMPL AS EMPL, PHONE AS PH)
        FOR CDB EMP
        FOR LDB L2
DEFINE RELATION R1 (EMPL, PH) FOR CDB EMP
                               FOR LDB L1
                               FOR PDB PDB1
DEFINE RELATION R2 (EMPL, PH) FOR CDB EMP
                               FOR LDB L1
                               FOR PDB PDB1
DEFINE RELATION R3 (EMPL, PH) FOR CDB EMP
                               FOR LDB L2
                               FOR PDB PDB2
DEFINE VIEW EMPLOYEE AS
        NOJOIN * ( R1, R2, R3)
```

Figure 12
Database Schema Conflict Resolution (cf. with (5))

6.6 DATA VALUE CONFLICT - DATA INCONSISTENCIES

This conflict arises when data retrieved from two local databases for the same logical data item is inconsistent. Data inconsistency does not necessarily mean that retrieved data is incorrect. In Example 3, both formation names were correct even if they were inconsistent. This particular data discrepancy can be solved, either by generating two different logical data item names to treat the data semantically different or by supplying the user with both data items values and letting the user decide a correct value for the data item. The DBA can exercise either of these options using the ADDS data definition language.

Another source of data inconsistency occurs in the attempt to match two local database records that contain time-dependent information. For example, if a company has several branches and in each branch an employee database. If an employee is transferred from one branch to another, the employee record for that employee will not necessarily match. This and similar cases of data inconsistency are solved by defining an integrated database as a result of algebraic operations on local databases.

Data inconsistency may also occur when one of the local databases contains inconsistent data. In this case the DBA, by determining a consistent local database source, ignores data from the unreliable database. This can be achieved by projecting logical data items from a reliable database and performing an outer join or join operation. The natural join or outer natural join operations should be exercised with caution since unreliable data values may occur in the same logical data item for local databases.

7. QUERY CONVERSION ALGORITHM

An ADDS user query can refer to a composite database view (universal query) or to a set of logical relations within a composite database (extended relational algebra query). We have already discussed an algorithm for the translation of a universal query into an equivalent extended relational algebra query. Now we present an algorithm that converts an ERA query directed to a specific CDB to a set of subqueries that operate against the supported databases. Here, we will present a simple case of query conversion when a query is of the form

$$R = Query\_expression.$$

The query conversion algorithm is described below.

1. All logical conditions of the Query_expression are converted to disjunctive normal form and a query parse tree is constructed so that the boolean expression at each node in the tree is no more than a single conjunctive expression.

2. Each node in the query parse tree contains an indication of whether or not the subtree defined by the node belongs to a single LDB.

3. Equivalent tree transformations are applied to compact the tree (i.e. grouping relations from the same LDB in the same subtree).

4. A query subtree marked with the "same LDB" flag is presented to a single DBMS query processor.

Figure 14 provides an example of an ADDS

Query Referencing Relations from One LDB

```
LR1:  SELECT WELLID, DEPTH
      FROM LR1
      WHERE DEPTH >= 1500 &
            DEPTH <= 1550
LR2:  SELECT WELLID, DEPTH, WELLNAME
      FROM LR2
      WHERE DEPTH >= 1500 &
            DEPTH <= 1550 &
            WOWNER = 'AMOCO'
LR3:  SELECT WELLID, DEPTH, GRDEN
      FROM LR3
      WHERE DEPTH >= 1500 &
            DEPTH <= 1550
```

Figure 14
Query Conversion Example

query conversion. In the example, the ERA query of Figure 4 is converted into an equivalent set of subqueries for the physical databases defined in Figure 2.

8. CONCLUSIONS

In this paper we described database integration problems in the heterogeneous database environment and presented the solutions that are incorporated into the ADDS system. We defined the notions of composite databases, logical databases, physical databases and base relations to provide a consistent treatment of all database models. The ADDS data model, query language and data definition language were discussed and solutions to integration problems within ADDS were outlined. ADDS users may formulate queries against composite database views using universal query expressions or formulate queries against logical relations using extended relational algebra expressions. We describe an algorithm to convert a user query into a set of equivalent subqueries referring only to logical relations from the same logical database.

The ADDS pilot system was first implemented in 1984. A version of ADDS that incorporates most of the ideas discussed in this paper is currently being implemented.

REFERENCES

1. Landers, T., Rosenberg, R. L., An Overview of MULTIBASE, Proceedings of the 2d International Symposium on Distributed Databases, Berlin, 1982.

2. Batini, C., Lenzerini, M., Moscarini, M., Views Integration, in Methodology and Tools for Data Base Design, Ceri, S., (Ed.), North-Holland, 1983.

3. Smith, J., Smith, D., Database Abstractions: Aggregation and Generalization, ACM TODS, 2, 2, 1977.

4. Bussolati, U., Ceri, S., Antonellis, V., Zonta, B., Views Conceptual Design, in Methodology and Tools for Data Base Design, Ceri, S., (Ed.), North-Holland, 1983.

5. Dayal, U., Hwang, H. Y., View Definition and Generalization for Database Integration in MULTIBASE, Proceedings Berkley Workshop on Distributed Data Management and Computer Networks, 1982.

6. El-Masri, R., Semantic Integrity in DDTS, Honeywell report HR-80-274, 1980.

7. Motro, A., Virtual Merging of Databases, PhD Thesis, The Moore School of Engineering, University of Pennsylvania, 1981

8. Date, C. J., The Outer Join, Proceedings of the Second International Conference on Databases, London, 1983.

9. Staniskis, S., Kaminski, W., Kowalewski, M., Krajewski, K., Mezyk, S., Turco, G., Architecture of the Network Data Management System, in Distributed Data Sharing Systems, Schreiber, F., Litwin, W., (Ed's), North-Holland, 1984.

10. Breitbart, Y., Tieman, L., ADDS - Heterogeneous Distributed Database System, in Distributed Data Sharing Systems, Schreiber, F., Litwin, W., (Ed's), North-Holland, 1984.

11. Katz, R., Goodman, N., View Processing in MULTIBASE, in Entity-Relationship Approach to Information Modelling and Analysis, Chen, P., (Ed.), North-Holland, 1981.

12. Codd, E., F., Extending the Data Base Relational Model to Capture more Meaning, ACM TODS, 4, 4, 1979.

Integrating heterogeneous databases

W Staniszkis

Problems of heterogeneous database integration are presented and the principal user requirements, together with design and implementation issues are discussed. A general model of a Multidatabase Management System (MDBMS) based on a relational data model is presented. Structure and organisation of the MDBMS software are discussed in detail. Finally, the multidatabase system design problems and the future development trends are presented.

Introduction

The growing maturity of Database Management Systems (DBMSs) and techniques has led to a substantial growth in investment in corporate data resources. The current potential of information processing systems and the sophistication of user requirements have created a strong need for integration of data resources at the corporate as well as government administration levels. The increasing backlog of Data Processing (DP) applications precludes the possibility of re-implementing existing systems, in order to create new centralised databases supporting the required integration of data.

Typically, a large organisation has a number of different centralised DBMSs and many geographically distributed databases. In some cases, computer networks based on heterogeneous hardware are used within the same organisation. Hence, integration of data resources requires distributed data management capabilities that are sufficiently powerful to cope with the situation outlined above.

Intensive research and development work in the area of multidatabase systems, including those to be implemented in the heterogeneous hardware environment, has been stimulated by the growing user demand.

A Multidatabase Management System (MDBMS) may be defined in terms of the following characteristics:

1 *Integration of heterogeneous databases:* this implies that the underlying databases, accessible through the system, are managed by different DBMSs and may represent diverse logical data models.

2 *Distribution:* the fact that data is not resident at the same site (processor) and that all sites are linked via a geographical or local network.

3 *Logical correlation:* the fact that data has some properties that tie it together, so that it may be represented by a meaningful, common data model.

The first characteristic distinguishes the MDBMSs from distributed DBMSs, although both types of system belong to a wider class, namely the distributed data-sharing systems. The two types of system above have many common characteristics, yet they are sufficiently diverse, in terms of their objectives and potential utilisation, to merit separate treatment.

Distribution may not always be a necessary condition to justify an application of a MDBMS. Clearly, there exist cases where different centralised DBMSs are present at a single site, and a multidatabase system may be used to provide for the required integration of data. However, the lack of distribution capabilities would be a serious limitation as far as most applications are concerned.

Logical correlation implies existence of a common logical data model with its corresponding data language. Since many different data models already exist, corresponding to the various centralised databases accessible in the realm of a multidatabase system, the necessary mappings between those data models and the common data model of a MDBMS must be provided. This is the major distinguishing factor between the multidatabase and the distributed database management systems. In the case of the latter, a common logical data model is applied and the data is physically distributed.

At present there exists little user experience in the area of the multidatabase systems, and the existing applications may be considered, at best, to be experimental prototypes. However, the limited experience suggests a number of principal user requirements.

The following requirements have already been reported as desirable in *(STA1–STA3)*:

1 The data model that supports a non-procedural, end-user friendly data language.

2 The complete distribution transparency providing for the manipulation of data, as if the user were accessing a unique centralised database.

3 The local data model transparency relieving the user of the complexity of dealing at the same time with many diverse logical data models.

4 The explicit support for definition of data abstractions providing means for correct representation of the multidatabase system semantics.

5 Minimal interference with the local processing of the centralised databases included in a multidatabase system.

Current objectives of multidatabase systems, exemplified by the user requirements listed above, show that interrogation functions take precedence over the distributed update capabilities. In many cases, allowing the multidatabase system users to update the underlying centralised databases would be considered too much of an interference in the local applications. However, update capabilities based on transaction processing may be useful, and they feature in some of the current MDBMS prototypes. This creates serious technical problems, particularly in the area of concurrency control. We shall discuss problems associated with multidatabase transaction processing in more detail later.

Most of the currently implemented systems have adopted the relational data model as the global data model. In some cases, mappings from network and hierarchical data models are supported. Extensions of the relational data structure definition facilities have also been proposed to provide explicit support for data abstraction.

Since multidatabase systems utilise already existing databases, the possible interference of the global and local functions may be considered from two perspectives: the need to modify existing database design to support the multidatabase system needs, and the degradation of the local application performance resulting from additional workload generated by a multidatabase system.

Modification of existing database systems to meet the specific requirements of the multidatabase systems users would seldom be permitted. This fact has a determining influence on the multidatabase system design methodology.

The need to minimise the multidatabase system workload causes the processing cost, rather than the response time, to be the principal goal of query optimisation. Apart from the query optimisation strategy, this fact has an important influence on implementation of the MDBMS user interfaces.

Typically, a MDBMS would support the following data abstraction architecture:

1 *The global schema.* The global schema constitutes the principal integration level, It comprises all logical data structure objects resulting from data abstraction and integration processes performed on the data objects defined in the local database schemata. This level provides an integrated view of the underlying databases, supporting, in most cases, distribution and data model transparency.

2 *The user schema.* The user schemata correspond to the concept of the external schema of the ANSI/SPARC DBMS architecture. They comprise all the user view and snapshot definitions.

3 *The local schema.* The local schemata, defined in the host DBMS data description language, represent the logical data structure of the underlying local databases to be integrated into a multidatabase system.

4 *The auxiliary schema.* The auxiliary schema is stored, in some cases fragmented, in all sites of a computer network. It comprises data model mapping and other information related to the local resources, as well as information used to resolve incompatibilities of the local databases and the respective host DBMSs.

In the majority of multidatabase systems the global schema is replicated in all sites of the computer network. This fact and the need to access data residing in distinct, geographically distributed databases creates new problems in the area of database administration and design.

In the following section we present a number of MDBMSs, mostly developed as research prototypes. Subsequently, the principal features of a generalised MDBMS architecture and implementation principles are discussed. Finally, problems related to multidatabase system design and the future trends in multidatabase management technology are presented.

Current research and development work

The state of the art survey of the distributed database management technology has been given in *(STA4,STA5)*. Both types of system, namely the distributed database and the multidatabase system, have been presented. We shall briefly summarise information regarding the most important developments in the area of MDBMSs.

A representative sample of the current research and development work includes such systems as ADDS *(STA6,STA7)*, MERMAID *(STA8–STA10)*, MULTIBASE *(STA11,STA12)*, NDMS *(STA13)*, SIRIUS-DELTA *(STA14)*, DQS *(STA15)*, and AIDA *(STA16)*.

A Distributed Database System (ADDS)

ADDS has been developed at the Amoco Production Company, US with the prime objective of linking oil exploration databases installed in the computer network of IBM mainframes. The global schema is relational and the system integrates INQUIRE, IMS/MVS, and SQL/DS databases. The global query facility provides for distribution and local data model transparency. Global queries are mapped into a collection of local queries, expressed in the host DBMS's query language, and the local query functional incompatibilities are resolved by query post-processing. Query optimisation criteria are the communication cost and the local database processing cost. Distributed transaction processing is not supported in the system.

MERMAID

MERMAID is a testbed system developed at the System Development Corporation, US to integrate relational databases in a local network of VAX and SUN workstation computers. The relational databases currently accessible through the system are INGRES, ORACLE, and the Britten-Litton IDM database machine. The global schema is relational and it also contains the auxiliary information. A single query processor accepts a number of relational data languages, namely SQL, QUEL and ARIEL. Query processing is based on an intermediate language Distributed Intermediate Language (DIL) designed to support distributed query processing. Query optimisation is based on the communication cost and the query optimisation algorithm is sensitive to data fragmentation and replication. Distributed transaction processing is not supported.

MULTIBASE

MULTIBASE has been developed at the Computer Corporation of America to support retrieval of data from heterogeneous, distributed databases. The global schema is based on the functional data model and DAPLEX is supported as the data language. A global query is decomposed into a set of local queries that are executed by the host DBMSs. Query post-processing is used to resolve the incompatibilities of the local query languages. Fragmentation is not managed directly; however, it is possible to use derivation mechanisms to generate global data from local data objects. Thus, when several local databases autonomously store local data objects, which can be regarded as portions of the same global data object, the global schema includes that global data object and does not make any reference to its components. In this sense the fragmentation transparency is supported. Query optimisation is divided into two distinct steps, namely the global and local optimisation phases. The global optimisation algorithm minimises the communication cost and attempts to utilise the potential of parallel processing. The local optimisation algorithm minimises the response time of the host DBMS data retrieval operations. Distributed transaction processing is not supported.

Network Data Management System (NDMS)

NDMS has been developed at CRAI, Italy to provide a facility for retrieval and distributed processing of data residing in distinct, pre-existing databases and data files installed in a heterogeneous computer network. The current version of the system operates on a network of IBM and VAX computers integrating local databases supported by ADABAS, IMS/VS, IDMS DB/DC, RODAN and INGRES database management systems. The global schema, replicated in all sites of the computer network, is relational with SEQUEL supported as the data language. User schemata are supported by the view definition mechanism of SEQUEL and both permanent, as well as temporary, snapshots may be defined. The auxiliary schema comprises mapping definitions controlling materialisation of global schema relations. Query processing is based on an intermediate data manipulation language designed to exploit the inherent parallel execution capabilities.

A centralised query planner generates a query plan, defined as a sequence of the intermediate language operations, resulting from the query optimisation algorithm. The goal function of the query optimisation algorithm is minimisation of the overall query processing cost, including the communication cost as well as the CPU and I/O operation costs. Query post-processing is not necessary, since all local database accesses are performed via the host DBMS data access modules developed in the respective data manipulation languages. Distributed transaction processing is supported and the concurrency control approach is based on the two-phase commit protocol and the corresponding host DBMS facilities.

SIRIUS-DELTA

A part of the SIRIUS project, initiated in 1977 at INRIA, France, has been devoted to development and experimentation with multidatabase system architectures. Approach to the multidatabase system architecture, developed within the project, is characterised by a different treatment of the database integration problem. It is believed that the distribution transparency is not necessary in the multidatabase system and that the localisation of data embodies important semantic knowledge. A data language MALPHA, based on the assertion-type language ALPHA *(STA17)*, has been developed to support the multidatabase operations. The data definition language describes the structure and dependencies, integrity constraints and privacy dependencies. A collection of relational databases is considered to be a relational multidatabase. The multidatabase update operations are also supported by MALPHA.

Distributed Query System (DQS)

DQS has been developed at CRAI, Italy as a commercial system based on the research and development experience stemming from NDMS development work. It provides facilities for distributed query processing on an integrated collection of heterogeneous databases residing in a Systems Network Architecture (SNA) network of IBM mainframes. The system is integrated with the CICS teleprocessing environment and currently supports integration of databases controlled by IMS/VS, IDMS DB/DC and ADABAS database management systems. Integration of operating system access method files, that is VSAM, is also supported. The global schema is relational and SEQUEL has been implemented as the distributed query language. Distributed transaction processing is not supported.

Architecture for Integrated Data Access (AIDA)

AIDA has been developed at the System Development Corporation, US. It allows the user of one or more existing databases stored under one or more relational DBMSs to access data using a common language, either ARIEL or SQL. AIDA includes two components that have been developed within the MERMAID project—the MERMAID testbed and the ARIEL language and translator. A similar approach has also been adopted with respect to query optimisation. The important feature of the system is an attempt to integrate the distributed data, text, image, voice, and knowledge processing.

The above presentation indicates clearly that most of the systems do not match the principal user requirements formulated in the first section of this paper. This is the result of the evolving multidatabase system technology and the differing objectives of the various organisations sponsoring the research and development work. Although the relational data model prevails as the global schema representation, many systems do not support heterogeneous data models of the underlying databases. They are still considered to be MDBMSs, because integrated access to databases managed by diverse DBMSs is supported.

In most cases, distributed transaction processing is not supported. This is caused by unresolved problems of concurrency control in the MDBMS environment. The difficulty results from the fact that MDBMSs utilise the host DBMSs on the level of user interfaces, that is on the query language or the data manipulation language level. Hence, it is impossible to apply most of the concurrency control algorithms developed for the distributed database management systems.

The lack of cooperation between local and global locking mechanisms may, for example, lead to undetectable global deadlocks. A detailed presentation of concurrency control problems in MDBMS environment may be found in (STA18,STA19).

General model of the multidatabase system architecture

The general model of the multidatabase system architecture is presented in terms of the data abstraction architecture and the logical system architecture.

Data abstraction architecture

The data abstraction architecture, shown in Figure 1, presents the various data abstraction levels that must be supported in a multidatabase system.

The underlying local databases may be represented by an arbitrary data model, as required by the data description language of the corresponding host DBMS. Mappings between the local data models and the global schema data model are automatically supported and materialisation of the required relation, other than the snapshot relation, is done during query execution. One may say that the global schema represents, in this sense, a virtual database. Assuming that the relational data model is supported by the global schema, two different relation types may be defined. Base relations produced as aggregation of the logical data structure objects of the underlying database and derived relation represent aggregations or generalisations of the base relations. The collection of base and derived relations represents the global schema of the MDBMS, in the same way as the logical schema of a relational DBMS represents the centralised relational database.

The first data abstraction level consists of the base relations derived directly from the local databases. A base relation may be extracted from one local database. All the necessary data model mappings are performed at this level of the MDBMS.

Since any of the generally used data models may be represented at the local database level, all necessary mapping transformations must be supported. Let us discuss the network/relational data model mapping as an example of the required transformations.

Two different approaches to the network/relational data model mapping have already been proposed in MDBMSs. The first approach, discussed in (STA20), is based on dynamic construction of the base relation materialisation algorithm. The second approach, proposed in (STA13), introduces a mapping definition language that determines the required materialisation algorithm. Both the above approaches have been defined for the CODASYL DBMS environment and they assume that the materialisation algorithms are constructed in the host programming language and the CODASYL Data Manipulation Language. Theoretical foundations for the network/relational data model mapping may be found in (STA21).

Dynamic materialisation requires interpretation of the base relation schemes and the CODASYL database schema. The materialisation algorithm is determined by the local query optimiser. A general class of tree queries has been defined and an optimisation algorithm, synthetising efficient programs for these queries, has been proposed. The problem of selecting the cheapest strategy for processing of a given query is resolved by a heuristic optimisation algorithm.

The mapping language approach places the responsibility for construction of an efficient materialisation algorithm on the mapping definition specifier. An arbitrary navigational algorithm may be specified for

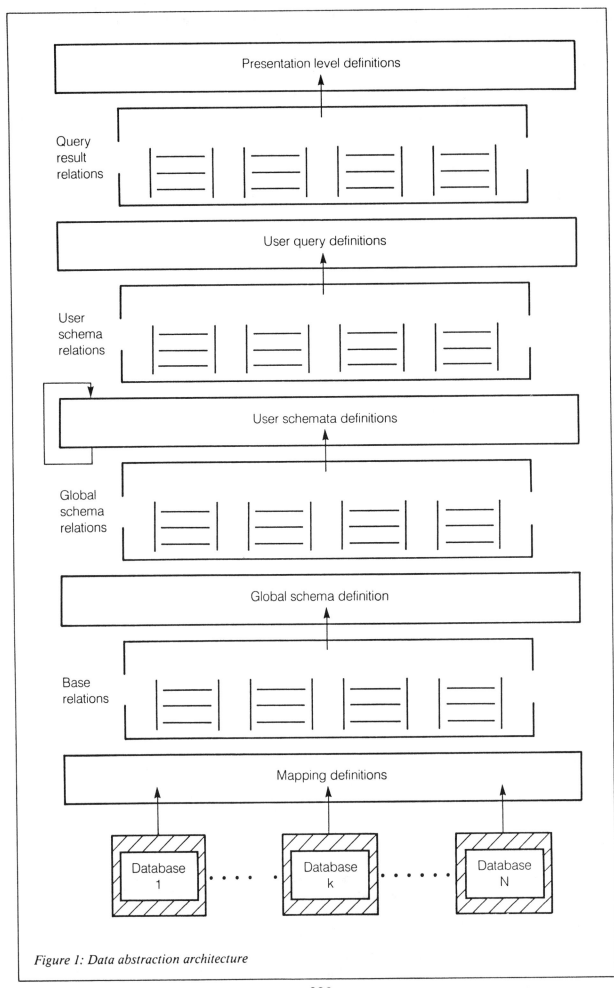

Figure 1: Data abstraction architecture

materialisation of a base relation. One of the advantages of this approach is the enhanced control over data extraction operations from any of the local databases. An example of a mapping definition, using the mapping definition language implemented in NDMS, is shown in Figure 2.

The above mapping definitions represent aggregation data abstractions, in the sense that we construct the higher level named objects (relations) representing a relationship (or relationships) between the lower level objects.

Two types of aggregation abstractions may be defined: the complete aggregations and the partial aggregations. The complete aggregation relations comprise tuples that must be materialised, only when all underlying data objects are present on the instance level. This means that no null values are allowed for any of the relation attributes. The partial aggregation relations must include at least values of attributes that belong to the prime key of the relation and may contain null values for all other attributes.

An outline of the materialisation algorithm for the SUPPLY relation, resulting from the mapping definition shown in Figure 2, is presented in Figure 3.

As we have stated earlier, the global schema comprises both the base relation schemes and the derived relation schemes. We shall discuss definition of the derived relation schemes based on the SEQUEL data definition mechanism. Derived relations represent aggregation, generalisation and restriction abstractions defined over the base relations. Note, that at this point, we introduce a mechanism for supporting the distribution transparency. Earlier, we have achieved the data model transparency by introducing the appropriate mapping mechanisms materialising the base relations.

Aggregation abstractions are defined as joins over two or more base relations coupled with the required projection and restriction operations. Restriction abstractions are defined as relational queries over one base relation. The respective query blocks are comprised in the view definition used to create the derived relation scheme. Generalisation abstractions are defined either as exclusive IS A hierarchies, thus conforming to the definition of the generalisation abstraction given in *(STA22)*, or as non-exclusive IS A hierarchies. In the

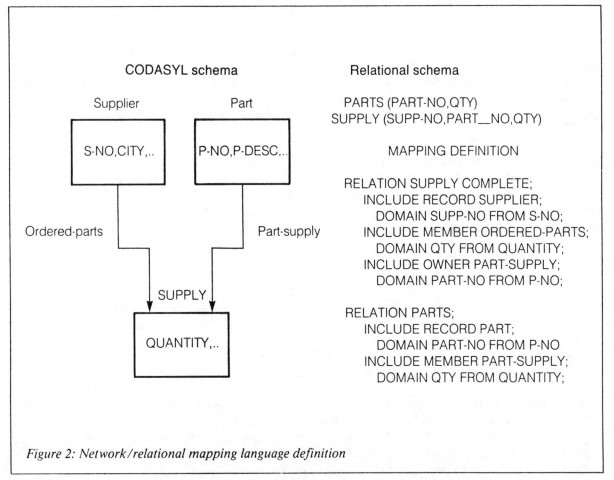

Figure 2: Network/relational mapping language definition

```
For all SUPPLIER records do
    Find next SUPPLIER record [in AREA]
    Extract data item S-NO
    For all SUPPLY records in ORDERED-PARTS set do
        Find next SUPPLY record in ORDERED-PARTS set
        Extract data item QUANTITY
        Find owner record in PART-SUPPLY set [record PART]
        Extract data item P-NO
        Materialise tuple of relation SUPPLY
    End
End
```

Figure 3: Materialisation algorithm for the SUPPLY relation

latter case, all the well-defined relation rules, given in *(STA22)*, hold, but the rule requires the sets of the lower level objects to be disjoint.

Reasons for introducing the non-exclusive generalisation abstractions are the subject of a detailed presentation given in *(STA3)*. It seems that the need to integrate databases defining different aspects of the same real life objects will be frequent in the case of multidatabase systems. Both types of generalisation abstractions may be supported explicitly by the opportune modification of SEQUEL, or any other data language, view definition mechanism. The extended view definition statement of SEQUEL is shown in Figure 4.

Implementation of generalisation views differs according to the generalisation type. The exclusive generalisation relations are materialised as a union of projections of the underlying generic relations. In this case, the TYPE function may be specified as the rightmost attribute of the view relation giving the name of the underlying generic relation. The non-exclusive generalisation relations are materialised as a projection of the outer equi-join *(STA23,STA24)* on the prime key attributes of the underlying generic relations.

The following generalisation specification rules must be observed:

1   Prime key attributes must be specified (by underscore) in the view relation. These attributes must agree on name and type with the prime key attributes of the underlying generic relations.

2   Attributes, defined in the attribute name list of the exclusive generalisation clause, must also be defined in all of the underlying generic relations. The name and type correspondence must be observed.

3   Attributes, defined in the attribute name list of the non-exclusive generalisation view relation, must also be defined in at least one of the underlying generic relations. The type correspondence must be observed. If a numeric attribute appears in more than one underlying generic relation, then the arithmetic mean will be computed as its value during materialisation of the view relation. Non-numeric attributes may not appear in more than one generic relation.

```
define__view          :: =  DEFINE [perm__spec] VIEW
                             relation__name (attr__list) [,TYPE]
                             AS view__specification

view__specification   :: =  query__block I generalisation__block

generalisation__block :: =  [EXCLUSIVE] GENERALISATION
                             (attr__list) [MEAN (attr__list) ]
                             OF relation__name__list
```

Figure 4: Format of the extended SEQUEL define__view statement

The multidatabase system users are granted explicit or implicit access rights to the global schema relations. They may either pose queries directly against the global schema relations, or define the relational views. An arbitrary number of nested view definition levels may be defined in the user schema as aggregation, restriction and generalisation abstractions. Users may grant explicit or implicit access rights with respect to their user schema relations to other users of the multidatabase system at the same computer site.

Snapshots of relations may be used, being either transient or permanent snapshots. During their life span the snapshot relations are accessible to all users holding the appropriate access rights. The transient snapshots are created during a user session and they are accessible only during the same session. They are physically destroyed upon completion of the current user session. The permanent snapshots are maintained for an undetermined length of time. They may either remain unchanged, or be periodically refreshed by the system. The snapshot recreation interval must be specified in the perm__spec option of the corresponding view definition statement.

Logical system architecture

A multidatabase management system installed in a computer network consists of two principal components; the MDBMS software and the system dictionary. The control software provides all necessary data management and data communication services and the system dictionary comprises all necessary data and environment definitions. The multidatabase system users are accessing the system at their respective nodes. A schematic representation of a multidatabase system architecture is shown in Figure 5.

Mirror images of the MDBMS software must be installed at all sites of a computer network containing databases to be integrated into a multidatabase system. If heterogeneous computer system hardware environments are supported by the MDBMS, as in the case of NDMS, functionally equivalent versions of the control software must be developed for each computer system environment.

The system dictionary may be seen as a distributed database, managed by the MDBMS, comprising data descriptions pertaining to the respective schema levels as well as the multidatabase system user descriptions and the data administration information.

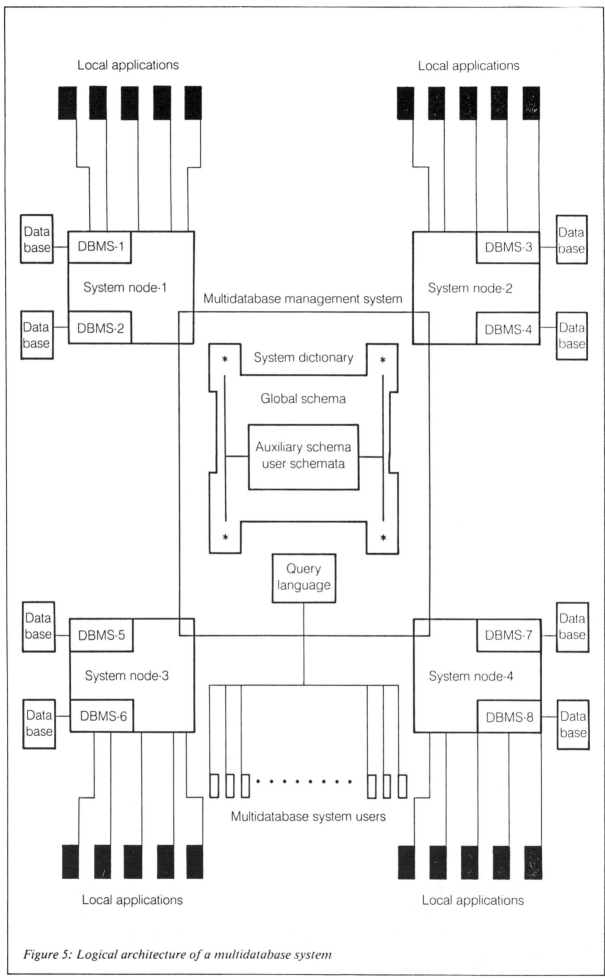

Local applications

Local applications

Data base — DBMS-1 — System node-1

Data base — DBMS-2

Data base — DBMS-3 — System node-2

Data base — DBMS-4

Multidatabase management system

* System dictionary *

Global schema

Auxiliary schema user schemata

* *

Query language

Data base — DBMS-5 — System node-3

Data base — DBMS-6

Data base — DBMS-7 — System node-4

Data base — DBMS-8

Multidatabase system users

Local applications

Local applications

Figure 5: Logical architecture of a multidatabase system

240

The global schema is replicated in all system nodes, because of the requirement to access the base relation schemes during the query translation and optimisation phases. Partitioning of the global schema would result in significant delays during the query acceptance phase of the query processing cycle.

The user schemata are partitioned according to the user location within the computer network. This imposes a slight restriction on the multidatabase system use by allowing system users to pose queries only at their native nodes. A feature to accept foreign users at other system sites, while processing their queries in the native sites, may be introduced as a possible solution to the problem.

The auxiliary schema is partially replicated and partially partitioned among the system nodes. The replicated information characterises distribution of the global schema relations and provides the corresponding statistical information. The partitioned information pertains to the mapping information required for materialisation of the base relations.

Databases, managed by the respective DBMSs, are concurrently used by the local applications and accessed by the MDBMS data manipulation functions. The respective MDBMS functions, extracting data to materialise the base relations, are seen by a local DBMS as an additional application task.

User definitions comprise authorisation information as well as the possible restrictions, such as the expected query size, the working storage size, etc, that may be imposed on the users by the system node data administrator.

Distribution of data administration functions resulting from the above multidatabase system environment calls for an additional level of coordination. Such a level may be created by a body, comprising all individuals responsible for the local databases and the multidatabase system node administration, setting up and enforcing the necessary system-wide rules and regulations.

Multidatabase system implementation

Implementation of a MDBMS may be presented in terms of the system node software structure. We have mentioned earlier that the control software is replicated as mirror images, in the case of homogeneous computer systems, or functionally equivalent software systems, in the case of heterogeneous computer systems, in all multidatabase system nodes. In either case, the principal software structure and interfaces are the same in all system nodes.

The system node software structure as implemented in NDMS *(STA13)* is presented in order to provide a concrete example of a possible approach to the MDBMS implementation. In the case of NDMS, functionally equivalent control software has been developed for the various computer system hardware/software environments. The schematic representation of the NDMS node software structure is shown in Figure 6. The end-user interface comprises a set of processors providing services for the various user functions required in the multidatabase system environment.

The Environment Definition Compiler provides facilities to define the various system node characteristics and resource restrictions. All host DBMSs and the source databases, to be accessed in the object node, are also defined. The native user characteristics, including their names, locations, security levels and resource restrictions, are specified.

The Mapping Definition Compiler (MDC) is an interactive facility to create the base relation mapping rules with respect to the various source databases. Different Mapping Definition Languages are supported by MDC to accommodate the variety of the source database data models supported within a multidatabase system.

The SEQUEL compiler allows the end-users to create the user schemata, in the form of SEQUEL views, and to formulate relational queries. The privacy of user views is maintained via the SEQUEL grant mechanism. The compiler checks the syntactic and the semantic consistency of a query and, if the query is correct, stores the query tree in the queue.

The command processor provides commands used to manage the user session, redefine the user screen and edit system statements. The query control commands are provided to investigate the query status and to fetch the query results from the working storage. An end user may, unless restricted by the node

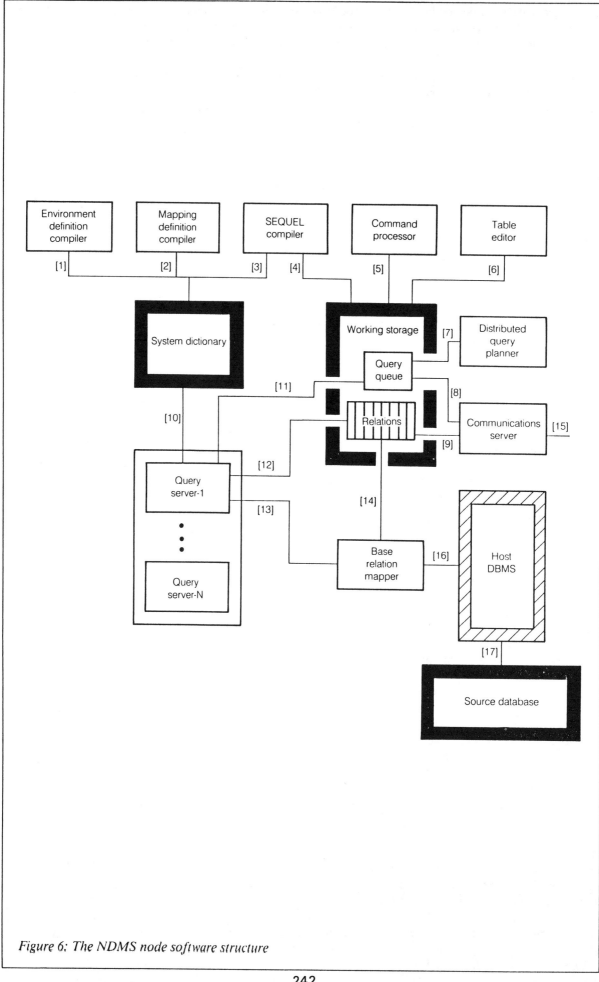

Figure 6: The NDMS node software structure

administrator, input an arbitrary number of queries into the system. As soon as the query passes the acceptance procedure, the user terminal becomes free to interact with the system.

The table editor provides facilities to define presentation of query results. An unedited query is presented in the standard tabular form. The users may define new headers, column display attributes, and sort the resulting table. The final version of a result table may either be printed on the system printing device, or be unloaded as a sequential file for further processing.

All information stored in the system may reside either in the system dictionary, or in the working storage. The system dictionary comprises all schema and environment information as well as system statistics. The working storage is used as a repository of relations, being the final query result tables, the snapshots and the intermediate relations. The query queue, comprising the query trees and query programs, is stored in the working storage.

The distributed query planner processes query trees to produce query programs to be subsequently distributed, in the form of query subprograms, among the respective system nodes. Query programs are optimised, on the basis of the communication, the CPU and the I/O costs, and decomposed into a required number of subprograms. A detailed discussion of the NDMS distributed query optimisation may be found in (STA25).

The communications server sends and receives messages comprising query subprograms as well as final or intermediate query results. It provides a unique interface with the host TP monitor used within a particular system node.

Query programs, and consequently query subprograms, are generated in an intermediate data manipulation language that implements the relational algebra operations defined in the query tree. The distributed relational operations are also implemented in the intermediate language.

The query server is a processor implementing the intermediate data manipulation language. An arbitrary number of query servers, subject to the node resource restrictions, may be concurrently active. Each query server acts as an independent processor executing intermediate language operations stored in the query queue. All intermediate language operations, with the exception of the materialisation operation, are executed on relations stored in the working storage. The execution synchronisation within a given query subprogram is controlled with the use of a precedence matrix. Hence, it is possible to manage concurrent execution of intermediate language operations within a single query subprogram, as well as within all query subprograms stored in a query queue. The query queue may be organised according to the predefined priority scheme. Query processing in NDMS has been presented in (STA25).

One of the intermediate data manipulation functions pertains to the base relation materialisation operation. The base relation mapper, developed for each specific host DBMS, accesses the source databases via the corresponding DBMS data manipulation language, and materialises the base relation tuples according to the corresponding mapping rules. Separation of the mapping processes from the query server facilitates development of interfaces to new DBMSs and file systems.

Any number of host DBMSs may be concurrently accessed within a given system node, provided that all the required mapping and resource definitions have been entered into the system dictionary.

The control information and data flow within the system node is summarised in Figure 7. Both the system dictionary and the working storage reside on the auxiliary storage devices. This allows sufficient flexibility in the system shutdown and warm restart procedures and ensures that minimum processing is lost in the case of system failure.

Design of multidatabase system applications

Distributed database design has been the subject of many research projects over the last five years. An overview of the research results has been published in (STA26). Design of distributed databases entails all classical steps of centralised database design, namely the conceptual, the logical, and the physical phases of database design.

The logical phase of the distributed database design is augmented, with respect to its centralised database

243

Label	Process input	Process output
[1]	Environment definition elements used to validate new statements	Environment definition elements resulting from new statements
[2]	Source database schema elements from the host DBMS data dictionary used to validate new base relation mapping definitions	Base relation mapping definitions
[3]	Base relation and view definition involved in a user query or view definition	User view and privacy grant definition
[4]		Query tree resulting from a user query
[5]	Query queue information and result tables	
[6]	Result tables	Edited result tables
[7]	Query trees	Query programs
[8]	Query subprograms	Query subprograms
[9]	Relations	Relations
[10]	Base relation mapping rules and resource information	
[11]	Intermediate data manipulation language operations	
[12]	Relations	Relations
[13]	Materialisation parameters	
[14]		Base relation tuples
[15]	Messages input into the system node	Messages output from the system node
[16]	Source database records	
[17]	Source database pages	

Figure 7: Information flow in the NDMS node

counterpart, with fragmentation design. The fragmentation design determines how global relations are subdivided into horizontal, vertical and mixed fragments. The fragmentation design has been presented in (STA27–STA30).

The physical database design level entails, in the case of a distributed database, the fragment allocation design. This determines how distributed relation fragments are mapped to physical images. The design phase includes decisions regarding fragment replication. The mathematical problem of optimally distributed data over computer network has been widely analysed in the context of distributed file systems, and, more recently, in the context of distributed database systems (STA31–STA36). Results of the above research efforts helped to establish allocation criteria, as well as the mathematical foundations, for potential software tools aiding distributed database designers.

A comprehensive proposal of a distributed database design methodology has recently been presented in (STA4). There are several reasons why a different design methodology is needed for design of multidatabase systems. The principal characteristics of the MDBMS that determine the multidatabase system design process are as follows:

1 *Integration of pre-existing databases:* the principal objective of a multidatabase system is to integrate pre-existing databases residing in a computer network. Since such databases are used and maintained by local applications, operating outside the scope of a MDBMS, and the data may be owned by many different organisdations, it is neither feasible to implement any change in the logical/physical data structure, nor to change the location of data in the various databases. As a result of the above constraints neither the fragmentation, nor the fragment allocation design phases are feasible in the case of the multidatabase system design methodology.

2 *Integration of heterogeneous data models:* this seems to be the most difficult step in the global schema design. It requires mapping of semantics represented in the local database schemata into a common data model underlying the global schema. The process of extracting the local database semantics and integration of the local schema abstractions into the global schema relations corresponds to the conceptual, and partially to the logical, phase of the distributed database system design methodology.

3 *Distributed query processing:* the objectives of the distributed query processing support design is to minimise the query processing cost, including both the processing cost experienced by the local computer system node and the cost of data transmission. In the DDBMS environment this would entail the fragment allocation design and the physical data structure design. In the case of multidatabase systems, it seems unlikely that any physical reorganisation of the already existing local databases would be permitted, and, for obvious reasons, fragment allocation is not feasible.

As a result of the above requirements a specific design methodology, pertaining to the multidatabase system design requirements, must be developed. A preliminary proposal of such a methodology has been presented in (STA37). The multidatabase system design methodology comprises the following design phases:

1 *Requirements analysis:* the principal objective of a multidatabase system is to allow distinct user communities to share data resources distributed over a set of heterogeneous databases residing in a computer network. The system is not to be a substitute for the local database applications providing the respective users with the required application support. It is rather to create an image of a 'superdatabase' representing the required level of abstraction with respect to the local databases and thus substantially enlarge the information space available to the multidatabase system users. Hence, the requirements analysis must define the boundaries of the global schema, as well as the specific, application-dependent, view requirements of distinct user groups. Such requirements must subsequently be reconciled with the availability of data in the source databases.

2 *Global schema design:* the global schema must represent semantics of the 'superdatabase' data to be abstracted from the underlying local databases and to reconcile all semantic conflicts that may exist on the required abstraction level. The principal steps are the analysis of the local database semantics, construction of the intermediate conceptual data models based on a unique formal representation, integration of the partial conceptual data models, and decomposition of the integrated conceptual data model into a set of global schema relation schemes.

3 *Application schemata design:* application schemata represent the higher abstraction level with respect to

245

the global schema. Each user community is to share an application schema supported by the node administrator acting as their representative versus other user communities as well as providing all necessary local support. All necessary transformations are expressed as relational views. The enhanced performance requirements are also considered at this stage and they may be resolved by introducing the data storage redundancy. The redundant storage requirements are defined in terms of permanent view (snapshots).

4 *Auxiliary schema design:* the auxiliary schema comprises the local database schemata global schema mapping rules controlling base relation, materialisation at the query execution time, the query optimisation criteria and the quantitative description of base relations. The mapping rules are distributed over the computer network sites and their definition is the responsibility of the local database administrators. The principal criteria for mapping rule definitions are the expected performance characteristics of the host DBMS base relation mappers executed during processing of distributed queries. The query optimisation criteria reflect the relative cost of the various processing resources, namely the relative CPU, I/O, and data transmission costs, as well as the main memory constraints at each site. The query optimisation criteria are replicated at all sites of the computer network. The quantitative descriptions of base relations are to be automatically derived from the source databases with the use of a statistical data analysis function. The quantitative information is replicated at all sites.

Future development trends

Although little production level application experience exists at this moment, the present commercial software product development projects in the area of MDBMS, supported by the various user requirement and marketing studies, are indicative of the emerging new data management software technology.

It seems that the commercial systems, presently under development, will reflect the present state of the art of prototype systems presented in this paper. The major issue in this area is the increase of portability of the MDBMS software, both in the sense of new underlying DBMSs and the new computer system hardware/software environments.

Increased portability will be achieved through standardisation of the MDBMS node software architecture, comprising both the interfaces and functionalities. It seems that about 80 per cent of the MDBMS control software is independent of the specific computer system hardware/software environment and may be directly ported to other environments. The remaining internal system functions must be designed and implemented according to the technical characteristics of the specific computer system hardware/software environment.

Problems that are still outstanding, both in terms of research results and the development work, fall into the following areas; high-level man/machine interfaces, multidatabase system design and implementation methodologies and tools, and system control function algorithms, mainly in the area of query and transaction processing.

The high-level man/machine interface must provide facilities appropriate to the different levels of skill and experience of the variety of end users working in the multidatabase system environment. It should also provide development staff with a comprehensive set of application development tools, thus simplifying the task of producing new applications.

The growing number of multidatabase systems and the inherent complexity of data and function mappings will stimulate efforts in the area of design methodologies and tools. This will cover both the semantic and functional design areas and the performance optimisation and tuning area.

Query processing requires further improvements in the area of distributed query optimisation. The present architecture of the MDBMS node software, in particular the intensive use of intermediate storage, opens new possibilities in the area of query processing. One of the examples may be the dynamic construction of index structures supporting the relational algebra operations.

Transaction processing may only be applied in production level systems if satisfactory solutions in the areas of multidatabase updates and distributed concurrency control are found and implemented. The principal problem of implementing multidatabase updates is that of providing means to enforce the global and local integrity constraints. The concurrency control algorithms must consider the functional incompatibility of concurrency control mechanisms of the underlying DBMSs.

Acknowledgements

The author is grateful to all his colleagues, in particular to M Kowalewski, S Mezyk, W Kaminski, G Turco and T Mostardi, who worked with him at CRAI in the area of multidatabase management systems. Without their collaboration he would not have been able to gain the experience that allowed him to write this paper. The author is also indebted to David Bell and all collaborators in the CEC MAP project for many in-depth discussions concerning the multidatabase system design and implementation problems.

STA1
Staniszkis W et al
'Network data management system—general
architecture and implementation principles'
Proc 3rd Intl Conf on 'Engineering software'
Imperial College of Science and Technology
London UK
(Apr 1983)

STA2
Dayal U and Hwang H Y
'View definition and generalisation for database
integration in multibase: a system for
heterogeneous distributed databases'
Proc 6th Berkeley workshop on 'Distributed data
management and computer networks'
(May 1982)

STA3
Dayal U
'Processing queries over generalisation hierarchies
in a multidatabase system'
Proc 9th VLDB Conf
Florence Italy
(1983)

STA4
Ceri S and Pelagatti G
'Distributed databases—principles and systems'
McGraw-Hill Book Co
(1984)

STA5
Staniszkis W
'Distributed database management, state of the art
and future trends'
Proc 8th Intl Seminar on
'Database management systems'
Piestany Czechoslovakia
(Oct 1985)

STA6
Breitbart Y J and Tieman L R
'ADDS—heterogeneous distributed database
system'
Proc 3rd Intl Seminar on
'Distributed data sharing systems'
F A Schreiber and W Litwin (eds)
Parma Italy
(1984)
North-Holland Publishing Co
(1985)

STA7
Breitbart Y, Olson P L and Thompson G R
'Database integration in a distributed

heterogeneous database system'
Proc Intl Conf on 'Data engineering'
Los Angeles US
(5-7 Feb 1986)
IEEE Computer Society
(1986)

STA8
Brill D, Templeton M and Yu C
'Distributed query optimization in MERMAID:
a front-end to data management systems'
Proc Intl Conf on 'Data engineering'
Los Angeles US
(Apr 1984)

STA9
Templeton M et al
'An overview of the MERMAID system—a front-
end to heterogeneous databases'
Proc 16th Annual Electronics and Aerospace Conf
Washington DC US
(Sep 1983)

STA10
Templeton M et al
'MERMAID—experiences with network
operation'
Proc Intl Conf on 'Data Engineering'
Los Angeles US (5-7 Feb 1986)
IEEE Computer Society (1986)

STA11
Smith J M et al
'MULTIBASE—integrating heterogeneous
distributed database systems'
Proc AFIPS NCC vol 50
(1981)

STA12
Landers T and Rosenberg R L
'An overview of MULTIBASE'
Proc 2nd Symposium on 'Distributed databases'
H-J Schneider (ed) Berlin (Sep 1982)
North-Holland Publishing Co (1982)

STA13
Staniszkis W et al
'Architecture of the network data management
system'
Proc 3rd Intl seminar on 'Distributed data sharing
systems'
F A Schreiber and W Litwin (eds)
Parma Italy (Mar 1984)
North-Holland Publishing Co
(1985)

STA14
Litwin W et al
'SIRIUS systems for distributed data management'
Proc 2nd Symposium on 'Distributed databases'
H-J Schneider (ed) Berlin (Sep 1982)
North-Holland Publishing Co
(1982)

STA15
'Distributed query system, functional specification'
CRAI Rende (CS) Italy
(1985)

STA16
Templeton M et al
'Introduction to AIDA—a front-end to heterogeneous databases'
To appear in a IEEE publication

STA17
Codd E F
'A database sublanguage founded on the relational calculus'
Proc of 1971 SIGFIDET workshop
(11-12 Nov 1971) San Diego US
ACM (1971)

STA18
Gligor V D and Luckenbaugh G L
'Interconnecting heterogeneous database management systems'
IEEE Computer vol 17 no 1
(1984)

STA19
Gligor V D and Popescu-Zeletin R
'Concurrency control issues in distributed heterogeneous database management systems'
Proc 3rd Intl Seminar on 'Distributed data sharing systems'
F A Schreiber and W Litwin (eds)
Parma Italy (Mar 1984)
North-Holland Publishing Co (1985)

STA20
Dayal U and Goodman N
'Query optimization for CODASYL database systems'
Proc ACM/SIGMOD '82 Intl Conf on
'Management of data'
(1982)

STA21
Zaniolo C
'Design of relational views over network schemas'
Proc ACM/SIGMOD '79 Intl Conf on

'Management of data'
(1979)

STA22
Smith J M and Smith D C P
'Database abstractions: aggregation and generalisation'
ACM TODS vol 2 no 2
(June 1977)

STA23
Codd E F
'Extending the database relational model to capture more meaning'
ACM TODS vol 4 no 4
(Dec 1979)

STA24
Date C J
'The outer join'
Proc 2nd Intl Conf on 'Databases'
Cambridge UK (Sep 1983)
Wiley Heyden Ltd (1983)

STA25
Staniszkis W et al
'NDMS query planner'
In 'NDMS working papers' W Staniszkis (ed)
CRAI Research rep 84-24
Rende Italy
(Oct 1984)

STA26
Ceri S, Pernici B and Wiederhold G
'An overview of research in the design of distributed databases'
Database Engineering vol 7 no 4
(Dec 1984)

STA27
Ceri S, Negri M and Pelagatti G
'Horizontal partitioning in database design'
Proc ACM/SIGMOD '82 Intl Conf on
'Management of data'
(1982)

STA28
Ceri S, Navathe S B and Wiederhold G
'Distribution design of logical database schemata'
IEEE Transactions on Software Engineering
vol SE-9 no 4 (1983)

STA29
Davenport R A
'Design of distributed database systems'
The Computer J
vol 24 no 1 (1981)

STA30
Navathe S B, Ceri S and Wiederhold D J
'Vertical partitioning algorithms for database design'
ACM TODS
vol 9 no 4
(Dec 1984)

STA31
Ceri S, Martella G and Pelagatti G
'Optimal file allocation in a computer network: a solution method of the knapsack problem'
Computer Networks vol 6 no 5
(1982)

STA32
Dowdy L W and Foster D V
'Comparative models of the file assignment problem'
ACM Computing Surveys
vol 14 no 2 (1982)

STA33
Fisher M L and Hochbaum D S
'Database location in computer networks'
J ACM vol 27 no 4 (1980)

STA34
Irani K B and Khabbaz N G
'A methodology for the design of communication networks and the distribution of data in distributed supercomputer systems'
IEEE Transactions on Computers
vol C-31 no 5 (1982)

STA35
Lam K and Yu C T
'An approximation algorithm for a file-allocation problem in a hierarchical distributed system'
Proc ACM/SIGMOD '80 Intl Conf on 'Management of data'
(1980)

STA36
Saccà D and Wiederhold G
'Partitioning in a cluster of processors'
Proc 9th VLDB Conf
Florence Italy
(1983)

STA37
Mostardi T and Staniszkis W
'Multidatabase system design methodology'
CRAI Research rep 85-27
CRAI Rende (CS) Italy
(1985)

Heterogeneous Distributed Database Management: The HD-DBMS

Invited Paper

The proliferation of different DBMS and advances in computer networking and communications have led to increasing heterogeneous distributed DBMS network scenarios. Major heterogeneity problems and challenges include: different database models, syntactically and semantically different DBMS, different types of controls (recovery, etc.), etc. We address herein the long-range goal for a heterogeneous distributed DBMS (HD-DBMS) to be able to support a network in which any user in any node can be given an integrated and tailored view or schema, while in reality the data may reside in one single database or in physically separated databases, managed individually by the same type of DBMS (by the only one the user understands) or by different DBMS.

We cite the major approaches to data sharing and accessing: from the primitive commercial file and database unload/load and PC download, to common interfaces on top of existing DBMS, to the R&D and prototype efforts toward the long-range desires. Commercial availability of the more encompassing thrusts may become a reality with the mounting problems, opportunity costs, and demand for data sharing in the heterogeneous world. Major research and development projects in this arena are leading toward some partial attainment of the long-range objective.

The UCLA HD-DBMS project is highlighted herein, with a presentation of its status, progress, and plans. It is a longer range project, with the unique feature of allowing any user in the network to use a preferred database model and DML to access or update any data in the heterogeneous network. HD-DBMS is to provide a multilingual interface to heterogeneous distributed databases.

I. INTRODUCTION

The use of different generalized database management systems (DBMS) has proliferated in recent years. As a result, the heterogeneous distributed database management system scenario has emerged. An example is shown in Fig. 1. A variety of large and small computers and even personal computers, most of them with their own and incompatible DBMS, may be tied together in a network as shown. Satellite communication may be involved between distant nodes. Local networks of computers might be involved, such as at

location X in the figure. Database machines may be involved in managing the database(s) at a node, or in a local network.

The heterogeneous database environment has emerged in many organizations, governmental environments, and computer networks due to

a) the proliferation of databases
b) the proliferation of different DBMS
c) the proliferation of a variety of minicomputers and personal computers
d) the emergence of networks tying together heterogeneous hardware and software
e) advances in data communications
f) distributed databases
g) lack of overall (not just local) database planning and control.

This environment adds to all the challenges and problems for the homogeneous distributed environment the problems of heterogeneity of DBMS: different data models (network, hierarchical, relational, etc.), syntactically and semantically different DBMS (e.g., even within the relational model family there are significant differences between SQL and QBE), different types of controls in each GDBMS (e.g., backup and recovery, locking and synchronization, etc.). It is desired that a future heterogeneous distributed DBMS (HD-DBMS) provide not only distribution transparency but also heterogeneity transparency.

The example, in Fig. 1, shows four databases involved: at location X there is a database managed by a relational DBMS and another managed by a network DBMS (e.g., a CODASYL System) on another local computer, and at two other remote locations there are two separate databases, each managed by a hierarchical DBMS such as IMS. With current technologies every user accessing any database is expected to use the facilities and abide by the syntactic and semantic regulations of the DBMS which created each database, unless some interface software is developed by the installation. Although some such interface software is, of necessity, being developed frequently by user installations, thus far it allows only cosmetic variations from the syntax and semantics of the DBMS managing the particular database.

Manuscript received October 22, 1985; revised November 26, 1986.

The author is with the Computer Science Department, University of California, Los Angeles, CA 90024, USA, and with Computomata International Corp., Los Angeles, CA 90025, USA.

IEEE Log Number 8714292.

Reprinted from *Proc. IEEE*, vol. 75, no. 5, pp. 588–600, May 1987.

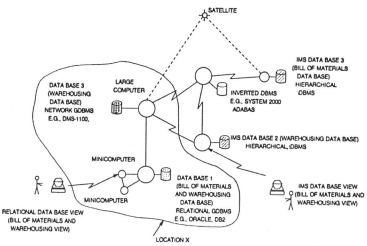

Fig. 1. Heterogeneous database management system scenario—an example.

What would be greatly desired to enhance the attractiveness and usefulness of sharing data resources in a heterogeneous network, as shown in Fig. 1, is the ability for a user to access any database as if it were managed under any one of the DBMS at one central location. Thus a user could have access to any database through a relational view at one of the minicomputers in the local network at location *X*, while another set of users, at nodes where IMS databases reside, could have access to any database as if it were managed by IMS. Ideally, a user anywhere could look at any database through his favorite DBMS, whether or not it was the preferred one at his site.

There will be, of course, many users who will confine their database accesses to a local database managed by the local DBMS. In fact, they will undoubtedly constitute the majority of the bulk applications. However, there is a growing population of users across the heterogeneous scenario whose needs we address herein.

In a nutshell, the ideal long-range goals would be for an HD-DBMS to be able to support a network in which any user in any node can be given an integrated and tailored view or schema, while in reality the data may reside in one single database or in physically separated databases, managed individually by the same type of DBMS (by the only one the user understands) or by a different DBMS. No HD-DBMS with such full capabilities is available today. There are many unsolved problems, and others remain to be uncovered. However, major research and development projects in this arena are leading toward some partial attainment of the previous long-range objectives.

Section II outlines the range of approaches to the heterogeneous challenge, from the extreme of database unload/load, to a common interface for DBMS, to the top of the line and long-range R&D and prototype efforts. Section III outlines the UCLA HD-DBMS project and progress striving for the longer range goals.

II. Approaches to Communication in a Heterogeneous Environment

A. File and Database Unload/Load

One extreme and simplistic approach to accessing data in a heterogeneous environment is to physically

1) unload the data from the source hardware/software environment, then
2) store them in a common format understood and handled by both source and target environments, and
3) load them into the target environment.

This approach in fact has been used to unload/load data files across heterogeneous environments for several years. The common format has been usually ASC II. In a number of cases, specialized types of data are unloaded/loaded via common formats specially designed and tailored to carry data descriptions and other semantic information from source to target. Examples are satellite telemetry data, geographical data types, etc.

With the emergence and proliferation of 1) personal computers and the many different types (IBM PC, Apple's McIntosh, etc.), 2) Local Area Networks (LANs), and 3) incompatible software packages (spread sheets, word processors, file and database managers, etc.), the need for unload/load has increased. There is an increasing number of commercial "file transfer" programs whose task is to help transfer files from one machine to another, providing increasing levels of help and transparency over the many details that heterogeneity springs onto the unload/load process. An examination of the generalized file transfer technology commercially available shows that the data that can be easily transferred are essentially sequential files. Even random-access files are not easily transferable. The transfer of more sophisticated files such as indexed sequential files, e.g., VSAM in large IBM operating systems, is not transparent and usually is not automated (try, for example, to transfer such files between Honeywell and IBM environments). A usual approach is to unload such indexed files to sequential files, stripping all indexing and other vendor-specific control information, use the sequential ASC II file transfer route, and load into the equivalent version (including indexing) on the target environment. Conversion software houses and specialists are usually necessary to do this.

Simplistic unload/load or file transfer programs are of little help in a database environment. All the crucial relatability know-how, indexing, and/or hashing, would be lost in converting the database into a number of individual sequential ASC II files. The process of loading the database into the target environment would involve new database definitions, new indexing definitions, invocation of loading utilities that might require special formating over the files being transferred, etc. In all, it is a practically most difficult process. Try converting a CODASYL database schema and contents from any vendor you select to IMS or *vice versa*.

Specialized Database Load/Unload: A number of pioneering efforts on the subject of "file description and translation" in a true database environment were started in the 1970s, [38] and others. Other more recent efforts include IBM's Express [42]. Due to commercial interests, a number of specialized database unload/load packages have been developed by a number of vendors. The predominant ones are

1) those that unload from a nonrelational database system and load to a relational database system;
2) those that "download" a database or portions of a database from a mainframe computer to a smaller computer or PC.

The subtle difference between these two types of packages is that the latter are more numerous, usually less sophisticated, and generally download into sequential ASC II files for input to simple file handlers such as spread sheets, graphics packages, etc.

Among the most frequently cited mainframe database load/unload software bridges are IMS's Extract to unload portions from an IMS database and load it as an equivalent SQL/DS or DB2 database [22], and Honeywell's PDQ facility to unload portions from an IDS/DM IV database to a relational IQ database (essentially SQL) [19].

There is a growing number of mainframe-PC data downloading packages. In fact, a growing number of DBMS vendors now offer such capability from their DBMS to sequential files for use at the PC level. In a number of cases the download may be invoked from the PC, and data are then downloaded from the database into the following:

a) ASC II or DIF format for use with popular spreadsheets, word processors, and even the dBase relational micro DBMS; an example is Informatics' Answer/DB for downloading IMS data [23]-[25], and its 123/Answer, and dBase/Answer packages that translate the ASC II files retrieved by Answer/DB into the proper internal format of these packages.

b) Special vendor format for use with the vendor's own PC software packages; an example is Cullinet's facility to download data from its IDMS/R database into its PC Goldengate software packages (including graphics, spreadsheets, etc.) [12].

A fundamental problem or challenge with downloaded data is, since it is a redundant copy of mainframe data, the maintenance of consistency or synchronization in an updating environment. The usual current commercial approach is to download and propagate pertinent updates from the main database periodically, and either a) not permit updating from the PC level or b) permit updating on the PC level and not reflect the updates "upstream."

B. Relational Interfaces to DBMS

One of the hopes of the advocates of relational database management is that it will be widely adopted. The success and attractiveness of relational data management has led to many commercial relational DBMS. Relational micro-DBMS now predominate at the PC level. Furthermore, there is a tendency for various vendors to provide a relational interface or view on top of their existing nonrelational DBMS. Examples of this are Cullinet's IDMS/R providing a relational interface to the internal CODASYL IDMS database [11], and Honeywell's PDQ permitting a relational interface to operate directly on the native CODASYL IDS/DM IV database (or, as another option, on a copy of the IDS/DM IV database) [19]. A few vendors have first provided a relational interface on a native nonrelational system and then have redone it into a more native relational system.

Unfortunately, there is no relational standard. Although the relational structure and relational calculus and algebra are the common thread, and IBM's SQL and QBE may be largely taken as *de facto* standards, the fact is that there are many variations of SQL and QBE. Except for the simpler read-only command SELECT . . . FROM . . . WHERE . . . , there are noticeable variations in other areas, such as on updating commands whose semantics and integrity controls vary greatly among implementations. Thus a standard relational interface among DBMS vendors has not evolved, and it appears that it will not evolve. Nevertheless, there will be a common general way of structuring databases and supporting operations, specifically project and join. Furthermore, relational interfaces for DBMS and mainframe to PC bridges may be exercised jointly in some cases. For example, download data from the mainframe nonrelational database via its relational interface into the PC environment, where the copy might be manipulated via another relational DBMS (like the dBase family).

In spite of the relational DBMS differences, the interconnection of DBMS with relational interfaces may be augmented further by a network-wide "generalized relational" interface that may provide a user at any node in Fig. 1 transparency over the relational DBMS differences. Such "generalized relational" interface will not have the challenge of mapping schemas between different models, and translating between widely different database access languages; it only has to be concerned with relatively simpler differences between the various relational interfaces of each DBMS in the network. Such generalized relational interface or front-end to a distributed relational DBMS network is exemplified by the SDC project outlined in the article by Templeton *et al.* in this issue.

C. Research and Prototype Projects

A number of longer range R&D and prototype projects are aimed at achieving the goals cited in the Introduction. They do not entail data unload/load or download, nor the existence of relational DBMS or relational interfaces to every DBMS in the network. Such long-range projects address and perform in various ways the mapping or translation of database structures and corresponding data-accessing language commands illustrated in Fig. 2. Most projects approach this by introducing intermediate database model and database access language levels. Both the types of intermediate models and languages and the number of levels vary, with the number of levels usually ranging from three to five depending on the project. Major efforts include UCLA's HD-DBMS project [4] the main focus of Section III;

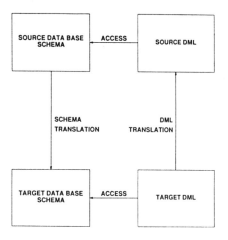

Fig. 2. Relationship between schema translation and DML translation.

Computer Corporation of America's MULTIBASE [13], [14], [29], [31], [44]; INRIA's heterogeneous SIRIUS-DELTA [17]; and Informatics' MARK V DAG [24]. In addition to these projects, a number of authors have also addressed the challenge [1], [18], [26]–[28], [30], [33], [36], [45], [46].

The majority of the current research and development efforts and initial commercial support expected simplify the task by requiring every user to communicate using a common language and data model [MULTIBASE, DAG, SIRIUS-DELTA]. A frequent choice is a relational model [SIRIUS-DELTA]. MULTIBASE further simplifies the task for a more near-term achievable system by handling only read type of global database requests; all updates are managed locally by individual sites. The complexity and restrictions of updating through user views in relational DBMS is acknowledged. The initial commercial version of MULTIBASE may be available in the near future. It will provide distribution transparency and heterogeneity transparency for read-only global queries using DAPLEX as a common language and data model [43]. (See the article by Chan et al. in this issue which includes a synopsis of DAPLEX.) In contrast, HD-DBMS provides a multilingual interface to heterogeneous distributed databases, while these other systems provide only a monolingual interface to heterogeneous distributed databases.

DAG (Distributed Application Generator) [24] intends to be a generator of applications and also of the necessary DBMS commands embedded in the application program to access databases managed by IMS and/or SQL/DS. The database view to the application is a logically integrated hierarchical IBM database, although it may be composed of portions residing in several separate IMS and/or SQL/DS databases at different sites and under different IBM operating systems and data communications software (CICS, IMS/DC).

III. THE UCLA HD-DBMS PROJECT

A. Overall Architecture

The UCLA HD-DBMS project is a multi-year, long-range project started in the late 1970s. Since 1983 part of the project has involved collaboration and support from Informatics General Corp. (now Sterling Software). Several publications on it have appeared in the open literature [4]–[6], [20], [35]. This section provides a status of the project, progress, and near-term plans.

The HD-DBMS strives to achieve the major long-range goals cited in Section I, not constraining the user to a common arbitrary language nor to read-only queries; however, it is a very-long-range possibility, beyond the more achievable MULTIBASE and SIRIUS-DELTA tasks. Its primary focus is on the heterogeneity challenge, not on the database physical distribution challenge taken up by other efforts assuming a homogeneous or common DBMS environment.

The HD-DBMS approach entails a *global* (network-wide) *conceptual model* of data and a global *internal model* of data. The global conceptual mode is a highly logical model of the information content of the integrated system. It is used as a vehicle in the process of understanding user queries and decomposing them to extract information from individual databases. The *global internal model* is the access-path oriented model of the structure of the integrated system showing precisely the data structures and access paths actually available (e.g., network-wide access routes, local database relationships, inter-database relationships, etc.), but independent of a specific implementation. The global internal model is the union of the internal models of each participating database. It is used as a vehicle in the process of identifying the specific access paths through the different databases that should be followed to answer user queries, while shielding the user from the need to know the intricacies of the access path implementation and physical storage of data. The global internal model identifies major elements outside the realm or interests of each local DBMS: relationships between entities in different DBMS, logical replication, and perhaps physical replication of entities and relationships in heterogeneous databases.

An extension of the ER model proposed by Chen [7] is fundamentally used for the conceptual level, rather than other models [1], [2]. Our model for the internal level [20] is an evolution of our earlier proposal [35]; it was inspired by and includes ingredients from DIAM (Data Independent Accessing Model) [32], [39], and [40].

Other significant efforts toward heterogeneous DBMS networks propose providing users with either a *new* model view, typically a relational view (MARK V DAG a hierarchical view), of every database, and one query language to be eventually translated into search programs to access the actual databases. A crucial difference between our project and others is that we wish to permit each user or program at a node to view and access data in the database model and language *desired* rather than force learning another language or reprogramming for another model and language. The desired languages would be constrained to a few, of course, but not to only one in a given database model.

Fig. 3 shows the proposed system architecture. The *global query translator* processes the query initially submitted by a user and, with the knowledge of the virtual database model associated to that query, translates it to the form acceptable by the global conceptual model (an ER model) and global internal model. The query is then decomposed by a *query decomposer* and *access path selector*, a translator, into the appropriate subquery(ies). The subquery(ies) will then have to be translated into the query language or data manipulation language of a specific DBMS, so as to then be pro-

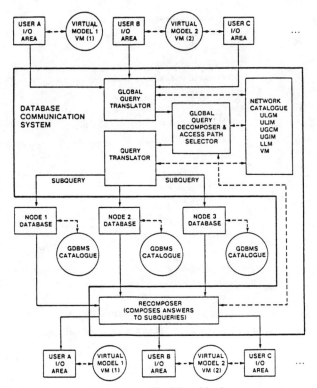

Fig. 3. System architecture and building blocks to support communication in a heterogeneous database environment.

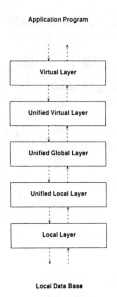

Fig. 4. Layered architecture for the HD-DBMS.

cessed by the corresponding node(s) to extract the information from the specific physical database(s) involved. The answers to the subquery(ies) are then joined together and reformatted by the *query composer*, a translator, according to the virtual database model. The result is the answer to the original query based on the user's virtual model.

There will be, of course, many users who will confine their queries locally to a given physical database managed by a given DBMS. They will undoubtedly constitute the majority of the bulk volume applications. In this case, the local DBMS will process their queries directly and completely. The global query translator, the query decomposer and access path selector, and the query composer will not be needed for such cases.

HD-DBMS Layered Architecture: A number of important catalogs or directories and mapping or translation procedures for data structures and data access commands are necessary. Fig. 4 shows the five different layers of our architecture and their associated models. The local layer contains the physical databases actually stored. The outermost layer is the collection of virtual databases as seen by the users of the heterogeneous database network. The outermost layer is the database network. The user deals with the outermost level, called the *virtual* model (VM), and the system should handle all the necessary mapping to extract information from the local physical databases.

Following Fig. 4:

1) An application program database view is defined using the data definition language of a host DBMS. This view is defined to the HD-DBMS at the virtual layer (VL).

2) An application program query (DML or query command) enters the virtual layer and is transformed by the HD-DBMS into a unified virtual layer (UVL) query. This layer is

an ER representation of the application program's virtual layer view.

3) The UVL query is then mapped into a unified global layer (UGL) query. The UGL is an ER conceptual representation of the entire heterogeneous database. It represents the union of individual unified local layer (ULL) database views.

4) The UGL query is transformed into a set of one or more ULL queries and an access plan. A ULL definition exists for each physical database. Externally, a ULL definition of a physical database is an ER view of that database. Internally, ULL access path specifications exist for data within a single physical database and for each interdatabase relationship between two or more physical databases.

5) A ULL query is transformed into a local layer (LL) DBMS dependent query, and then sent to the local DBMS. The ULL queries are performed according to the precedence established by the access plan.

Once the results of the original query are obtained, the data are translated back through the layered architecture

CREATE TABLE PART	(	P# CHAR(5)	NON-NULL,	/*	PART NUMBER	*/
		PD CHAR(25)	NON-NULL,	/*	PART DESCRIPTION	*/
		CL CHAR(2)	NON-NULL,	/*	PART CLASSIFICATION	*/
	)					
CREATE TABLE WH	(	W# CHAR(5)	NON-NULL,	/*	WAREHOUSE NUMBER	*/
		WD CHAR(25)	NON-NULL,	/*	WAREHOUSE DESCRIPTION	*/
	)					
CREATE TABLE PW	(	P# CHAR(5)	NON-NULL,	/*	PART NUMBER	*/
		W# CHAR(5)	NON-NULL,	/*	WAREHOUSE NUMBER	*/
		QTY DECIMAL(5)	NON-NULL	/*	QUANTITY ON HAND	*/
	)					
CREATE TABLE PSTR	(	P#A CHAR(5)	NON-NULL,	/*	ASSEMBLY PART NUMBER	*/
		P#C CHAR(5)	NON-NULL,	/*	COMPONENT PART NUMBER	*/
		QTY_USED		/*	QUANTITY OF THE	*/
		DECIMAL(5)	NON-NULL	/*	COMPONENT PART	*/
				/*	CONTAINED IN THE	*/
				/*	ASSEMBLY PART	*/

Fig. 5. DB1 definition: An SQL relational database.

into the form expected by the application program. This involves both structural and data translation.

B. Example Heterogeneous Database Network

The following is an example of a close-to-reality heterogeneous database network. It will be used in subsequent sections.

The scenario consists of four databases under different DBMS: SQL (two databases), CODASYL, and IMS. Each of the databases is defined in Figs. 5–8. Fig. 9 presents the unified global conceptual ER model (UGCM) that covers the four databases; note that the partitioned global conceptual model shows the contribution of each of the four databases to the UGCM.

```
SCHEMA      NAME IS DB2.
AREA        NAME IS DB_AREA.
RECORD      NAME IS PART.
            LOCATION MODE IS CALC HASH - P#.
               USING P# IN PART.
               DUPLICATES NOT ALLOWED.

            WITHIN DB_AREA.

            02 P# TYPE IS CHAR  5.
            02 PD TYPE IS CHAR 25.
            02 CL TYPE IS CHAR  2.
RECORD      NAME IS WH.

            WITHIN DB_AREA.

            02 W# TYPE IS CHAR  5.
            02 WD TYPE IS CHAR 25.
SET         NAME IS INVENTORY.

            OWNER IS PART.

            MEMBER IS WH.

            MANDATORY AUTOMATIC.

            ASCENDING KEY IS W# IN WH.

            DUPLICATES ARE NOT ALLOWED.

            SET OCCURENCE SELECTION IS THRU
            LOCATION MODE OF OWNER.
```

Fig. 6. DB2 definition: A CODASYL network database.

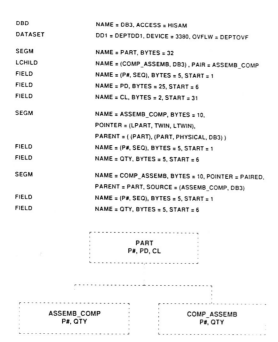

Fig. 7. DB3 definition: An ISM/DB hierarchical database.

```
SCHEMA NAME IS PART-WAREHOUSE

AREA NAME IS DATA-AREA

RECORD NAME IS PART

LOCATION MODE IS CALC HASH - P# USING

P# IN PART DUPLICATES ARE NOT ALLOWED.

WITHIN DATA-AREA

02 P#     : TYPE IS CHAR 16

02 PD     : TYPE IS CHAR 20

02 CLASS : TYPE IS CHAR 1

RECORD NAME IS WH

02 W#     : TYPE IS CHAR 5

02 WD     : TYPE IS CHAR 16

02 QTY   : TYPE IS DEC 6

SET NAME IS INVENTORY

OWNER IS PART

MEMBER IS WH

MANDATORY AUTOMATIC

ASCENDING KEY IS W# IN WH

DUPLICATES ARE ALLOWED

SET OCCURRENCE SELECTION IS LOCATION MODE OF OWNER
```

Fig. 8. DB4 definition: A CODASYL network database.

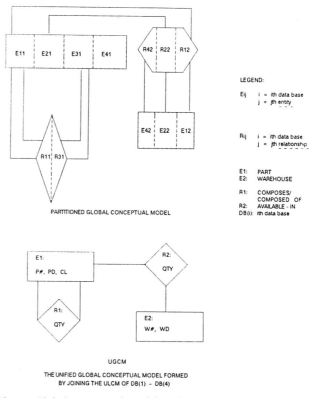

Fig. 9. Global conceptual model in the HD-DBMS.

A sample of queries issued at the virtual conceptual model is shown in Fig. 10, with a trace of the data accessed through the various heterogeneous databases.

C. Database Mapping/Translation

The UGCM is the conceptual model of the integrated database. It is formed by the union of the ULCMs of the participating databases, and any inter-database relationships. A VM can be derived from the UGCM so that a VM

QUERY 1:

FIND THE STOCK STATUS OF THE PART WITH P# = 112

NOTES:

The stock level may be found in DB(1), DB(2)
and DB(4), each under a different GDBMS

QUERY 2:

FIND THE STOCK STATUS OF THE COMPONENTS OF THE
ASSEMBLY WHOSE P# = 112.

NOTES:

Each component is stored in several warehouses

All components and their stock levels at all
warehouses are requested

Bill of material data bases and warehousing -
inventory data bases need to be accessed
to obtain the answer

DB(1) or DB(3) have bill of materials information
to be obtained first, so as to then search
DB(1), DB(2) and DB(4) for stock levels of
the component parts

Fig. 10. Sample queries.

is independent of the organization or physical disposition of the underlying database(s). Thus a number of crucial database mappings or translation procedures are needed. These translations in a few cases may be more like reformatting. The mappings should be kept at least in the network data dictionary/catalog, Fig. 3.

The data model (schema or subschema) mappings or translations have been identified or developed thus far, from the user view through the various data model layers, to the individual DBMS and back to the user. We assessed our work and work by others in the field and opted for using algorithms for the following specific translations proposed by Dumpala and Arora [15]:

Mapping Relational Schema into ER Schema
Mapping Network Schema into ER Schema
Mapping Hierarchical Schema into ER Schema
Mapping ER Schema into Relational Schema
Mapping ER Schema into Network Schema
Mapping ER Schema into Hierarchical Schema

These algorithms are ready for implementation.

The following is just an example of the mapping between relational and ER schemas. A relation in a relational schema will correspond to one of the following ER constructs:

- an entity
- a *k*-ary relationship
- a binary relationship with attributes (1:N or N:1)
- an M:N binary relationship set without attributes
- an entity, plus key attributes of some other entities.

Thus a relational query targeted at a relation will be translated into different query commands at the ER level, depending on which of the above data constructs are involved. More on this in Section III-E.

D. Query/DML Translation

The terms "data manipulation language (DML)" or "query language" shall be used synonymously to refer to any of the data access languages of the major types of DBMS: CODASYL DML, relational SQL, or IMS DL/1. The terms "database request" and "query" will also be used synonymously.

As per Fig. 4, the queries made by a user on a VM should be translated to the equivalent queries at the UGCM level, then at the UGIM level, then at the ULIM level, and finally at the LLM level for processing by the particular DBMS involved; the answer is then composed or reformatted to adhere to the original VM level. Thus a number of crucial mappings or translation procedures is needed. Fig. 2 shows the relationship between schema translation and DML translation. We provide our progress in the following sections.

1) The ER DML Global Conceptual Language: The HD-DBMS architecture uses an ER DML as the global conceptual language (GCL), at the unified global conceptual level. This is the DML into which all virtual layer DMLs are translated. This is also the DML whose queries are decomposed and distributed to various local physical databases. Two of the most important justifications for a GCL are the following. First, a GCL reduces the number of translations (both schema translation and DML translations) necessarily within a distributed database system. It is easy to understand that, without a GCL, $m \times n$ translators would be needed in an HD-DBMS that has n physical databases and supports m virtual model databases, while with a GCL, only $m + n$ translations would be needed. Secondly, a GCL allows for a single, conceptual view of the whole database, which, in reality, consists of a group of heterogeneous physical databases.

Functional Requirements of a GCL: The single most important functional requirement of a GCL is that it be semantically "rich" enough to express queries from all the virtual level DMLs. This means that, for any existing virtual level DML, any DML statement may find its equivalent in the GCL. It is not necessary to have a one to one correspondence between the GCL and other virtual level DMLs so long as the GCL is able to express any statement expressed by a virtual level DML. How do we know if a GCL meets this requirement? There has not been a satisfactory answer to this question despite various attempts that have been made. One of them is the introduction of the term "completeness" [3], [36]. Informally, a DML is complete if, for a database, any piece of information stored in the database can be retrieved using that DML. A GCL that is complete should meet this requirement. Unfortunately, there is no consensus on the definition of completeness for an ER based DML.

In addition to the above requirement, it is desirable for a GCL to be as independent of the physical aspects of the database as possible. The reason for this is that a GCL is a DML against a conceptual database only. This requirement alone excludes the possibility of using a procedural type DML (record-at-a-time DML) as GCL since a procedural DML ties itself too closely to the physical aspect of a database.

There are thus two choices for a GCL: 1) an algebraic type of DML, and 2) a calculus type of DML. There have been several proposals for "ER algebra" in the literature [8], [36]. All those proposals are clearly inspired by the relational algebra proposed by Codd [9], [10]. However, the situation is different in the ER model as opposed to the relational model. In the relational model, only the data entity is a relation. All the operations in the relational algebra apply to relations only. The result of any relational algebraic operation is also a relation. In contrast, there are two basic data entities in the ER data model: entity and relationship. Semantically, they are different. An algebra that applies on two data entities is considerably more difficult to define than one that applies on a single data entity since as the number of data entities increases the types of the output data entity and their semantic meanings seems to grow rapidly. The area of ER algebra is still at its infant stage. More research is needed to find a good definition of ER algebra. Consequently, we have not adopted any existing ER algebra for the GCL.

The ER DML: Our choice for GCL is a calculus type language. Fig. 11 shows a summary of the GCL. We call it cal-

1. GET (a-list) WHERE (qual)

2. ADD entity (av-list)

3. DELETE (entity) WHERE (qual) or

   DELETE (entity) WHERE (entity-1 [NOT] IN entity-2)

4. MODIFY entity (av-list) WHERE (qual)

5. CONNECT entity-1 (qual) TO entity-2 (qual)

   IN (relation) [WITH (av-list)]

6. DISCONNECT entity-1 (qual) FROM entity-2 (qual)

   IN (relation)

Here (a-list) refers to a list of attributes, not necessarily associated with the same entity, and (av-list) refers to a list of attribute:value pairs. The (qual) defines the qualification clause which consists of qualifications of attributes (possibly from different entities), comparison operators (=, <, >), logical joins (AND or OR) and relation names. In addition, the (qual) and ADD (av-list) may contain a nested GET command. Optional clauses are enclosed in square brackets ([]).

Fig. 11. The ER DML global conceptual language.

culus type because there is a natural correspondence between this type of DML and the relational calculus. A fundamental aspect of a calculus-based DML is the notion of the tuple variable. In relational calculus, tuple variable is a variable that ranges over some named relation. In a calculus type ER DML (i.e., the proposed GCL), the 'a-list' in the GET statement plays the similar role. An 'a-list' is a variable that ranges over a specified set of 'paths,' where a path is a traversal of an ER diagram. The results from our research have demonstrated that, with a few modifications, most DML (DL/1, CODASYL DML, SQL, and relational algebra) against the corresponding data model (hierarchical, network, relational) find their equivalence in this GCL. Therefore, this GCL satisfies the first requirement posed earlier. This GCL has little, if anything at all, to do with the physical aspects of the database, which is the second requirement.

In arriving at our required ER DML, we also analyzed four earlier relational-type languages proposed by other authors: EAS-E [34], GORDAS [16], ERL [21], and DAPLEX [29], [43]. EAS-E is very English-like, but seems best suited for an interactive query language rather than a good intermediary language. DAPLEX is the query language based on the CCA functional data model. GORDAS is a read-only query language. However, the GET command it uses seems very powerful, and so our language patterns the GET command after GORDAS. Our language is very similar to ERL. ERL claims to be a complete query language (READ, INSERT, MODIFY, DELETE), but there are a few features we dropped. The language presented will be seen to approach a relational language with the major addition of commands using inter-entity relations.

2) Query/DML Translation Algorithms: We have identi-

fied characteristics and requirements of algorithms to translate between the various model and language layers of Fig. 4. *Our major approach/objective is to develop a "DDL/DML compiler–compiler work bench" from which we can more easily develop the desired translations.* Thus we have completed translation algorithms for:

- Hierarchical IMS DL/1 (except logical database and Fast Path commands) into the ER DML
- CODASYL DML into the ER DML
- Relational Algebra into the ER DML
- Relational SQL into the ER DML.

Some of this work, that focusing on the translation from SQL to ER DML, is presented in [6]; examples of it are provided in the next section.

Translation algorithms for the following are now being developed:

- ER DML into relational SQL
- ER DML into hierarchical DL/1
- ER DML into CODASYL DML.

Our next task is to start prototype implementation of a subset of the following algorithms for proof of concept:

CODASYL DML into ER DML into SQL
SQL into ER DML into CODASYL DML.

Small programs in languages such as COBOL and C with CODASYL DML and SQL embedded in them would be used to test the translation paths.

E. SQL to ER DML Translation and Examples

Herein we provide some insight into the translations involved, by outlining SQL/DS to ER DML translation. The translation environment and scheme from SQL/DS to ER DML has the following characteristics:

- It is composed of a set of 10 basic rules.
- Each SQL statement is one of six types of commands.
- Each SQL statement applies to one of five types of relations.
- A rule may, in turn, cause other rules to be invoked.

Fig. 12 outlines the translation matrix. It portrays the ten rules that compose the overall SQL to ER DML translation

TYPE OF COMMAND / TYPE OF RELATION	SINGLE MAPPING	NESTED MAPPING	SINGLE MAP. WITH MORE THAN 1 REL.	DATA INSERTION	DATA DELETION	DATA UPDATE
TYPE 1 RELATION	RULE 1	RULE 4	RULE 3	RULE 5	RULE 7	RULE 10
TYPE 2 RELATION	RULE 2	RULE 4	RULE 3	RULE 6	RULE 8	RULE 11
TYPE 3 RELATION	RULE 2	RULE 4	RULE 3	RULE 6	RULE 8	RULE 11
TYPE 4 RELATION	RULE 2	RULE 4	RULE 3	RULE 6	RULE 8	RULE 11
TYPE 5 RELATION	RULE 1 OR 2	RULE 4	RULE 3	RULE 5 + 6	RULE 9	RULE 9 + 10 + CONNECT

Fig. 12. SQL to ER DML translation scheme matrix.

algorithm. Our translation covers all SQL DML commands except "group-by" and "aggregate" functions which we may add later.

Let us look at three example translations. Fig. 13 provides two sample ER schemas and corresponding relational sche-

SCHEMA 1

R1 (P#, PD, CL)
R2 (W#, WD)
R3 (P#, W#, QTY)
R4 (P#.1, P#.2, QTY)

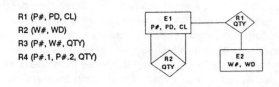

SCHEMA 2

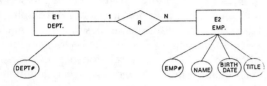

R (EMP#, DEPT#, NAME, BIRTH – DATE, TITLE)

Fig. 13. Sample schema and corresponding relational schema.

mas. Figs. 14–16 provide three DML translation examples. The translation scheme for SQL read-type commands follows, explaining in detail the Examples in Figs. 14 and 15, and much of Fig. 12. The translation detail for all SQL commands appears in [6].

In our data model translation strategy, adapted from [15], a relation in a relational schema corresponds to one of the five following ER constructs:

1) An Entity
2) A *k*-ary relationship
3 A binary relationship with attributes (1:*N* or *N*:1)
4) An *N*:*M* binary relationship set without attributes
5) An entity, plus key attributes of some other relations.

We shall call the respective relations type 1, type 2, $\cdots$, and type 5 (see Fig. 13). We now discuss, for each type of relation, how a single mapping involving such a relation can be mapped into the ER DML.

Type 1 Relation: In this case, a relation, *R*, with attributes *A*1, *A*2, $\cdots$, *An*, corresponds to exactly an entity, *E*, with attributes *A*1, *A*2, $\cdots$, *An*. For example, for the following relation in a relational schema:

Relation: EMP(EMPNO,NAME,DNO,SAL)

there exists an entity in the ER schema having the following format:

Entity EMP(EMPNO,NAME,DNO,SAL).

The attribute names need not be exactly the same so long as their semantics remain the same, for example, SAL in the relation versus SALARY in the entity.

The translation of an SQL query involving this type of relation into the ER DML is straightforward since in both data models only one data entity is involved (a relation in the

Example 1:

- Single mapping with more than one relation
- Accessing sample schema 1
- Using rule 3
- SQL statement

SELECT	P#, W#, WD
FROM	R1, R2, R3
WHERE	R1.P# = '100'
AND	R1.P# = R3.P#
AND	R3.W# = R2.W#

ER statement

GET (P#, W#, WD) WHERE
(E1 R2 E2 & E1.P# = '100')

Fig. 14. Example of SQL to ER DML translation.

Example 2:

- Nested mapping
- Accessing sample schema 1
- Using rule 4
- SQL statement

SELECT	*
FROM	R1
WHERE	P#IN
SELECT	P#
FROM	R3
WHERE	W#='W123'

- ER statement

This intermediate statement is generated first:

GET(P#) WHERE (R2 & R2.W#='W123')

This is the final statement (with the previous statement nested in the WHERE clause):

GET(P#,PD,CL) WHERE (E1 R2 & E1.P# =
GET(P#) WHERE (R2 & R2.W#='W123'))

Fig. 15. Example of SQL to ER DML translation.

Example 3:

- Update
- Type 5 relation
- Accessing sample schema 2
- Using rule 9, 10
- SQL statement

UPDATE	R
SET	DEPT#='D23' & TITLE='ENG'
WHERE	EMP#='E10493'

- ER statement

DISCONNECT E2(EMP#='E10493') FROM E1 IN R12

MODIFY E2(TITLE='ENG') WHERE (E2.EMP#='E10493')

CONNECT E2(EMP#='E10493') TO E1(DEPT#='D23') IN R12

Fig. 16. Example of SQL to ER DML translation.

relational model and entity in the ER model). The following rule is designed to guide such translation:

Rule 1: For a single mapping involving a type 1 relation, generate a GET statement in the ER DML. The a-list in the GET statement takes the form of the select_clause in the single mapping. The WHERE clause in the GET statement includes two parts. The first is the name of the entity involved. The second takes the form of the WHERE_clause in the single mapping.

Type 2 Relation: A type 2 relation in the relational schema corresponds to a *k*-ary relationship in the ER schema. An attribute of a type 2 relation is either one of the attributes of that *k*-ary relationship or one of the key attributes of the entities connected by the *k*-ary relationship. The rule for translating a single mapping involving a type 2 relation into the ER DML is as follows:

Rule 2: For a single mapping involving a type 2 relation, generate a GET statement in the ER DML. The a-list in the GET statement takes the form of the select_clause in the single mapping. The WHERE clause in the GET statement includes two parts. The first consists of the corresponding relationship name and the names of the *k*-entities connected by this relationship. The second part takes the form of the WHERE_clause in the single mapping.

Type 3 Relation: A type 3 relation in the relational schema comes from (being mapped from) a binary relationship with attributes in the ER schema. The binary relationship is of either type $1:N$ or type $N:1$, but not of type $N:M$, which is mapped into a type 4 relation. An attribute of a type 3 relation is either one of the attributes of the binary relationship or one of the key attributes of the two entities this binary relationship connects. Clearly, the relationship in this case (binary) is a special case of that in the previous case (*k*-ary). Therefore, the translation of a single mapping involving a type 3 relation can be done by using rule 2.

Type 4 Relation: A type 4 relation in the relational schema corresponds to an $N:M$ binary relationship in the ER schema. Again, this is a special case of a *k*-ary relationship. The translation of a single mapping involving a type 4 relation can, therefore, also be done by using rule 2.

Type 5 Relation: In order to understand the formation of a type 5 relation, the concepts of *source* and *target* entities need to be introduced. Let $E1$ and $E2$ be the entity sets involved in relationship set R, of type $1:N$. Then $E1$ is referred to as the source entity set and $E2$, the target entity set. When an ER schema is mapped into a relational schema, for each type $1:N$ relationship set without attributes, a type 5 relation is created in the relational schema. The attributes of the type 5 relation consist of all the attributes of the target entity plus the key attribute of the source entity. To translate a single mapping involving a type 5 relation into the ER DML, the three clauses (SELECT, FROM, and WHERE) of the single mapping are examined first; if the key attribute of the source entity appears in one or more of the clauses, then

rule 2 is used to guide the translation, otherwise rule 1 is used.

Single Mapping Involving More than One Relation: Using the rules developed so far, we are able to translate a single mapping involving a single relation into the ER DML. These rules alone have limited use since most queries, when expressed in terms of SQL, involve more than one relation. Let us discuss how this kind of multi-relation mapping can be mapped into the ER DML.

To start, we note that at the global conceptual model level we have an ER schema which is a connected ER diagram. By connected we mean that any two entity sets in the diagram are connected via some relationship sets and some entity sets. This is important to our developing the translation rules since this guarantees that there is at least some directed (through a single relationship set) or indirected (through more than one relationship set and some entity sets) relationship between any two relations in the relational schema. This suggests that we should try to find such relationship when we have a single mapping that involves more than one relation. As we have indicated earlier, a relation in the relational schema corresponds to one of the five ER segments (part of an ER diagram) in the ER sechema. For a single mapping involving more than one relation, we first find all ER segments in the ER schema corresponding to those relations in the single mapping. Once we have all the ER segments, we find a traversal of the ER diagram that includes all the ER segments. This traversal will then contain the relationship between the relations in the single mapping. The next thing to do is to connect the qualifier (WHERE clause) in the single mapping into the qualifier on the traversal (part of the ER diagram that encompasses all the ER segments). The following rule summarizes the above and can be used to guide the translations of a single mapping involving more than one relation into the ER DML.

Rule 3: For a single mapping involving more than one relation, each of which is of one of the five types, generate a GET statement in the ER DML. The a-list of the GET statement takes the form of the select_clause in the single mapping. The WHERE clause of the GET statement includes two parts. The first part contains the traversal of the ER schema. The second part takes the form of the WHERE_clause in the single mapping. The traversal of the ER schema is generated by first finding the corresponding ER segments for the relations in the single mapping and then taking part of the ER diagram that includes all the ER segments

Example: See the example in Fig. 15.

Nested Mapping: With SQL it is possible to use the result of a mapping in the WHERE clause of another mapping. This operation is called nested mapping. Nested mappings are not restricted to only two levels. When processing a nested mapping, the innermost mapping is executed as though it were a single mapping; the result of the mapping is passed to the outer mapping and the outer mapping then proceeds as though it were given a set of constants in place the inner mapping. This continues from the innermost mapping out until it reaches the outermost mapping. Similarly, the ER DML (the Global Conceptual Language) allows for the embedment of a GET statement in the WHERE clause of another GET statement. This nested GET statement feature makes it possible to map a nested mapping in SQL into the ER DML. The following rule guides such a translation.

Rule 4: For each nested mapping, generate a nested GET statement in the following manner. Working from the innermost mapping out, for each mapping seen, which is a single mapping, generate a GET statement using the rules described earlier for single mappings. If the current single mapping has a single mapping in its WHERE clause, which should have been mapped into a GET statement due to the fact that we work from inside out, then the WHERE clause of the current GET statement is combined with the inner GET statement to form the new WHERE clause. This process continues until the outermost mapping is mapped into the ER DML.

Example: See the example in Fig. 16.

We stress that the overall translation approach in our HD-DBMS effort will hold even if the source relational language and the target ER DML were to vary. This has been one of our requirements. Thus the translation would be extended to other relational materializations. The same holds for the other types of DML and corresponding translation schemes within our scope.

F. View Update

While we have stated the ideal long-range goals, we have identified problems that may impose limits on the types of user views of the databases and particularly on the types of data accessing commands that may be issued from the VM user level. We have sorted out the various problems, assessed the possibility and cost of solution, identified the limitation on types of commands and data model mapping if such problems are not solved, and outlined possible solution approaches. As an example, the magnitude of foreseen and unsolved problems appears to have led most efforts to not to permit updating a database, even while forcing each user wishing access to a heterogeneous database to abide by a new or common model and query language.

The "view update" problem in relational systems is one major problem in the distributed heterogeneous case even if relational systems are not involved; constraining the differences permitted betweeen user views and local logical models alleviates the problem and makes it more solvable. We have now formally identified the rules of the game to permit 1) updating commands to various degrees and 2) differences in mapping between the user view and the underlying participating database schemas, while preserving integrity constraints. We first assessed actual view updating in IMS, SQL/DS, DB2, Oracle, Ingres, and QBE. We also analyzed paper approaches proposed by various authors.

We are now designing the mechanisms for DBAs or users for logically and easily expressing various limitations or controls on the types of user views, data accessing commands, and updates so as to preserve stated integrity controls and various degrees of transparency of distribution

and heterogeneity. The role of the Prolog language or of some of its mechanisms as an internal mechanism to formally express such controls are being considered. We are now identifying the translation of such controls to corresponding controls (DDL and/or application programs) on specific DBMS.

We have identified the major issues referred to as the "view update problem" and also most of the required integrity controls or database update decisions that DBAs or users must make to solve most, it not all, realistic view update problems.

G. Futher Features

A very brief synopsis of work we have done in two major areas follows.

Protocols: We have identified the protocol information needed to implement the HD-DBMS. In developing these protocols, the logical components within the HD-DBMS to implement these protocols were also defined. The protocols defined describe the information exchange needed to enable the various logical components of the HD-DBMS handshake or communicate so as to maintain data integrity in the system and also to handle the translations. The protocols allow the components to implement: queries and/or updates on data within the system; aborts on queries/updates; delayed updates; broadcasting and handling systems status (as in up/down/recovering).

In addition to defining the protocols, the format by which the protocols travel between the logical components was also defined. Ample example scenarios of events within the HD-DBMS have been created. Each scenario contains detailed illustration of the protocols needed to handle the event and the sequence in which they are used.

Internal Model: A major model of the HD-DBMS is the internal model, both at the global and the local levels. A generalized database access path model has been defined for the purpose of representing relationships between data entities in the HD-DBMS [20]. This data model, termed the Generalized Data Access Graph (GDAG), is a major architectural component. The GDAG is maintained by the HD-DBMS as part of the network data dictionary (catalog). It encompasses the capability of modeling the access paths of the three major data models, via a common data independent notation. A salient capability is the modeling of inter-database relationships using an equivalent notation.

IV. CONCLUDING REMARKS

We have outlined the language desiderata for data sharing and accessing in the increasing scenarios of heterogeneous databases. We have cited the major approaches to data sharing and accessing: from the primitive commercial file and database unload/load and PC download, to common interfaces on top of existing DBMS, to the R & D and prototype efforts toward the long-range goals. Commercial availability of the more encompassing thrusts may become a reality with the mounting problems, opportunity costs, and demand for data sharing in the heterogeneous world.

The HD-DBMS project is highlighted herein, with a presentation of its status, progress, and plans. It is a longer range project, with the unique feature of allowing any user in the network to use his preferred database model and DML to access any data in the heterogeneous network; another distinguishing feature, thus far, is its support for updating, not only for read-type accessing.

Prototype implementation of the HD-DBMS for proof of concept will follow. The first thread probably will be to translate:

- from a CODASYL DML at the virtual level into ER DML into SQL
- from SQL at the virtual level into ER DML into CODASYL DML.

Prototyping will first face read-only commands and immediately thereafter updating commands. A robust data dictionary will be used, undoubtedly extending its model, to implement the crucial network-wide dictionary/catalog.

We intend to use graphical mouse-oriented tools to paint ER database models. ER data definitions and graphical ER diagrams should eventually be generated automatically from existing DDLs, and DDLs should be generated automatically also from ER data definitions and graphical ER diagrams. Schema integration into the global conceptual model should be semi-automated; the reverse process should also be automated.

Although the flavor of presentation is "bottom-up," that is, starting with existing individually designed heterogeneous databases, the system is also targeted for new databases being designed globally from the start, and then being distributed in the heterogeneous environment. The latter will be a growing case as the flexibility of heterogeneous distributed systems becomes available.

ACKNOWLEDGMENT

The author wishes to acknowledge the contribution of the following past and current members of the HD-DBMS project: E. Nahouraii and M. H. Pirahesh (IBM Corp.), J. Ben-Zvi and J. Horowitz (Informatics), G. Chen (Hughes Aircraft), W. Johnson (Lockheed), A. Chen, and G. Wang. The collaboration and support of Informatics General Corporation is appreciated. Finally, he wishes to thank the two anonymous reviewers for their comments.

REFERENCES

[1] M. Adiba and D. Portal, "A cooperations system for heterogeneous data base management systems," *Informat. Syst.*, vol. 3, no. 3, pp. 209–215, 1978.

[2] J. R. Abrial, "Data semantics, in *Conf. Proc. IFIP-TC2 Working Conf. on Data Base Management* (Cargese, Corsica, Apr. 1974), J. W. Klimbie and L. Koffeman, Eds. Amsterdam, The Netherlands: North-Holland, 1974.

[3] P. Atzeni and P. P. Chen, "Completeness of query languages for the entity-relationship model," in *Proc. 2nd Int. Conf. On Entity-Relationship Approach*, P. P. Chen, Ed., ER Institute, 1981.

[4] A. F. Cardenas and M. H. Pirahesh, "Database communication in a heterogeneous database management system network," *Informat. Syst.*, vol. 5, no. 1, pp. 55–79, 1980.

[5] ——, "The E-R model in a heterogeneous data base management system network architecture," in P. Chen, Ed., *Proc. Int. Conf. on Entity-Relationship Approach to System Analysis and Design*. Amsterdam, The Netherlands: North-Holland, 1980, pp. 577–583.

[6] A. F. Cardenas and G. Wang, "Translation of SQL/DS data access/update into entity/relationship data access/update," in *Proc. 4th Int. Conf. on the E-R Approach* (Chicago, IL, Oct. 28–30, 1985).

[7] P. P. Chen, "The entity-relationship model—Toward a unified view of data," *ACM Trans. Database Syst.*, vol. 1, no. 1, Mar. 1976.

[8] ——, "An algebra for a directional binary entity-relationship model," in *Proc. 1st IEEE COMPDEC* (Los Angeles, CA, Apr. 1984), pp. 37–40.

[9] E. F. Codd, "A relational model of data for large shared data banks," *Commun. ACM*, vol. 13, no. 6, 1970.

[10] ——, "Relational completeness of data base sublanguages," in *Data Base Systems*, R. Rustin, Ed. Englewood Cliffs, NJ: Prentice-Hall, 1972.

[11] Cullinet Software Inc., "IDMS/R, summary description," Westwood, MA.

[12] Cullinet Software Inc., "Goldengate, summary description," Westwood, MA.

[13] U. Dayal and H. Y. Hwang, "View definition and generalization for database integration in a multidatabase system," *IEEE Trans. Software Eng.*, vol. SE-10, no. 6, pp. 628–645, Nov. 1984.

[14] U. Dayal, "Query processing in a multidatabase system, in *Query Processing in Data Systems*, W. Kim, D. Reiner, and D. Batory, Eds. New York, NY: Springer-Verlag, 1985.

[15] S. R. Dumpala and S. K. Arora, "Schema translation using the entity-relationship approach," in *Proc. 2nd Int. Conf. on Entity-Relationship Approach*, P. P. Chen, Ed., ER Institute, 1981.

[16] R. Elmasri and G. Wiederhold, "GORDAS: A formal high-level query language for the entity-relationship model," in *Proc. 2nd Int. Conf. on Entity-Relationship Approach* (Washington, DC, 1981).

[17] A. Ferrier and C. Stangret, "Heterogeneity in the distributed database management systems SIRIUS-DELTA," in *Proc. 8th Int. Conf. on Very Large Data Bases* (Mexico City, Mexico, Sept. 8–10, 1982), pp. 45–53.

[18] V. D. Gligor and G. L. Luckenbaugh, "Interconnecting heterogeneous data base management system," *IEEE Computer*, vol. 22, pp. 33–43, Jan. 1984.

[19] Honeywell Information Systems, "Relational query/interactive query reference manual," Manual #DR52.

[20] J. Horowitz and A. F. Cardenas, "Relationships in a heterogeneous distributed database environment," submitted for publication in *Informat. Syst.*

[21] H. Y. Hwang and U. Dayal, "Using the entity-relationship model for implementing multiple model database system," in *Proc. 2nd Int. Conf. on Entity-Relationship Approach*, P. P. Chen, Ed., 1981.

[22] IBM Corp., "SQL/DS, concepts and facilities," Reference Manual GH24-5013.

[23] Informatics General Corp., "Answer/DB reference manual," Canoga Park, CA.

[24] Informatics General Corp., "Distributed application generator, technical system description," Canoga Park, CA.

[25] Informatics General Corp., "Lotus/Answer," "Visi/Answer," and "dBase II/Answer," Reference Manuals, Canoga Park, CA.

[26] J. Iossiphidis, "A translation to convert the DDL of ERM to the DDL of System 2000," in *Proc. Int. Conf. on Entity-Relationship Approach to System Analysis and Design*, P. P. Chen, Ed. Los Angeles, CA, 1979).

[27] B. E. Jacobs, "On database logic," *J. ACM*, vol. 29, no. 2, pp. 310–332, Apr. 1982.

[28] R. H. Katz, "Database design and translation for multiple data models," Ph.D. dissertation, UC Berkeley, 1980.

[29] R. Katz and N. Goodman, "View processing in multibase—A heterogeneous database system," in *Entity-Relationship Approach to Information Modeling and Analysis*, P. P. Chen, Ed., ER Institute, 1981.

[30] R. H. Katz and E. Wong, "Decompiling CODASYL DML into relational queries," *ACM Trans. Database Syst.*, vol. 7, no. 1, pp. 1–23, 1982.

[31] T. A. Landers and R. L. Rosenberg, "An overview of multibase," in *Distributed Databases*, H. J. Schneider, Ed. Amsterdam, The Netherlands: North-Holland, 1982.

[32] M. Levin, "The DIAM theory of algebraic access graphics," Sterling Systems, Inc., Denver, CO, 1980.

[33] Y. D. Lien, "Hierarchical schemata for relational databases,"

ACM Trans. Database Syst., vol. 6, no. 1, pp. 48–69, Mar. 1981.

[34] H. M. Markowitz, A. Mallhota, and D. P. Pazel, "The ER and EAS formalisms for system modeling, and the EAS-E language," in Proc. 2nd Int. Conf. on Entity-Relationship Approach (Washington, DC, 1981).

[35] E. Z. Nahouraii, L. O. Brooks, and A. F. Cardenas, "An approach to data communication between different GDBMS," in Proc. 2nd Int. Conf. on Very Large Data Bases (Brussels, Belgium, Sept. 1976).

[36] C. Parent and S. Spaccapietra, "An entity-relationship algebra," in Proc. 1st IEEE Conf. on Data Engineering (Los Angeles, CA, Apr. 24–27, 1984), pp. 500–507.

[37] L. S. Schneider "A relational query compiler for distributed heterogeneous databases," IFIP TC 2.6, NASWG, Jan. 1977.

[38] SDDTG of CODASYL Systems Committee, "A stored data definition language for the translation of data," Informat. Syst., vol. 2, no. 3, 1977.

[39] M. E. Senko, E. B. Altman, M. M. Astrahan, and P. L. Fehder, "Data structures and accessing in database systems," IBM Syst. J., vol. 12, no. 1, 1973.

[40] M. E. Senko, "DIAM as a detailed example of the ANSI/SPARC architecture," in Proc. IFIP-TC2 Working Conf. Modeling in Data Base Mangement Systems (Freudenstadt, Germany, Jan. 1976), G. M. Nijssen, Ed. Amsterdam, The Netherlands: North-Holland, 1976.

[41] N. Shu, B. Housel, and V. Lum, "CONVERT: A high level translation definition language for data conversion," IBM Corp. Res. Rep. RJ 1500, San Jose, CA, Jan. 1975.

[42] N. Shu et al., "EXPRESS: A data extraction, processing and restructuring system," ACM Trans. Database Syst., vol. 2, no. 2, June 1977.

[43] D. W. Shipman, "The functional data model and the language DAPLEX," ACM Trans. Database Syst., vol. 6, no. 1, pp. 140–173, Mar. 1981.

[44] J. M. Smith et al., "MULTIBASE—Integrating heterogeneous distributed database systems," in Proc. 1981 Nat. Computer Conf. Reston, VA: AFIPS Press, pp. 487–499.

[45] G. Sockut, "A framework for logical-level changes within data base systems," IEEE Computer, vol. 23, pp. 9–27, May 1985.

[46] E. Wong and R. H. Katz, "Logical design and schema conversion for relational and DBTG databases," in Proc. Int. Conf. on Entity-Relationship Approach to System Analysis and Design, P. P. Chen, Ed., Los Angeles, CA, 1979.

Query Processing in Heterogeneous Distributed Database Management Systems

M. P. REDDY, B. E. PRASAD, AND P. G. REDDY

Abstract—A growing number of applications demand the integration of various islands of existing information resources. Heterogeneous distributed database management systems have been designed to integrate and to provide uniform interface to pre-existing databases implemented with different database management systems. In this paper an attempt has been made to identify the problem in developing such systems. Special focus is on processing strategies adopted in eight prototypes viz., MULTIBASE, MERMAID, ADDS, PRECI*, IMDAS, NDMS, MRDSM, and IISS, which are at various stages of implementation. Although the ultimate aim of the designers of these systems is to develop a complete transaction processing mechanism, they have so far been successful in implementing query processing mechanisms only. To make these systems commercially viable, and to make them more appealing to the users, a mechanism for processing global updates still remains to be developed.

1. INTRODUCTION

THE aim of a heterogeneous distributed database management system (HDDBMS) is to provide uniform interface to nonintegrated databases implemented with different database management systems. Many applications in any organization require data from more than one existing database. These databases are designed independently because of

(a) diverse data processing requirements of various divisions of the organization which are beyond the processing capacity of any single database management system,
(b) lack of a central database administrator to coordinate independent working groups to develop an integrated system suitable for all of them, and
(c) unavailability of efficient distributed database software. Vendors of different machines supply different database management packages, which are incompatible with each other in many aspects. Each database has its own data model to express the database schema, and this model can be accessed only by its particular retrieval language.

Many difficulties arise in formulating and processing retrieval requests that require data from more than one database. While the benefits of integrated distributed databases and their implementation through homogeneous distributed databases are well understood, it is neither financially feasible nor operationally advisable to throw away all the existing

M. P. Reddy, B. E. Prasad, and P. G. Reddy are with the School of Mathematics and Computer/Information Sciences, University of Hyderabad, Hyderabad-500 134, India.

information systems, and develop an integrated system in their place.

To mitigate the problems mentioned above, the concept of heterogeneous distributed database management systems (HDDBMS) has evolved. Such systems use ideas derived from homogeneous distributed database management systems, with subtle differences because of differences in the design process for the two environments. Homogeneous distributed databases are designed using the top-down approach [1]; a global database, which satisfies the needs of an entire organization, is designed, and this database is fragmented and distributed over various sites in such a way that the overall maintenance of the database is cost-effective; further, all these fragments of the database are implemented at their respective sites using the same DBMS software. On the other hand, design of an HDDBMS uses the bottom-up approach [6]–[21]; all the existing databases of the organization are used to come up with a uniform interface that makes the user have the illusion of having one centralized database management system for the entire organization.

In the homogeneous distributed database environment, data can be globally managed [2]–[5], and global deadlocks can be detected and resolved easily using a homogeneous concurrency control mechanism. Apart from processing global queries and updates, the facilities of location transparency and replication transparency are provided to the user. Such facilities cannot be readily provided in a heterogeneous distributed database environment because of the peculiar problems described in the next section. Next, the general architecture of a HDDBMS is presented in Section 3. The architecture and query-processing strategies of eight existing HDDBMS prototypes are discussed in Section 4. Future directions and conclusions are presented in Section 5.

2. PROBLEMS OF QUERY PROCESSING IN HETEROGENEOUS DDBMS

A good heterogeneous distributed DBMS must be able to access, aggregate, and update information maintained in multiple databases through a single uniform interface, without the need to change existing databases, and without disturbing local applications. This objective is difficult to attain because of differences at several levels as described in the following subsections.

2.1. Difference in Data Models

Since data of ingredient databases have been stored using different data models, conversion of schema from one data

Received August 2, 1988; revised Nov. 8, 1988.

model to other data models becomes necessary to respond to any query involving more than one database of different data models.

2.2. Differences in Data Manipulation Languages (DML)

Different DBMSs support different data manipulation languages. So a query stated by the user in a global data manipulation language must be translated into a relevant DML of the corresponding database.

2.3. Schema Integration

Since the constituent databases have been designed and implemented independently, there are inherent data incompatibilities. These data incompatibilities are of two kinds: 1) qualitative data incompatibilities, and 2) quantitative data incompatibilities.

2.3.1 Qualitative Data Incompatibilities

Some of the qualitative data incompatibilities are as follows:

- *Scale differences:* This incompatibility arises when the same attribute of an entity is stored in different databases in different units. For example, the attribute "LENGTH" of an entity may be stored in terms of centimeters in one database, and as inches in another database.
- *Level of abstraction:* This incompatibility is encountered when information about an entity is stored in dissimilar levels of detail in two databases. For example, "LABOR-COST" and "MATERIAL-COST" may be stored separately in one database, and they may be combined together as "TOTAL-COST" in a second database.
- *Inconsistency in naming objects:* This can be further divided into the following two subclasses, as follows:
  i) *Synonyms:* This inconsistency occurs when classes with different names represent the same concept. For example, the term "DOMESTIC-CUSTOMER" in one database may refer to the same set of entities as the term "BUYERS" in another database.
  ii) *Homonyms:* This inconsistency is observed when the classes with same name represent different concepts. For example, the attribute "SALARY" in one database might mean a weekly salary, whereas it may imply monthly salary in another case.

2.3.3. Quantitative Data Incompatibilities

As databases are managed independently, the values of the same quantitative attribute of an entity stored in different databases may be different from each other. This inconsistency complicates query-processing procedure. For example, suppose the attribute "weight" of a particular ship is 50 tonnes in one database and 60 in another (this difference may be because the ship is unloaded in the first case, and loaded in the second case). To answer the query "get the names of all ships weighing less than 55 tonnes," the query processor must be equipped with a mechanism to deal with such inconsistent parameters. Inconsistency in the value of an attribute maintained in multiple databases arises due to:

i) various databases storing the attribute to different levels of accuracy;

ii) underlying assumptions about the attribute, such as loaded weight and unloaded weight, and

iii) lack of ability to implement global concurrency control algorithms in heterogeneous environments.

2.4. Expressive Power of Local Operators

The power of various data manipulation languages varies over a wide scale. Whereas high level data manipulation languages such as DAPLEX offer set-at-a-time capabilities, low level languages, such as those based on CODASYL models focus on record-at-a-time facilities. Also, some database management systems do not provide temporary storage for intermediate results. This disparity in system functionality increases the complexity of query optimization software.

Designers of HDDBMS must deal with all the problems mentioned above. The components of a general HDDBMS architecture are discussed in the following section.

3. GENERAL ARCHITECTURE OF HDDBMS

An HDDBMS consists of the following components:

- Uniform user interface
- Command translator
- Data translator
- Integration database
- Query optimizer.

3.1. User Interface

The user interface accepts the query from the user, supplies the results of the query and other information to the user, and insulates the user from the idiosyncracies of individual database management systems. The user interface must be flexible enough to guide the naive user to properly formulate his or her query, as well as to support professionals to retrieve information with speed and efficiency.

3.2. Command Translators

The command translator accepts the query and translates it into the query language understood by the underlying database management systems. There are two approaches for designing a command translator. One approach is to provide the user with a global query language, and the other is to allow the user to state the query in a local query language. In the first approach, translators are required to transform the query entered using a global query language to corresponding subqueries in local query language on corresponding local schemata. In the second approach, the query stated in the local query language on the external schema must be translated into the intermediate query language on the global schema. Finally, the latter query on global schema must be translated into the subqueries on local schemata in their corresponding query languages. While in the second approach the user need not learn the global query language, the number of translators required to be developed is larger than in the first approach.

3.3. Data Translators

The user views the heterogeneous distributed database as a single database with a common representation for the data elements that pertain to the same domain. However, data may have different representations in different databases. Data retrieved with the purpose of selectively joining two databases or for use in a final report must be translated into the global representation. The data translation process typically involves the transformation of data types, structures, units, and formats of the data, from native local representations to the global representation.

3.4. Integration Database

The integration database contains the information required to resolve the data incompatibilities among the component databases. Various types of data incompatibilities were described previously in Section 2.3 of this paper.

3.5. Query Optimizer

Query processing involves both transmission and local processing. The transmission effort can be minimized by reducing the amount of data to be moved among the sites; this issue is handled by the global query optimizer. The minimization of local processing effort is handled by the local query optimizer. The advantage of having two optimizers is that the global optimizer can be designed without delving into too many details of component database management systems.

The flow of information among the components described above is as follows. The user interface accepts the query from the user. If it is a valid query, it is sent to the global optimizer. The global optimizer breaks the query into subqueries such that each subquery can be answered by a single database. The command translator receives these subqueries in the global query language, and translates them into the local query language of the corresponding database. Each translated subquery is simplified before generating the optimal access path for execution. All the intermediate results that are generated by these subqueries are assembled and, if necessary, processed further to prepare the final result of the query.

In the following section, we study eight existing prototypes of HDDBMS to see how the above components are used in various architectures.

4. Prototypes of Heterogeneous Distributed Database Management Systems

In this section, we present the schema architecture and query processing strategies of eight existing prototypes of HDDBMS. These are: MULTIBASE [6], [7], MERMAID [8], [9], ADDS [10], PRECI* [11], [12], [13], [14], IMDAS [15], [16], NDMS [17], MRDSM [18], [19], [20], and IISS [21]. The basic features of these systems are studied and compared in [22]. In this paper, the focus is on the query processing aspect.

4.1. MULTIBASE

MULTIBASE is designed by Computer Corporation of America (CCA) to provide a logically integrated, retrieve-only, user interface to a physically nonintegrated distributed database environment. It provides single query language,

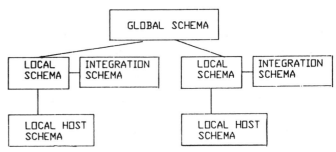

Fig. 1. Architecture of MULTIBASE.

location transparency, and resolves data incompatibilities. However, no tool is available either to ensure consistency across databases or to provide global update facility to users.

The architecture of MULTIBASE has three levels of schemata: a Global Schema (GS) at the top level; an Integration Schema (IS) and one Local Schema (LS) per local database at the middle level; and one Local Host Schema (LHS) per local database at the bottom level, as shown in Fig. 1.

The local host schemata are the original existing schemata defined in local data models and managed by the local DBMS. Each of these LHS is translated into a local schema defined in the functional data model. The LS and the IS are mapped via a view-mapping into the global schema. The GS allows users to pose queries against what appears to be a homogeneous and integrated database.

The query processing mechanism of MULTIBASE is shown in Fig. 2.

The total responsibility of query processing is shared by the Global Data Manager (GDM) and the Local Database Interface (LDI). The GDM contains a translator, an optimizer, a decomposer, a filter, a monitor, and an internal DBMS. In the GDM, the transformer accepts the global query stated by the user in DAPLEX query language, and produces a DAPLEX query on local schemata and the auxiliary database schema. This transformed query is sent to the optimizer which produces a global execution strategy that combines local processing and data movement steps. The decomposer takes a transformed global query and separates it by local database site, thereby producing DAPLEX single-site queries. The filter reduces the decomposed queries by removing from them the operations that are not supported by the local host DBMS. In such a case, the optimizer will design an alternative strategy. Once the strategy of execution is fixed, the control is passed to the monitor. The monitor oversees the execution of the strategy developed by the optimizer. It initiates single-site DAPLEX queries at appropriate LDIs, combines the data returned by the LDIs, and formats the output as requested by the user. The internal DBMS, which supports all DAPLEX capabilities, is used to store the results of DAPLEX single-site queries, and to perform all the required steps of the final query.

The LDI contains a local query optimizer and a translator. The local optimizer of LDI examines the DAPLEX single-site query, determines a local query processing strategy that will rapidly answer the query, and the translator transforms these single-site DAPLEX queries into its local DML. These local queries retrieve the necessary data from the local host

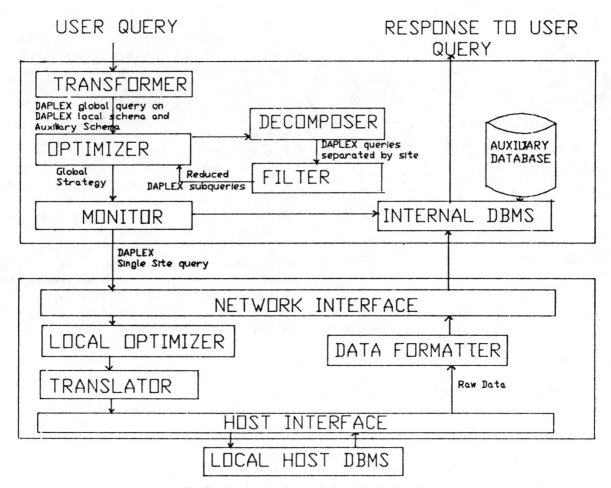

USER QUERY

RESPONSE TO USER QUERY

TRANSFORMER

DAPLEX global query on
DAPLEX local schema and
Auxiliary Schema

OPTIMIZER

Global
Strategy

DECOMPOSER

DAPLEX queries
separated by site

Reduced
DAPLEX subqueries

FILTER

AUXILIARY
DATABASE

MONITOR

INTERNAL DBMS

DAPLEX
Single Site query

NETWORK INTERFACE

LOCAL OPTIMIZER

DATA FORMATTER

Raw Data

TRANSLATOR

HOST INTERFACE

LOCAL HOST DBMS

Fig. 2. Query processing mechanism of MULTIBASE.

database, and these data are loaded into the internal DBMS. The internal DBMS processes the intermediate results and prepares the final result.

One peculiar aspect of MULTIBASE is that it has the database management system called internal DBMS to process the intermediate results. This concept of having an internal DBMS simplifies the process of integration. The overall architecture facilitates the integration of a new database with the existing components of MULTIBASE without much effort. So, the design goals of generality, extendability, and compatibility of MULTIBASE are achieved using this architecture. In MULTIBASE, main stress is given to integration rather than to query optimization.

4.2. MERMAID

System Development Corporation, a part of UNISYS, has developed a prototype named MERMAID, which is a front-end to three relational database management systems that run on a network of computers. At present, MERMAID supports relational DBMSs only, but its four-layer schema is designed to include nonrelational DBMSs as well.

The architecture of MERMAID contains three different major processes: the user interface, the distributor, and one DBMS driver for each database to be accessed. All information about component databases, users, host computers, and the network is contained in a data dictionary/directory (DD/

D), which is stored in a database and is accessed through a special driver. The user environment has an ARIEL or SQL parser and a translator that produces the query in DIL (Distributed Intermediate Language). The distributor contains the optimizer and the controller. The distributor optimizes the query, breaks it into single-site subqueries with the help of information present in DD/D, and sends the subqueries to their corresponding database drivers. Each database driver contains a translator that transforms the subquery in DIL to the DBMS query language.

The logical schema architecture of MERMAID is depicted in Fig. 3. The subschema layer represents the user view based on the global schema. The user view can be represented in a relational or semantic model. The global schema represents the global view of all the data defined in the distributed local schemata. It is represented in the relational model. The distributed local schema represents the external view of the local database in relational data model. The local database schema can be represented in any data model. Since the local schemata currently supported are all relational, there is no distinction between the distributed local schema and the local schema. However, this four-layer schema architecture is intended for future expansion to include nonrelational DBMSs as well.

The query processing strategy is depicted in Fig. 4. The user builds an ARIEL or SQL query in the user environment.

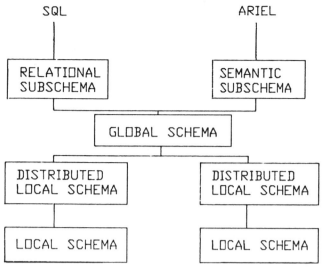

Fig. 3. Architecture of MERMAID.

This query is then parsed and validated by the translator, and if the query is valid, it is sent to the distributor. The controller reads the query, and passes it to the optimizer, which plans the execution. The DIL query may need to be decomposed into several subqueries, and the controller sends the subqueries to one or more DBMS drivers. Each DBMS driver translates the DIL (sub)query into the local DBMS query language, and sends it to the DBMS for retrieval of the necessary data. The results returned to the driver may be in the form of a report, or they may be a relation that must be sent to another driver. When the final report has been assembled at a site, the controller directs the driver at that site to send the report to the user interface.

The designers of MERMAID have assumed that most of the commercially available databases are either relational, or at least available with relational interface. More importance is given to query optimization than to integration of different data models. An extended SDD-1 semi-join algorithm is used for query optimization, and it has been further extended to support fragmented and replicated relations. A replicated algorithm derived from distributed INGRESS has been developed and tested. Based on the assumption that CPU overheads dominate the network costs, this algorithm uses fragmented relations to maximize the amount of parallelism in operations.

As in MULTIBASE, there is no internal DBMS to process intermediate results. MERMAID makes use of one of the component database management systems to process the intermediate results. Research is still continuing in the areas of object management, security, and the design of a deductive inference engine which could add inference capabilities to the system.

4.3. Amoco Distributed Database System (ADDS)

ADDS is a HDDBMS prototype developed by the Amoco Oil Company. The conceptual architecture of ADDS is capable of integrating relational, network, and hierarchical databases. The current version of ADDS is used to retrieve data from hierarchical and relational databases only. ADDS provides location transparency in both batch and interactive processing modes.

In ADDS, there is no global schema. Instead, a number of schemata called Composite Database Schemata (CDBs) can be constructed and defined using local schemata called Logical Database (LDB). Each LDB is a transformed version of one or more local databases called Physical Databases (PDB). All the CDBs are placed in a directory. The user can choose a CDB, define a view, and query on this view. Also, the user can define his or her CDB schema. The schema architecture of ADDS is shown in Fig. 5.

The basic components of ADDS are the User Interface (UI), the ADDS directory, the Task Master (TM), the Request Manager (RM), the Server, and the component databases. The UI provides security for the corporate databases by requiring a password to enter the ADDS environment. It establishes the ADDS environment as specified by the user, and provides menus to the new users. Experienced users can bypass the menu mode and make queries directly on the views defined on the CDB schema. The UI also checks the syntax, parses the query into logical database subqueries, and forwards the parsed query to the Request Manager.

The TM is activated by the user's request for service. It performs resource management and allocation, monitors task status by requiring periodic reports, and takes remedial actions in case of failure.

The Request Manager consists of filter, optimizer, scheduler, merger, and formatter. The filter receives the user's query and decomposes it into subqueries. It analyses each subquery to determine if all the operators in the subquery can be processed by the particular DBMS; if not, it replaces the unsupported operators with a corresponding set of statements that are supported by the host DBMS. If the equivalent statements are not available for an operator on a host DBMS, the ADDS function calls can be used to support the unsupported operation. Information on operators and ADDS functions are available for each DBMS in the directory. The optimizer determines a processing strategy by considering the idiosyncrasies of various DBMSs (e.g., the need to use ADDS functions for unsupported operations), and the different communication costs of local vs remote DBMS linked by communication lines with different speeds. The scheduler implements the query strategy developed by the optimizer. Subqueries that can be processed in parallel are sent to the appropriate database server. Relations formed by each subquery are returned to the scheduler, which enters the relation into the user's relational database, or sends them to another server if further processing is required.

The flow of information through various ADDS components is pictorially represented in Fig. 6. The user's query is analyzed by the UI for its correctness using ADDS directory information. At this stage, the UI determines the number of Parallel Task Processes (PTP) required. A request for PTP is sent to the TM, which allocates the required resources, and assigns these tasks to the RM. The RM prepares subqueries for each LDB, schedules the data retrieval, and sends subqueries to the allocated task processes. A server is started for each LDB within the open CDB. The server translates the ADDS subquery into the local DBMS language, executes the translated query, and returns data to the Request Manager for

268

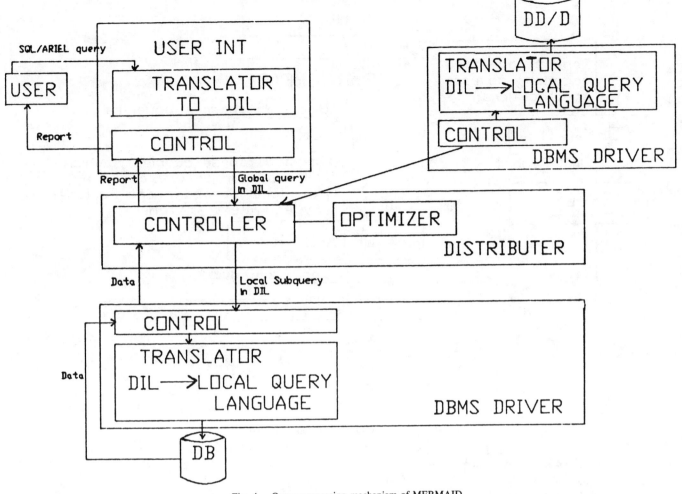

Fig. 4.   Query processing mechanism of MERMAID.

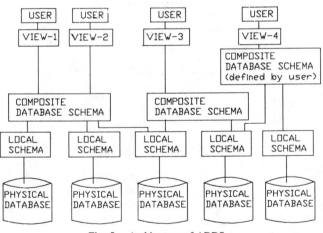

Fig. 5.   Architecture of ADDS.

merging with data from other LDBs. Relations are created from the output of subqueries.

This prototype provides a friendly user interface. It provides menus to the naive user, and experienced users can bypass these menus to pose their queries. It provides interactive and batch processing modes to the user. Usage of relations for the storage of intermediate results gives the user explicit control on relational algebra to reduce retransmission of data

whenever a series of similar requests are to be entered. Future enhancements include supporting update transactions, ADDS-to-ADDS communications, and tools for automatic CDB creation.

4.4. PRECI*

PRECI* is a prototype developed at the University of Keele. The schema architecture of PRECI* is as shown in Fig. 7. One peculiar aspect of PRECI* is its support of two varieties of nodes: inner nodes and outer nodes. Inner nodes provide the best available service to global users through global database schema and global external schema, and also facilities like location transparency and replication transparency. These facilities are not available for data at outer nodes because only data from inner nodes can participate in global schema.

In the architecture shown in Fig. 7, the lowest layer NES represents the nodal external schema which can be used by the local user. NDS is the nodal database schema. Each nodal DBMS must support at least a minimal subset of PAL language, viz., selection, projection, join, division, union, and difference. The Participation Schema (PS) describes the nodal data along with various authorization controls. Each participation schema has a version number which is updated each time

269

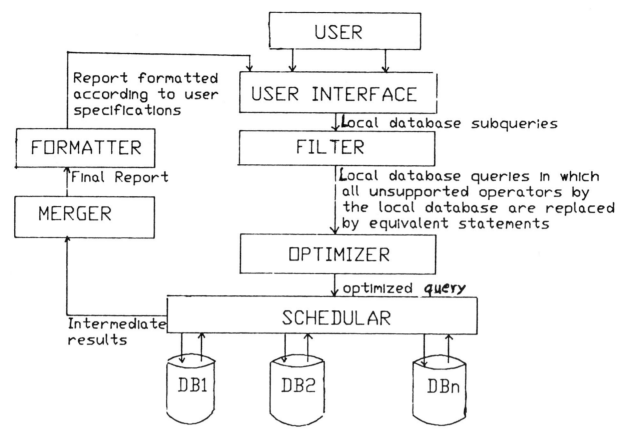

Fig. 6. Query processing mechanism in ADDS.

the PS is changed. The knowledge that is required to resolve data inconsistencies and the details of replication of data are stored in a separate database called the Subsidiary Database (SDB), which is managed by SDBMS (Subsidiary Database Management System) under the control of the DDBMS at each node. The GDS is formed by the PS of the inner nodes. The GDS supports integration data and metadata, which are stored in SDB. The GDS itself does not provide an integrated view. Instead, all conversion formulae and other relevant information are stored. The desired integration is carried out at the Global External Schema (GES).

The query processing mechanism of PRECI* is graphically shown in Fig. 8. The user query is validated at the originating node by the Global Query Processor (GQP) using the GES in the case of inner nodes, and the PS in the case of outer nodes, along with appropriate authorization checks. The query is then resolved into a set of intermediate subqueries by the optimizer, taking into account the availability of replicated data, availability of operators, and, finally, the communication costs. Considering these facts the GQP prepares a query tree, in which each subtree represents one or more subqueries for each selected execution node. Then the GQP prepares plans for subquery execution, one for each subquery. This plan consists of pre/post-execution instructions, relevant input/output data structures, and a list of actions to be invoked on specified execution.

The query plan generated by the GQP for each subquery is passed on to the Global Subquery Processor (GSP). The principal task of the GSP is to transform a subquery into one or

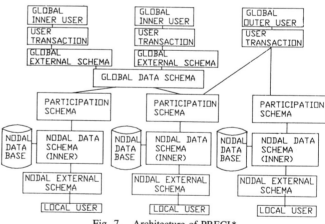

Fig. 7. Architecture of PRECI*.

more nodal queries, and submit them to the next stage for compilation. There are two reasons why a subquery may require further splitting or transformation. First, one of the operations of a subquery may be of a type that can be performed only by the SDBMS, but not by the NDBMS. Second, if the NDBMS does not support a PAL interface, the subquery must be transformed into the relational language supported at that node. The GSP eventually generates a nodal query plan which includes compilation or execution instructions.

The Nodal Query Processor (NQP), which is a part of the NDBMS, receives the nodal query plan, and retrieves the necessary data from the nodal database. These results are processed further, if required, and transmitted to the user.

270

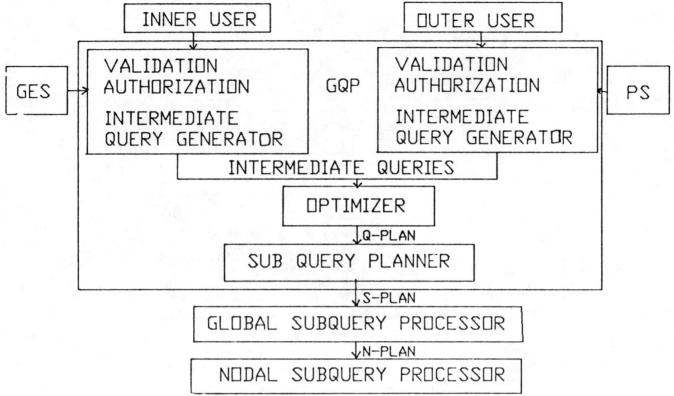

Fig. 8. Query processing mechanism in PRECI*.

The designers of PRECI* have aimed at a high degree of parallelism. While final processing is done at a result node as in MULTIBASE, PRECI* facilitates parallel-processing at multiple nodes. The designers of PRECI* are planning to implement global updates on base relations.

4.5. IMDAS

The Integrated Manufacturing Database Administration System (IMDAS) has been developed by the National Bureau of Standards of the United States, recently renamed as the National Institute of Standards and Technology. IMDAS supports only relational databases meant for manufacturing systems. The computing environment consists of a network of heterogeneous component systems acquired from various vendors. The system design envisages that the integrated database contain all data needed for control; in addition, this database should serve as a medium through which the component systems communicate with one another. IMDAS provides local autonomy, which is essential in a manufacturing environment, because the control and data systems must provide for the independent testing and modular integration of new equipment and control software.

The scheme architecture of IMDAS contains four layers as shown in Fig. 9. At the bottom level of the IMDAS are data repositories such as commercial DBMSs. These DBMSs are logically clustured into groups. The interface between DBMSs of each group and the rest of the IMDAS is provided by the Basic Data Administration System (BDAS). With the use of a dictionary describing the distribution of data at subordinate BDAS, the Distributive Data Administration System (DDAS) takes responsibility for all such hosts and their corresponding data. In order to resolve conflicts between various DDAS, a single system is designated as the Master DAS (MDAS).

The query processing mechanism is shown in Fig. 10. The user queries are received by DDAS, and converted into an IMDAS-internal form, which is used for all communications between MDAS, DDASs, and BDASs. By consulting the dictionary that describes how data are distributed at local BDASs, the DDAS performs query mapping. If the data are outside the scope of responsibility of the DDAS, it will send the transaction to the MDAS. If the transaction is completed, it is returned to the DDAS, and then to the user. The DDAS may also receive queries from the MDAS in order to complete the processing of another DDASs query. Once the DDAS has decided where to access the data required for a query, it schedules the query based on other activities in the system. If this involves distribution of different tasks to several BDAS, the scheduling and execution may occur in parallel, provided there are no conflicts. Data retrieved from each BDAS are assembled by the data assembly service of DDAS and ultimately supplied to the user.

The architecture of IMDAS is more suited to provide nodal autonomy, which is defined as a highly essential feature of the factory automation information system. IMDAS allows global updates on base relations only. Present research is on intelligent classification of data by service requirements, and on the design and placement of the integrity and concurrency control mechanism for different classes of data.

4.6. NDMS

The Network Data Management System (NDMS) is a prototype HDDBMS developed by CRAI, Italy. This system provides the user with a unified relational view of data and a single-relational query language. Local databases can be updated by the coordinated distributed processing application.

271

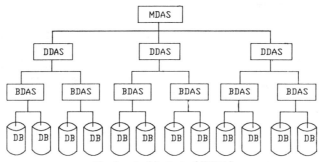

Fig. 9. Architecture of IMDAS.

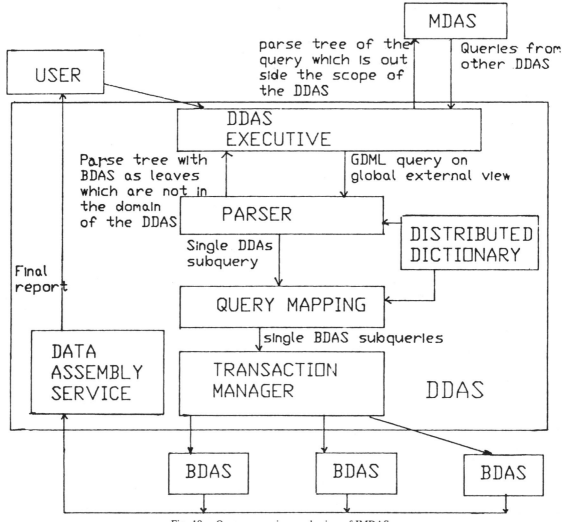

Fig. 10. Query processing mechanism of IMDAS.

It provides data integration of underlying databases, and solves all problems of data incompatibility.

The schema architecture of NDMS has three layers: the NDMS internal schema, the application schema, and end user views, as shown in Fig. 11. The NDMS internal schema is comprised of base relations defined as aggregations over the local databases. Mapping languages are available for the network and hierarchical data models. The view-definition mechanism of the host relational DBMS is used to define the respective aggregations. Naming conventions and semantic constraints are used to resolve the potential semantic conflicts that may arise during the internal schema definition resulting

from semantic incompatibilities between the local databases. The Nodal Data Administrators are responsible for NDMS applications at each node, and they define relational views using the SEQUEL view-definition mechanism, as a collection of data abstraction over the NDMS internal schema. The defined relational views are granted to the end users, who, in turn, may define their own specific data abstractions.

The query processing mechanism of NDMS is depicted in Fig. 12. The NDMS query processing strategy is comprised of three main elements; the intermediate storage structure, the query optimization, and the query execution.

Algebraic query tree transformation is performed to reduce

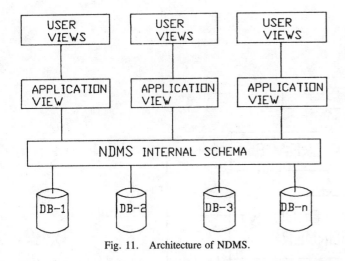

Fig. 11. Architecture of NDMS.

the size of intermediate query results. The SEQUEL query tree produced as a result of the algebraic transformation is processed by the query planner. The objective of the query planner is to produce an optimized query program, which is subsequently decomposed into a number of query subprograms. These subprograms are executed at the respective NDMS nodes, with the help of query optimization algorithms coupled with specialized storage organization. A special storage organization called Vectorial Data Representation (VDR), which is a hybrid transposed file organization, is used to increase the efficiency of local query processing and intersite relational operations. The query program and the resulting subprograms generated by the query planner are in the form of a sequence of the VDR data manipulation functions. These query subprograms are sent to the query server of their respective NDMS node. The query server receives the query subprogram from the queue, processes VDR functions in it, and stores the results in the intermediate storage. Once all these query subprograms are processed, all these intermediate results are merged and supplied to the user.

One special aspect of NDMS is its use of VDR data structure to store intermediate results. The designers are planning to design end user query interface to provide the graphic query interface and distributed design application tools. Research is continuing in the design of more sophisticated concurrency control mechanism for NDMS.

4.7. MRDSM

Multics Relational Data Store Multibase (MRDSM) has been developed by INRIA (France) to support multiple databases designed using the MRDS relational database management system of Honeywell. Heterogeneity is dealt with at the semantic level by providing uniform access to all databases implemented with same DBMS. The global query language, MDSL, is an extended version of DSL, which is the data manipulation language of MRDS.

The schema architecture of MRDSM is shown in Fig. 13. The global schema does not exist in MRDSM. Users can create conceptual schema known as multischema with elements from local database schemata.

The query processing mechanism is shown in Fig. 14. A

query in MDSL is received by the multiple query decomposer, which produces a Multidatabase Execution Plan (MEP) that consists of a set of monodatabase queries with interdatabase operations. The MEP is decomposed by the elementary multidatabase query decomposer by removing interdatabase operations that cannot be performed locally, producing single database queries. These single database queries are passed on to the execution plan processor. The execution plan processor initiates the MRDS single-DB queries at appropriate DBs, and collects partial results into the Working Database (WDB). Further processing is performed on intermediate results, which are loaded into the WDB, and the final result is transmitted to the user.

This system differs from most other prototypes described in this paper by not providing any global schema. The designers feel that providing a global schema is difficult even for a small number of databases because of the differences in data models, and other semantic conflicts. The second reason is that there is no general technique available for implementing updates through global schema. Another interesting aspect of this prototype is the application of knowledge processing techniques to simplify query expressions.

4.8. IISS

The Integrated Information Support System (IISS) is a prototype of a heterogeneous distributed database management system designed by the General Electric Company for the U.S. Air Force. This system has been designed to provide integrated data management facilities and distributed processing capabilities for heterogeneous databases resident on heterogeneous computer systems. This computing environment is to be used in three distinct manufacturing areas: shop floor management, decision support, and material requirement planning.

IISS supports databases designed using relational and network data models. The global data model used by IISS to support integrated application is $IDEF_1$ which is an ER-based model. The schema architecture of IISS is shown in Fig. 15. The lowest layer is the local host schema expressed in the data model of the local host database management system. The conceptual schema represents the data presented in all component databases of IISS expressed in $IDEF_1$. The external schema is a subset of conceptual schema defined based on the data requirement of a user to support the user application process. The user can pose a query to the corresponding external schema by an application process. The application process is a program in COBOL with embedded NDML (Neutral Data Manipulation Language) commands.

The query processing mechanism of IISS is shown in Fig. 16. Presently, IISS is not supporting ad hoc queries. Users can retrieve information only via application processes. The application process is a COBOL program including an NDML statement, which implements the logic of the intended application. The integrated application program is precompiled to transform the NDML statements into procedures which can be executed by the local host DBMS. The problems associated with the aggregation and data transforms pertaining to the distributed environment are also resolved by the precompiler.

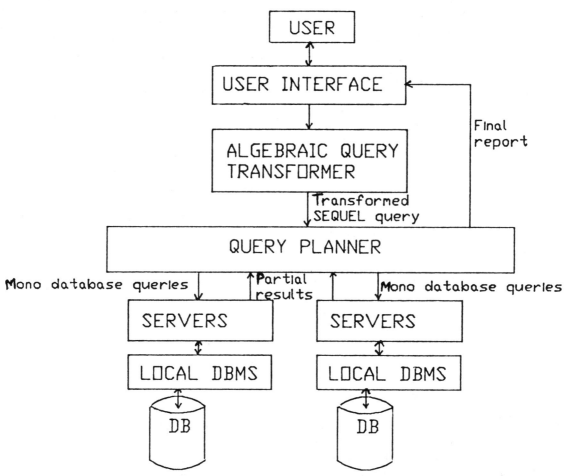

Fig. 12.   Query processing mechanism in NDMS.

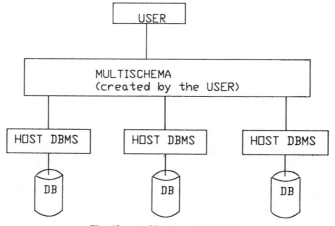

Fig. 13.   Architecture of MRDSM.

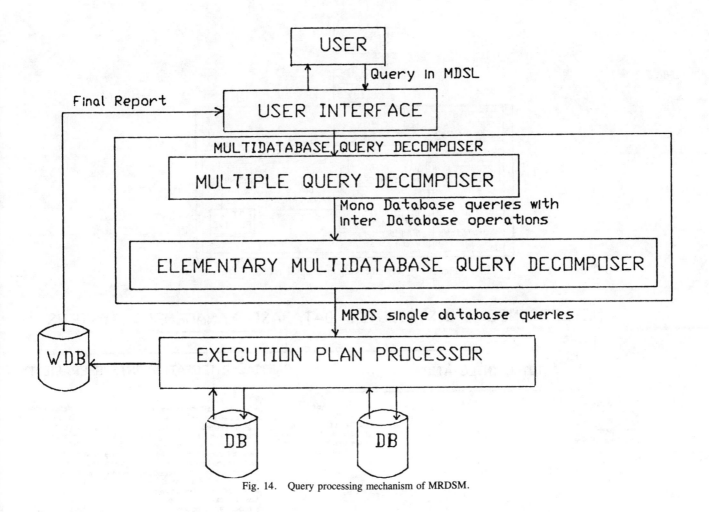

Fig. 14.   Query processing mechanism of MRDSM.

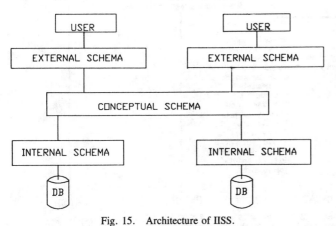

Fig. 15.   Architecture of IISS.

In the precompiler, the multinode NDML query, which is written against the external schema of the application, is transformed into its conceptual equivalent by the external schema/conceptual schema transformer (ES/CS). The resulting multinode conceptual NDML query is analyzed, and an optimized decomposition/aggregation strategy is formulated. This strategy reflects the storage characteristics of the distributed databases as expressed by the internal schemata. The multinode conceptual NDML query is decomposed into a set of single database NDML queries. For each single data NDML query processor, an internal access mechanism path is generated. The access path reflects the data structuring characteristics of the database holding the data. This information is derived from the internal schema of the database. A COBOL procedure based on the access path determined is then automatically generated. This COBOL procedure is nondatabase-manager-specific (although it reflects the data structure of a specific database), and as such it contains generic CODASYL data manipulation statements. In addition to the logic required to carry out the data retrieval operations, the query processor contains the logic required to transform the data retrieved from the internal format and units into the format and units specified by the conceptual schema. Once the generic query processor has been generated, the generic CODASYL data manipulation languages are replaced by the specific data manipulation statements recognized by the target database manager. The query aggregators perform the JOIN and PROJECT operations required to assemble the data specified by the distributed query. The data aggregators aggregate data presented to them in conceptual format and units. Likewise, aggregators present data to other aggregators in the same format. However, the last aggregator routes the aggregated data to the conceptual/external transformer. This module also performs the format and unit transformations required to return data in external/conceptual formats, and units to the querying application process. The distributed query processing mechanism specified by the precompiler is controlled and monitored by the query scheduler. This module monitors the status of various query processors, data aggrega-

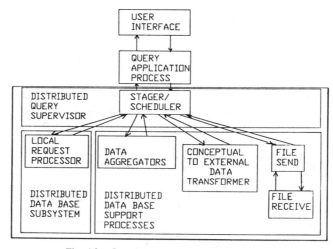

Fig. 16.   Query processing mechanism in IISS.

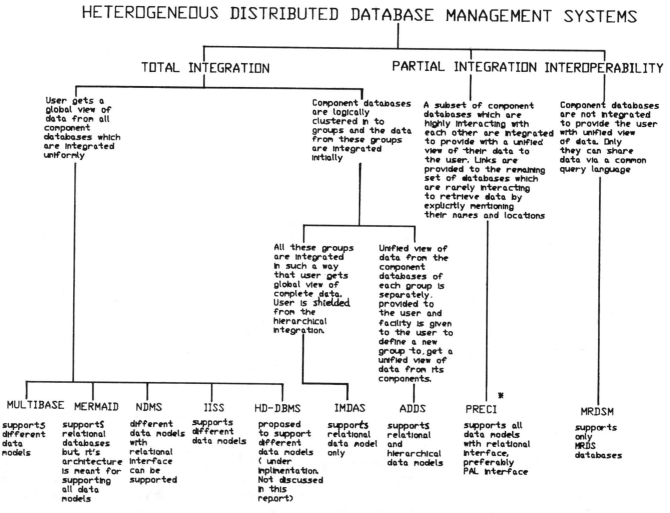

Fig. 17.   Classification of HDDBMS.

tors, and the conceptual-to-external transformer involved in distributed query processing.

5. CONCLUSIONS AND FUTURE DIRECTIONS

The prototypes discussed in the previous section can be broadly divided, based on their philosophy of integration, into three categories: total integration, partial integration, and interoperability. Total integration aims at giving the illusion that data of all component databases are stored under a centralized database management system; such integration provides a unified view, or global view, of all data to the user, who can pose his or her query on this global schema. At the other extreme, interoperability does not provide such a global schema; the user is presented with functions in visibly distinct schemata, which bear resemblance to schemata in existing databases. The intermediate category of partial integration is a hybrid of total integration and interoperability. It provides the global view for data of some component databases while, in other cases, the user must explicitly provide the location of the required data. The various prototypes discussed can be classified into these three broad categories, as depicted in Fig. 17.

It would be pertinent here to make some concluding observations about differences between homogeneous and heterogeneous systems. Since the design of a homogeneous DDBMS involves a top-down approach, replication is provided by the database designer considering the ratio of update transactions to query transactions [23]. The consistency is maintained by the global concurrency control mechanism. Replicated copies increase the availability and make query processing simpler and cost-effective. But the bottom-up approach followed in the design of heterogeneous DDBMS does not provide any control over the duplication of data. Since one of the objectives of an HDDBMS is to provide complete local autonomy to local DBMS sites, any change to the existing mechanism for concurrency control and recovery at local DBMSs must be ruled out. Distributed artificial intelligence techniques [24] may be used in designing a global concurrency control mechanism which uses concurrency control mechanisms of local databases as its components. Once the consistency among duplicated copies is guaranteed, the advantage of redundant information in query processing [25] can be exploited.

Semantic knowledge about the attributes domain [26], [27], [28] can be used to increase the efficiency of query processing in the HDDBMS environment. Knowledge about special processors attached to local DBMS, like database machines, finite element analyzers, etc., can also be used to increase query processing efficiency. Considerable efficiency can be achieved by keeping the knowledge of all local integrity constraints at the global level in order to reject all unqualified queries right at global level.

Query processing in an HDDBMS is inherently complex because of heterogeneity in the data model, in architecture, and in function. As such, it is desirable to develop a semantically-rich data model, and to use it as a global data model to achieve standardization in system architecture, components, and functions. Adoption of a common global data model, and standardization of other design procedures, will greatly simplify the task of integrating heterogeneous systems.

ACKNOWLEDGMENTS

The authors would like to thank Dr. Amar Gupta for his inputs on an earlier version of this paper. M. P. Reddy is financially supported by the University Grants Commission, New Delhi, under a Junior Research Fellowship.

REFERENCES

[1] Ceri, S. and G. Pelagatti, *Distributed Databases: Principles and Systems.* New York, NY: McGraw-Hill Computer Science Series, 1985.

[2] Traiger, I., *et al.*, "Transactions and consistency in distributed database management system," *ACM-TDOS,* vol. 7, no. 3, 1982.

[3] Bernstein, P. A. and N. Goodman, "Concurrency control in distributed database systems," *ACM Computing Surveys,* vol. 13, no. 2, 1981.

[4] ——, "A sophisticated introduction to distributed database concurrency control," presented at *Eighth VLDB,* Mexico City, 1982.

[5] Kohler, W. H., "A survey of techniques for synchronization and recovery in decentralized computer systems," *ACM Computing Surveys,* vol. 13, no. 2, 1981.

[6] Landers, T. and R. L. Rosenberg, "An overview of MULTIBASE," presented at *Second Symp. on Distributed Databases,* Berlin, W. Germany, Sept. 1982.

[7] Smith, J. M., *et al.*, "MULTIBASE—integrating heterogeneous distributed database system," in *Proc. of AFIPS,* vol. 50, 1981.

[8] Templeton, M., *et al.*, "MERMAID—A front-end to distributed heterogeneous databases," Tech. Rep., System Development Corporation, Santa Monica, CA., 1986.

[9] Templeton, M., D. Brill, A. Chen, S. Dao, and E. Lund, "MERMAID experience with network operation," presented at *IEEE Int. Conf. Data Eng.,* Los Angeles, CA, Feb. 1986.

[10] Breitbart, Y. J. and L. R. Tieman, "ADDS—Heterogeneous distributed database system," presented at *3rd Int. Seminar on Distributed Data Sharing Syst.,* Italy, Mar. 1984.

[11] Deen, S. M., *et al.*, "The design of a canonical database (PRECI*)," *Computer J.,* vol. 24, no. 3, 1981.

[12] Deen, S. M., R. R. Amin, and M. C. Taylor, "Query decomposition in PRECI*," presented at *3rd Int. Seminar on Distributed Data Sharing Syst.,* Italy, Mar. 1984.

[13] Deen, S. M., R. R. Amin, G. O. Ofori-Dwumfuo, and M. C. Taylor, "The architecture of a generalized distributed database system—PRECI*," *Computer J.,* vol. 28, no. 3, 1985.

[14] Deen, S. M., R. R. Amin, and M. C. Taylor, "Implementation of a prototype for PRECI*," *Computer J.,* vol. 30, no. 2, 1987.

[15] Libes, D. and E. Barkmeyer, "IMDAS: An overview," Draft Rep., Integrated Systems Group, NBS, Gaithersburg, MD, 1986.

[16] Barkmeyer, E., *et al.*, "An architecture for distributed data management in computer integrated manufacturing," Rep. No. NBSIR 86-3312, NBS, Jan. 1986.

[17] Staniszkis, W., *et al.*, "Architecture of the network data management systems," presented at *3rd Int. Seminar on Distributed Data Sharing Syst.,* Italy, Mar. 1984.

[18] Litwin, W. and A. Abdellatif, "Multidatabase interoperability," *Computer,* Dec. 1986.

[20] Wong, K. K. and P. Bazex, "MRDSM: A relational multidatabase management system," presented at *3rd Int. Seminar on Distributed Data Sharing Syst.,* Italy, Mar. 1984.

[21] *Integrated Information Support Systems (IISS) Report,* Rep. No. SDS 620140000, ICAM, Materials Laboratory, Air Force Systems Command, Wright-Patterson AFB, Feb. 1983.

[22] Bhalla, S., B. E. Prasad, Amar Gupta, and S. E. Madnick, "A framework and comparative study of distributed database management systems," Working Paper No. 1981-88, Sloan School of Management, MIT, Feb. 1988.

[23] Muro, S., *et al.*, "Evaluation of the file redundancy in distributed database systems," *IEEE Trans. Software Eng.,* vol. SE-11, no. 2, Feb. 1985.

[24] Ju-Yuan *et al.*, "An architecture for control and communications in distributed artificial intelligence systems," *IEEE Trans. Syst., Man, Cybernetics,* vol. SMC-15, no. 3, May/June 1985.

[25] Wong, E., "Dynamic re-materialization: Processing distributed queries using redundant data," presented at *Fifth Int. Berkeley Workshop on Distributed Data Management and Computer Networks,* 1981.

[26] King, J. J., "QUIST: A system for semantic query optimization in relational databases," presented at *Seventh VLDB,* 1982.

[27] Chakarvarthy, U. S., D. H. Fishman, and J. Minker, "Semantic query optimization in expert systems and database systems," in *Proc. First Int. Workshop on Expert Database Syst.,* Kiawah Island, SC, Oct. 1984.

[28] Jarke, M., "External semantic query simplification: A graph-theoretic approach and its implication in Prolog," in *Proc. First Int. Workshop on Expert Database Systems,* Kiawah Island, SC, Oct. 1984.

Part 4
Auxiliary Issues

THIS concluding part of the book presents four auxiliary issues related to integration of dissimilar systems.

In the first paper of this part, Paul Thompson presents a framework for integrating the three major reference models for information engineering. He also describes the PRECISE approach to engineering information systems. Another model for information mapping is described by Ramey and Brown in [1].

Next, Patricia Dwyer and James Larson describe their experiences with a distributed database testbed system. This system was developed for evaluating alternative approaches and algorithms for managing information stored in several databases on different systems.

In the following paper, Lynette Hirschman emphasizes the importance of natural language interfaces for large-scale information processing. After examining all the relevant technologies, she concludes that during the next seven years, we should witness major advances in our ability to interact with computer-based information systems via natural language, both written and spoken.

In the last paper, Deborah Estrin discusses the unique usage-control requirements that characterize most situations involving integration across organizational boundaries. She describes a conceptual model for implementing usage controls in interorganizational networks. Such controls enable organizations to implement a strategy that allows only selected pieces of information systems to be accessed on an external basis.

The organizational and strategic issues related to integration of information systems across organizational boundaries have been analyzed by Nohria and Venkatraman in [2]. The key conceptual elements in the analysis and establishment of interorganizational networks are summarized in Table I, and the structural properties of such networks are shown in Table II. They emphaisze that issues such as assignment of coordinating role, ownershap, and estblishment of standards play an unusually critical role in a heterogeneous environment.

Based on the current trends in the areas of databases, expert systems, connectivity, natural language interfaces, speech recognition, information engineering, and other relevant areas, it appears that the 1990s will witness major strides in the field of integration of dissimilar information systems, with a number of organizations opting to introduce this nascent, commercially-available technology. Just as the evolution of integrated database management technology displaced conventional piecemeal programming approaches in the 1960s, similarly the new information integration approaches will lead

TABLE I
CONCEPTUAL ELEMENTS IN THE ANALYSIS OF NETWORKS

ELEMENT	CRITERIA
1. Delimitation of a relevant organizational field	— Functional interdependence — Exchange/transactional interdependence — Relevant analytical boundary such as geography, industry, etc.
2. Selection and definition of nodes	— Level of aggregation; individuals, groups, organizations, communities, nations, etc. — Distinguish between inter- and intra-organizational transactions — Distinguish between multiple roles and statuses
3. Type of linkage	— Transactional; expressive, instrumental, cognitive or objective — Organizational interpenetration; joint membership, joint programs, joint ventures, etc.
4. Nature of links	— Strength — Intensity — Symmetry — Reciprocity — Formalization — Standardization — Frequency — Loose vs Tight — Direct vs Indirect — Multiplexity
5. Modalities (cultural context) of network formation	— Normative context; competitive, contingent cooperation, or mandated cooperation
6. Historical context of network formation	— Place and time of network formation enter into explanations

to a significantly different computational environment by the year 2000 A.D.!

REFERENCES FOR PART 4

[1] Ramey, T. L. and R. R. Brown, "Entity link key attribute semantic information modeling: the Elka model," in *Technical Opinions Regarding Knowledge-Based Integrated Information Systems Engineering*, A. Gupta and S. Madnick, Eds., MIT, Cambridge, MA, 1987, pp. 171–199. (NTIS and DTIC Accession Number A 195857).

[2] Nohria, N. and N. Venkatraman, "Interorganizational information systems via information technology: A network perspective," in *Strategic, Organizational, and Standardization Aspects of Integrated Information Systems*, A. Gupta and S. Madnick, Eds. MIT, Cambridge, MA, 1987, pp. 171–199. (NTIS and DTIC Accession Number A 195855).

TABLE II
STRUCTURAL PROPERTIES OF NETWORKS

STRUCTURAL PROPERTY	EXPLANATION
A. Overall Network	
1. Size	Number of individuals participating in the network
2. Density	The ratio of potential ties to actual ties
3. Connectivity	The degree to which members of the network are linked to one another through direct or indirect ties. (A maximally dense network is fully connected, but full connectivity is also compatible with low density.)
4. Clustering	The number of dense regions in a network
5. Hierarchy	Degree to which members direct unreciprocated ties to other members
6. Reachability	Average number of links between any two individuals in the network
B. Network Partitions	
1. Cohesiveness	Partitions of networks that interact maximally with each other and minimally with others
2. Equivalence	Organizations in each partition share similar relations with organizations in other blocks whether or not they are connected to each other
C. Nodes	
1. Liaisons	Nodes with maximal interaction with members of other groups or liaisons, but not with any particular group
2. Bridges	Group members who are linked to other groups directly
3. Gatekeepers	Group members who serve as interface with non-group members
4. Isolates	Nodes that have the least number of links with other members of the network
5. Centrality as measure of activity	Total direct nominations in a network
6. Centrality as measure of betweeness	Nominations in pathways of connectivity
7. Centrality as measure of closeness	Distance from different clusters

BIBLIOGRAPHY FOR PART 4

[1] Appleton, D. S., "Very large projects," *Datamation,* Jan. 1986, pp. 63–70.

[2] Bachman, C. W. and R. G. Ross, "Toward a more complete model of computer-based information systems," *Computers and Standards,* vol. 1, 1982, pp. 35–48.

[3] Breitbart, Y., *et al.,* "Performance evaluation of a simulation model for data retrieval in a heterogeneous database environment," in *Proc. 1984 IEEE Conf. on Trends and Applications,* pp. 190–197.

[4] Gray, J. N. and M. Anderton, "Distributed computer systems: Four case studies," *Proc. IEEE,* May 1987, pp. 719–733.

[5] Hackathorn, R. D. and J. Karimi, *Comparative Evaluation of Information Engineering Methods,* Working Paper, University of Colorado at Denver, Feb. 1986.

[6] Lee, D. T., "Decision support in a distributed environment," in *Proc. National Computer Conf.,* Las Vegas, NV, July 9–12, 1984, pp. 447–488.

[7] Nijssen, G. M., "From databases towards knowledge bases,"

DBMSs-Technical Comparison. Maidenhead, UK: Pergamon Infotech Limited, 1983, pp. 114–131.

[8] Sarin, S. K. and N. A. Lynch, "Discarding obsolete information in a replicated database system," *IEEE Trans. Software Eng.,* vol. SE-13, no. 1, Jan. 1987, pp. 39–47.

[9] Shaw, M. J., "A knowledge-based framework for distributed decision support systems," in *Proc. Sixteenth Ann. Pittsburgh Conf. on Modeling and Simulation,* vol. 16, part 3, Apr. 1985, pp. 831–836.

[10] Sirbu, M. and K. Hughes, "Standardization of local area networks," presented at the *Fourteenth Ann. Telecommun. Policy Res. Conf.,* Airlie, VA, Apr. 1986.

[11] Steinberg, C., "Data retrieval in a distributed telemetry ground data system," *Data Eng.,* vol. 10, no. 3, Sept. 1987, pp. 53–59.

[12] Tanenbaum, A. S. and R. V. Renesse, "Distributed operating systems," *ACM Computing Surveys,* vol. 17, no. 4, Dec. 1985, pp. 419–470.

[13] Thompson, P., "Natural language analysis, information modeling, and database engineering," in *Proc. of Eighteenth Hawaii Int. Conf. on Syst. Sci.,* 1985, pp. 500–514.

Reference Models for Information Engineering

PAUL THOMPSON

Abstract—This paper describes three important reference models and one engineering framework for data sharing and exchange. It relates reference models to standards activities, and shows how to integrate them. This integration is not widely recognized. This paper also gives examples of technical models to illustrate the content of an engineering framework approach in the context of engineering and manufacturing enterprises.

OVERVIEW

First, we present an overview of the current state of industrial automation and the need for information engineering techniques. Then, we discuss three reference models for standards activities: The ISO/Open Systems Interconnection, the ISO/Conceptual Schema Concepts, and the ANSI/Three Schema Architecture. Next, we present the PRECISE* engineering framework for data-driven conceptualization, specification, design, and development. We illustrate this framework with two technical models. Finally, we describe directions for future work.

ASSESSMENT OF THE CURRENT SITUATION

Historical Trends and Pressures

Economic Developments—Today's engineering and manufacturing enterprises face new economic developments. We see increasing pressure from competitors, unstable interest and foreign exchange rates, increasing speed of technology transfer, low offshore labor costs, new materials and processes, changing markets, new environmental laws, and so on.

The pace of economic change shows clearly in the record numbers of new business start-ups, mergers, and bankruptcies of the last few years.

Information System Developments

Industrial Automation—Two important technological changes for the engineering and manufacturing community are the dramatic decrease in the cost of, and the enormous increase in capability of, information systems hardware and software. These two forces drive the change from an industrial age to a mixed industrial/information age.

As a result, information systems hardware and software are becoming very important to managers, engineers, and factory workers of all kinds, and this importance is reflected at many levels.

First, we are designing more intelligence into the end product of the enterprise, for example, digital dashboards, voice warnings, and computer controlled ignition and diagnosis in new automobiles. This intelligence provides added value to the product.

Second, we are putting more automation into the design and manufacturing processes for better quality, and more flexible and more efficient production. Examples are assembly robots, flexible manufacturing cells, engineering design analysis programs, expert system diagnosis, product and configuration databases, CAD/CAM/CAE support tools, and so forth.

Third, we are transmitting more data electronically between the enterprise, its divisions, suppliers, and customers. We are wiring together the "islands of automation" inside and outside the enterprise. Even firms which have believed automation was too expensive for them are now being dragged into the information age as their important customers insist upon electronic data exchange.

Computers and Information Systems Science: Yesterday and Today—In the early days we spent our time on algorithms to crunch numbers, and on building data processing systems to track the accounting figures. We located data processing systems in the administrative offices, away from the day to day activities of the enterprise. We considered computers a separate department. We did not consider them to be part of our business, engineering, and manufacturing processes.

Today, we are concerned with databases, expert systems, graphics, communications, and on-line integrated systems. Engineering and manufacturing divisions, not the administrative offices, are now taking the lead in developing and installing advanced computer applications. We are bringing advanced automation directly to the workers.

In the past, it was sufficient for a programmer to learn a scientific or business programming language to do useful work. Today, the computer specialist has to be an expert in many information system technologies and modeling techniques.

Need for Advanced Information Engineering

However, despite the power of today's computer hardware, we continue to have problems developing applications that meet the user's and organization's needs. Information systems construction remains a complex, labor intensive, high-risk operation.

Some reasons for development problems include:

- Good work demands a thorough understanding of both the user's world and the computer world. (One barely has time to be an expert in even one of these areas.)

Reprinted with permission from *First Symp. Knowledge-Based Integrated Info. Sys. Eng.,* Feb. 1987.
© Copyright 1987 MIT.

- Rapid technological advances quickly outdate our current knowledge.
- Vendors promote their own unique systems, ignoring or diluting standards.
- The technology of computers is so fascinating that many of our best people become experts in the technology before, and instead of, understanding the problems they have to solve.
- The enormous labor required to build and debug the systems of the past acts as a brake on the introduction of new work methods and development solutions. (We call this the legacy problem.)

Of all development problems, one problem stands out: the difficulty of truly integrating systems so that the various parts work together intelligently and synergistically.

It is not hard to buy stand-alone applications. It is not hard to wire the hardware together. But it is very hard to get the systems to communicate intelligently with each other. And it is very hard to build them sound enough that they can grow and change with the enterprise without rewrites.

Information engineering is that branch of information systems science that offers some solutions to these problems. Information engineering is an approach to building integrated systems based on reference models and modeling methodologies. Information engineering builds sound, truly integrated systems.

Information engineering develops sound, integrated information systems the same way our best companies build their own complex products: by using an engineering process to determine objectives and requirements, to specify and analyze designs, to prototype products before production, and to manage the process by objectives, costs, and schedules.

Like other forms of engineering, information engineering uses modeling and analysis technologies appropriate to the development phase. These modeling and analysis technologies come from basic information science fundamentals.

Reference models capture and delineate these principles for ease of learning, discussion, and standard-making.

Information Engineering Reference Models

A reference model prescribes the important, fundamental form of a subject area. It identifies major concepts, functions, purposes, and building blocks. A reference model sets direction for future project and standards work activities. These work activities may develop one or more standards under the reference model.

Here, we discuss three categories of reference models used in information engineering. The standards reference models originate from national and international standards activities. Most deal with data organization or communication. Engineering framework models identify needed technical models and the organization of people and activities necessary to accomplish effective work efforts. The technical reference models specify analysis and design techniques to analyze problems and specify solutions. Most technical models have a strong graphical component.

We discuss below a few of the more important examples of each kind.

TABLE 1
ABBREVIATIONS

ANSI	American National Standards Institute
BRM	Binary Relationship Model
CAD	Computer Aided Design
CAE	Computer Aided Engineering
CAM	Computer Aided Manufacturing
CCITT	Consultative Committee on International Telegraphy and Telephony
CDC	Control Data Corporation
CS	Conceptual Schema
DBMS	Database Management System
EAR	Entity Attribute Relationship
ES	External Schema
FFM	Functional Flow Model
FM	Functional Model
IA	Information Analysis
IE	Information Engineering
IEEE	Institute of Electrical and Electronic Engineers
IPL	Interpreted Predicate Logic
IS	Internal Schema
ISO	International Standards Organization
LAN	Local Area Network
NIAM	Nijssen's Information Analysis Method
OSI	Open Systems Interconnection
SPARC	Study Planning and Requirements Committee
SQL	Structured Query Language
TC97/SC5/WG3	Technical Committee-Subcommittee-Working Group

Major Standards and Models

The ISO Open Systems Interconnection Model [1], [2], [3]

The Open Systems Interconnection Reference Model is a result of work by the International Standards Organization (ISO) and the Consultative Committee on International Telegraphy and Telephony (CCITT). Its purpose is to bring order into the connection of distributed computer systems and the exchange of messages among them.

The ISO/OSI model partitions the communications process into seven layers to provide modularity and ease standardization. Lower layer functions deal with physical communications and links. The higher layer functions deal with functionality and protocols.

More people are probably aware of this model than the other two models. When an organization reaches the point that it wants to tie together distributed computers (often from different vendors), it needs a communication model. This model permits it to evaluate vendor offerings. It gives some assurance that the investment in communication hardware and software will not be wasted.

The ISO/OSI Model

The seven layers are:

1. physical—electrical and physical connections; network topology.
2. data link—format of discrete message frames; control of error between 2 nodes; layer 2 guarantees correct message transmission.
3. network—routing of packets between networks of multi-link paths; flow regulation and status messages.
4. transport—reliable transparent multilink paths; physical addresses; layer 4 guarantees correct packet transmission.
5. session—communication between user programs; device names instead of addresses.
6. presentation—data restructuring; encryption; how applications enter the network.
7. applications—services for application programs; for example, electronic mail.

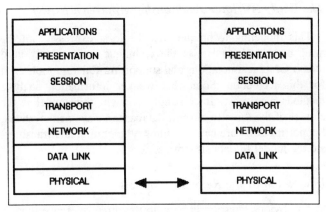

Fig. 1.   The OSI 7 layer model.

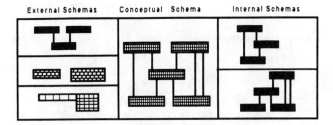

Fig. 2.   The ANSI/SPARC 3 schema architecture.

IEEE 802 Standards

Experts have found it easy to agree upon standards for the lower layers (1–3) of this architecture. Indeed, the Institute of Electrical and Electronic Engineers (IEEE) LAN-802 Standards Committee has proposed three different standards for these layers:

1. 802.3 baseband or broadband transmission over a bus architecture using carrier-sense multiple-access with collision detection. This is the basis of the Xerox Ethernet and the IBM PC Network.
2. 802.4 token-passing bus architecture.
3. 802.5 token-passing ring architecture, such as the IBM Token-Ring Network.

The ANSI/SPARC 3-Schema Architecture [4], [5]

In 1977, the Study Planning and Requirements Committee (SPARC) of the American National Standards Institute (ANSI) published a report on requirements for database systems. This report has since become known as the three schema architecture report. In the database world this report has enormous (and still growing) influence.

Previously, all database management proposals defined the properties of data in one database schema with some permitted subsetting into subschemas. These proposals were limited and not powerful enough to handle engineering and manufacturing enterprise problems, or to achieve data independence.

The ANSI/SPARC committee recognized the need for three schema types to express three different views of the data. Today most people agree that a three schema architecture is absolutely essential to integrated information systems.

The three schemas are:

- *One conceptual schema*—A conceptual schema models the enterprise view of the data. The conceptual schema comprises the "what" of the enterprise data. The conceptual schema must carry the semantics of the data to permit intelligent database systems.
- *Multiple internal schemas*—An internal schema describes the physical structure of the data on one or more computers, using various database structuring packages. Internal schemas comprise the "how" of efficient physical data storage. With an internal schema, one can tune an

application *after* it is running. Also, one needs to change only the internal schema, not the program code. This provides run-time efficiency and development productivity.
- *Multiple external schemas*—An external schema describes the user's view of the data (or his or her program's view of the data). External schemas comprise the "how" of data usage. Different groups within the enterprise want to view the data differently. They can, when they use external schemas. Also, some applications run better with a relational table view of data, and some with a record-at-a-time network view of data. A programmer can design the best external schema for his or her application.

Relationship of ANSI/SPARC 3-Schema Architecture to Database Standards

At present, the only database language standard is SQL. SQL is both an ANSI and ISO standard. The CREATE TABLE statements of SQL correspond to an ANSI conceptual schema, although a very simple one, and a semantically weak one. Other SQL statements create tabular views. These are somewhat equivalent to the ANSI external schema. SQL has no internal schema.

The ISO Conceptual Schema Concepts [6], [7]

The most important ANSI/SPARC schema is the conceptual schema. The conceptual schema constitutes both a model of the enterprise and an information contract between the modelers and the implementers of a database system. To be effective one needs a powerful conceptual schema. With it one can build intelligent database systems, reduce development costs, and provide a stable platform for various applications.

Also it is important to have an equally powerful information analysis method for the design of the conceptual schema.

ISO committee TC97/SC5/WG3 studied conceptual schema needs. They derived a set of concepts and principles for the conceptual schema, and a set of assessment guidelines for conceptual schema proposals. The committee also considered and evaluated three candidates for the conceptual schema language. Working on a common case study, they documented the principles of the three candidates and evaluated their power. Fig. 3 summarizes the results of their study and evaluation.

The Interpreted Predicate Logic Model (IPL)

IPL was the most expressive of the three models compared. Based on predicate logic and mathematical notation, it was

	EAR	BRM	IPL
Propositions modeled	25	40	47
Based on	Data	Semantics	Math
Graphical notation	X	X	
Tools	X	X	

Fig. 3. Comparison of conceptual schema models.

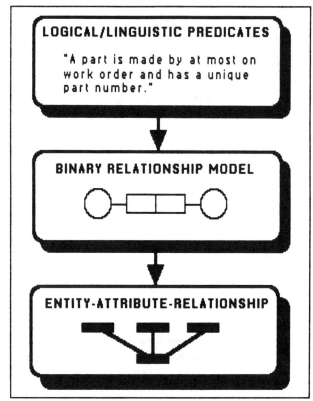

Fig. 4. The ISO conceptual schema concepts.

able to describe the entire universe of discourse of the sample problem.

However, IPL has some serious limitations. It does not have a graphical notation, it does not have software tool support, and it does not come with an information analysis method. The degree of mathematization makes the model attractive to mathematicians, but acts as a barrier to less highly trained practitioners.

The Binary Relationship Model (BRM)

This modeling technique is more semantically expressive than IPL. It comes with a rich and interesting graphical notation, a strong information analysis methodology, and supporting software tools for aid in analysis and database engineering. The model has basic but powerful and graphical constraint rules based on set theory. It also has an advanced constraint language (not documented in the report) which is as powerful as IPL.

Supporting software can automatically categorize entities, analyze references, migrate keys, fully normalize relations, and generate database schemas.

The Entity Attribute Relationship Approach (EAR)

This modeling technique was the least expressive of the three compared, and it is the technique most widely used today. Graphical notations and supporting software tools exist for this technique. Somewhat weaker information analysis methods also exist. Interestingly enough, this model is the closest of the three to current database management systems. Supporting software can provide key migration and transliterate the model to data structures.

Integration of the Reference Models

An obvious question is how do the three reference models relate, since standards work does not exist in isolation. Project and information engineers have to use their results in a consistent step-by-step approach to development and deployment. Isolated and unconnected reference models would be of little practical use.

Integration of OSI and 3-Schema Models—The highlights of the OSI and 3-schema models are: .

1. The OSI model is an architectural model for DATA EXCHANGE. The 3-schema model is an architecture model for DATA SHARING. Data which are exchanged are data in motion. Data which are shared are data at rest. At a certain level of abstraction the user is unconcerned whether the data received originated in a shared database or is exchanged (transmitted) from a remote user. The user is concerned with the message, not the medium.
2. The OSI model describes "how" the data is physically transported.
3. The 3-schema model describes:
   - HOW users and programs view the data (external schema).
   - WHAT the data means (conceptual schema).
   - HOW the computer stores the data (internal schema).

The OSI model and the internal schema both describe the physical format and access of data. (The OSI Model describes the format in great detail because it aims for open systems. The internal schema is just the top structure of a physical data structuring. The lower levels are a private part of the vendors' database management systems.)

It is clear that the integration point for the two models is the internal schema. In a data sharing environment, the user will store the data in a database. The user (or his or her friendly database engineer) will describe that database with an internal schema. In a data exchange environment, the user (or the friendly communications expert) will conduct the communication through the OSI 7 layer model.

Looked at from another point of view, one can consider the external and conceptual schemas as being layers 8 and 9 in the current open systems architecture.

Integration of ISO/Conceptual Schema (CS) [8], [9]

Whereas the previous two reference models prescribed computer hardware and software architectures, the ISO/

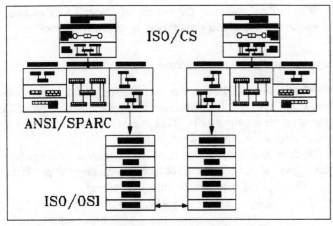

Fig. 5. Integration of the three reference models.

conceptual schemas is more a developmental approach, or at least can be viewed as such. We can use the results of the ISO/CS report to put together an information analysis approach, and link the resulting conceptual schema to the ANSI/SPARC conceptual schema.

The purpose of good information analysis is to develop a rigorously correct, consistent, understood, and agreed-upon problem-oriented conceptual schema. This conceptual schema is both a formal description of the user's information problem, and a prescription for any database design.

A problem-oriented conceptual schema resulting from an information analysis determines the construction of the database conceptual schema, if one wishes to use database technology. The same problem-oriented conceptual schema can just as easily determine a frames structure or an object-oriented database design, one needs knowledge-base technology. It can even help the individual decide between the two!

One well-tested way of conducting an information analysis is to collect user statements of the meaning of data in their environments, integrate these statements into a semantic network so that all relationships are clear, and then carefully construct a data model from the resulting knowledge. Although it is unlikely that the ISO committee had this method in mind when it examined the three candidate models, the models do lend themselves to this approach.

We can construct an information analysis method using the ISO candidate models as follows:

1. Collect user statements or predicates. Analyze these user predicates for fact and rule content. The Interpreted Predicate Model provides a formal mathematical symbolism for this analysis.
2. Integrate these statements into a semantic network to show relationships and to check for consistency. The binary relationship model provides formal graphical and lexical symbolism for this work.
3. Transform the binary network into a data model. The Entity Attribute Relationship data model provides a good mechanism for recording data design decisions.
4. If one is going to share data, then transform the data model into a database conceptual schema. Next, determine the external schemas and internal schemas based on access needs.

5. Or, if one desires to exchange data, determine the products and standards to be used according to the OSI model. Then determine a neutral conceptual schema and any external schemas needed.

Framework Models [10]

A framework describes in general terms the steps involved in information engineering, and identifies the modeling techniques or classes of techniques to be used. A framework is a model of models.

There are very few consistently thought-out framework approaches published today. As far as we know Control Data Corporation (CDC) is the only company that has documented such an approach. We will describe their approach here.

CDC calls their product PRECISE* Information Engineering. The PRECISE approach to engineering information systems consists of a framework, a project guide model, methodologies, techniques, tools, training, and consulting services.

The PRECISE* framework satisfies many of the requirements placed on an information engineering approach. This framework covers all steps from the strategic planning down to detailed design. It balances input from strategic planners, domain experts, and technical engineers. It relates activity analysis and design to data analysis and design. It combines modeling techniques at the conceptual level with data-driven design and implementation.

The outline of the framework is simple but important for its balance. There are three levels: strategic, tactical, and technical. Within each level are four models. The upper two models document the "what" and the lower two models document the "how." The right two models document the "data" and the left two models document the "activity."

Strategic Information Engineering

Strategic information engineering models the enterprise. It determines its information needs and requirements for information systems.

The Enterprise Model—The function model is a hierarchy of the enterprise functions and their information needs. It is independent of current organizational structure, current methods, and current technology. The function model forms a stable foundation for the specification and development of information systems capable of surviving both environmental and technological changes.

The entity model defines the objects of major interest to the enterprise, and the relationships between objects and functions.

The Planning Model—Since the development of an integrated information system is a major effort, PRECISE* determines separate and managable project efforts based on the results of the modeling, dependencies, immediate critical needs, and resource availability. It puts these together in the application plan and the subject database plan.

Tactical Information Engineering

Tactical information engineering develops thorough and accurate specifications of all user requirements needed to meet

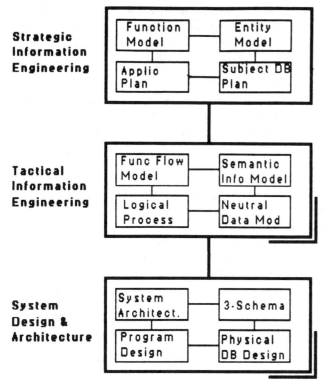

Strategic Information Engineering

| Funtion Model | Entity Model |
| Applic Plan | Subject DB Plan |

Tactical Information Engineering

| Func Flow Model | Semantic Info Model |
| Logical Process | Neutral Data Mod |

System Design & Architecture

| System Architect. | 3-Schema |
| Program Design | Physical DB Design |

Fig. 6. PRECISE* information engineering.

strategic and tactical objectives. This phase repeats for each project effort, until the set of integrated requirements specifications is complete.

Tactical information engineering distinguishes between a domain and the information system within the domain.

Domain or Object System Modeling—The function flow model is a refinement of the function model developed during the strategic planning activity. For the functions that fall within the scope of a particular project, PRECISE* determines and documents the subfunctions, environments, and flows.

The Semantic Information Model is a rich semantic network that, as the name implies, concentrates on the meaning of information rather than on data structure. It contains object types, fact types, and all-important protective constraints. PRECISE* uses a unique methodology. It begins with everyday natural language of the domain experts and steps through an exact linguistic analysis until it reaches the semantic network.

Information System Modeling—The logical process model defines the scope of the information system and specifies the logic of processes to support functions. Functions decompose into either manual processes or automated processes. The model includes information stores, frequency of occurrence, response time requirements, triggers, and authorization.

PRECISE* generates the neutral data model from the semantic information model by strict rules that preserve the model integrity independent of any database structure or product. The neutral data model provides a richness of data structure equal to or beyond any database management product now available. The thoroughness of the data structure enables one to select the most suitable database manager.

To further enhance the value of models, PRECISE* prescribes a validation prototyping to confirm the models.

System and Data Architecture

The system and data architecture phase translates specifications into a design. It builds more refined and detailed models based on the previous work. This phase repeats as necessary to yield implementable software projects.

System and data architecture distinguishes between the modeling of the technical solution (technology dependent), and the physical solution (product dependent).

The Technical Solution—PRECISE* organizes the specifications of subsystems, procedures, programs, subprograms, etc., into the system architecture model. Guided by the function model, logical processes group to form run units. Existing systems map into the design, and interfaces connect the old and new. With the help of users, design engineers design screens and reports. Creating the system architecture also involves evaluating technical alternatives, and selecting distributions of system components and local and remote communications means. On the data side, the three-schema model separates the enterprise definition of the database from physical storage characteristics and usage views of the data. The external schemas derive their data and navigational needs from the logical processes. In turn, the internal schemas derive their data needs from distribution analysis, and their access mechanisms from the need to support external schemas' joins and navigation, and also from conceptual schema constraint checking.

A design prototype verifies that user interfaces (screen and report layouts) are not only acceptable, but will increase the productivity of the end user. When needed, the system design and architecture phase investigates an application's potential performance with a performance prototype or benchmark.

The Physical Solution—The program design and the physical data model develop detailed, product specific designs. These models specify in detail how to use selected products. Detailed program design goes down to a pseudocode level using data-driven design techniques. The physical data model describes how to store the data. It describes the files, keys, indices, sequences, physical file placement, etc.

Technical Models [11]

To illustrate how the various technical models fit into an information engineering framework, we select and describe two models from the Tactical Information Engineering phase. These are newer and more effective conceptual models than the reader may be acquainted with. For each model, we describe its purpose, the concepts modeled, and the process used to create it.

Functional Flow Model

Purpose of a Functional Flow Model—A functional flow model represents the engineering, manufacturing, and management functions essential to the enterprise, and the flows between those functions. This model is independent of any

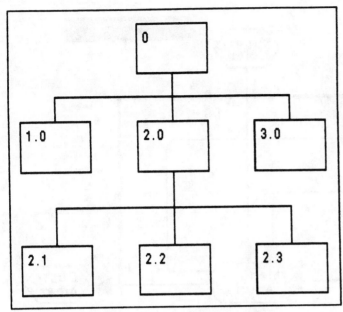

Fig. 7. Functional decomposition.

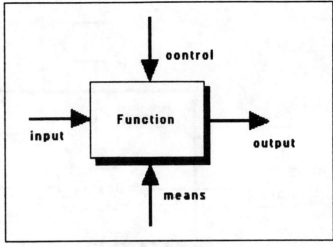

Fig. 8. Types of flows.

specific physical computer system implementation and any specific organizational structure.

With a functional flow model one can quickly grasp the scope and important interrelationships of a domain. The functional flow model concepts include:

Function Box—a function of the enterprise. We make no distinction between automated and manual activities, because what one finds automated today might not be fitting for tomorrow, and what is manual today might be automated tomorrow. Functions decompose into subfunctions.

Environment Box—a source or destination outside the boundary of the domain under study. An environment could be the government, a customer, or other parts of this enterprise.

Flow Line—a flow of material or information between functions or between environments and functions. Flow lines always connect a box at each end. They never split, join, or remain unattached.

Flows can connect in four ways to functions: input, control, means, and output.

- Input flows are consumed by the function to create the output.
- Output flows are produced by the function.
- Control flows affect or direct the processing of the function.
- Means flows are the mechanisms which support the function.

Means can be material (such as a group of persons or a tool), or immaterial (such as a body of knowledge or philosophy). It is important that any means documented in a functional model be truly necessary, and not just the part of the current situation.

There are three kinds of flows:

- Material flows
- Information flows
- Energy flows.

Functional Flow Abstractions

The functional flow model contains three abstractions:

1. Abstraction from detail. The hierarchy of composition, decomposition abstracts from the bottom level details.
2. Abstraction from physical mechanisms. The activities modeled are truly functional. They contain no details of manual or automated implementation.
3. Abstraction from time. The flows do not start or stop. They flow constantly. There are no stores for delaying and batching the flows.

How to Construct a Functional Flow Model

How does one make a functional flow model? We have tried several ways before concluding that the following steps work best:

1. Do a top-down decomposition of the functions—Since functions are the heart of the flow model it is important to get them right first. Analysts and users often change their minds on the decomposition as they learn more. It is easy to change a decomposition. It is hard to change a flow model. As such, decomposition goes faster than a flow model.

Follow-on efforts often concentrate on only part of the model. Avoiding flow models for these out-of-scope parts saves time. Analysts must put much mental effort and many hours of diagramming into making flow models. There is a natural reluctance to change the model even if they find a better functional decomposition.

2. Select the level for making the flow model—It is not necessary or desirable to make a flow model for every level of decomposition. Choose carefully.

3. Do a bottom-up construction of the flows—Bottom level functions are small units whose behavior is specific and

287

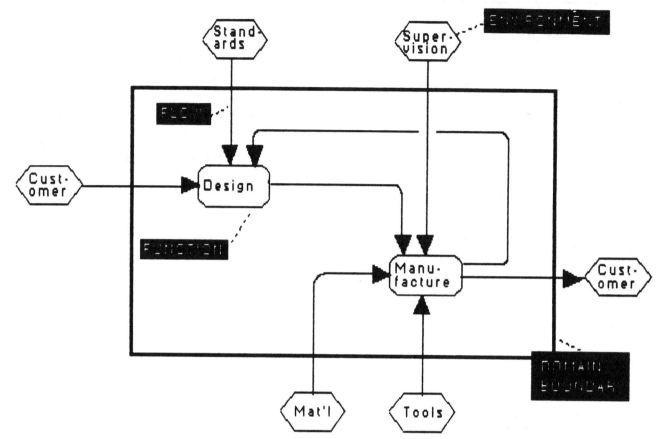

Fig. 9. Functional flow model concepts.

obvious. If the model builder needs to determine the flows, he or she can go to the specific person or group responsible for the function. At the high level, the responsibility for functions is more diffuse. It is difficult to find who can help.

Bottom level in-flows and out-flows are more specific. Higher level flow contents are necessarily more vague. One can compose flows and functions mechanically because the parts are identified. One will find it more difficult to decompose because the parts are unknown. Theoreticians recommend flow models with 5–9 functions per piece. We do not. Our practical experience shows that many analysts need and can absorb diagrams of 20 or more functions. The detail of these diagrams is necessary to their understanding. An artificial limitation only increases ambiguity.

4. Iterate as necessary.

Binary Semantic Models [8], [9]

Purpose of a Binary Semantic Model—A binary semantic model represents all object types, fact types, and integrity constraints of the domain. The binary model documents the meaning of the data in engineering, manufacturing, and management functions. The PRECISE* binary semantic model is the same as the ISO binary relationship model.

Binary Semantic Modeling Concepts

Object Type—person, place, object, thing, event, etc.
Solid Circle—represents a concept type: the intentional

definition of any "real world" object or event. Example: PART.
Dashed Circle—represents a symbol type: a set of names, numbers, codes or descriptions which refer to the concepts. Example: PART-NUMBER and PART-NAME.

Often there is no one-to-one relationship between concept types and symbol types. One finds some concepts with more than one symbol used to refer to them (for example PART-NAME and PART-NUMBER). Some concept types have no officially recognized symbol types (for example, a remount corrective operation in the manufacturing process may not have an identification).

Fact Type—a named specific relationship type between two object types.
Idea Type—is an information bearing relationship between two concept types. Each concept plays a role in the relationship. The roles go in the boxes next to the corresponding concept types. The presence of both roles permits reading the relationship in either direction.
Bridge Type—is a naming relationship connecting a concept type with a symbol type. We call it a bridge type because it bridges between the concepts and the representations for these concepts.
Subtype—subtype and supertype relationship. Two solid concept circles connected by a straight line with an arrowhead. The arrow points to the supertype. For example, a QUALITY-TEST is a subtype of a TEST.

288

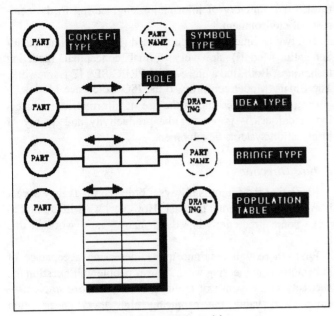

Fig. 10. Binary semantic model concepts.

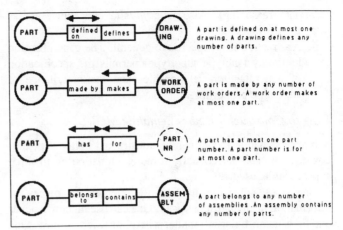

Fig. 11. Simple uniqueness constraints.

Constraints—restriction rules on the information structure states or transitions to preserve integrity. Constraints are formal knowledge rules about natural laws or enterprise policy. We show constraints with dashed lines.

For example, there may be an enterprise rule that one must officially release a part before it can be manufactured. This is a constraint. Likewise, there is a "law" of nature that a person may have only one age. This too is a constraint.

An intelligent database management system enforces these constraints when programs add to or delete information from the database. It uses these constraints to guarantee the quality, usefulness, and consistency of the information. With constraint enforcement, no user can accidentally or deliberately introduce nonsensical or inconsistent information.

In traditional systems, constraint enforcement has been undocumented, nonformal, and haphazard. Lack of constraint checking has greatly increased the cost of traditional development and use.

A few commonly occurring constraint types are:

Subtype Exclusion—two or more subtypes are mutually exclusive.
Subtype Total—the union of two or more subtypes equals the total supertype.
Role Uniqueness—a role or combination of roles is unique.
Role Subset—the population of the objects involved in role1 must be a subset of the population of the objects involved in role2. Role subset specifies precedence.
Equivalence of Path—two different paths from object type 1 to object type 2 give the same result.

Binary Semantic Model Abstractions

1. Abstraction from instance to type (object types and fact types).
2. Abstraction from name to concept (concept types versus symbol types and more involved references).

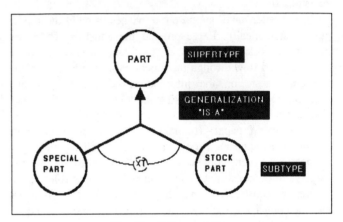

Fig. 12. Subtype notation.

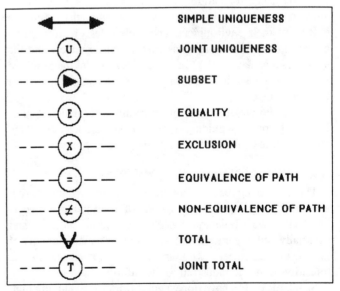

Fig. 13. Constraint notation.

3. Abstraction from particular viewpoints. All viewpoints are equally valid. There is no one entity preferred over another. Normalization does not impose a database technology viewpoint.
4. Abstraction from data oriented structures (symbolic, not

289

data reasoning). Also, every valid conceptual access path is modeled.

5. Abstraction from specific to general. The generalization hierarchy (subtype-supertype) permits the specification of generalization relationship, and the inheritance of supertype properties.

How to Construct a Binary Semantic Model

A binary semantic model can be constructed bottom-up, top-down, or middle-out. Usually some combination of all three approaches is used.

One does not have to find the elementary pieces of information in any particular way. One can use them whenever one finds them. It doesn't matter where, or when, or how. One has this flexibility because the model can handle elementary concepts. It doesn't force the individual to take design decisions first.

On the other hand, suppose one wishes to build the model more systematically. Large projects demand this. There are many methods and they all work. One can, for example, trace and analyze a flow through the functional flow model. Or one can concentrate on the information needed by just one function. Or one can use another method.

One can build the binary semantic model graphically, using large sheets of paper. (Interactive graphics tools are now beginning to appear). First, draw objects and their subtype connections. Then, connect ideas and bridges to the objects. Finally, draw constraints connecting objects and roles. As a diagram is constructed, one constantly checks its correctness and meaning by verbalizing the symbols in English, and by using population tables.

Interviewing is the most common technique people used in the initial stages of building a binary semantic model. Users are at ease explaining in English the information they need, the objects of their environment, and their rules of information behavior. Later in the analysis users begin to understand the symbolic language of the binary semantic model diagram and want to help make it. Users can learn the technique in a short training course.

During the initial stages a professional information analyst is very helpful in guiding user discussions, keeping them focused on the subject, and explaining the techniques.

SUMMARY AND CONCLUSIONS

The increasing use of automation in the manufacturing industries is causing the development of information engineering techniques. Techniques such as building models, and especially building the right model, are now a major activity of information engineers who are helping companies in the transition from the industrial to the information age.

Standards bodies have done a good work in developing high level, conceptual models: the Open System Interconnection 7-layer model, the ANSI/SPARC 3-Schema, and the ISO Conceptual Schema models.

Information engineering frameworks and practical guide models for applying information engineering models incorporate reference models. The PRECISE* Information Engineering framework model illustrates one vendor's mature approach to effective delivery of information engineering in the commercial environment.

The two technical models discussed (Functional and Binary Semantic Models) are very formal conceptual modeling techniques. Both find a place in the PRECISE* IE framework. The Binary Model conforms to the ISO Reference Model.

Project experience shows the use of information engineering techniques is improving the productivity and quality of information systems development.

Future Directions

Predicting the future is always a little risky—as they say, it is much safer to predict the past. However, we will attempt to make some predictions based on many years' work in this field.

First, there will continue to be increasing acceptance of information engineering work. Fewer people will question the necessity and expense of building models *before* implementation, and value the capturing high level specification knowledge.

Second, we will develop tools to capture and analyze models, to present them lexically and graphically, and to generate designs and implementations directly from the models. We will make these tools graphically oriented for maximum communication value. Also, we will design these tools with the very methods they support.

Third, information engineering will draw on ideas and tools from artificial intelligence (AI). IE practitioners will come to recognize that rule-based knowledge is as important as functional and information knowledge, and will develop or adapt methods to model rules. They will begin to use AI tools such as object oriented programming and object oriented databases, and AI workstations. The IE tool builders will use AI techniques in their tools.

In turn, the AI researchers will realize the need for a knowledge engineering methodology to build large scale expert systems. They will eventually see that information engineering has the technical models for domain analysis, and the framework concepts for handling large projects. They will adopt many information engineering models as part of the techniques of knowledge acquisition.

We are just at the start of a revolution in the manufacturing industry and in society. It promises to be an interesting experience.

ACKNOWLEDGMENTS

I have benefited greatly from design meetings and joint work with the members of Control Data's Information Engineering Technology Center: Joan Milloy, Denny Mikkelson, Jon Stonecash, Jim Anderson, Roger Thyr, and Necito Delacruz; and from in depth discussions with Dr. Sjir Nijssen, Dr. Robert Meersman, Frans van Assche and Baba Piprani; and from many customers and students.

REFERENCES

[1] *Information Processing Systems, Open Systems Interconnection Basic Reference Model.* New York, NY: American National Standards Institute.

[2] Odrey, N. G. and R. Nagel, "Critical issues in integrating factory automation systems," *CIM Review*, vol. 2, no. 2, Winter 1986.

[3] Lefkon, D., "A LAN primer," *Byte*, pp. 147–154, July 1987.

[4] Interim Report, ANSI/SPARC Study Group on Data Base Management Systems, 1975.

[5] *The ANSI/X3/SPARC DBMS Framework Report of the Study Group on Database Management Systems*, AFIPS, 1977.

[6] "Concepts and terminology for the conceptual schema and information base," Van Griethuysen, Ed., ANSI pub. no. N197, 1982.

[7] "Assessment guidelines for conceptual schema language proposals," Van Griethuysen and King, Eds. ISO TC97/SC21/WG5-3 1985.

[8] Thomson, P., "Natural language analysis, information modeling and database engineering," presented at *Eighteenth Annual Hawaii Systems Conf.* Jan. 1985.

[9] van Wintraecken, J. J., *Informatie analyse volgens NIAM in theorie en praktijk*. Control Data and Academic Press, (English edition 1988).

[10] PRECISE* Information Engineering Overview, Pub. Nr. 76070010, Control Data Corporation, Minneapolis, MN 1986.

[11] PRECISE* Information Engineering Textbook, Control Data Corporation, Information Engineering Technology Center (IETC), Jan. 1987.

Some Experiences with a Distributed Database Testbed System

PATRICIA A. DWYER AND JAMES A. LARSON

Invited Paper

DDTS (Distributed Database Testbed System) was developed for the purpose of evaluating alternative approaches and algorithms for managing data stored in several databases on different machines. An overview of the system and information architectures of DDTS, as well as an example of the execution of a distributed request, are presented. The results of experiments with three query optimization algorithms are summerized. Our approach for dealing with semantic integrity constraints in a distributed system is reviewed. By sacrificing the enforcement of semantic integrity constraints that span sites, DDTS can be used as a federated distributed database management system.

I. INTRODUCTION

Most of the operational databases in use today are centralized, i.e., the data are stored on a single computer. Many enterprises have several centralized databases located on different computers for reasons including the following:

- The enterprise itself is geographically distributed.
- The total information requirement is too large to be maintained by a single centralized DBMS.
- Several databases were developed separately for historical reasons, for example, different divisions of the enterprise developed overlapping databases separately.
- The introduction of personal computers to the enterprise has resulted in the establishment of several small databases.

Many organizations need to have rapid and reliable global access to data maintained by these separate databases. Currently, this is quite difficult. To do this, a user must perform five tasks:

1) Determine the computers that contain the data to be accessed.
2) Formulate several queries, to be executed on the different computers.

Manuscript received August 6, 1985; revised October 3, 1986.
The authors are with the Honeywell Corporate Systems Development Division, Golden Valley, MN 55427, USA.
IEEE Log Number 8714295.

3) Copy or transfer the results to a single computer for merging.
4) Combine and merge the results.
5) Extract from the combined results the answer to the original request.

These tasks can be time-consuming, tedious, and error-prone and are candidates for automation in a *Distributed Database Management System* (DDBMS). The DDBMS software performs the above five tasks on behalf of the user making the original request.

The goal of the Distributed Database Management System (DDBMS) Project at Honeywell's Computer Sciences Center (CSC) was to design and build a system for the purpose of evaluating alternate approaches and algorithms for managing data stored in several databases on different machines. The system, known as DDTS (Distributed Database Testbed System) [5], [9] provides the apparatus through which hypotheses can be analyzed and quantitative models validated.

This paper is organized as follows: Section II is a minitutorial describing the architecture of DDTS, while Section III summarizes a series of experiments conducted on DDTS dealing with distributed query optimization. Section IV discusses a research effort that we have abandoned, the automatic enforcement of semantic integrity constraints that span sites in a DDBMS. Section V discusses the next generation of DDBMS that we are investigating.

From its conception DDTS has been considered to be a testbed and not a prototype such as SDD-1 [26]. While the distinction between a testbed and a prototype can at times be small, it is important during design and implementation; the latter emphasizing efficiency and simplicity; the former modularity and flexibility, whenever possible. Even a testbed, however, must be built upon certain architectural foundations (e.g., a single conceptual schema of the database, and the definition of a transaction). Choices must be made in order to build the apparatus. The architecture of DDTS is not intended to be unique (although it is in some areas); rather, readers should notice that we have built upon

Reprinted from *Proc. IEEE*, p. 633–648, vol. 75, no. 5, May 1987.

previous ideas [15], [18], [26], [27] as experimental science often does and too frequently computer science does not.

II. DDTS Achitecture Overview

The underlying structure of DDTS can be described briefly in terms of an information architecture and a system architecture. The information architecture describes the types of schemas and their relationships while system architecture describes the important processing modules and their relationships.

A. Information Architecture

The ANSI/SPARC Study Group in database management systems has proposed a framework [15] consisting of three

levels of database description (schemas) which are designed to provide the data independence. The three schema levels are as follows:

- *External Schema*: to describe a user's view of the database.
- *Conceptual Schema*: the logical description of the portion of the real world being modeled by the database.
- *Internal Schema*: the description of the database representation structure.

The ANSI/SPARC proposal appears to offer an ideal framework for providing data independence. Multiple user views defined in terms of heterogeneous data models can be specified as multiple external schemas. The format of a database and its internal representation structures can be

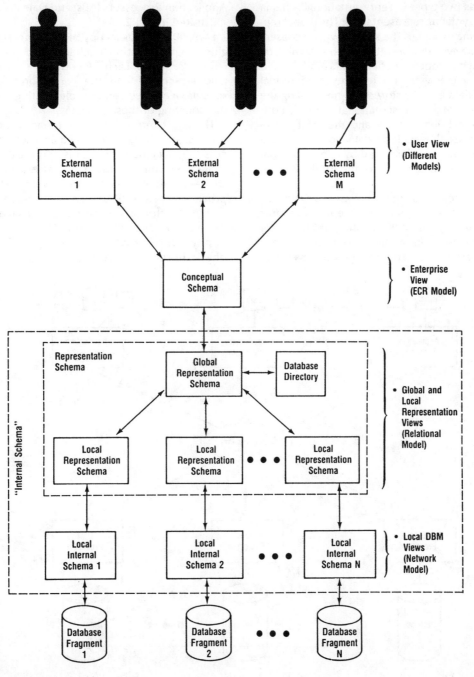

Fig. 1. DDTS information architecture.

defined by the internal schema. Finally, the conceptual schema provides for a semantic specification of the conceptual information for an enterprise, which is stable in that it is independent of implementation concepts.

For a distributed DBMS even more schema levels are needed, especially if the system supports heterogeneous data models and languages. The ANSI/SPARC three-schema architecture has been extended to a five-schema architecture of DDTS [5], [9] illustrated in Fig. 1. The conceptual schema is a semantic model of the total database content. At present, external schemas are not implemented, so users view the database via the conceptual schema. The conceptual schema is expressed using the Entity–Category–Relationship model of data [8] an extension of the Entity–Relationship data model of Chen [3]. The conceptual schema also describes semantic integrity constraints to be enforced by DDTS. DDTS has two types of representational schema for describing the syntactic representation: The global representational schema describes the system-wide representation and provides a system-wide interface to all local database managers that is independent of the data models used by the local database managers. The local representational schema describes data actually stored at a node using the same syntax as the global representational schema. Both the global representational schema and the local representational schema use the relational data model. The data stored in each node are also described by a local internal schema, which uses the data model of the local database manager.

To use DDTS to access existing databases, a Database Administrator must first build a local representational schema from the description of the existing database. We refer to this existing description as the local internal schema. After all of the local representational schemas have been built, they are "integrated" to form the global representational schema. During the integration process, differences in local names and structures of replicated data are resolved [22]. Next, the conceptual schema, which describes semantic integrity constraints that are to be enforced by DDTS, is designed. This type of "bottom-up" approach is needed to design a global schema for multiple, existing databases.

B. System Architecture

The DDTS system architecture is based on a model of distributed computing in which a set of abstract processors execute sets of concurrent processes [19]. Local processes (within the same processor) and remote processes communicate via message exchange. DDTS consists of a set of Application Processors (APs) and Data Processors (DPs), as illustrated in Fig. 2.

Each AP contains a copy of the conceptual schema, the global representational schema, and the local representational schemas. Each DP contains it own local representational schema and the corresponding local internal schema. We are currently implementing utilities to manage the updating of these schemas.

The APs control the user interfaces and manage transactions, and the DPs manage data. Each AP has a lead process that accepts user log-ins and creates a process (the GORDAS Command Interface process) for each user. Each DP has a lead process that accepts requests for transaction processing at the DP, and creates a process (the Local Execution Monitor process) for each transaction request. The APs and DPs are software processors–logical abstractions of physical processors. The APs and DPs are allocated to physical processors during system configuration. A com-

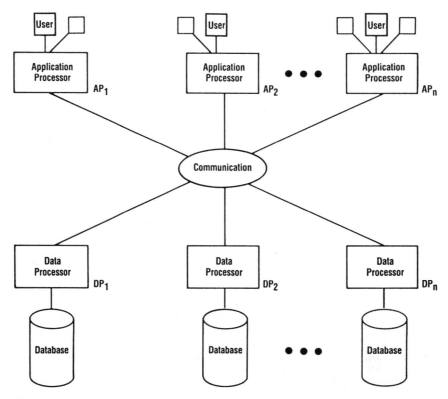

Fig. 2. DDTS system architecture.

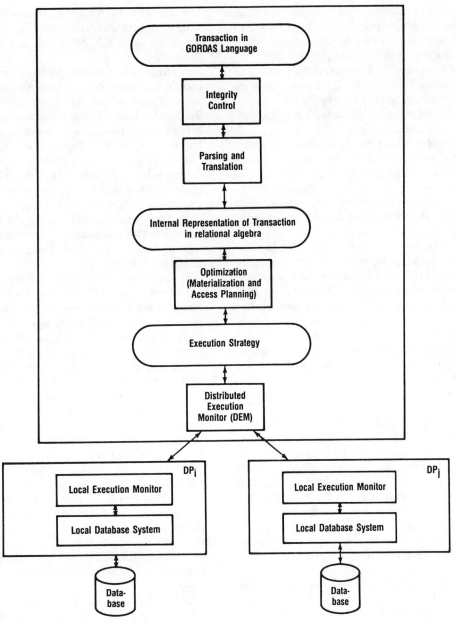

Fig. 3. DDTS processors.

munications subsystem transfers messages between processes.

DDTS is partitioned into the following set of subsystems, illustrated in Fig. 3:

- GORDAS Command Interface (GCI)
- Translation and Integrity Control (TIC)
- Materialization and Access Planning (MAP)
- Distributed and Local Execution Monitors (DEM/LEM)
- Local Operations Module (LOM)
- Communications Processor (CP)
- Instrumentation and Demonstration (TRACER)

The following subsections highlight the functionality of each of these DDTS subsystems.

1) GORDAS Command Interface: A DDTS user can enter transactions consisting of multiple retrieval and update requests expressed in GORDAS, a high-level query language [8]. Transactions that are executed frequently may be "compiled" and stored for later execution. The GORDAS

Command Interface (GCI) provides the interactive end-user interface to DDTS. A GCI process is spawned for each user that logs into an AP. GCI provides transaction definition functions, including DEFINE and DELETE, and transaction execution functions, including COMPILE and EXECUTE. A conversational transaction text editor is built into GCI.

2) Translation and Integrity Control: Before a GORDAS transaction is executed, the GORDAS requests in the transaction must be translated to an internal representation for processing by the Translation and Integrity Control (TIC) module. The internal representation is nonprocedural and has features of both the relational algebra and the relational calculus. It is similar to an internal representation of SQL, the language for System-R [1]. A lexical scanner and recursive-descent parser translate the GORDAS requests into this internal form and check that they are well formulated with respect to the conceptual schema. A rudimentary data dictionary is consulted during this process. References to entity types, attributes, and relationships in the GORDAS requests are mapped to references to relations and attributes in the relational form. At present, all of the GORDAS language can be parsed, although translation of certain requests (nested queries) is not fully implemented.

TIC is intended to automatically insert run-time checks in a GORDAS transaction to ensure that the transaction does not violate the database's semantic integrity constraints. The automatic enforcement of semantic integrity constraints is further discussed in Section IV.

3) Materialization and Access Planning: After a transaction has been translated by TIC, materialization and access planning (MAP) is performed to derive a strategy for efficiently processing the transaction in the distributed system. DDTS MAP presents a new transaction optimization technique combining data flow analysis and traditional distributed query optimization techniques.

Transaction optimization differs from the more familiar query optimization in that update requests and control constructs (e.g., IF-THEN-ELSE) may appear in the transaction and limit the range of optimization. In DDTS, *data flow analysis* techniques are used to group retrieval and update requests into operation blocks that serve as units of optimization, and to determine an order dependency of requests within each block. The blocks are formed based on the control constructs in the transaction (e.g., THEN-part and ELSE-part of an IF). The blocks are then optimized independently using normal distributed query optimization techniques.

The optimization algorithm currently implemented in DDTS finds a *materialization* (a data selection plan) that minimizes transmission cost by selecting data copies closest to the user's AP. A minimum cost *execution strategy*, which attempts to maximize parallelism, is found based upon that materialization. The final result is formed at a "result DP," which is the one chosen most often in the materialization. Any unary relational operations (e.g., SELECT, PROJECT) are performed at the node where the data reside. Materialization and access planning are discussed further in Section III.

4) Distributed and Local Execution Monitors: The Distributed Execution Monitor (DEM) carries out the distributed execution of a transaction based upon the execution stategy created by MAP. A DEM creates a set of Local Execution Monitors (LEMs) at the DPs involved in the transaction. Conceptually, the LEMs are slave extensions to the DEM process dedicated to the user at the AP. A DEM then communicates directly with its own set of LEMs. This extended dedicated process structure was chosen over a dedicated server-process structure to obtain greater parallelism.

The DEM synchronizes the LEMs involved in the transaction execution via message exchange. The DEM will send compile and/or execute requests to initiate the processing of a transaction at the LEMs. (If a transaction is to be compiled only, the DEM stores the execution strategy and operation blocks generated by TIC and MAP for later execution.) Based on status information returned by the LEMs during execution, the DEM decides to commit or abort the transaction. DDTS uses a one-phase commit protocol during transaction compilation and a two-phase commit protocol during transaction execution. In case of concurrency control conflict that may result in deadlock, the DEM will cause the effects of the transaction to be rolled back, and the

transaction to be restarted. Three different deadlock prevention algorithms have been implemented: a "no-wait" algorithm, and the WAIT-DIE and WOUND-WAIT algorithms [24].

A transaction that attempts to update data at a failed node cannot start execution. A failure during the execution of a transaction is detected by the distributed execution monitor, which instructs the remaining local execution monitors to abort their local processing and use the recovery technique specific to the local database manager to back out the incomplete transaction. When the failed site recovers, the local execution monitor detects that no global commit was received and uses the recovery technique specific to the local database manager to back out the incomplete transaction. DDTS uses the unanimous agreement algorithm [18] for update of replicated data. Because this algorithm updates all the copies or none of them, it ensures unlimited consistency.

5) Local Operations Module: The Local Operations Module (LOM) of each DP acts as an interface between the LEM and the local DBMS. As part of this interface, LOM is responsible for local translation and optimization of subtransactions that have been assigned to the DP by MAP. The LOM translates subtransaction requests in the internal representation to data manipulation requests in the language of the local DBMS. In DDTS, the local DBMS is IDS-II [13], which uses the CODASYL network model. If the translation is to be compiled only, the translated requests are stored for later execution.

Local translation of the subtransaction is combined with a local optimization to minimize the number of disk accesses required during execution. At present, only minor optimization techniques have been implemented (e.g., identification of CALC keys in selection predicates). A more sophisticated optimization algorithm for DDTS is described [23] which builds a binary operation tree for the subtransaction and attempts to recognize particular subtrees of relational requests, each of which can be optimized by a specific procedure written in the IDS-II data manipulation language.

6) Communications Processor: The Communications Processor (CP) at each node is a logical processor that implements the abstraction of ports (the DDTS message queues) used by AP and DP processes at a physical site. The CP implements the port abstraction in terms of the available functions and services of the underlying network. Most of the time, these functions are provided directly by the transport services of the local or geographic network, with the CP providing an address mapping function from logical DDTS port names to physical port names.

There are currently three ports defined for each AP, the command response port, the data response port, and the reliability monitor port, and two ports defined for each DP, the command port and the information port. The command response port is used for messages that indicate successful completion of requested subcommands; the data response port is used for messages that return data to the AP; and the reliability monitor port is used for messages that report status and error conditions to the AP. The DP command port is used for receipt of all subcommands from the AP; and the information port is used for receipt of data sent between DPs to satisfy subcommand requests.

Originally, local ports were realized directly by the local

mail facility of the GCOS6 operating system. A port was implemented as a mailbox (message queue) of the same name. Extensions to local mail were made in order for a process to communicate with a remote port. Those messages destined for a remote port are placed in a generic mailbox associated with the remote port's processor. A lower level (software) CP forwarded these messages over an ad hoc communication network to the Communications Processor at the remote node. The receiving CP then deposited the message into the final destination mailbox. The original communications network was fabricated by a set of point-to-point serial links between all Level 6s.

Two different communication networks are currently supported by DDTS. The first is based on a Local Area Network (LAN) with the Ungermann–Bass Net/One Ethernet Data Link Service [30]. Xerox's Internet Transport Protocols (ITP) Internetwork Datagram Protocol [31] is used for communication over the Ethernet LAN. The second network is a long-haul communication system, Honeywell's Distributed Systems Architecture (DSA) [14]. DSA provides ISO Session Level support.

7) Instrumentation and Demonstration: To make DDTS useful as an experimentation tool, we developed DDTS metering and instrumentation facilities in a tool called TRACER. TRACER supports the collection of experimental data at various predefined points in the system execution, i.e., at various *event* occurrences. TRACER "probes" (analogous to breakpoints) are placed in the system software at points of interest; the probes define potential events. The experimenter is able to define, interactively, a set of actions to perform upon an event occurrence. Typically these actions cause the display of system state data, including event name, time of day, process name, and additional event-specific data. These data may be displayed on a terminal, written to a file, or transmitted within a message to a particular port. TRACER also supports system tracing for distributed debugging and system demonstration.

C. An Example of Transaction Processing in DDTS

To better understand transaction processing in DDTS, an example will be presented. The simplified personnel database has only one external schema, which is also the conceptual schema. It is based on Honeywell's entity-category-relationship (ECR) data model, an extension of the conventional entity-relationship data model.

The ECR model's view of the world consists of entities and relationships among them. An entity represents some object in the real world. An entity type is a collection of similar entities; each entity belongs to exactly one entity type. A category is used to define the role that entities play in relationships with other entities in the database. For example, in Fig. 4, some employees play the role of full-time employees.

Relationships identify the specific entities that are related to one another. In Fig. 4, "ownership" relates full-time employees with divisions. For this particular relationship, the arrow used in the schema indicates that each employee must be related to exactly one division in the database; however, a division may employ several full-time employees. This exemplifies the integrity constraints that are particularly easy to express in the ECR model. Note that in some cases an entity type (division) and its role-defining category

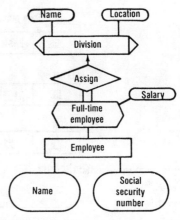

Fig. 4. Example conceptual schema.

(owning division) may be combined to simplify the schema. Entity types, categories, and relationships may have attributes, such as those shown in the circles of Fig. 4. These provide information about their members.

The conceptual schema for the simplified corporate personnel database (Fig. 4) has two entity types: DIVISION and EMPLOYEE. The DIVISION entity type has the attributes NAME and LOC; the EMPLOYEE entity type has attributes NAME and SSN (Social Security number). FULL-TIME EMPLOYEE, a subset of EMPLOYEE, includes those employees who work full time and has the attribute SALARY. ASSIGN is a relationship that shows the assignment of full-time employees to divisions. Each full-time employee must be assigned to exactly one division.

Fig. 5 shows the global representation schema, a set of relations that corresponds to the ECR conceptual schema.

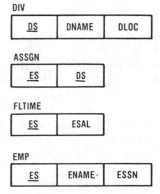

Fig. 5. Example global representation schema.

The attributes ES and DS are internally generated keys for the EMP and DIV relations, which represent the EMPLOYEE and DIVISION entity types, respectively.

Fig. 6 shows a possible set of local representation schemas in a distributed DBMS with two DPs. Fig. 7 shows the CODASYL DBTG network's local internal schemas for the same two DPs.

By following a transaction as it is processed by the distributed DBMS, one can see how each schema is used and why different data models are appropriate at different stages of processing. In general, the data model used at a particular stage of processing lends itself to the processing performed at that stage.

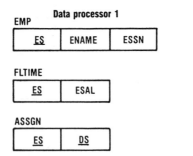

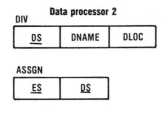

Fig. 6. Example local representation schemas.

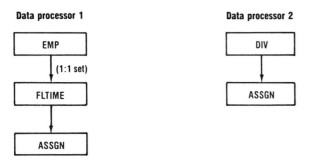

Fig. 7. Example local internal schemas.

The process is illustrated in Fig. 8. An application program or interactive user submits a transaction to an AP in terms of an external schema. The first task of the AP is to translate the transaction from the external schema to the conceptual schema. This generally involves a change in data model. Since the external and conceptual schemas are identical in this example, the transaction is already in terms of the conceptual schema. The AP then translates the transaction from the conceptual schema to the global representation schema, inserting commands into the transaction to enforce integrity constraints expressed in the conceptual schema.

Associated with the global representation schema is such information as the partitioning and replication of the data among the DPs, file sizes, and access-path descriptions that are independent of the implementation. Using this information, the AP selects the DPs to process the transaction, as well as the data copies they will use. It also recognizes opportunities for parallel execution of operations within the transaction.

The result is a set of data-manipulation commands for each DP participating in the transaction. The AP transmits these commands to the DPs and coordinates their execution, ensuring that the transaction either terminates successfully or aborts and restores the data at all DPs.

When a DP receives commands to be executed as part of a transaction, it first translates the commands into the data-manipulation commands of its local internal schema. The translation can include local optimizations, which takes advantage of access-path information, and any special hardware or software at the site to improve performance. The local DBMS then executes the commands.

Several stages of processing are required to execute a transaction in this distributed DBMS. For an *ad hoc* query, all processing must be done when the user submits the query. To improve performance, application programs can be compiled and stored for later execution by the DPs. The compile step may include all of the processing, except actual data manipulation by the DPs, under the supervision of the APs. Currently, site and data-copy selection are done at compilation time. In the case of site failures, site and data-copy selection are repeated at execution time by reprocessing of the transaction by MAP.

The five-schema information architecture for a distributed DBMS thus supports reliable execution, data independence, multiple external views with dissimilar data models, and heterogeneous underlying local DBMSs. It provides a uniform scheme to enforce the integrity constraints specified in the conceptual schema. It also supplies each transaction-execution stage with just the level of information it requires.

D. Initial Demonstration

The implementation of the initial phase of DDTS was successfully demonstrated during the summer of 1982 (using the MOD600 GCOS operating system) and again in the summer of 1983 (using the MOD400 GCOS operating system). A single AP and two DPs were configured on the system, physically located on two Level 6 minicomputers (Fig. 9). The AP was able to support multiple users, and each DP managed a different "half" of the distributed database. A demonstration package received TRACER messages to update a graphical display of the DDTS system state.

E. Current Version of DDTS

After the initial version of DDTS was demonstrated, improvements were made to the system in order to increase the performance. DEM/LEM was redesigned to decrease the number and size of the control messages. The initial communications subsystem based upon an RS-232 point-to-point serial connection was replaced by the Xerox ITP and the Honeywell DSA protocols. In the initial version of DDTS, a user logged into an AP. For each transaction, LEM tasks were spawned at each DP required by the transaction. After execution of the transaction, the tasks were deleted. We determined that spawning a task was a significant bottleneck in the system. In the current version of DDTS, a user logs into an AP and at this time LEM tasks are spawned at each DP. The user can submit multiple transactions, and the LEM tasks are not deleted until the user logs out of the AP. The response time for the current version of DDTS is approximately one order of magnitude less than the response time of the initial version.

The next section describes a series of experiments conducted on DDTS. This series of experiments dealt with alternative strategies for distributed transaction optimization.

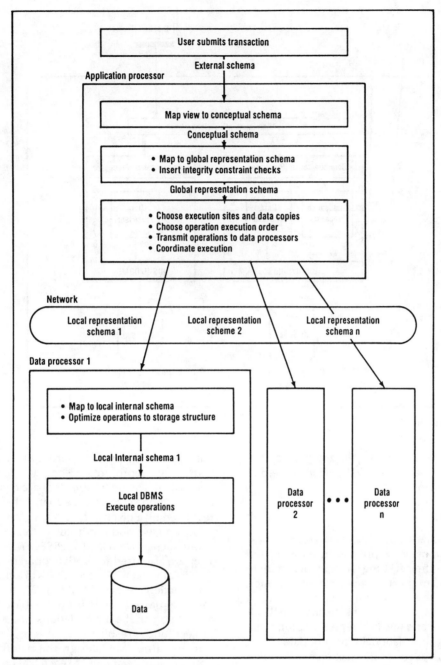

Fig. 8. Processing a request in DDTS.

III. Materialization and Access Planning

The Materialization and Access Planning (MAP) for a distributed query, update, or transaction is an important part of the processing of the query, update, or transaction. Materialization and access planning result in a strategy for processing a query, update, or transaction in the DDBMS. Materialization consists of selecting data copies used to process the query, update, or transaction. This step is necessary since data may be stored at more than one site on the network. Access planning consists of choosing the execution order of operations and the actual execution site of each operation.

A MAP algorithm selects a good materialization for all data in the query, update, or transaction. Three different access planning methods have been implemented: Gen-

eral-Response, General-Total, and Initial Feasible Solution (IFS) [1]. General-Response and General-Total build optimal execution strategies using a cost function of the communications costs. Both methods optimize communications costs through the use of semijoins. Local processing costs are not considered. General-Response builds an execution strategy with minimum response time, the time elapsed between the start of the first transmission and the time at which the result arrives at the required computer. General-Total builds an execution strategy with minimum total time, the sum of the time of all transmissions. IFS is a straightforward approach that does not perform any optimization.

This section presents the system environment of the DDTS system that is relevant to the MAP process. The five issues discussed are the internal data model, the execution strategy language, the type of data distribution, the level

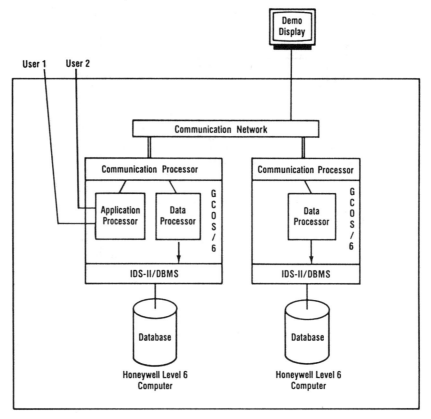

Fig. 9. Initial implementation of DDTS.

of distribution transparency, the usage characteristics, the transaction management facilities, DDTS performance, and suggestions for future work.

A. Internal Data Model

In DDTS, MAP is applied to queries, updates, and transactions whose operations are expressed in terms of the global representation schema. Using location information, MAP produces an execution strategy that contains operations against the local representation schemas. Each LOM translates its operations to operations against an IDS/II schema. Both the global and the local representation schemas are defined using the relational model of data.

In DDTS, the query, update, or transaction expressed in GORDAS is translated to an internal nonprocedural representation. The internal representation of queries was an important problem. We developed a hierarchical representation for individual queries using the traditional binary and unary relational algebra operations. However, this representation turned out to be overly restrictive. For example, when three relations *A*, *B*, and *C* are joined, the representation forced us to join two of the relations and then join the result to the third relation. This unnecessary ordering of operations was eliminated by considering multiple binary operations of the same type as a cluster, which are optimized as a unit. Our current representation has features of both relational algebra and relational calculus. It is similar to an internal representation of SQL, the language defined for System-R [2].

The internal representation that is output from the GORDAS translator and input to the MAP module is a set of cluster trees. There is a cluster tree per query or update in a transaction. For queries, there is one cluster tree input. A cluster tree represents a compacted tree of a query or update [29]. The operations that are commutable are combined into one cluster node so that the optimization is not restricted by a given order.

The non-leaf nodes in a cluster tree are used for set operations such as UNION, INTERSECTION, and DIFFERENCE. They are also used for update operations such as DELETE, INSERT, and MODIFY. The leaves of a cluster tree represent combinations of SELECT, PROJECT, and JOIN operations. Each leaf has a variable list of the base relations involved, a condition on the base relations, and a list of attributes to project for the result.

In the current MAP design, the materialization and query optimization are applied to each leaf node in a cluster tree. For cluser trees with non-leaf set nodes, the location of the final result of each leaf is used to decide where the set operation is to occur. For cluster trees with non-leaf updates, the update is performed at all sites containing the relation. The record identifiers of the records to be updated are transmitted to all sites.

B. Execution Strategy Language

The output of the MAP algorithm is an execution strategy. This strategy contains the operations that are to be distributed among the sites involved in the execution of the query, update, or transaction, and contains commands used by the DEM to coordinate the execution. The operations to be distributed among the sites are expressed against the local representation schemas. These include a move command that instructs the data processor to move a temporary relation to another data processor. Each command may have preconditions, commands that must be executed previous to the execution of the command. By using the commands and the preconditions, a query tree can be built. An important implementation issue is the management of temporary data (temporary relations in DDTS). We initially took a simplified approach and stored all temporary information in memory segments up to 32K bytes in length. This is too restrictive for queries involving large relations. Spooling of large, temporary data to secondary storage is now supported.

MAP is applied to queries, updates, and transactions expressed in terms of the relational model of data. The input to MAP is an internal SQL representation, and the output from MAP is a distributed relational algebra representation.

C. Type of Distribution

The type of data distribution affects the MAP process in three ways. The first is whether the data are locally or geographically distributed, the second is whether the data are replicated, and the third is whether the data are partitioned.

Both the materialization and access planning algorithms used in the MAP process depend on whether data are locally or geographically distributed. Materialization and access planning algorithms may be divided into two classes. The first class finds a minimum-cost execution strategy based on a given materialization, and the second class finds a minimum-cost materialization based on a given execution strategy [11], [121]. The access planning algorithms used in DDTS are General-Response, General-Total, and Initial Feasible Solution (IFS) [1]. These algorithms belong in the first class. That is, a materialization for all data has been chosen before the access planning algorithm builds an execution strategy.

The materialization algorithm chooses a site for all data in the query. The algorithm used depends on whether the data are locally or geographically distributed. In a geographically distributed environment, a "closest in distance" type of algorithm may be used. For each relation, the DP site chosen is the one that is "closest" to the user's AP. In a locally distributed environment, distance is not a major factor, so a clustering algorithm may be better. A DP site is chosen based upon the number of relations required for the transaction that are available at the site. The site with the most number of relations is chosen first. If there are any remaining relations required, the next site with the most number of the remaining relations is chosen next. This algorithm continues until all relations have been materialized. Both algorithms have been implemented on DDTS.

The access planning algorithm also depends on whether the data are locally or geographically distributed. Access planning algorithms try to minimize a cost function of some type. A typical cost function is given by

$$cost = communication\ costs + processing\ costs.$$

The communication costs are a function of the amount of data transmitted on the network. The processing costs are a function of the disk access and CPU costs at each site in the network. General-Response and General-Total assume that processing costs are negligible with respect to communication costs. As a result of this assumption, execution strategies are produced that decrease the amount of data to be sent at the expense of computation. This assumption is more valid in a geographically distributed network than in a locally distributed network. This hypothesis was tested

by experimentation with DDTS, and was found to be correct.

The DDTS architecture supports both local and geographic distribution. Experiments with General-Response and General-Total should use both types of distribution. The need for an algorithm that includes processing costs, such as that proposed in [4], can be determined based on the performance of General-Rsponse and General-Total in these experiments. The results of the DDTS experiments that support the inclusion of local processing costs for the DDTS system environment are presented in [6] and summarized in Section III-G.

While the access planning algorithms do not depend on whether data are replicated, the materialization algorithm depends on whether data are replicated. This algorithm chooses copies of data needed to execute the query, update, or transaction from the various sites. If the data are not replicated, there is no choice to make and the materialization is predetermined. The MAP algorithm includes a simple materialization algorithm that chooses sites based on the number of relations needed by the query, update, or transaction located at each site. It chooses these sites with the most relations needed by the query, update, or transaction. This algorithm can be easily extended to choose sites based on the number of records or bytes needed by the query, update, or transaction.

Both the materialization and the access planning algorithms depend on the type of data partitioning. In the relational model, data can be partitioned in several ways:

1) *By schema:* A schema is a description of the relations and attributes in a database. At this level of partitioning, each database resides at a single site and cannot be distributed among the sites.

2) *By relation:* The relations in a schema can be distributed among the sites. All rows and columns of a relation are stored at the same site.

3) *By row (horizontally):* The rows (tuples) in a relation can be distributed among the sites.

4) *By column (vertically):* The columns (attributes) in a relation can be distributed among the sites.

5) *By row and column:* The rows and columns in a relation can be distributed among the sites.

The materialization and access planning algorithms assume that partitioning by relation is supported. Additional work will be needed if the other types of partitioning are to be considered.

In conclusion, the type of distribution supported by the MAP algorithm is geographically distributed data, with replication, and partitioning by relation. The MAP algorithm can be used with locally distributed data, but it may not produce satisfactory results because local processing costs are not considered. Additional work on the MAP algorithm is needed to support vertical and horizontal partitioning.

D. Level of Distribution Transparency

The level in the system where knowledge of data location is available affects the MAP process. In DDTS, the data location information is used to map between the global representation schema and the local representation schemas. At each AP, the MAP algorithm has access to the global representation schema, the necessary local representation schemas, and the data location information.

In the current implementation of DDTS, the global representation schema, the local representation schemas, and the data location information are replicated at all APs. Alternatively, the necessary data could be partitioned and distributed among the DPs [17]. In this case, the data used by MAP must be collected from the DPs before the MAP process begins.

E. Usage Characteristics

The type of usage of the system affects the MAP process. In DDTS, the user interfaces with the system by using the GORDAS query and update language. The user can build a transaction that consists of one or more query or update requests.

The current MAP algorithm handles queries, updates, and transactions of one or more queries or updates. Queries are decomposed using the materialization and access planning algorithms. Updates are decomposed by first building an execution strategy that builds a temporary relation of the tuple identifiers of the tuples to be updated. Commands are then added to the execution strategy to move this list of tuple identifiers to each site that has the relation to be updated, and to update the relation. Transactions of one or more query or update requests are decomposed in a similar manner. Execution strategies are built for each query or update independent of one another. An improvement would be to recognize common subexpressions in the transaction. This would reduce the number of temporary relations built.

A necessary extension to the proposed MAP algorithm is to process control constructs. Work has been done on decomposing the IF-THEN-ELSE-ENDIF control construct [7]. An algorithm was developed on DDTS that handles the IF-THEN-ELSE-ENDIF, but it uses a simple access planning algorithm. Further research is still necessary in this area.

The MAP provides an open-ended number of user interfaces. The proposed MAP algorithm is well-suited for queries, but it decomposes updates and transactions nonoptimally.

F. Transaction Management Facilities

The Reliable Transaction Processing project [24] at CSC addressed the problem of providing reliable, serializable, and highly available transaction execution in a distributed database management system. Site recovery logic and a commit protocol are used to provide reliability; a distributed concurrency control algorithm is used to provide serializability; and a data replication control algorithm is used to provide highly available transaction execution. For reliability, DDTS currently uses a one-phase commit protocol during transaction compilation and a two-phase commit protocol during transaction execution. For serializability, three distributed deadlock prevention algorithms have been implemented: a "no-wait" algorithm, and the WAIT-DIE and WOUND-WAIT algorithms [25]. For replication control, the unanimous agreement algorithm [18] is used. In this technique, the closest or fastest copy is used for read accesses, and every copy is used for write accesses.

The MAP algorithm is largely independent of the methods used to provide reliable transaction processing in DDTS. These activities occur during transaction execution, well after the MAP process has occurred. The materialization algorithm chooses the sites of all relations in the query or transaction. The execution strategies generated

for a transaction may be stored for later execution. Each subquery is sent to the local site where it is stored. Upon site failure, the MAP process must be re-executed for transactions involving the failed site. Site failure information must be available to the materialization algorithm, so that it can select new sites for use in the transaction.

The materialization algorithm handles replicated data at the granularity of relations. For a query, if a relation is replicated at more than one site, the materialization algorithm chooses a single copy. For an update, all copies are chosen, and the execution strategy contains an update command for each chosen copy. The data replication control algorithm ensures that the consistency of the replicated data copies is maintained in the presence of failures. The MAP process must be re-executed if a site containing data to be accessed in an execution strategy become unavailable at the chosen site but are still available at another site.

G. DDTS Performance

Two Honeywell Level 6s with the GCOS6 MOD 4 operating system were utilized for the DDTS experiments. One Application Processor (AP2) and one Data Processor (DP2) reside on one Level 6; one Data Processor (DP1) resides on the other Level 6. The configurations of the Level 6s were not identical. For example, one Level 6 has cache memory, while the other does not.

The experiments were performed using two different communication systems. In the first system, the communication network is realized by an RS-232 point-to-point serial link between the Level 6s with maximum transmission speed of 9600 Bd. A Communications Processor (CP) based on the GCOS6 MOD400 mail system resides on each Level 6 and is responsible for communication between APs and DPs and among the DPs. The second configuration uses a LAN with the Ungermann–Bass Net/One Ethernet Data Link Service [30]. The ITP datagram protocol [31] provides an interface for the DDTS send, receive, connect, and disconnect communication primitives.

This section summarizes the experimental results that are common to both communications subsystems followed by a discussion of the experimental results due to differences between the two subsystems. A detailed description of the experimental design and results is given in [6].

1) The elapsed real time spent in MAP is negligible compared to the time spent in distributed compilation and execution. The time spent in DEM is at least 98 percent of the response time. The time in DEM increases rapidly as the size of relations, number of relations, and number of attributes per relation accessed increases, due to increases in local execution time, execution time communications costs, and compile time communications costs. Local compile time is relatively constant.

2) In DDTS, we can compile transactions and save the execution strategies for later execution. If the cost of compiling a transaction is negligible compared to the cost of executing the transaction, we may want to use MAP algorithms that are more dynamic and balance workloads. Both the cost of compiling and the cost of executing a query are complex functions of the size of relations, number of relations, number of attributes per relation accessed, and the distribution of relations. For the same distribution, the cost of executing a query increases much more rapidly with the size of relations accessed than the cost of compiling a query,

302

and therefore the dynamic MAP algorithms may be desirable if large relations are accessed. Both the costs of compiling and executing a query increase rapidly with the number of relations and/or number of attributes per relation. The effect on communications time is much greater when the AP and DP are on physically separate computers.

3) General-Response and General-Total always chose the same solution for the data distributions and workloads used. They chose the best solution in most cases; the best solution was frequently the initial feasible solution because of the small sizes of the relations in the database. They chose the wrong solution in some cases because they used the wrong cost equations for communications and they did not consider local processing costs.

4) The load and capacity of the Level 6s are very important to overall performance. For some queries, it is more efficient to use a DP physically located on a different Level 6 than the same Level 6 as the AP. As the size and/or number of relations accessed increases, the communications costs increase and negate this effect. The configuration of the Level 6 (i.e., the existence of cache memory) influences the performance of DDTS by making one DP superior to another.

5) There is a constant overhead associated with each query. Its magnitude depends on the Level 6 configuration and load.

The experimental results related to the differences in the communications subsystems are summarized below:

The access planning algorithms, General-Response and General-Total, optimize a cost function that represents the communication costs. This function is assumed to be a linear function of the message size

$$\text{communication cost} = m * \text{size} + b.$$

The cost functions for communication from a processor at site 1 to a processor at site 2, a processor at site 2 to a processor at site 1, and a processor at site 2 to a processor at site 2 for both communication systems were obtained.

Plots of the communication time versus message length for a single message for the RS-232 based communication system are illustrated in Fig. 10. Plots of the data for the Local Area Network based system are illustrated in Fig. 11.

The performance of a DDBMS depends on whether the data are locally or geographically distributed. In general,

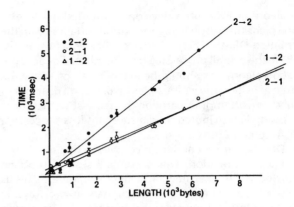

Fig. 11. Communication time versus message length for a single message for the Local Area Network based communication system.

access planning algorithms try to minimize a cost function of some type. A typical cost function is given by

$$\text{cost} = \text{communication costs} + \text{processing costs}.$$

The communication costs are a function of the amount of data transmitted on the network. The processing costs are a function of the disk access and CPU costs at each site in the network. General-Response and General-Total assume that processing costs are negligible with respect to communication costs. As a result of this assumption, execution strategies are produced that decrease the amount of data to be sent at the expense of computation.

The relative contributions to response time of local execution time and communication time for the LAN based system and the RS-232 based system differ greatly, as expected. The local processing time is the same for both systems; the difference in the relative contribution to response time is due to the difference in communication time. For both communication systems, the communication time is a linear function of the message size. These functions can now be used in the access planning algorithms. The local processing costs are negligible compared to the communication costs for the RS-232 based system; the local processing costs are greater than the communication costs for the LAN based system. The increase in the total local processing time for General- (Response and Total) must be accounted for in the LAN based system. The average increase was 1 ms as compared to a maximum decrease of 0.6 ms in total communication time for the experimental design used. In contrast, the maximum decrease in communications time for the RS-232 based system was 15 ms, and the local processing time increase was negligible.

The performance benefits to be gained by using General-Response or General-Total instead of IFS depend on the transmission speed of the communication line, the size of the relations that are accessed, and the frequency of join operations. For the relations accessed in our experiments, the IFS algorithm is sufficient for the LAN based system; performance benefits are realized for the RS-232 based system. As larger relations are accessed, the performance benefits are realized for the LAN based system. The results for the RS-232 based system can be generalized to a geographically distributed system in which the communication times are at least as slow.

We have observed that the distributed query optimiza-

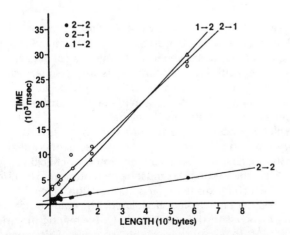

Fig. 10. Communication time versus message length for a single message for the RS-232 based communication system.

tion algorithm will often develop distributed query execution plans that result in high activity at certain sites in the distributed DBMS. These sites occasionally act as bottlenecks to the overall processing. The distributed query optimization algorithms should be extended to consider the current activity at the various sites involved in a distributed request and attempt to partition the request so that more processing is distributed to idle sites and less processing is distributed to busy sites.

In DDTS each AP contains a complete copy of all data dictionary information. This presents a storage problem when the AP is executed on a microcomputer. This is resolved by trimming the data dictionary in two ways: a) identifying information from the conceptual schema and global representation schema that describes only data that will be accessed at that AP, and storing only that information at the AP, or b) storing all of the data dictionary at one or more DPs. When an AP needs data dictionary information, it sends a data access request to the DP, which returns the necessary data dictionary information. Fetched data dictionary information is buffered in the AP until overlayed with new data dictionary information.

H. Suggestions for Future Work

Three areas of future work are suggested: advanced experimentation, simulation, and new MAP algorithm research.

Two areas of advanced experimentation are suggested: DDTS tuning and system and database parameter variation. DDTS tuning involves further identification of the DDTS bottlenecks and improvement of DDTS software in an effort to increase the performance of DDTS. This effort would result in a thorough understanding of a distributed database system's performance. Software modifications that would result in improvements to DDTS performance based on the initial experimental results are as follows:

1) Modify the cost functions used by MAP to be the actual communications costs functions measured. Modify MAP so that it does not assume that the cost of sending a message from A to B is the same as sending a message from B to A. Use the cost functions in the process of choosing a result DP, so that the MAP materialization algorithm does not assume that it costs the same to send a message of the same size from any DP to any AP.
2) Extend MAP to include local processing costs during both the materialization and access planning phases. Information about the configuration and loads of the DPs should be included. This effort is also part of the new MAP algorithm research area.

The second area of advanced experimentation is system and database parameter variation. Due to time and system constraints, the system and database parameters were varied over a small range of possible values. Specifically, the number of network nodes, multiprocessing levels, database size and content were fixed. The workloads were query only with 1 to 3 relations being accessed per query. The possible database distributions were limited by 2 network nodes and 5 relations. The following additional experiments are suggested:

1) Vary the number of network nodes using the current DDTS system configuration and database size and content.

Use the same workloads and database distributions used in the initial experiments.
2) All of the above experiments are initially performed with a single user. A follow-on to each experiment is allowed for more than one user.

The second area of future work is simulation. A simulation model of a distributed database system is a flexible tool that can be used to predict the performance of the distributed database system and the MAP algorithms in different system and database environments. In addition, new, alternative MAP algorithms can easily be added to the model, so that they can be compared with previously evaluated MAP algorithms.

The experimental data obtained on the implemented distributed database systems for varying system and database parameters can be used to validate the model. The model in turn provides an easy way to use the experimental data. The model can be used in the development of future DDBMS products to predict the performance of the products in different system and database environments.

The third area of future work is new MAP algorithm research. Based upon the experimental results, one important area of research is identified: the extension of the MAP cost function to include local execution costs and to do dynamic load balancing. The MAP algorithm will need information about the local system configurations and loads. Some information, such as the existence of cache memory, can be used at compile time. The load information is dynamic and a dynamic materialization algorithm will be necessary. Further research into dynamic MAP algorithms, and MAP algorithms that perform access planning before materialization is necessary. The latter algorithm provides the ability to do access planning at compile time and materialization at run time.

IV. Enforcing Global Semantic Integrity Constraints

DDTS was originally designed to automatically enforce semantic integrity constraints that involve data at two or more DPs. This section reviews the advantages and disadvantages for automatically enforcing such constraints. Section V outlines an alternative type of DDBMS that overcomes these disadvantages by neglecting to enforce semantic integrity constraints that span DPs.

A. Semantic Integrity Constraints

A semantic integrity constraint is a description of a condition that the database must always obey. Semantic integrity constraints are derived from the meaning of data. Many kinds of semantic integrity constraints are possible, including constraints on the value of a single data item, constraints on values of data items in the same record, and constraints among data items in several records.

A global semantic integrity constraint involves records in more than one DP. To enforce global semantic integrity constraints, the results of semantic integrity checking performed at the various DPs must be communicated to a single DP which makes the final determination as to whether the constraint is satisfied or violated. The communication costs involved in the enforcement of semantic integrity constraints that span sites can be expensive. This expense can be reduced by approaches that include the following:

Avoid constraints that cross sites. Cluster all of the records involved in a constraint at the same DP. However, if a record is involved in several constraints, then all records involved in any of those constraints must reside at the same DP. It is even conceivable that clustering records together that are involved in common constraints results in one large cluster and no distribution is possible.

Reduce constraint checking. Reduce the amount of constraint checking necessary by considering how all of the commands in a transaction interact and then check only those constraints that can be violated by the transaction as a whole. (Allowing multiple update commands per transaction is necessary because one update statement often cannot make all the changes necessary to bring the database from one consistent state to another.) Elmasri and Moore [21] have designed an algorithm for semantic integrity check generation that examines all of the operations in a transaction and the database objects upon which the operation is applied. A transaction graph is created for the transaction, connecting operations that are applied to related schema objects. For each operation applied on a schema object, a list of constraints that may be violated is generated. A set of checking operations is inserted into the transaction. These operations guarantee that the combination of all operations of a transaction leave the database semantically valid even if individual operations leave the database in an invalid state. By combining several checking operations within a transaction, the total number of checks is thus reduced.

No enforcement. Do not automatically enforce the semantic integrity constraints that involve records at more than one DP. If violations are likely to occur infrequently or a violation of the constraint is not very harmful, then it may not be economically justifiable to enforce the constraint.

B. Problems Resulting from Enforcing Global Semantic Integrity Constraints

DDTS requires that a single global conceptual schema be defined that describes all of the data in all participating database management systems. This is necessary in order that all database updates can be examined by TIC and modified if necessary so that all global semantic integrity constraints that cross sites can be enforced. This results in the following problems:

1) In order for a local transaction against a local database to be examined by TIC, it must be translated to GORDAS, and then translated back to the original language before being executed by the local database management system.

2) Because of the large number of types of global semantic integrity constraints that can exist, the TIC semantic integrity constraint enforcement algorithm is large and complex, and also expensive to execute.

3) The additional commands inserted into the transaction by TIC are executed each time the transaction is executed. These additional commands result in extra compute time even when they do not detect a global semantic integrity constraint violation.

4) Local DBAs have no control over who accesses the local database. This control has been transferred to the DBA responsible for creating external schemas for the APs and who specifies semantic integrity constraints that span sites.

5) Global semantic integrity constraints are not needed

in many situations. DDTS can be used to retrieve data from multiple pre-existing, independent databases in a manner similar to Multibase [16]. In such a retrieve-only system, no semantic integrity constraints need be specified because updates are not possible. Even if limited updates are permitted as in Mermaid [28] because of the independent nature of the databases, semantic integrity constraints that span databases may not exist. If they do exist, it may not be cost-effective to enforce them.

For these reasons we have elected not to implement global semantic integrity constraints in DDTS. By removing the need to specify and enforce global semantic integrity constraints, much of the motivation for maintaining a single global conceptual schema disappears. By removing the conceptual schema, DDTS can become a federated DDBMS.

V. DDTS as a Federated DDBMS

We define the term *federated* DDBMS [20] to be a loosely coupled collection of databases which users access using a common interface. In a federated database, there is no global schema that describes all of the data in all of the databases; instead, there are several unified schemas, each describing portions of databases for use by a class of users.

Fig. 12 illustrates the proposed revision to the DDTS information architecture. Basically this revision changes the DDTS information architecture as follows:

- Drop global conceptual schema (and the ability to specify semantic constraints).
- Replace the global representational schema by several unified schemas.

A *unified schema* describes data from one or more DPs. Several different unified schemas may exist at an AP, one for each class of users. This strategy is very flexible in that it may allow one class of users to access all of the data, and several classes of users to access different subcollections of the data. New unified schemas may be added for new classes of users. Existing unified schemas may be deleted at any time.

By sacrificing the requirement of enforcing global semantic constraints it is possible to minimize the four problems listed in Section IV-B.

1) Local transactions do not need to be processed by TIC, and thus do not have to be translated twice; they can be executed directly against the local database.

2) The cost of executing the semantic integrity constraint checker is removed.

3) Transaction execution is faster because commands to check for global semantic integrity constraints are eliminated.

4) The local DBA controls accesses to the local database, control which appears to be very important for political and social reasons.

Federated database management systems provide a natural migration for several existing centralized DBMSs. Initially each centralized DBMS has one conceptual schema which describes all of the data in its database. The local DBA replaces the conceptual schema by one or more local representational schemas (each describing only a portion of the local internal schema). Users then define unified schemas that map to several local representational schemas, each from a different database.

The authors doubt that several existing centralized

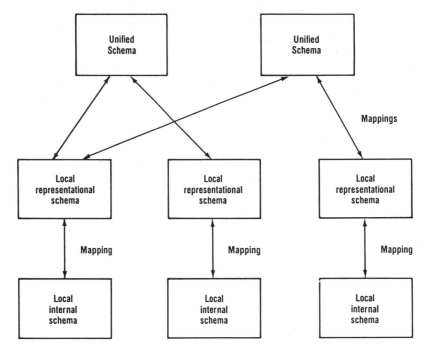

Fig. 12. DDTS information architecture as a federated distributed database management system.

DBMSs can be converted directly to a tightly coupled DDBMS such as DDTS that has a single global conceptual schema that describes all data in the participating database. An intermediate stage such as a federated DBMS appears desirable, if enforcement of semantic integrity constraints that cross sites is not required.

It is interesting to note that a federated DBMS will contain all of the subsystems of DDTS, with the exception of TIC. Additional modules will be needed to aid the DBAs to create unified schemas. Our work towards software aids to help the DBA generate unified schemas is outlined in [10].

VI. CONCLUSION

DDTS has been and will continue to be a valuable tool in evaluating approaches to the various problems of DDBMS. In this paper we have summarized some of the experiments conducted with DDTS, specifically those evaluating three materialization and access planning algorithms. The DDTS architecture is not able to support the needs of enterprises with several existing databases that must be shared but not tightly coupled. These needs can best be met by a federated DBMS whose information architecture may differ from, but whose system architecture is quite similar to that of DDTS.

In general, our experiences with DDTS have served to a) demonstrate the feasibility and utility of distributed databases, and b) refine DDTS into a useful and efficient distributed DBMS.

ACKNOWLEDGMENT

Many people worked on the design and implementation of DDTS. C. Devor, R. Elmasri, A. Hevner, K. Kasravi, E. Onuegbe, M. Pham, J. Richardson, S. Rahimi, M. Smith, M. Spinrad, J. vanDruten, J. Weeldreyer, and others laid the groundwork and built the testbed from which the results contained in this paper were derived.

REFERENCES

[1] P. M. C. Apers, A. R. Hevner, and S. B. Yao, "Optimization algorithms for distributed queues," *IEEE Trans. Software Eng.*, vol. SE-9, pp. 57–68, Jan. 1983.
[2] M. M. Astrahan and D. D. Chamberlin, "Implementation of a structured English query language," *Commun. AMC*, vol. 18, pp. 580–588, Oct. 1975.
[3] P. P.-S Chen, "The entity-relationship model: Towards a unified view of data," *ACM Trans. Database Syst.*, vol. 1, no. 1, pp. 9–36, Mar. 1976.
[4] W. W. Chu and P. Hurley, "Optimal query processing for distributed database systems," *IEEE Trans. Comput.*, vol. C-31, no. 9, Sept. 1982.
[5] C. Devor and J. Weeldreyer, "DDTS: A testbed for distributed database research," in *Proc. ACM Pacific Conf.*, Nov. 1980.
[6] P. A. Dwyer, "An experimental evaluation of materialization and access planning in a distributed data base testbed system," 1985, submitted for publication. (Available as Tech. Rep. from Honeywell Computer Sciences Center, 1000 Boone Avenue North, Golden Valley, MN. 55427.)
[7] P. A. Dwyer and A. Hevner, "Transaction optimization in a distributed database testbed system," in *Proc. IEEE Computer Society's 7th Int. Computer Software and Applications Conf.* (Chicago, IL, Nov. 1983). (Also available as Honeywell Corporate Technology Center, Computer Science Tech. Rep. CTC-83-38, Sept. 1983.)
[8] R. Elmasri, A. Hevner, and J. Weeldreyer, "The category concept: An extension to the entity-relationship model," *Data Knowledge Eng.*, vol. 1, no. 1, 1985.
[9] R. Elmasri, C. Devor, and S. Rahimi, "Notes on DDTS an apparatus for experimental research in distributed database management systems," in *Sigmod Rec.*, vol. 11, no. 4, pp. 32–49, July 1981.
[10] R. Elmasri, J. A. Larson, S. Navathe, and T. Sashidar, "Tools for view integration," *Database Eng.*, vol. 7, no. 4, pp. 28–33, 1984.
[11] A. Hevner and S. Yao, "Query processing in a distributed databases," *IEEE Trans. Software Eng.*, vol. SE-5, May 1979.
[12] A. R. Hevners, "Transaction optimization on a distributed database system," in *Proc. 2nd Symp. on Reliability in Distributed Software and Database Systems* (Pittsburgh, PA, July 1982).
[13] Honeywell Information Systems, *GCOS6 IDS/II User's Guide*, Waltham, MA, Nov. 1978.

[14] Honeywell Information Systems, Inc. *DSA Concepts*. Westwood, MA, publ. DM34, Jan. 1983.

[15] A. Klug and D. Tsichritzis, Eds., *The ANSI/X3/SPARC Report of the Study Group on Data Base Management Systems*. Reston, VA: AFIPS Press, 1977.

[16] J. Landers and R. L. Rosenberg, "An overview of multibase," in *Distributed Data Bases*, H.-J. Schneider, Ed. New York, NY: Elsevier, North-Holland, 1982, pp. 153–183.

[17] J. A. Larson, "A data dictionary for a distributed DBMS," Honeywell Computer Sciences Tech. Rep. CTC-83-30 8212, Mar. 1983.

[18] B. M. Lindsay *et al.*, "Notes on distributed database," IBM Res. Rep. RJ2571, San Jose, CA, 1979.

[19] B. Liskov, "Primitives for distributed computing," in *Proc. 7th Symp. on Operating System Principles* (ACM, Pacific Grove, CA, Dec. 1979), pp. 33–42.

[20] D. McLeod and D. Heimbinger, "A federated architecture for database systems," in *AFIPS Conf. Proc.*, vol. 49 (National Computer Conf., 1980), pp. 283–289.

[21] R. E. Moore, "An algorithm for automatic generation and insertion of semantic integrity checks into database transactions," Masters thesis, Dep. Computer Sci., Univ. of Houston, TX, Aug. 1983.

[22] S. B. Navathe, R. Elmasri, and J. A. Larson, "Integrating user views in database design," *IEEE Computer*, vol. 19, no. 1, pp. 50–62, Jan. 1986.

[23] E. Onuegbe, S. Rahimi, and A. Hevner, "Logical query translation and optimization in a distributed system," in *Proc. Nat.*

[24] J. P. Richardson, M. D. Spinrad, and M. G. Smith, "An overview of reliable transaction processing in DDTS," Honeywell Corporate Computer Sciences Center, Computer Science Tech. Rep. HR-82-268, pp. 17–38, Nov. 1982.

[25] D. J. Rosenkrantz, R. E. Stearns, and P. M. Lewis, "System level concurrency control for distributed database systems," *ACM Trans. Database Syst.*, vol. 3, no. 2, pp. 178–198, June 1978.

[26] J. Rothnie *et al.*, "Introduction to a system for distributed databases (SDD-1)," *ACM Trans. Database Syst.*, vol. 5, no. 1, pp. 1–17, Mar. 1980.

[27] M. Stonebraker, "MUFFIN: A distributed database machine," Rep. UCB/EUDERL-M79/28, Electronics Research Lab., Univ. of California, Berkeley, CA 1979.

[28] M. Templeton, D. Brill, A. Chen, S. Dao, and E. Lund, "Mermaid—Experiences with network operation," in *Proc. IEEE Data Engineering Conf.* (Los Angeles, CA, Feb. 5–7, 1986), pp. 292–300.

[29] J. D. Ullman, *Principles of Database Systems*. Rockville, MD: Computer Sci. Press, 1982.

[30] Ungermann-Bass, Inc., *Net/One Ethernet Data Link Service Reference Manual*, Santa Clara, CA, publ. 870 11524A, Feb. 1983.

[31] Xerox Corp., *Internet Transport Protocols*, Stanford, CT, publ. XSIS 028112, Dec. 1981.

Computer Conf. (Anaheim, CA, May 1983), pp. 229–239. (Also available as Honeywell Corporate Technology Center, Computer Science Tech. Rep. HR-82-269, Nov. 1982.)

Natural Language Interfaces for Large-Scale Information Processing

LYNETTE HIRSCHMAN

1. INTRODUCTION

THIS paper outlines the role and availability of natural language processing in managing large scale information processing applications. The use of natural, as opposed to formal, languages is a key ingredient in facilitating human-machine communication, where "natural language" is taken to mean use of either spoken or written language, by the human and by the machine. Use of natural language raises the machine nearer the human level, rather than expecting the human to accommodate to the level of the machine. The vision in the discussion that follows is of *intelligent machine assistants* aiding the human decision maker in assimilating, organizing, storing, accessing, and integrating vast amounts of data. Without this assistance, it is clear that decision making will be labor-intensive, uneven in quality, slow, expensive, and probably insufficiently informed for optimal decision-making.

To date, natural language processing (NLP) has had very limited impact on interfaces to large-scale applications. This technology is only now maturing to the point where commercial applications are feasible; we expect major breakthroughs in the next five to ten years in: 1) providing custom systems for natural language access to distributed information systems; 2) capture of information in natural language (NL) form for building information systems; 3) providing limited "toolkits" which can be customized by end users for limited NL interface applications; 4) combining NL techniques with other media: icons, menus, pointing devices, to provide succinct high-level interfaces; and 5) supporting communication via *spoken* language, especially speech recognition, but also speech generation, in addition to written language. Realistically, a robust broad-coverage speech system is not likely to be available for at least six to eight years. However, there are a number of important applications of NL that are likely to be available within a five-year horizon. This paper will describe the state of the art, and identify some key applications with near-term payoff.

Although the obvious applications of NLP are to user interfaces, there are some other important contributions that this area will provide. For example, one of the major issues emphasized in the Highlights of the Knowledge-Based Integrated Information Systems Engineering Project [11] is the ability to define a "global" semantics for distributed databases. A study of how people talk about the data in such databases can provide the underpinnings to such a mapping. The semantics required to formulate an NL front-end may capture much of the global semantics required by such a system.

The specific issue of temporal processing is significant enough to merit special mention. In a dynamic situation, especially a decision support application, it is critical to be able to capture temporal information, retrieve it, reason about it, and talk about it. NL researchers have been among the chief groups addressing this issue, and their work can make major contributions to the processing of temporal relations. This paper will discuss some of the ongoing work in this area in Section 6.1.

2. DIMENSIONS OF NATURAL LANGUAGE PROCESSING

This section describes various dimensions of natural language processing applications. These dimensions can be summarized as follows:

1) *Directionality of communication,* human to computer (understanding) and computer to human (generation). In addition, although the focus is on natural language, we will discuss several "mixed" approaches, which rely on techniques other than NL techniques. In particular, Section 3.2 discusses combining information retrieval techniques with natural language techniques; and Section 5 discusses combining graphics, menu, and mouse interfaces with natural language.

2) *Written versus spoken language,* for both recognition and generation. Although spoken language generation has reached a reasonable level of sophistication, spoken language understanding remains a very difficult issue: speaker-independent continuous speech understanding with a nontrivial vocabulary size (2000+ words) is still several years away. One of the critical issues here will be the ability of a speech understanding system to adapt to the speech of different users. Many systems require extensive training for each new user; the training requirement for future systems will decrease, as research makes progress in ability to model a range of users and to provide rapid speaker adaptation.

3) *Size of domain,* ranging from a very narrow domain, covering very limited topics, to completely unconstrained discourse. To date, the major successes have been achieved by constraining the domain of discourse to a narrow, well-defined topic (e.g., newspaper stories about Cyrus Vance, database queries to a database with information on Fortune 500 companies, spoken text

Reprinted with permission from *First Symp. Knowledge-Based Integrated Info. Sys. Eng.,* Feb. 1987.

editing commands, etc.). A constrained domain limits vocabulary, limits lexical ambiguity, and limits the kind of things that can be talked about, making it possible to build a reasonably detailed domain model. As the domain expands or as multiple domains are covered, problems of domain modeling and lexical ambiguity can become severe. Although some systems attempt to cover an application area rather than a domain (e.g., checking business correspondence for grammatical correctness in EPISTLE [22], [14]), coverage of broad domains significantly increases the complexity of the problem.

4) *Complexity of utterance,* ranging from single sentence to complex multiparagraph discourse. The difficulty grows in complexity as the task moves from single sentence utterances requiring relatively little in the way of discourse processing machinery, to complex discourse, which requires an elaborate set of modules for processing discourse relations, including machinery to carry along discourse context, as well as modules for reference resolution, temporal reasoning, and reconstruction of contextually implicit information. This applies to both recognition and generation.

Application types fall into three basic classes, which cut across the dimensions enumerated above. The three classes are:

a) information access
b) information capture
c) mixed initiative interactions (human-machine dialogue).

The first class of application, *information access,* is what usually comes to mind when discussing natural language interfaces to data/knowledge bases. This is the application area where commercial products are becoming available (e.g., Intellect, Q&A, Themis). The key requirement for information access is the use of natural language understanding to translate a natural language request into a DB/knowledge base query. The minimum requirement is ability to understand single sentence utterances. A more sophisticated interface would add the capability to understand a series of queries, including the ability to handle pronouns and ellipsis, but such a system requires substantially less sophistication than a system for information capture (see discussion below). Natural language generation can be used to enhance intelligibility of the answers in certain situations [15], as well as to offer feedback and/or explanations.

Information capture emphasizes the ability to understand paragraph and multiparagraph input. This requires a substantially more sophisticated system than simple query processing. Information capture via natural language has been an active area of research for over fifteen years, and is rapidly maturing. One indication of this is the *Message Understanding Conference,* which was held in San Diego in 1987. The goal of that conference was to demonstrate and compare capabilities of various message processing systems, given a Navy domain of intelligence messages (RAINFORMS). Given the state of the technology, it seems likely that there will be systems routinely capturing natural language text input in limited domains within the next five to seven years (e.g.,

medical reports [12], equipment failure reports [19], [7], intelligence messages [1], and bank telex messages [18]).

The third area, *mixed initiative* or *dialogue interaction,* requires the most sophistication, since it is a more open-ended situation which requires that the machine adapt to a variety of user responses for help or information. It requires an ability to handle connected discourse (as does the information capture application); it requires an ability to generate coherent explanations for its answers; and, finally, it requires an ability to provide "cooperative responses" to a range of users, including users who become increasingly sophisticated as they gain familiarity with the system. This in turn requires the ability to model the users of the system, and to update these models over time.

3. INFORMATION ACCESS VIA NATURAL LANGUAGE

Accessing information (e.g., databases or knowledge bases) via natural language is the most widely known application of natural language, probably because it is the only one that has had some significant commercial distribution in the form of systems such as Intellect, Q&A, and Themis. In addition, there are several powerful research systems, including SRI's TEAM system [9], and BBN's IRUS system [34]. By allowing a user to write queries in English, rather than in a formal query language, the information in the DB becomes more easily accessible to a wider community of users.

Accessing information via natural language raises a host of issues and implementation questions:

Portability—Can the system be ported to a different DB? To a different DBMS? To a different hardware/software environment?

Coverage—What portion of the language does it cover? Is this portion enough for users to stay inside it? Do users have to be trained to stay inside the language subset?

Reliability—What mistakes does the system make? Can it reliably recognize its own failure to understand? How does it help the user to "fix" a request that it hasn't understood? How does the system handle something outside the DB domain?

Intelligibility—How does the system feed the information back to the user? Does it offer an explanation? Does it request additional information in cases of ambiguity? Does it catch false assumptions on the part of the user?

System Integration—How does the system fit into the overall data processing architecture? Does it require special hardware/software? Can it be integrated into other facilities (report generation tools, pointing devices, etc.)? Can the system be used to access distributed databases? Knowledge bases?

3.1. Requirement for Access to Distributed Database Systems

The current systems provide only a very small portion of the capabilities outlined above. In addition, for complex decision-making applications, it is not clear that access to individual databases in isolation, by whatever means, addresses the information processing problem. What is really required is intelligent access to heterogeneous distributed data management systems, since in many applications, data may be distributed, for historical reasons, across a number of different systems; finding a solution will involve accessing different kinds of data from the different systems and aggregating the data (using some kind of inference or reasoning procedure), and finally displaying the answer(s) in an appropriate fashion. The ideal architecture would then be a powerful natural language capability interfacing to an expert distributed database system, which would be able to retrieve data from different DBs and reason about it.

Since a natural language DB interface must define a mapping between the database semantics and the semantics of a given language, it is also natural to look to natural language processing techniques to aid in defining a "global" semantic mapping. In particular, the kind of information that a natural language interface needs, namely the aggregation (part-whole) hierarchy and the specialization/generalization (is-a) hierarchy, are two important methods of organizing information in defining database semantics. Natural language and DB technology need to interact in this area, to improve tools for providing a generic semantic description of databases that can be used both for global schema definition and NL interfaces.

3.2. Browsing through Large Databases

For some applications, what is required is not retrieval of a specific set of facts, but the ability to "browse" through the database. This is particularly important when 1) the user does not know exactly what information is needed, and 2) the volume of data is very large, so that a query might retrieve unmanagable amounts of data. This would be typical, for example, of search using key words, where the user tends to formulate retrieval requests based on feedback from the system. For example, if a retrieval request to a database containing equipment failure reports for all reports about *tapes* retrieves several thousand entries, the user will want to narrow the search to *bad magnetic tapes*, to retrieve only those reports of direct interest. Alternatively, if an initial request for *mag tape* retrieves nothing, the user might want to generalize the query to a search for *bad tapes*, or possibly may rephrase the query entirely, to retrieve the desired data.

To date, there has been interest in natural language techniques as applied to information retrieval problems, but few successful systems (even research systems) based on any kind of linguistic processing have been realized. One successful natural language front-end to an information retrieval system is the NLM CITE system [5], which provides a natural language interface to MEDLINE, a major medical bibliographic information retrieval system.

Even more experimental are the systems used to encode information for use as index terms in retrieval. The RECONSIDER system [32] offers an interesting approach based on the *structured text* found in *Current Medical Information and Technology (CMIT)*. The techniques in RECONSIDER are not linguistic, but exploit the regularities in CMIT to create inverted files of co-occurring terms, used for retrieval of diseases associated with symptoms. Limited natural language techniques have also been applied to generation of subject indexes [33] and to chemical reaction databases [28].

Although augmenting information retrieval with natural language techniques has received some attention, it is still an underexplored area that could have significant near-term payoff. For example, one strategy might be to use key word search to retrieval sentence units containing a particular word, followed by natural language processing, to determine whether the key word is in the appropriate context. By getting feedback from the user about which occurrences were or were not of interest, it would be possible for the system to build a profile of "interesting" occurrences, such that it could screen progressively more occurrences of the key word on its own.

These questions provide an initial framework for the evaluation and comparison of the various natural language systems currently under development.

4. Information Capture via Natural Language Understanding

The second major area of application is information capture: the ability to use natural language processing techniques to convert free-form textual information into a database or knowledge base. Such an application is sketched in Section 4.3 of the Knowledge-Based Integrated Information Systems Development Methodologies Plan where NLP is used to process formal information model statements in the IDEF framework [3].

There is a long history of research in this area, although information capture is a substantially more difficult task than query processing, due to the greater syntactic variety, including (for messages) telegraphic style, the necessity of handling referring expressions, and the need to handle discourse phenomena, such as discourse coherence, time, reference resolution, and recovering contextually implicit information.

Some of the early efforts in the area of text processing were done by the Linguistic String Project at New York University, which investigated processing of various types of medical reports [29], [30], [8]. Successors to this work include a joint Unisys-NYU effort, focused on the processing of Navy maintenance reports (CASREPSs) [7], [25]. Other efforts in this area include Schank's research [31], the NOMAD system developed by Granger at UC Irvine [6], Lebowitz' *Researcher* system [17], and Logicon's MATRES system [23].

These systems all share some features, at least in terms of input/output specifications. Input is free text; output is a representation of the information in terms of (quantified) predicates with arguments, represented in terms of case-frames, e.g., a verb followed by its (thematic role) arguments, as in *repair(agent(engineer),patient(compressor))*. In systems that handle time, there is generally the concept of an event or state, with an associated predicate-argument structure and a time (span) [26].

The possible applications of such processed text are numerous. Just as natural language queries can be mapped into DB retrieval requests, predicate argument structures can be converted in DB update requests (although handling of quantification and temporal modifiers raises some issues here). Other approaches include summarization [19] and simulation, and generation of index terms for information retrieval.

5. Mixed Initiative Dialogue

The third (and most sophisticated) type of human-machine interaction is the "mixed initiative dialogue," where machine and human collaborate in a conversational mode to achieve a particular goal [10].

This kind of system can be seen as an outgrowth of other scenarios discussed earlier. For example, a truly cooperative response, even in something like a DB query setting, would consist of a user interacting with (a machine version of) an expert DB administrator, who would aid the user (and possibly instruct the user) in how to obtain the particular information desired.

To achieve this kind of interaction, a range of capabilities is needed. For example, text generation will clearly be involved as soon as there is any kind of "conversation." It will be particularly important in providing explanations or instructions to the user.

A key element of task-oriented dialogue is the notion of progression from some initial state to a final state where a given task has been completed. The system must maintain a model of the changes over time, as the task moves from initial state to completion. Somewhat independent of this, the user will be learning about the task, especially if the system provides explanation and instruction—thus the machine will need to maintain a model not only of the state of task completion, but of information already presented to the user—that is, a dynamic model of the state of the user.

The concept of user modeling is even more important if the primary purpose of the system is to aid or instruct a range of users. In this case, the system must infer from the user's questions (or perhaps from some preliminary information furnished explicitly by the user) what the user's state of expertise is. This will enable the system to furnish the most relevant amount and depth of information to the user.

Intermediate between a fully automated system that learns as it interacts with the user, and a "dumb" system that cannot adapt to the user, is the notion of *machine-aided* task execution. This has been the dominant paradigm, for example, in the machine-aided translation systems, but is also applicable to other areas, such as financial transactions, intelligence stations, automatic zip-code assignment, etc. In a machine-aided setting, the machine performs what tasks it can without human help, but recognizes a class of inputs as being outside the set of information supplied. In such a system, the NL system would process the inputs and notify the operator of those transactions that it cannot process. The system could supply the information required to identify the transaction, and characterize the parameters which it used to recognize this as information it could not process. The operator would then interact to complete the processing (or at least eliminate the problem), and the "new" information would be added to the knowledge base (if appropriate), further extending the operations performed by the system. The interface might use speech synthesis to alert the operator and explain the status, but could then resort to more classic interfaces to accept additional inputs.

In addition to the notion of "mixed initiative dialogue," it is important to mention mixed media interaction, where the system (and the user) select the medium most appropriate to the type of information. For example, the user may want to point to an area on a map (using the mouse), in order bring up a tabular display of data about the area on the map, and then ask a question, in natural language, about some of the data in the display. Similarly, the system might "answer" a question about the location of an object on a map by *highlighting* the location of the object on the map. This notion of "seamless multimedia" interfaces is an active area of research at several institutions (CMU, ISI, BBN).

6. Spin-Offs from Natural Language Research

Aside from the types of human-machine interaction explored in the earlier sections, there are a number of areas that have great relevance outside strict natural language applications. These areas deserve special mention, because the research here may have broad applicability even when no natural language interface is involved.

6.1. Temporal Processing

The first of these is the processing of temporal information. Time is obviously a highly visible and important part of communication through language. It is communicated through a variety of linguistic devices, including verb tense (*The bus left* vs. *The bus leaves*), aspect (*The bus has left* vs. *The bus left*), adverbial expressions (*The bus left on Sunday*), verb semantics (*The bus' departure preceded the loading of the cargo*), subordinate clauses (*The bus left after they arrived*), and other related devices, such as causal statements (*The bus stopped because it was out of gas*).

By exploring the ways in which time is expressed in natural language, linguists have uncovered a rich variety of temporal relations [2], [27]. The ability to represent these relations and to update a knowledge base as it changes over time are clearly issues with relevance not just to natural language processing, but to any system that tries to represent a dynamic situation. Change over time also has extremely important implications for the database world, although conventional DB systems do not allow any sophisticated reasoning about temporal relations between events. This will clearly be a major research area for knowledge representation and databases in the next few years.

6.2. User Modeling

The area of user modeling, although mentioned in connection with mixed initiative dialogue systems, clearly is not limited to natural language interaction. The notion of user modeling is essential to the successful design of human-machine interfaces.

There are two dimensions to user modeling: the modeling of a range of users of a system, in order to tailor responses to the appropriate type of user [16]; and the ability of a given user to learn over time, so that information once given need not be repeated over and over again: explanations may become more succinct, for example.

The first kind of user modeling, namely detecting the level of a user, is somewhat analogous to fault diagnosis—the system needs to "diagnose" the level of the user, based on limited (and sometimes inconsistent) information.

311

The second aspect of user modeling will need to model the change in the user's state over the course of the interaction. In particular, such a user model needs to maintain its context, where the context consists of previously exchanged information. This will be changing continuously over the course of the dialogue. Failure to incorporate at least limited user modeling will lead to systems that seem very "dumb" and repetitive, as well as inflexible or unfriendly.

6.3. Tools for Global Semantics

The ideal user interface to a distributed, heterogeneous database system would provide the user with a uniform view of the information contained in the system: a global DB semantics. The construction of such a global semantics is a complex task; it involves reconciling different views of the data, different implicit semantics, different units of measure, etc.

Since natural language interfaces must also model a kind of global semantics, which relates language constructs to general semantic classes and relationships in the domain, the tools developed for modeling semantics in natural language may well provide a useful "global semantics" for heterogeneous databases. One useful strategy may be to define two levels of semantics—a general semantics, used for supporting the natural language interface, and a second "global DB semantics," which is defined by a mapping from the general concepts to those concepts and relationships supported by specific distributed databases. The relationship between the semantics needed for natural language and the kind of semantics needed for a global DB semantics is an interesting open research issue.

6.4. Knowledge Acquisition

At the heart of both expert systems applications and natural language applications is the issue of knowledge acquisition: how to get the domain-specific knowledge into the system. It is clear that advances in this area will also affect the DB area, since the same techniques used in expert systems can be used to structure databases, and to input information into databases. Section 4 discussed information capture using natural language techniques, but based on the assumption that one already had a natural language system running in a given domain. Here the issue is: how to get that system running.

For natural language systems, it is necessary to acquire both linguistic and general domain knowledge. There is extensive research now on building a range of tools to aid in this process. The first level of tool is a knowledge representation framework that permits the user to model various "second order" relationships in a domain, e.g., part-whole, and type relationships. A second level tool would prompt the user to generalize this information, and would check for missing and inconsistent information. More advanced tools might perform generalizations and analogies on their own, given novel problems and sets of data, to provide limited "machine learning." The success of expert systems technology long-term (and also natural language interfaces) will depend heavily on the availability of such tools to ease the knowledge acquisition process.

7. Conclusion

The preceding sections have discussed a variety of uses for natural language interfaces, as well as some tools that continued research in this area will make available. This section will provide a brief discussion of the timetable for such results.

7.1. Information Access

There are now commercial systems providing limited natural language access to databases. The language coverage is not very broad, and the systems are limited in their ability to flag and explain their errors. However, this technology is currently available and will continue to improve. It is clear that natural language interfaces have not created a sudden demand for more such systems. This is because typing natural language into a system, though perhaps more friendly for the naive user than a DB retrieval request, is still cumbersome. For natural language interfaces to become truly successful, it will be necessary to provide speech recognition, so that a user can *speak*, rather than type, to get information out. Speech recognition is still a very fragile technology, though enormous gains have been made in signal processing hardware and software. It seems likely that as researchers link the signal processing back-end with the linguistic/semantic frameworks developed for text processing, we should begin to see reasonable continuous speech recognition (in limited domains) in the next 4–8 years.

7.2. Information Capture

There are only very limited "custom systems" available today for information capture from natural language (for example, the bank telex system ATRANS, developed by Cognitive Systems [18]). However, this technology is maturing and over the next few years, there should be a number of custom systems developed to capture information from various types of messages. We are also seeing the first natural language "toolkit," namely Carnegie Group's Language-Craft. Although LanguageCraft leaves much to be desired, it is an interesting first step in providing users with a limited tool set from which to build natural language interfaces (this is mostly aimed at building query interfaces, but has been used to build limited text processing interfaces as well—as mentioned in the Knowledge-Based Integrated Information Systems Development Methodologies Plan, Section 4.3 [3]).

For this class of application, there are still two serious problems: coverage of the system, and the issue of acquiring sufficient domain-specific knowledge. In general, most current systems have a fairly limited coverage of the language; those systems which have a broader coverage have problems with robustness and maintainability, particularly if the system is to be maintained by nonlinguists. The portability issue is being addressed in a number of ongoing research efforts, including work by Hirschman [13], Ballard [4], Moser [24], among others. However, tools in this area are still quite primitive and require substantial expertise on the part of the user. It will still be three to five years before we see good sets of tools to support portability of large scale systems.

It seems likely that we will see a steady growth in custom applications and an increasing number of "toolkits" over the next three to five years. In this area, there is less of a need to couple the system to speech recognition, since there are huge volumes of written material routinely transmitted; however, the ability to accurately capture spoken language would revolutionize various applications. For example, the introduction of a "talking typewriter," which transcribes spoken input, would have an significant impact on the office automation area. The commercial market here is enormous, and we are already seeing the first attempts at introducing such products.

7.3. Mixed Initiative Dialogue

The mixed initiative dialogue places the greatest demand on the system, to not only understand, but to generate reasonable responses. In the past, generation hs been handled largely by canned or template-driven responses. However, there is substantial research going on in text generation, and there are now research systems capable of doing generation for specific tasks [21], [20]. However, these systems are still research systems, and it would require substantial work to turn them into a commercially marketable "toolkit." The obvious next step is to couple generation systems with speech synthesis systems to provide spoken output; these advances will be taking place in the next year or two.

The area of mixed initiative dialogue will prove to be an extremely useful one as expert systems applications become more widespread. Such systems will also play a major role in computer-aided instruction. Again, the addition of speech recognition and generation will probably make an enormous difference in user acceptance and utility of such systems.

In general, the next five years to seven years should prove to be a pivotal period in the deployment of natural language interfaces. As speech technology develops to the point where spoken language can become the medium of interaction, the demand for such interfaces will probably increase dramatically. It is clear that the technology is maturing to the point where it will be able to provide order of magnitude improvements in the human/machine interface, and any system of the future will almost certainly include the ability to interact with the system via natural language, both written and spoken.

REFERENCES

[1] Meyers, A., "VOX—An extensible natural language processor," in *Proc. IJCAI-85*, Los Angeles, CA, 1985, pp. 821–825.

[2] "Maintaining knowledge about temporal intervals," *Comm. ACM*, vol. 26, no. 11, 1983, pp. 832–843.

[3] *Knowledge-Based Integrated Information Systems Development Methodologies Plan*, A. Gupta and S. Madnick, Eds., Sloan School of Management, MIT, Cambridge, 1987. (NTIS and DTIC Accession Number 195851).

[4] Ballard, B., "TELI," in *Proc. 24th Ann. Conf. Assoc. Computational Linguistics*, 1986.

[5] Doszkocs, T. E. and B. A. Rapp, "Searching MEDLINE in English: A prototype user interface with natural language query, ranked output, and relevance feedback," in *Proc. ASIS Ann. Meeting*, Knowledge Industry Publications, 1979, pp. 131–139.

[6] Granger, R. H., C. J. Staros, G. B. Taylor, and R. Yoshii, "Scruffy text understanding: design and implementation of the NOMAD system," in *Proc. Conf. Applied Natural Language Processing*, 1983, pp. 104–106.

[7] Grishman, R. and L. Hirschman, "PROTEUS and PUNDIT: research in text understanding," *Computational Linguistics*, vol. 12, no. 2, pp. 141–145.

[8] ——, "Question-answering from natural language medical data bases," *Artificial Intelligence*, vol. 11, 1978, pp. 25–43.

[9] Grosz, B., "TEAM: A transportable natural-language interface system," in *Proc. Conf. on Applied Natural Language Processing*, Santa Monica, CA, Feb., 1983, pp. 39–45.

[10] ——, "Focusing and description in natural language dialogues," in *Elements of Discourse Understanding*, A. Joshi, B. Webber, and I. Sag, Eds., Cambridge, MA: Cambridge University Press, 1981, pp. 84–105.

[11] Gupta, A. and S. Madnick, *Knowledge-Based Integrated Information Systems Engineering: Highlights and Bibliography*, Sloan School of Management, MIT, Cambridge, MA, 1987. (NTIS and DTIC Accession Number A195850).

[12] Hirschman, L., G. Story, E. Marsh, M. Lyman, and N. Sager, "An experiment in automated health care evaluation from narrative medical records," *Computers and Biomedical Res.*, vol. 14, 1981, pp. 447–463.

[13] Hirschman, L., "Discovering sublanguage structures," in *Sublanguage: Description and Processing*, R. Kittredge and R. Grishman Eds. Hillsdale, NJ: Lawrence Erlbaum Assoc., 1986.

[14] Jensen, K., G. E. Heidorn, L. A. Miller, and Y. Ravin, "Parse fitting and prose fixing: getting a hold on ill-formedness," *Computational Linguistics*, vol. 9, nos. 3–4, 1983, pp. 147–160.

[15] Kalita, J. K., M. L. Jones, and G. I. McCalla, "Summarizing natural language database responses," *Computational Linguistics*, vol. 12, no. 2, 1986, pp. 107–124.

[16] Kass, R. and T. Finin, "Rules for the implicit acquisition of knowledge about the user," in *Proc. of AAAI-87*, Seattle, WA, 1987.

[17] Lebowitz, M., "Researcher: An experimental intelligent information system," in *Proc. Ninth Int. Joint Conf. Artificial Intelligence*, 1985, pp. 858–862.

[18] Lytinen, S. and A. Gershman, "ATRANS: Automatic processing of money transfer messages," in *Proc. of AAAI-86*, Philadelphia, PA, 1986, pp. 1083–1088.

[19] Marsh, E., H. Hamburger, and R. Grishman, "A production rule system for message summarization," in *Proc. 1984 National Conf. on Artificial Intelligence*, Oakland University, Rochester, MI, 1984.

[20] McDonald, D. D. and J. Pustejovsky, "Tags as a grammatical formalism for generation," in *Proc. 23rd Annual Meeting ACL*, Chicago, IL, 1985, pp. 94–103.

[21] McKeown, K. R., *Text Generation: Using Discourse Strategies and Focus Constraints to Generate Natural Language.* Cambridge, MA: Cambridge University Press, 1985.

[22] Miller, L. A., G. E. Heidorn, and K. Jensen, "Text-critiquing with the EPISTLE system: An author's aid to better syntax," in *Proc. Nat. Comp. Conf.*, AFIPS Press, Arlington, VA, 1981, pp. 649–655.

[23] Montgomery, C. A., "Distinguishing fact from opinion and events from meta-events," in *Proc. Conf. Applied Natural Language Processing*, Santa Monica, CA, Feb. 1983, pp. 55–61.

[24] Moser, M. G., "Domain dependent semantic acquisition," in *Proc. First Conf. Artificial Intelligence Applications*, Denver, CO, 1984, pp. 13–18.

[25] Palmer, M. S., D. A. Dahl, R. J. [Passonneau] Schiffman, L. Hirschman, M. Linebarger, and J. Dowding, "Recovering implicit information," presented at Proc. of the 24th Annual Meeting of the Association for Computational Linguistics, Columbia University, NY, Aug. 1986.

[26] Passonneau, R. J., "Situations and intervals," in *Proc. 25th Annual Meeting of the Assoc. for Computational Linguistics,* Stanford, July, 1987, pp. 16–24.

[27] ——, "A computational model of the semantics of tense and aspect," *J. Computational Linguistics*, vol. 14, June 1988, pp. 44–60.

[28] Reeker, L. M., E. M. Zamora, and P. E. Blower, "Specialized information extraction: Automatic chemical reaction coding from English descriptions," in *Proc. Conf. on Applied Natural Language Processing*, Santa Monica, CA, Feb. 1983, pp. 109–116.

[29] Sager, N., "Natural language information formatting: The automatic conversion of texts to a structured data base," in *Advances in Computers*, M. C. Yovits and M. Rubinoff, Eds. New York, NY: Academic Press, 1978, pp. 89–162.

[30] ——, *Natural Language Information Processing: A Computer Grammar of English and Its Applications.* Reading, MA: Addison-Wesley, 1981.

[31] Schank, R. C., J. L. Kolodner, and G. DeJong, "Conceptual

information retrieval," in *Information Retrieval Research*, R. N. Oddy *et al*. Ed. London: Butterworth and Co. Ltd., 1981, pp. 94–116.

[32] Tuttle, M. S., D. D. Sherertz, M. S. Blois, and S. Nelson, "Expertness" form structured text? RECONSIDER: A diagnostic prompting program," in *Proc. Conf. on Applied Natural Language Processing*, 1983, pp. 124–131.

[33] Vladutz, G., "Natural language text segmentation techniques applied to the automatic compilation of printed subject indexes and for online database access," in *Proc. Conf. on Applied Natural Language Processing*, 1983, pp. 136–142.

[34] Weischedel, R., *et al*., "BBN laboratories: research and development in natural language processing in the strategic computing program," *Computational Linguistics*, vol. 12, no. 2, 1986, pp. 132–136.

Controls for Interorganization Networks

DEBORAH ESTRIN, MEMBER, IEEE

Abstract—Interorganization computer networks support person-to-person communication via electronic mail; exchange of cad/cam data, software modules, or documents via file transfer; input to an order-entry or accounting system via a database query and update protocol; and use of shared computational resources via an asynchronous message protocol or remote login. In most such interorganization arrangements, the set of resources that an organization wants to make accessible to outsiders is significantly smaller than the set of resources that it wants to remain strictly-internal (i.e., accessible to employees of the organization only). In addition, because the potential user is a person (or machine) outside the boundaries of the organization, the damage associated with undesired use can be high. Because of these characteristics, *Interorganization Networks* (*ION's*) have unique usage-control requirements.

This paper describes a conceptual model for implementing usage controls in ION's. In the first half of the paper we review usage control requirements in networks that cross organization boundaries. Our analysis suggests that category sets and nondiscretionary control mechanisms can be used to isolate strictly-internal facilities from ION facilities, and distinct ION's from one another. The second portion of the paper focuses on the problem of authentication in ION's, which is an essential component of the proposed control mechanisms.

Index Terms—Access control, authentication, network interconnection, network security.

I. USAGE CONTROL REQUIREMENTS IN ION's

INTERORGANIZATION computer networks support person-to-person communication via electronic mail; exchange of cad/cam data, software modules, or documents via file transfer; input to an order-entry or accounting system via a database query and update protocol; and use of shared computational resources via an asynchronous message protocol or remote login. In most such interorganization arrangements, the set of resources that an organization wants to make accessible to outsiders is significantly smaller than the set of resources that it wants to remain strictly-internal (i.e., accessible to employees of the organization only). In addition, because the potential user is a person (or machine) outside the boundaries of the organization, the damage associated with undesired use can be high. Because of these characteristics, *Interorganization Networks* (*ION's*) have unique usage-control requirements. This section analyzes these requirements and sets the stage for Section II of the paper in which we describe our approach based on non-discretionary controls. Section III elaborates on the authentication mechanisms needed to support our proposal.

Unlike traditional simple security requirements, the goal is not simply to prohibit access by outsiders; some outside access is explicitly desired. The goal is to support access to certain machines, services, and processes, while preventing access to all other internal facilities. In addition, because the function of the internal network predates and dominates that of the ION, interconnection must not interfere with internal operations. Therefore, it is not acceptable that ION facilities be physically isolated from all strictly-internal resources for this would interfere with internal communications and resource access. We want to implement *logical networks* that can be isolated from one another yet share physical resources (see Fig. 1).[1] Similarly, when two organizations interconnect, it may be inappropriate to impose a connection between the other organizations to which each was interconnected previously. In other words, the new ION may overlap physically with the existing ION's, but it must not form a transit path between those organizations that desire to remain isolated from one another (such as *B* and *C* in Fig. 2).

A. Constraints on the Solution

ION participants typically want to make only a subset of their internal resources accessible to outsiders; and in most cases, the default condition for external access is *no* access. There are two *obvious* ways to support access to certain resources while preventing access to all other resources. The first is to physically isolate those resources that are to be made externally accessible from those that are to remain strictly internal [see Fig. 3(a)]. The second is to increase access controls on *all* systems on the *internal* network so that no system allows external access unless it is explicitly approved to do so [see Fig. 3(b)]. Both solutions support controlled interconnection; however, the constraints described below make both approaches unacceptable as general solutions.

First, in most cases, the function of the internal network predates and dominates that of the interorganization network. Moreover, typically, the purpose of an internal network is to facilitate communication and resource sharing. Increased internal usage controls that are tailored to restrict outsiders may interfere with this objective. In addition, the administration of most networks is intentionally decentralized. Consequently, it is very difficult to assure conformance with new policies such as accessibility of internal resources to outsiders. Internal networks also

Manuscript received May 15, 1986.

The author is with the Department of Computer Science, University of Southern California, Los Angeles, CA 90089.

IEEE Log Number 8611570.

---

[1] The term logical network refers to a collection of computational resources and applications that communicate with one another. Logical networks operate on top of physical networks which are composed of communication links and switches.

Reprinted from *IEEE Trans. Software Engineering*. pp. 249–261, vol. SE-13, no. 2, Feb. 1987.

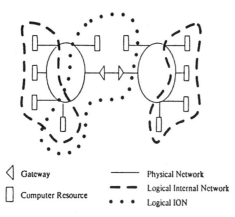

Fig. 1. Overlapping logical networks: the ION shares physical resources with the two organizations' internal networks. However, at the logical level, the ION is isolated from the strictly-internal facilities.

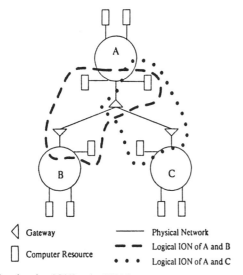

Fig. 2. Overlapping ION's: the ION between *A* and *B* shares physical resources with the ION between *B* and *C*. However, at a logical level the two ION's are not connected to one another, i.e., *B* cannot communicate with *C* via *A*.

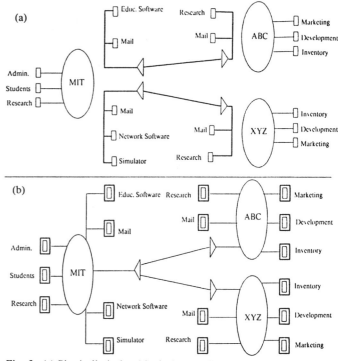

Fig. 3. (a) Physically isolated logical networks. (b) Modified access controls on all internal systems.

grow incrementally by adding connections to other internal networks as well as single machines. Therefore, it is hard to determine whether such additions introduce resources into the internal network that do not conform to network-wide policy. Finally, in order for resource owners or users to enforce a security policy they must be educated as to its purpose and operation. Educating all resource owners and users in a decentralized network is hard to accomplish once, let alone every time an external link is established.

A solution based on physical isolation may be acceptable for some special cases, but, given these constraints, it is not a general solution because it imposes excessive restrictions on communication and integration between externally accessible and internal systems. For example, in Fig. 5 XYZ Inc. provides MIT with access to some research facilities. Physical isolation would imply that these internal research facilities could not be integrated with the XYZ's internal development system. Similarly, if to protect itself from customers a supplier had to phys-

ically isolate customer-accessible online order-entry systems from the internal inventory system, the supplier would forego one of the main benefits of online order-entry—the potential for integration of order processing and inventory control. The second obvious solution described above is also unacceptable as a general solution. The constraints summarized imply that strictly-internal resources which have nothing to do with the interconnection not be required to take any action such as modifying security mechanisms, in order to be protected from external access. A requirement to take explicit security action when an external link is added violates several of the constraints listed. First, the access controls implemented may impose on internal communication and resource sharing. Second, modifying all internal systems is an exceedingly costly proposition in most mid- to large-sized organizations. Finally, even if such a cost could be justified, given decentralized management of internal facilities and/or interconnections, it is not feasible to assure conformance of all systems with new interconnections.

If internal security levels are high, all users have limited capabilities, and therefore the extent of damage that would result from treating external users as internal is contained. Nevertheless, there remain two reasons why internal security measures must be augmented in the presence of interorganization interconnection, even if the existing internal access control measures are conservative and nondiscretionary, to begin with. First, in most environments, internal needs are best met by open access to *some* shared internal resources which nevertheless should not be accessed by outsiders; in the same way that small office supplies often are freely accessible to employees.

Second, the design of a security mechanism depends critically upon an accurate model of the user population. External connections that are implemented incrementally under decentralized management may undermine the assumptions on which some internal security mechanisms were developed previously. Requirements for increased internal security also raise issues for divisions within a single organization. Divisions that wish to communicate and share resources but that wish to remain autonomous and control access to local resources encounter tensions between connectivity and autonomy or liability that are analogous to the general ION issues described here.

In summary, only the administrators of the external link (i.e., the ION gateway) and the internal resources that are made explicitly accessible should be required to take security action; in accordance with organization-wide policies or guidelines, perhaps. Owners of all other internal resources should be assured that their facilities are not accessible to outsiders. In other words, the management of a strictly-internal resource should not have to rely on its own discretionary action for restriction of external access to its facilities. *This requirement suggests the use of nondiscretionary access controls to isolate strictly-internal resources and networks from the ION without relying on the discretion or explicit action of strictly-internal resource owners.*

II. Nondiscretionary Controls for ION's

There are three essential differences between the nondiscretionary access controls called for here, and those traditionally employed in military security systems [2]–[4]. First, in the case of military systems the most common use of nondiscretionary controls is to restrict the flow of information from higher classification levels to lower ones; i.e., no read up, by a lower classification level of a higher one, and no write down, by a higher classification of a lower one. In ION's, of equal or greater concern is preventing outsiders from *invoking* proprietary, expensive, or scarce resources that are supposed to be strictly internal. In traditional terms, control of invocation concerns unauthorized disclosure, modification, and denial of *resources;* whereas, information flow control concerns only unauthorized disclosure of *information.* Although many commercial and government institutions are extremely concerned about the outgoing flow of information, in this paper we focus on invocation control because it has received far less attention in the past.

Second, the nondiscretionary invocation controls that have been developed are designed to protect the integrity of the *invoker*, not the *invoked* [5], [6]. For example, the integrity rating of a program indicates the level of assurance that the program does not contain any trojan horses. Based on these ratings, the simple integrity policy allows a user to invoke programs of *equal-or-greater* integrity only; i.e., the mathematical dual of the basic security policy [5]. In contrast, we are trying to protect each ION participant in its role as service *provider*, not *user*. To do

so, we must protect the provider from unauthorized disclosure, modification, and denial of resources. Therefore, we want a policy that prevents a program from being invoked by a user that does not have an adequate integrity rating. The invocation policy should allow a user to invoke services of *equal-or-less* integrity only. Rotenberg [7] was also concerned with protecting information providers but did so only in the form of controlling information flow, i.e., unauthorized disclosure of information. He assumed that all services necessarily returned information, and that information flow controls would prevent the returning of information to unauthorized users. In current-day network environments there exist facilities that do not necessarily return information or that do so only after the resources have been expended or an irreversible action has been taken (e.g., gateways, print servers, robotic devices, order-entry systems.) In this environment, control of invocation is needed in order to protect the owners of such services. A related issue is that in the communication applications addressed here the distinction between object and subject is not meaningful because both participants in a communication take on both roles. Consequently the distinction between clearance and classification is not useful.

Most systems that enforce nondiscretionary policies enforce confinement between categories of information. In other words, information can flow from a source to a destination only if the destinations category set contains *all* of the elements contained in the source's category set. The third distinction between traditional nondiscretionary controls and those proposed here is that organizations would like to support *overlapping* logical networks (see Fig. 1). In order to do so, the nondiscretionary controls enforced on network communications should implement a relaxed rule, namely, that information can flow from a source to a destination so long as the source's and destination's category sets *overlap*, i.e., have a nonempty intersection. As is described later, this intersect restriction on network communications would then be complemented with traditional system-level controls in those systems made accessible. These issues are summarized in Fig. 4.

Based on these characteristics and requirements, we suggest that special network entry points, *ION gateways*, implement nondiscretionary invocation controls. ION gateways are logical gateways that mediate and control the forwarding of messages from outsiders into the internal network.[2] Each organization operates its own ION gateway. Therefore, communication between any two ION participants involves two ION gateways. In addition, ION facilities which can be communicated with by outsiders must implement discretionary or nondiscretionary controls to protect other non-ION resources. Finally, because organizations communicate with multiple external

---

[2]ION gateways may be composed of multiple physically distributed components, e.g., a packet forwarder, policy filter, authentication server.

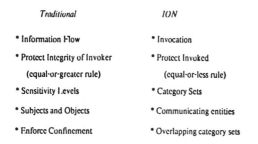

Traditional	ION
• Information Flow	• Invocation
• Protect Integrity of Invoker	• Protect Invoked
(equal-or-greater rule)	(equal-or-less rule)
• Sensitivity Levels	• Category Sets
• Subjects and Objects	• Communicating entities
• Enforce Confinement	• Overlapping category sets

Fig. 4. Comparison of traditional nondiscretionary controls and the requirements encountered in ION's.

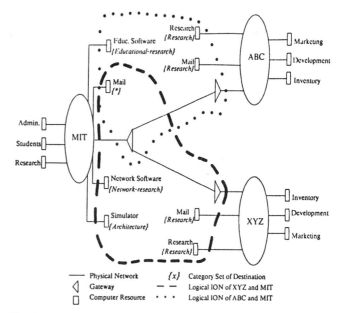

Fig. 5. Example of an Interorganization Network: one ION exists between MIT and XYZ and another ION exists between MIT and ABC. Both ION's overlap physically yet are isolated logically from the internal networks of the three organizations.

organizations, and these interorganization relationships are not hierarchically related to one another, the access rights should be based on category sets (compartments) and not sensitivity levels.

The participating organizations can tailor the strength of the gateway's implementation to suit their security requirements. These requirements will vary with the value of the online information and resources, as well as the nature of the interorganization relationships. One way to formulate the general requirement is to require that the level of monitorability and accountability equal that of telephone and paper communication.

In the following sections we describe two example ION's and discuss how nondiscretionary controls can be implemented in the ION gateways and ION facilities without modification to strictly-internal facilities.

A. Examples

The following two examples illustrate how nondiscretionary invocation controls could be used to protect the resources of interconnected organizations. The first example is from the perspective of MIT. The second is from the perspective of ABC Inc. These examples are *representative* of existing activities. However, the details have been changed somewhat to illustrate several points in a single example; therefore the examples are *hypothetical*, not actual, cases.

MIT has connected some of its internal computer facilities to those of two of its industrial sponsors, ABC and XYZ who happen to be competitors of one another (see Fig. 5). The connections are intended to support exchange of software modules, access to some unique computational resources, and electronic mail. ABC has access to a host on which an MIT research group is developing educational software. XYZ has access to a different host on which another MIT research group is developing network software. XYZ also has access to a design simulation program developed by yet another group of researchers at MIT. In addition, both ABC and XYZ have access to electronic mail communications. For the sake of this example, we assume that both ABC and XYZ invoke the various services (i.e., file servers for software distribution, simulator, and mail distribution) by sending appropriately formatted messages through the gateway, and the servers return the requested data via the same gateway to

the requesting organization. Aside from these ION resources, MIT has other strictly-internal computer-based facilities: administration, student accounts, other research projects, gateways to other networks, etc.

In this example there are *five* logical networks that need to be isolated from one another; where logical network refers to a set of computer resources that are intended to communication and interwork. The two logical ION's are shown in Fig. 5, one between MIT and ABC, and the second between MIT and XYZ. In addition, each of the three organizations has a logical internal network which each organization should be able to isolate from the ION's. Note that there is no logical ION between ABC and XYZ because none of their facilities are intended to communicate or interwork. In order to isolate ION from strictly-internal facilities, and the XYZ ION facilities from the ABC ION facilities, MIT can implement the following controls:

1) Implement a single ION gateway and prohibit direct connection of all internal machines to outside organizations. Equip the gateway with an authentication mechanism to certify the source of each message.

2) Assign appropriate category sets to each of the ION facilities, and no category sets to strictly-internal ones. MIT assigns the category set {Educational-research} to the host used for development of educational software, the set {Network-research} to the host used for development of network software, {Architecture} to the design simulator, {*} to its electronic mail system to indicate all, and {Strictly Internal} to all other internal systems. See Fig. 5. If an internal facility is not registered at all the gateway assumes that it is not accessible via this entry-exit point. The category information is assigned to internal re-

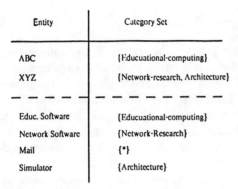

Entity	Category Set
ABC	{Educational-computing}
XYZ	{Network-research, Architecture}
Educ. Software	{Educational-computing}
Network Software	{Network-Research}
Mail	{*}
Simulator	{Architecture}

Fig. 6. MIT's gateway table containing category set information.

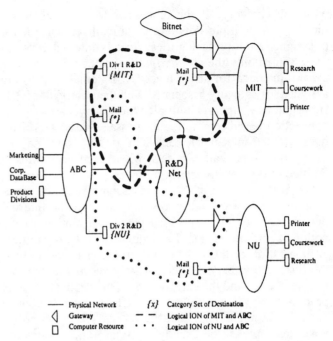

Fig. 7. Example of an Interorganization Network: one ION exists between ABC and MIT, and another ION exists between ABC and NU. Both ION's overlap physically yet are isolated logically from one another and from a third ION, Bitnet, to which MIT is connected.

sources but the information is maintained in MIT's gateway, see Fig. 6.

3) The ION gateway checks the category set of the source $\{Ci\}_s$ and of the destination $\{Ci\}_d$ of each message and forwards the message to the intended destination *if and only if* $\{Ci\}_s$ *Intersect* $\{Ci\}_d$ does not equal null-set $\{\ \}$ (referred to as the *Intersect* rule).

4) Equip the internal ION facilities (software distribution servers, electronic mail server, and design simulator) with discretionary or nondiscretionary controls to enforce application-specific controls (e.g., restrictions based upon the filename of a file request), isolate non-ION files and processes, and prevent transit between the ABC ION and the XYZ ION's.

Similarly, ABC and XYZ each label their own research hosts and inventory systems with the category set {MIT} only, and implement gateways with message authentication and the *Intersect* rule. *Note that each organization assigns category labels to incoming messages for interpretation by its own facilities. Therefore, although naming must be consistent within each organization, it need not be consistent throughout the ION as a whole.*

Our second example is from the perspective of one of the computer manufacturers, ABC, that connects its internal network to a nation-wide network of computer research and development (R&D) laboratories. Informal person-to-person research communication transpires with a large subset of all the organizations on the network. In addition, there are two universities, MIT and Northeastern (NU), with which ABC is conducting two separate joint studies, one with each of its major research divisions. In conjunction with these studies, ABC supports some file transfer and remote job entry with these two organizations only. To support such tailored connections, ABC assigns the category sets {MIT} and {NU} to Division 1's and 2's respective R&D systems, and all three organizations assign the wild-care category set {*} to their respective mail servers. See Fig. 7. The mail server is thereby made accessible to all network members, whereas the joint-development facilities are made accessible to the select parties only. As described above, the gateway authenticates messages, implements the *Intersect* rule, and ION facilities are equipped with discretionary or nondis-

cretionary controls to isolate non-ION processes and files. For the most part, the two universities, MIT and NU, are not concerned about protecting internal resources. One exception is that MIT has another gateway to a special network, Bitnet, which in turn connects to the European Academic Research Network (EARN) that interconnects European research institutions. In order for MIT to remain on Bitnet, it must guarantee that no nonuniversity parties send mail or other traffic to international destinations over the subsidized network.[3] For this purpose, MIT implements the *Intersect* rule in its gateway to the R&D net, assigning wild card category sets to entire regions of its internal network that it wants to be globally accessible, but assigning the Bitnet gateway the strictly-internal category only.

B. Implementation

In general, the following controls should be implemented by each ION participant. A more detailed description is provided elsewhere [1].

First, an ION participant must define categories and assign to each ION machine or process the set of categories (compartments) for which it is to be used. For example, the organization may define a category for each ION in which it is a participant.[4] If a process is intended for external access by members of a single ION (e.g., an order entry system for customers), then the process is assigned

[3]This restriction to university parties is necessary in order to conform with policy requirements of the European PTT's.

[4]If different external entities in an ION are to be given different capabilities, then subgroups are defined and each subgroup is assigned its own category set.

only that category. If the process is to be accessed by members of multiple ION's (e.g., a mail server), then it is assigned multiple categories. Strictly-internal services are assigned only the *strictly internal* category since they are not intended for any ion access. External entities are assigned the category associated with their particular ION. If the gateway supports multiple types of invocation (e.g., connection-based remote login, message-based server requests, electronic mail), each ION or subgroup may be assigned multiple category sets, where each set applies to a different type of invocation.

Given these category sets and assignments, the organization allows external invocations to enter the internal domain only through specified gateways; similar to the notion of entry points [7]. Each gateway forwards (routes) an invocation to the indicated destination if and only if the *Intersection* between the category set of the external invoker $\{Ci\}_s$ and the category set of the destination ION process $\{Ci\}_d$ is not nullset, $\{ \}$. The gateway's control policy does not require that the category sets of the invoker and invoked be exactly the same, i.e., it does not necessarily enforce confinement. Each ION application enforces additional controls which restrict flows across categories; see below. Strictly-internal entities (processes, programs, mail-boxes, machines, etc.) are assigned a category set of {strictly internal} only, and are therefore not accessible to any external groups. In addition, if an internal process or machine is not registered, it is not accessible via the ION gateway. The mechanism can be implemented using a nondiscretionary access control list for each ION process, where the list contains groups that are allowed to access the process. Internal invocations originate within the organization's domain, do not enter through gateways, and therefore are not subject to these nondiscretionary controls. In addition to maintaining category information for each outside ION or subgroup, the ION gateway must know where to route incoming and outgoing messages based on the destination address, as to traditional gateways.

Finally, the ION participant must implement discretionary or nondiscretionary controls within ION facilities. ION facilities must enforce application-specific controls that the gateway can not enforce itself (e.g., restrictions on the dollar amount of a purchase order or the filename of a cad/cam file request). In addition, ION facilities that reside in overlapping logical networks must prevent information or invocations from flowing between ION and non-ION entities, and between different ION entities. A range of traditional system security mechanisms can be employed. *System level controls complement the controls on network communications, i.e., at the network boundary.*

The result of these mechanisms is that no external invocations can be sent to entities that are not explicitly registered as accessible to outsiders. In addition, the ION participant can specify which categories of external users may access each ION process.

C. Information Flow

In many cases, information flow controls on outgoing traffic may be needed as well. If an organization is unable or unwilling to rely on existing policies to discourage employees from exporting confidential information via the ION, the organization may require additional information flow controls. For example, some features of computer-based communications remove direct employee discretion from the generation of ION messages, such as automatic distribution lists. A user who sends a message to a distribution list typically does not know which individuals are on the list; the user knows only that they share a common interest. If one of the addressees on the list is located outside of the organization, an employee may export information without realizing it and therefore without considering relevant company policies. In addition, an ION participant may enforce controls on outgoing flows if it must conform to policies imposed by other ION participants (e.g., Bitnet's no transit requirement described earlier in the MIT-ABC-NU example), or if it must pay for outgoing flows on a usage-sensitive basis. For many interorganization networks invocation control is needed for incoming traffic whereas information flow control is needed for outgoing traffic. Therefore, the two do not conflict with one another as they often do when both apply to traffic flowing in the same direction [6].

Some information flow controls can be implemented using category sets and the *Intersect* rule: internal user A can send a message/file X to external user/resource B if and only if $\{C\}_a$ and $\{C\}_b$ have a nonempty intersection. However, more elaboration is needed and capabilities will vary with the type of control mechanisms available internally. For example, if internal systems implement nondiscretionary controls that mark objects with security labels, the gateway can control outgoing information flow based on the security level of the message content as well as the category set of the message creator. Because each organization implements its own gateway, each can integrate existing internal labeling systems into its ION gateway.

In summary, the gateway authenticates, labels, and maintains information on category sets while most of the rest of the internal systems can go on unchanged. Because of the gateway's central role, there are a number of important design issues which require further elaboration but which we will only mention here. One is that the gateway and ION entities are programs that must be "trusted" by the organization that owns them. However, each ION participant can make its own decision as to the investment and trust that it will place on its ION gateway. The general requirement is to raise the level of monitorability to that of non-ION communication channels (e.g., telephone and paper). Therefore, organizations' security requirements vary according to the value of online information and resources, as well as the nature of the interorganization relationships. The second issue is that the gateway must authenticate the source of a request/message in order to properly evaluate its category set. A range of tools, of varying strength, can be used, from third-party authentication servers to one-time encryption keys. Although participants need not use a common authentication scheme internally, they must agree on the authentication protocol used by their respective gateways, as described in Section III.

D. Confinement and the Role of System-Level Controls

The above discussion and examples illustrate how a nondiscretionary policy based on a relaxed *intersection* rule can be used to isolate logical networks without imposing either physical isolation or increased access controls on all internal systems. Before concluding, it is important to emphasize the role of system-level controls in those systems that an organization does include in the ION. First, as was stated earlier, it is essential to the security of critical strictly-internal systems to implement controls in all ION systems to prevent external traffic from traveling via the ION system to strictly-internal systems or systems belonging to other ION's. Although such system-level controls depend on traditional security techniques, the task may be very difficult, depending upon the application involved. In particular, the larger in number and more varied are the tasks performed by the system, the harder it is to certify or audit system-level controls. At the same time, if the system is used for strictly-internal purposes as well, the overhead experienced by internal users must be minimized.

Despite these difficulties, an intersection rule on communication flows could be combined with confinement rules at the ION-system level to achieve confinement in the larger network system. For instance, in the first example (see Fig. 5), MIT provides both ABC and XYZ with access to its electronic mail delivery system. At the communications level, an intersection policy is enforced so that both customers can communicate with the order-entry system. As indicated in Fig. 6, ABC has category set {Educational-research}, XYZ has category set {Network-research,Architecture}, and the mail system has category set { }. If a traditional confinement policy were implemented, XYZ would be unable to communicate with the simulator because the simulator's category set is not a superset of XYZ's category set. Moreover, the confinement rule would prevent the mail system from sending online messages back to either of the companies because neither of the companies' category sets is a superset of the mail system's category set. By equipping the ION gateway with a nonempty intersection rule instead of a strict confinement rule, the desired communication between customers and the order-entry system is achieved. However, because the rule governing communications has been relaxed, the order-entry system must take responsibility for preventing flows across, what are intended to be, *isolated* logical networks—that between MIT and ABC and that between MIT and XYZ. In other words, the mail system needs to enforce the traditional confinement policy to prevent information and invocation flow (message based) between ABC and XYZ entities. Although the security of such a scheme depends critically upon the security of the system-level controls employed, the approach described throughout this paper structures the problem so that security risks can be isolated and managed by the organizations involved. In other words, although we have not eliminated the problems that are common to all computer system security (e.g., certifiability, overhead cost, etc.), we have developed an approach to access controls in ION's for which the security risks are as tractable as traditional computer system access controls. And we have done so without violating organization constraints such as minimizing interference with internal resource sharing.

III. Security and Authentication in Interorganization Networks

Previous sections did not address vulnerabilities introduced by ION communication that *is sanctioned* by official policies. In other words, discussion has focused mainly on how to tailor ION's to include only those resources desired by the organizations and did not address the risks associated with converting a manual information or resource channel into an automated one. In many cases the risks may be fundamentally altered in the absence of extremely costly measures, where cost is measured in both dollars and convenience of use. On the other hand, in many applications it is adequate to accept the risks if they can be identified and assessed *a priori* and monitorability and auditability are adequate.

Two aspects of ION communications that are inherently more risky than traditional voice or paper communications are the difficulty of authenticating information about the source and destination of communications, and the ability to cause internal mechanisms to behave contrary to the intended procedure. In general, human boundary-spanners are more cost-effective at both tasks than are machines because of the flexibility with which humans can combine multiple sources of information and detect suspicious or unordinary events. Often these procedures are not conscious or are at least hard to codify. The majority of this section discusses authentication in ION's. The last portion addresses the second issue which resembles the Trojan Horse phenomenon.

A. Authentication Requirements

The controls outlined in previous sections rest upon assigning categories or rights according to the organization affiliation of the source and destination. If the source and destination information can be falsified, then the controls are not effective. More accurately, they are not effective if they can be falsified *without detection* before or after the fact. Therefore, environments in which the risk of falsified source information is significant will require mechanisms to authenticate that a communication is from the entity it claims to be from. A range of authentication mechanisms can be used. In some cases the gateway may rely on the correct operation of the communication system, i.e., that the communication system does not accept mislabeled communications from sources and does not change the information in transit. Such reliance may be reasonable if the organizations employ a third party whose reputation depends upon proper operation and whose own accounting interests rely on proper identification of sources. Similarly, the gateway may rely on the fact that the source will not be able to receive replies to its messages if the source address is not correct. If falsification is not detectable through malfunction of this kind, the gateway may require a more explicit authentication mechanism. For example, a predefined password, ticket, or key may be used to authenticate a source to the gateway. Finally, ION participants can employ a third party mechanism to dynamically authenticate a source using session keys or ticket mechanisms. These alternatives are discussed in the following sections. It is also necessary to authenticate that the destination is who the source believes it to be. The latter function is more easily left to the reliable operation of the communication delivery system. Since the delivery system for incoming communication belongs to the organization, it is more reasonable for it to be trusted. In the case of outgoing communication, the authentication mechanisms described above must be employed to achieve the same level of trust.

An interesting problem that is not solved by any of these authentication mechanisms is message encapsulation and forwarding. Message forwarders can cause a message to appear to have a different organization affiliation than that of the message originator. However, we assume that message forwarders must take responsibility for their actions and if messages are encapsulated in such a way as to mask the name of the originator, it is the responsibility of the forwarder to declare itself as a mail gateway/tunnel and conform to organization guidelines (e.g., implement usage controls) [8]. Therefore, as part of the guidelines specifying the ION usage controls that each ION gateway must implement, an organization must make clear that automatic forwarding of mail off of the internal network constitutes gateway behavior.

The remainder of this section describes authentication requirements and protocols for ION's. Neeham–Schroeder type authentication tools are shown to satisfy the authentication requirements outlined in the usage control model [10]. The primary ideas presented here are that internal authentication mechanisms need not necessarily be modified to comply with interorganization requirements, and that multiple classes of authentication are desirable.

In order to enforce the desired policies and controls, and to comply with contract agreements, interconnecting organizations must be able to authenticate one another. The main purpose of authentication in this domain is to assure *accountability* should some behavior transpire that is in violation of contracts.

There are two types of authentication required:

- First, when one organization contacts another for the first time, the organizations must authenticate that each is legitimate. For example, when a new client contacts a vendor, the vendor typically checks the client's credit rating just as the client has checked the vendor's credibility in the market. In this case, the new computer-based transaction mechanisms should allow organizations to assess one another via third parties in the same formal way that is done currently via telephone and paper.

- Second, each time an organization contacts another, it must authenticate that it is the organization that it claims to be. When an established client contacts a vendor to reorder some item by telephone or paper mail, both parties typically have informal or formal procedures for assuring each other that they are who they claim to be. For example, purchasing agents recognize one another's voices, or rely on the letterhead of invoices and letters, or call back the requester at the claimed organization. In this case, the new mechanisms must substitute for what are often informal procedures via telephone or postal mail.

In both cases, different levels of authentication are appropriate for different organizations and types of transactions. For example, the larger the proposed purchase, the more confident the vendor will want to be that the customer has an adequate credit rating and that it is who it claims to be. Similarly, the larger the purchase, the more confident the client will want to be that the vendor will be able to uphold its end of the agreement—delivery date, quantity, quality, service, etc.

The goal of this discussion is to specify how two or more organizations can make use of trusted third parties to authenticate one another without having to modify internal systems and protocols, with the exception of the ION gateway. The methods proposed fit well with the model of usage controls described in earlier sections. The discussion begins with a list of assumptions about organizations' and third party facilities. Initiation authentication is then described, followed by transaction authentication, and multiple levels of service for both types of authentication.

B. Assumptions

Several assumptions are made about the ION participants' internal facilities. First, each organization[5] A has an internal authentication server AS_a that it, A, trusts to authenticate individuals *within* organization A. Contracts between ION participants specify that an organization A is responsible for the integrity of the information provided by AS_a. A second assumption is that an organization should be able to participate in ION authentication using existing internal authentication mechanisms. Although the organization might choose to intensify such mechanisms in the presence of new liabilities for correctness, it re-

---

[5] An organization is defined here as a set of entities that are willing to trust and be represented to other organizations by a single authentication server and gateway.

mains an internal decision. Finally, organizations are assumed to have a known and small number of ION gateways (we will assume 1 for simplicity). All packets that enter or exit an organization's internal network must pass through one of these official ION gateways. Much of the function described below for the ION gateways can be offloaded to special policy servers to improve the gateway's packet-forwarding performance. However, for simplicity all functions will be treated as a part of a single logical gateway, even though they may be physically separated.

Several assumptions are made with respect to third party services as well. First, each organization has many ION-supported relationships, each of which is governed by a separate contract. If no third party is employed, authentication must be handled on a pairwise basis. Since authentication fundamentally depends on sharing a secret, each organization would have to keep track and guard as many secrets as there are organizations it communicates with. The benefit of employing a third party is not the traditional space considerations, but rather the liability associated with guarding each of the secrets. In addition, minimizing the number of organizations that one trusts with a secret makes it is easier to certify that the secret is being kept. Also, if the communicating organizations are competitors or otherwise mistrustful of one another, the third party can act as a buffer between them. The function of the third party is twofold. The first is to provide information about organizations to one another when they interact for the first time. The second function is to certify that a particular transaction/connection/message/packet is from the *organization* that it says it is from. It is left to the source organization's AS to certify that the communication is from the claimed individual, i.e., x, within the organization A. Different levels of service (of *guarantee*) are available for different types of organizations, transactions, and relationships. Any two (or more) organizations that want to be able to authenticate messages from one another must agree on a single mutually trusted third party. Actually, the scheme below could be extended to allow the participants to use different third parties [9] but for simplicity we will assume that they agree on a single one.

C. Initiation Authentication

If transactions are carried out *online* it makes economic sense for organizations to be able to initiate relationships with one another online as well. For example, a computer manufacturer may buy a certain chip by sending online price queries to a collection of suppliers and initiating a purchase with the lowest bidder. In this case, the selected supplier will want to check the credit rating of the new client just as it does when a first-time purchase is proposed over the phone or on paper.

In the paper and voice world a wide range of requirements and corresponding procedure exist for evaluating the legitimacy or credit of a new client. We will discuss this further in subsection III-F. For now, we will assume

that the third parties that a supplier traditionally checks with are accessible online. If they are not, then the supplier must use traditional media for evaluating new clients.

The general approach to initiation authentication is described in terms of a new client A proposing to purchase something from a supplier B.

When the supplier receives a message it checks the source listed on the order against a list of known entities, i.e., initiated clients. If the source does not appear on the list, the supplier sends an authentication request to one of several third parties employed for this purpose. A may send a suggested third party's name along with the original message if A anticipates the need for initiation authentication. Along with the name of the claimed entity A, B includes the criteria according to which the AS should evaluate A, e.g., credit rating. B may set the criteria according to the destination of the message (i.e., the level of risk, or value of information or product residing at the destination), or the size of the request.[6] If the source is not registered with any of the third parties employed by the supplier, the purchase order may be rejected or a message returned saying that registration with third party X is required. It is then up to the customer to reinitiate the purchase after establishing its identity with X. If the third party does have the client registered, the third party returns its evaluation of the client (e.g., credit rating, or perhaps just an assurance that the client is a real company) to the supplier. The supplier adds the client to its list of initiated clients along with the evaluation. The supplier also records the name of the third party that was able to provide the information about the client. From this point on the client is initiated until the supplier decides to recheck the evaluative information.

Following is an example of a dialog that could be used to implement initiation authentication as described above:
1) $A \rightarrow B$: purchase order
2) $B \rightarrow AS$: A, evaluation criteria
3) $AS \rightarrow B$: A, evaluation
4) $\{ B \rightarrow A$: m, register with $AS \}$
5) B adds A, evaluation, AS address to known-entity list

At this stage the organization that the purchase order *claims* to be from is initiated as a legitimate entity to do commerce with. However, the supplier still needs to know that the purchase order in fact came from that organization. In addition, in the future, when the initiated client sends other purchase orders, the supplier must be able to authenticate that the purchase orders are from the claimed client for which the supplier maintains credit rating information, etc. What is needed is a mechanism for authenticating that a particular transaction is from the claimed party. The following subsection describes an approach to *transaction authentication*.

---

[6]In the latter case, gw_b would have to pass the purchase order to some service in order to determine the appropriate evaluation criteria since it is based on something other than the source and destination of the message, which is the only information the gateway has direct access to.

D. Transaction Authentication

Assuming that a client has been initiated and is now a registered client with the vendor, each transaction must be authenticated. This subsection outlines the approach and describes a simple protocol for transaction authentication and implementation issues.

A protocol for ION authentication will be described for two organizations, A and B, who want to authenticate messages from one another. However, we assume that both organizations communicate with many other organizations as well so that the approach must scale well. After each organization has registered itself and a secret key with a common third party, a Needham and Schroeder protocol is used to authenticate the organizations and provide communicating pairs with session keys so that they can authenticate messages from one another [10].

Before describing the protocol, we should emphasize why a third party is employed in this dynamic phase of authentication. As long as each organization is maintaining information about the other, each pair of communicating organizations could exchange a secret key with which to authenticate one another. Our rationale for employing a third party is that there is significant overhead in protecting a secret. Given that organizations have many correspondents (i.e., other organizations that they transact with), it is significantly more manageable for an organization to safeguard a single key to communicate with a third party than it is to safeguard n keys, one for each of its n correspondents. Note that the concern is not for space, since as mentioned, some contract or other information is already stored for almost every correspondent. Rather, the concern is for the nuisance associated with safeguarding secrets. For this reason, a third party is employed for transaction authentication.

The protocol begins when an individual x in organization A sends a message to y in organization B; x and y may be people or machines. The message header lists the source and destination organizations and individuals. All messages travel in and out of A and B via gw_a and gw_b, respectively. If B considers there to be no need (i.e., no risk associated with open access to y), it may forward the message to y unauthenticated. However, if B wants to control external access to internal resource y, then for this discussion we will assume that B uses nondiscretionary controls and assigns category labels to incoming messages, as was described. Because B assigns a category label according to the source of the message, B wants to authenticate the source, i.e., make sure that the source listed in the message header really generated the message. Functionally, this means that the organization listed in the header will take responsibility for the message.

To authenticate the source organization, B sends a message to the third party that it has listed as the one to use to authenticate messages from A; we will call this third party authenticator AS_{ab}. (We assume that during initiation authentication described above, the two parties identified a mutually trusted third party.) B asks AS_{ab} for a key

with which to authenticate A and subsequent messages sent by A during this session. B also returns the message m to gw_a saying that authentication is required. When gw_a receives the returned, unauthenticated message from gw_b it asks its internal AS_a to authenticate x. B also authenticates y through a conversation with its internal AS_b.

AS_{ab} sends gw_b a session key E_{ab} along with the session key encrypted in A's private key E_a; included also is a timestamp and an identifier of B. The entire message includes a timestamp or nonce and is encrypted under B's private key E_b. Both organizations' addresses and private keys have been stored with AS_{ab} previously when A and B registered with AS_{ab}. AS_{ab} uses these secret keys to authenticate the organizations. B then sends A the session key encrypted in A's secret key. B does not have A's secret key, but was given the encrypted session key by AS_{ab}. B is guaranteed by AS_{ab} that only A will be able to read this message. Similarly, A is guaranteed by AS_{ab} that any message identifying B along with a session key encrypted under A's secret key must have originated with AS_{ab} and that only B has been given a copy of the session key. A and B now each have a copy of the session key and are guaranteed by AS_{ab} that any message encrypted under key can be read by the other organization, only. Finally, to protect against replays by an intruder, A and B carry out a simple handshake, e.g., exchanging the current date and time.

Both gateways store the session key and gw_a resends the message m from x encrypted with the key. Both gateways encrypt all subsequent communication between x and y with the session key until the session ends or either party decides to reauthenticate. gw_b is assured that any messages arriving under that key came from gw_a and gw_a relies on internal authentication to assure that the message came from party x within A. Similarly, gw_a is assured that only someone in B can receive the message, since only gw_b can decrypt the message, and gw_b relies on its internal authentication to assure that the message goes to y, only.

The dialog that corresponds to this protocol is listed below.

1. $x \rightarrow GW_b$: m
2. $GW_b \rightarrow AS_{ab}$: (B, A)
3. $GW_b \rightarrow GW_a$: m, error-unauthenticated
4. $GW_a \rightarrow AS_a$: x and $GW_b \rightarrow AS_b$: y
5. $AS_{ab} \rightarrow GW_b$: $E_b(A, E_{ab}, E_a(B, E_{ab}, T))$
6. $GW_a \rightarrow GW_a$: $E_a(B, E_{ab}, T)$
7. $GW_a \rightarrow GW_b$: $E_{ab}(I)$
8. $GW_b \rightarrow GW_a$: $E_{ab}(I - 1, J)$
9. $GW_a \rightarrow GW_b$: $E_{ab}(J - 1)$

In summary, using their secret keys (e.g., E_a and E_b), each organization can authenticate itself to the trusted third party in order to request a session key. The gateways use this session key to authenticate the source and destination organizations of each message. The organizations take responsibility for authenticating the destination within their respective organizations, based on existing internal authentication mechanisms. Consequently, AS_{ab} is liable if organization A or B is incorrectly authenticated, whereas AS_a and AS_b are liable if x or y are not who they claim to be. This characteristic is significant because it allows an organization with tight physical security to dispense completely with internal authentication if it so chooses.

E. Implementation

The following changes are required to implement this protocol among organizations with heterogeneous internal networks:

Third Party:

1) A method for distributing keys between organizations and trusted third parties is needed so that the trusted third party can authenticate the organization.

ION Gateway:

1) The gateway must maintain a list of trusted third parties so that when an unauthenticated message arrives from another organization, the gateway knows where to go to request authentication. The gateway must also store the private key used to authenticate its organization to trusted third parties. In addition the gateway maintains the known-entities list which includes evaluation information and mutually trusted third party for each initiated organization.

2) Encryption in the gateway. *No* internal entities need to encrypt messages for the purpose of authentication. Each gateway must store the session keys and associate them with the appropriate incoming and outgoing packets; e.g., by assigning the source, destination pair and the key to a virtual or physical port.

3) The gateway must be able to ask the authentication mechanism to authenticate the source of an outgoing message (i.e., generated internally).

Note that the individual persons or machines that originate messages need not be concerned with this procedure other than responding to authentication challenges from the internal AS. The gateway handles external authentication requests, retransmission of the first message in a session, as well as all encryption.

Several of the functions that logically are done in the gateway when a session is first authenticated may be offloaded to different hardware in order to improve the efficiency of forwarding packets that belong to ongoing sessions. However, if the level of authentication is such that sessions consist of one message only (e.g., authenticating electronic mail), there is little savings. On the other hand, if each packet in a mail, remote login, or file transfer session is authenticated individually, the overhead may be great and warrant offloading. Therefore, the appropriate engineering depends on the level of interconnection, i.e., whether the gateway is a packet forwarding gateway or an application level gateway in which application protocols are terminated.

To offload this function to a server, the protocol would be modified as follows. When the first packet in a session arrives it is assumed to be unauthenticated and is forwarded to the ION policy server which sits in the destination organization (B in the above example). The policy server carries out the protocol listed above for the gateway (gw_b in the above example). The gw automatically forwards all unauthenticated incoming packets to the policy server during this dialog with the third party ION authenticator (AS_{ab}). Once the source organization is authenticated and the session key is obtained, the ION policy server sets the port in the gateway to authenticated and sets the session key. From then on packets arriving to that port in that key will be forwarded to the destination(s) for which they were authorized (determined by the rights assigned to the source organization, see [11]), until the session is closed or until either side decides to reauthenticate. In either event, the policy server resets the port and session key entries. The policy server could also handle the initiation protocols for authenticating new clients.

As organizations adopt more sophisticated internal authentication mechanisms, such as badge readers, the discrepancy between internal and external authentication levels will grow. If internal facilities and applications assume that authentication involves the sophisticated internal mechanism instead of a less sophisticated external mechanism, it may be inappropriate to tell the application that an ION user is "authenticated" in the same way that internal users are. The ION gateway must compensate for the lower level of authentication of external users by taking responsibility for their authentication, or by adopting additional mechanisms, assuming the internal application cannot be updated to accommodate multiple levels of authentication.

F. Multiple Levels of Service

Different types of transactions require different degrees of confidence in the authenticity of the client. And, different strengths of authentication require different types of equipment and facilities. When the highest level of authentication is not available, some lower level of authentication may be adequate. If a purchase order arrives for $10 000 worth of goods, the supplier must be relatively confident that the client is legitimate and in fact made the order, before the order is acted upon; the cost associated with incorrect authentication is high. However, if a smaller client sends a purchase order for $100 worth of goods, relatively little authentication may be necessary and the facilities needed for the protocol described above may not be available. Therefore, it would be nice to support intermediate services, i.e., multiple levels of service.

One method for offering a "second-class" authentication scheme is to rely solely on initiation type authentication as described below.

The protocol begins when A sends a message to B. We assume that A has no encryption capabilities at all.

Initiation authentication is only slightly affected by the lack of encryption capabilities. If A is not on B's known-entity list then B contacts a (set of) third party(ies) to authenticate the existence of organization A and to evaluate it. Assuming B contacts a third party that does have A registered, that third party returns to B values of the requested evaluation criteria along with a flag indicating the level of authentication that A can support; for example, first-class to indicate that A has encryption capabilities and can carry out the protocol described earlier, and second-class to indicate that A has no capabilities and must rely on passwords sent in the clear to authenticate itself to the third party.

Transaction authentication can no longer rely on a Needham–Schroeder protocol if A has no encryption or decryption capabilities. Therefore, when B asks the third party to authenticate a particular transaction or message from A (either the first transaction or later ones), the third party informs B that only second-class transaction authentication is available. One procedure that the third party could use in the absence of encryption would be to ask the source of the message to B (presumably A) to resend the password that it submitted upon registration. If the resent password matches A's registered password, the third party could send a message to B indicating that the third party believes the source of the message is in fact A. Similarly, the third party could authenticate B and inform A that the third party believe that the destination is B. In both cases, the third party must include the authentication level rating, second-class. A and B can then decide whether to accept or reject this level of authentication for the proposed transaction. The primary risks are that there is no session key for the parties to authenticate themselves to one another directly and there is no control over an impostor intervening in the transaction after it has begun. In addition, passwords are subject to interception because they are sent to the third party in the clear.

For certain types (low risk) of transactions and communications, this limited level of assurance may be acceptable, and preferable to no authentication at all to the extent casual impostors are detected or discouraged. However, it is vital that both parties keep track of the level of authentication in use. For example, if in the middle of a transaction A proposes to increase a purchase order by an order of magnitude, B should know that only second-class authentication is being used and reject the suggestion if it sees fit.

G. Internal Authentication

Before concluding it is worth emphasizing that although organizations do not have to modify their internal authentication mechanisms in order to support ION authentication, interorganization connects can heighten the need for reliable internal authentication mechanisms. The mechanisms described in this paper allow an organization to decouple internal and external authentication. However, if an organization's internal authentication mechanisms are weak or nonexistent, the ability to authenticate external entities leaves several problems unaddressed.

First, using the protocols described above, an organi-

zation is liable for requests that its gateway allows to flow to the outside world, i.e., by passing a message the gateway has asserted its belief that it was generated by an authorized program or user. Just as an organization needs to guard against employees writing fraudulent or excessive paper purchase orders, so it must guard against fraudulent or excessive online purchase orders. Many organizations have extensive authentication procedures in place with respect to traditional paper purchase orders, certainly more extensive than they have for electronic mail. An ION participant must recognize the need to augment traditionally weak electronic mail authentication with something better suited to the application.

A second concern that impinges on internal authentication requirements regards incoming communication. For example, an internal order-entry system that accepts online orders from customers via the gateway relies on the gateway to authenticate that the originator of the order belongs to the organization that it claims to belong to. However, if the level of trust on the internal network is low, the order-entry system will need to authenticate that the requests that claim to be from outsiders actually are coming from the ION gateway. If this authentication does not take place then an internal user could spoof the order-entry system by sending a message that claims to be from the ION gateway.

In summary, offloading responsibility for external authentication to the ION gateway is desirable because it decouples external from internal authentication. However, such decoupling may also be dangerous if the organization does not carefully reevaluate assumptions made about the trustworthiness of the internal environment. In the absence of external interconnection, the cost of unauthenticated communications may have been deemed less than the expense of authentication mechanisms. Interorganization connections change the parameters of the equation and should lead ION participants to reevaluate their internal as well as their external authentication mechanisms.

H. Subverting Access Controls

The first security issue outlined in the introduction to this section is similar to the trojan horse phenomenon; namely, that special commands or control characters can be embedded in a communication and cause the receiving machine to behave in a way in which its operating organization did not intend it to behave. For example, control characters can be embedded in a text message which is then sent for display on the screen by a person's mailreader. If the recipient's display terminal interprets these control characters as pseudocommands (e.g., to clear the screen, interrupt the current program, interpret the following text as a command, etc.), the text message can turn an otherwise passive communication medium into an active one. In other words, the remote machine can be made to take some action aside from delivering and displaying text to a human. A similar problem arises with some text formatters that interpret a piece of text as a command if it is preceded by special characters. As with the display system that interprets control characters as commands, the formatter interprets these special characters as commands and transforms a passive channel into an active one. In order to guard against such misuses, the gateway must filter messages for control sequences. This requires that the gateway be able to recognize a control sequence. Therefore, generic control characters and commands can be filtered at the gateway, while system-specific ones may require filtering at the end-points.

In summary, organizations can initiate relationships with one another using third parties to authenticate one another's identity and desired credit information, can carry out transactions using third parties to authenticate that the transaction request travels from and to the claimed party, and finally, both of these activities can be carried out at the appropriate authentication cost level.

IV. CONCLUSION

In conclusion, our analysis suggests that category sets and nondiscretionary control mechanisms can be adapted to satisfy usage control requirements in interorganization networks; namely, to isolate the strictly-internal facilities from the ION facilities, and distinct ION's from one another. We also demonstrated how to adapt authentication mechanisms to support controls across organization boundaries. The proposed approach to interconnection has implications for network interconnection and gateway design, in particular the level of interconnection [12]. Further research is needed to understand the range of applications for which the proposed modifications might be suited, the implications for nondiscretionary security models, and implementation of third party authentication services.

ACKNOWLEDGMENT

I thank B. Baldwin, C. Landwehr, S. Lipner, D. Reed, J. Saltzer, S. Sluizer, and J. Sutherland for insightful comments and suggestions on drafts of this paper.

REFERENCES

[1] D. Estrin, "Access to inter-organization computer networks," Ph.D. dissertation, Dep. Elec. Eng. and Comput. Sci., Massachusetts Inst. Technol., Cambridge, Aug. 1985.
[2] P. Karger, "Non-discretionary access control for decentralized computing systems," S.M. thesis, Dep. Elec. Eng. Comput. Sci., Massachusetts Inst. Technol., Cambridge, May 1977; also available from M.I.T. Lab. Comput. Sci., Tech. Rep. TR-179.
[3] C. Landwehr, C. Heitmeyer, and J. McCleen, "A security model for military message systems," *ACM Trans. Comput. Syst.*, vol. 2, no. 3, pp. 198-222, Aug. 1984.
[4] D. Bell and L. LaPadula, "Secure computer systems," Mitre Corp., Tech. Rep. ESD-TR-73-278, June 1974.
[5] K. Biba, "Integrity considerations for secure computer systems," Mitre Corp., Tech. Rep. ESD-TR-76-372, Apr. 1977.
[6] S. Lipner, "Non-discretionary controls for commercial applications," in *Proc. of the 1982 Symp. Security and Privacy*, IEEE Comput. Soc., Oakland, CA, Apr. 1982, pp. 2-10.
[7] L. Rotenberg, "Making computers keep secrets," Ph.D. dissertation, Dep. Elec. Eng. and Comput. Sci., Massachusetts Inst. Technol., Cambridge, Feb. 1974; also available from M.I.T. Lab. Comput. Sci., Tech Rep. TR-115.
[8] D. Cohen and J. Postel, "Gateways, bridges, and tunnels in computer mail," in *Local Networks, Strategy and Systems. Proc. Localnet '83*, Online Ltd., Northwood, UK, 1983, pp. 109-123.
[9] S. Routhier, "An improved authentication server for inter-computer communication," S.B. thesis, Dep. Elec. Eng. Comput. Sci., Massachusetts Inst. Technol., June 1983.
[10] R. Needham and M. Schroeder, "Using encryption for authentication in large networks of computers," *Commun. ACM*, vol. 21, no. 12, pp. 993-999, Dec. 1978.
[11] D. Estrin, "Non-discretionary controls for inter-organization networks," in *Proc. 1985 Symp. Security and Privacy*. Silver Springs, MD: IEEE Comput. Soc. Press, 1985, pp. 56-61.
[12] ——, "Inter-organization networks: Implications of access control requirements for interconnection protocols," in *ACM SIGCOMM '86 Symp. Commun. Architectures and Protocols*, New York, 1986.

Author Index

A

Abdellatif, A., 213
Amin, R. R., 191
Appleton, D. S., 6

B

Barkmeyer, E., 176
Batini, C., 72
Bernstein, P. A., 163
Breitbart, Y., 135, 221
Brill, D., 200

C

Cardenas, A. F., 251
Cha, S. K., 113
Chaudhuri, S., 113
Chen, A. L. P., 200

D

Dao, S. K., 200
Dayal, U., 163
Deen, S. M., 191
DeMichiel, L., 113
Dwyer, P. A., 292

E

Estrin, D., 315

G

Gligor, V. D., 35
Goodman, N., 163

H

Hasan, W., 113
Heimbigner, D., 46
Hirschman, L., 308
Hutchinson, N., 24

K

Krishnamurthy, V., 176

L

Lam, H., 176
Landers, T., 163
Larson, J. A., 292
Lenzerini, M., 72
Lin, K. W. T., 163
Litwin, W., 144, 213
Luckenbaugh, G. L., 35
Lund, E., 200

M

MacGregor, R., 200
Manola, F., 126
McLeod, D., 46
Mitchell, M., 176

N

Navathe, S. B., 72
Notkin, D., 24

O

Ofori-Dwumfuo, G. O., 191
Olsen, P. L., 221

P

Prasad, B. E., 264
Pu, C., 150

Q

Qian, X., 113

R

Rathman, P. K., 113
Reddy, M. P., 264
Reddy, P. G., 264

S

Sanislo, J., 24
Schwartz, M., 24
Shuey, R., 11
Silberschatz, A., 135
Smith, J. M., 163
Staniszkis, W., 231
Su, Y. W., 176
Swami, A., 113

T

Taylor, M. C., 191
Templeton, M., 200
Thompson, G. R., 135, 221
Thompson, P., 281
Tirri, H., 144

W

Walker, M. G., 113
Ward, P., 200
Wiederhold, G., 11, 113
Winslett, M., 113
Wong, E., 163

Subject Index
(Number denotes first page of article.)

MDAS (Master Data Administration System), 176
MDBMS (Multidatabase Management System), 231
Memory residence, 113
Menu interfaces
  open-ended, 113
MERMAID database, 200
Metadata, 191
Mixed initiative dialogue, 308
Models
  CODASYL, 163
  file, 163
  functional flow, 281
  IMDAS, 176
  relational, 163, 281
  semantic, 281
  technical, 281
MRDSM, 264
Multidatabases, 264
  implementation, 231
  interoperability, 213
  management, 144
  MRDSM, 159
  software, 159
  transaction management, 135
Multibase systems, 163
  management, 231
  software, 159, 163, 231
Multiple inheritance, 113

N

Natural languages
  information access, 308
  interfaces, 279, 308
NDMS (Network Data Management System), 231, 264
Negotiation, 46
Networks
  analysis, 279
  interorganization, 315
  structural properties, 279
Nodal autonomy, 191
NQP (Nodal Query Preprocessor), 191

O

Object encapsulation, 126
Object-oriented databases
  applications in information systems, 126
Office information, 46
Optimization
  global, 163
  local, 163
O-vectors
  hierarchical certification, 150

P

PRECI database system, 191, 264
Preintegration, 72
Private branch exchanges (PBX), 11
Protocols
  application-level, 35
  data transfer, 35

Q

Queries
  conversion algorithms, 221

elementary, 213
incomplete, 213
interdatabase, 213
multiple, 213
Query execution, 191
Query languages, 150, 213
  ADDS, 221
Query optimization, 113, 200, 264
Query processing, 159, 231
  architecture, 113, 163
  HDDBMS, 264
Query translators, 163, 251

R

Reference models
  for information engineering, 281
Resource management
  information, 6

S

Schema integration
  DBMS, 72
Schemas
  CODASYL, 231
  conforming, 72
  database, 213
  diversity, 72
  export, 46
  global databse, 191, 200
  importation, 46
  integration, 72, 163
  participation, 191
  PRECI, 191
  private, 46
Semantics
  binary models, 281
  global, 308
  integrity constraints, 113, 292
Serialization
  concurrency control, 150
Software systems, 1, 6
  multibase, 159, 163
Standards
  database, 281
Superdatabases, 33, 150
  declarative interface, 150
  glue, 150
  recovery, 150

T

Testbed systems
  distributed database, 292
Timestamp based methods, 144
Time warp mechanisms, 144
Transaction managers and management, 292
  distributed, 35
  in multidatabases, 135
Transactions
  authentication, 315
  concurrency, 150
  global, 135, 150
  graphs, 135
  local, 135
  processors, 191, 292
  safe, 144

Amar Gupta (SM'85) is Principal Research Associate at the Sloan School of Management, Massachusetts Institute of Technology, Cambridge. He holds a bachelor's degree in electrical engineering from the Indian Institute of Technology, Kanpur, a master's degree in management from the Massachusetts Institute of Technology, and a doctorate in computer technology from the Indian Institute of Technology, New Delhi. He conducted the research for his doctorate dissertation at three prestigious universities in India, England, and the United States.

Dr. Gupta has been involved in research, management, and publishing activities since 1974. Since joining M.I.T. in 1979, he has been active in the areas of multiprocessor architectures, performance measurement, distributed homogeneous and heterogeneous data bases, expert systems, personal computers, and transfer of information technology. He serves as a consultant to a number of corporations, government agencies, and international bodies on various aspects of computer technology, and is an active technical advisor to several international organizations and committees.

Dr. Gupta is the Chairman of the Technical Committee for Microprocessor Applications of the IEEE Industrial Electronics Society, and Assistant Chairman for several annual IECON conferences. He was also involved with the Very Large Data Base Conference (VLDB '87), held in England in 1987. He received the Rotary Fellowship for International Understanding in 1979 and the Brooks Prize (Honorable Mention) in 1980.

He has written more than 50 technical articles and papers, and produced seven books.

Dr. Gupta is a permanent resident of the United States, and expects to be approved for U.S. citizenship by the time this book is published.